Making History Count

A Primer in Quantitative Methods for Historians

Making History Count introduces the main quantitative methods used in historical research. The emphasis is on intuitive understanding and application of the concepts, rather than formal statistics; no knowledge of mathematics beyond simple arithmetic is required. The techniques are illustrated by applications in social, political, demographic, and economic history.

Students will learn to read and evaluate the application of the quantitative methods used in many books and articles, and to assess the historical conclusions drawn from them. They will see how quantitative techniques can open up new aspects of an enquiry, and supplement and strengthen other methods of research. This textbook will also encourage students to recognize the benefits of using quantitative methods in their own research projects.

Making History Count is written by two senior economic historians with considerable teaching experience on both sides of the Atlantic. It is designed for use as the basic text for taught undergraduate and graduate courses, and is also suitable for students working on their own. It is clearly illustrated with numerous tables, graphs, and diagrams, leading the student through the various key topics; the whole is supported by four specific historical data sets, which can be downloaded from the Cambridge University Press website at www.cambridge.org/9780521806633.

CHARLES FEINSTEIN is Emeritus Professor of Economic History and Emeritus Fellow of All Souls College, Oxford. His publications include *National Income, Expenditure and Output of the United Kingdom, 1855–1965* (1972), *British Economic Growth, 1856–1973* (with R. C. O. Matthews and J. Odling-Smee, 1982), and *The European Economy between the Wars* (with Peter Temin and Gianni Toniolo, 1997).

MARK THOMAS is Associate Professor of History at the University of Virginia. His publications include *Capitalism in Context: Essays on Economic Development and Cultural Change* (ed., with John A. James, 1994), *Disintegration of the World Economy between the Wars* (ed., 1996), and *The Economic Future in Historical Perspective* (ed., with Paul David, 2002).

Making History Count

A Primer in Quantitative Methods for Historians

CHARLES H. FEINSTEIN
AND MARK THOMAS

CAMBRIDGE
UNIVERSITY PRESS

CAMBRIDGE UNIVERSITY PRESS
Cambridge, New York, Melbourne, Madrid, Cape Town, Singapore, São Paulo

Cambridge University Press
The Edinburgh Building, Cambridge CB2 8RU, UK

Published in the United States of America by Cambridge University Press, New York

www.cambridge.org
Information on this title: www.cambridge.org/9780521806633

First published 2002

A catalogue record for this publication is available from the British Library

Library of Congress Cataloguing in Publication data
Feinstein, C. H.
   Making history count : a primer in quantitative methods for historians /
   Charles H. Feinstein and Mark Thomas.
      p.   cm.
   Includes bibliographical references and index.
   ISBN 0-521-80663-1 (hc) – ISBN 0-521-00137-4 (pbk.)
      1. History–Statistical methods. 2. History–Methodology. 3. Historical models.
   I. Thomas, Mark, 1954- II. Title.

D16.17 .F45 2001
902'.1–dc21   2001035660

ISBN 978-0-521-80663-3 hardback
ISBN 978-0-521-00137-3 paperback

Transferred to digital printing (with corrections) 2008

Contents

Part II Samples and inductive statistics

Figures

Tables

Panels

Preface

We would like to express our deep appreciation to Daniel Benjamin, Levis Kochin, Timothy Hatton, Jeffrey Williamson, George Boyer, and Richard Steckel for agreeing to our use of their work for the case studies, which are a central feature of the approach we have adopted for this book. We are particularly grateful to Boyer, Hatton, and Steckel for providing us with the unpublished data that we have used throughout the text and exercises to illustrate quantitative procedures, and for allowing us to reproduce their data sets on our web site. We have also received very helpful comments from a number of our colleagues, notably James Foreman-Peck, Jane Humphries, Sharon Murphy, and Richard Smith. We owe a special debt of gratitude to Joachim Voth, who read the entire text with great care and sent us many thoughtful criticisms and suggestions. None of these scholars has any responsibility for any errors of procedure or interpretation that remain.

We particularly wish to acknowledge the contributions of generations of students who took our courses in quantitative methods in Oxford and Charlottesville. They showed that intuitive appreciation of the importance and limitations of quantification in history could be developed by undergraduates and graduates from a wide range of intellectual and disciplinary backgrounds. The approach adopted in the present text was originally designed primarily for students who had no prior knowledge of statistics, and who were in many cases initially hostile to, or intimidated by, quantitative procedures. It was, above all, their positive response, their success in applying these methods in their own work, and their helpful comments that motivated us to develop the text for a larger readership.

Our final debt is to our families, for their encouragement, forbearance, and general support during the long period over which this book has evolved.

PART 1

Elementary statistical analysis

CHAPTER 1

Introduction

1.1 Aims of the book

This text has three principal objectives. The first is to provide an elementary and very informal introduction to the fundamental concepts and techniques of modern quantitative methods. A primer cannot be comprehensive, but we will cover many of the procedures most widely used in research in the historical and social sciences. The book is deliberately written at a very basic level. It does not include any statistical theory or mathematics, and there is no attempt to prove any of the statistical propositions. It has been planned on the assumption that those reading it have no retained knowledge of statistics, and very little of mathematics beyond simple arithmetic.

It is assumed that the material in the book will be taught in conjunction with one of the several statistical packages now available for use with computers, for example, *SPSS for Windows, STATA, MINITAB*, or *SAS*. By using the computer to perform all the relevant statistical calculations and manipulations it is possible to eliminate both the need to learn numerous formulae, and also the tedious work of doing laborious calculations. However, if the computer is going to provide the results, then it is absolutely essential that the student should be able to understand and interpret the content and terminology of the printouts, of which figure 1.1 is a typical specimen, and the second objective of the book is to achieve this.

This leads naturally to the third and most important objective. The book is throughout concerned to relate the quantitative techniques studied to examples of their use by historians and social scientists, and by doing this to promote the understanding and use of these methods. In the following section we introduce four specific studies that will be deployed throughout the book, but – at appropriate points in the text – we also refer readers to other examples of the application of quantitative methods to historical and other issues. A student who studies this text will not be able

Variables Entered/Removed[b]

Model	Variables Entered	Variables Removed	Method
1	FARMERS, CHILDALL, LONDON, WEALTH, GRAIN[a]		Enter

a. All requested variables entered.

b. Dependent Variable: RELIEF

Model Summary

Model	R	R Square	Adjusted R Square	Std. Error of the Estimate
1	.532[a]	.283	.271	6.84746

a. Predictors: (Constant), FARMERS, CHILDALL, LONDON, WEALTH, GRAIN

ANOVA[b]

Model		Sum of Squares	df	Mean Square	F	Sig.
1	Regression	5638.346	5	1127.669	24.050	.000[a]
	Residual	14300.769	305	46.888		
	Total	19939.116	310			

a. Predictors: (Constant), FARMERS, CHILDALL, LONDON, WEALTH, GRAIN

b. Dependent Variable: RELIEF

Coefficients[a]

Model		Unstandardized Coefficients		Standardized Coefficients	t	Sig.
		B	Std. Error	Beta		
1	(Constant)	11.352	1.718		6.609	.000
	GRAIN	.301	.089	.204	3.363	.001
	CHILDALL	5.609	1.030	.271	5.445	.000
	WEALTH	-.276	.179	-.081	-1.544	.124
	LONDON	-4.156E-02	.010	-.234	-4.110	.000
	FARMERS	5.873	2.131	.158	2.756	.006

a. Dependent Variable: RELIEF

Figure 1.1 Illustration of SPSS print-out of regression results

to claim that she is a fully qualified statistician. However, she should have the confidence to read chapters or articles which use quantitative methods, to understand what the authors have done and why they have done it, and to make her own critical evaluation of the procedures used and the historical conclusions drawn from the statistical results.

Students should also be able to see from the case studies and other examples how the use of quantitative methods can open up new aspects of an enquiry and can supplement and strengthen other methods of research. We hope that they might then appreciate how their own research projects might benefit from the application of these methods, and take their own first steps in this direction.

The book is designed to be used both as the basic text for taught courses and for students working on their own without an instructor. In planning the content and sequence of the chapters, one of our primary considerations has been to keep the material in the early chapters at a very elementary level. Many of those for whom this book is intended will naturally be somewhat wary about taking a course in quantitative methods, but if they find that they can make substantial progress in understanding some of the basic statistical concepts they will gain confidence in their ability to handle the slightly more difficult material in later chapters. There is a small price to be paid for this approach, since it means that correlation and regression are covered twice: first without any statistical theory (in chapters 3 and 4) and then again in greater depth (in chapter 8). However, the text has been used for a number of years to teach a class taken almost exclusively by statistical novices who initially approached the course with deep suspicion, and experience has shown that this strategy is very successful.

It is, of course, also possible for instructors to follow the material in a different sequence, or – depending on the time available and the level it is desired to achieve – to omit certain topics altogether. For example, chapter 7 on non-parametric methods has been included because these procedures are often appropriate for the sort of problems faced by historians; and it has been placed at this point in the text because it makes a useful complement to the discussion of the standard principles of hypothesis testing in chapter 6. However, a course designed primarily to provide a very basic introduction to regression analysis in 10 sessions might skip this. It might, for example, start with chapters 2–6 and 8–9, add material on dummy variables from chapter 10 and on the basic aspects of non-linear regression from chapter 12, and then cover the appropriate applications in the case studies in chapters 14 and 15.

This would be sufficient to give students a good grounding in some of the main aspects of regression methods, and should enable them to cope with many examples of the use of these methods in the historical literature. However, the omission of chapter 11 would mean that they would not have acquired any knowledge of either the serious problems which can arise when the assumptions underlying the standard regression model (discussed in chapter 9) are violated, or the associated procedures for diagnosing and – where possible – correcting for these violations. This would also be a substantial weakness for any students who wished to apply these methods to their own research. One alternative, for students able to start with some knowledge of very elementary statistics and wishing to aim a little higher (while still limited to 10 sessions), would be to skip chapters 1–4 and 7, and work through chapters 5–6 and 8–15.

The normal text and tables are supplemented by material in boxes and panels. *Boxes* are used to highlight the fundamental definitions and concepts, and should be studied closely. *Panels* are used to provide explanations or information at a slightly more advanced level than the rest of the text. The panels should be helpful for some readers, but those who omit them will not be at any disadvantage in understanding the remainder of the text. In addition to footnotes (referred to by a letter), we have also used endnotes (referred to by a number) where it seems desirable not to burden the main text with lengthy annotations. Endnotes typically consist either of lists of references to further examples of the applications of statistical methods to historical topics, or of technical points which need not distract all readers although they may be useful to some.

We have given a formula for all the basic concepts even though the book is written on the assumption that the computers will provide what is required for any particular statistical operation. It is usually possible to set out these formulae in various ways, but we have always chosen the variant that best explains the essential nature of the concept, rather than one that facilitates computation (and we avoid the complication of alternative versions of the same formula). We recognize that many readers will not be accustomed to working with symbols, and so may be uncomfortable initially with this method of setting out information. However, the multi-part nature of many concepts means that a formula is the most concise and effective 'shorthand' way of showing what is involved, and we would strongly urge all readers to make the small initial effort required to learn to read this language; the rewards for doing so are very substantial.

1.2 The four case studies and the data sets

Throughout the book we will make frequent reference to four data sets that were compiled and used by historians to investigate specific historical issues.[a] In order to illustrate and practise the various techniques discussed in subsequent chapters we will normally draw on one of these data sets, and the results will be reproduced and discussed in depth in chapters 14 and 15, by which time readers will have encountered all the procedures used in these studies. We are extremely grateful to the authors for their agreement to the use of their statistical material and for making available their unpublished data. These data sets are not reproduced in this book but can be accessed without charge on the Cambridge University Press web site at www.cambridge.org/9780521806633. Further instructions for downloading the data are given on the web site.

A brief outline of the issues raised in these studies is given in appendix A, together with a description of each of the individual statistical series that make up the data sets. In all cases we refer to each series in a data set by a short name given in capital letters, and since some computer programs limit series titles to eight letters we have adopted that restriction. Even when abbreviated these names should be reasonably self-explanatory (for example, BRTHRATE or IRISHMIG) and they are much easier to remember and interpret than symbols. Where the authors we are quoting have used a similar convention we have generally adopted their names; where they have not done so we have created our own.

In addition to these primary data sets, most chapters include references to other examples of the application of the given procedures by historians. These illustrations are designed both to reinforce understanding of the techniques and to show the range of issues that have been addressed by historians with the aid of quantitative methods. The text also uses imaginary data where it is desirable to have very simple numbers in order to illustrate basic concepts or to make calculations without the need for a computer.

1.3 Types of measurement

Measurement is the assignment of numbers or codes to observations. The measurements we work with can be classified in various ways. In this introductory section we note a number of basic terms and distinctions.

---

[a] The four studies are George Boyer, *An Economic History of the English Poor Law*, Cambridge University Press, 1990, chapters 4 and 5; Timothy J. Hatton and Jeffrey G. Williamson, 'After the famine: emigration from Ireland, 1850–1913', *Journal of Economic History*, 53, 1993, pp. 575–600; Daniel K. Benjamin and Levis A. Kochin, 'Searching for an explanation for unemployment in interwar Britain', *Journal of Political Economy*, 87, 1979, pp. 441–78; and Richard H. Steckel, 'The age at leaving home in the United States, 1850–1860', *Social Science History*, 20, 1996, pp. 507–32.

1.3.1 Cases, variables, and values

A data set consists of a series of units or **cases** each of which has one or more characteristics, known as **variables**. For each variable there is a sequence of varying observations, each with its own particular **value**. The cases are the basic unit for which the measurements are available, and there are two main types (see §1.3.2). They can be individuals, households, firms, towns, churches, votes, or any other subject of analysis; or they can be weeks, quarters, years, or any other period of time for which a data series is available.

In the English Poor Law data set:

Cases: The cases are 311 English parishes (identified by a number).

Variables: There are 15 variables for each parish. These include, for example, the *per capita* relief expenditure of each parish (RELIEF), the annual income of adult male agricultural labourers in the parish (INCOME), and the proportion of unemployed labourers in the parish (UNEMP).

Values: For the RELIEF variable the values for the first five parishes are (in shillings): 20.4, 29.1, 14.9, 24.1, 18.2, etc.[b]

In the data set for annual emigration from Ireland:

Cases: The cases are the 37 successive years from 1877 to 1913.

Variables: There are five basic variables for each year. These are the rates per 1,000 of the population emigrating from Ireland (IRISHMIG), the foreign and domestic employment rates (EMPFOR and EMPDOM), the foreign wage relative to the domestic wage (IRWRATIO), and the stock of previous emigrants (MIGSTOCK).

Values: For the main emigration variable (IRISHMIG), the values of this rate for the first five years are: 7.284, 7.786, 8.938, 18.358, and 15.238.

1.3.2 Cross-section and time-series variables

A set of measurements that applies to a single case at different periods of time is referred to as a **time series**. The series in the data sets dealing with migration from Ireland from 1877 to 1913, and with unemployment and benefits in Great Britain each year from 1920 to 1938, are both examples of annual time series.

A set of measurements that applies to different cases at a single point in time is referred to as a **cross-section**. The data set for children leaving home is a cross-section, with values for each variable for each child in the sample in 1850.

---

[b] The data on relief expenditure shown for the 24 Kent parishes in the data set are given to 3 decimal places (i.e. have 3 figures after the decimal point). In the text the values for the first five parishes are **rounded** to 1 decimal place.

It is also possible to combine cross-section and time-series data to create what is known as a **panel** or **longitudinal** data set. The second of the two data sets for Irish emigration (see part (b) of table A.3 in appendix A), which has values for the variables for a cross-section of 32 counties for each of the four census dates (1881, 1891, 1901, and 1911), is an example of panel data. The process of combining the values for the cross-section over time is referred to as **pooling** the data.

In principle, time series are used to study changes *over time*, and cross-sections to study differences *between cases* (for example, families, parishes, or countries) at a particular date. However, it is not always possible to obtain the necessary time series for periods in the past, and historians sometimes attempt to infer how relationships might have changed over time by looking at differences in a cross-section for a more recent date. For example, the patterns of household expenditure of low-income families in a modern cross-section might be used to infer something about overall patterns of expenditure at an earlier date when all families had lower incomes.[c]

1.3.3 Levels of measurement

We can distinguish the following three **levels** or **scales** of measurement. Each has its own properties and the nature of the statistical exercises that can be performed depends on the level of the data.

Nominal measurement

This is the lowest level and conveys no information about the relations between the values. Each value defines a distinct category but can give no information other than the label or name (hence **nominal** level) of the category. They are sometimes also referred to as **categorical** variables.

For example, a study of migration to urban areas might include as one of the variables the birthplace of the migrants. These towns or villages cannot be ranked or placed in any order in terms of their value as place of birth (though they could be by other criteria such as size, or distance from the migrants' final destination).

Ordinal measurement

This applies when it is possible to **order or rank** all the categories according to some criterion without being able to specify the exact size of the interval between any two categories.

---

[c] A similar procedure is adopted by Boyer, *Poor Law*, p. 126 to explain the increase in relief expenditure over time on the basis of cross-section variations in expenditure across parishes.

This is a very common situation with historical data and can occur for one of three reasons:

- The relevant variables are often *ordinal by definition*. For example, an analysis of the labour force might classify workers as unskilled, semi-skilled, skilled, and professional. We could agree that skilled workers ranked above semi-skilled, and semi-skilled above unskilled, but could not say anything about the distance between the categories.
- *Lack of data might impose an ordinal scale* even when a higher level would, in principle, be possible. For example, in a study of education it would in principle be possible to measure the number of years spent at school by each member of the labour force, but the surviving records may state only whether or not they completed five years' primary education, and if they did whether they then went on to secondary school. We would thus have to treat 'schooling' as an ordinal variable with three values: 'less than five years', 'five years', and 'secondary or above'.
- The third reason for using ordinal scales might be doubts about the *accuracy of the data*. In a study of wealth, for example, we might decide that the actual values reported by property owners were too unreliable to use, but that we could safely order them on the basis of, say, three values: large, medium, and small.

Interval or ratio measurement[1]

These measurements have all the properties of an ordinal scale. In addition it is now possible to measure the *exact distance between any pair of values*. This level of measurement is thus truly quantitative, and any appropriate statistical procedure can be applied to values on an interval or ratio scale.

Values measured on such a scale may be either **continuous** or **discrete** (discontinuous). A continuous variable, such as height or income, is measured in units that can be reduced in size to a theoretically infinite degree, limited only by the sensitivity of our measurement procedures. Discrete variables, by contrast, can take only a limited number of pre-determined values (most commonly whole numbers) and occur when we are counting indivisible units such as cotton mills or people.

1.3.4   Populations and samples

The term **population** (or universe) refers to all possible observations. If, for example, we were interested in the number of cotton mills in New England in 1880, the 'population' would consist of all mills in existence at that date.[2] In a few cases historians might have such information if, for example, a complete census of textile mills had been taken at the relevant date. Normally, however, we would have only a **sample**.

The characteristics of the population variables are known as **parameters**, those of the sample variables as **statistics**. Parameters are fixed values at any point in time and are normally unknown. Statistics, on the other hand, are known from the sample, but may vary with each sample taken from the population. The extent of such variation from sample to sample will depend on the homogeneity (uniformity) of the population from which it is drawn.[d]

A crucial feature of any sample is whether or not it is **random**. A random sample satisfies three basic conditions. First, *every item* in the population (parishes in England and Wales, voters in an election, cards in a deck of cards) has *an equal chance of appearing in the sample*. Secondly, *every combination of items* has an equal chance of selection. Thirdly, there is independence of selection: the fact that any one item in the population has been selected has *absolutely no influence on whether or not any other item will be selected*.

When the sample is drawn **with replacement** the same item can be selected more than once; for example, after a card is drawn it is put back in the deck. If the sample is drawn **without replacement** the item can be selected only once. Almost all use of sampling in historical analysis is sampling without replacement. Each parish, each voter, each cotton mill is sampled only once when the data set is being compiled.

The proper procedures to be followed in constructing samples, whether the sampling should be random or some other type, such as stratified or cluster sampling, and the size of the sample required for any particular project are complex subjects which go beyond the scope of this book and specialized texts should be consulted.[3]

1.3.5 Dummy variables

A variable that cannot be measured can still be used in quantitative work by assigning values representing each of two (or more) categories. This is known as a **dummy variable**. In the simplest case, where there are only two possible values (equivalent to yes or no) the dummy variable is formed by setting the positive values equal to 1 and the negative values to 0. There are a number of these in the Poor Law data set – for example, whether or not the parish pays child allowances and whether or not it has a workhouse.

---

[d] Harold Wilson, Britain's only statistically informed prime minister, once remarked that he needed to sip only one spoonful from a plate of soup to know whether it was too hot to drink.

They can also be used in time-series analysis – for example, years in which there was a war might be given a value of 1, while peacetime years are assigned a value of 0. In more complex cases there could be more than two categories. For example, a study of voting behaviour might divide the electorate into four categories according to whether in the previous election they had voted Democrat, Republican, or Independent, or had not voted.

This procedure effectively transfers the information into a numerical form (albeit a limited one) and makes it possible to apply standard statistical tools to the variable. For fuller discussion of the use of dummy variables see §10.1 and also chapter 13.

1.4 Simple notation

The use of symbols may deter some readers, but they are a very convenient form of shorthand and if properly defined are not difficult to understand. They are used sparingly in this book, mainly to supplement more cumbersome verbal statements and to bring out the essential features of some of the concepts. The following notes introduce the simple conventions adopted.

It is customary to refer to **variables** by the letters X and Y. For each variable there would be a sequence of observations, each of which would have its own particular value. For example, the values in a sequence of 5 observations for X could be listed as

$$X_1, X_2, X_3, X_4, \text{ and } X_5$$

More generally, if there were n observations this could be written as

$$X_1, X_2, \ldots, X_n$$

and if it is desired to indicate that we are referring to any one particular observation without specifying which it is, we normally use a subscript i

$$X_i$$

It is sometimes necessary to refer to a **constant** rather than a variable, that is to a value which is fixed. Such constants are usually denoted by the initial letters of the alphabet – for example, a, or its Greek equivalent, α (alpha).

Summation

The symbol used to refer to the total (or sum) of all the observations in the sequence is the Greek letter capital sigma, Σ

Thus instead of writing $X_1 + X_2 + X_3 + X_4 + X_5$ we could write

$$\sum_{i=1}^{5} X_i$$

This is an instruction to add all the values in the series from $i=1$ to $i=5$. If it is obvious which values are included this may be simplified to

$$\Sigma X$$

Differences

The symbol used to refer to the difference between two series is the Greek letter capital delta, Δ

Thus if instead of referring to the successive values of an annual variable X, it is desired to refer to the change in these values from year to year, this is done by writing

$$\Delta X$$

Time and time lags

If it is desired to indicate that the variable refers to a specific year (or other period of time), the convention is to use the subscript t. Thus X_t would indicate the current period, X_{t-1} the previous period, and X_{t+1} the follow-ing period.[e] X_{t-1} is known as a **lagged variable**.

Population and sample

The characteristics of the population are usually denoted by Greek letters, and those of samples from that population by Roman letters. For example, the standard deviation of the population (this term will be defined in §2.3.2) is designated by σ (lower case Greek sigma) and the standard devia-tion of the sample by s.

1.5 The equation of a straight line

We shall refer at numerous points to **linear,** or straight-line, relationships. A straight line can be represented algebraically by an equation of the form

$$Y = a + b\,X$$

where X and Y are any two variables, and a and b are any two constants.

This equation tells us that each value of Y is equal to some constant, a,

---

[e] The equation on p. 581 of Hatton and Williamson, 'Emigration', refers to current and previous years in this way.

plus the value of X multiplied by another constant, b.[f] The precise position of the straight line will then change depending on the specific values given to a and b.

This is illustrated in figure 1.2 (a) for the particular case where a = 2 and b = 3. The equation thus becomes

$$Y = 2 + 3X$$

- a is the **intercept**. It determines the level at which the straight line crosses the vertical axis and is the value of Y when X = 0. In figure 1.2 (a) the line intercepts (cuts) the vertical axis at 2.
- b is the **slope** of the line. It tells us by how much Y changes for every change of 1 unit in X. In figure 1.2 (a) Y rises by 3 units on the vertical axis every time there is a change of 1 unit in X on the horizontal axis.

The **sign** of b is also important. In figure 1.2 (a), b is positive, so Y *rises* as X rises. By contrast, in the following equation, b is negative

$$Y = 10 - 2X$$

so Y *falls* by 2 units for every increase of 1 unit in X , as shown in figure 1.2 (b).

1.6 Powers and logarithms

1.6.1 Powers

(a) For any number, X, the statement 'multiply X by itself n times' is written X^n. The technical term for this is: 'raise the number X to the nth **power**.' 'n' is called the **exponent**. Thus

$$X^1 = X; \qquad X^2 = X \times X; \qquad X^3 = X \times X \times X, \qquad \text{and so on}$$

Note that $X^0 = 1$.[g]

---

[f] Multiplication can be represented in various ways. Thus the statement 'a multiplied by b' can be written as: a × b, as a . b, as a(b), or simply as ab. The order of multiplication makes no difference: ab is exactly the same as ba.

If one of the terms to be multiplied has more than one component then these must be placed in brackets; for example b(a + c) tells us to add a to c and then multiply the result by b. It is essential to complete the operation in brackets *before* the multiplication.

Similarly for division, the statement 'a divided by b' can be written as a ÷ b, or as a/b or as $\frac{a}{b}$, but here the order is critical. a/b is not the same as b/a. The term above the line is called the **numerator**, and the term below the line the **denominator**.

[g] If the reason for this is not immediately clear, consider the second example in paragraph (d) below.

Figure 1.2 Graph of a straight line

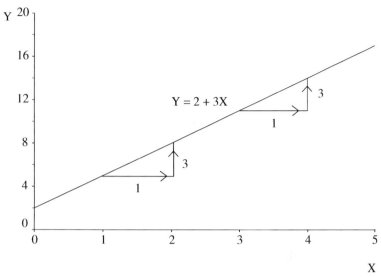

(a) With positive slope Y rises by 3 units when X increases by 1 unit

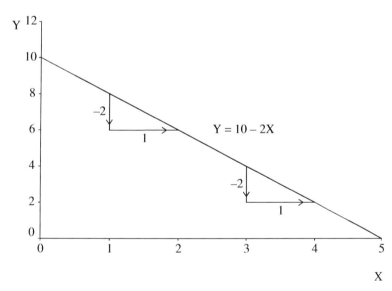

(b) With negative slope Y falls by 2 units when X increases by 1 unit

(b) If the exponent is negative, the result is obtained by *dividing 1* by the number raised to the same positive power. Thus

$$X^{-1}=1/X^1=1/X; \qquad X^{-2}=1/X^2, \quad \text{and so on}$$

(c) We may also be interested in multiplication of powers. The product of a number (X) raised to a power (say, 2) and of the same number raised to another power (say 3) is obtained by *adding* the exponents. Thus

$$X^2 \times X^3 = X^{2+3} = X^5 = X \times X \times X \times X \times X$$

(d) Just as multiplication of powers is done by addition, so division of powers is done by subtraction

$$\frac{X^3}{X^2}=X^{3-2}=X^1=X$$

Also

$$\frac{X^3}{X^3}=X^{3-3}=X^0=1$$

(e) Finally, the exponent of a number may be a fraction, in which case the result is obtained as follows

$$X^{\frac{1}{2}}=\sqrt[2]{X}; \qquad X^{\frac{3}{4}}=(\sqrt[4]{X})^3; \qquad \text{and so on}^h.$$

1.6.2 Logarithms

For every positive number there is a corresponding **logarithm** (log). It is equal to the *power to which a given base must be raised to equal that number.*
Take, for example, the number 100 and the base 10. Then

the log of 100 to the base 10 = 2

because

$$10^2=100$$

i.e. the base 10 raised to the power 2 = 100

Logs can be calculated for any base greater than 1. Base 10 was originally widely used, but with computers the base generally adopted is not 10 but a constant with special mathematical properties known as e, equal to 2.71828 (to 5 decimal places).[4]

Logs to the base e are known as **natural logs**, and unless we explicitly state that we are using logs to base 10, all references in the remainder of this book are to natural logs. The proper abbreviation for natural logs is 'ln', but 'log' is also frequently used and since it is easier to recognize what it refers to we have also adopted this term. Thus if you see a statement such as

---

[h] If the term to be raised to a power is given in brackets it is again essential to first complete the operation in brackets. For example $(a-b)^2$ is calculated by deducting b from a and then squaring the remainder; this is not the same as a^2-b^2.

log INFTMORT, it refers to the natural log of the series in the Poor Law data set for infant mortality.

When logarithms are used in a calculation, the result can always be converted back to ordinary numbers by obtaining the corresponding **exponential** (of a natural log) or **anti-log** (of a log to base 10). As long as that is done consistently, the final result is unaffected by the choice of base.

Calculations using logs

Logs were originally used extensively as a simpler way of doing certain calculations, because it follows from their definition that:

(i)   The *product* of two numbers (X and Y) can be found by *adding* their logs, and then taking the exponential of the result

$$\log (X \times Y) = \log X + \log Y$$

(ii) *Division* of one number by another can be done by *subtracting* their logs, and then taking the exponential of the result

$$\log \left(\frac{X}{Y} \right) = \log X - \log Y$$

(iii) A number can be *raised to a power* by *multiplying the log of that number by the exponent*, and then taking the exponential of the result

$$\log (X^n) = n \times \log X$$

Since square roots and other radicals can be expressed as exponents in the form of a fraction (see §1.6.1) they can also be calculated by multiplying the log of the number by the appropriate fraction, and then taking the exponential of the results

$$\log(\sqrt{X}) = \log (X^{\frac{1}{2}}) = \frac{1}{2} \log X$$

$$\log(\sqrt[4]{X}) = \log (X^{\frac{1}{4}}) = \frac{1}{4} \log X$$

and so on.

1.6.3 Logs as proportions and ratios

The use of logs for calculations has now been largely superseded by computers, but they remain important because of their other properties; in particular, the fact that *they represent proportional rather than absolute changes*. The basis for this statement is shown in panel 1.1.

Logs can also be used to measure the ratio of one series to another. The aim here is not to calculate the value of that ratio in ordinary numbers (as described in §1.6.2) but to have a measure in logs of the ratio.

Panel 1.1   The log of a variable represents proportional changes in that variable

A fundamental property of logarithms is that the *absolute change in the log* of any variable corresponds to the *proportionate* change in that variable.

To illustrate this, consider the following simple example. In column (2), Income is rising by 2 per cent in each period, so the proportionate change in the series, given in column (3), is always 0.02. The natural log of Income is shown in column (4), and the absolute change in this series in column (5). The absolute change in the log of Income in column (5) is constant at 0.0198, corresponding to the constant proportionate change in Income itself in column (3) of 0.02.[*]

(1)	(2)	(3) Change in col. (2) as a proportion	(4)	(5) Absolute change in col. (4)
Period	Income		Log (Income)	
1	100	...	4.6052	...
2	102	0.02	4.6250	0.0198
3	104.04	0.02	4.6448	0.0198
4	106.1208	0.02	4.6646	0.0198
5	108.24322	0.02	4.6844	0.0198

One very useful consequence of this property of logs is that it makes it possible to graph a time series for any variable on a proportionate basis by converting it to logs. When a statistical program is used to plot such a graph it typically offers the choice of making the vertical axis either **linear** or **logarithmic**. If you select the former the program will plot the original values of the variable; if you select the latter (usually referred to as a **log scale**) it will convert the values to logs and plot these.

In the linear form, each absolute increment will be the same: the distance on the vertical axis between, say, 100 and 200 units will be exactly the same as the distance between 800 and 900. This can give a very misleading impression. The change from 100 to 200 represents a doubling of the series; the change from 800 to 900 is an increase of only 12.5 per cent.

[*] It may also be noted that the constant proportionate change in the series is *approximately but not exactly* equal to the constant absolute change in the log of the series. If the constant absolute change in the log of the series is converted back to ordinary numbers (by taking the exponential) the result is *exactly* equal to 1 + the proportionate change. Thus, in this example, the unrounded change in column (5) is 0.0198026, and the exponential of this is exactly 1.02.

By contrast, if the graph is plotted on a logarithmic vertical scale, each proportionate increment will be the same. Thus the distance between 100 and 200 units will be equal to the distance between 800 and 1,600 units, and so on. This conveys a much more accurate impression of the growth of the series.

There is an example of this procedure in the article by Benjamin and Kochin on unemployment.[i] As indicated in table A.4 in appendix A, they use the variable DEMAND to indicate the effects of aggregate demand on unemployment. DEMAND is measured by the *proportionate* deviation of output from its trend value (the higher the proportion, the stronger the demand), where the variable for output is NNP and its trend value is NNP*. We thus have

DEMAND = the ratio of NNP to NNP* = $\log$ NNP $-$ $\log$ NNP*

In the same way a multiplicative relationship between two series can be expressed as the sum of their logs and, as we shall see in chapter 12, logs also play an important part in regression analysis.

1.7 Index numbers

Many of the series used in quantitative analysis take the form of index numbers of the changes in either prices or quantities. Common examples of the former include indices of producer (or factory-gate) prices for industrial products, of retail prices for consumer goods, of wage rates, and of share prices such as the NASDAQ or the FTSE100. Among the latter are indices of industrial or agricultural production, or of total gross national product (GNP), indices of real wages, and indices of the quantity of goods imported.[j]

These indices are constructed from time series on prices and quantities, working either directly with these data or using them in the form of price and quantity **relatives**. Such relatives look exactly like index numbers because they also have one item in the series shown as 100. However, they are merely series that have been converted from an absolute to a relative basis; they do not provide any additional information that is not already contained in the original series on which they are based.

---

[i] Benjamin and Kochin, 'Unemployment', pp. 452–3.

[j] Quantity indices are also referred to as volume indices, or as indices 'in real terms'. A national accounts series such as GNP expressed in monetary units 'at constant prices' (or 'in constant dollars') is also a form of quantity index.

By contrast, a proper **index number** combines information on the changes in prices (or quantities) to create a series that cannot be directly measured in any other way. For example, if an historian has collected information on the changes over time in the prices of a representative selection of goods and services purchased by working-class consumers, she could employ an appropriate procedure to construct an index number of the overall change in their cost of living. There is no way in which she could measure the 'cost of living' directly.

Index numbers play a prominent role in many aspects of historical research and debate. To give just three examples: the index of the prices of consumables and of builders' wage rates compiled by Phelps Brown and Hopkins for the seven centuries from 1260 to 1954 has been used by numerous scholars to indicate the influence of changes in prices and wages during this period.[5] Successive versions of an index of industrial production have been at the heart of the long-running controversies about the pace and pattern of economic growth in Britain during the industrial revolution and in the later slow-down at the end of the century.[6] Indices measuring the relationship between the prices received by Britain, the United States, and other advanced countries for the manufactured goods sold to countries on the periphery, and the prices they paid for the food and raw materials purchased from the periphery, lie at the centre of heated debates about the nature of the relationship between the two groups of countries.[7]

Index numbers are commonly applied in historical research, not only in the representation of the movement of aggregate prices, wages, or output, but also as components of more complex models of historical processes. In this role they have many of the attributes of a 'black box', in that it is extremely hard to determine what is responsible for the behaviour of a particular index number over time, and the researcher is implicitly putting faith in the person(s) who constructed the index. Unfortunately, not all index numbers warrant this faith, either because of the low quality of their ingredients, or because the recipe for their making has not been followed properly.

Given the general significance of index numbers, and given our overall strategy in this book of explaining, rather than assuming, it seems important to provide guidance on how index numbers are constructed and why. This may enable readers to gain some deeper understanding of their limitations, and so provide some basis for scrutinizing the series used by historians. However, since none of what follows in this book requires a knowledge of index numbers, we have postponed the discussion to appendix B, at the end of the book.

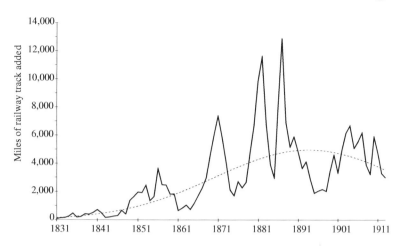

Figure 1.3 Miles of railway track added in the United States, 1831–1913 with fitted trend

1.8 Trends and fluctuations

Many of the time series that are of interest to historians display a combination of long-term growth or decline and short-term fluctuations. This applies, for example, to economic series such as the tonnage of ships built or index numbers of wholesale prices; to demographic series such as birth or marriage rates; and to social series such as the number of indictable offences reported to the police or the number of deaths from suicide. Both features – the trend and the cycle – are well illustrated by the annual data on the miles of railway track added in the United States from 1831 to 1913 (see the solid line in figure 1.3).

The secular **trend** in a series represents the broad pattern of movement that is sustained in the same direction over long periods of time. It may be interpreted as the general direction of movement ignoring all shorter-term variations, and may indicate either long-term growth or decline, or it may be broadly stable, with neither growth nor decline. In figure 1.3 the trend in railway construction indicated by the broken line is initially upward for some six decades, and then turns downward from the 1890s.

Superimposed on the long-run trend are varying types of **fluctuation** of shorter duration. If a series is available for periods shorter than a year it may show more or less regular **seasonal** fluctuations. These may occur as a direct result of the weather (sales of fuel higher in the winter, building activity higher in the summer) or of seasonal harvests, as with grain or cotton. Or they may reflect the indirect impact of the seasons on social habits, as seen in the tendency for marriages in pre-industrial pastoral communities to take place after the spring season of lambing and calving. Holidays taken at Christmas and Easter also cause regular seasonal fluctuations.

Annual series typically show less regular fluctuations. These are of broadly two types. They may reflect some recurrent cyclical pattern such as the business cycle experienced in many economies. This typically consisted of a downswing in trade, employment, and other indicators of economic activity from peak to trough, followed by an upswing to the next peak, the whole cycle usually lasting for between seven and 10 years. These economic cycles were in turn an important influence on a range of social, political, and demographic variables such as marriage rates and elections.[8] Fluctuations in economic activity of considerably longer duration – by some accounts as long as 60 years – have also been detected by some scholars, but are more controversial.[9]

Alternatively, the fluctuations may be completely irregular, occurring either in response to exceptional events such as wars or floods, gold discoveries or dramatic new inventions, that affect either the country itself or its major trading partners. Or they may simply be random variations in an individual series as a consequence, for example, of idiosyncratic human behaviour.

Some discussions of the analysis of time series suggest that it is possible to split the series into these different components, producing separate series for the trend, seasonal fluctuations (where applicable), regular fluctuations, and a residual of irregular movements. However, some of the procedures suggested for splitting year-to-year movements into regular and irregular fluctuations are very unsatisfactory, and can actually generate spurious fluctuations which were not present in the original series, while others are mathematically very complex and well beyond the level of this text.[10] For annual series we prefer, therefore, to make only a single division into long-run trend and short-term fluctuations, and in the following section we will describe a method for doing this.

1.8.1 Measuring the trend by a moving average

There are two main procedures for determining the trend in a time series. The simplest is to calculate a **centred moving average**. The other involves fitting a trend line to the data by regression analysis. This is a more reliable but also a more complex procedure, and we must defer its introduction until we have developed the necessary procedures in subsequent chapters, though we may note that the trend line in figure 1.3 was obtained in this way.[11]

The procedure for deriving a moving average is very straightforward. It is calculated directly from the original time series by choosing an appropriate number of years (for an annual series, or months for a monthly series) and calculating the average of the series for those years. The selected period of time is then moved forward one year, and the average calculated for that new period, and so on until the series is completed.

It is conventional to choose an odd number of years for the moving average, so that as each average is struck it can be allocated to the central year of the time period to which it relates. The longer the period that is chosen, the more the fluctuations will be smoothed out, but the choice must depend to some extent on the length of the underlying time series.

If dealing with time series covering several centuries, as Wrigley and Schofield were in their investigation of the long-term trends in English fertility and mortality, an average as long as 25 years may be appropriate.[12]

For shorter series, averages of between five and 11 years are common, and the more regular the periodicity in the underlying series, the more effectively a moving average covering the same period will smooth out the series. For example, if the series had alternating peaks and troughs, both occurring every nine years with unfailing regularity, a nine-year moving average would completely eliminate the cycle and leave only a smooth trend. Unfortunately such regularity is seldom if ever encountered in historical data.

We can illustrate the procedure by calculating an 11-year moving average for the first 20 years of the data on railway construction in the United States (see table 1.1). To obtain the 11-year moving average we start with the original series for railway miles added in column (1) of table 1.1. In column (2), the average of the first 11 years 1831–41 is calculated. This is $(72 + 134 + \ldots + 516 + 717)/11 = 319.3$, and so 319.3 is placed opposite the middle of the 11 years, 1836, to give the first item in the moving average. The average of the next 11 years, 1832–42 ($= 357.4$) is then allocated to 1837, and so on until the column ends with the average for 1840–50 ($= 610.8$), placed opposite 1845.

We have already noted that one defect of moving averages is that they are capable of creating spurious cyclical fluctuations. This is a very serious weakness when the procedure is intended to identify shorter cycles in the data, but matters less if the aim is merely to indicate the long-term trend. A second weakness of the moving average is evident from the illustration in table 1.1: the procedure leaves blank years at the beginning and end of the sequence, and it is thus impossible to examine the precise relationship between the original data and the trend for these missing years.

A further problem can be seen from a comparison of the 11-year

Table 1.1 Calculation of 11-year moving average and deviations from trend, miles of railway track added in the United States, 1831–1850

	(1)	(2)	(3)	(4)
	Original series	*Trend*	*De-trended series*	
	Railway miles added	Centred 11-year moving average	Original data as % of trend	Deviation of original data from trend as % of trend
1831	72			
1832	134			
1833	151			
1834	253			
1835	465			
1836	175	319.3	54.8	−45.2
1837	224	357.4	62.7	−37.3
1838	416	359.6	115.7	15.7
1839	389	363.4	107.1	7.1
1840	516	363.6	141.9	41.9
1841	717	348.4	205.8	105.8
1842	491	393.2	124.9	24.9
1843	159	409.0	38.9	−61.1
1844	192	495.6	38.7	−61.3
1845	256	610.8	41.9	−58.1
1846	297			
1847	668			
1848	398			
1849	1,369			
1850	1,656			

Notes:
(1) Brinley Thomas, *Migration and Economic Growth*, Cambridge University Press, 1954, p. 288.
(2) See text.
(3) $= (1)/(2) \times 100$.
(4) $= [(1) - (2)]/(2) \times 100$.

moving average shown in figure 1.4 (a) with the fitted trend in figure 1.3. It is immediately evident that the former does not smooth out the fluctuations as successfully as the latter. It would, of course, be possible to take an even longer number of years, say 25, but only at the cost of still longer periods at the beginning and end of the series for which there would be no trend value. One additional disadvantage of the moving-average procedure is that it has no mathematical form independent of the data from which it is constructed, and so cannot be extrapolated by formula to cover earlier or later periods. Despite these weaknesses it is very simple to construct and has been widely used by historians.

We have so far referred to centred moving averages, but it is also possible to construct other forms of moving average. In particular, if the focus of interest is the experience of the most recent years, it would be appropriate to calculate an average of (say) the last five years in the series at any given date, and to place the average against that date. This series would then be moved forward one year at a time, so that at each date it provided a measure of the movements in the underlying series over the last five years. The 'tracking polls' used to provide a rolling measure of the most recent poll results during the course of an election are one variant of this. More elaborate variants might attach greater importance to the experience of the most recent years by calculating a weighted average (see §2.2.2), with progressively diminishing weights for the more distant years.

1.8.2 Measuring the fluctuations by the ratio to the trend

Having calculated the long-run trend in the series by means of a moving average or a fitted trend, it is then possible to derive a **de-trended series** that measures the remaining fluctuations.[13] This can be done by simply calculating the absolute deviation from trend, i.e. the absolute difference between the original series and the trend. This is satisfactory if the underlying series is broadly constant over time, but not if it is changing in value. In the latter case, for example, if the series were increasing strongly, a deviation of (say) 10 units that might seem relatively large at the beginning of the series would be relatively small by the end. It is generally better, therefore, to measure the **ratio of the original series to the trend** by expressing it as a percentage of the trend.

This is done in column (3) of table 1.1, by dividing the original series by the centred 11-year moving average. Years such as 1838 and 1841, when railway construction was booming and the series was above its trend, have values greater than 100; years such as 1836 and 1843, when construction

Figure 1.4 Miles of railway track added in the United States, 1831–1913

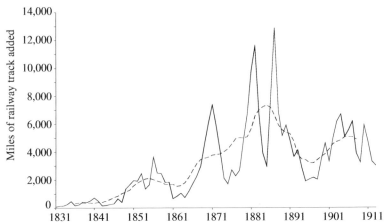

(a) Original series with 11-year moving average

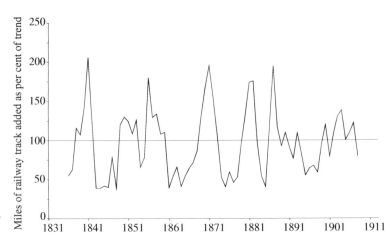

(b) De-trended series

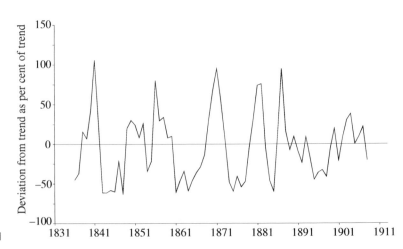

(c) Percentage deviation from trend

was depressed and below its trend, have values below 100. The trend has been removed from the series, and what is left in column (3) is the remaining component: the regular and irregular fluctuations. The corresponding de-trended series calculated with the 11-year moving average is shown in figure 1.4 (b).[k]

Much the same result can be obtained by calculating the **percentage deviation from the trend.** This is equal to the absolute difference between the trend and the original series, expressed as a percentage of the trend, as is done in column (4) of table 1.1 and figure 1.4 (c). This is also a de-trended series and will show exactly the same fluctuations as column (3). The only difference is that the former fluctuates around a mean of 100 per cent and the latter around a deviation of 0 per cent.

When dealing with monthly time series, or other periods of less than a year, it is possible to make separate estimates of the seasonal variations and to separate these from the residual cyclical and irregular fluctuations. Such seasonal adjustment plays no part in any further work in this text, but it is a useful illustration of the way in which historical data – for example a series for birth rates or for agricultural production – can be decomposed into these three elements: long-run trend, recurrent seasonal fluctuations, and residual fluctuations, thus enabling the historian to analyse separately each of these contributions to the overall change in the series. A brief account of one simple seasonal adjustment procedure is set out in panel 1.2 for those who wish to see how this three-way split is made.[14]

---

[k] Since the ratio of two series can be calculated as the difference between their respective logarithms, a de-trended series can also be derived in this way, as with the DEMAND variable measured by Benjamin and Kochin, 'Unemployment', pp. 452–3 (see also §1.6.3).

Panel 1.2   Decomposition of a time series into trend, seasonal factors, and residual fluctuations

This panel describes a simple procedure for splitting a time series into trend, seasonal factors, and residual fluctuations, using quarterly data on bankruptcy in England for 1780–84 to illustrate the calculations.* The original data for the five years are set out with a column for each quarter in row (1) of table 1.2. The trend is calculated as a 25-quarter moving average over the longer period 1777–87 (so that there are trend values for all quarters from 1780 I to 1784 IV), and is given in row (2).

Row (3) gives the original series as a ratio to the trend for each quarter and this reveals the seasonal pattern in the bankruptcy statistics. The main seasonal feature is clearly the persistently low level in the third quarter of the year. Hoppit attributes this primarily to the strong favourable effect of the grain harvest on a wide range of activities and to the higher level of building. Conversely, bankruptcies were at their highest in the winter months, and this is also reflected in the ratios for the first and fourth quarters in row (3).

The temptation at this point is to calculate the average of the quarterly ratios for the five-year period, but a more accurate measure is obtained by calculating the ratio of the five-year totals for the original series and the trend. This is given in row (4). Row (5) then makes a minor correction to these ratios; the average of the four quarterly ratios in row (4) is 0.9721, and each quarter must be multiplied by 1/0.9721. As a result of doing this, the average of the corrected adjustment factors in row (5), weighted by the five-year total of the trend, is exactly equal to 1. This in turn ensures that the total number of bankruptcies over the five years is not changed by the seasonal adjustment to the component quarters.

The original series is then divided by the adjustment factors in row (5) to give the seasonally adjusted series. As can be seen in row (6), the low autumn levels are raised and the higher levels in the other three quarters are all reduced. This series thus reflects both the trend in bankruptcy and the remaining irregular fluctuations from quarter to quarter *after the seasonal variations have been removed.*

---

* The data are taken from Julian Hoppit, *Risk and Failure in English Business, 1700–1800,* Cambridge University Press, 1987, pp. 187–96. For his own de-seasonalized series Hoppit used a 61-quarter moving average, so our results are not exactly the same as his, though the differences are small. For his interesting discussion of the short-term fluctuations in bankruptcy see *ibid.,* pp. 104–21.

The final adjustment, made in row (7), also eliminates the trend, thus leaving only the irregular fluctuations in a de-trended and de-seasonalized series. Since in this case there was little movement in the trend over these years (see row (2)), the series in row (7) does not diverge much from the series in row (6).

The decomposition of the original data into the three elements is now easily checked. For example, for the first quarter of 1780, if we multiply the trend (row (2)), by the recurrent seasonal factor (row (5)), and by the residual fluctuation (row (7)), and divide the result by 100 we get ($133.32 \times 1.093 \times 83.03$)/100 = 121, which is the value of the original series in row (1).

Table 1.2 Calculation of a seasonally adjusted series, bankruptcy in England, 1780–1784

	QI	QII	QIII	QIV
(1) Original series, number of bankruptcies ($=$ B)				
1780	121	117	74	123
1781	116	110	97	128
1782	151	144	110	144
1783	148	144	101	128
1784	148	145	94	150
(2) Trend: 25-quarter moving average ($=$ T)				
1780	133.3	133.2	131.8	132.7
1781	132.7	131.6	127.6	127.8
1782	126.2	125.5	123.6	125.0
1783	124.5	126.2	125.0	126.9
1784	127.1	127.7	127.4	129.0
(3) Ratio of original series to trend ($=$ B/T)				
1780	0.908	0.879	0.562	0.927
1781	0.874	0.836	0.760	1.002
1782	1.197	1.147	0.890	1.152
1783	1.189	1.141	0.808	1.009
1784	1.165	0.738	0.738	1.162

Table 1.2 (*cont.*)

	QI	QII	QIII	QIV
(4) Initial seasonal adjustment factors				
Five-year totals, 1780–4				
Original series	684	660	476	673
Trend	643.72	644.12	635.40	641.40
Ratio of original to trend	1.063	1.025	0.749	1.049
(5) Corrected seasonal adjustment factors ($=S$)				
	1.0931	1.0541	0.7707	1.0794
(6) Seasonally adjusted series ($=B/S=T\times R$)				
1780	110.7	111.0	96.0	113.9
1781	106.1	104.3	125.9	118.6
1782	138.1	136.6	142.7	133.4
1783	135.4	136.6	131.1	118.6
1784	135.4	137.6	122.0	139.0
(7) Residual fluctuations in de-trended and de-seasonalized series ($=B/(T\times S)=R$)				
1780	83.0	83.4	72.9	85.9
1781	80.0	79.3	98.6	92.8
1782	109.5	108.8	115.5	106.7
1783	108.8	108.3	104.8	93.4
1784	106.5	107.7	95.7	107.7

Notes:
(1) Hoppit, *Risk and Failure*, pp. 195–5.
(2) 25-quarter moving average calculated on quarterly series for 1777–87.
(3) $=$ Row (1)/Row (2).
(4) The five-year total of row (1) divided by the five-year total of row (2).
(5) The quarterly correction factors in row (4) average 0.9721, and each is raised by 1/0.9721. This ensures that the five-year total for row (6) will be the same as for row (1).
(6) $=$ Row (1)/Row (5) $\times$ 100.
(7) $=$ Row (1)/(Row (2) $\times$ Row (5)) $\times$ 100.

Notes

[1] Many statistical textbooks treat these as two separate levels of measurement, with the ratio as the highest level. The distinction between them is that the interval level does not have an inherently determined zero point. However, this issue is hardly ever encountered in historical research; the example usually given relates to temperature scales in which 0° is an arbitrarily defined point on the scale but does not represent an absence of temperature.

[2] In some contexts it might be appropriate to think of an **infinite** as opposed to a **finite** population. In the case of the mills this would consist of all the mills which might hypothetically ever have been constructed in the past or which will be constructed in future; see further §9.2.3 below.

[3] For a brief introduction to general sampling procedures, see H. M. Blalock, *Social Statistics*, 2nd edn., McGraw-Hill, 1979. R. S. Schofield, 'Sampling in historical research', in E. A. Wrigley (ed.), *Nineteenth-Century Society, Essays in the Use of Quantitative Methods for the Study of Social Data*, Cambridge University Press, 1972, pp. 146–90, is an excellent discussion of sampling procedures in an historical context.

[4] It is not necessary to know any more about the constant e, but for those who are curious it is equal to the limiting value of the exponential expression

$$\left(1 + \frac{1}{n}\right)^n$$

as n approaches infinity. For example, if n is taken as 10,000, e = 2.71815, and taking higher values of n will not change the first three decimal places. The value of 2.71828 was calculated by taking n as 1,000,000.

[5] Henry Phelps Brown and Sheila V. Hopkins, 'Seven centuries of the price of consumables, compared with builders' wage rates', *Economica*, 23, 1956, reprinted in Henry Phelps Brown and Sheila V. Hopkins, *A Perspective of Wages and Prices*, Methuen, 1981, pp. 13–59. For a consumer price index for the United States for 1774–1974, see Paul A. David and Peter Solar, 'A bicentenary contribution to the history of the cost of living in America', *Research in Economic History*, 2, 1977, pp. 1–80.

[6] The first index of industrial production in Britain was compiled by Walther G. Hoffmann, *British Industry, 1700–1950*, Basil Blackwell, 1955. There have been several subsequent alternative indices, including Phyllis Deane and W. A. Cole, *British Economic Growth 1688–1959*, Cambridge University Press, 1962; W. Arthur Lewis, *Growth and Fluctuations, 1870–1913*, Allen & Unwin, 1978; N. F. R. Crafts, *British Economic Growth during the Industrial Revolution*, Cambridge University Press, 1985; and Robert V. Jackson, 'Rates of industrial growth during the industrial revolution', *Economic History Review*, 45, 1992, pp. 1–23. The corresponding index for the United States is Edwin Frickey, *Production in the United States 1860–1914*, Harvard University Press, 1947.

[7] For an excellent introduction to the debate about the terms of trade see John Spraos, 'The statistical debate on the net barter terms of trade between primary commodities and manufactures', *Economic Journal*, 90, 1980, pp. 107–28.

[8] Among the classic studies of business cycles are T. S. Ashton, *Economic Fluctuations in England, 1700–1800*, Oxford University Press, 1959; A. D. Gayer, W. W. Rostow and A. J. Schwartz, *The Growth and Fluctuation of the British Economy, 1790–1850*, Oxford University Press, 1953; and Arthur F. Burns and W. C. Mitchell, *Measuring Business Cycles*, NBER, 1947.

[9] Solomos Solomou, *Phases of Economic Growth, 1850–1973, Kondratieff Waves and Kuznets Swings*, Cambridge University Press, 1987, is a sceptical investigation of the evidence for these longer fluctuations in Britain, Germany, France, and the United States.

[10] One such technique is known as spectral analysis; for a brief non-mathematical introduction see C. W. J. Granger and C. M. Elliott, 'A fresh look at wheat prices and markets in the eighteenth century', *Economic History Review*, 20, 1967, pp. 257–65.

[11] The procedure for fitting a simple linear trend is described in §4.2.5. The more widely used trend based on a logarithmic transformation is explained in panel 12.1 of chapter 12, and other non-linear trends (such as the one illustrated in figure 1.3) are introduced in §12.4.

[12] E. A. Wrigley and R. S. Schofield, *The Population History of England 1541–1871*, Edward Arnold, 1981, pp. 402–53.

[13] Examples of historical studies based heavily on patterns determined by such a distinction between the trend and the cycle include Brinley Thomas, *Migration and Economic Growth*, Cambridge University Press, 1954; A. G. Ford, *The Gold Standard 1880–1914, Britain and Argentina*, Oxford University Press, 1962; and Jeffrey G. Williamson, *American Growth and the Balance of Payments 1820–1913, A Study of the Long Swing*, University of North Carolina Press, 1964.

[14] There are alternative methods for calculating seasonally adjusted series using more advanced statistical techniques; one such method is described in panel 12.2 in §12.4.

CHAPTER 2

Descriptive statistics

This chapter presents an introduction to the key elements of **descriptive statistics**: the ways in which quantitative information can be presented and described. The first step in the analysis of quantitative data is its organization and presentation in tables and graphs. The basic features of the data – such as its central or most common values and the way the observations are distributed around these central values – can then be summarized in various ways.

2.1 Presentation of numerical data

2.1.1 Frequency distributions

Quantitative data in their raw form consist of a series of numbers or categories. For example, the Poor Law data on *per capita* relief expenditure in 1831 by the 24 parishes in Kent could be set out in its original sequence as in table 2.1, with the data rounded to one decimal place.

Even with 24 observations it is difficult to get much sense of the data in this form. It would help a little if the values were arranged in ascending or descending order of magnitude (known as an **array**). This would immediately show the highest and lowest values and give some indication of the most common level of payment, but with a large number of observations it would still be hard to interpret the information in this form.

A much clearer picture can be obtained if the data are re-arranged as a **frequency distribution**. This is the most common form in which data are summarized and presented. With a discrete variable (see §1.3.3) it makes sense to measure the frequency of occurrence of *each* of the values. For example, if a lecturer had set an examination with nine questions, she might find it informative to compile a frequency distribution showing how many candidates had answered each question.

However, this is less appropriate for a continuous variable such as the

Table 2.1 *Per capita* expenditure on relief in 24 Kent parishes in 1831 (shillings)

20.4	29.1	14.9	24.1	18.2	20.7
8.1	14.0	18.4	34.5	16.1	24.6
25.4	12.6	13.3	27.3	29.6	13.6
11.4	21.5	20.9	11.6	18.2	37.9

payments of relief, since we would not normally be interested in minute differences, e.g. in finding out how many parishes paid 18.1 shillings, and how many paid 18.2 shillings, etc. Instead we choose appropriate **class intervals** and note the frequency of the occurrence of payments in each class.

For table 2.2 we have chosen seven class intervals, each with a width of 5 shillings; so that all the payments in the first interval are equal to or greater than 5 shillings (abbreviated to ≥5) but less than 10 shillings (< 10); those in the next are equal to or greater than 10 shillings but less than 15 shillings, and so on.[1] The **frequency** is shown in column (3) and the **relative frequency** in column (4). In order to show how the frequency is derived the underlying tally is shown in column (2), but this would not normally be included in a frequency table. The relative frequency shows the share of the

Table 2.2 Frequency, relative frequency, and cumulative frequency of *per capita* relief payments in Kent in 1831

(1) Class intervals (shillings)	(2) Tally	(3) Frequency (*f*)	(4) Relative frequency (%) (*f*/n × 100)	(5) Cumulative frequency	(6) Cumulative relative frequency (%)
≥5 but <10	1	1	4.2	1	4.2
≥10 but <15	++++ 1 1	7	29.2	8	33.4
≥15 but <20	1 1 1 1	4	16.6	12	50.0
≥20 but <25	++++ 1	6	25.0	18	75.0
≥25 but <30	1 1 1 1	4	16.6	22	91.6
≥30 but <35	1	1	4.2	23	95.8
≥35 but <40	1	1	4.2	24	100.0
		$\overline{24}$	$\overline{100.0}$		

Note:

In column (1) ≥ stands for 'equal to or greater than', and < for 'less than'.

observations in each class interval. In table 2.2 this is expressed as a percentage of the total (adding to 100), but it could equally well be a proportion (adding to 1).

It is sometimes also useful to know the **cumulative frequency** of a variable. This gives the number of observations which are less than or equal to any selected value or class interval. The **cumulative relative frequency** gives the corresponding proportions or percentages. For example, we can see from column (5) of table 2.2 that *per capita* relief payments were less than 20 shillings in 12 Kent parishes, and from column (6) that this represented 50 per cent of the parishes.

By summarizing the data in the form of a frequency distribution some information is lost, but it is now much easier to get a clear idea of the pattern of relief payments in the Kent parishes.

Number and width of the class intervals

The precise number and width of the class (or cell) intervals in a frequency table is a matter of judgement. Too many narrow intervals and the pattern is again obscured; too few and too much information is lost. For example, in relation to table 2.2, covering a sample of 24 parishes, having (say) 2 classes would tell us very little, whereas 20 classes would be little improvement on the presentation of all the data in table 2.1. A rough rule of thumb is that it is usually best to have between five and 20 classes, depending on the number of observations.

It is preferable if the width can be made uniform throughout. Classes of unequal width (e.g. 10 – 14.9, 15 – 24.9, 25 – 29.9) are confusing to the reader and a nuisance in computations. However, this is not always possible. For example, when there are a few extreme values (as in data on wealth holdings) the intervals may have to be changed to accommodate the very uneven distribution.

It is sometimes necessary to work with open-ended classes, e.g. 'under 10 shillings' or '50 shillings and over'. However, if the data were given in this form in the original source this can cause problems in calculations that require a figure for the mid-point of the class intervals (as in §2.4). At the lower end it may not be plausible to assume that the values are (roughly) evenly distributed all the way down to a lower bound of zero. At the upper end, in the absence of information about the values in excess of the lower limit given for the open-ended class, the best that can be done is to make an informed guess about the likely values within this class.

Figure 2.1 Bar chart of number of workhouses in selected counties in 1831

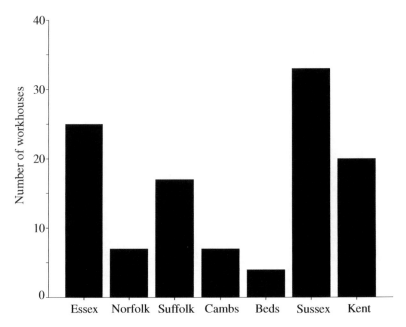

2.1.2 Bar charts and histograms

It is often useful for both statistician and reader to present results in a form that can be interpreted visually. Two common methods of doing this with frequency distributions are bar charts and histograms.

Bar charts are commonly used to present data on the frequency distribution of qualitative data, or data which falls into discrete categories. Thus the number of workhouses in the sample parishes in seven counties in the south and south-east of England could be represented in a bar chart such as figure 2.1, in which there is a bar for each of the selected counties, and the *height* of each bar indicates the number (or frequency) of workhouses reported in the Poor Law data set. There is no statistical convention relating to the width of each bar, though it is visually more appealing to present bars of common width for each category equally spaced.

Histograms are used where the frequencies to be charted are grouped in class intervals. Each bar (or rectangle) represents either the absolute number or the proportion of cases with values in the class interval. To illustrate the construction of histograms we will use the Poor Law data on *per capita* relief payments by all 311 parishes. The information is set out in table 2.3 using eight class intervals, each with a width of 6 shillings. The number of parishes in each class is given in column (2), the corresponding

Table 2.3 Frequency of *per capita* relief payments in 311 parishes in 1831

(1) Class intervals (shillings)	(2) Frequency	(3) Relative frequency	(4) Cumulative relative frequency
≥0 but <6	6	1.93	1.93
≥6 but <12	78	25.08	27.01
≥12 but <18	93	29.90	56.91
≥18 but <24	63	20.26	77.17
≥24 but <30	46	14.79	91.96
≥30 but <36	17	5.47	97.43
≥36 but <42	5	1.61	99.04
≥42 but <48	3	0.96	100.00
	311	100.00	

Note:
In column (1) ≥ stands for 'equal to or greater than', and < for 'less than'.

relative frequency in column (3), and the cumulative relative frequency in column (4). The relative frequencies in column (3) are shown with a total of 100. It would make no difference if they were all divided by 100 and summed to 1.

Since there is by construction a strictly proportional relationship between the absolute frequency in column (2) and the relative frequency in column (3) – the latter is always exactly a fraction of the former (in this case, equal to $1 \div 311$) – it will make no difference whatsoever to the appearance of the histogram whether we plot it using column (2) or column (3).

If it is possible to keep all class intervals *the same width*, then the visual impact of the histogram is effectively determined by the height of each of the rectangles. Strictly speaking, however, it is the *area* of each bar that is proportional to the absolute or relative frequency of the cases in the corresponding class interval.

The first two versions of the histogram for the *per capita* relief payments by all 311 parishes in figure 2.2 are of this type. In (a) there are eight class intervals as in table 2.3, each with a width of 6 shillings; in (b) the number of intervals is increased to 23, each with a width of only 2 shillings. For (b) the horizontal axis is labelled by the mid-point of each range.

Figure 2.2
Histograms with
different class
intervals for *per
capita* relief
payments in 311
parishes in 1831

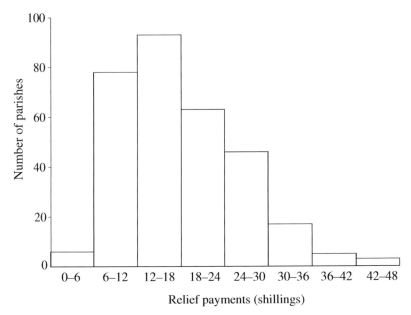

(a) With 8 equal class intervals, each 6 shillings wide

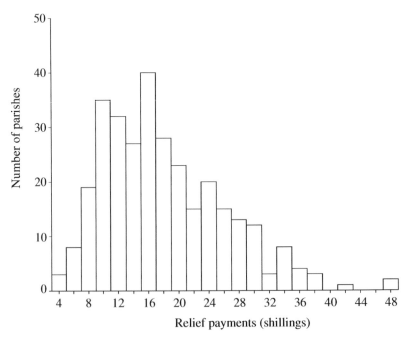

(b) With 23 equal class intervals, each 2 shillings wide

Figure 2.2 (*cont.*)

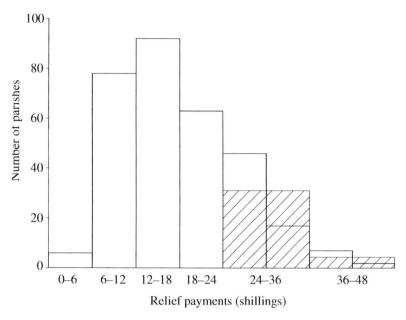

(c) With 6 class intervals of unequal width

In this case we could select these (or other) class intervals with equal widths because we have the data for every individual parish in the data set. But what would we do if the data had already been grouped before it was made available to us, and the class intervals were not of equal width? Assume, for example, that the information on relief payments in the 311 parishes had been published with only six class intervals, the first four with a width of 6 shillings as in table 2.3, and the last two with a width of 12 shillings (i.e. with absolute frequencies of 63 and 8, and relative frequencies of 20.26 and 2.57).

Since the *width* of these last two intervals has been *doubled*, they must be shown on the histogram with their *height* set at only *half* that of the 6 shilling intervals. The *areas* (i.e. width × height) of the two sets of intervals will then be proportional. In figure 2.2 (c) the original eight-class equal-width histogram of figure 2.2 (a) is reproduced, with the alternative rectangles for the two wider class intervals superimposed on the last four intervals.

The height of the first of these 12-shilling intervals is set at 31.5, equal to half the 63 parishes in this class; the height of the second at 4, equal to half of the eight parishes in this final class. It is easy to see that when done on this basis the area of each of the new rectangles is exactly equal to that of the two corresponding rectangles in the previous version.

The advantage of the histogram in such situations is thus that despite the change in width of the intervals it is still possible to represent either the absolute or the relative frequency of the cases in each class interval by comparison of the *area* of their rectangles. Because it is the area rather than the height that is proportional to the frequency, it is always wise when looking at a histogram to refer first to the horizontal axis to ascertain the widths, and not to be misled by the visual impact of the height of each of the columns.

2.1.3 Frequency curves

Imagine a line that is drawn so that it passes through the mid-point of each of the class intervals of a frequency distribution for a *continuous* variable such as *per capita* relief payments. This graph is called a **frequency polygon.** If the histogram is like the one in figure 2.2 (a), with relatively few cases and wide class intervals, the polygon will look very different to the histogram. There will be numerous triangles that fall within the polygon but lie outside the histogram, and others that are outside the polygon but inside the histogram. However, if we look closely at figure 2.3 (a), in which the two graphs are shown on the same diagram, we see that all these triangles form exactly matching pairs, so that the area under the two graphs is *exactly* the same.

Now assume that we can gradually reduce the width of the class intervals to take full advantage of the whole scale over which a continuous variable is measured.[a] As we increased the number of rectangles in the histogram and narrowed their width, we would find that the shape of the polygons drawn through the mid-points of the rectangles approximated more and more closely to a smooth curve. We would ultimately get a perfectly smooth **frequency curve.**

It was noted in §2.1.2 that the relative frequencies in column (3) of table 2.3 could be treated as if they summed to 1, and also that the areas of the rectangles making up a histogram are proportional to the relative frequencies. Since together the rectangles cover all the class intervals, the *total area under the histogram* can also be thought of as equal to 1. We have now seen how we might in principle obtain a perfectly smooth frequency curve, and that the area under such a curve is identical to the area under a histogram. Thus the total *area under the frequency curve* can also be thought of as equal

---

[a] We also need to assume that we can increase the number of cases we are dealing with (i.e. that we can work with very much larger numbers than the 311 parishes in our Poor Law data set). By increasing the number we avoid the irregularities in the distribution that might occur with small numbers of cases in narrow class intervals.

Figure 2.3 *Per capita* relief payments in 311 parishes in 1831

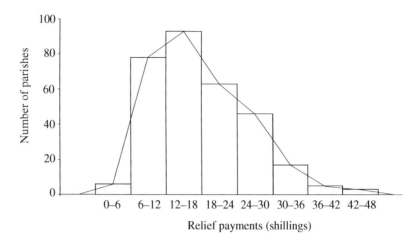

(a) Histogram and frequency polygon

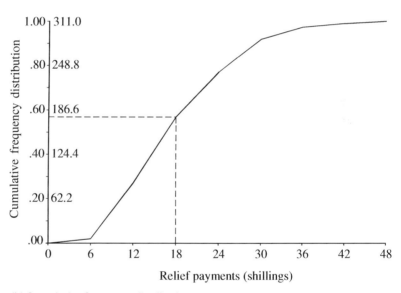

(b) Cumulative frequency distribution

to 1. This simple but important idea of the area under a smooth frequency curve will be extremely useful in relation to the normal distribution, a concept which plays a major part in many of the statistical techniques we employ later in this book.

A different form of frequency polygon can also be used to display the **cumulative frequency distribution** defined in §2.1.1. This diagram (also known as an **ogive**) is illustrated in figure 2.3 (b) with the data from column (4) of table 2.3 for the *per capita* relief payments by the 311 parishes. The scale shown on the horizontal axis indicates the *upper* limit of the successive class intervals, and that on the vertical axis indicates both the cumulative relative and cumulative absolute frequency. (The values for the latter are obtained by cumulating column (2) of table 2.3.)

The curve of the cumulative frequency distribution traces either the proportion or the number of cases that are *less than* the corresponding value of the variable shown on the horizontal axis. Since there is an exact correspondence between the absolute and relative frequencies, the two graphs are identical. For example, the position marked off by the broken lines in figure 2.3 (b) indicates that relief payments of less than 18 shillings per person were made by 177 parishes, corresponding to a proportion of 0.569 (56.9 per cent). The s-shape is characteristic of such cumulative frequency diagrams.

2.2 Measures of central tendency

If we refer again to the data set in table 2.1, there are 24 observations, each giving the *per capita* expenditure on relief in one of the Kent parishes in 1831. Grouping the data in class intervals in a frequency table (such as table 2.2), and plotting this as a histogram, provides a more helpful indication of some features of the data, but this is neither a convenient nor a precise way in which to *summarize* the information. In order to achieve this we need to determine three aspects of the data:

(a) Which are the *central* (i.e. the most common or typical) values within the distribution?

(b) How is the distribution *spread* (dispersed) around those central values?

(c) What is the *shape* of the distribution?

Each of these features can be described by one or more simple statistics. These are the basic elements of descriptive statistics, and together they provide a precise and comprehensive summary of a data set. We shall now look at each in turn.

There are three principal measures that are used to locate the most common or most typical cases. They are referred to collectively as **measures of central tendency.**

2.2.1 The mean, the median, and the mode

(a) The **arithmetic mean**, also called the arithmetic average, is obtained by adding up all the values and dividing this total by the number of observations.[b] It is usually denoted by $\overline{X}$ (X bar) when referring to a sample, and by μ (lower case Greek mu) for the corresponding population. Thus

$$\overline{X} = \frac{\Sigma X}{n} \tag{2.1}$$

where n is the number of observations in the data set for which there are values for the variable, X.[c]

(b) The **median** is the value that has one-half of the number of observations respectively above and below it, when the series is set out in an ascending or descending array. Its value thus depends entirely on whatever happens to be the value of the observation in the middle of the array; it is not influenced by the values of any of the other observations in the series.

For example, if there are five observations, the median is the value of the third observation, and there are two cases above this and two below. When there is an even number of observations, the average of the two middle observations is taken as the median.

(c) The **mode** is the value that occurs most frequently (i.e. is most fashionable). When data are grouped in class intervals the mode is taken as the mid-point of the category with the highest frequency. In a frequency distribution the mode is represented by the highest point on the curve. A distribution may have more than one mode; one with two modes is described as **bimodal.**

---

[b] This measure is frequently referred to simply as the mean. When no further qualification is given the term 'mean' can be understood to refer to the arithmetic mean. However, it is also possible to calculate other means, such as a **geometric mean**, and when there is any possibility of confusion the full titles should be used. The geometric mean is calculated by multiplying all the values and taking the appropriate root: thus if there are five terms in a series $(X_1, X_2, \ldots, X_5)$ the geometric mean would be the fifth root of their product:

$$\sqrt[5]{X_1 \times X_2 \times X_3 \times X_4 \times X_5}$$

[c] We will follow the convention of using lower case n to refer to the number of observations in a sample. The symbol for the corresponding number in the population is upper case N.

The three primary measures can be illustrated with the following simple data set containing seven observations set out in ascending order:

> 3, 5, 5, 7, 9, 10 and 45
> The arithmetic mean $= \Sigma X/n = 84/7 = 12^d$
> The median $= 7$
> The mode is 5

The most useful of these measures for most purposes are the mean and the median. The mean is generally to be preferred because it is based on all the observations in the series, but this can also be its weakness if there are some extreme values. For example, in the series just given the mean is raised by the final very large value, whereas this observation has no effect on the median. It is a matter of judgement in any particular study whether or not to give weight to the extreme values in reporting a measure of central tendency. For the data on RELIEF in table 2.1 the mean is 20.3 and the median 19.4.

The mode is the only one of these three measures that can be used with either nominal or ordinal level measurements.

2.2.2   Weighted averages and standardized rates

The simple mean defined in §2.2.1 effectively treats all n observations as having equal importance, and is the measure of central tendency most often referred to in statistical work. However, for certain purposes it may not be appropriate to give the same weight to each observation when some observations represent a larger share of the relevant total than others. For example, if the aim were to measure the average change in prices of various farm products between 1920 and 1938, it would not be appropriate to give the same weight to minor products (such as pumpkins) as to major products (such as wheat).

To illustrate a very useful alternative procedure we will take the data for CNTYMIG in the Irish emigration data set (for simplicity we restrict the example to the first four counties and round the data to 1 decimal place). To begin with, consider only the data in columns (1) and (2) of table 2.4 for 1881.

It is immediately evident that there are considerable differences in the rate of migration per 1,000 of population from these four counties, and that the one with the lowest rate – Dublin – also has the largest population.

---

^{d} The geometric mean is 8.02, indicating that the extreme value (45) has less effect on this measure than on the arithmetic mean.

Table 2.4 Population and migration for four Irish counties in 1881 and 1911

	(1)	(2)	(3)	(4)
	1881		1911	
County	Population (000)	CNTYMIG (per 1,000)	Population (000)	CNTYMIG (per 1,000)
Carlow	46.6	29.0	36.3	5.9
Dublin	418.9	6.8	477.2	2.3
Kildare	75.8	19.8	66.6	4.4
Kilkenny	99.5	11.9	75.0	4.9

Arithmetic mean of CNTYMIG in $1881 = \dfrac{29.0 + 6.8 + 19.8 + 11.9}{4} = \dfrac{67.5}{4} = 16.9$

Weighted arithmetic mean of CNTYMIG in $1881 =$

$\dfrac{(29.0 \times 46.6) + (6.8 \times 418.9) + (19.8 \times 75.8) + (11.9 \times 99.5)}{46.6 + 418.9 + 75.8 + 99.5} = \dfrac{6884.7}{640.8} = 10.7$

Conversely Carlow has the highest rate of migration but the smallest population. If we ignore these differences in the migration rates and size of the counties and calculate the simple mean we get an average of 16.9 migrants per 1,000 (as shown at the foot of table 2.4).

If we wish to take these differences into account, we must instead use a **weighted arithmetic mean**. This requires that each county is given an appropriate weight, in this case its population size in 1881. The weighted mean is then calculated by multiplying each rate of migration by its weight, and dividing the total of these products by the sum of the weights. The calculation is set out at the foot of table 2.4, and the result is 10.7 per 1,000. This is considerably lower than the unweighted mean, and gives a much more accurate measure of the overall rate of migration from these counties.

More generally, the formula for a weighted mean, $\overline{X}'$, is

$$\overline{X}' = \frac{\Sigma(w_i X_i)}{\Sigma w_i} \tag{2.1a}$$

where w_i is the appropriate weight for each observation, X_i, in the series.

We will also introduce one particular form of weighted average that is very widely used in demographic and medical history, the standardized rate.

If we look at the 1911 data in columns (3) and (4) of table 2.4 we see that the emigration rates have fallen sharply in all four counties, and that the population in Dublin has increased since 1881 while that in the other three counties has fallen. The weighted average rate of CNTYMIG for 1911 is only 3.0.

However, this decline as compared to 10.7 in 1881 is partly a result of changes in migration from the individual counties, and partly a result of changes in the relative importance of the different counties. If we wish to get a summary measure of the rate of emigration which is *unaffected by the population changes* we can calculate a **standardized rate**. In this case we would ask, in effect: what would the 1911 rate have been if the distribution of the population by county were fixed at the proportions of 1881? The answer is obtained by weighting the four 1911 county rates by their respective 1881 populations, and is 3.2.

This procedure has very wide application, with the possibility of standardizing a variety of rates for one or more relevant factors. For example, crude birth rates per 1,000 women are frequently standardized by age in order to exclude the effects of changes in the age composition of the female population. Crude death rates per 1,000 of the population might be standardized by both age and occupation; suicide rates by both geographical region and gender; marriage rates by social class; and so on. In every case the standardized rate is effectively a weighted average of a particular set of specific rates such as the age-specific birth rates or the age- and occupation-specific death rates.

2.2.3 Percentiles, deciles, and quartiles

It was noted in §2.2.1 that the median is calculated by taking the value in an array above and below which there are one-half of the observations. Exactly the same principle can be applied for other measures, but taking other fractions.

(a) **Quartiles:** Instead of dividing the observations into two equal halves we can divide them into four equal quarters. The first quartile is then equal to the value that has one-quarter of the values below it, and three-quarters above it. Conversely the third quartile has three-quarters of the values below it, and one-quarter above. The second quartile has two quarters above and two quarters below, and is thus identical to the median.

(b) **Percentiles and deciles:** Other common divisions are percentiles, which divide the distribution into 100 portions of equal size, and deciles, which divide it into 10 portions of equal size. So if you are told at the end of your course on quantitative methods that your mark is at the ninth decile, you will know that nine-tenths of the students had a lower mark than you, and only one-tenth had a better mark.

The fifth decile and the fiftieth percentile are the same as the median; the 25th and 75th percentiles are the same as the first and third quartiles.

2.3 Measures of dispersion

Knowledge of the mean or some other measure of central tendency tells us something important about a data set, but two sets of numbers can have the same mean and still be markedly different. Consider, for example, the following (fictitious) numbers relating to the profits (in dollars) earned by two groups of five farmers in counties A and B:

County A: 14, 16, 18, 20, and 22
County B: 2, 8, 18, 29, and 33

Both these series sum to 90 and have the same mean of 18 dollars, but it is immediately obvious that the spread of numbers around this shared central value is very much greater in the second county. Our view of the risks and rewards of farming in the two regions would be influenced accordingly, and we would want to include some indication of this factor in any summary statement about farm incomes.

To do this we need some measure of the **dispersion** or spread of the data around its central value, and there are a variety of different ways such a measure can be constructed.

2.3.1 The range and the quartile deviation

(a) The **range** is a very crude measure of dispersion and is simply the difference between the highest and lowest value in the series. Its obvious weakness is that it is based entirely on these two extreme values, and takes no account whatsoever of all the other observations.

(b) The **quartile deviation** (or inter-quartile range) is a slightly better measure. Instead of representing the range as the difference between the maximum and minimum values it measures the distance between the first and third quartiles (see §2.2.3). It is sometimes divided by 2 and called the **semi-interquartile range**. In either form it is thus a measure of the distance covered by the middle half of all the observations, and is less sensitive to extreme values of the distribution than the range. However, it still ignores a considerable part of the data, and it does not provide any measure of the variability among the cases in the middle of the series.

The remaining measures of dispersion avoid both these weaknesses.

2.3.2 The mean deviation, the variance, and the standard deviation

If the objective is to get a good measure of the spread of *all* the observations in a series, one method which suggests itself is to find out how much each value differs from the mean (or some other central or typical value). If we then simply added up all these differences, the result would obviously be affected by the number of cases involved. So the final step must be to take some kind of average of all the differences.

The three following measures all do this in varying ways.

(a) The **mean deviation** is obtained by calculating the difference between each observation (X_i) and the mean of the series ($\overline{X}$) and then finding the average of those deviations.

In making this calculation the *sign* of the deviation (i.e. whether the value of the observation is higher or lower than the mean) has to be ignored. If not, the sum of the positive deviations would always be exactly equal to the sum of the negative deviations. Since these two sums would automatically cancel out, the result would *always* be zero.

The mean deviation does take account of all the observations in the series and is easy to interpret. However, it is less satisfactory from a theoretical statistical point of view than the next two measures.

(b) The **variance** uses an alternative way of getting rid of the negative signs: it does so by calculating the *square* of the deviations.[e] It is then calculated by finding the mean of the squared deviations. This is equal to the sum of the squared deviations from the mean, divided by the size of the sample.[f]

THE VARIANCE

The variance, s^2, is equal to
the *arithmetic mean of the squared deviations from the mean.*

The formula is thus

$$s^2 = \frac{\Sigma(X_i - \overline{X})^2}{n}$$
(2.2)

---

[e] Taking squares solves the problem because one of the rules of elementary arithmetic is that when a negative number is multiplied by another negative number the result is a positive number; e.g. $-4 \times -4 = +16$.

[f] When we get to the deeper waters of chapter 5 we will find that the statisticians recommend that n should be replaced by n − 1 when using sample data in the calculation of the variance and certain other measures. We will ignore this distinction until we reach that point. Note, however, that if you use a computer program or calculator to check some of the calculations done 'by hand' in chapters 2–4 you will get different results if your program uses n − 1 rather than n. The distinction between the two definitions matters only when the sample size is small. If n = 30 or more there would be practically no difference between the two estimates.

Table 2.5 Calculation of the sample variance for two sets of farm incomes

	(1)	(2)	(3)	(4)	(5)	(6)
		County A			County B	
	X_i	$(X_i - \bar{X})$	$(X_i - \bar{X})^2$	X_i	$(X_i - \bar{X})$	$(X_i - \bar{X})^2$
	14	-4	16	2	-16	256
	16	-2	4	8	-10	100
	18	0	0	18	0	0
	20	2	4	29	11	121
	22	4	16	33	15	225
Sum	90	0	40	90	0	702
n = 5						
Mean ($\bar{X}$)	18			18		
Variance (s^2)			8			140.4

The calculation of the variance for the simple data set given above for the hypothetical farming incomes in the two counties is set out in table 2.5.

The variance of County A $= 40/5 = 8$, while that of County B $= 702/5 = 140.4$, and is very much greater. Note that the result of squaring the deviations from the mean is that the more extreme values (such as incomes of 2 dollars or 33 dollars) have a very large impact on the variance.

This example was deliberately kept very simple to illustrate how the variance is calculated and to show how it captures the much greater spread of incomes in County B. In a subsequent exercise we will take more realistic (and larger) samples, and use a computer program to calculate the variance.

The variance has many valuable theoretical properties and is widely used in statistical work. However, it has the disadvantage that it is expressed in square units. In the farm income example we would have to say that the variance in County A was 8 'squared dollars', which is not very meaningful. The obvious way to get rid of these awkward squared units is to take the *square root of the variance*. This leads to our final measure of dispersion.

(c) The **standard deviation** is the square root of the variance. Thus:

The standard deviation in County A equals $\sqrt{8} = 2.8$ dollars
The standard deviation in County B equals $\sqrt{140.4} = 11.8$ dollars

THE STANDARD DEVIATION

The standard deviation, s,

is equal to
the *square root of the*
arithmetic mean of the squared deviations from the mean.

The formula is thus

$$s = \sqrt{\frac{\Sigma(X_i - \overline{X})^2}{n}} \qquad (2.3)$$

The standard deviation is the most useful and widely used measure of dispersion. It is measured in the same units as the data series to which it refers. Thus we can say that the mean income in County A is 18 dollars, with a standard deviation (s.d.) of 2.8 dollars. Such results will often be reported in the form: $\overline{X} = 18$, s.d. $= 2.8$, or in even more summary form as: $\overline{X} = 18 \pm 2.8$.

The standard deviation can be thought of as the average or typical (hence standard) deviation from the mean. Thus it will be seen that in County A the deviations from the mean (see column (2) of table 2.5) vary between 0 and 4, and the standard deviation is 2.8. Similarly in County B the spread of the deviations in column (5) is from 0 to 16, and the standard deviation is 11.8. The standard deviation thus lies somewhere between the smallest and largest deviation from the mean.

The variance and the standard deviation have several mathematical properties that make them more useful than the mean deviation. Both play an extremely important role in many aspects of statistics.

2.3.3 The coefficient of variation

The standard deviation is calculated in the same units (e.g. of weight or length or currency or time) as the series to which it refers. This makes it specific to that series, and means that it is difficult or misleading to compare the *absolute* standard deviations of two series measured in different underlying units. This would also be true even with the same unit, if that is used for values where there is a substantial change in level.

For example, we might discover that in 1914, when the mean weekly wage of adult male workers in the United Kingdom was £1.60, the standard deviation was £0.30; and that in 1975 when the mean was £75, the standard deviation was £17.50 (these are very rough approximations to the actual data). Because growth and inflation has completely altered the level of wage payments, it is impossible to tell from this whether the dispersion of wages was larger or smaller in the later period.

To do this we need a measure of *relative rather than absolute variation.* This can be obtained by dividing the standard deviation by the mean. The result is known as the **coefficient of variation,** abbreviated to CV (or cv)

$$CV = s/\overline{X} \tag{2.4}$$

The two estimates for CV are, therefore, $0.3/1.6 = 0.19$ and $17.5/75 = 0.23$ and it is evident that the variation of wages has increased slightly.[g]

2.4 Measures of central tendency and dispersion with grouped data

In the preceding description of the procedures for computation of the measures of central tendency and dispersion it was taken for granted that the full set of values was available for all the cases. It may be, however, that for some projects the relevant information is available only in the form of **grouped** data. Imagine, for example, that instead of the individual data for relief payments in each of the 311 parishes, the only information that survived in the historical record was the grouped data of table 2.3. Certain additional *assumptions* would then be required in order to calculate the measures of central tendency and dispersion.

The results obtained for grouped data on these assumptions will not be exactly the same as those that we would get if we had all the individual data. However the inaccuracies will generally be minor unless the class intervals are very wide or there are serious errors in the values attributed to the open-ended classes.[h]

2.4.1 The median and mean with grouped data
In order to calculate the median, mean, and other measures with such grouped data it is necessary to make some assumptions about the distribution of the unknown individual cases *within* the class intervals. For the median, quartiles, and similar measures the conventional assumption is that the cases are all spread *at equal distances* within their respective intervals.

---

[g] CV is sometimes expressed as a percentage. In the above example multiplying by 100 would give results of 19 per cent and 23 per cent, respectively.

[h] The scale of the possible differences is illustrated by question 1 in the exercises at the end of this chapter.

To illustrate this procedure, consider the data on *per capita* relief payments in table 2.3. Since there are 311 parishes, the median parish will be the 156th. There are 84 parishes in the first two class intervals, so we need another 72 to reach the median parish, and it will thus fall somewhere in the third class interval, which has a lower limit of 12 shillings. There are a total of 93 parishes in that class interval and, by assumption, they are spread at equal distances along the interval of 6 shillings. The median parish will therefore occur at the value equal to 12 shillings plus 72/93 of 6 shillings, or 16.6 shillings.[i]

For measures involving the mean, the corresponding assumption is that all the cases within the group have a value equal to the *mid-point* of the group. Thus we take a value of 15 shillings for all 93 parishes in table 2.3 with relief payments between 12 and 18 shillings, and similarly for the other intervals.[j]

Let us denote each of these mid-points by X_i, and the frequency with which the cases occur (as shown in column (2) of table 2.3) by f. These two values can then be multiplied to get the product for each class interval, fX_i. The sum of those products is thus ΣfX_i, and the formula for the mean with grouped data is then this sum divided by the sum of the frequencies, Σf

$$\bar{X} = \frac{\Sigma fX_i}{\Sigma f} \qquad (2.5)$$

There are two points to note with regard to this formula. First, for the data in table 2.3, the denominator in this formula, Σf, is 311, which is precisely what n would be when calculating the mean with ungrouped data using the formula in (2.1). Secondly, the procedure is exactly equivalent to the weighted arithmetic mean introduced in §2.2.1, as can be readily seen by comparing this formula with the one in (2.1a). The mid-points of the class intervals correspond to the observations in the series, and the frequencies become the weights.

2.4.2   The variance and standard deviation with grouped data

The calculation of the variance with grouped data then involves the following steps. Find the deviations of each of the mid-points from this mean value $(X_i - \bar{X})$; square each of these terms $(X_i - \bar{X})^2$; and multiply this by the corresponding frequency, f, to obtain the product $f(X_i - \bar{X})$. The variance is then equal to the sum of these products divided by the sum of the frequencies

---

[i] This result is rounded to 1 decimal place. Note that a result can never be more precise than the data on which it is based.

[j] If there are any open-ended classes (e.g. if the last class in table 2.3 had been reported only in the form of a lower limit of 'equal to or greater than 42 shillings') it would be necessary to make an intelligent guess as to a sensible value for the mid-point.

$$s^2 = \frac{\Sigma f(X_i - \overline{X})^2}{\Sigma f} \tag{2.6}$$

The standard deviation can similarly be calculated as the square root of the variance

$$s = \sqrt{\frac{\Sigma f(X_i - \overline{X})^2}{\Sigma f}} \tag{2.7}$$

2.5 The shape of the distribution

2.5.1 Symmetrical and skewed distributions

The final aspect of the distribution that is of interest is its shape, i.e. the way in which the data are distributed around the central point. The distribution around the mean may be symmetrical or it may be skewed either to the left or to the right.

In §2.1.3 we noted that if we have a sufficiently large number of cases for a variable measured on a continuous scale, and if these cases are then grouped in sufficiently narrow class intervals, a line drawn through the mid-point of each of the class intervals ultimately becomes a perfectly smooth frequency curve.

One subset of such smooth frequency curves is perfectly symmetric. This applies to the **rectangular distribution**, in which case the proportion of frequencies in each of a succession of equally spaced intervals is identical, and also to the **pyramidical distribution**.[2] The most important member of this family of *perfectly smooth and symmetrical* frequency curves is also *bell-shaped* and is known as the **normal curve**, illustrated in figure 2.4 (a). Because the curve is symmetrical and unimodal, the mean, median, and mode are all identical. The normal curve plays a very large part in this book and will be discussed more fully in §2.6.1.

Other families of distribution are smooth but *not symmetrical*. For example, a distribution may be *skewed to the right*, as in figure 2.4 (b), where there are large numbers of small or medium values and a tail stretching to the right with a small number of very large values (**positive skewness**). Examples of such positive skewness are often found with data on income distribution or holdings of land and other property, and on the size of firms. Data on the age of marriage or on the number of births per married women would also be positively skewed.[k]

Alternatively, a distribution may be *skewed to the left*, as in figure 2.4 (c),

---

[k] Such distributions are sometimes loosely referred to as **log-normal**. A true log-normal distribution is one that is strongly positively skewed when the data are entered in ordinary numbers and normally distributed when the data are converted to logs.

Figure 2.4
Symmetrical and
skewed frequency
curves

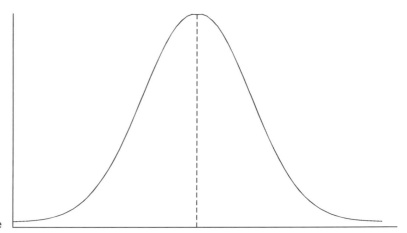

(a) The normal curve

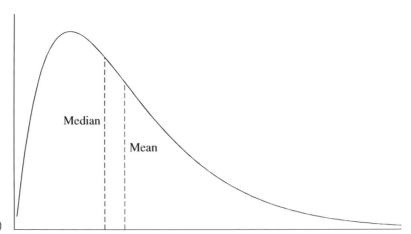

(b) Smooth curve
skewed to the right
(positive skewness)

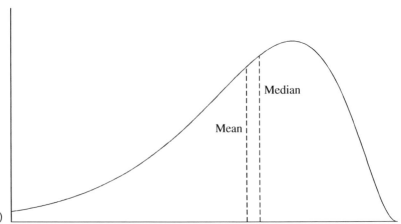

(c) Smooth curve
skewed to the left
(negative skewness)

with a tail made up of a small number of very low values (**negative skewness**). This would be characteristic of data on the age of death in Britain or the United States in any normal peacetime year. There would be a small number of deaths at low ages as a result of accidents and illness, but the great majority would occur at ages 60–90 and the right hand tail would effectively end abruptly a little above age 100.

2.5.2 Measures of skewness

Measures of skewness should be independent of the units in which the variable is measured, and should be zero when the distribution is perfectly symmetrical so that there is no skewness. One simple measure of the extent to which a distribution is asymmetrical (skewed) is given by the relationship between the mean and the median: the greater the skewness the larger the difference between the mean and the median. If the distribution is positively skewed, the mean will be raised by the large values in the right-hand tail of the distribution, whereas the median is unaffected by these extreme values. The mean will thus be larger than the median. Conversely, if the distribution is negatively skewed, the mean will be smaller than the median. A very rough indication of the presence of either positive or negative skewness in any particular distribution can thus be obtained by a comparison of the mean and median of a distribution.

A simple measure based on these features is a variant of the Pearson coefficient of skewness

$$\text{Skewness} = \frac{3(\text{Mean} - \text{Median})}{\text{Standard deviation}} \qquad (2.8)$$

This satisfies the two criteria mentioned above and would lie between -3 and $+3$, though these limits are seldom encountered in practice.

Statistical packages tend to use more precise measures based on the deviations of the individual observations from the mean. In one such measure, these deviations are cubed, and expressed in terms of the number of standard deviations, also cubed. The arithmetic mean of this term is then calculated. The formula is thus

$$\frac{\Sigma(X_i - \overline{X})^3/s^3}{n} \qquad (2.9)$$

2.6 The normal distribution

2.6.1 Properties of the normal distribution

Since the *perfect* normal curve is a theoretical distribution based on an infinitely large number of observations it can be only approximated by *actual* frequency distributions, but we will find many examples of random variables that show a very good approximation to the theoretical normal distribution. We will also find that the normal distribution has a number of remarkable properties.

A variable is defined as a **random variable** if its numerical value is *unknown until it is observed*; it is not perfectly predictable. The observation can be the outcome of an experiment such as tossing a coin or planting seeds, or it can be the measurement of a variable such as height, the price of wheat, or the age of marriage. If it can take only a finite number of values (for example, the number of births per married women is limited to positive whole numbers such as 0, 1, 2, or 3) it is called a **discrete** random variable. If it can take any value (within a relevant interval) it is called a **continuous** random variable.

The normal curve is defined by an equation involving two constants and the mean and standard deviation of the distribution of a continuous random variable, X. The equation gives the value of Y (the height of the curve, shown on the vertical axis) for any value of X (measured along the horizontal axis). Y thus measures the frequency with which each value of X occurs. Although the form of this equation is considerably more complicated than the one used in §1.5 for a straight line ($Y = a + bX$), the principle is exactly the same. We select the values for the constants, in this case they are π (lower case Greek pi, approximately 3.1416) and e (approximately 2.7183), plug in the changing values for the variable(s) in the equation (in this case the values for X), and calculate the corresponding values for Y.

The normal curve is not a single, unique, curve. All normal curves will have the same smooth and symmetrical bell-like shape, but there are very many different normal curves, each defined by its particular mean and standard deviation. Two normal curves may have the same spread (standard deviation) but different means, in which case the one with the larger mean will be further to the right along the horizontal (X) axis, as in figure 2.5 (a). Or they may have the same mean but different standard deviations, in which case the one with the larger standard deviation will be spread out more widely on either side of the mean, as in figure 2.5 (b). Or both means and standard deviations may be different, as in figure 2.5 (c).

When a statistical program is used to plot a histogram for any particular data set it can also be requested to add the particular normal curve

Figure 2.5 A family of normal curves

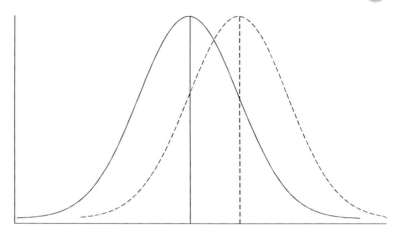

(a) Different means but the same standard deviation

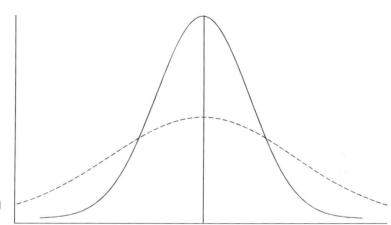

(b) The same mean but different standard deviations

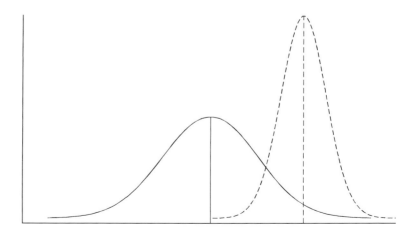

(c) Different means and standard deviations

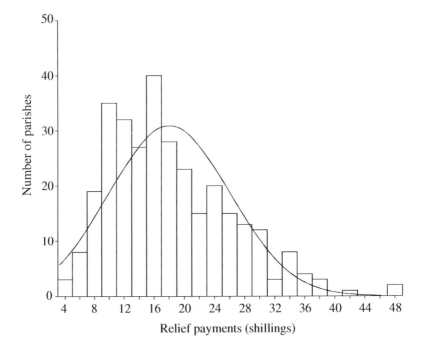

given by the mean and standard deviation of that data. It is thus possible to see how far the data conform to the normal distribution. This is done, for example, in figure 2.6 with the histogram of parish relief payments previously shown in figure 2.2 (b), and it can be seen that it is a reasonably good approximation.

The fact that many actual distributions approximate the theoretical normal distribution enables statisticians to make extensive use of the properties of the theoretical normal curve. One obvious property that we have already noted implicitly is that the mean, median, and mode are all equal; they coincide at the highest point of the curve and there is only one mode.

A second property of considerable importance relates to the area under the normal curve. Irrespective of the particular mean or standard deviation of the curve it will always be the case that *a constant proportion of all the cases will lie a given distance from the mean measured in terms of the standard deviation.* It is thus possible to calculate what the proportion is for any particular *distance from the mean expressed in terms of standard deviations (std devs).*

Since the distribution is perfectly symmetrical we also know that exactly one-half of the above proportions are to the right of (greater than) the mean and one-half are to the left of (smaller than) the mean.

Three particular results, specified in the following box, are of special interest.

SPREAD OF THE NORMAL CURVE

90 per cent of all cases are within **1.645 std devs** either side of the mean, leaving 5 per cent in each of the two tails

95 per cent of all cases are within **1.96 std devs** either side of the mean, leaving 2.5 per cent in each of the two tails

99 per cent of all cases are within **2.58 std devs** either side of the mean, leaving 0.5 per cent in each of the two tails

---

These proportions are illustrated in the three panels of figure 2.7.

In the above description, particular areas were selected given in convenient whole numbers. It is equally possible to select convenient whole numbers for the number of standard deviations to be taken either side of the mean, in particular:

- The distance of ± 1 **std dev** from the mean covers **68.26 per cent** of all cases
- The distance of ± 2 **std devs** from the mean covers **95.46 per cent** of all cases
- The distance of ± 3 **std devs** from the mean covers **99.73 per cent** of all cases

To fix this extremely important property of the normal distribution in your mind, consider an example of a roughly normal distribution that should already be intuitively familiar. If you are told that the mean height of a large sample of male students at the University of Virginia is 6 feet ($'$) and the standard deviation (std dev) is 5 inches ($''$), you could apply the characteristics stated above and would find that:

- *Roughly two-thirds* are between 5$'$ 7$''$ and 6$'$ 5$''$ tall (the mean ± 1 std dev)
- That only a small minority, *less than 5 per cent,* are shorter than 5$'$ 2$''$ or taller than 6$'$ 10$''$ (the mean ± 2 std devs)

Figure 2.7 Areas under the normal curve

(a) 1.645 standard deviations either side of the mean covers 90 per cent of the area. This leaves 5 per cent in each tail.

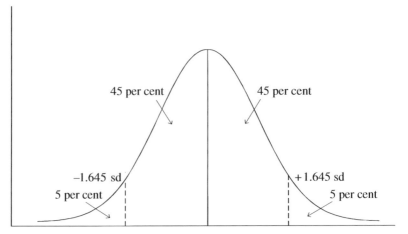

(b) 1.96 standard deviations either side of the mean covers 95 per cent of the area. This leaves 2.5 per cent in each tail.

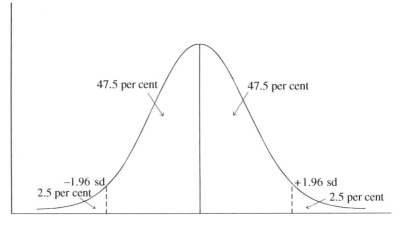

(c) 2.58 standard deviations either side of the mean covers 99 per cent of the area. This leaves 0.5 per cent in each tail.

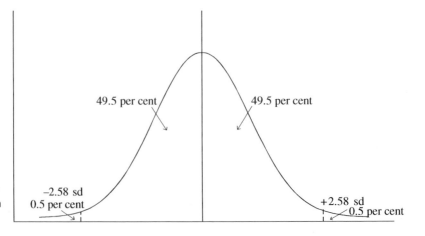

- There are effectively *none* below 4′ 9″ or above 7′ 3″ (the mean ±3 std devs).[1]

These results should seem plausible, and should help you to understand how to interpret information about the standard deviation for (approximately normal) distributions that are less familiar than heights.

This leads directly to the idea that areas under the normal curve can be thought of in terms of the number of standard deviations.

2.6.2 The standard normal distribution

We have seen (§2.6.1) that there is a large family of normal curves, each defined by its particular mean and standard deviation. Because there are so many different normal curves it is helpful to *standardize* them.

To do this, note that one way to measure the distance from the mean of the distribution to any point above or below the mean is to ask how many standard units that distance represents. Thus with the height example used in the previous subsection, where the mean was 6′ and the standard deviation was 5″, we could say that if a student measured 6′ 11″ his height was 2.2 standard deviations above the mean.

This idea of the *distance from the mean* $(X - \bar{X})$ *expressed in units of standard deviations* can be generalized to standardize any normal distribution. The result creates a new variable, designated Z, and the distribution of Z is referred to as the **standard normal distribution**

$$Z = \frac{(X - \bar{X})}{s} \tag{2.10}$$

A very important feature of this *standardized* distribution is that the mean must, by definition, always be zero, and the standard deviation must always be equal to 1. This is illustrated in table 2.6, where a hypothetical (and approximately normally distributed) series for the heights of a sample of 40 male students is given in column (1), and the corresponding standardized distribution (Z) in column (4). (The distances exactly 1 or 2 standard deviations above and below the mean are highlighted.) Columns (2) and (3) give the information required to calculate Z and the standard

---

[1] For those more accustomed to think in metric units, the equivalent units are a mean of 180 cm and a standard deviation of 13 cm. The height of roughly two-thirds of the students is thus between 167 and 193 cm, and fewer than 5 per cent are either shorter than 154 cm or taller than 206 cm.

Table 2.6 Heights of a sample of 40 male students and the standardized distribution

(1) Xi Height in inches	(2) $(X_i - \bar{X})$	(3) $(X_i - \bar{X})^2$	(4) $(X_i - \bar{X})/s$ $= Z$	(5) $(Z_i - \bar{Z})^2$ $= Z^2$
61.1	−10.9	118.81	−2.18	4.75
62.0	−10.0	100.00	−2.00	4.00
63.5	−8.5	72.25	−1.70	2.89
64.7	−7.3	53.29	−1.46	2.13
65.3	−6.7	44.89	−1.34	1.80
66.3	−5.7	32.49	−1.14.	1.30
67.0	−5.0	25.00	−1.00	1.00
68.0	−4.0	16.00	−0.80	0.64
68.2	−3.8	14.44	−0.76	0.58
68.3	−3.7	13.69	−0.74	0.55
68.5	−3.5	12.25	−0.70	0.49
69.2	−2.8	7.84	−0.56	0.31
69.3	−2.7	7.29	−0.54	0.29
70.0	−2.0	4.00	−0.40	0.16
70.3	−1.7	2.89	−0.34	0.12
70.7	−1.3	1.69	−0.26	0.07
71.4	−0.6	0.36	−0.12	0.01
71.7	−0.3	0.09	−0.06	0.00
72.0	0.0	0.00	0.00	0.00
72.4	0.4	0.16	0.08	0.01
72.6	0.6	0.36	0.12	0.01
72.8	0.8	0.64	0.16	0.03
72.9	0.9	0.81	0.18	0.03
73.4	1.4	1.96	0.28	0.08
73.7	1.7	2.89	0.34	0.12
73.9	1.9	3.61	0.38	0.14
74.1	2.1	4.41	0.42	0.18
74.3	2.3	5.29	0.46	0.21
74.5	2.5	6.25	0.50	0.25
75.4	3.4	11.56	0.68	0.46
75.6	3.6	12.96	0.72	0.52
76.3	4.3	18.49	0.86	0.74
76.5	4.5	20.25	0.90	0.81
77.0	5.0	25.00	1.00	1.00
77.3	5.3	28.09	1.06	1.12
77.5	5.5	30.25	1.10	1.21
78.8	6.8	46.24	1.36	1.85
80.3	8.3	68.89	1.66	2.76
81.2	9.2	84.64	1.84	3.39
82.0	10.0	100.00	2.00	4.00
Σ 2,880.0	0.00	1,000.00	0.00	40.00

n = 40

deviation of Z is calculated in column (5). The mean of Z is seen to be 0 and the standard deviation is 1.00.[m]

It will also be seen how the standardized distribution maps the initial distribution, so that the mean value of the original series ($=72$ inches) corresponds to the mean value of the standardized distribution ($=0$). Similarly, a distance of 1 standard deviation above or below the mean in the original distribution ($\bar{X} \pm 1$ std dev $= 72 \pm 5 = 67$ or 77 inches) corresponds to values of $Z = \bar{Z} \pm 1$ std dev $= 0 \pm 1 = -1$ or $+1$. In the same way a distance of 2 standard deviations above or below the mean (62 or 82 inches) corresponds to values of $Z = -2$ or $+2$.

Statisticians have compiled tables that show the proportion under the standardized curve for all values of Z. The proportions in these tables apply to the perfect *theoretical* distribution, but for any actual distribution that is approximately normal the proportions will be roughly the same. An extract from such a table of the standard normal distribution is reproduced in table 2.7.[n]

In this particular version the area under the curve is subdivided in five different ways, so that five different proportions of the total area are given for each *positive* value of Z. Since the curve is perfectly symmetrical the proportions for the corresponding *negative* values of Z would be exactly the same.

The five different proportions in columns (2)–(6) are:

(a) The cumulative proportion up to Z.
(b) The proportion from the mean to the specific positive value of Z. (Since the total proportion to the left of the mean $=0.5$, this is always *0.5 less than the value in (a)*.)
(c) The proportion in the right-hand tail beyond Z. (Since the total proportion under the curve $= 1$, this is always *1.0 minus the value in (a)*.)
(d) The proportion in both tails given by the positive and negative value of Z. (This is always *twice the proportion in (c)*.)
(e) The central proportion excluding the two tails defined by the positive and negative values of Z. (Since the total proportion under the curve $= 1$, this is always *1.0 minus the value in (d)*.)

[m] The calculations are as follows: The mean height for these students $= \bar{X} = \Sigma X/n = 2{,}880/40 = 72.0$. The variance of the heights $= s^2 = \Sigma(X_i - \bar{X})^2/n = 1{,}000/40 = 25.00$, and so the standard deviation of these heights $= s = \sqrt{25} = 5.00$. This standard deviation is then used in column (4) to calculate Z. For Z, $\Sigma Z/n = 0.00/40 = 0.0$, and this is used in column (5) to calculate the variance of $Z = \Sigma(Z_i - \bar{Z})^2/n = 40/40 = 1.00$. The standard deviation is therefore $\sqrt{1.00} = 1.00$.

[n] A more complete table covering all values of Z can be consulted in D. V. Lindley and W. F. Scott, *New Cambridge Statistical Tables*, Cambridge University Press, 2nd edn., 1995, p.34, and in most general statistics books.

Table 2.7   Areas under the standard normal curve for selected values of Z

(1) Selected values of Z	(2) Cumulative area up to Z	(3) Area from mean up to Z	(4) Area in one tail beyond Z	(5) Area in both tails beyond Z	(6) Central area
0.00	0.5000	0.0000	0.5000	1.0000	0.0000
0.20	0.5793	0.0793	0.4207	0.8414	0.1586
0.40	0.6554	0.1554	0.3446	0.6892	0.3108
0.60	0.7257	0.2257	0.2743	0.5486	0.4514
0.80	0.7881	0.2881	0.2119	0.4238	0.5762
1.00	0.8413	0.3413	0.1587	0.3174	0.6826
1.20	0.8849	0.3849	0.1151	0.2302	0.7698
1.28	**0.8997**	**0.3997**	**0.1003**	**0.2006**	**0.7994**
1.40	0.9192	0.4192	0.0808	0.1616	0.8384
1.60	0.9452	0.4452	0.0548	0.1096	0.8904
1.645	**0.9500**	**0.4500**	**0.0500**	**0.1000**	**0.9000**
1.80	0.9641	0.4641	0.0359	0.0718	0.9282
1.96	**0.9750**	**0.4750**	**0.0250**	**0.0500**	**0.9500**
2.00	0.9772	0.4772	0.0228	0.0456	0.9544
2.20	0.9861	0.4861	0.0139	0.0278	0.9722
2.40	0.9918	0.4918	0.0082	0.0164	0.9836
2.58	**0.9951**	**0.4951**	**0.0049**	**0.0098**	**0.9902**
2.80	0.9974	0.4974	0.0026	0.0052	0.9948
3.00	0.9986	0.4986	0.0014	0.0028	0.9972
3.20	0.9993	0.4993	0.0007	0.0014	0.9986
3.40	0.9997	0.4997	0.0003	0.0006	0.9994
3.60	0.9999	0.4999	0.0001	0.0002	0.9998
3.80	0.9999	0.4999	0.0001	0.0002	0.9998

Note:
The two-tailed area in column (5) refers to both the positive and the negative values of Z.
Source: Lindley and Scott, *Statistical Tables*, p. 34 for column (2); other columns as explained in the text.

You will find that authors usually give only one of these five possible proportions, and different authors choose different proportions. This divergence in the way the table is printed is confusing, and means that if you want to use one of these tables you must first establish the form in which the information is presented.

The proportions are normally given to 3 or 4 decimal places. It is often more convenient to think in terms of percentages, and these are obtained by multiplying the proportions by 100 (i.e. moving the decimal point 2 places to the right): for example, $0.500 = 50$ per cent.

Once the form in which the data are presented in any particular table is clarified, it is a simple matter to find the proportion up to or beyond any given value of Z. Take, for instance, the student in table 2.6 with a height of 77 inches. This corresponds to a value for $Z = 1.0$, and is thus 1.0 standard deviations from the mean height of 72 inches. From column (4) of table 2.7 it can be seen that the proportion greater than this value of Z is 0.1587, or 15.9 per cent. Since there are 40 students this indicates that if the heights of this sample are normally distributed there should be approximately six students (15.9 per cent of 40) taller than this one. Table 2.6 in fact has six taller students.

Notes

[1] Note that the precise class intervals depend on the extent to which the underlying data have been rounded. The data in table 2.1 were rounded to 1 decimal place, so the true upper limit of the first class interval in table 2.2 would be 9.94 shillings. All values from 9.90 to 9.94 would have been rounded down to 9.9 shillings, and so would be included in the interval ≥ 5 but < 10. All values from 9.95 to 9.99 would have been rounded up to 10 shillings, and so would be included in the interval ≥ 10 but < 15.

[2] If a perfect die is thrown once the probability of obtaining a six is 1/6, and the probability of obtaining each of the other face values from 1 to 5 would be exactly the same, so these outcomes would represent a rectangular distribution. A pyramid-shaped distribution would be obtained for the probability of each value if the die were thrown twice. With each successive throw beyond two the distribution moves towards the bell-shape of the normal curve. For the corresponding successive distributions when the probabilities relate to tossing increasing numbers of coins, see figure 5.1.

2.7 Exercises for chapter 2

All exercises in this and subsequent chapters may be solved by computer, unless the question states specifically that they should be done *by hand.*

1. Extract the data on INCOME for Cambridgeshire (County 5) by parish from the Boyer relief data set.

    (i) *By hand,* use these data to construct:
    - An array
    - A frequency distribution using 5 class intervals of equal width of £5, beginning at <£20
    - A frequency distribution using 10 class intervals of equal width of £2, beginning at <£20
    - A frequency distribution using 16 class intervals of equal width of £1, beginning at <£20.

    (ii) Which frequency distribution provides the information on Cambridgeshire incomes in the most useful fashion?

    (iii) What difference does it make if you round the income figures to 1 decimal place before constructing the frequency distributions?

    (iv) What difference does it make if you round the income figures to the nearest whole number before constructing the frequency distributions?

    (v) Instruct the computer to construct a histogram with 10 intervals. Are the resulting class intervals the same as for the relative frequency distribution in (i) above? Explain your finding.

2. Take the WEALTH variable for every parish in the Boyer relief data set.

    (i) Calculate the following statistics:
    - Upper, lower, and middle quartiles
    - 10th and 90th percentiles
    - Range
    - Mean, median, and mode
    - Variance
    - Standard deviation
    - Coefficient of variation.

    (ii) Plot a histogram of WEALTH with: (a) 31 intervals and (b) 11 intervals.

    (iii) Plot a bar chart of mean WEALTH in each of 21 counties. (*Hint*: use COUNTY for the category axis.)

Comment on the relationship between the different measures of central tendency and dispersion, and discuss what they tell you about wealth in these parishes.

3. Using Boyer's birth rate data set, calculate the means and standard deviations of INCOME, BRTHRATE, and DENSITY, counting each parish as a single observation. Now calculate the means and standard deviations of the same variables, with each parish weighted by its population (POP). How would you explain the difference between the two measures? Is there any reason to prefer one set of measures to the other?

4. The following table provides data on the percentage of women in England and Wales, aged 10 and above, who worked outside the home in 1911 and 1991, classified by age and marital status. It also shows the percentage of women in each age group who were married in 1911 and 1991, as well as the age structure of all women, single or married, in the two years.

	1911				1991			
Age	% single women working	% married women working	% all women married	% women by age	% single women working	% married women working	% all women married	% women by age
<15	10.4	0.0	0.0	11.8	–	–	–	–
<20	69.5	13.4	1.2	11.3	54.7	47.2	2.0	6.2
<25	77.6	12.9	24.2	11.3	75.8	62.3	22.9	9.1
<35	73.7	10.6	63.2	21.0	75.7	62.2	62.8	18.4
<45	65.3	10.6	75.3	16.9	75.4	72.4	78.5	16.8
<55	53.5	10.5	70.9	12.3	73.0	70.5	79.9	13.9
<65	36.6	8.8	58.4	8.2	35.9	38.0	72.5	12.6
<75	18.7	5.7	37.5	5.1	4.9	5.1	53.6	11.9
≥75	6.3	2.3	16.1	2.1	1.1	1.5	23.2	11.2
ALL	50.4	10.3	44.6	100.0	46.0	53.0	56.1	100.0

Note:
Single includes single, widowed, and divorced women. Married refers to currently married women.

Sources: Census of Population, England and Wales, 1911 and 1991.

   (i) What proportion of ALL women were in paid employment in (a) 1911? (b) 1991?
   (ii) How much of the overall change in the proportion of ALL women working between 1911 and 1991 was due to:

(a) The changing proportion at work among single and married women. (*Hint*: evaluate the level of female market work if the distribution of married and single women working had remained the same as in 1911.)

(b) The changing age structure of the female population.

(c) The changing age at marriage among women.

Write a brief paragraph setting out what the table and your calculations indicate about the changing patterns of women's involvement in paid employment.

5. Let us suppose that the data on WEALTH for the 311 parishes in the Boyer relief data set have been aggregated in the original source to produce the following table:

Average wealth per person (£)	Number of parishes	Population
⩾0 but <2	14	26,023
⩾2 but <3	44	90,460
⩾3 but <4	83	123,595
⩾4 but <5	58	76,421
⩾5 but <6	48	48,008
⩾6 but <7	25	19,811
⩾7 but <8	16	11,086
⩾8 but <9	6	3,820
⩾9 but <10	9	5,225
⩾10	8	2,634
ALL	311	407,083

Note:
No other information is available.

(i) Calculate total wealth in each class interval using (a) the number of parishes, and (b) the population, as the weighting system. What assumptions did you make about the level of wealth per person in each class interval and why?

(ii) Calculate the mean, median, mode, upper and lower quartiles, variance, standard deviation, and coefficient of variation for total wealth.

(iii) Change your assumption about the level of wealth per person in the top and bottom classes and recalibrate the measures of central tendency and dispersion. Which measures are most sensitive to changes in the measurement of average wealth? Explain your answers.

6. Using the WEALTH data from Boyer's relief data set:

(i) Calculate the average level of wealth per person for each county. Repeat the exercise of question 5, using both the number of parishes and the number of people in each county to calculate total wealth.

(ii) Compare the measures of central value and dispersion with those produced by question 5. Identify and account for any discrepancies. How do your results in questions 5 and 6 compare to the results of question 2?

Is the loss of information in these various permutations serious? How might we evaluate any loss of information?

7. Instruct the computer to produce histograms of the following variables from the Boyer data set on births:

BRTHRATE
INFTMORT
INCOME
DENSITY

(i) In each case, inspect the shapes of the histograms and assess whether the data are normally distributed, negatively skewed, or positively skewed. Record your findings.

(ii) Now ask the computer to calculate the degree of skewness in each of these variables. Compare these results to your own findings.

8. The LONDON variable in the Boyer data set is measured by assigning to each parish in a given county the same distance from the centre of London as the mid-point of the county, in miles. This is likely to create a bias in the measurement of distance for each parish. Why? How will the bias affect the measured mean and standard deviation of the variable LONDON, relative to its 'true' value? How might you test for the extent of any differences?

9. We are interested in determining which parishes are the most and least generous providers of relief to the unemployed poor. How might we construct such a variable from the data in the RELIEF file?

10. A random sample of 1,000 women was found to have a mean age of first marriage of 23.6 years with a standard deviation of 3 years. The ages can be assumed to be normally distributed. Use the table of the standard normal distribution (table 2.7) to calculate:

   (i) How many of the women were first married between 20 and 29 years?

  (ii) What was the minimum age of marriage of the oldest 5 per cent of the sample?

(iii) What proportion of the women married at an age that differed from the mean by more than 1.8 standard deviations?

CHAPTER 3

Correlation

3.1 The concept of correlation

This chapter is devoted to one of the central issues in the quantitative study of two variables: *is there a relationship between them*? Our aim is to explain the basic concepts, and then to obtain a measure of the *degree* to which the two variables are related. The statistical term for such a relationship or association is **correlation,** and the measure of the strength of that relationship is called the **correlation coefficient.**

We will deal first with the relationship between ratio or interval level (numerical) variables, and then look more briefly in §3.3 at the treatment of nominal and ordinal level measurements.[a] In this initial discussion we ignore the further matters that arise because the results are usually based on data obtained from a sample. Treatment of this important aspect must be deferred until the issues of confidence intervals and hypothesis testing have been covered in chapters 5 and 6.

If there is a relationship between the two sets of paired variables (for example, between the level of relief expenditure (RELIEF) and the proportion of unemployed labourers (UNEMP) in each of the parishes, or between EMPFOR, the annual series for foreign employment and IRMIG, the number of immigrants from Ireland), it may be either positive or negative. When there is **positive correlation,** high values of the one variable are associated with high values of the other. When there is **negative correlation,** high values of the one variable are associated with low values of the other. In each case the closeness of the relationship may be strong or weak.

The third possibility is, of course, that there is no consistent relationship: high values of one variable are sometimes associated with high values of the other, and sometimes with low values.

---

[a] These different levels of measurement were explained in §1.3.3.

3.1.1 Correlation is not causation

It must be stressed at the outset that *correlation does not imply causation.* It is only some appropriate theory that can provide a hypothesis that might lead us to believe that there is a causal relationship between two variables.

An empirical finding that there is an association does *not* imply that changes in the one variable are causing the changes in the other, however high the degree of correlation. Even if we have reason to believe that there is a causal relationship, the fact of a high degree of correlation does not in itself prove causality, although it may be regarded as another piece of evidence in support of the underlying hypothesis.

It is very easy to get an association between two variables even when there is no plausible hypothesis that might cause one to influence the other. This can occur either coincidentally, because the two variables are independently moving in the same directions, or – more commonly – because the movements in both variables are influenced by some (unspecified) third variable.

Over a period of years there might, for example, be a strong positive correlation between sales of umbrellas in New York and the number of slugs counted in the city parks. But this would occur only because both are influenced by how much rain has fallen; the umbrellas do not actually cause the proliferation of slugs. The simultaneous decline of the birth rate and of the number of storks in Sweden as a result of industrialization is a more famous example.

Correlation of this sort is called **spurious** or nonsense correlation, but as noted by Wonnacott and Wonnacott, it would be more accurate to say that the correlation is real enough, and that it is the naive inference of cause and effect which is nonsense.[b]

3.1.2 Scatter diagrams and correlation

The best way to explore the form and extent of any association between two variables is to plot them on a **scatter diagram** (or scatter plot). This is a chart in which one variable is measured on the vertical axis, and the other on the horizontal axis.

Each point on the diagram represents a pair of values of the two variables. In a time series, each pair relates to the same time period (for example, UNEMP and BENEFITS, British unemployment rates and benefit payments, in a given year, say 1925). In a cross-section, each pair relates to the same case (for example, CNTYMIG and AGRIC, emigration rates and the proportion of the male labour force in agriculture, in each Irish county). Some illustrative scatter plots are shown in figure 3.1, with the two variables referred to simply as X and Y.

---

[b] T. H. Wonnacott and R. J. Wonnacott, *Introductory Statistics,* 5th edn., John Wiley, 1990.

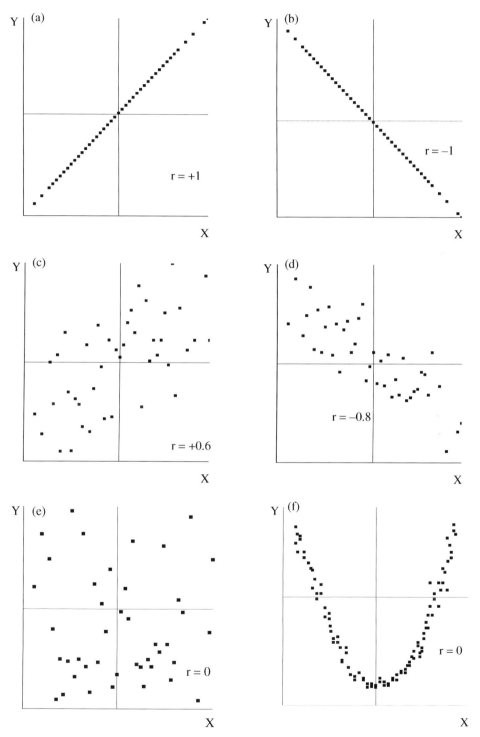

Figure 3.1 Scatter diagrams showing different strengths and directions of relationships between X and Y

Perfect correlation

In the upper panel, plot (a) on the left has perfect positive correlation, and plot (b) on the right shows perfect negative correlation. In each case all the points fall on a perfectly straight line.

Such very strong association would seldom, if ever, be encountered in the social sciences. It might, however, occur in a controlled physical experiment; for example, X in plot (a) might be a measure of the flow of water into a closed tank, and Y the height of the water in the tank.

Positive and negative correlation

In the middle panel, plots (c) and (d) again illustrate positive and negative correlation, but here the degree of association is somewhat weaker. In (c) high values of X are generally associated with high values of Y, and low values of X with low values of Y, though with some exceptions, giving a modest positive correlation. In (d) there is a stronger negative correlation: most high values of X are associated with low values of Y, and low values of X with high values of Y.

No linear relationship

The lower panel shows two examples where there is no linear relationship. They are, however, very different. In (e) on the left there is no relationship of any kind: the plots are all over the graph. In (f) on the right there very clearly is a relationship, but it is not a linear (straight-line) one; it is U-shaped.

Plot (f) is important as a reminder that the techniques for the measurement of association that we are examining here (and until chapter 12) relate only to **linear** relationships. Nevertheless, we will find in practice that there are a great many interesting relationships that are, at least approximately, linear. So even with this restriction, correlation is a very useful technique.

As an illustration of an historical relationship, a scatter diagram based on the data for 24 Kent parishes reproduced in table 2.1 is given in figure 3.2. UNEMP is shown on the (horizontal) X axis and RELIEF on the (vertical) Y axis.

3.1.3 Outliers

Note that one of the points in figure 3.2 (in the top right) is very different from all the others. This is known as an **outlier**. One of the advantages of plotting a scatter diagram before proceeding to more elaborate procedures

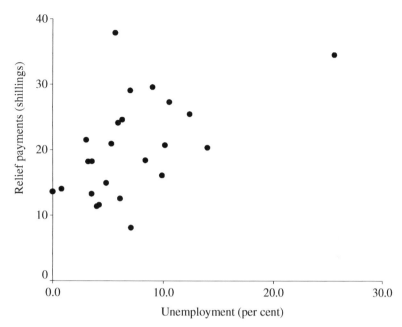

Figure 3.2 Scatter diagram of relief and unemployment, 24 Kent parishes in 1831

is that it immediately reveals the presence of such outliers. The first step should always be to check the data to ensure that the outlier is a genuine observation and not an error in the original source or in the transcription of the data. If it is genuine then its treatment in further analysis is a matter of judgement and there is no simple rule.

If more is known about the circumstances creating the outlier it may be decided that these represent such exceptional circumstances that the case will distort the principal purposes of the study, and alternative procedures should be invoked. This might apply, for example, when two time series have been plotted on a scatter diagram and it is realized that the outlier represents a year in which there was some abnormal extraneous event such as a war or a prolonged strike. In a regional cross-section it may be found that the particular area includes a major city and that this is distorting the results of what is intended to be primarily a study of rural areas.

Alternatively, it may be judged that despite the extreme values the outlier is a fully representative case and should remain as one of the observations in the analysis and in the calculation of further statistical measures.

These and other issues relating to the treatment of outliers are considered in §11.3.4.

3.2 The correlation coefficient

A scatter diagram is an excellent way to get a good visual impression of the presence or absence of a relationship between two variables. But if we want to make a more precise statement about the degree of association we have to use the numerical measure known as the **correlation coefficient.**[c]

3.2.1   Measuring the strength of the association

This measurement of the strength of the association between two interval level variables is designated by the symbol r. It is constructed so that it can take any value in the range from -1.0 to $+1.0$:

> $r = -1.0$ indicates perfect negative correlation
> $r = +1.0$ indicates perfect positive correlation
> $r = 0$ indicates the complete absence of any (linear) correlation.

In figure 3.1, r equals 0.6 for the modest positive relationship in plot (c), and it equals -0.8 for the stronger negative relationship in plot (d). If we calculate the correlation coefficient for UNEMP and RELIEF in the 24 Kent parishes in figure 3.2 the result is found to be 0.52.

THE CORRELATION COEFFICIENT

The correlation coefficient, r,

is a measure of the
degree of linear relationship between two variables.

The value of r may be positive or negative,
and is independent of any specific units.

r will always be between 0 and -1.0 for negative correlation,
and between 0 and $+1.0$ for positive correlation.

The *higher the value of r,*
the stronger is the relationship
between the two variables.

---

[c] Or, more formally, as the Pearson product-moment correlation coefficient.

In calculating r, the variables X and Y appear symmetrically. Interchanging the data for X and Y would not change the results in any way. So the coefficient can tell us only the degree of association between the two variables. An historian might have reason to believe that two variables that show a strong relationship are also causally related, so that one of the variables is influenced by the other. But he cannot learn anything from the correlation coefficient about which of the two might be exercising the influence, and which responding to it.

3.2.2 Derivation of the correlation coefficient, r

At this stage it would be possible simply to hand over to the computer and leave an appropriate statistical program to apply the appropriate formula and calculate r, the correlation coefficient. However, it is desirable to probe a little further in order to develop a better grasp of the ideas lying behind the calculation of the coefficient. These ideas are of great general importance to an understanding of the quantitative methods we shall be using, both here and in many of the subsequent exercises involving regression analysis.

The central issue to be addressed is the measurement of the association between two variables, X and Y. As we have seen, the relationship can be summarized as follows:

	Values of X	Values of Y
Positive correlation:	large or small	large or small
Negative correlation:	large or small	small or large

We have also seen in figure 3.1 that when there is perfect positive or negative correlation, the points cluster along the straight line (plots (a) or (b)). The further the points deviate from this line the weaker is the correlation between the two variables, until we reach the case in plot (e) where there is no possible single line that would be a good fit through all the points.

To get a numerical measurement it is necessary to give a more precise content to the scheme set out above, and to this sense of deviations from the line of perfect correlation. What do we mean by 'large' or 'small' for any particular pair of variables? Given the techniques that have already been

Figure 3.3
Deviations from the
mean

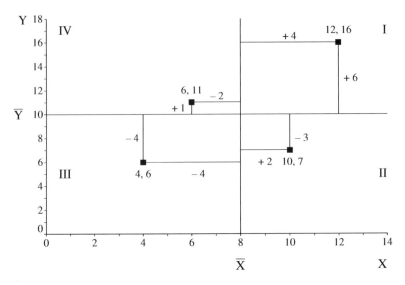

explored in developing the measures of dispersion in §2.3, one obvious possibility would be to think in terms of the size of the respective **deviations from the mean.**

The crucial first step in the calculation of the correlation coefficient is thus to obtain the deviations of each value of X from the mean of the series for the X variable ($\overline{X}$), and the deviations of each value of Y from the mean of that series ($\overline{Y}$).

In order to be able to see exactly what is involved, consider a very simple example, with only 4 pairs of observations:

X_i	Y_i
4	6
6	11
10	7
12	16
Mean: $\overline{X}=\underline{8}$	$\overline{Y}=\underline{10}$

These four sets of points are plotted in figure 3.3, which is divided into four quadrants by drawing a horizontal line through the mean value of Y ($\overline{Y}=10$) and a vertical line through the mean value of X ($\overline{X}=8$).

The first pair of values (4, 6) appears in quadrant III, with both observations below their respective means. Thus both deviations from the mean are negative. To get a measure of the *combined* value of the deviation of both X and Y from their respective means we can either:

add the two deviations to get their *sum*: $-4 + -4 = -8$

or multiply the deviations to get their *product*: $-4 \times -4 = +16$.[d]

Multiplication has certain advantages, and this is the procedure adopted. It then follows that the pairs of values in each quadrant can be classified as follows:

- Any pair of values in quadrant I will have *both values above* their respective means, and both deviations from the mean will be positive. So the product of the deviations for all such points will be *positive*.
- Any point in quadrant III will have *both values below* their respective means, and both deviations from the mean will be negative. So the product of the deviations for all such points will also be *positive*.
- Any pair of values in quadrants II and IV will have *one of the pair above its mean and one below*, and so one deviation will be positive and the other negative. So the product of the deviations for all such points will be *negative*.

The basic element in the measure of association (r) is thus obtained by *adding up all the products of the deviations from the mean*. Two further steps are then required to get the final measure:

(a) We have obtained the total of the combined deviations from the mean by adding up (summing) all the products of the deviations from the mean. But this measure is obviously affected by the *number* of cases in the data set: the larger the number the bigger the sum. To correct for this we divide by the number of cases; this is equivalent to taking an average of the product of the deviations. The resulting measure is called the **covariance** of X and Y, or COV (XY).

(b) The covariance is measured in the units in which X and Y are measured, and is thus awkward to use. If the units were changed (for example from feet to metres) this would cause an inappropriate change in the covariance. In order to correct for this, the covariance is divided by both the standard deviation of X and the standard deviation of Y, thus neutralizing the specific units in which X and Y happen to be measured.

---

[d] If one negative number is multiplied by another negative number the product is positive; if a negative number is multiplied by a positive number the product is negative.

COVARIANCE

The covariance of two variables X and Y is equal to

the sum of the products
of their deviations from their respective means,

divided by
the number of cases.

$$COV(XY) = \frac{\Sigma(X_i - \overline{X})(Y_i - \overline{Y})}{n}$$ (3.1)

We thus get the final formula for the correlation coefficient.

THE CORRELATION COEFFICIENT, r

For two variables, X and Y,
the correlation coefficient, r, is equal to
the covariance of X and Y
divided by
the product of the
standard deviation of X and the standard deviation of Y

$$r = \frac{COV(XY)}{s_X \cdot s_Y}$$ (3.2a)

This can also be written as[1]

$$r = \frac{\Sigma(X_i - \overline{X})(Y_i - \overline{Y})}{\sqrt{\Sigma(X_i - \overline{X})^2} \times \sqrt{\Sigma(Y_i - \overline{Y})^2}}$$ (3.2b)

r is thus independent of any specific units of measure. Unlike the mean or the standard deviation a change in the units in which the variables are measured would have no effect on the value of r. The calculation of r is illustrated for the simple four-case sample data set at the foot of table 3.1.

There should now be no difficulty in understanding intuitively the properties of the correlation coefficient:

Table 3.1 Calculation of the coefficient of correlation for a sample of four (imaginary) values of X and Y

	(1)	(2)	(3)	(4)	(5)	(6)	(7)
			Deviations from means		Deviations squared		Product of deviations
	X_i	Y_i	$(X_i - \bar{X})$	$(Y_i - \bar{Y})$	$(X_i - \bar{X})^2$	$(Y_i - \bar{Y})^2$	$(X_i - \bar{X}) \times (Y_i - \bar{Y})$
	4	6	−4	−4	16	16	+16
	6	11	−2	1	4	1	−2
	10	7	2	−3	4	9	−6
	12	16	4	6	16	36	+24
Sum	32	40	0	0	40	62	+32
Mean	8	10					

$$\text{Standard deviation of X} = s_X = \sqrt{\frac{\Sigma(X_i - \bar{X})^2}{n}} = \sqrt{\frac{40}{4}} = 3.16$$

$$\text{Standard deviation of Y} = s_Y = \sqrt{\frac{\Sigma(Y_i - \bar{Y})^2}{n}} = \sqrt{\frac{62}{4}} = 3.94$$

$$\text{COV(XY)} = \frac{\Sigma(X_i - \bar{X})(Y_i - \bar{Y})}{n} = 32/4 = 8.0$$

$$\text{Correlation coefficient} = r = \text{COV (XY)}/s_X s_Y$$
$$= 8/(3.16 \times 3.94) = 0.64$$

- It will be low when there is no strong relationship between the variables, because in that case there will be a scatter of points in all the quadrants. When the products are added together the positive values in I and III will cancel out the negative values in II and IV, reducing the size of the measure of association. The more evenly the points are scattered over the positive and negative quadrants the closer the coefficient will be to 0.
- The value of r will be large and positive (close to +1.00) when there is a strong positive association between the two variables, because in that case most of the pairs of values will fall in quadrants I and III, and there will be little offsetting effect from points in the negative quadrants.[2]
- The value of r will be large and negative (close to −1.00) when there is a strong negative association, because in that case most of the pairs of values will fall in quadrants II and IV, and there will be little offsetting effect from points in the positive quadrants.

If it is possible to establish that there is a strong (positive or negative) correlation between any two variables, and if there is some theoretical reason to assume that one variable (Y) is influenced by the other (X), then this suggests the possibility that if we know the values of X, we can say something about the likely values of Y. This cannot be done by correlation techniques, but requires the further stage of regression analysis, which we take up in chapter 4.

3.2.3   Interpreting a correlation coefficient

How should we interpret a correlation coefficient? We have already suggested a fundamental rule of interpretation, namely that correlation must not be confused with causation. When an r of 0.75 is recorded between two variables, it indicates that they are related to each other, but it does not tell us anything about the nature of the relationship. It could be that changes in one variable were responsible for the behaviour of the other; however, it could also be that both variables were influenced by the movement of a further, unidentified, variable.

But even if we have decided this issue, there are other points to consider. How, for example, should we judge a particular value of r? One pair of variables may exhibit an r of 0.75, while r for another pair might be measured as 0.25. Are these large or small values? It is standard to apply adjectives indicating the strength of association, such as 'weak', 'moderate', or 'strong', but it should also be recognized that such terms are not absolute. An r of 0.75 might be considered high or low, depending on what was expected before the calculation was made.

Imagine, for example, that we have a sample of students from an historical statistics course. We record two pieces of information for each student, height and weight, and analyse this together with indicators of their performance in the statistics class. We would not expect that height and class performance would be highly correlated; indeed, our expected value would be close to zero. On the other hand, we would expect there to be a strong correlation between height and weight, perhaps on the order of 0.8.

When we analyse correlation coefficients, we must consider the results in the light of our expectations. Were we to find that height and class performance were correlated with r of 0.3, while height and weight were correlated with r of 0.50, we ought to consider the first figure to be high, and the second low, relative to expectations. We should also try to understand why such unexpected results occurred. The same principle applies to historical data. We should try to establish criteria for judging the strength of an association that go beyond a mere mechanical reporting of the correlation coefficients themselves.

A further point to bear in mind when interpreting correlation coefficients is that differences between values of r are not fully symmetric. A higher value of r clearly indicates a higher correlation between the two variables, but the difference between an r of 0.3 and one of 0.5 is not necessarily the same as the difference between 0.5 and 0.7. The relationship between r and the strength of association is not an absolutely linear one.

Finally, we should note that the strength of association between two variables may be affected by the way in which the information on the variables is collected. It is often noted that time-series data tend to exhibit higher values of r than do cross-section data on the same variables. It is, moreover, often suggested that the primary reason for a higher correlation in the time-series comparison is that it reflects the influence of a third variable, namely time. But this is not quite right.

It is certainly true that were we to compare two series (such as population and house-building in the United States in the nineteenth century) we would anticipate a high correlation because both series are trending upwards. It is also true that if we were to compare population levels and house-building rates across regions in, say, 1850, we would expect a lower correlation. Partly this reflects the removal of the influence of time, but the difference is mostly due to the additional influence of a myriad of local factors that affect the pattern of both variables. These would include income levels, migration rates, city building and zoning regulations, the responsiveness of local builders, and so on.

Most time-series data tend to focus on aggregate observations, such as the national rate of house-building and population growth over time, which expunges all the local variation from the statistics. With cross-section analysis, the local variation is included, generating a greater degree of deviation in both X and Y and resulting in a lower r between them.

3.2.4 An illustration of the use of correlation coefficients

For an illustration of the use of correlation coefficients in historical research we turn to the work of Dorothy Thomas, one of the pioneers in the quantitative analysis of social statistics. In a study based on a London PhD and published in 1925 she undertook a comprehensive investigation of the relationship between the business cycle and social conditions in Britain between 1854 and 1913.[e]

Her measure of the business cycle was based on seven series indicative of

---

[e] Dorothy Swaine Thomas, *Social Aspects of the Business Cycle*, Routledge, 1925. The book includes a reprint of part of a paper written jointly with W. F. Ogburn in 1922, when she was at Columbia University, in which a similar analysis was made for the United States using data for 1870–1920.

business conditions, including the value of total exports, unemployment, production of pig iron and of coal, and raw material prices. For each of these she found the secular trend by fitting a suitable curve, calculated the percentage deviation of the series from the long-run trend, and then divided the deviations from trend by their standard deviation to obtain a standardized series.[f] These standardized cycles in each series were then averaged to obtain the overall measure of fluctuations in the 'British business cycle'. A similar procedure was followed for each of the series of social statistics she wished to investigate, and correlation coefficients were calculated.

She also considered the possibility of delayed responses, as a result of which a peak or trough in the business cycle would not make its impact in the same year, but might do so a year or more later. To allow for this she calculated the correlation coefficient between the two series with both measured for the same year, and also with the social indicator lagged by one, two, or three years. The study was further extended by making separate calculations for subperiods to see whether any change in the relationship over time could be detected.

Some of the main results are reported in table 3.2. The positive correlation for, say, marriage rates, indicates that years in which there was a boom in business activity were also years in which the number of marriages was above trend. The negative correlation on suicide rates indicates an inverse relationship: the higher the level of business activity the smaller the proportion of population committing suicide relative to the trend.

The implication of this extended exercise was clearly that the fluctuations in the social statistics were influenced by those of the business cycle. However, Thomas was aware that this was not necessarily a direct influence. She noted explicitly (p. 162) that 'causality cannot be claimed merely on the basis of the coefficients of correlation' and discussed the possibility of indirect influences.

For example, her discussion of the correlation between the business cycle and the birth rate recognized that this might in part be due to the close connection between the cycle and the marriage rate, and between the marriage rate and the birth rate. Similarly, the inverse correlation of the cycle with the rate of illegitimate births was attributed to the restriction of marriage during depressions and its expansion during booms; and she suggested that the lagged positive correlation with infant mortality might be the result of the increase in alcohol consumption during times of

---

[f] For the procedure for calculating the deviations from trend see §1.8. Her method of fitting a trend is the one explained in §12.4.

Table 3.2 Coefficients of correlation with the British business cycle, 1854–1913[a]

	(1) Same year	(2) Social series lagged one year[b]
Marriage rates	+0.67	+0.45
Birth rates	−0.07	+0.29
Illegitimate birth rates	+0.07	−0.26
Death rates[c]	+0.04	+0.31
Infant mortality rates[d]	+0.04	+0.28
Suicide rates	−0.50	−0.47
Divorce rates	−0.02	0
Emigration rates		
Total	+0.48	+0.14
To United States	+0.77	+0.59
Per capita consumption		
Beer	+0.30	+0.45
Spirits	+0.36	+0.60
Prosecutions for drunkenness[e]	+0.33	+0.54
Pauperism[f]		
Indoor	−0.32	−0.52
Outdoor	−0.11	−0.32
All indictable crimes[e]	−0.25	+0.09
Crimes against property[e]		
Without violence	−0.25	+0.02
With violence	−0.44	−0.37

Notes:
[a] The series generally cover a period from the mid-1850s to 1913, but in a few cases the initial date is later than this. The majority cover only England and Wales but those for consumption of alcohol and for emigration relate to the whole of the United Kingdom.
[b] Except for birth rates, which are lagged by 2 years.
[c] Excluding deaths from epidemic diseases.
[d] Excluding deaths from diarrhoea.
[e] Per 100,000 population.
[f] Number of paupers relieved indoors (i.e. in workhouses) or outdoors (i.e. in their own homes) per 1,000 population.
Source: Dorothy Swaine Thomas, *Social Aspects of the Business Cycle*, Routledge, 1925

prosperity. Her comments on the size of the coefficients show that she was also sensitive to the issues of interpretation discussed in the previous subsection.

Thomas included in her discussion a comparison with the corresponding results obtained for the United States. Marriage rates were found to follow business conditions even more closely ($r = +0.81$) than in England and Wales. The positive correlation between the cycle and the lagged death rate was 'contrary to expectation' but was also found in the United States ($r = +0.49$); and both countries showed the same positive correlation between the cycle and lagged infant mortality rates, with a somewhat higher coefficient in the United States ($+0.43$).

One of the more interesting contrasts was the relationship of divorce rates to the cycle. In England and Wales there was no relationship between the two series ($r = -0.02$), whereas in the United States they were highly correlated ($r = +0.70$). The absence of correlation in the former case was attributed to the fact that divorce was expensive and restricted to a small class of wealthy people who were not much affected by the business cycle.

Thomas concluded from her investigation that there was good evidence that the business cycle caused repercussions in various other spheres of social activity, and that the interrelationship between these social phenomena raised questions for social theorists as to the part played by group influences on individual actions. She thought her study 'brings to light tendencies of great interest for the social reformer' and that, above all, it points strongly to the need for further research.[3]

3.3 Spearman's rank correlation coefficient

The measure of correlation which has been discussed is appropriate when working with data that have interval or ratio levels of measurement. An alternative measure, known as **Spearman's rank correlation coefficient**, r_s, is used:

(a) for data that can only be measured on an ordinal scale; or
(b) where ranks have been allotted to data which were originally measured on an interval scale, but the point of interest lies in their rank; or
(c) where the margins of error in interval level data are so large that it is advisable to confine attention to the ranking rather than the actual values.

Like the correlation coefficient, r, the rank correlation coefficient, r_s, takes values ranging from $+1.0$, when there is perfect agreement between the rankings, to -1.0, when there is perfect disagreement. It equals 0 when there is no relationship whatsoever.

The method of calculation is very simple. Each of the two variables is placed in rank order, starting with rank 1 for the highest (or lowest) value. The difference in ranks for each pair, designated D_i, is calculated. These differences are then squared and the sum of the squared differences is used in the following formula, where n equals the number of pairs[g]

$$r_s = 1 - \frac{6\Sigma D_i^2}{n(n^2 - 1)} \qquad (3.3)$$

This measure of correlation was used by Simon Szreter in an examination of the fall in fertility which started in England and Wales in the late nineteenth century.[h] Among his key variables is a measure of completed fertility, classified by the occupation of the husband. This is defined as the number of children born alive to the present marriage by 1911.[i] At the head of the list (rank 1), with the lowest completed fertility, were barristers with an average of 3.16 children born to their marriages; at the other end of the list (rank 195) were coal miners working at the face, with an average of 7.60.

As one element in his very wide-ranging study of the relationship between fertility and social class, occupation, and employment status, Szreter looks at the extent to which this ranking of occupations according to the limitation of fertility within marriage was correlated with a second ranking, reflecting the alternative strategy of prudential marriage: limiting fertility by delaying the age at which the female married. For this index the lowest rank was scored by the occupation with the largest proportion marrying at older ages.

For all occupations, the Spearman coefficient between completed fertility and prudential marriage shows a strong positive correlation of +0.799. However, when Szreter calculated the coefficient for five separate quintile groups (ordered by the completed fertility ranking) he found very interesting differences. For example, for the 39 occupations in the first quintile (those that had most effectively limited births within marriage), the rank correlation coefficient was −0.06. By contrast, for the 39 occupations in the fifth quintile (those with the highest fertility), it was +0.433.

For occupations in this quintile with the highest fertility there was thus a reasonable degree of consistency in their behaviour: in general they were

---

[g] Note that precisely the same result could be produced by using formula (3.2b) but the Spearman coefficient is much simpler to calculate when dealing with ordinal data.

[h] Simon Szreter, *Fertility, Class and Gender in Britain, 1860–1914*, Cambridge University Press, 1996. The issues to which we refer are analysed in chapter 7, especially pp. 335–50. The main source for the data is table 35 in the *Fertility of Marriage Report* in the 1911 Census of Population.

[i] The main measure refers to couples married in 1881–5 when the wife was aged 20–24; Szreter also uses data for families formed at earlier and later ages of marriage and dates.

Table 3.3 Fifth-quintile male occupations rank ordered by completed fertility and female age at marriage

(1) Occupation	(2) Rank by completed fertility	(3) Rank by female age of marriage	(4) Square of difference in rank
Boilermakers	1	21	400
Brass, bronze workers	2	5	9
China, pottery manufacture	3	12	81
Stone – miners, quarriers	4	2	4
Tanners, curriers	5	13	64
Plasterers	6	20	196
Refuse disposal	7	27	400
Ironfoundry labourers	8	10	4
Plaster, cement manufacture	9	22	169
French polishers	10	30	400
Steel – manufacture, smelting, founding	11	9	4
Bricklayers	12	24	144
Road labourers	13	16	9
Gas works service	14	8	36
Oil (vegetable) – millers, refiners	15	28	169
Navvies	16	14	4
Agricultural labourers i/c of horses	17	3	196
General labourers	18	15	9
Agricultural labourers i/c of cattle	19	1	324
Shipyard labourers	20	35	225
Shepherds	21	6	225
Agricultural labourers	22	18	16
Fishermen	23	34	121
Bargemen, lightermen, watermen	24	39	225
Brick, terracotta makers	25	19	36
Dock, wharf labourers	26	25	1
Coal – mineworkers above ground	27	23	16
Builders' labourers	28	11	289
Glass manufacture	29	31	4
Masons' labourers	30	7	529
Coalheavers, coal porters	31	29	4
Tinplate manufacture	32	4	784
Ship – platers, riveters	33	33	0

Table 3.3 (*cont.*)

(1)	(2)	(3)	(4)
	Rank by	Rank by	Square of
	completed	female age	difference
Occupation	fertility	of marriage	in rank
Iron – miners, quarries	34	38	16
Bricklayers' labourers	35	17	324
Coal – mineworkers below ground	36	37	1
Puddlers – iron, steel rolling mills	37	26	121
Pig iron manufacture –(blast furnace)	38	32	36
Coal – mineworkers at the face	39	36	9
			5604

Source: Szreter, *Fertility*, Appendix C, pp. 612–13. The rank order is given in Appendix C for all 195 occupations and the occupations in the fifth quintile were re-ranked from 1 to 39 for this table.

not controlling fertility either by birth control within marriage or by late marriage. This was also true within the fourth quintile. By contrast, within the three lower fertility quintile groups there was an almost complete absence of a relationship between age at marriage and completed fertility. A considerable number of these occupations were thus achieving low fertility within marriage despite also marrying at a relatively young age.

The procedure for calculating the coefficient is illustrated with the data for the fifth quintile in table 3.3. The two rankings are given in columns (2) and (3), and the difference in ranking is obtained and squared in column (4). ΣD^2, the sum of the squared differences, is found to be 5,604. N is 39, so $N^2(N-1)$ in the denominator is 59,280. Inserting these values in (3.3) gives

$$r_s = 1 - \frac{6 \times 5,604}{59,280} = 1 - 0.567 = 0.433$$

Notes

[1] The second expression is obtained by filling in the formulae for COV (XY) and the two standard deviations. Note that when this is done all the terms in n cancel out. The formula for COV (XY) above the line is divided by n; while those for S_x and S_y below the line are each divided by the square root of n, and the product of $\sqrt{n} \times \sqrt{n}$ = n. Thus, both numerator and denominator are divided by n, and so it is eliminated from the formula.

[2] It is beyond the scope of this text to prove that r can never be greater than 1, but it is

perhaps intuitively evident that if there is *perfect* correlation between X and Y so that all the points lie on a straight line, then there will be a *constant* ratio between every pair of values of X and Y. Let us call this ratio b (as in the equation for a straight line, Y $= a + bX$, in §1.5). The ratio between the means of X and Y, and between their deviations from their respective means, must then also be equal to b. All the terms in $(Y - \bar{Y})$ in the formula for r can thus be replaced by $(X - \bar{X})$. If this is done, the numerator and the denominator in the formula both become $b\Sigma(X - \bar{X})^2$, and so $r = 1$.

[3] Later work, also using correlation coefficients, has generally tended to confirm Thomas' findings. See, for example, Jay Winter, 'Unemployment, nutrition and infant mortality in Britain, 1920–50', at pp. 240–45 and 255–6 in Jay Winter (ed.), *The Working Class in Modern British History*, Cambridge University Press, 1983, pp. 232–56, on the inverse relationship between infant mortality and unemployment; and Humphrey Southall and David Gilbert, 'A good time to wed? Marriage and economic distress in England and Wales, 1839–1914', in *Economic history Review*, 49, 1996, pp. 35–57, on the negative correlation between marriage and unemployment (with no lag) in a sample of towns. For a graphical analysis of the incidence of criminal behaviour in England and Wales between 1805 and 1892 see V. A. C. Gattrell and T. B. Hadden, 'Criminal statistics and their interpretation', in E. A. Wrigley (ed.), *Nineteenth-Century Society, Essays in the Use of Quantitative Methods for the Study of Social Data*, Cambridge University Press, 1972, pp. 363–96. Their finding that 'more people stole in hard times than good', while the rate of violent crime was stimulated by 'high wages and high employment' and a consequent 'higher consumption of liquor' also supports Thomas.

3.4 Exercises for chapter 3

1. Calculate *by hand* the correlation coefficient between the following pairs of observations:

Regional grain prices in England, 1691–1692:
(shillings per quarter)

	Wheat	Oats
Thames Valley	43.4	15.1
Eastern	36.3	13.4
Midland	32.7	9.7
Southern	40.0	12.3
South-Western	39.9	10.9
Northern	29.7	8.8

Source: A. H. John, 'The course of agricultural change, 1660-1760', in L. Pressnell (ed.), *Studies in the Industrial Revolution*, University of London, 1960, p. 136.

2. Plot scatter diagrams of the following pairs of variables in the Boyer relief data set.

> UNEMP and DENSITY
> LONDON and INCOME
> GRAIN and RELIEF

(i) In each case, use visual inspection to determine whether the data are uncorrelated, positively correlated, or negatively correlated, and indicate the probable strength of the association. Record your results.

(ii) Now calculate the correlation coefficient. Compare these calculations with the results of your visual inspection.

3. Plot a scatter diagram of the data on UNEMP and BENEFIT from the Benjamin–Kochin data set. Are there any outliers? Calculate the correlation coefficient between these two variables, including and excluding the outlier. What does this calculation tell us about the importance of this unusual observation?

4. Plot a scatter diagram for the variables RELIEF and UNEMP for the 28 Essex parishes in the Boyer relief data set. Are there any outliers? What criteria did you use to identify any unusual observations? Compare the correlation coefficients for the data with and without any outliers. Interpret your results.

5. The following data have been extracted from Angus Maddison's compilation of national income statistics for the nineteenth and twentieth centuries (*Monitoring the World Economy, 1820-1992*, OECD, 1995, p. 23). What are the correlation coefficients between the levels of income in 1820 and 1870; 1870 and 1913; and 1820 and 1913?

Income per person (constant (1990) US dollars) in:	1820	1870	1913
Austria–Hungary	1,295	1,875	3,488
Australia	1,528	3,801	5,505
Canada	893	1,620	4,213
France	1,218	1,858	3,452
Germany	1,112	1,913	3,833
Netherlands	1,561	2,640	3,950
United Kingdom	1,756	3,263	5,032
United States	1,287	2,457	5,307

A critic judges that the probable margins of error in the national income data, especially for 1820 and 1870, make it 'advisable to confine attention to the ranking rather than the actual values' of income per person. In response, calculate the Spearman rank correlation coefficient for each pair of years and compare the results to your previous calculations. Do the comparisons validate the critic's judgement?

6. Calculate the Spearman rank correlation coefficients for the following pairs of variables in the Irish migration data set for 1881:

> URBAN and ILLITRTE
> CATHOLIC and RELIEF
> URBAN and AGRIC

Calculate the Pearson correlation coefficients for the same pairs of variables. Interpret your results, being sure to indicate which measure is more appropriate and why.

CHAPTER 4

Simple linear regression

The aim in this chapter is to extend the analysis of the relationship between two variables to cover the topic of regression. In this introductory discussion we will deal only with **linear** (straight-line) relationships between *two* variables (**bivariate regression**). In chapter 8 this analysis will be extended to include more than two variables (**multiple** or **multivariate regression**), and **non-linear** relationships will be discussed in chapter 12. As with the discussion of correlation, problems arising from the use of sample data are deferred until the issues of confidence intervals and hypothesis testing are covered in chapters 5 and 6.

4.1 The concept of regression

In the discussion of correlation in chapter 3 we emphasized that no distinction was made between the two variables, X and Y, and that interchanging them would have no effect on the correlation coefficient. In the present chapter we change procedure and introduce a fundamental distinction between the two variables.

4.1.1 Explanatory and dependent variables

It will often be the case that we have some theoretical reason to think that movements in one of the variables are *influenced by* movements in the other.

In that case, the convention is to use X for the variable that is *having the influence*, and Y for the variable that is *influenced*.

We could write that as

Y is influenced by X

or, more formally,

$$Y = f(X)$$

which says that Y is some **function** of X.

Y is then referred to as the **dependent variable** and X as the **independent or explanatory** (Xplanatory!) **variable.**[1] When these are plotted in a scatter diagram the dependent variable (Y) is always shown on the vertical axis and the explanatory variable (X) on the horizontal axis.

We might, for example, have two time series, one showing the number of crimes of theft committed each year in the nineteenth century, and the other showing the average price of wheat in that year. The hypothesis would be that people are more likely to steal when times are hard, and the price of wheat is taken as an indicator of the prevailing economic conditions.[a] In this case it is very clear that if there is a relationship the price of wheat will be the explanatory variable (X) and the number of crimes the dependent variable (Y); there is no reason to think that the frequency of crime could influence the wheat price.

However, the decision as to which is the explanatory variable is not always so simple. It will often happen that there is a **mutual interaction** between the two variables. A cross-section study of the relationship between the level of national income per head in a sample of countries, and the expenditure on education by those countries, might find a good correlation. That relationship could occur either (a) because richer countries were able to spend more on education than poor countries; or (b) because high levels of education increased worker productivity and raised the level of national income. More advanced regression techniques would then be needed to investigate these possibilities.

In their study of the impact of benefits on unemployment in inter-war Britain, Benjamin and Kochin consider the possibility that they may have 'interpreted the direction of causation incorrectly, that is, the high level of unemployment may be the cause of the high benefit-to-wage ratio rather than the reverse'. This could happen if, say, the British parliament had been influenced by the extent of unemployment to provide improved benefits. However, they conclude that causation in this direction was not a major problem for their analysis.[b]

Having established this terminology for the two variables we can now take up the concept of regression.

4.1.2 The questions addressed by regression

When we examined the relationship between two interval or ratio level variables (X and Y) in the discussion of correlation, the two main questions addressed were:

[a] For a quantitative historical analysis of a relationship of this type see Douglas Hay, 'War, dearth and theft in the eighteenth century', *Past and Present*, 95, 1982, pp.117–60.

[b] Daniel K. Benjamin and Levis A. Kochin, 'Searching for an explanation for unemployment in interwar Britain', *Journal of Political Economy*, 87, 1979, pp. 453–4.

(a) Is there any *relationship* or *association* between X and Y?
(b) If so, how *strong* is that association, and is it positive or negative?[c]

Once we have established that there is a close relationship between them (and have some reason for thinking that it is not a spurious relationship) we are likely to want to explore two further questions. These are:

(c) What is the *precise nature of the relationship* between X and Y, and how exactly will Y change when X changes by a specified amount?
(d) *How much of the change* (variation) in Y is explained by the specified change in X?

With these questions we are moving beyond issues of mere association to issues of causation, in which changes in one variable *cause* changes in the other.

Regression cannot establish causality, but it can tackle the fundamental issue of *how* the two variables are related. Question (c) is equivalent to asking: What is the *predicted value* of Y for any given value of X? The answer is obtained by fitting an appropriate **regression line** to the data on X and Y. The answer to question (d) is given by calculating the **coefficient of determination (r^2)**. We examine each of these procedures in turn.

4.2 Fitting the regression line

The procedure for fitting a line poses three issues.

4.2.1 How do we define a line?

Recall from §1.5 that a straight line is defined by a general equation of the form

$$Y = a + bX \qquad (4.1)$$

where a and b are constants.

This equation tells us that for any value of X:

$$Y = \textit{the value of a plus b times the value of X}$$

In fact we need to know only two values of X and Y to draw a straight line since, by definition, all points given by the equation lie on the *same* straight line.

As shown in figure 1.1 (see §1.5), b measures the **slope** of the line.

---

[c] An initial visual answer to the first of these questions was obtained in §3.1.2 from a scatter diagram. The correlation coefficient (r) was introduced in §3.2 as the measure of the strength and direction of the association.

If b is *positive*, the line slopes *upward*:   when X rises there is a rise in Y

when X falls there is a fall in Y

If b is *negative*, the line slopes *downward*: when X rises there is a fall in Y

when X falls there is a rise in Y

The larger b is, the steeper the slope, and thus the larger the magnitude of the change in Y for any given change in X.

In the specific context of regression, b is known as the **regression coefficient,** and the basic purpose of a great deal of quantitative analysis is directed to the task of establishing the regression coefficients for particular relationships. It is this coefficient that ideally quantifies the influence of X on Y and enables us to 'predict' how Y will change when X changes.

A primary objective of the quantitative historian and social scientist is thus to test the propositions (hypotheses) suggested by relevant theories in order to discover whether predicted relationships between sets of variables are supported by the data. And, if they are, to measure the regression coefficients in order to give substance to the theory by specifying exactly how the dependent variable is affected by the explanatory variable.

4.2.2   What criterion should be adopted for fitting the line?

We have a cluster or 'swarm' of points, each based on one pair of observations of the two variables. We want to find the *line* which is the 'best fit' through all these pairs of values, i.e. which best describes the linear relationship between X and Y.

If the two variables were perfectly correlated (as in plots (a) and (b) in figure 3.1), it would be easy to do this, since all the points would lie on a single straight line. But that hardly ever occurs. Instead we are more likely to have a spread of points, such as that shown by the RELIEF and UNEMP variables for the 24 Kent parishes in figure 3.2.

There are various possible ways in which the deviations of each point from a line through the middle of the cluster could be measured. The method normally adopted is to calculate the *vertical* distance from each point to the regression line.[2] This is illustrated in figure 4.1 for our simple four-case example from §3.2.2.

What the regression line does is, in effect, to *predict* the values of Y that will be given by the corresponding values of X. A new symbol, $\hat{Y}$ (Y hat), is used to designate this value of Y predicted by the regression line.

Because the correlation is not perfect, most – or all – of the actual Ys will lie some distance from the line, and thus from their predicted value. These

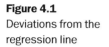

Figure 4.1
Deviations from the
regression line

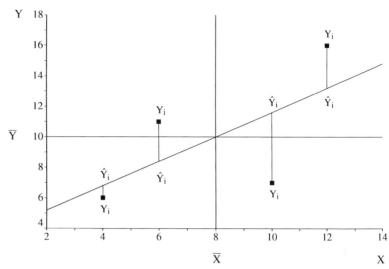

deviations of the *actual* Ys from their *predicted* values are known as **residu-**
als. The advantage of taking the *vertical* distance from the line as the measurement of this deviation or residual $(Y_i - \hat{Y}_i)$ is that it can then be
compared directly with the corresponding vertical deviation of the point
from the mean – this was the distance adopted in §3.2.2 as the measure of
the total deviation.

However, if the residuals are calculated in this way the positive and negative values will automatically cancel out. The sum of all the deviations
below the best fitting regression line will equal the sum of all those above
the line. The position would thus be comparable to the one encountered in
measuring dispersion by the mean arithmetic deviation in §2.3.2. There is
a further difficulty: more than one line can be found which satisfies the
condition of equality of positive and negative vertical deviations from the
line.

The way to get round both these problems is to take the *square* of these
deviations, $(Y_i - \hat{Y}_i)^2$. Since we are interested in all the points in the data set,
we then take the *sum* of these squared deviations from the regression line,
$\Sigma(Y_i - \hat{Y}_i)^2$. There is only one line that minimizes this *sum of squares of the*
vertical deviations, and it is this line that is selected as the 'best fit'.

To show this visually, figure 4.2 repeats figure 4.1, but this time with
the actual squares drawn on each of the deviations for the four pairs of
observations.

Figure 4.2 Least
squares deviations
from the regression
line

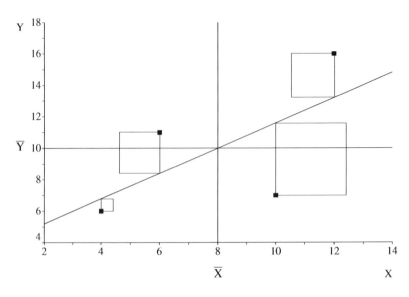

THE REGRESSION LINE

For two variables, X and Y,
the 'best fitting' regression line is defined as the line that

minimizes
the sum of the squares of the vertical deviations
of all the pairs of values of X and Y
from the regression line.

Because of this criterion, the basic procedure is known as **ordinary least squares** regression (frequently abbreviated to OLS).

4.2.3 How do we find this best fitting line?

The formal procedure for minimizing the sum of the squares requires the use of differential calculus, and the details need not concern us. The procedure yields the two formulae needed to calculate the regression line which satisfies the least squares criterion: one for the regression coefficient or slope, b, and the second for the intercept, a.

THE REGRESSION COEFFICIENT

The regression coefficient, b, is the
slope of the regression line

$$b = \frac{\Sigma(X_i - \overline{X})(Y_i - \overline{Y})}{\Sigma(X_i - \overline{X})^2}$$

(4.2)

The components should be familiar, and in fact b equals the covariance of X and Y, divided by the variance of X.[d]

Given b, the intercept, a, can be quickly found from the second formula:

$$a = \overline{Y} - b\overline{X}$$

(4.3)

To increase familiarity with this procedure it will be helpful to work through the simple four-case data previously given in table 3.1. The calculation of the regression line for these pairs of values is set out in table 4.1. All the necessary information was given in table 3.1, but is repeated here for convenience.

With larger data sets one of the statistical computer packages can be used to do the necessary work. For example, for the RELIEF and UNEMP data for the 24 Kent parishes, it applies these formulae to derive the best fitting regression line, giving a = 14.9 and b = 76.4. This regression line is shown in figure 4.3.

4.2.4 The regression of Y on X versus the regression of X on Y

When estimating the strength of the association between two variables it was observed that the coefficient of correlation (r) is wholly symmetrical: the correlation of X with Y is always identically equal to the correlation of Y with X (see §3.2.1).

Such symmetry is *not* present when the regression coefficient, b, is estimated. As shown above, the variance of X is part of the calculation of b, but the variance of Y is not. It is thus essential to distinguish between:

- The *regression of Y on X,* in which *X is the explanatory variable* by reference to which Y can be predicted; and
- The *regression of X on Y,* in which *Y is the explanatory variable* by reference to which X can be predicted.

---

[d] The terms for n in the covariance and the variance cancel out and so do not appear in the formula given for b in (4.2).

Table 4.1 Calculation of the regression coefficient for four values of X and Y

	(1)	(2)	(3)	(4)	(5)	(6)	(7)
			Deviations from means		Deviations squared		Product of deviations
	X_i	Y_i	$(X_i-\bar{X})$	$(Y_i-\bar{Y})$	$(X_i-\bar{X})^2$	$(Y_i-\bar{Y})^2$	$(X_i-\bar{X}) \times (Y_i-\bar{Y})$
	4	6	−4	−4	16	16	+16
	6	11	−2	1	4	1	−2
	10	7	2	−3	4	9	−6
	12	16	4	6	16	36	+24
Sum	32	40	0	0	40	62	+32
Mean	8	10					

$$b = \frac{\Sigma(X_i - \bar{X})(Y_i - \bar{Y})}{\Sigma(X_i - \bar{X})^2} = 32/40 = 0.80$$

$$a = \bar{Y} - b\bar{X} = 10 - (0.8)(8) = 3.60$$

For any given data set these two regressions are *not* the same. If we have reason to be interested in both these forms of a mutual inter-relationship (as in some of the examples discussed in §4.1.1), two separate regression equations have to be found.

The two regressions will have different intercepts and different slopes. If, for example, the two variables are expenditure on education and national income, the amount by which national income grows, when there is an increase in expenditure on education, will not be the same as the amount by which expenditure on education increases, when there is a rise in national income.

4.2.5 Fitting a linear trend to a time series

In §1.8 we discussed the distinction between the long-run trend and short-term fluctuations in a time series. We described a simple method for measuring the trend by means of a moving average, but noted that this procedure suffered from a number of weaknesses. We can now improve on this by using our regression technique to **fit the trend**.

Essentially all that is involved in doing this is that the series for which we wish to find the trend is taken as the dependent variable, and *time is treated*

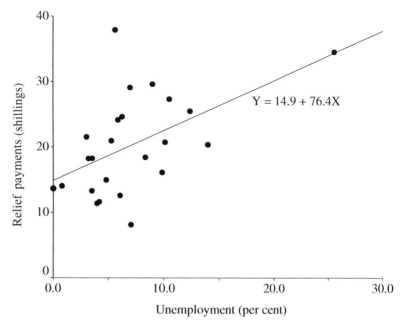

Figure 4.3 Scatter diagram of relief and unemployment with regression line, 24 Kent parishes in 1831

$Y = 14.9 + 76.4X$

as the explanatory variable. The 'names' of the actual years covered by the series (1920, 1921, and so on) have no significance in this context, and we would in the end obtain the same results if we substituted any other sequence of numbers that increased by 1 unit each year. The choice of units for the measure of time will, however, affect the size of the regression coefficients, as we show below.

Given X and Y, the intercept, a, and the regression coefficient, b, can be derived by the standard procedure given in §4.2.3, and these two constants define the trend line. To illustrate the technique we will use the series for NNP (real net national product in £ million at 1938 factor cost) from the Benjamin and Kochin data set.[3] We do so in two forms: in the first we use the actual dates (1920–38) as the measure of time (YEAR); in the second we replace these by the numbers 1–19 (TIME).

When we use YEAR as the explanatory variable, the regression line fitted by our computer package is

$$Y = -132{,}130.60 + 70.54\,\text{YEAR}$$

When we use TIME as the explanatory variable, the regression is

$$Y = 3{,}236.33 + 70.54\,\text{TIME}$$

We see that the two results have the same slope but very different intercepts. In both forms the trend line will rise by £70.54 million every year (i.e. for every increase of 1 unit in either measure of time). But we are trying to obtain the trend in NNP and so need to know the position of the line in relation to this series.

If we take the first year 1920, the equation with YEAR tells us that the predicted value of the line ($\hat{Y}$ in the terminology of §4.2.2) will be $-132,130.6 + (70.54 \times 1920)$, which is £3,307 million. For the same year, the alternative equation with TIME tells us that $\hat{Y}$ will be $3,236.33 + (70.54 \times 1)$, which is again £3,307 million. We will similarly get the same result for every other year, whichever form of the regression we use. The contrast is nevertheless a useful reminder of the need to think about the units in which the dependent and explanatory variables are measured before drawing any conclusions from a regression. We return to this issue in §4.3.3.

The use of simple linear regression is in many respects an improvement on the moving average procedure. There are no missing years at the beginning and end of the series, the trend is perfectly smooth, and – if desired – it could be extrapolated to earlier or later years. However, the method is itself subject to the important limitation that it can generate only a linear trend, and can thus be used only when inspection of the data indicates that a straight line is appropriate. In this case, as can be seen in figure 4.4, the linear trend does fit the data well. However, if there is clearly evidence of a non-linear trend, then the calculation must be made with slightly more advanced methods, notably the log-linear (semi-logarithmic) trend that will be described in chapter 12 (see especially panel 12.1).

4.3 Measuring the goodness of fit

The procedure for obtaining the regression line for any pair of variables, X and Y, has now been established. There will always be one regression line which we can fit to a given data set by applying the ordinary least squares (OLS) criterion. By definition it is the best linear fit that can be achieved on that criterion.

However, that still leaves the crucial research question: *How good a fit is it?* It may be the *best* fit there is, but is it a *good* fit?

4.3.1 Explained variations and unexplained variations (residuals)

Asking how well the line fits the data points is equivalent to asking: *How much of the variation in Y is explained by this regression line?* In the ideal case of perfect correlation, all the points would lie exactly on the line, and the regression line would 'explain' 100 per cent of the variation in Y. If we know how X changes, we could say by *exactly* how much Y will change.

Figure 4.4 Net national product, United Kingdom, 1920–1938 and linear trend

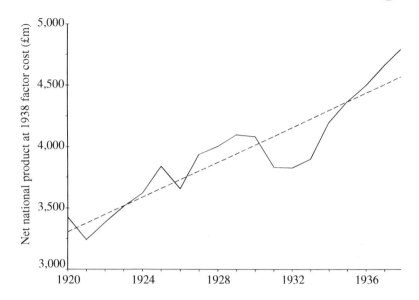

In history and the social sciences we always have to settle for something less than this. However powerful the selected explanatory factor may be, there will always be a variety of other factors – both systematic and random – which will also affect the behaviour of the dependent variable (Y).

It is thus necessary to have a measure of how successful the regression line is in explaining (in the limited sense of 'accounting for') the movements in Y. This measure is known as the **coefficient of determination** (r^2) and is equal to the square of the correlation coefficient. The value of r^2 is always between 0 and 1.[e] The closer it is to 1, the larger the proportion of the variation in Y that has been 'explained' by the movements in the explanatory variable, X.

The statistical package will quickly find r^2 for us, but in order to see more clearly what is happening it will be useful to look briefly at the underlying logic of the calculation.

The objective is to find a measure of the success with which the movements in Y are explained by the movements in X. We thus need some way to specify these movements in Y, and we take for this purpose the *deviation from the mean* for each value in the series. The justification for this is that if we knew nothing about the factors determining the behaviour of Y, our 'best guess' for the value of any individual case, Y_i would have to be that it would be equal to the mean of the series, $\bar{Y}$.

---

[e] Since r cannot be greater than ± 1, r^2 cannot be greater than 1^2, and $+1 \times +1 = -1 \times -1 = 1$.

Figure 4.5
Explained and
unexplained
deviations

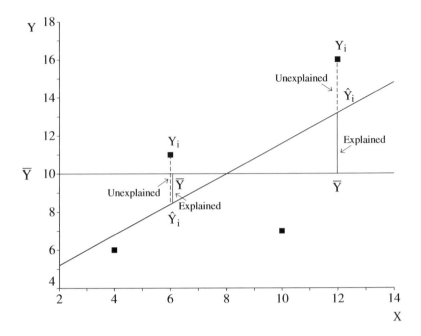

The regression line should enable us to improve on this estimate by pre-dicting the value of Y for any given value of X. As noted earlier, the symbol $\hat{Y}$ is used to designate this *predicted* value. There are thus three possible values of Y to be considered:

$$Y_i = \text{the value of any particular observation}$$

$$\bar{Y} = \text{the mean value of all the observations, and}$$

$$\hat{Y}_i = \text{the value of } Y_i \text{ predicted by the regression line.}$$

The relationship between them is illustrated in figure 4.5, using again the data for our simple four-case example from table 4.1. The graph shows the four points together with:

(a) a horizontal line drawn through the mean value $\bar{Y}$; and
(b) the regression line, $\hat{Y}_i = 3.60 + 0.80\, X_i$.

The deviations (or variations) for each value of Y can then be analysed as follows:

$$(Y_i - \bar{Y}) = \text{the } total \text{ deviation}$$

$$(\hat{Y}_i - \bar{Y}) = \text{the part of the deviation predicted or ‘}explained\text{’ by the regression line}$$

$$(Y_i - \hat{Y}_i) = \text{the } residual \text{ or part left } unexplained = (Y_i - \bar{Y}) - (\hat{Y}_i - \bar{Y})$$

This decomposition of the deviations or variation is illustrated in figure 4.5 for two of the four cases: those where $X = 12$ and $Y = 16$, and where $X = 6$ and $Y = 11$. In the former the regression line comes between the mean and Y_i, and the total deviation is a straightforward sum of the explained and unexplained components. However, for the latter point, Y_i is above both the mean and the predicted value, so that the value predicted by the regression line actually takes us even further from the value of Y_i, leaving an unexplained residual which is larger than the total deviation.

On the basis of this form of decomposition of the deviations we can now turn to the construction of a measurement of the goodness of fit.

4.3.2 The coefficient of determination, r^2

It is – as usual – preferable to work with the *squares* of the deviations, and since we are interested in the outcome over all pairs of values, it is again necessary to *sum* all the cases. Fortunately, the decomposition given above also holds when we take the *sum of squares*. We can thus write:

$$\Sigma (Y_i - \bar{Y})^2 \quad = \quad \Sigma (\hat{Y}_i - \bar{Y})^2 \quad + \Sigma (Y_i - \hat{Y}_i)^2 \qquad (4.4)$$

Total variation $=$ Explained variation $+$ Unexplained variation

Alternative terms are sometimes used. The total variation may be called the **total sum of squares.** The explained variation may be called either the **explained sum of squares** or the **regression sum of squares,** and the unexplained variation may be called either the **residual sum of squares** or the **error sum of squares.**

Equation (4.4) provides the means to measure the **coefficient of determination.**

THE COEFFICIENT OF DETERMINATION

The coefficient of determination, r^2,

is the *proportion of the total variation that is explained by the regression line.*

r^2 is equal to the ratio of the *explained* sum of squares to the *total* sum of squares.

$$r^2 = \frac{\Sigma (\hat{Y}_i - \bar{Y})^2}{\Sigma (Y_i - \bar{Y})^2} \qquad (4.5)$$

Table 4.2   Calculation of the coefficient of determination for four values of X and Y

(1)	(2)	(3)		(4)	(5)	(6)	(7)
Variables		**Predicted value of Y**		**Explained Deviation**		**Total Deviation**	
X_i	Y_i	$a + bX_i$	$= \hat{Y}_i$	$(\hat{Y}-\bar{Y})$	$(\hat{Y}-\bar{Y})^2$	$(Y_i-\bar{Y})$	$(Y_i-\bar{Y})^2$
4	6	$3.6+0.8\,(4)$	$= 6.8$	-3.2	10.24	-4	16
6	11	$3.6+0.8\,(6)$	$= 8.4$	-1.6	2.56	1	1
10	7	$3.6+0.8\,(10)$	$= 11.6$	$+1.6$	2.56	-3	9
12	16	$3.6+0.8\,(12)$	$= 13.2$	$+3.2$	10.24	6	36
32	40			0.0	25.60	0	62

Note:
For column (3) a = 3.60 and b = 0.80 as calculated in table 4.1.

r^2 = Explained deviation/Total deviation
= 25.60/62 = 0.41

We can now apply this measure to our basic parish example. For RELIEF and UNEMP in Kent we get an r^2 of 0.275. Unemployment is thus able to account for only 27.5 per cent of the variation in payments by these parishes, and the greater part of the variation has thus to be explained by other factors. These could include the generosity of the ratepayers, the different systems of child allowances, the level of income from wages and other sources such as allotments, the extent of sickness, and the proportion of old people in the parish.

The actual details of the calculation of r^2 for the simple four-case data set are shown in table 4.2.

4.3.3 Some intuitive implications

We conclude this section by exploring the relationship between the regression coefficient, b, and the coefficient of determination, r^2. When we derived the best fitting line in §4.2.3, it was noted that the formula given for the regression coefficient, b, in an equation of Y on X, was equal to the covariance of X and Y, divided by the variance of X.

Similarly, in §3.2.2, when we derived the coefficient of correlation between X and Y, it was noted that r could be written as the covariance of X and Y, divided by the product of the standard deviation of X and the standard deviation of Y (see (3.2a)). It is worth writing both of these out as equations

$$b = \frac{\text{COV}(XY)}{s_X^2} \tag{4.6}$$

$$r = \frac{\text{COV}(XY)}{s_X s_Y} \tag{4.7}$$

The first of these two equations can easily be re-written as

$$b = \frac{\text{COV}(XY)}{s_X s_Y} \times \frac{s_Y}{s_X} \tag{4.6a}$$

and if the first of these terms in (4.6a) is replaced by r we have

$$b = r \times \frac{s_Y}{s_X} \tag{4.8}$$

This states that the regression coefficient is equal to the correlation coefficient (the square root of the coefficient of determination) multiplied by the ratio of the standard errors of Y and X. Three intuitive results follow immediately from (4.8).

First, if $r = 0$, then b must also be 0.

Secondly, although r is independent of the units of measurement of X and Y, b is not. To return to our earlier example, if RELIEF expenses were measured not in shillings but in pounds, the standard error of X would fall to one-twentieth of its level (since there are 20 shillings to a pound). The correlation coefficient, r, would remain unchanged. Thus, b would be 20 times larger in this alternative regression. This is an example of a **scalar** effect, which arises when a variable is revalued consistently across all observations.[f]

The scalar effect of changing the denomination of a variable can be very useful to researchers. Let us imagine, for example, that a PhD student is interested in the demographic origins of homelessness in the United States in the 1930s and considers urban size to be a major influence. She therefore collects cross-section data on homelessness and total population for each city. If she decided to regress the proportion of each city's population who were homeless in 1930 on the number of individuals in each city according to the US Census of that year, she would find that the coefficient, b, would be very small, on the order of 0.00000001.[g]

---

[f] Note that the relationship between YEAR and TIME in the regression fitted to NNP in §4.2.5 is not consistent in this sense: the ratio of 1920 to 1 is very different from the ratio of 1938 to 19.

[g] Assume that there are five cities, with populations of 3,400,000, 5,000,000, 1,500,000, 500,000, and 200,000. Proportions of homelessness are 0.03, 0.06, 0.02, 0.01, and 0.0085. From this, we can calculate that $s_y = 0.018814$; $s_x = 1,823,623$; $r = 0.97$; and $b = 0.00000001$.

Presenting the coefficient in this way would be cumbersome. Were she to express homelessness as a percentage rather than a proportion of the population (e.g. 5.0 per cent, rather than 0.05), b would rise to 0.000001. Alternatively, were she to express urban size in millions of residents, b would rise to 0.01. If she combined both these scalar transformations of the data, b would become 1.

This final result indicates that, according to the regression, a city that is 1 million people larger than another would experience a 1 per cent increase in homelessness. This second result has exactly the same meaning as the original version, in which an increase in population from one city to another of one person increased the proportion of homelessness by one-millionth of a per cent. However, the second version is clearly very much easier to think about and work with.

It is thus important to look at the units of measurement of the dependent and explanatory variables before drawing strong inferences about the historical importance of an estimated regression coefficient.

Thirdly, the size of the coefficient, b, will be influenced by the relative size of the variation of X and Y, even when the two variables are expressed in the same units (e.g. both X and Y are proportions, or they are both denominated in the same currency unit). As should be clear from (4.8), for any given value of r, the larger the ratio of s_Y to s_X, the larger will be the regression coefficient, b.

To illustrate, assume that X and Y are highly correlated, say with $r = 0.9$. If the values of X are very highly clustered (so that s_x is relatively low), while those of Y are more spread out (so that s_Y is relatively high), the regression coefficient, b, will be high, indicating a steep regression line of Y on X (see figure (4.6(a)). Alternatively, if X varies a great deal around its mean, while Y is more tightly distributed, the ratio of s_Y to s_x will be lower than in the previous case and b will be small, indicating a shallow regression line (see figure (4.6(b)). At the extreme, if there is no variation in X (so that s_x is zero), the regression line will be vertical (b is infinite). If there is no variation in Y (so that s_Y is zero), the regression line will be horizontal (b is zero).

It is thus essential to pay attention to the variation of the regression variables before evaluating the regression as a whole. If there is little or no variation in the explanatory variable (low s_x), it is not going to explain much of the behaviour of the dependent variable. The regression model will have little explanatory power. On the other hand, if there is little or no variation in the dependent variable (low s_Y), there is little to be explained, and applying a formal regression model may be a case of 'using a sledgehammer to crack a nut'.

Figure 4.6 The relationship between the correlation coefficient, r, the regression coefficient, b, and the standard deviations of X and Y

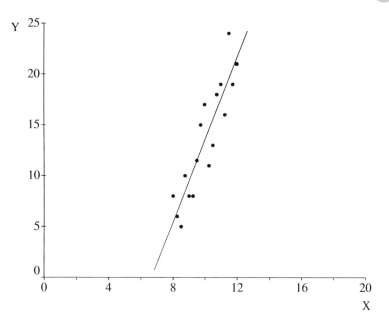

(a) When s_x is low relative to s_y

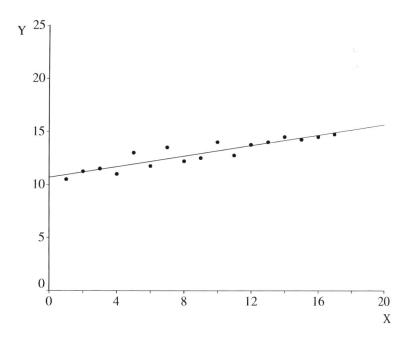

(b) When s_x is high relative to s_y

Figure 4.7
Ballantine for a
simple regression
with one
explanatory variable

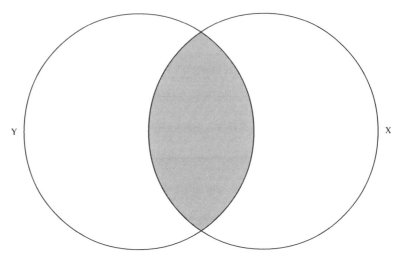

4.4 Introducing the Ballantine

One way of presenting this somewhat technical material in a more intuitive format is with the aid of a diagram known as the **Ballantine**.[4] The Ballantine for the case of simple regression with one explanatory variable is presented in figure 4.7. The two variables, X and Y, are each represented by a circle, the areas of which represent their respective variances.

In figure 4.7, we have assumed that the variances of X and Y are equal and have therefore drawn the circles to be the same size. The shaded area in the diagram shows the overlap between the two variables. This overlap (or union) of the two circles indicates the extent to which the variance of X explains the variance of Y. It is equal to r^2, the coefficient of determination. In this case, the shaded area is 30 per cent of the total area of Y's circle: the coefficient of determination is thus 0.3.

That part of the variance that cannot be explained by the regression is shown by the unshaded part of each circle, which in this case is equal to 0.7. The greater the degree of overlap, the more of the variation of Y is explained by the variation of X. If the two circles overlap completely, X explains Y completely and the coefficient of determination is 1. Conversely, if the two circles do not overlap at all, then the two variables are completely independent and the coefficient of determination will be 0.

The Ballantine of figure 4.7 is a very stylized representation of regression analysis. In particular, it sets the variances of X and Y to be equal. Normally, of course, this would not be the case: each variable will have a different variance.[5] How does this difference in the relative size of the variances affect our understanding of the Ballantine? In order to understand this, let us delve into the derivation of the Ballantine a little further, with the aid of our simple regression model from §4.2 based on the data given in table 4.1.

The variances of X and Y can be calculated as 10 and 15.5, respectively (from columns (5) and (6)); thus, in the Ballantine representation of this regression, Y would have a larger circle than X. The covariance between X and Y is 8.0 (from column (7)). The covariance is a measure of how far the two variables move together, or covary; this is the statistical equivalent of the shaded area in figure 4.7.

The size of the shaded area relative to the total area of each circle is equal to the ratio of the covariance to the variance of X and Y, respectively. The coefficient of determination is simply the product of these two ratios. Thus

$$r^2 = \frac{8}{10} \times \frac{8}{15.5} = 0.41$$

This result is thus the same as the one calculated in a different way in table 4.2.

In the bivariate case, the Ballantine also incorporates all the information necessary to calculate the regression coefficient. Recalling that r is simply the square root of the coefficient of determination, and that the standard deviations of X and Y are equal to the square roots of their respective variances, we can use (4.8) to calculate the regression coefficient, b, as

$$b = \sqrt{0.41} \times \frac{\sqrt{15.5}}{\sqrt{10}} = 0.64 \times \frac{3.94}{3.16} = 0.80$$

which is the same figure that is derived in table 4.1.

In later chapters, we shall use the Ballantine to explore the complexities of regression analysis. In future, we shall always draw the circles with the same area, and ignore the complications involved in having variables with different variances. Therefore, when looking at the Ballantines in later chapters, it should be remembered that they are an analytical device, rather than a precise depiction of the structure of any regression and its component variables.

Notes

[1]   The dependent variable may also be referred to as the regressand, or as the explained, endogenous, or target variable. The explanatory variable can similarly be referred to as the regressor or the predictor, or as the independent, exogenous, or control variable.

2   Alternative possibilities would be to measure either the horizontal distance or the distance represented by a line drawn at right angles to the regression line.

3   Note though that this is not the form of trend actually used by Benjamin and Kochin. They calculated a so-called log-linear trend by a procedure we will explain in panel 12.1 in chapter 12.

4   The Ballantine was originally introduced by Jacob and Patricia Cohen, *Applied Multiple Regression/Correlation Analysis for the Behavioral Sciences*, Lawrence Erlbaum Associates, 1975, to discuss correlation coefficients, and later mis-spelt and extended by Peter Kennedy to the analysis of regression techniques, Peter E. Kennedy, 'The "Ballentine": a graphical aid for econometrics', *Australian Economic Papers*, 20, 1981, pp. 414–16.

5   One way to conceptualize the Ballantine with equal circles is to assume that all variables have been standardized by the Z transformation, so that all variances are forced to one.

4.5 Exercises for chapter 4

1. Which is the explanatory variable and which the dependent variable in the following combinations?

> Height and weight
> Birth rate and marriage rate
> Unemployment and poverty
> Rainfall and crop yields
> Rate of unemployment and level of relief expenditures in parishes in Southern Britain
> Government spending on welfare programmes and the voting share of left-liberal parties

In which of these cases might you expect a mutual interaction between the two variables?

2. Using the following values of X and Y:

> X: 4, 8, 12, 16
> Y: 10, 10, 3, 7

Calculate *by hand*:

> The regression coefficient, b
> The intercept, a
> The total sum of squares
> The explained sum of squares
> The residual sum of squares
> The coefficient of determination.

3. In the table below, (2) is an imaginary series. (3) is the official (*London Gazette*) market price of wheat, rounded to the nearest 5 shillings. (4) is a hypothetical series.

(1)	(2) Number of popular	(3) Price of wheat	(4) Number of
Year	disturbances	(shillings per qtr)	shipwrecks
1810	20	105	12
1811	50	95	23
1812	60	125	32
1813	40	105	22
1814	20	75	8
1815	10	65	7
1816	30	75	17
1817	30	95	17
1818	20	85	8
1819	40	75	18
1820	20	65	8
1821	20	55	8

  (i) *By hand*, calculate the correlation coefficient for wheat prices and the number of disturbances.

  (ii) *By hand*, find the equation for the regression line for wheat prices and the number of disturbances. (*Hint*: think first about which is the appropriate explanatory variable.)

 (iii) Plot the corresponding scatter diagram and regression line.

 (iv) By hand, calculate the correlation coefficient for number of shipwrecks and the number of disturbances.

  (v) Compare the coefficients calculated in (i) and (iv).

Write a short note interpreting your results.

4. Using the Hatton–Williamson data set on Irish migration by county, determine how much of the total variance in FAMSIZE in 1911 is explained by the behaviour of:

     CATHOLIC

     AGE

     ILLITRTE

Interpret your results.

5. Run simple regressions on the Benjamin–Kochin data set of

> UNEMP on BENEFITS, 1920–39
> UNEMP on DEMAND, 1920–39

Record the coefficients and standard errors. Plot the residuals from each regression. What do they tell you about the extent to which 1920 is an outlier? Re-run these regressions dropping 1920. Record the coefficients and standard errors and plot the residuals.

6. Critics of your analysis of disturbances and wheat prices in question 3 suggest the following errors in the statistics:

   (i) The number of disturbances in 1819 was 60 not 40.
  (ii) The price of wheat in 1819 was 70 not 75.
 (iii) All the figures on the number of disturbances have a margin of error of plus or minus 10 per cent.
 (iv) The figures of wheat prices are too low, since they represent market prices received by farmers, not retail prices paid by workers; retail prices are 25 per cent higher in each year.

Draw up a statistical response to all of these criticisms. Generate new results where applicable.

7. Use the methodology of §4.4 to calculate *by hand* the coefficient of determination and the regression coefficient from the data in question 2. What do your results tell you about the limitations of this approach?

8. In a bivariate regression of Y on X, the variance of the dependent variable is 100, while the variance of the explanatory variable is 4. The covariance of X and Y is 2.

   (i) Draw the Ballantine that illustrates the regression, being careful to draw the variances of X and Y in due proportion. Calculate the values of b and r^2 in this model.

In a second regression, the variance of X is 100 and the variance of Y is 4.

  (ii) Draw the Ballantine that illustrates the regression; calculate the values of r^2 and b.
 (iii) How do you explain any differences between your answers for (i) and (ii)?

PART II

Samples and inductive statistics

CHAPTER 5

Standard errors and confidence intervals

5.1 Introduction

The previous chapters have been concerned with a review of basic descriptive statistics. We now move to the much more important topic of **inductive statistics**. This chapter and chapter 6 will be devoted to an exploration of some of the implications of working with data from samples. The basic purpose of inductive statistics is to make it possible to say something about selected characteristics of a **population** on the basis of what can be inferred from one or more **samples** drawn from that population (see §1.3.4).

Samples can be obtained in various ways. Typically, the historian works with information extracted from surviving documents such as parish registers, manuscript census schedules, household inventories, farm accounts, private diaries, and records of legal proceedings. She will usually be working with a sample of such records, either because that is all that was ever available (only some people keep diaries), or because only some of the original documents have survived, or because the records are so detailed that it would be too expensive and time-consuming to extract all the information they contain.

Whenever sample data are used it is necessary to pose the fundamental question: How good are the results from the sample? How much can we learn about the population as a whole from the data available to us, and with what confidence? The overall answer to these questions involves three separate issues that must be considered briefly before turning to the statistical aspects.

(a) Is the sample of records that has survived representative of the *full set of records* that was originally created?

(b) Is the sample drawn from the records representative of the *information in those records*?

(c) Is the information in those records representative of a *wider population* than that covered by the records?

We may consider two categories of source material. In the first, evidence for the entire set of records is recoverable (as would normally be true of census manuscripts, parliamentary debates, certain of the records of legal proceedings, and certain parish registers), in which case the two remaining issues are (b) and (c). Dealing with (b) is a matter of adopting an appropriate sampling method. As long as each member of the population is equally likely to be selected, so that the sample is random, (b) will be achieved.[1]

The judgement with respect to (c) will depend on the nature of the records concerned. Census schedules should cover the entire population, though certain groups may be under-represented because they are, or choose to make themselves, less visible to the enumerators. Surviving records of various forms of taxation (for example, hearth and poll tax returns, income taxes, and probate inventories) will often be complete and are a valuable source for historians, but they typically omit a substantial part of the population: usually the poor, often women, always those who managed to evade assessment. Parish registers may provide data that are representative of members of the established church, but not of dissentients such as Methodists or Quakers; or the parishes for which registers survive may not be representative of all parishes in the country. Court records may not be representative of all the individuals falling within the court's jurisdiction if the costs of initiating legal proceedings were prohibitive for some. This group of issues under (c) is thus a matter for careful consideration in relation to each particular source.

The second category of sources consists of cases where the surviving records are highly fragmentary (e.g. private diaries, business records, household inventories) so that there are problems with respect to (a). In that case care needs to be taken to establish that the source provides a reliable guide to the original population, before proceeding to address (b) and (c). For some sources this can be done by comparing key characteristics of the surviving records to some known attributes of the population. If these characteristics are generally consistent, this may be enough to establish representativeness.[2]

Sometimes the comparison indicates that records survive for some parts of the population more frequently than for others (e.g. that business records survive more often for bigger firms than for smaller ones). In such cases, it may be possible to develop sampling strategies to counteract the bias in the surviving data and create a more representative data set. Finally, there may be cases where it is not possible to establish the *bona fides* of the surviving data at all, either because there is no basis for comparison with the population (e.g. household inventories) or because the data are clearly not representative (e.g. private diaries in an era of limited literacy).

We do not suggest that statistical analysis of unrepresentative evidence is uninteresting, but in what follows we are assuming that the sample is representative of the population in all three of the dimensions mentioned, such that we can apply the logic of inferential statistics to recover information about the population attributes from the sample available to us.

Once representativeness has been established, we can focus on the nature of the sample results. So, when we ask, 'How good are the results obtained from the sample?', we are asking, in effect, whether the same results would have been obtained if a different sample had been used.

Unfortunately, it is normally not possible to find out by drawing more samples (either because the information is not available or because the exercise would be too expensive). Instead we have to rely on statistical theory to tell us about the probability that the results we have obtained can be regarded as a true reflection of the corresponding characteristics of the underlying population. Our task is thus to learn how we can make **inferences** about various **parameters** of the population, given what we know from the sample **statistics** (see §1.3.4).

In particular, in this chapter we will consider how to achieve a given probability that a specified range or **confidence interval** around the sample statistic will cover the true (unknown) value we wish to estimate; and in chapter 6 we will explore the closely related topic of the procedure for **testing statistical hypotheses**. If we were considering only one variable, these statistics might be, for example, estimates of the mean and standard deviation of the sample. If we were dealing with the relationship between samples of data for two variables, we might have sample statistics for the correlation and regression coefficients.

As noted before (§1.4), Greek letters are usually used to denote characteristics of the population, while Roman letters are used for the corresponding estimates from samples from that population. The Greek and Roman symbols we will use in this and other chapters are set out below.

SYMBOLS FOR CHARACTERISTICS OF THE POPULATION AND ASSOCIATED SAMPLES

Characteristic	Population	Sample
Mean	μ	$\bar{X}$
Variance	σ^2	s^2
Standard deviation	σ	s
Proportion	π	p
Correlation coefficient	ρ	r
Intercept for regression line	α	a
Regression coefficient	β	b
Number of cases	N	n

5.2 Sampling distributions

To introduce the subject of confidence intervals we will confine our attention to estimates of a *sample mean*. All the points that are made would apply equally to any other measure derived from the sample, such as a proportion or a correlation coefficient.

Take, for example, the information on BRTHRATE in 1826–30 in the Poor Law data set consisting of a sample of 214 English parishes. The mean rate was 15.636 births per 100 families. There were, however, over 15,000 parishes in England at that time. So the fundamental question that has to be considered is: if the population mean is μ (lower case Greek mu),

How good is this sample mean, $\bar{X}$, as an estimator of μ?

At this point probability becomes crucial to the procedure and would be studied intensively in a formal statistics course. Although we are not going to do this, we must take just a fleeting glance at what is involved in order to get an intuitive understanding of some basic features of the procedures we will use.

5.2.1 Sampling distributions and point estimates of the population mean

To answer our fundamental question about the reliability of the sample mean it is necessary to introduce the concept of a **sampling distribution**. In this case we are dealing with the **sampling distribution** of the **sample mean**, but there would be a corresponding sampling distribution for every other statistic derived from a sample, for example, the **sampling distribution** of the **sample regression coefficient**. To understand this notion of a sampling distribution it is essential to appreciate that it is one of *three* distinct – though related – distributions.

- The first is the **population distribution**. The information required for this is not actually available in the case of BRTHRATE. However, it would, in principle, have been possible to obtain and plot a distribution of BRTHRATE for *all* parishes in England. On the horizontal (X) axis this would show the range of values recorded for births per 100 families. On the vertical (Y) axis it would show the total number (or proportion) of parishes in England that had recorded each successive rate.

  Some birth rates would occur very infrequently; these would be shown at the extremes of the distribution, either to the left if they were very low rates, or to the right if they were exceptionally high. Other rates would occur very frequently, particularly those close to the mean, and these would be plotted near the centre of the distribution.

- The second is the **distribution of the particular sample** drawn from this population. For this we actually have the relevant data on the mean BRTHRATE for the sample of 214 English parishes and could plot the distribution. On the horizontal axis this would show the range of values recorded for births per 100 families. On the vertical axis it would show the number (or proportion) of parishes in the sample that had recorded each successive birth rate.

- The third is the **sampling distribution of the sample mean**. This is rather different in character from the first two. Imagine that there is not just one sample of 214 parishes, but a very large number of successive random samples of that size, each drawn from the same population.[a] For every separate sample the *mean* BRTHRATE shown by that sample could be calculated.

  We could then plot a distribution of these *sample means*. On the horizontal axis this would show the range of values recorded for the mean BRTHRATE. On the vertical axis it would show the number (or proportion) of samples that had produced each value of the mean. This hypothetical distribution is called the sampling distribution of the sample mean.

---

[a] Strictly, it should be *all possible* samples of the given size.

For a practical illustration of the concept of the sampling distribution, see questions 7 and 8 in the exercises for this chapter.

More generally, it can be defined as shown in the following box.

SAMPLING DISTRIBUTION

A sampling distribution
is the *distribution of a sample statistic*
that would be obtained if

a large number of random samples of a given size
were drawn from a given population.

Note that this sampling distribution is not observed empirically. It is the *hypothetical* distribution that *would be obtained* if a large number of samples were taken from a given population. This notion of a sampling distribution can now be applied to some fundamental propositions in statistical theory.

5.3 Four fundamental statistical propositions

Four fundamental propositions relating to the sample results can be derived from statistical theory. They are known collectively as the Central Limit Theorem, and in this text these are simply accepted gratefully without further enquiry into their mathematical foundations.

5.3.1 The Central Limit Theorem

1 (a) If the population has a normal distribution the sampling distribution of a known sample mean ($\bar{X}$) will also be normal; and

  (b) even if the population distribution is *not* normal, the sampling distribution of $\bar{X}$ will nevertheless be approximately normal, provided that the sample size is sufficiently large.[b]

2 (a) The mean of the sampling distribution of the sample means will be equal to μ, the unknown population mean.

---

[b] A sample size of 10 or 20 will often be enough for this purpose, but anything less than 30 is usually treated as a *small* sample. The reason for this is discussed in §5.4.2.

  (b) *On average,* the known sample mean ($\overline{X}$) will be equal to the mean of
      the sampling distribution.
  (c) It therefore follows that, *on average,* the known sample mean ($\overline{X}$) will
      be equal to μ, the unknown population mean.

   The value of the sample mean can thus be taken as a **point estimate** of
the population mean.[c] Naturally any individual sample is likely to be a little
above or below the population mean. The second contribution made by
statistical theory enables us to calculate by how much any single sample is
likely to miss the target.

3 (a) The estimation error for any given point estimate, $\overline{X}$, is determined
       by the shape of the sampling distribution.

   The flatter the sampling distribution, the more the possible values of $\overline{X}$
will be spread out, and the wider the distance between any given $\overline{X}$ and μ.
Conversely, the greater the clustering of sample means, the less the likely
estimation error of any given $\overline{X}$ relative to μ. Because the standard deviation of the sampling distribution thus indicates the range of possible error
in estimating μ owing to differences between samples, it is commonly
referred to as the **standard error**.

THE STANDARD ERROR

The estimated
standard deviation of the sampling distribution
is known as
the Standard Error.

This may be abbreviated to SE.

  (b) The size of the standard error depends on the size of the sample being
      drawn from the population. As the sample size increases, the more
      clustered will be the array of sampling means around the population
      mean, μ, and the smaller will be the estimation error attributable to
      any given sample mean, $\overline{X}$.

   The ideal formula for the standard error of the sample mean is $\sigma/\sqrt{n}$,
where σ (lower case Greek sigma) is the standard deviation of the

---

[c] A **point estimate** is a single value. The alternative is an **interval estimate** covering a range of
values and thus making a less precise claim to identify the single (unknown) population value.

population distribution, and n is the size of the sample. Unfortunately, however, this formula requires the value of the population standard deviation (σ), and we usually do not know this. Once again the theorem comes to the rescue.

4 The standard deviation of the sample (s) can be taken as the best estimate of the population standard deviation (σ). The standard error of the sample mean can thus be calculated by substituting s for σ in the previous formula to produce:[3]

$$\text{Standard error of the sample mean} = s/\sqrt{n} \qquad (5.1)$$

This equation enables us to calculate the error involved in adopting $\overline{X}$ as an estimate of μ, *on the basis of information known only from the sample itself.*[d]

THE STANDARD ERROR OF A SAMPLE MEAN

The best estimate
of the standard error of a sample mean,
i.e. of the standard deviation
of the sampling distribution of a sample mean, is

$$\frac{s}{\sqrt{n}} \qquad (5.1)$$

where s is the standard deviation of the sample
and n is the size of the sample.

For the BRTHRATE variable, s$=4.505$ and n$=214$, so the **standard error** of the sample mean is $4.505/\sqrt{214}=0.308$.

You will often see these characteristics of a sample summarized in one expression, namely that the value of $\overline{X}$ is equal to:

$$\overline{X} \pm \frac{s}{\sqrt{n}} \qquad (5.2)$$

---

[d] As noted in chapter 2, computer programs and calculators may calculate the standard error using n-1 rather than n. The reason for doing this is explained in §5.4.2. The distinction between the two definitions matters only when the sample size is small. If n$=30$ or more there would be practically no difference between the two estimates.

This expression provides information on both the measured mean of a sample and its standard error. In the case of BRTHRATE, the information would be displayed as:

$$BRTHRATE = 15.636 \pm 0.308$$

We have thus far derived the standard error *of the sample mean*. Standard errors can also be calculated for other sample statistics; it is necessary, therefore, to indicate which standard error is being reported in any case. This is often accomplished by adding the symbol for the characteristic in brackets after the abbreviation SE (for standard error); so for the sample mean it would be $SE(\overline{X})$. At a later point in this chapter (see §5.6) we will give the formulae for the standard error for some other common sample statistics.

On the basis of these four theoretical propositions, we are able to use statistics derived from a sample to estimate the value of a population parameter and to indicate how accurate we consider the estimate to be. In §5.5, we will use these simple rules to construct intervals within which we believe our estimate of the unknown population mean to fall, and to calculate the probability that we will be correct in this belief.

However, we are not yet ready for this. We must first spend some time developing the procedures for calculating the confidence interval, and we do this in §5.4. It is also necessary to pay some more attention to the meaning of the sample being drawn, and one important aspect of this is discussed in panel 5.1.

5.4 Theoretical probability distributions

In §5.3.1, we used the Central Limit Theorem to show that $\overline{X}$ is on average equal to the population mean, μ, and that its sampling distribution is normally distributed with an estimation, or standard, error equal to $s/\sqrt{n}$, where s is the standard deviation of the sample and n is the sample size. Before we use that information to construct confidence intervals around our sample estimate of $\overline{X}$ we should spend a little time reviewing and extending our understanding of the normal distribution.

5.4.1 Empirical and theoretical frequency distributions

It may be helpful to begin by recapitulating some of the material presented in chapter 2. When we first encountered the normal curve and its standardized version, the standard normal distribution, in §2.6 we were dealing with **frequency distributions**, i.e. with the number of occurrences of particular values of a continuous **random variable**.

Panel 5.1   Sampling with and without replacement

Almost all sampling theory is concerned with the process of **sampling with replacement**. Each drawing of an observation to create the sample is made over the entire population. Every observation has the same probability of being sampled with each successive drawing. In the simple case of drawing a card from a pack, sampling with replacement requires that a card once drawn be placed back into the pack, available for a repeat draw.

In historical research, however, once an observation is drawn, it is normally excluded from successive drawings. Every observation has the chance of being sampled once, but no observation can be sampled more than once. Thus, when a historian draws a 10 per cent sample of households from the US Census in 1860 in order to analyse the pattern of wealth holding, he will probably draw every tenth observation from the list of census manuscript schedules. Once a household is chosen, it cannot be chosen again. Likewise, each parish in Boyer's data set is chosen only once. These are examples of **sampling without replacement**.

Some statistical texts imply that sampling without replacement significantly distorts the application of inferential statistics. A standard example is the probability of drawing aces from a deck of cards. The expectation of drawing an ace from a virgin deck is 1 in 13; if cards are continually replaced after selection, this probability will remain the same in successive draws. This is the notion of **sampling independence**.

If, however, cards are not replaced, then the probability of selecting an ace in any given draw will not be independent of previous draws. In the second draw, for example, if an ace has already been chosen, the probability of selecting another falls to 1 in 17 (3 aces remain in 51 cards); if a different card is chosen in the first draw, the probability rises to 1 in 12.75 (4 in 51). In this example, the smaller the population, the greater the distortion.

If we had 1,000 decks, the removal of an ace in the first draw would reduce the chances of choosing an ace next time from 1 in 13 to 1 in 13.003, a fairly trivial change. The larger the population (or more accurately, the larger the ratio of the population to the sample), the less damaging is the use of sampling without replacement. If the population were assumed to be infinite in size, the problem would disappear completely.

So how detrimental is it to our use of statistical techniques that the historical procedure does not replicate the ideal sampling method of the statistics textbook? In practical terms, fortunately for the quantitative historian, the answer is that it does not matter much *as long as the population is reason-*

ably large compared to the sample. This is comforting; historians usually have to make do with samples that are too small, so it is not likely that they will often have to worry about samples which are too large.

For two of the most important statistics that we deal with in this chapter – the mean and standard error of the sampling distribution – we can be more precise. The following propositions may be stated without further proof:[*]

(a) The *mean* of the sampling distribution of the sample mean is unaffected by the shift to sampling without replacement, as long as the drawing of the sample is truly random.

(b) The *standard error* of the sampling distribution of the sample mean (as defined in (5.2)) will always be *smaller* when samples are drawn without replacement. This can be corrected by dividing the result obtained from the sample by

$$\sqrt{\frac{N-n}{N-1}}$$

where N is the size of the population and n the size of the sample.

If the sample is not more than about one-fifth of the population the correction needed is only 2–3 per cent of the standard error that would be obtained if the sample were drawn with replacement, and can generally be ignored. However, if the sample drawn without replacement is a larger fraction of the population than this, the correction should generally be made.

Correction is desirable in such cases because under-statement of the standard error will lead to a corresponding under-statement of the sampling errors and confidence intervals explained below (see §5.5), and may thus create a misleading impression of the reliability of the inferences that can be made on the basis of the evidence from the sample.

It is also important to take the correction factor into account when *comparing* the means from two different samples, especially when both are small relative to the population as a whole. Thus, if we wish to determine whether the mean birth rate in Kent parishes was higher than in Sussex parishes and whether this difference is statistically meaningful, we should recognize that both samples were drawn without replacement and construct the standard errors of the means accordingly. We shall return to this issue more formally in §6.7.1.

---

[*] For illustrations of these propositions see exercises 2, 3, and 5 at the end of this chapter.

We began with a normal curve, a purely theoretical curve specified mathematically by an equation involving the constants π and e, and the mean and standard deviation of the distribution. This was a perfectly smooth and symmetrical curve with a bell-shape. Different normal curves were illustrated in figure 2.5. It was noted that many real-life empirical values for specific variables such as height had a distribution that was a reasonable approximation to the normal distribution.

Then, in §2.6.2, we developed the idea that any normal curve could be *standardized*. For any particular observation in the sample, X_i, we could take the value of the sample mean ($\bar{X}$) as a *benchmark* with which to compare the observation. The distance of any observation from the mean of the sample was measured in units of the sample standard deviation. The result was called Z, defined as

$$Z = \frac{(X_i - \bar{X})}{s} \tag{5.3}$$

It was observed that the distribution of Z always has a mean of zero and a standard deviation of 1. The proportion under the curve (i.e. the proportion of the standardized distribution) up to or beyond any specific value of Z can be obtained from a published table (an extract from which was reproduced in table 2.7). This can be used to calculate the position of any given value relative to the rest of the distribution.

We now move from such empirical distributions and introduce the idea of a **theoretical probability distribution** of a random variable. We will first discuss such a distribution and then consider its standardized form. It is easiest to begin with a simple example for a **discrete** random variable (one which can take only a finite number of values), such as the number of heads that would be obtained in two tosses of a coin. A comprehensive list of all the possible combinations is:

First coin	Second coin
Tail	Tail
Tail	Head
Head	Tail
Head	Head

We can thus see that there is only a one in four chance of getting either no heads or two heads, and two in four chances of getting one head. If we think of these chances in terms of probabilities they can be summarized as follows:

Number of heads	Probability
0	1/4
1	2/4
2	1/4

Notice that the total of the probabilities is 1, because the three results exhaust all the possible outcomes. These results represent the **probability distribution** or **probability density function** for this particular discrete random variable: the number of heads obtained in two tosses of a coin.

Exactly the same ideas can be applied to a **continuous** random variable (which can take any value within a relevant range) such as GNP or age of marriage, though the mathematics needed to determine the probability distribution may be considerably more complicated. If such a probability distribution is depicted graphically, the value of the random variable, X, is measured along the horizontal axis, and the vertical axis shows the probability that X lies within some specified interval; for example, the probability that the age of marriage of a woman lies between 16.0 and 18.0 years.[4] The total area under the curve again exhausts all the possibilities and is equal to 1.

One particular form of such a curve is the very important **normal theoretical probability curve**. This looks exactly like the normal curve discussed and illustrated in chapter 2. It is also a perfectly smooth and symmetrical, bell-shaped, curve. The location and spread of the curve along the horizontal axis are similarly determined by its mean and standard deviation. It too has a standardized equivalent, Z, with mean equal to zero and standard deviation equal to 1. The way in which this shape is derived from the probability distribution of a discrete variable is explained in panel 5.2 and illustrated in figure 5.1.

It may, at first, seem rather confusing to regard a particular distribution as both an empirical frequency distribution and a measure of probability. However, this follows directly from the objective notion of **probability as long-run relative frequency**. This is, in effect, what is meant when it is said that the probability of getting a head when tossing a single coin is 1/2, or that the probability of getting an ace when one card is drawn from a pack of 52 is 1/13. We would not expect to get one ace every time we drew 13 cards from the pack, but if we drew a single card 13,000,000 times (from an ultra-durable pack) then we would expect the number of aces to be very close to – although *not* exactly equal to – 1,000,000.[5]

This standardized normal probability distribution has all the same properties as the standard normal curve discussed in §2.6.2. We can thus

Panel 5.2   Generating the normal theoretical probability curve

Why does the probability distribution of a random event take the shape of the normal curve? Let us use the case of the proportion of heads in a series of coin tosses to show the process.

The probability of producing a head in a coin toss is 0.5. Thus, after one coin toss, we would expect to produce either 0 heads or 1 head, each with a 50:50 probability. After two tosses, the probability structure changes. There are now four possible combinations of heads and tails: as noted in the text, the outcomes are such that there is a 1 in 4 chance of producing either 0 heads or 2 heads, and a 2 in 4 chance of producing 1 head.

With three tosses, the number of combinations increases to 8, for which the probabilities are:

0 heads: 1/8;   1 head: 3/8;   2 heads: 3/8;   3 heads: 1/8.

The average (or, in the language of probability theory, expected) number of heads is 1.5.*

As we increase the number of tosses, the probable number of heads will be distributed symmetrically around its mean of 0.5. But, with each additional coin toss, the tails of the distribution become more elongated. Thus, after 5 throws, the chances of producing either no heads or all heads falls to 1 in 32; after 10, to 1 in 1,024; after 15, to 1 in 32,768.** Moreover, as the number of tosses increases, so the distribution as a whole begins to spread out, as more combinations become possible and the variance of the distribution increases.

We show the process in figure 5.1, which reproduces the distribution of heads for 2, 4, 10, and 20 coin tosses. The gradual transition towards the familiar bell-shape of the normal distribution is clearly evident.

---

* This is in effect a weighted average (see §2.3.2) calculated as the sum of the number of heads multiplied by their respective probabilities:

$$\Sigma[(0 \times 0.125) + (1 \times 0.375) + (2 \times 0.375) + (3 \times 0.125)] = 1.5.$$

** Note that the number of possible permutations of heads and tails is equal to 2^n, where n is the number of separate coin tosses. No matter how many tosses, only one permutation in each sequence will be either all tails or all heads.

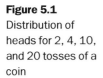

Figure 5.1

Distribution of heads for 2, 4, 10, and 20 tosses of a coin

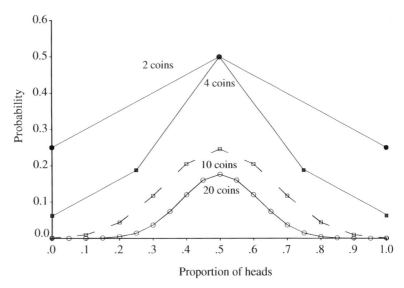

use the information in published tables such as table 2.7 to find the proportion of the distribution in the area defined by any value of Z. We might, for example, ascertain the proportion of the distribution up to or beyond a specific value of Z, and can then interpret that proportion as the *probability* of getting some given result that is greater than (or, if Z is negative, less than) that value of Z.

Similarly the proportion of the distribution lying between two specific values of Z can be interpreted as the probability of getting some result in the range defined by those two values. Each of these values of Z corresponds to some value in the original distribution before it was standardized, according to the definition of Z given by (5.3).

5.4.2 The Z- and t-distributions

We now extend the idea of a standardized theoretical probability distribution to apply to the *sampling distribution of a sample statistic*; for example, the sampling distribution of the sample mean discussed in §5.2. In this case the population mean, μ, is taken as the *benchmark* with which to compare the value of the mean derived from a sample, $\overline{X}$. The distance of the sample mean, $\overline{X}$, from this benchmark can be expressed in units of the standard deviation of the sampling distribution. As noted in §5.3, this particular standard deviation is known as the standard error (SE), and for a sample mean its value – as given in (5.2) – is $s/\sqrt{n}$. Using this SE to standardize the deviation of the sample mean from the population mean, we can define Z as

$$Z = \frac{(\overline{X} - \mu)}{s/\sqrt{n}} \tag{5.4}$$

We would thus obtain a separate value for Z for every sample we draw from a given population and for which we calculate a mean. These values of Z represent a theoretical **probability distribution**. If we depicted this on a graph the successive values of $\overline{X}$ would be measured along the horizontal axis, and the vertical axis would record the *probability* of obtaining those values. The total area under the curve again exhausts all the possibilities and is equal to 1.

However, in order to obtain this formula for Z, it was necessary to replace the unknown σ by the known sample standard deviation, s. Such substitution will almost always be necessary in historical research, because there is usually no way of knowing the population values. Unfortunately, the statisticians have established that this procedure is not entirely satisfactory. It turns out that $s/\sqrt{n-1}$ is a better estimate of the standard deviation of the sampling distribution than $s/\sqrt{n}$. The reason for this can be explained intuitively in terms of the concept of **degrees of freedom (df)**. This is discussed in panel 5.3.

As a consequence, an alternative standardized measure has been devised, which is known as *Student's t*, or simply *t*, where

$$t = \frac{(\overline{X} - \mu)}{s/\sqrt{n-1}} \tag{5.5}$$

Here, too, a separate value for *t* would be obtained for every sample drawn from a given population for which a mean was calculated. These values of *t* similarly represent a theoretical **probability distribution of a sample statistic**, known as the *t*-distribution.

The *t*-distribution is symmetric and bell-shaped, with mean and mode equal to zero. It is thus similar in appearance to the standard normal probability distribution, but its precise shape depends *solely* on a parameter, k, which is determined by the number of degrees of freedom (df) in the estimate of the population standard deviation. This equals $n-1$, i.e. df is one less than the size of the sample.

There is thus a different distribution – and so different probabilities – for each df, and the distribution is flatter (less peaked) and more spread out

Panel 5.3   The concept of degrees of freedom

The use of $s/\sqrt{n-1}$ rather than $s/\sqrt{n}$ in the formula for the t-distribution (5.5), can be explained intuitively in terms of the concept of **degrees of freedom**.

To introduce this concept, consider a simple example in which there is a series consisting of only three numbers, with a mean value of 4. If you were invited to choose the constituents of this series you would be able to choose any number you liked for the first *two* values, but once you had done that the final number would be determined for you. Say, for example, you chose first 1 and then 5. The third number would then be constrained to be 6; no other value would be consistent with your first two choices and a mean of 4. Using our standard notation we can say that if the number of items in a sample series (n), and the sample mean of that series ($\overline{X}$) are both known, then only $n-1$ of the items in the series are 'free' to take any value; there are only $n-1$ degrees of freedom (df). One degree of freedom has been lost.

Since the sample mean is used in the formula for the sample variance, 1 degree of freedom is lost and there are only $n-1$ 'free' observations involved in its calculation. This is what is meant by stating that there are only $n-1$ degrees of freedom (df). The same principle applies to the calculation of the standard deviation or the covariance.

We shall encounter this concept again in other contexts in later chapters (see §7.3 and §8.2). A general definition which applies to these and other measures is:

> The degrees of freedom of a statistic is the number of quantities that enter into the calculation of the statistic, minus the number of constraints connecting those quantities.[*]

[*] Peter E. Kennedy, *A Guide to Econometrics*, 3rd edn., Blackwell, 1992, p. 67.

the lower the number of df (see figure 5.2). However, the difference between successive t-distributions diminishes rapidly as the sample size (and so the number of df) increases, and the distributions become less spread out. After we reach about 30 df, the t-distribution approximates increasingly closely to the standard normal probability distribution.[6]

In principle, the t-distribution *is always superior* to the standard normal Z-distribution *when σ is unknown*, but its advantages are especially important when the sample size is small (less than about 30). In such cases the

Figure 5.2 The
t-distribution for
selected degrees
of freedom

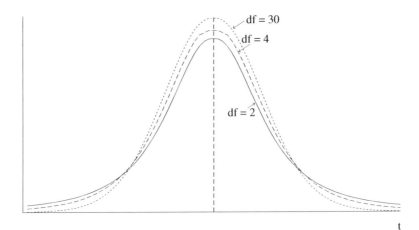

differences between the two distributions can have an important effect on
the decisions based on these distributions (such as those in §5.5 and §5.6 of
this chapter and in §6.4 and §6.5 of chapter 6). As the sample size increases
above this the differences between the two distributions cease to matter.

An extract from the published table for the theoretical *t*-distribution is
given in table 5.1, with the number of degrees of freedom specified in the
left-hand column. Note that the information is presented in a different form
from the table for the standard normal distribution. In table 2.7 we read
across from a specific value for Z to find the proportion of the total area
under the curve (i.e. the probability) relating to that value of Z. For example,
for $Z=1.96$ the proportion in one tail (column (4)) was 0.025 (2.5 per cent).

For the *t*-distribution the procedure is to read across from the number
of degrees of freedom in column (1) to find the value of t that leaves a
specified proportion in either tail of the distribution. For example, for 10 df
the value of t corresponding to the same proportion (probability) of 0.025
(2.5 per cent) in one tail is given in column (4) of table 5.1 and is found to
be $t=2.228$.

It can be seen from this example that, for small samples, the probability
of getting a result that is greater (or less) than some specific value is *higher*
with the *t*-distribution than with the standard normal distribution.[e]
Conversely, the probability of getting a result between any two values will be
lower with the *t*-distribution than with the standard normal distribution.

[e] With the standard normal distribution, if the probability of getting a result greater than $Z=1.96$
is 2.5 per cent, the probability of getting a result greater (further to the right) than that, such as Z
$=2.228$, would be less than 2.5 per cent, and thus less than the probability of getting that result
with the *t*-distribution.

Table 5.1 Distribution of t for selected degrees of freedom

(1)	(2)	(3)	(4)	(5)	(6)
			Value of t for which area in one tail is:		
df	0.10	0.05	0.025	0.01	0.005
1	3.078	6.314	12.706	31.821	63.657
2	1.886	2.920	4.303	6.965	9.925
3	1.638	2.353	3.182	4.541	5.841
4	1.533	2.132	2.776	3.747	4.604
5	1.476	2.015	2.571	3.365	4.032
6	1.440	1.943	2.447	3.143	3.707
7	1.415	1.895	2.365	2.998	3.499
8	1.397	1.860	2.306	2.896	3.355
9	1.383	1.833	2.262	2.821	3.250
10	1.372	1.812	2.228	2.764	3.169
11	1.363	1.796	2.201	2.718	3.106
12	1.356	1.782	2.179	2.681	3.055
13	1.350	1.771	2.160	2.650	3.012
14	1.345	1.761	2.145	2.624	2.977
15	1.341	1.753	2.131	2.602	2.947
16	1.337	1.746	2.120	2.583	2.921
17	1.333	1.740	2.110	2.567	2.898
18	1.330	1.734	2.101	2.552	2.878
19	1.328	1.729	2.093	2.539	2.861
20	1.325	1.725	2.086	2.528	2.845
21	1.323	1.721	2.080	2.518	2.831
22	1.321	1.717	2.074	2.508	2.819
23	1.319	1.714	2.069	2.500	2.807
24	1.318	1.711	2.064	2.492	2.797
25	1.316	1.708	2.060	2.485	2.787
26	1.315	1.706	2.056	2.479	2.779
27	1.314	1.703	2.052	2.473	2.771
28	1.313	1.701	2.048	2.467	2.763
29	1.311	1.699	2.045	2.462	2.756
30	1.310	1.697	2.042	2.457	2.750
32	1.309	1.694	2.037	2.449	2.738

Table 5.1 (*cont.*)

(1)	(2)	(3)	(4)	(5)	(6)
		Value of *t* for which area in one tail is:			
df	0.10	0.05	0.025	0.01	0.005
34	1.307	1.691	2.032	2.441	2.728
36	1.306	1.688	2.028	2.434	2.719
38	1.304	1.686	2.024	2.429	2.712
40	1.303	1.684	2.021	2.423	2.704
50	1.299	1.676	2.009	2.403	2.678
60	1.296	1.671	2.000	2.390	2.660
120	1.289	1.658	1.980	2.358	2.617
∞	1.282	1.645	1.960	2.326	2.576

Source: D. V. Lindley and W. F. Scott, *New Cambridge Statistical Tables*, 2nd edn., Cambridge University Press, 1995, table 10, p. 45.

The column headings in table 5.1 refer only to one tail, but because the distribution is symmetrical the area in both tails marked off by any given value of *t* is always exactly double the one-tailed area.[f] The value that marks off a specified tail in this way is called the **critical value** or **critical point**, and will feature prominently in chapter 6 (see §6.3.2).

5.5 Confidence intervals for a sample mean

After this digression into two of the core ideas of mathematical statistics, sampling distributions and probability distributions, we can now revert to the problem posed at the start of §5.2. If we know the sample mean, $\bar{X}$, how good is this as an estimator of what we really want to know, which is the population mean, μ?

Our first step towards an answer to this question is to fix a **confidence interval** around the estimate of the mean obtained from the sample.

---

[f] Similarly, the corresponding cumulative and central areas, or the area to the right of the mean – which were shown in table 2.7 – can easily be found, given that the total area = 1 and the area to the right (or left) of the mean = 0.5.

5.5.1 Interval estimates and margins of error

The second of the fundamental propositions in §5.3.1 stated that the sample mean, $\overline{X}$, could be taken as an estimate of the unknown population mean, μ. It was noted that although this would be correct on average, each individual sample would be likely to miss the target.

For this reason it is often preferable to replace the **point estimate** given by the single sample mean by an **interval estimate**. This interval is equal to the sampling error involved in relying on the sample mean. We can thus write

$$\overline{X} \pm \text{the sampling error} \tag{5.6}$$

We can also decide how large we want this margin of error to be. The interval can be made wider or narrower depending on how *confident* we want to be that the interval estimate we adopt does contain the true μ. Given the sample size, if it is desired to be more confident – at the cost of being less precise – a wider interval should be chosen, i.e. the sampling error would be increased.

The usual practice is to opt for a **95 per cent confidence interval**. This means that we expect to be correct 19 times out of 20 (or 95 times out of 100) that our interval estimate does include μ. Equally, of course, it means that we have to recognize that we will be wrong (in the sense that our interval estimate will not actually include μ) once in every 20 times. In other words, by choosing a 95 per cent confidence interval we are satisfied with a 95 per cent probability that the estimate will be correct.

It is important to note that this is *not* the same as saying that we can be 95 per cent confident that μ lies within the particular interval estimate derived from a single sample. The value of μ is fixed and cannot change; what can change is the value of $\overline{X}$ obtained from successive samples, and thus the range around $\overline{X}$ given by the confidence interval. With a 95 per cent confidence interval it is expected that only one in every 20 intervals derived from successive samples will not contain μ.

It is thus a statement of confidence in the *procedure* we are adopting, embracing all the (hypothetical) interval estimates we would obtain if we were able to repeat the calculations with a large number of samples of a given size.

5.5.2 Confidence interval for an estimate of a population mean

What size interval do we need in order to have the required degree of confidence that the range we are giving either side of the (known) sample mean will contain the (unknown) population mean?

More specifically, if we want a 95 per cent confidence interval (i.e. if we want a 95 per cent *probability*) how many *standard errors either side of the sample mean* do we have to add to achieve this degree of confidence?

We know from the Central Limit Theorem (see proposition 1 in §5.3.1) that the sampling distribution of the sample mean will be (approximately) normal. If it is necessary to use the sample standard deviation, s, in place of the population standard deviation, σ, then the table for the t-distribution (see table 5.1) can be consulted to find the value of t that leaves the specified proportion in the two tails of the distribution.[7] Thus to achieve 95 per cent confidence we have to exclude an area with 5 per cent in the two tails, equal to 2.5 per cent (usually given as a proportion, 0.025) in each of the tails.

95 PER CENT CONFIDENCE INTERVAL FOR A MEAN

An **interval estimate** of a population mean takes the form

$$\bar{X} \pm \text{sampling error.} \tag{5.6}$$

For the **95 per cent confidence interval** this can be stated as

$$\bar{X} \pm t_{0.025} \text{SE}(\bar{X}) \tag{5.7}$$

where $t_{0.025}$ is the value that excludes 2.5 per cent
in each of the two tails of the t-distribution
for any given sample size,

and SE($\bar{X}$) is the Standard Error
of the sampling distribution of the mean.

In §5.3 the standard error for BRTHRATE for the sample of 214 English parishes ($=s/\sqrt{n}$) was found to be 0.308 births around a mean rate of 15.636 births per 100 families. If we look up $t_{0.025}$ for the t-distribution for 213 degrees of freedom in table 5.1 we find (by interpolation) that the critical value is 1.971.[8]

The 95 per cent confidence interval for the *mean* birth rate (births per 100 families) of the population is thus

$$15.636 \pm (1.971 \times 0.308)$$
$$= 15.636 \pm 0.607$$

We are thus able to say that there is a 95 per cent probability that a range from 15.029 to 16.243 (i.e. from $15.636 - 0.607$ to $15.636 + 0.607$) births per 100 families will contain the (unknown) population mean.[g]

This is equivalent to saying that with the statistical procedure we are using we can expect our sample to provide confidence intervals that will include the population mean about 95 per cent of the time. If 20 samples were taken, it is probable that the inference about the population mean, μ, that we draw from the sample mean, $\overline{X}$, would be right 19 times and wrong once. Of course, if we only have one sample there is no way of knowing whether this is one of the 19 that gives the correct result, or the twentieth one that gives the wrong result!

If the prospect of getting the wrong result 5 per cent of the time is alarming then it is always open to the investigator to adopt a higher standard. Choosing a 99 per cent confidence interval would mean that the investigator could expect these (wider) intervals to include the unvarying mean about 99 per cent of the time.

A familiar variant of this problem usually occurs during an election when opinion polls are used to predict the proportion of the electorate that will vote for a particular party or presidential candidate.[h] In a run of such polls there are typically some that excite special interest by deviating substantially from the remainder in the series, but once it becomes apparent that they have not detected a sudden shift in opinion the pollsters acknowledge reluctantly that this deviant result was a 'rogue poll'.

In other words, this is one of the incorrect results that any sampling procedure is bound to produce if it is repeated sufficiently often. The frequency of rogue polls is systematically related to their sample size. The only way for the pollsters to reduce the probability of errors would be to work with larger samples, but that is often too expensive for their sponsors.

To see what the confidence interval would be for the mean BRTHRATE if the sample size were smaller, imagine that instead of the 214 parishes the sample had been confined to the 23 parishes for which information was found for Kent (county 1).[i] The mean BRTHRATE obtained from this sample was 18.547 with a standard deviation of 4.333. Since the sample size is small it is important to replace $\sqrt{n}$ by $\sqrt{n-1}$ in the formula for the

---

[g] If we used $s/\sqrt{n-1}$ rather than $s/\sqrt{n}$, the standard error would change imperceptibly to 0.309 and the confidence interval would be 15.636 ± 0.608.

[h] In this case the relevant sampling statistic is a proportion rather than a mean, but the statistical principle is the same.

[i] For those who recall that we worked with 24 Kent parishes in chapters 2–4 it may be helpful to note that those statistics related to the first Boyer data set for poor relief. The number of parishes in his birth rate data set is smaller, and in the case of Kent is 23.

standard error.[j] $SE(\bar{X})$ is therefore $4.333/\sqrt{22} = 0.924$. With a sample of this size there are 22 df, and if we look up table 5.1 for the t-distribution with 22 df we find a critical value for $t_{0.025}$ of 2.074.

Thus with this sample the 95 per cent confidence interval for the *mean* population birth rate is

$$18.547 \pm (2.074 \times 0.924)$$
$$= 18.547 \pm 1.916$$

On the basis of this sample we are thus able to say that there is a 95 per cent probability that a range from 16.631 to 20.463 births per 100 families will contain the (unknown) population mean. With the smaller sample we are able to place the population mean only within a fairly wide interval (with 95 per cent confidence).

If a higher standard of confidence were required (say, 99 per cent) the proportion to be excluded in each tail would be 0.005 (giving a total proportion of 0.01 or 1 per cent in both tails). For 22 df, the critical value is $t_{0.005} = 2.819$ (see column (6) of table 5.1) and the confidence interval for the population BRTHRATE would be correspondingly wider: 15.942 to 21.152 births per 100 families.

It should also be noted that there is no overlap between the 95 per cent confidence interval for the population mean birth rate obtained from the sample of 23 Kent parishes and the corresponding interval obtained earlier from the full sample of 214 parishes. The lower bound for the former (16.631) is actually higher than the upper bound for the latter (16.243). This is a sharp reminder that it would not be good sampling procedure to attempt to derive an estimate of the mean birth rate in England as a whole from a sample of parishes drawn exclusively from one county (see §1.3.4).

As should also be obvious, any confidence interval is directly affected by the size of the sample on which it is based. The larger the sample, the smaller will be the standard error, and hence the smaller the width of the interval. The alternative to achieving a higher standard of confidence at the expense of a wider interval is thus to increase the size of the sample where this is not precluded by considerations of cost or availability of data.

5.6 Confidence intervals for other sample statistics

An analogous procedure can be used to determine the confidence interval for any other result obtained from a sample, for example a proportion or a regression coefficient. In each case:

[j] See n. 3 (p. 144).

(a) There is a (hypothetical) **sampling distribution** of the sample statistic. (This important concept was discussed in §5.2.1 with reference to the sampling distribution of the sample mean, but it was noted that there would be a sampling distribution for every sample statistic.) The standard deviation from the mean of this sampling distribution is called the Standard Error (SE).

(b) The shape of that sampling distribution and the size of the sample determine how reliable the sample statistic is as an estimate of the corresponding population parameter.

(c) The required result can be expressed in terms of a confidence interval. For any given level of confidence (say, 95 per cent) the size of the interval is determined by

the selected probability of getting a result outside that range,
multiplied by
the relevant Standard Error.

5.6.1 Sample proportions

For a sample **proportion**, p, the standard error is given by

$$SE(p) = \sqrt{\frac{\pi(1 - \pi)}{n}} \qquad (5.8)$$

where π (lower case Greek pi) is the (unknown) proportion in the population. Because π is not known it is estimated by using the sample proportion, p, and the formula becomes

$$SE(p) = \sqrt{\frac{p(1 - p)}{n - 1}} \qquad (5.9)$$

The formula for the 95 per cent confidence interval for a sample size of (say) 41 (so df $= 40$) is thus

$$p \pm t_{0.025} \, SE\,(p)$$

$$p \pm 2.02 \sqrt{\frac{p(1 - p)}{n - 1}} \qquad (5.10)$$

5.6.2 Correlation coefficients

The correlation coefficient, r, was introduced in §3.2 as a measure of the strength of the relationship between two variables. At that stage the result was accepted without regard to the circumstances in which it was obtained.

In the light of the concepts discussed in this chapter it should now be clear that this is not satisfactory.

It is necessary to ask the same question about the correlation coefficient as about any other result obtained from a sample: is the value obtained for r simply the result of random (chance) features of the particular sample, or does it reflect systematic and consistent features of the relationship between the *population* of the two variables? In other words, if the correlation coefficient for the population mean is ρ (lower case Greek rho), is this sample correlation coefficient, r, a good estimator of ρ?

To answer this question in terms of confidence intervals we need to know the standard error of the correlation coefficient, SE(r). This is

$$SE(r) = \frac{1 - \rho^2}{\sqrt{n-1}} \tag{5.11}$$

Unfortunately, this formula is of limited use, both because the value of ρ is not usually known and because the sampling distribution of r is highly skewed unless the sample size is quite large (a sample of at least 100 is recommended). To replace it statisticians have developed a transformation, Fisher's z, which is obtained from r as follows[9]

$$z = \frac{1}{2} \log_e \left(\frac{1+r}{1-r} \right) \tag{5.12}$$

Fisher's z should not be confused with the Z values introduced in earlier chapters in relation to the standard normal distribution, and discussed again in §5.4 of this chapter. The two are completely different.

The sampling distribution of Fisher's z is approximately normal and its standard error is given by

$$SE(z) = \frac{1}{\sqrt{n-3}} \tag{5.13}$$

An illustration of Fisher's z used for a confidence interval for a correlation coefficient

To illustrate the procedure using Fisher's z, we will take the example from §3.2.1 where the coefficient of correlation between UNEMP and RELIEF for the 24 Kent parishes was found to be 0.5244 (to 4 decimal places). From (5.12)

$$z = \tfrac{1}{2} \log_e (1.5244/0.4756) = \tfrac{1}{2} \log_e (3.2052) = \tfrac{1}{2} (1.1648)$$
$$= 0.582$$

Then from (5.13)

$$SE(z) = 1/\sqrt{21} = 1/4.5826$$
$$= 0.218$$

Because z is approximately normally distributed we can use the standard normal distribution (rather than the t-distribution) so the 95 per cent confidence interval around z is given by

$$z \pm 1.96\,SE(z) = 0.582 \pm 1.96\,(0.218)$$
$$= 0.582 \pm 0.427$$

The confidence interval around z thus ranges from $+0.155$ to $+1.009$. To complete the exercise we then have to reverse the transformation and convert back to the corresponding values of r. This can be worked out using the formula in (5.12), and is also available in a published table, which gives the value of r corresponding to the lower and upper limits of the interval as 0.154 and 0.765, respectively.[k]

On the basis of this rather small sample of 24 parishes we thus require a quite wide range in order to be able to say that there is a 95 per cent probability that this confidence interval will contain the (unknown) population correlation coefficient.

There are two further points about this confidence interval that should be noted. First, it is not symmetrical about the correlation coefficient of 0.524: the upper limit of 0.765 is closer to r than the lower limit of 0.150. The reason for this is that the upper limit of r is 1, and this in turn constrains the upper limit of the confidence interval. If we had taken an example in which r was negative, the lower limit would be similarly constrained so that it could not exceed -1.

Secondly, the range given by the confidence interval around a positive value for z could be larger than the value of z, so that the lower limit of the range had a negative value. This would mean that the corresponding lower limit of r would also be negative. Say, for example, that the correlation coefficient obtained from a sample of 24 cases had a positive value of $+0.28$. At the 95 per cent confidence level the interval that we could expect to contain the true population correlation coefficient would stretch from -0.14 to $+0.61$, and would thus include the possibility of a negative correlation.

5.6.3 Regression coefficients

The estimated standard error for a regression coefficient involves some very important concepts that we will investigate in chapter 9. For the

---

[k] Lindley and Scott, *Statistical Tables*, table 17, p. 59.

present, we can simply note that SE (b), the standard error of a sample **regression coefficient** for the slope, b, of a regression line with only one explanatory variable, is

$$SE(b) = \sqrt{\frac{\Sigma(Y_i - \hat{Y})^2}{(n-2)\Sigma(X_i - \overline{X})^2}} \tag{5.14}$$

The formula for the 95 per cent confidence interval for the population regression coefficient, ß, and a sample size of (say) 32 (df = 30) is therefore

$$b \pm t_{0.025} SE(b) \tag{5.15}$$

Substituting the formula for SE (b) from (5.14) in this equation gives

$$= b \pm 2.04 \sqrt{\frac{\Sigma(Y_i - \hat{Y})^2}{(n-2)\Sigma(X_i - \overline{X})^2}} \tag{5.16}$$

In this chapter we have reviewed the formulae for the standard errors of the sampling distributions of a mean, proportion, regression coefficient, and correlation coefficient. These four statistics illustrate the basic principles. For other sample statistics your statistical program and computer will provide the required formula for the standard error and do the necessary calculations.

Notes

[1]   A full discussion of all the statistical (and financial) issues that arise in drawing an appropriate sample cannot be provided here. A brief introduction to the topic is given in the references given in §1.3.4. W. G. Cochran, *Sampling Techniques*, 3rd edn., Wiley & Sons, 1977, is a good example of a more comprehensive text.

[2]   This is the procedure adopted by Boyer in his analysis of the English Poor Law Data (*An Economic History of the English Poor Law*, Cambridge University Press, 1990, pp. 131, 149). Parishes that did not return relatively complete questionnaires to the Poor Law Commission were excluded from his sample. However, every parish returned some information and Boyer was able to compare these results with those for his sample to indicate that incomplete respondents were not systematically different from those that did reply in full. He thus decided that he could treat his data as though they were drawn from a random sample.

[3]   The statisticians actually make a subtle distinction here. Although they tell us that the sample standard deviation, s, is the best estimate of σ, they say that the best estimate of the standard deviation *of a sampling distribution* is not $s/\sqrt{n}$, but $s/\sqrt{n-1}$. If the sample size is large (more than 30) the difference made by using $s/\sqrt{n}$ rather than $s/\sqrt{n-1}$ in the denominator hardly matters, as can be seen by reworking the BRTHRATE example given below, but with smaller samples it becomes progressively more important. We will say more about this distinction in §5.4.2 and offer an intuitive explanation for it in panel 5.3.

4　We are told by the statisticians to refer in this way to the probability of a continuous random variable having a value within some specified *interval*, because the probability of any one specific value is always zero.

5　In this context, each card must of course be replaced immediately it has been drawn. The number of aces would not be expected to be exactly 1,000,000 with replacement because each draw is completely *independent*. Assume, for example, that at any point in the sequence of drawing the cards, the proportion of aces had fallen 20 below 1 in 13. The cards have no memory of the previous draws, and so there is absolutely no reason to expect that the next 20 draws will all be aces. At any stage, the probability for each succeeding draw is exactly the same as it was at the outset of the experiment: 1 in 13.

6　The variance of the *t*-distribution is given by the formula k/(k − 2), where k equals the number of df (= n − 1). This means that the larger the sample size (and hence k) becomes, the closer the variance is to 1, and hence the more closely the distribution approximates the standard normal probability distribution. As we know from §2.6.2, the standard deviation (and hence also the variance) of this standard normal distribution is also 1.

7　The *t*-distribution should be used in preference to the *Z*-distribution whenever σ is not known, irrespective of the sample size. However, it should be intuitively obvious that the difference between s and σ will be greater the smaller the size of the sample on which s is based, and so the use of the *t*-distribution is again especially important when dealing with small samples.

8　When the number of df is large it is recommended that interpolation should be harmonic. For an explanation see Lindley and Scott, *Statistical Tables*, p. 96.

9　An alternative version of (5.12) is sometimes quoted, which is not calculated in natural logs but in logs to the base 10 (see §1.6.2). This is

$$z = 1.1511 \log_{10}\left(\frac{1+r}{1-r}\right),$$

and gives the identical result. The value of Fisher's z for any given r can also be obtained from published tables, for example, Lindley and Scott, *Statistical Tables*, table 16, p. 58.

5.7　Exercises for chapter 5

1. If we have a perfect die the probability of getting each of the six faces on a single throw is exactly 1/6. Since the probability of getting each of the numbers from 1 to 6 is the same, the probability distribution for the throw of a single die is rectangular. We can take such a rectangular distribution as the population of all possible throws of a single die.

   (i) Calculate the sampling distribution of the means of samples based on throwing two dice.

  (ii) Calculate the sampling distribution of the means of samples based on throwing three dice.

(iii) Plot the distributions obtained in (i) and (ii) and give an intuitive explanation of why the distribution approximates more closely to the normal distribution as the sample size increases.

2. A **population** consists of the five numbers: 2, 3, 6, 8, and 11.

(i) Calculate *by hand* the mean and standard deviation of the population. (*Note*: this is the entire population; not a sample.)

(ii) Specify all possible samples of size 2 which can be drawn **with replacement** from this population, and calculate the means of each of these samples. (*Hint*: this means that you can have both 2, 3 and 3, 2 and also 2, 2, etc.)

(iii) Calculate the mean of the sampling distribution of means. Compare your result with the population mean.

(iv) Calculate the standard error of the sampling distribution of means. Compare your result with the value obtained from the formula $SE = \sigma/\sqrt{n}$.

(v) Comment on your results.

3. Take the same population as in question 2 and undertake the same exercises, but using the approach of sampling **without replacement**. Comment on your results, especially with regard to any contrasts and similarities with the answers to question 2.

4. Using the Boyer relief data set, calculate the mean and standard deviation of INCOME for the 24 Kent parishes:

(i) Calculate *by hand* the 90 per cent and 99 per cent confidence intervals for mean INCOME for the 24 Kent parishes. Compare your result with the confidence intervals given by your statistical program.

(ii) Calculate *by hand* the 99 per cent confidence interval for the proportion of Kent parishes with a workhouse. Compare your result with the confidence interval given by your statistical program. (*Hint*: treat this a mean.)

(iii) If the 95 per cent confidence interval for INCOME is calculated for a sample of 24 Kent parishes it is found to be 34.3625 ± 2.129. How many parishes would need to be included in the sample to reduce the 95 per cent confidence interval to ± 1? (You can take $t_{0.025} = 1.96$.)

(iv) By how many times would the sample need to be increased in order to reduce the confidence interval to one-eighth of the size of ± 1 adopted in question (iii); i.e. to 0.125? What general result can be derived from this?

(v) Calculate the 95 per cent confidence interval for the regression coefficient in the regression of RELIEF on UNEMP for all 311 parishes.

5. Calculate the standard error of parish population for Cambridge, Oxford, and Sussex using the Boyer relief data set. Use the methodology of panel 5.1 to correct the standard errors for the application of sampling techniques without replacement, noting that the number of rural parishes in each county in 1832 was 170, 295, and 155, respectively. Evaluate the significance of the revisions for this data set. Would the same conclusions apply if the total number of parishes in each county were (a) half as many and (b) a third as many as the numbers presented?

6. Boyer has demonstrated that the selected parishes in his relief and birth data sets are representative of all those who replied to the Poor Law Commission's questionnaires in 1832. But only a small proportion of all parishes in Great Britain replied to the request for information. In the case of Kent, 29 out of 404 rural parishes responded; Boyer used 24 of these answers to construct his relief sample. You wish to determine whether Boyer's parishes are typical of *all* Kent parishes in 1831, including those that did not respond to the questionnaires.

As a first step to testing for representativeness, you examine the relative size of the parishes in the sample and the population, to determine whether Boyer's parishes are atypically large or small. The Census of 1831 indicates that the average size of all rural Kent parishes is 965.75 persons, with a variance of 1632.5. How would you use this information to determine the validity of Boyer's sample? What conclusions do you draw?

7. In a file on the web site, identified as LOCAL, we have compiled data on the unemployment rate for adult males in July 1929; the data have been collected for each of the 664 local Employment Exchange districts in Great Britain. This data set may be considered the **population** for analysis of sampling procedures. Use this information to:

(i) Construct the population frequency distribution and measure the population mean and variance. Note whether the distribution is normal or skewed.

(ii) Draw 5 random samples of 5 local districts each and construct a sampling distribution of the mean unemployment rate. (*Hint*: you will need to use either a random number table, such as that given in Lindley and Scott, *Statistical Tables*, p. 78 or many other statistics texts; or a random number generator from your statistical program.)

(iii) How does the sampling distribution of the mean change as you increase the number of samples of 5 districts each from 5 to 10 to 20? What is the standard error of the sampling distribution in each case?

Note whether the distribution is normal or skewed.

8. As a further test of the nature of sampling distributions, use the LOCAL unemployment file on the web site to:

(i) Draw 5 random samples of 10 local districts each and construct a sampling distribution of the mean unemployment rate. Increase the number of samples (each of 10 districts) to 10 and then to 20, recording the information on the mean and standard error of the distribution. Note whether the distribution is normal or skewed.

(ii) Repeat this exercise using random samples of 20 local districts each, and compare your results to those in (i).

What conclusions do you derive from these two exercises about the correct approach to sampling?

CHAPTER 6

Hypothesis testing

6.1 Testing hypotheses

In chapter 5 we established how to determine the confidence intervals for a single result obtained from a sample. The next issue to be considered covers the situation where we wish to investigate a specific **hypothesis** relating to a result obtained from one or more samples.

With confidence intervals the *implicit* hypothesis is that the specified interval contains the required value. With hypothesis testing the hypothesis is made *explicit,* and can be framed so as to refer to particular values of the population statistic. It might, for example, be a hypothesis relating to a comparison of the results of two different samples. Or it might be a hypothesis about whether or not the result of a single sample can be considered as different from some specified value.

For example, RELIEF in the sample of Kent parishes has a mean value of 20.28 shillings with a standard deviation of 7.64 shillings. For Sussex the corresponding values are a mean of 26.04 shillings and a standard deviation of 8.04 shillings. The mean in Sussex was thus almost 6 shillings (28 per cent) higher than the mean in Kent.

This differential might have occurred, either

(a) because of *chance factors* and accidental irregularities reflected in the samples we happened to get from the two counties; or
(b) because there were *systematic and consistent* differences in the underlying structural features of the two counties; for example, in the sources of income available to labourers, the generosity of relief payments, or the incidence of poverty and sickness in the two areas.

The aim of **inductive statistics** is to enable us to decide which of these possibilities we should regard as more likely. If the answer is (a), the implication is that a similar differential would not be found if further samples were drawn from additional parishes in each county. If so, the apparent difference shown by the two existing samples of parishes is simply a reflection of random factors that are of no real interest to historians.

If the answer is (b), then it is a potentially interesting finding and historians of the Poor Law should proceed further to consider why *per capita* relief payments were some 28 per cent higher in Sussex than in Kent.

6.1.1   A simple illustration

In order to illustrate some of the central ideas in a more familiar context, consider the following simple story about four men, each of whom was arrested and charged with theft. The four cases are quite separate. The initial presumption is that each man is innocent until proved guilty. The jury have to decide whether to uphold or reject this presumption on the basis of the evidence presented to them.

The four cases, and the main evidence the prosecution have against the men arrested, are as follows:

(a) *Goods stolen from a house*: A noticed loitering outside the house a couple of days before the theft.
(b) *A robbery at a drug store*: B seen driving away from the store on the night of the robbery.
(c) *A break-in at an electrical goods warehouse*: C seen in the vicinity of the warehouse in the early evening and overheard boasting in a bar later on the same night that he had done a good evening's work and would soon have loads of money to spend.
(d) *A theft of jewellery and antiques*: D reported trying to sell the stolen goods to a second-hand dealer the following morning.

The jury rapidly acquitted A. They also acquitted B but only after a long discussion. C was found guilty but on a majority verdict. D was quickly and unanimously found to be guilty.

The jury's decisions can be interpreted as follows. In each case the question they had to ask themselves was: What is the chance that the man would have been doing what the police reported *if he was innocent?* If they judged the probability to be high, they would decide that he was innocent. If they judged it to be low, they would reject the presumption of innocence and find the man guilty. In making their judgement they have to recognize that if they set their probability standard too high they run the risk of acquitting a guilty man; if they set it too low they may convict someone who is innocent.

In these four cases the jury evidently drew their dividing line between high and low probability somewhere in the region between the chance of B being seen driving away from the store if he was innocent, and the probability of C being seen near the warehouse and then being overheard boasting in the pub if he was innocent. In A's case the likelihood of innocence was found to be very high, in D's it was obviously very low.

We will return to this story in §6.3.6.

6.1.2 The five stages of hypothesis testing

The essence of hypothesis testing is a decision about the plausibility of a particular outcome given by the sample information. This decision is reached by working through the following sequence:

(a) Decide the issue to be determined and *specify a hypothesis in an appropriate form for testing* (see §6.2).

(b) Select a *level of probability* on the basis of which it will be decided whether or not the hypothesis should be rejected (see §6.3).

(c) Select the relevant *test statistic* and its related *sampling distribution*. The test statistic expresses the specific result incorporated in the hypothesis (e.g. a mean or a regression coefficient) in a form suitable for comparison with the probability of all possible outcomes of that particular statistic. The sampling distribution gives that theoretical probability distribution for all the possible outcomes (see §6.4).

(d) Calculate the test statistic and compare this calculated value with the tabulated theoretical probability distribution in order to *reach a decision* about the hypothesis (see §6.5).

(e) *Interpret the results* of the decision (see §6.6).

In the subsequent sections we will explain each of these stages, and then in §6.7 we will illustrate three specific tests of hypotheses involving a difference of sample means, a correlation coefficient, and a regression coefficient.

6.2 The null hypothesis

It is a basic principle of inductive logic that a proposition can be refuted by one observation but cannot be proved. To take a famous example, the proposition that 'all swans are white' would have to be rejected if a single black swan was observed, but would not be proved by the sighting of a single white swan, or indeed even of a thousand.

Following from this principle, statisticians proceed by setting up a hypothesis that can be **rejected**. This is known as the **null hypothesis** and is referred to as H_0.

THE NULL HYPOTHESIS

The **null hypothesis** (H_0) specifies
the negative form of the proposition to be tested, for example,

there is *no difference* between two means or proportions,
or *no relationship* between two variables,
or a new drug *should not be* introduced because it has adverse side effects.

The **alternative** or **research hypothesis** (H_1)
specifies the opposite:

that there is a difference,
or there is a relationship,
or the drug should be introduced.

Notice that the null hypothesis should normally be framed in terms of the outcome that would be regarded by the researcher as *undesirable*: she would normally prefer to find that there *was* a relationship between the two variables or that the experiment *was* successful, or that the drug *should be* introduced.

The aim of research is then to determine whether or not the null hypothesis should be rejected. If the data used for this purpose are found to be inconsistent with the hypothesis it should be rejected. If the data are consistent with the hypothesis it should not be rejected. The language used is important: because of the principle stated at the beginning of this section the researcher must not claim that her experiment has established that the null hypothesis is correct or that it should be accepted. The appropriate response is that it is *not rejected*. The more frequently and successfully a hypothesis resists rejection in successive independent experiments, the better its status and the more it might be relied on, but it would still remain a hypothesis that could be rejected in some future experiment.

6.2.1 Other assumptions of the model

It is important to bear in mind that in setting up a null hypothesis to be tested, using data obtained from a sample, it is also necessary to make certain assumptions about:

(a) the underlying population from which the sample was drawn; and
(b) the research procedures used to obtain the sample data.

It is only if one is certain about (a) and (b) that it is possible to *isolate the null hypothesis* as the issue that is to be decided by the selected test.

One of the crucial questions with respect to (a) is whether or not the population distribution is approximately normal (i.e. if it looks approximately like the theoretical frequency curve described in §2.6). If it is, then one set of tests, in which this normality is assumed, is appropriate. If it is not, then another set, known as **non-parametric tests,** which will be introduced in chapter 7, must be employed. These latter tests do not assume a normal distribution and are also applicable to nominal and ordinal level data.

The crucial question with respect to (b) is whether or not the sample is truly **random**. (A brief indication of what is required to satisfy this condition was given in §1.3.4.) If the sample is not random, then it is essential to consider the extent to which there might be a **bias** in the data because of this. If there is a serious bias, the data are contaminated and the results cannot be relied on.

It may, nevertheless, be possible to argue that even though the sample is not random, the results are not invalidated. For example, as noted in chapter 5 (see n. 2), Boyer (*Poor Law*, p. 129) claims this for his data, on the grounds that the parishes that completed the returns to the Poor Law Commission from which his samples are drawn were not systematically different from those that did not.

6.3 How confident do we want to be about the results?

6.3.1 Two types of error and the null hypothesis

The basic idea underlying this fundamental statistical procedure is that it is not possible to achieve certainty in the decisions we make on the basis of incomplete or imperfect information. To introduce the topic consider a familiar non-statistical example: the everyday problem of a pedestrian trying to cross a busy road:

The more carefully he waits until he is sure it is safe to cross, the less likely he is to be run over. But if he tries to achieve maximum safety he might wait forever and would never get to the other side of the road.

There is thus an inescapable dilemma. If he minimizes the risk he maximizes delay; if he minimizes the delay he maximizes the risk. *Both problems cannot be avoided simultaneously.*

In statistics this dilemma is expressed in terms of two types of error, known respectively as **Type I** and **Type II**. There is always a trade-off between these: the more a statistician tries to eliminate one type, the more likely he makes the other.

TWO TYPES OF ERROR

Type I: Rejecting a true hypothesis.

Type II: Failing to reject a false hypothesis.

Illustration: an experiment with a new drug

The issue can be illustrated by the case of a trial for a new drug, where the null hypothesis (H_0) is that it should not be introduced because it may have very adverse side effects for many users. The research hypothesis (H_1) is that there are no serious side effects and it should be introduced.

There are then four possibilities:

(a) If the scientists *do not reject H_0 when it is true* (i.e. the drug does have adverse side effects) they will make the *correct decision*. The drug will not be introduced and no patients will suffer from the adverse effects.

(b) If they *reject H_0 when it is true* (and instead fail to reject H_1) they will make a **Type I error**: the drug will be introduced and some unfortunate patients will suffer the adverse effects.

(c) If they *do not reject H_0 when it is false* the drug will not be introduced. This will represent a **Type II error,** and the beneficial treatment the drug could have provided will be lost.

(d) If they *reject H_0 when it is false* (and instead fail to reject H_1) they will again make the *correct decision*: the drug can be introduced and patients will be treated without the risk of adverse side effects.

These possible outcomes can be summarized in the box below.

IMPLICATIONS OF REJECTING OR NOT REJECTING THE NULL HYPOTHESIS

| | Decision: | |
	Reject H_0	Do not reject H_0
H_0: True	Type I error	Correct
H_0: False	Correct	Type II error

If it was known whether H_0 was true or false it would, of course, be easy to make the correct decision: H_0 would never be rejected when it was true and would always be rejected if it was false. But since this cannot be known it is necessary to rely on statistical theory for guidance on the *probability* that H_0 is true, given the outcome of the research, and should not be rejected; or the probability that it is false, and should be rejected.

This in turn means that it is not possible to achieve complete *certainty* with respect to the validity of any particular research hypothesis (H_1). All that can be done is to establish whether or not the hypothesis is *probably* true in the light of the evidence. There is thus *always* some possibility that an error will be made in relation to this decision.

The crucial point is thus that this procedure is designed to assist the investigator to make a decision about the null hypothesis in the light of a specific event or result, while recognizing that this decision will be subject to the possibility of error.

The question the historian has to ask is: What is the probability that I would have obtained that result if the null hypothesis is correct? If there is a low probability then H_0 should be rejected. If there is a high probability then H_0 should not be rejected.

This then leads us to the further issue: What should be regarded as a high or low probability? This depends on the margin of error the investigator regards as appropriate in reaching a conclusion about the null hypothesis. We discuss this in the following subsection.

6.3.2 Significance levels and the critical region

In order to decide about this margin of error, the question the researcher has to consider is: What risk is she willing to take of making Type I and Type II errors? One crucial component of her answer will be the **significance level,** conventionally designated by α.

SIGNIFICANCE LEVEL

The significance level, α, of a decision
is *the probability* of making
a *Type I error.*

The more there is at stake in rejecting a true null hypothesis, the greater the need to select a low probability of making a Type I error, even though, as we have seen, this will increase the prospect of making a Type II error.

The probability of making a Type II error is designated as β. The probability of *not* committing a Type II error $(1 - \beta)$ is known as the **power (or efficiency) of a test** of the null hypothesis.

THE POWER OF A TEST

The power (or efficiency) of a test $(1 - \beta)$
is its ability *to avoid a Type II error.*

For any given sample size,
the greater the ability of a test to eliminate false hypotheses,
the greater is its relative power.

The critical region
The concept of the **critical region** is very closely related to that of the level of significance. The *lower* the level of significance, the *smaller* the critical region, the *less* the chance of making a Type I error, i.e. the *less* the probability of rejecting H_0 when it is true. The reason for introducing yet another unfamiliar term is that it illustrates the procedure, and so helps to clarify the rules to be followed in making the final decision.

THE CRITICAL REGION

The critical region constitutes
the set of unlikely (low-probability) outcomes
the occurrence of which would require
rejection of the null hypothesis.

Figure 6.1 The
critical region

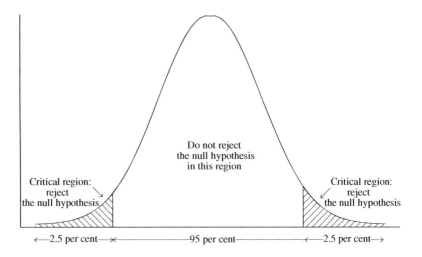

(a) A two-tailed test at the 5 per cent level of significance
     At this significance level the critical region covers 2.5 per cent of the area
     in each tail

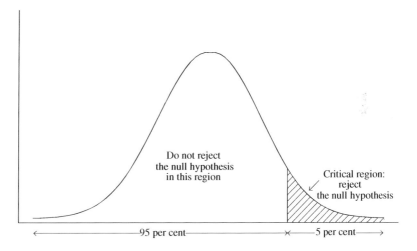

(b) A one-tailed test at the 5 per cent level of significance
     At this significance level the critical region covers 5 per cent of the area
     in one tail

A 5 per cent level of significance can thus be translated into a **critical region** covering 5 per cent of the area under the curve (shown in figure 6.1 (a) as the two shaded areas of 0.025 (2.5 per cent) in each of the two tails of the distribution), and a **non-rejection region**, covering the remaining 95 per cent. The **critical value** marks the border between the two regions.

As good social scientists our procedure should always be to make it difficult to reject the null hypothesis, H_0, and thus also difficult to fail to reject the research hypothesis, H_1. It is essential to proceed in this way even though (indeed, precisely because) we would actually like to reject H_0 and not reject H_1 because the alternative would be more intellectually interesting (or financially profitable). This good practice is achieved by selecting a small critical region.

The trade-off

There is, however, a price to be paid for this. Consider, for example, a comparison of the 1 per cent and 5 per cent significance levels. At the 1 per cent significance level the critical (rejection) region is smaller, and the non-rejection region is bigger, than at the 5 per cent level. Therefore, at the 1 per cent level, with a smaller critical region, there is less likelihood of a Type I error (rejecting H_0 when it is correct). But then there will automatically be a larger non-rejection region, which means there is more likelihood of a Type II error (not rejecting H_0 when it is false).

There is thus an inescapable trade-off: the less the chance of a Type I error, the greater the chance of a Type II error. The standard approach to hypothesis testing is to assume that Type I errors are *less desirable* than Type II errors and to proceed accordingly. For this reason, the power of a test is rarely invoked in empirical analysis. The conventional methodology instead focuses on setting the significance level and then choosing a method that minimizes the chances of committing a Type I error.

Thus in the example of the drug trial, the consequences of introducing a drug with adverse side effects are usually viewed as far more serious than the consequences of not introducing a drug with potential life-saving or life-enhancing properties.[1] This logic is reinforced by the recognition that, in general, it is very hard to identify the sampling distribution of the research hypothesis, and one cannot therefore easily observe the probability of committing a Type II error. As a rule, therefore, researchers are content to recognize the trade-off by not reducing α to extremely low levels, but beyond this little more is done or said.

6.3.3   One- and two-tailed tests

There is one further aspect of the critical region that must be clarified. In figure 6.1 (a) the critical region was divided equally between the left- and right-hand tails. But in principle the whole critical region could be shown either in the right-hand tail, as in figure 6.1 (b), or in the left-hand tail. The first refers to what is called a **two-tailed test**, the second (whether to the left or the right) to **one-tailed tests**.

Which of these should be used? The answer normally depends on whether or not the hypothesis being investigated tells the researcher something about the *direction* of the result. For example, the null hypothesis might simply state that there is no difference between two means. If so, there is nothing in the hypothesis about direction and a two-tailed test must be used.

Alternatively, the null hypothesis might state that the mean from the first sample is *larger* than the mean from the second. If so, it is only differences in that direction that are of interest, and a one-tailed test must be used. In this case the relevant tail naturally depends on the direction predicted by the hypothesis. If it is positive (larger than), it is the right-hand tail; if negative (smaller than), the left-hand tail.

H_1 is often expressed using the symbols $>$ for 'greater than' and $<$ for 'smaller than'. For example a researcher might state:

$$H_0: \mu_1 = \mu_2$$
$$H_1: \mu_1 > \mu_2$$

The direction of the arrowhead conveniently points to the direction of the tail to be selected.

To illustrate this procedure consider two (hypothetical) samples from which a demographer has derived figures for the mean age of marriage in England in 1780 and 1820. If she has reason to think there may have been a fall in the age of marriage over this period she is able to predict the direction of the change, and a one-tailed test is appropriate. H_0 would be that there is no difference between the two mean ages, and H_1 would be that $\overline{X}_{1820}$ was lower than $\overline{X}_{1780}$ ($H_1: \overline{X}_{1820} < \overline{X}_{1780}$).

If the mean age in 1820 is then found to be actually higher than in 1780 the result is clearly inconsistent with the idea of a fall in the age of marriage, and a test of the hypothesis is hardly necessary. But if it is lower, then the demographer has to decide whether or not to reject the null hypothesis of no difference and must concentrate attention on the left-hand tail.

Notice that the effect of selecting a one-tailed test is to increase the size of the relevant critical region for any given level of significance. This increases the probability of a result in the critical region and thus makes it *easier* to reject the null hypothesis. For this reason, one-tailed tests should be used only when there is a good *a priori* reason, *independent of the data being tested,* for investigating a directional hypothesis. And if a one-tailed test is adopted, the choice must be made *before* the results of the test are calculated.

6.3.4   Statistical versus historical significance

Despite the importance that is attached to this concept of statistical significance it is absolutely crucial to understand that it does *not* imply that the result is necessarily meaningful or significant – in the everyday sense of the word – for the researcher.

A typical null hypothesis for many statistical measures is that there is no relationship between two variables, or that the value of a coefficient is zero. If a measure is found to be statistically significant this establishes that the null hypothesis can be rejected, but not that the relationship matters or that the value of the coefficient is important in the context of the research. Statistical significance is determined partly by the strength of the relationship, or the extent of the difference between the coefficient and zero shown by the sample, and partly by the size of the sample. *If the sample size is large enough it is almost always possible to obtain a 'statistically significant' result.*

Thus, if it is established that a result is statistically significant, this indicates that it merits further consideration, *not that it is automatically to be regarded as an important or interesting finding.* That is a totally different question, and statistical significance must never be confused with **historical significance**, i.e. with the issue of what is substantial or important from the point of view of the historian.

Take, for example, the initial illustration in §6.1 of the difference between the mean values of RELIEF in Kent and Sussex, respectively 20.3 shillings and 26.0 shillings. A difference of this magnitude that was shown to be statistically significant at the 5 per cent level would be of considerable interest to historians of poverty and the Poor Law. If, however, the results had been 21.0 shillings in Kent and 21.1 shillings in Sussex the difference would be of little *historical* significance, even if it could be shown to be *statistically* significant at the 1 per cent level, or lower.

Similarly a regression coefficient may be found to be statistically significant, but be so small as to demonstrate that the explanatory variable has no practical effect on the dependent variable.[a]

6.3.5   Conventional significance levels and prob-values

The traditional procedure

The conventional levels of significance are 1 per cent, 5 per cent, and 10 per cent. For most research in history and the social sciences it has become the norm to adopt the 5 per cent level as appropriate. If a researcher has stated

---

[a] An important aspect of the analysis of any quantitative exercise is thus to examine the magnitudes of the regression coefficients and other results. This is discussed with several illustrations from the literature in chapters 14 and 15.

that she will adopt the 5 per cent level and then finds that her results are significant at the 1 per cent level, she will normally note this with special satisfaction, and the results might then be described as 'highly significant'.

If, however, the research related to something like the experiment to test a new drug for adverse side effects, it would be advisable for the drug company to require a higher degree of certainty that the drug was safe. It would thus be necessary to choose a lower level of significance in order to have an extremely low probability of making a Type I error (namely, reject-ing the null hypothesis of adverse effects when it was true, i.e. when the drug actually did have such effects). In such a crucial context a level even lower than 1 per cent might be appropriate.

It is an important principle of good research practice that the appropri-ate level should be decided *in advance*; it should not be influenced by the results once they have been obtained.

Significance levels can also be regarded as the complement of the confidence intervals discussed in chapter 5. If a null hypothesis is rejected at the 5 per cent level, i.e. with a 5 per cent probability of error in coming to this conclusion, this is exactly equivalent to saying that it lies *outside* the 95 per cent confidence interval. Conversely, if it is not rejected at the 5 per cent level, this is equivalent to saying that it falls *within* the 95 per cent confidence interval.

Significance levels and prob-values

The traditional procedure outlined above involved the selection of a specific significance level, in the social sciences typically 5 per cent. This can, however, be criticized as a rather arbitrary procedure. If the result falls just within the critical region corresponding to the 5 per cent level H_0 is rejected; if it falls just outside the region H_0 is not rejected, no matter how small the difference in the probability of these two outcomes. There is no valid justification for making such a distinction between significance levels of, say, 5.1 per cent and 4.9 per cent.

The origins of this procedure lay in a pre-computing age when the rele-vant probability distribution tables from which the levels were determined were expensive to reproduce and had to be kept simple. For example, a complete set of tables for the t-distribution (which was shown in abridged form in table 5.1), with all the information for every individual degree of freedom, would run to many pages.

With the advent of modern computers it is no longer necessary to use published tables. Modern statistical packages like SPSS and STATA can swiftly calculate all the necessary information, and their default procedure is to report the *actual probability* of the outcome, i.e. the precise critical value equal to the calculated test statistic. Hypothesis testing procedures have changed accordingly. Instead of indicating whether or not the test statistics fall within the critical region defined by one of the conventional significance levels, many researchers now report these actual probabilities. Researchers should still indicate, at least broadly, the level they regard as appropriate for their project, but their readers are given the fullest possible information and can make their own judgements about how the significance tests should be interpreted.

This actual probability is given under various headings, including **prob-value** or **p-value** or **Sig**. Thus a prob-value of 0.003 means that the probability of obtaining that result – if H_0 is true – is only 0.3 per cent. The smaller the probability, the stronger the case for rejecting H_0, so for most purposes this would mean that the null hypothesis could be rejected. A prob-value of 0.053 would mean that the probability of obtaining that result if H_0 is true is 5.3 per cent. If the conventional 5 per cent significance level were being strictly followed, this would lead to a decision that H_0 should not be rejected, but a different judgement might be made depending on the context and the size of the sample.

PROB-VALUE OR p-VALUE

Prob-value or p-value
(or sig or statistical significance)

is the probability
that the outcome observed would be present

if
the null hypothesis were true.

6.3.6   The critical region and the four cases of theft

It may help to consolidate understanding of the concepts introduced in the preceding sections if we revert now to the story in §6.1.1 of the four men charged with theft. The presumption of innocence is equivalent to the null hypothesis. The four types of evidence represent the sample statistical results in the light of which the null hypothesis is to be rejected or not rejected. The dividing line between the non-rejection and critical regions is implicit rather than explicit, but the majority of the jury clearly located it somewhere between the higher probability of B being seen driving away from the drug store if he was innocent and the lower probability of C being seen near the warehouse and then being overheard boasting in the bar if he was innocent.

A's case falls well into the non-rejection region: there is a very good chance (high probability) that he could have been noticed outside the house a couple of days before the theft even if he was innocent. Conversely, D's case is well into the critical region: the jury obviously thought that there was very little chance (very low probability) that he would have been trying to sell the stolen goods to a dealer the morning after the theft if the presumption of his innocence were true. A low probability thus leads to rejection of the null hypothesis.

Note that Type II errors (failing to reject the null hypothesis when it is false) do not come into this story at all. The emphasis in the Anglo-American legal system on the notion of reasonable doubt is consistent with setting a low significance level, α (but not *too* low, since it is reasonable rather than absolute doubt that is at issue). In other words, these judicial systems are primarily concerned to avoid making Type I errors: finding accused persons guilty when they are innocent.

However, in jurisdictions in which the rights of the accused are less sacrosanct, or in a situation where it is seen as more important to avoid cases where the guilty are acquitted, the judicial system might be more concerned to avoid Type II errors: finding the accused innocent when they are actually guilty. In these circumstances it is considered more important to lock up potential wrongdoers without too much concern for any infringement of their civil rights if they are indeed innocent. A prime example of this in the case of the United Kingdom was the policy of internment of suspected terrorists during the 1980s. The movement towards parole denial in certain categories of crime in the United States (especially involving violence against children and sexual deviancy) may be viewed similarly.

6.4 Test statistics and their sampling distributions

We have now stated a null hypothesis, and selected an appropriate significance level and critical region (or used a statistical program to determine its probability equivalent). The next stage in the procedure is to select the relevant *test statistic* and its related *sampling distribution*.

6.4.1 The basic ideas

The null hypothesis refers to one of the basic statistical measures derived from one or more samples. This sample measure (or sample statistic) might be, for example, a mean or median, a proportion, a variance, a correlation or regression coefficient, or a comparison of observed and expected frequencies.

For every such sample statistic it is necessary (a) to calculate a test statistic and (b) to ascertain the sampling distribution for that statistic.

- The **test statistic** expresses the specific result calculated from the sample data in a form suitable for comparison with the sampling distribution.
- The **sampling distribution** is associated with a **theoretical probability distribution for** all possible outcomes of that particular test statistic.

The concept of a sampling distribution of a sample statistic was introduced in §5.2. In that instance the concept was illustrated by a discussion of the sampling distribution of the sample mean, but exactly the same ideas apply to any other statistic derived from a sample. For any such sample statistic or measure there is a corresponding sampling distribution, i.e. the distribution of the value of that statistic which would be obtained if the statistic was calculated repeatedly on the basis of a large number of random samples.

The statisticians calculate these sampling distributions on the basis of mathematical reasoning that we do not need to consider. Each of these sampling distributions has specific properties (for example, its mean and standard deviation).

These will generally agree more or less closely with the corresponding properties of one of a number of *theoretical* probability distributions, for example, the standard normal distribution. We can also rely on the statisticians to tell us which sampling distributions correspond to which theoretical distributions.

In fact, several different sampling distributions follow the *same* theoretical distribution. So we do not use a different theoretical distribution for each individual test statistic. Two of the theoretical probability distributions and associated tests that are most widely used in research in history and the social sciences are those for Z and t, both of which were introduced in §5.4.2.

In the following sections we will first look briefly at the test statistics associated with these two distributions, and then complete our discussion of hypothesis testing.

6.4.2 Z- and t-tests

The first two theoretical probability distributions we encountered were the standard normal (or Z-) distribution and the closely related t-distribution (see §5.4.2).

In the case of a mean, for example, the essence of the theoretical Z-

distribution was that the value of the population mean, μ (mu), was taken as the *benchmark*, and the deviation (or distance) from that benchmark of a particular sample mean, $\bar{X}$, was expressed in terms of the standard deviation of the sampling distribution of the sample mean.

This standard deviation of a sampling distribution was given the special name of **standard error.** It is commonly designated by the abbreviation SE followed by the statistic to which it relates. Thus for a sample mean it would be $SE(\bar{X})$, for a sample regression coefficient it would be $SE(r)$, and so on. The question thus posed is: How many standard errors from the benchmark is the value of the mean obtained from the given sample?

It was stated in §5.3 that $SE(\bar{X})$ is equal to $\sigma/\sqrt{n}$. So in order to answer that question, it would be necessary to know the population standard deviation (σ), but that information is hardly ever available. However, as explained in §5.4.2, if the sample size is large enough (generally taken to be more than 30), we can use the standard deviation of the sample, s, as an estimate of σ. The standardized deviation of the sample mean from the population benchmark can then be measured as

$$Z = \frac{(\bar{X} - \mu)}{SE(\bar{X})} = \frac{(\bar{X} - \mu)}{s/\sqrt{n}} \tag{6.1}$$

The table for the proportionate areas under the curve of the standard normal distribution can then be used to assess the probability of getting a particular value greater (or less) than Z, or the probability of getting a particular value within some range, for example from the mean to Z.

The alternative *t*-distribution replaces $s/\sqrt{n}$, by a better estimate of the standard error, $s/\sqrt{n-1}$, to give

$$t = \frac{(\bar{X} - \mu)}{SE(\bar{X})} = \frac{(\bar{X} - \mu)}{s/\sqrt{n-1}} \tag{6.2}$$

It was further noted that although the *t*-distribution is, in principle, always superior to the *Z*-distribution when σ is unknown, its advantages are especially important when the sample size is less than about 30.

We can now apply these distributions to our primary theme of hypothesis tests. In what follows we refer, for simplicity, to the *t*-tests, since historians often have to work with small samples, but the same fundamental ideas apply to both *Z*- and *t*-tests.

The basic idea behind the main test statistics is exactly the same as in the above review of the theoretical distributions, except that in the context of hypothesis tests it is *the value specified in the null hypothesis* that is taken as the benchmark. In a test of a sample mean this would typically be the value of the population mean as in (6.2).[2] In a test of a sample regression coefficient the null hypothesis might be that there is no association between the variables, so the benchmark is r equals zero; and so on.

The result of this standardized deviation from the benchmark is often referred to as t_{calc}.[b] So (6.2) might be written as

$$t_{calc} = \frac{(\overline{X} - \mu)}{SE(\overline{X})} = \frac{(\overline{X} - \mu)}{s/\sqrt{n-1}} \qquad (6.2a)$$

For other sample statistics there would be a corresponding calculation, with an appropriate estimate for the standard error of the sampling distribution of the given statistic. A number of examples of such alternative test statistics will be given in §6.7. The table for the areas under the curve of the t-distribution (see table 5.1) can then be used to assess the probability of getting a particular value greater (or less) than that test statistic, t_{calc}.

We thus have two values that have to be compared. One is the test statistic, t_{calc}, calculated by means of an appropriate formula such as (6.2a) from the *actual* sample data available to the researcher. The other is the *theoretical* probability distribution of t (or Z) indicating the values that would be obtained from an infinite number of random samples.

This fundamental principle for the calculation of test statistics can be applied much more widely, i.e. it need not be limited to means or to a single sample. The more general form of these test statistics can be given as

$$t_{calc} = \frac{\text{Sample estimate} - \text{Null hypothesis}}{SE} \qquad (6.3)$$

STATISTICS FOR *t*-TESTS

The test statistic, t_{calc}, equals:

the deviation of the sample statistic from
the value for that statistic *specified in the null hypothesis*

divided by
the standard error (SE)
of the sampling distribution of that statistic:

$$t_{calc} = \frac{\text{Sample estimate} - \text{Null hypothesis}}{SE} \qquad (6.3)$$

[b] The corresponding test statistic calculated for a Z-test would be Z_{calc}, and so on. An alternative notation uses an asterisk to distinguish the test statistic; thus t^*, Z^*, etc.

The test statistic given by (6.3) is used if the null hypothesis relates to some specific non-zero value. This would apply if relevant values are given by some other source; for example, if it is known from past experience that the proportion of students failing their statistics course is 15 per cent, and it is desired to test whether the current failure rate of 17 per cent is indicative of a deterioration in performance. Alternatively, the specific value might be derived from a theoretical proposition regarding, say, the slope of the regression coefficient; for an illustration of the case where the null hypothesis is b = 1 see §6.7.3.

However, if – as is often the case – the null hypothesis is that the value is zero, then the second term in the numerator can be eliminated, and the formula reduces to the simpler form known as the *t*-**ratio**

$$t_{calc} = \frac{\text{Sample estimate}}{\text{SE}} \tag{6.4}$$

---

t-RATIOS

Where the null hypothesis is that the value of the sample statistic $= 0$ the test statistic, t_{calc}, becomes:

the ratio of
the sample estimate
to
the standard error (SE) of the sampling distribution of that statistic:

$$t_{calc} = \frac{\text{Sample estimate}}{\text{SE}} \tag{6.4}$$

In general we can rely on our statistical software to provide the required formula for SE and thus to calculate the various test statistics, but we will look at some examples of the procedure in relation to differences between two sample means, and to correlation and regression coefficients, in §6.7.

6.5 Making a decision

We are now ready to take the final step in the testing of a hypothesis. We have selected an appropriate sampling distribution and test statistic, and have decided on the significance level and whether it should be a one- or two-tailed test. We proceed as follows:

1. Calculate the test statistic (e.g. t_{calc}) from the sample data using the relevant formula.
2. Compare this result with the corresponding tabulated sampling distribution, the theoretical probability of getting a result *greater than* the selected critical value given by the choice of significance level and critical region(s).
3a. If the calculated statistic is larger than the specified theoretical probability (and thus falls in the critical region) the *null hypothesis is rejected*: see figure 6.2 (a).
3b. If it is smaller than the specified theoretical probability (and thus falls in the non-rejection region) the *null hypothesis cannot be rejected*: see figure 6.2 (b).

The logic of this procedure should be clear from the preceding discussion. The fundamental principle is that H_0 should be rejected only if the results obtained from the sample *are unlikely to have occurred if H_0 is true.* What is meant by 'unlikely' has been decided in advance by the selection of the significance level and critical region.

To recapitulate the full procedure, consider again the case of the drug trial:

- H_0 is that the drug should not be introduced because it has adverse effects.
- The company should reject H_0 only if the results obtained from the trial are extremely unlikely to have occurred if H_0 is true.
- The theoretical distribution defines the critical region of results that are extremely unlikely to occur.
- If the test result falls in this region, H_0 can be rejected.

- If it falls in the much larger non-rejection region, H_0 cannot be rejected and the drug should not be introduced.

More generally, the statistical packages calculate the probability that the observed relationship found in the given data set would be present if H_0 is true. The *lower* the prob-value the *less likely* it is that such a result would be obtained *if H_0 were true.* So if a very *low* prob-value (or equivalent term) is reported the null can be rejected.

This procedure is often found to be rather confusing. There are a number of reasons for this, and it may help to remember the following points:

- First, a *low level of significance* (probability) corresponds to a *high value for the test statistic* which takes it towards or into the tails of the

Figure 6.2 A one-tailed hypothesis test at the 5 per cent level of significance

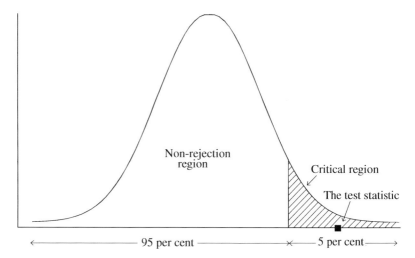

Non-rejection region

Critical region

The test statistic

←————————— 95 per cent —————————×——5 per cent——→

(a) Rejection of the null hypothesis
    The test statistic is *greater than* the critical value: H$_0$ is rejected

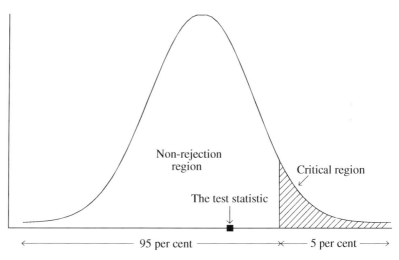

Non-rejection region

Critical region

The test statistic

←————————— 95 per cent —————————×——5 per cent——→

(b) Failure to reject the null hypothesis
    The test statistic is *less than* the critical value: H$_0$ cannot be rejected

distribution, and thus towards or into the critical region where the probability is low.

● Secondly, when this occurs and the test statistic is in the critical region, the procedure is to reject the null hypothesis, which sounds depressing. But remember that H$_0$ is usually specified as the *undesirable* outcome, so rejection of the null is actually good news for the researcher.

6.6 Interpreting the results

The final stage in the process is the interpretation of the results. Once the statistical program has tested the hypothesis the important task is to consider the implications of the result.

Assume, for example, that the test was designed to see whether or not emigration from Ireland (IRISHMIG) was associated with the level of employment in the United States and other foreign destinations (EMPFOR). H_0 would then be that there was no association. If H_0 *cannot be rejected* it follows that the research hypothesis, H_1, must be rejected. The conclusion would have to be that there is no association, at least so far as this can be tested with the particular data set you have used. However, if H_0 *is rejected*, then the researcher can proceed to consider the further implications of the research hypothesis, H_1, that there is an association – i.e. that emigration was influenced by employment opportunities in the receiving countries.

It is worthwhile to stress again the point made in §6.3.4. A finding that a result is 'statistically significant' does *not* mean that it is important to an historian. All that has been established is that the result is unlikely to have arisen by chance given the degree of relationship that exists between the variables and the size of the particular sample that was tested.

However, if the magnitudes show that the result is of interest, the research can proceed underpinned by statistical support for the view that there is an association between IRISHMIG and EMPFOR. The researcher must then apply her historical knowledge and understanding to consider why this association applied, and what consequences follow from it for her analysis of the determinants of Irish emigration.

6.7 Three illustrations of the use of *t*-tests

To complete this chapter on hypothesis tests we will take three common sample statistics to illustrate the use of *t*-tests. The first is a test of the difference between two sample means, the second a coefficient of correlation between two variables, and the third a regression coefficient.

6.7.1 A *t*-test for a difference of means

This first illustration would normally be done with a statistical computer package that would report the various values derived in the remainder of this section. The reason for working through an example in this more laborious way is that the process should help to explain what the computer is doing and give you a better feel for the procedure.

We use the data for RELIEF for the counties of Kent and Sussex referred to at the beginning of this chapter, and the issue to be considered is whether the difference of 5.76 shillings between the sample means is statistically significant. If so, it is clearly large enough to be also historically interesting. The relevant summary statistics are:

	Kent	Sussex
Sample size (n_1 and n_2)	24	42
Mean (shillings) ($\overline{X}_1$ and $\overline{X}_2$)	20.28	26.04
Standard deviation (s_1 and s_2)	7.641	8.041
SE of the mean ($=s/\sqrt{n}$)	1.560	1.241

The null hypothesis is that there is no difference between the two sample means:

$$H_0: \mu_1 = \mu_2$$

and the test statistic is formally:

$$t_{calc} = \frac{\overline{X}_1 - \overline{X}_2 - (\mu_1 - \mu_2)}{SE(\overline{X}_1 - \overline{X}_2)} \qquad (6.5)$$

But if, as the null hypothesis states, $\mu_1 = \mu_2$, then $\mu_1 - \mu_2 = 0$, and (6.5) reduces to:

$$t_{calc} = \frac{\overline{X}_1 - \overline{X}_2}{SE(\overline{X}_1 - \overline{X}_2)} \qquad (6.6)$$

It is then necessary to apply an appropriate formula to obtain the value of $SE(\overline{X}_1 - \overline{X}_2)$. This involves a further procedure that is explained in panel 6.1. The result in this instance is found to be 2.021. This value can then be used in (6.6).

$$t_{calc} = \frac{\overline{X}_1 - \overline{X}_2}{SE(\overline{X}_1 - \overline{X}_2)} = \frac{-5.761}{2.021} = -2.850$$

We can now complete the procedure by comparing this value for t_{calc} with the theoretical *t*-distribution given in table 5.1. In this case the number of degrees freedom (df) is $(n_1 + n_2 - 2) = 64$. For 64 df and a two-tailed test at the 5 per cent significance level the critical value is just under 2.000. t_{calc} is substantially greater than this and so falls well within the critical region. Thus H_0 can be rejected.

If a statistical computer program is used in place of table 5.1 it is possible to be more precise. It reports that the prob-value is actually 0.006, thus indicating that the probability of getting a *t*-statistic of -2.85 when H_0 is

Panel 6.1   Calculation of the standard error of the difference between two sample means

The calculation of $SE(\bar{X}_1 - \bar{X}_2)$ in the denominator of (6.6) depends on whether or not the variances of the (unknown) underlying populations from which the two samples are drawn, σ_1^2 and σ_2^2, can be assumed to be equal. (A special test, known as the F-test, can be applied to test the null hypothesis, $H_0: \sigma_1^2 = \sigma_2^2$)*.

If this null hypothesis cannot be rejected, the population variances can be assumed to be equal, and the information from the two samples can be pooled. The formula for the **pooled** estimate of that common variance (s_p^2) uses information from *both* samples as follows.

$$(s_p^2) = \frac{(n_1 - 1)s_1^2 + (n_2 - 1)s_2^2}{n_1 + n_2 - 2} \tag{6.7}$$

$$= \frac{(23)(7.641)^2 + (41)(8.041)^2}{24 + 42 - 2}$$

$$= \frac{1342.8523 + 2650.965}{64} = 62.403$$

This pooled variance (s_p^2) can then be used in the formula given in (6.8) to calculate the SE of the difference between the two sample means:

$$SE(\bar{X}_1 - \bar{X}_2) = \sqrt{\frac{s_p^2}{n_1} + \frac{s_p^2}{n_2}} \tag{6.8}$$

$$= \sqrt{\frac{62.403}{24} + \frac{62.403}{42}} = \sqrt{2.600 + 1.486} = 2.021$$

What is done if the outcome of the F test is that the null hypothesis of no difference between the variance of the populations *can* be rejected? In that case it has to be assumed that the population variances are unequal and the information from the two samples cannot be pooled. It is then necessary to use each of the separate sample variances in the calculation of the SE. The formula for the standard error is then:

---

* The F-test will be introduced in §9.3.1: it is applied to the testing of equal sample variances in question 6 in the exercises for chapter 9. An alternative test for equality of sample variances, known as Levene's test, is used by SPSS.

$$SE(\bar{X}_1 - \bar{X}_2) = \sqrt{\frac{s_1^2}{n_1} + \frac{s_2^2}{n_2}} = \sqrt{2.433 + 1.539} = 1.993 \qquad (6.9)$$

This is marginally smaller than the result with the pooled variance, and the SE of the difference between the means will be marginally larger.

However, it must be noted that if the alternative correction for unequal variances does have to be applied, it is also necessary to correct for a change in the number of degrees of freedom to be used in testing the SE for statistical significance. The correction, which arises from the inefficiency of the additive formula (6.9) as an estimate of $\sigma_{\bar{x}_1 - \bar{x}_2}$, may be quite large.

Thus, in the case of the comparison between Kent and Sussex, the number of degrees of freedom for the case of unequal variances is 35, compared to a figure of 64 under the assumption of equal variances.[4] A comparison of the critical *t*-values at the 5 per cent significance level in these two cases (1.98 for 64 df; 2.04 for 35 df) indicates that the need to correct for unequal variances tends to make the *t*-test more stringent. The smaller the samples, the greater the effect of the correction.

that there is no difference between the means is only 0.6 per cent. This is very low and so the null hypothesis can be rejected at a markedly lower significance level than 5 per cent.[3]

6.7.2 A *t*-test for a correlation coefficient when the null hypothesis is zero correlation

Consider, for example, the Irish emigration data for the census year 1881. If we use a statistical program to measure the correlation between migration (CNTYMIG) and the degree of population pressure indicated by average family size (FAMSIZE) the coefficient, r, is found to be +0.528. The null hypothesis would be that there is no association between these two variables, H_0: $\rho = 0$, where ρ is the population correlation coefficient. We will apply a 1 per cent significance level to test this null hypothesis.

As explained in §6.4.2, when the null hypothesis to be tested is that the value of the population coefficient is zero, the numerator of the test statistic reduces to $r - 0 = r$. This is divided by the standard error (SE) of r to give the *t*-ratio or *t*-statistic

$$t_{calc} = \frac{r}{SE(r)} \qquad (6.10)$$

To work this out we need to know SE(r), the standard error of a correlation coefficient (i.e. the standard deviation of the sampling distribution of all the correlation coefficients that would be derived from an infinite number of random samples). The statisticians have calculated that for *the special case of ρ = 0*

$$SE(r) = \sqrt{\frac{1 - r^2}{n - 2}} \tag{6.11}$$

where r is the correlation coefficient and n is the size of the sample, i.e. the number of pairs of values of X and Y for which the strength of the association is being tested.[5]

Substituting this formula for SE(r) in the previous equation gives the test statistic in the following box.

THE TEST STATISTIC FOR A CORRELATION COEFFICIENT

When ρ = 0, the test statistic
for a correlation coefficient, r, is

$$t_{calc} = \frac{r - \rho}{SE(r)} = \frac{r - 0}{SE(r)}$$

$$= \frac{r}{\sqrt{\dfrac{1 - r^2}{n - 2}}} = \frac{r\sqrt{n - 2}}{\sqrt{1 - r^2}} \tag{6.12}$$

with n − 2 degrees of freedom.

---

t_{calc} is then compared with the theoretical probability of getting such a result as indicated by the *t*-distribution (which was described in §5.4.2), and a decision made about whether or not the null hypothesis should be rejected at the chosen significance level.[c]

For the correlation of CNTYMIG with FAMSIZE in 1881 across a sample of 32 counties this would give

---

[c] The Spearman rank correlation coefficient (r_s) was introduced in §3.3 as an alternative measure of correlation for use with ordinal or ranked data. For large samples (probably above 30 and

$$t_{calc} = \frac{0.528 \times \sqrt{32 - 2}}{\sqrt{1 - (0.528)(0.528)}} = \frac{0.528 \times 5.477}{\sqrt{0.721}}$$

$$= \frac{2.892}{0.849} = 3.406$$

From table 5.1 we see that for $n - 2 = 30$ degrees of freedom the critical value for a two-tailed significance level of 1 per cent (0.005 in one tail) is 2.750. t_{calc} is considerably greater than this and thus lies well within the critical region, so the null hypothesis can be rejected at the 1 per cent level.[6]

6.7.3 A *t*-test for a regression coefficient

One of the most important results of regression analysis is the sign and size of the regression coefficient, b, for the explanatory variable. A major aspect of the evaluation of a model is thus the test of the reliability of such coefficients. This vital procedure is encountered on numerous occasions in the literature of the social sciences.

The null hypothesis in relation to the regression coefficients would be that there is no relationship between X and Y: any change in the explanatory variable, X, has no effect on the dependent variable, Y. In the case of simple regression with only one explanatory variable this is equivalent to saying that the regression coefficient for the population, β, is zero; the regression line is absolutely horizontal, it has no slope.

Once again we have to decide how good our sample regression coefficent, b, is as an estimator of β. Under the null hypothesis of β = 0, the numerator of the test statistic reduces to $b - 0 = b$. The value of b is then divided by SE(b), the standard error of the coefficient (i.e. the standard deviation of the sampling distribution of regression coefficients obtained from an infinite number of random samples), to give the *t*-**ratio**

$$t_{calc} = \frac{b}{SE(b)} \tag{6.13}$$

SE (b) was given previously in (5.14) in §5.6.3, and is repeated here

$$SE(b) = \sqrt{\frac{\Sigma(Y_i - \hat{Y}_i)^2}{(n - k)\Sigma(X_i - \overline{X})^2}} \tag{6.14}$$

certainly above 50), the statistical significance of r_s can be gauged by the statistic, $z = r_s \sqrt{n - 1}$, using the procedure introduced in §2.5.2. For smaller samples, a special table must be used, such as that provided by Sidney Siegel and N. John Castellan, Jr., *Nonparametric Statistics for the Behavioral Sciences*, 2nd edn., McGraw-Hill, 1988, pp. 360–1.

where k is the number of parameters. In a simple regression k would be 2 (the intercept and one explanatory variable). This formula for SE(b) is then substituted in (6.13) to derive the test statistic, t_{calc}.

THE TEST STATISTIC FOR A REGRESSION COEFFICIENT

If the null hypothesis is that
there is *no relationship*
between the dependent variable
and a specified explanatory variable,

the test statistic for the regression coefficient, b,
on that explanatory variable is the *t*-ratio:

$$t_{calc} = \frac{b - 0}{SE(b)} = \frac{b}{\sqrt{\dfrac{\Sigma(Y_i - \hat{Y}_i)^2}{(n - k)\Sigma(X_i - \overline{X})^2}}} \tag{6.15}$$

---

t_{calc} can then be compared with the theoretical value of the *t*-distribution in the usual way and a decision reached with regard to the null hypothesis.

Before working through an illustration of this test, there are a few additional points that should be mentioned in relation to *t*-tests for regression coefficients. The first relates to a widely used rule of thumb. Reference to the table of the *t*-distribution shows that for a two-tailed test at the 5 per cent level of significance the value of *t* is very close to 2 for sample sizes of 20 or more (see column (4) of table 5.1). (This is the small-sample equivalent of the statement in §2.6.1 that 1.96 standard deviations cover 95 per cent of a normal distribution, leaving 5 per cent in the two tails.)

This leads to a very convenient rule of thumb for establishing the statistical significance of a regression coefficient without undertaking more formal calculations. If the *t*-ratio (i.e. the ratio of the regression coefficient to its standard error) is equal to 2 or more, the relationship between that explanatory variable and the dependent variable is statistically significant at the 5 per cent level.

Secondly, it is also straightforward to test other null hypotheses regarding the relationship between the dependent and explanatory variables; for example, that β has some specified value, say 1.[7] This simply requires the insertion of that value in the numerator in place of the zero, so the test statistic becomes

$$t_{calc} = \frac{b - 1}{\sqrt{\dfrac{\Sigma(Y_i - \hat{Y}_i)^2}{(n - k)\Sigma(X_i - \bar{X})^2}}} \tag{6.16}$$

Thirdly, irrespective of the value attributed to β under the null hypothesis, the evaluation of t_{calc} against the theoretical distribution is conventionally done using a two-tailed test. This implies that no *a priori* view has been specified regarding the sign of the regression coefficient.

However, it is very often the case that the researcher's specification of the model does embody a view of what the sign of the coefficient will be; in other words that he does have a theoretical expectation about whether a change in the explanatory variable in question will cause the dependent variable to rise or to fall. If so, he is interested in the *direction* of the result (see §6.3.3) and a one-tailed test would be more appropriate.

It is important to remember the distinction between statistical and historical significance when evaluating these *t*-statistics. All the points that we have made thus far relate to the issue of statistical significance. It may well be that even though the *t*-statistic is large enough to establish that the coefficient is significantly different from zero, the result is nevertheless of no interest to the historian. This could be because the regression coefficient, while clearly non-zero, is too small to have historical relevance; or because the range of the coefficient (as indicated by the confidence interval) is so wide that it provides no helpful guidance as to the likely effect of the variable on the historical event; or because the correlation between the two variables is spurious and only accidentally significant.

Finally, note that the procedure for testing hypotheses about the intercept of the regression line, a, is essentially the same, though there is a slight difference in the calculation of its standard error, SE(a) which we need not reproduce here. It is automatically given in the results calculated by most statistical computer programs.

Illustration of the t-test for a regression coefficient

To illustrate the application of this very important test we will derive the regression coefficient for the regression of unemployment (UNEMP) on the replacement rate given by the ratio of unemployment benefits to wages (BWRATIO) in the data set on inter-war unemployment in Britain. This is a simplified version of the model developed by Benjamin and Kochin that is discussed in chapter 15 because we have only one explanatory variable.

We would normally leave the calculations to the computer, but in order to illustrate the procedure we will work them out 'by hand'. The values required for this are shown in table 6.1, omitting the intervening stages

Table 6.1 Calculation of the regression coefficient and *t*-ratio for the regression of
UNEMP on BWRATIO

	(1)	(2)	(3)	(4)	(5)	(6)
			Product of deviations of X and Y from their means	Deviation of X from its mean squared	Predicted value of Y	Deviation of Y from its predicted value squared
	UNEMP Y_i	BWRATIO X_i	$(X_i-\bar{X})(Y_i-\bar{Y})$	$(X_i-\bar{X})^2$	$\hat{Y}$	$(Y_i-\hat{Y})^2$
1920	3.90	0.15	3.105	0.100	8.740	23.430
1921	17.00	0.24	−0.749	0.051	10.149	46.933
1922	14.30	0.37	−0.058	0.009	12.184	4.477
1923	11.70	0.40	0.134	0.004	12.654	0.910
1924	10.30	0.42	0.159	0.002	12.967	7.112
1925	11.30	0.48	−0.032	0.000	13.906	6.791
1926	12.50	0.48	−0.016	0.000	13.906	1.977
1927	9.70	0.48	−0.053	0.000	13.906	17.690
1928	10.80	0.50	−0.096	0.001	14.219	11.690
1929	10.40	0.50	−0.109	0.001	14.219	14.585
1930	16.10	0.53	0.152	0.004	14.689	1.992
1931	21.30	0.54	0.556	0.005	14.845	41.665
1932	22.10	0.50	0.279	0.001	14.219	62.110
1933	19.90	0.51	0.268	0.002	14.376	30.520
1934	16.70	0.53	0.189	0.004	14.689	4.046
1935	15.50	0.55	0.150	0.007	15.002	0.248
1936	13.10	0.57	−0.062	0.011	15.315	4.905
1937	10.80	0.56	−0.270	0.009	15.158	18.994
1938	12.90	0.56	−0.075	0.009	15.158	5.099
Sum			3.472	0.222		305.173
Mean	13.70	0.467				

Source: For (1) and (2) see the data set for inter-war unemployment.

$(Y_i-\bar{Y})$, $(X_i-\bar{X})$, and $(Y_i-\hat{Y})$. The first step is to calculate the value of the
regression coefficient, b, and the intercept, a, using the formulae given in
(4.2) and (4.3) in §4.2.3. This gives

$$b = \frac{3.472}{0.222} = 15.64$$

and

$$a = 13.70 - 15.64(0.467) = 6.40$$

The regression equation is therefore

$$\text{UNEMP} = 6.40 + 15.64\,\text{BWRATIO}$$

t_{calc} can then be calculated using the formula in (6.15)

$$t_{calc} = \frac{15.64}{\sqrt{\dfrac{305.173}{(19-2)0.222}}} = \frac{15.64}{\sqrt{80.860}} = \frac{15.640}{8.992}$$

$$= 1.74$$

As the final step in the procedure this value for t_{calc} is compared with the theoretical t-distribution (summarized in table 5.1). In this case the number of degrees freedom (df) is $(n-2) = 17$. For 17 df and a two-tailed test at the 5 per cent significance level the critical value is 2.110. Since t_{calc} is *less than* this it falls well within the non-rejection region, and H_0 cannot be rejected.

If a statistical computer program is used in place of table 5.1 it is possible to be more precise. For this regression it reports that the prob-value for the explanatory variable is actually 0.101. This indicates that the probability of getting a t-statistic of 1.74 when H_0 is that there is no relationship between UNEMP and BWRATIO is as much as 10.1 per cent. The null hypothesis would thus fail to be rejected even if the significance level had been set at 10 per cent.

Notes

[1] A classic illustration of the consequences if such an approach is not adopted was the case of Thalidomide. This anti-nausea drug was introduced in the 1950s for the benefit of pregnant women, but was later demonstrated to have caused substantial numbers of severe birth defects among the children of those who took the drug. Note that in the wake of such cases, the legal rules of liability certainly intensify the preference for significance over efficiency among drug companies.

[2] Since we have laid stress on the fact that the population standard deviation, σ, is typically unknown, it might legitimately occur to you to ask how we know the value of the population mean, μ. The answer would be that we very seldom do know what μ is, and the test statistics historians calculate are normally variants of (6.2a) that do *not* involve hypotheses about the value of a single mean, and thus do not involve μ. See, for example, §6.7.

[3] For a number of applications of a difference of means test by an historian see Ann Kussmaul, *Servants in Husbandry in Early Modern England*, Cambridge University Press, 1981, pp. 57–9 and 64–5. For example, she has two samples giving information on the distances travelled by servants between successive hirings in the late eighteenth century. The larger sample, based on the Statute Sessions held at Spalding (in

Lincolnshire), indicates a mean distance for male servants of 12.32 km. The figure calculated from the smaller sample, based on settlement examinations (held to determine entitlement to poor relief) in Suffolk, was 8.24 km. The two estimates were found to differ significantly ($p = 0.0031$). Kussmaul also uses the corresponding procedure to test for differences of proportions.

[4] The corrected number of degrees of freedom will be calculated automatically by the computer, using the formula:

$$df = \frac{\left(\dfrac{s_1^2}{n_1} + \dfrac{s_2^2}{n_2}\right)^2}{\left(\dfrac{s_1^2}{n_1}\right)^2\left(\dfrac{1}{n_1 + 1}\right) + \left(\dfrac{s_2^2}{n_2}\right)^2\left(\dfrac{1}{n_2 + 1}\right)} - 2$$

rounded to the nearest whole number.

[5] The fact that the hypothesis being tested is that $\rho = 0$ must be emphasized. It is only when this is true that it is possible to apply the formula for the standard error given in (6.11). In all other circumstances it would be necessary to use the alternative formula for SE(r) and transformation of r into Fisher's z outlined in §5.6.2.

[6] For extensive use of tests of the significance of correlation coefficients see Dorothy Swaine Thomas, *Social Aspects of the Business Cycle*, Routledge, 1925. As mentioned in §3.2.4, Thomas measured the correlation between the business cycle and a number of social variables such as births, marriages, and crime. For each of the numerous coefficients she also calculated a standard error corresponding to (6.11) (though with n rather than n − 2 in the denominator), and stated that she would take as 'a test of significance that r should be as much as three times the value of this expression' (p. 178). This would be more than sufficient to cover the 1 per cent significance level, and is thus a very conservative standard (compare the rule of thumb mentioned in §6.7.3 for a ratio of two as an approximation to the 5 per cent level).

[7] This null hypothesis would be appropriate, for example, in a study of market integration. If a standardized commodity such as wheat is sold in two neighbouring markets, say Liverpool and Manchester, and these markets are linked by trade, then one would expect any move in price in one market to be closely followed in the other market. In these circumstances, a regression of the price in Liverpool on the price in Manchester should show a regression coefficient of unity. For an application of this approach to international markets (for which it is also necessary to take account of tariffs and transport costs) see Donald N. McCloskey and J. Richard Zecher, 'How the gold standard worked, 1880–1913', pp.192–4 in Donald N. McCloskey, *Enterprise and Trade in Victorian Britain*, Allen & Unwin, 1981, pp. 184–208.

See also the analysis of the prices quoted for three British stocks on the London and Amsterdam stock exchanges in the eighteenth century in Larry Neal, *The Rise of Financial Capitalism*, Cambridge University Press, 1990, pp.120–32. The rationality of the market prices is established by showing that when the share price is regressed on the present value of the expected future dividends the coefficient 'is statistically significant in each case and is very close to the theoretical value of 1.0' (p. 131).

6.8 Exercises for chapter 6

1. Identify the null hypothesis and research hypothesis for the following cases:

   (i) The death rate from tuberculosis was the same in Britain and the United States in the 1920s.

   (ii) Death rates from tuberculosis fell in Britain between 1920 and 1950.

   (iii) Death rates from tuberculosis in the United States in 1930 were systematically related to the level of urbanization.

   (iv) Tuberculosis is caused by consumption of raw, untreated milk.

   (v) The American Civil War generated a significant increase in total iron production to make armaments.

   (vi) The American Civil War caused no change in the level of iron production in the United States.

Which of the hypotheses are directional and which are not?

2. Write a brief essay assessing the relevance of Type II errors in historical research. Under what circumstances are Type II errors likely to be important? Are there situations in which the possibility of a Type II error can safely be ignored?

3. Test the following hypotheses using Hatton and Williamson's cross-section data on Irish emigration by county:

   (i) The correlation between Catholicism and family size was statistically significant in 1881, but not in 1911.

   (ii) The correlation between housing density and degree of urbanization was statistically significant in 1881, but not statistically different from -0.5.

   (iii) The chances of finding a county with an average family size of less than four children is less than 5 per cent; however, the chances of finding a county with an average family size of more than six children is greater than 5 per cent.

   (iv) The proportion of the Irish population who could not read or write in 1911 was the same as in 1881.

   (v) The decline in the Irish emigration rate between 1881 and 1911 was dramatic. Every county in 1911 fell outside the 99 per cent confidence interval for the migration rate in 1881.

4. Calculate *by hand* the value of t_{calc} for the regression coefficient of disturbances on wheat prices in chapter 4, question 3. Compare this with the appropriate test statistic, being sure to identify the correct numbers of degrees of freedom. Does this suggest that the regression coefficient is statistically significant?

5. The example in the text of the difference of means test of relief payments in Kent and Sussex does not take into consideration the fact that these data were collected by **sampling without replacement**. Using the procedures introduced in chapter 5, recalculate the example incorporating the finite population correction. Report your results. Does the correction weaken or strengthen the conclusions reached in the text? Explain your conclusions. Can any general rules be learned from this example?

6. Use the Boyer relief data set to test the hypothesis that workhouses in Southern England were more likely to be built in parishes with more aggregate wealth at their disposal (you will need to construct a new variable that measures total wealth per parish; this can be achieved by multiplying average wealth by parish population).

(i) Apply a difference of means test of this hypothesis. Interpret your results in the light of the maintained hypothesis.

A critic of your analysis of the relationship between wealth and the workhouse notes that the distribution of total wealth by parishes is not even approximately normally distributed. Indeed, the critic observes that the distribution is log-normal (see §2.4.1).

(ii) Generate bar charts of total wealth and the log of total wealth by parish to assess these criticisms. Then repeat (i) with the log of total wealth. Does this cause you to amend your evaluation of the maintained hypothesis that wealthier parishes were more likely to build workhouses?

(iii) Is there a more straightforward answer to your critic, that does not involve recalculation of the data? (*Hint*: remember the Central Limit Theorem.)

7. Generate the means and standard deviations of BRTHRATE for parishes in Bedfordshire, Buckinghamshire, Essex, and Sussex from Boyer's birth data set.

(i) Use the data to test for equality in the average level of births per 100 families in Bedfordshire and Essex, assuming equal variances in the two counties. Note the relative size of the standard deviations of the birth rate for the two counties. What difference does it make to your conclusions if you treat the population variances in the two counties as unequal rather than equal?

(ii) Use the data to test for equality in the average level of births per 100 families in Buckinghamshire and Sussex. Once again, there is a notable difference in the standard deviation of the birth rate between the two counties. What difference does it make to your conclusions if you treat the population variances in the two counties as unequal rather than equal?

What lessons can be drawn from these two examples about the importance of correcting for unequal variance when carrying out difference of means tests?

8. Let us assume that more responses to the Poor Law questionnaires have been discovered in the depths of the Public Record Office. Reassuringly, all the means and standard deviations of the variables remain the same, both for the entire sample, and also for the individual counties.

  (i) With this new evidence in hand, you decide to reassess the results of question 7. The number of observations has been increased, such that there are now 35 parishes reported for Bedfordshire and Essex; 37 parishes for Buckinghamshire, and 45 for Sussex.
 (ii) What do you find when you repeat the exercise? How would you explain any change in the results?
(iii) What do the results of questions 7 and 8 tell us about the robustness of the t-test for difference of means between samples?

9. In Steckel's data set on the patterns of leaving home in the United States, 1850–60, there are two variables. YNGERFAM and OLDERFAM, that record the number of younger and older children in each household.

  (i) Calculate the mean and standard deviation of each variable.
 (ii) You wish to record the total number of children in the household. Create a new variable, TOTALFAM. Calculate the mean and standard deviation of the new variable.
(iii) Compare the mean and standard deviation of TOTALFAM with the means and standard deviations of YNGERFAM and OLDERFAM. What do these comparisons tell you about the additivity of these measures of central tendency?

10. In a revision of Benjamin and Kochin's analysis of inter-war unemployment in Britain, a researcher addresses the question of the separate effects of benefits and wages on unemployment. He wishes to test whether the impact on unemployment of a change in the benefit level (BENEFITS), holding the wage rate constant, was the same as a change in the average wage (WAGES), holding the benefit rate constant. He also wishes to test whether the coefficient on the benefit rate is significantly different from

unity (i.e. $b_1 = 1$), and whether the coefficient on DEMAND is significantly different in this specification from the one reported in (14.2).

The result of the revised regression is (t-statistics in parentheses):

$$UNEMP = -3.127 + 0.461 \text{ BENEFITS} + 0.081 \text{ WAGES} - 96.492 \text{ DEMAND}$$
$$(0.29) \quad (3.41) \qquad\qquad (0.60) \qquad\qquad (9.10)$$

What are the answers to the researcher's hypotheses?

CHAPTER 7

Non-parametric tests

7.1 Introduction

Historians cannot always work with problems for which all the relevant data are based on quantitative measurements. Very often the only information available for analysis relates to the number of cases falling into different categories; the category itself cannot be quantified.[a] Thus household heads might be classified according to their sex, political affiliation, or ethnicity. Wars might be grouped into epic, major, and minor conflicts. Women might be subdivided by their religion, the forms of birth control they practised, or the socio-economic status of their fathers.

Alternatively the historian might have data that can be ranked in order, but the precise distance between the ranks either cannot be measured or is unhelpful for the problem under consideration. One example might be a ranking of all the universities in the country by a newspaper combining on some arbitrary basis a medley of criteria such as the quality of students admitted, library expenditure per student, and total grants received for research. Another might be a ranking of the power of politicians in an assembly on the basis of some measure of their influence on voting in the assembly.[1] Similarly, an historian of religion might construct a ranking of the intensity of religious belief of the members of a community according to the frequency of their church attendance in a given period.

In all such cases it is not possible to apply the techniques of hypothesis testing described in chapter 6. There are two fundamental reasons why **parametric** tests such as Z and t cannot be used.[b] First, these statistical tests

---

[a] In the terminology of §1.3.3 the information is at the nominal level of measurement, as opposed to the interval or ratio level of most economic data.

[b] Statistical tests such as Z and t (or the F-test that will be introduced in §9.3) are known as **parametric** tests because they test hypotheses about specific parameters (characteristics of the population) such as the mean or the regression coefficient.

cannot be made with nominal or ordinal levels of data, they require variables that are measured on an interval scale. With nominal level data it is simply not possible to perform any of the basic operations of arithmetic such as would be needed to calculate a mean. With some forms of ordinal level data, for example, the ranking of politicians on the basis suggested above, it might be possible to perform such operations, but the interpretation of the results would be problematic. The successive differences between any two 'scores' are not true intervals with substantive meaning, and consequently the interpretation of test results, such as the position of the test statistic in relation to the critical region, may be misleading.

Secondly, the parametric tests assume that the sample observations satisfy certain conditions, in particular, that they are drawn from populations that are approximately normally distributed (see §6.2.1).

To take the place of the parametric tests in situations where they are not appropriate, a large battery of **non-parametric** tests has been developed. These can be applied to nominal or ordinal level data, and require the minimum of assumptions about the nature of the underlying distribution. It is thus appropriate to use a non-parametric test when there is reason to think that the relevant population distribution is not normal (or its exact form cannot be specified). This is particularly likely to be the case when dealing with small samples.

The fundamental principles of hypothesis testing outlined in chapter 6 apply equally to the various non-parametric tests. It is again necessary:

- to specify a null hypothesis
- to select a significance level and critical region
- to calculate a test statistic
- to compare this with the theoretical probability given by the sampling distribution for that statistic.

There are a number of non-parametric tests that are quite widely used, and are available with several statistical computer programs. We will begin in §7.2 by discussing three such tests that can be used in relation to comparisons between data from two small samples using ranked (ordinal level) data. Inevitably, there is a price to be paid for the advantages of these non-parametric tests, and this is considered briefly in §7.2.4.

In the following section, §7.3, we introduce another non-parametric test of statistical significance known as χ^2 (lower case Greek chi, pronounced ki-squared). This is a very widely used test for dealing with data classified into two or more categories. §7.4 describes a very useful non-parametric test than can be applied to establish whether or not events in a sample occur in a random sequence. Two further tests that can be used to determine the goodness of fit of an actual distribution in comparison with some specified alternative are briefly noted in §7.5.

As with numerical (interval level) measures, the preceding tests relating to statistical significance are only part of the story. If an association is found to be statistically significant it is also necessary to establish the strength of that association, and §7.6 discusses some of the non-parametric measures which are available for this purpose.

All the non-parametric tests discussed in §7.2–§7.5 establish critical values that determine whether or not the null hypothesis should be rejected (see §6.3.2). For small samples these are usually based on exact sampling distributions for the relevant test statistic, and there are published tables of the critical values for a range of combinations of sample size and desired significance level.[c] For larger samples the test may rely on an approximation to a particular sampling distribution that becomes more precise as the size of the samples increases.

The tables of critical values have to a large extent been superseded in recent years by computer programs, with the benefits noted in relation to parametric tests in §6.3.5. The programs are able to cover all sample sizes, and in addition to calculating the required test statistic will also report the corresponding prob-value. This will be either the exact prob-value or its large-sample approximation. However, reference to the published tables helps one to get a better feel for the way in which critical values change with sample size or number of degrees of freedom, and we will generally discuss both methods of reaching a decision.

The topics in this chapter build on ideas developed in previous chapters, but are not themselves required for the topics covered in the later part of this book. They could be skipped by students whose main interest is in the subject of regression taken up in the subsequent chapters.

7.2 Non-parametric tests for two independent samples

We will look at each of these first three tests in the context of two **independent** samples.[d] The definition of independence has two components. As *between* the samples, it means that the units selected for the first sample are completely independent of those selected for the second sample. (The

[c] Tables are given in D. V. Lindley and W. F. Scott, *New Cambridge Statistical Tables*, 2nd edn., Cambridge University Press, 1995, for all the tests referred to in this chapter.

[d] In addition to these tests for two *independent* samples there are other non-parametric tests for two *related* samples (i.e. those that are not independent), or for three or more samples, usually referred to collectively as *k* samples. There are also tests for a single sample, and three examples of these tests will be discussed in §7.4 and §7.5.

alternative would be two **related** samples, as in a medical trial when every person in one sample has a family relation in the other sample, or the same person is used in 'before and after' samples. Such related samples hardly ever occur in the data available to historians.) The second aspect of independence applies *within* each sample, and requires that each unit is independent of every other unit within that sample.

The essential principle behind all three of these tests for two independent samples is quite straightforward. Each test consists of an intuitively obvious way of comparing the results from the two samples in order to decide whether or not they come from underlying populations with exactly the same distribution, and hence can be treated as coming from the same population. In some cases only the general nature of the distribution can be considered; in others it is possible to compare more specific features such as the mean or variance.

The null hypothesis in each case is that there is no difference between the two samples: the two distributions are identical and come from the same population. The research hypothesis (H_1) might be simply that the two distributions are not identical, leading to a two-tailed test. Or H_1 might specify something about the direction of the difference leading to a one-tailed test in the specified direction. For example, this difference might relate to the mean or some other measure of central tendency, in which case H_1 would be that the values of one sample are larger (smaller) than the values of the other.

In order to highlight the principal features of the three tests we have created four variants of an artificially simple data set, and will use this to illustrate the comparison of two samples with each of the tests. The data set relates to two independent samples of newly enrolled students, 10 from Harvard and 10 from Yale. Each student was ranked by an impartial panel from 1 (highest) to 20 (lowest) on the basis of subjective assessments of their intellectual ability and application. The four variants (I, II, III, and IV) of the rankings are given in table 7.1. The advantage of this imaginary example is that it enables the tests to be illustrated in relation to a wider range of possible distributions than would normally be encountered in practice.

7.2.1   The Wald–Wolfowitz runs test

This is the simplest of the three tests. The two samples are combined and the values from each sample are ranked in either ascending or descending order. Are Harvard and Yale admitting their students from the same underlying population, or is there a statistically significant difference in the academic quality of their intake? The procedure for answering this question by

Table 7.1 Rankings of two independent samples of students (imaginary data, four variants)

University	I	II	III	IV
Harvard	1	1	1	1
Harvard	2	2	2	3
Harvard	3	3	3	5
Harvard	4	4	4	7
Harvard	5	5	9	9
Harvard	6	11	10	11
Harvard	7	12	11	13
Harvard	8	13	13	15
Harvard	9	14	14	17
Harvard	10	20	20	19
Yale	11	6	5	2
Yale	12	7	6	4
Yale	13	8	7	6
Yale	14	9	8	8
Yale	15	10	12	10
Yale	16	15	15	12
Yale	17	16	16	14
Yale	18	17	17	16
Yale	19	18	18	18
Yale	20	19	19	20

means of a runs test would be to list the 20 observations in rank order. If the symbols H and Y are used to designate the respective samples, the list for variant III of table 7.1 – ranked in descending order – would look like this:

HHHH YYYY HHH Y HH YYYYY H

Each sequence of the same letter constitutes a *run*. In the above illustration there are a total of seven runs: 4 in H and 3 in Y.

The basic idea behind the test is that if the underlying distributions are identical, the letters representing the two samples will be randomly scattered all through the list, creating *large numbers of short runs*. On the other hand, if the underlying distributions are different, the ranks from one of the samples are likely to predominate in some parts of the list, and those from the other sample in other parts, giving rise to *a small number of long runs*.

The test cannot say anything about how the distributions might differ

– it might be, for example, with respect to either the location (mean or median) or the shape (dispersion or skewness) of the distribution, or to both. It is thus mainly useful as a quick and easy test when the focus of interest is not on the specific features of the distribution but only on detecting a general difference.

The null hypothesis is that there is no difference between the two samples, i.e. they come from the same population. Even if no direction is predicted, the runs test is effectively a one-tailed test because H_0 *can be rejected only if there are a small number of long runs.*[e] However a direction may be predicted in advance; for example, the research hypothesis might be that one sample would have a higher ranking than the other. This would be a possible reason for selecting a lower significance level, such as 2.5 per cent, thus forming a smaller critical region and so making it harder to reject the null hypothesis.

The test statistic, r, is the number of runs and can be counted very easily. Given the choice of significance level and the test statistic, the decision can be made on whether or not to reject the null hypothesis. These final steps in the test can be performed on the computer by your statistical software, though for small samples it may be as quick to carry out the work by hand. There is no need to memorize the formulae the computer will apply, but they are discussed below so that those who wish to increase their understanding can see how the results are obtained. It is also useful to show explicitly that this non-parametric procedure belongs to the same family of test procedures as those already discussed in chapter 6.

If the samples are small (neither more than 20), the exact sampling distribution for the number of runs, r, can be calculated for different combinations of sample size, and is given in a published table.[f]

If the sample sizes are larger than this, the Central Limit Theorem (see §5.3.1) applies and the sampling distribution of r is approximately normal.[g] The standardized value of Z is calculated from the mean, μ_r, and standard deviation, σ_r, of the sampling distribution of the number of runs, r.

---

[e] This is an exception, therefore, to the general principle stated in §6.3.3 that a one-tailed test should be used only when direction is predicted.

[f] Lindley and Scott, *Statistical Tables*, table 18, pp. 60–2. The table is in two parts, the upper and lower percentage points (corresponding to the left- and right-hand tails of the distribution), but for the present test it is only the latter we are interested in. (The upper percentage points are required when the runs test is used below for the one-sample test of randomness, for which both tails may be relevant; see §7.4.)

[g] Recall from §5.3.1 that it is possible for the distribution of a *sampling distribution* to be approximately normal even when the underlying *population* from which the samples are drawn is not assumed to be normal.

THE WALD–WOLFOWITZ RUNS TEST

For *large* samples (either n_1 or n_2 greater than 20)
the sampling distribution of the test statistic, r,
is approximately normal,
with mean

$$\mu_r = \frac{2n_1 n_2}{n_1 + n_2} + 1, \tag{7.1}$$

and standard error, SE(r)

$$= \sigma_r = \sqrt{\frac{2n_1 n_2 (2n_1 n_2 - n_1 - n_2)}{(n_1 + n_2)^2 (n_1 + n_2 - 1)}} \tag{7.2}$$

The standardized value Z_{calc} can thus be derived in the usual way by calculating the difference in units of standard errors between the actual number of runs given by the particular sample, and the theoretical mean given by the sampling distribution.[h]

**THE STANDARDIZED TEST STATISTIC FOR THE
WALD–WOLFOWITZ RUNS TEST**

This is

$$Z_{calc} = \frac{r - \mu_r}{\sigma_r} \tag{7.3}$$

To make the test decision, the resulting Z_{calc} is compared with the theoretical sampling distribution. For small samples this is given by the special table; for large samples the table for the standard normal distribution (partially reproduced in table 2.7) is used.[i]

An illustration of the runs test
To illustrate the nature of this test, the runs given by each of the four variants of the imaginary data are shown in the upper panel of table 7.2.

[h] Compare the initial definitions of Z_{calc} and t_{calc} in §6.4.2.
[i] For the complete table of the normal distribution see Lindley and Scott, *Statistical Tables*, table 4, pp. 34–5.

Table 7.2   The Wald–Wolfowitz runs test

1 Data: Four alternative series of runs for two independent samples
(students from Harvard (H) and Yale (Y), imaginary ranked data from table 7.1)

I	II	III	IV
(2 runs)	(5 runs)	(7 runs)	(20 runs)
H	H	H	H
H	H	H	Y
H	H	H	H
H	H	H	Y
H	H	Y	H
H	Y	Y	Y
H	Y	Y	H
H	Y	Y	Y
H	Y	H	H
H	Y	H	Y
Y	H	H	H
Y	H	Y	Y
Y	H	H	H
Y	H	H	Y
Y	Y	Y	H
Y	Y	Y	Y
Y	Y	Y	H
Y	Y	Y	Y
Y	Y	Y	H
Y	H	H	Y

2 Test statistics, significance values, and results

(1)	(2)	(3)	(4)		(5)
	Test	Standardized			
	statistic	value	Significance		
Series	r	Z	(1-tailed) *		Decision
I	2	−3.905	0.0000	(0.0%)	Reject H$_0$
II	5	−2.527	0.0045	(0.45%)	Reject H$_0$
III	7	−1.608	0.0513	(5.13%)	Cannot reject H$_0$
IV	20	4.365	1.0000	(100.0%)	Cannot reject H$_0$

Note:
* Probability of obtaining this value of *r* if the null hypothesis is correct. Both sample sizes are less than 20, so the exact distribution of the test statistic can be used rather than the normal approximation.

Variants I and IV illustrate two extreme possibilities: in I every observation for Harvard is above any observation for Yale and there are thus only 2 long runs; in IV the observations alternate perfectly creating 20 short runs. Columns II and III cover intermediate possibilities with 5 and 7 runs, respectively.

We look first at the procedure when this decision is made on the basis of published tables and then at the results obtained from the computer program. For the present test we will adopt the 5 per cent level with no direction predicted. If we enter the table for the lower percentage points of the distribution we find that for two samples, both of size 10, the critical value for the 5 per cent level is 6. Any value of the test statistic, r, *less than or equal to 6 will fall in the critical region, and the null hypothesis should be rejected.* For any value of r greater than 6 the null hypothesis cannot be rejected.

As should be intuitively obvious, the null hypothesis that there is no difference between the samples is easily rejected in the case of I (2 runs) and is not rejected in the case of IV (20 runs). The two remaining cases are less obvious: the result of the test is that H_0 is rejected for II (with 5 runs), but cannot be rejected for III (with 7 runs).

The exercise is now repeated using a computer program and the standardized values of the test statistic, Z_{calc}. The test statistic, r, is reported for each variant in column (2) of the lower panel of table 7.2, and the value of Z_{calc} obtained by the computer in column (3).[2] The corresponding significance level for a one-tailed test and the final decision are reported in columns (4) and (5). Because we are working with small samples the program is able to calculate the *exact* significance based on the sampling distribution corresponding to the critical values in the published tables. With larger samples it would report the approximate significance based on the normal distribution.

The significance levels for I (2 runs) and IV (20 runs) are, respectively, 0.0000 (zero probability of getting this result if H_0 is true) and 1.000 (100 per cent probability of getting this result if H_0 is true), so H_0 can easily be rejected for the former but cannot be rejected for the latter. For II (5 runs) the significance level is 0.45 per cent, indicating as before that H_0 must be rejected. By contrast, for III (7 runs) the significance level of 5.13 per cent falls just outside the conventional 5 per cent critical region, and H_0 cannot be rejected at this level.

7.2.2 The Mann–Whitney U-test

This test is similarly based on the ranking of the observations in the two samples. It is a popular test of whether or not there are differences between the sample means (or of some other measure of location), but can also be used as a test for differences in dispersion or skewness. The basic idea is that if the underlying distributions are identical, the ranking of the observations from the two samples will be broadly similar. If they are not identical, the ranks of the one sample will be predominantly higher (or lower) than those of the other. This difference might occur because, for example, the mean of one sample was above the mean of the other, or because one sample was more spread out than the other.

The null hypothesis is thus that the two distributions are identical. The research hypothesis might either be simply that they are different (a two-tailed test); or, more specifically, that the rank values from one of the distributions are predominantly higher (lower) than those from the other (a one-tailed test in the specified direction).

The hypothetical ranking of the 20 students from Harvard and Yale is again used to illustrate the procedure, which is as follows:

(a) Combine both samples, and rank the students in ascending (or descending) order from 1 to 20.[j]
(b) Take the lowest rank in one of the samples (if the samples differ in size it is usual to take the smaller but this does not affect the result – we will take the Harvard sample), and count *the number of students with higher ranks* than this in the second sample (Yale). Repeat this for each successive rank in the Harvard sample.
(c) Add the results of this counting exercise for all 10 Harvard students. This sum is the test statistic, U.
(d) Compare U with the appropriate theoretical sampling distribution to test the probability that the observed difference in ranks could have come from the same distribution.

The **Wilcoxon rank sum** test is a variant of the Mann–Whitney test that simply counts the sum of the ranks of the smaller (or first) sample. This sum, W, is the test statistic, and there is a fixed relationship between W and U.[3] Furthermore, the exact significance levels of W and U are the same, so the two tests always give the same result.

The relevant calculations for the subsequent stages of this test are again given in order to clarify what the computer does if asked to perform the test. If the samples are small (neither more than 20) it is possible to use

---

[j] If the underlying scores result in a tie, the rank allocated is the mean of the ranks that would have otherwise been allocated to the tied scores. If the tie is *within* one of the samples the calculations are otherwise unaffected; if it is a tie *between* samples a correction to the formula for Z_{calc} is required.

a special table that gives the exact sampling distribution for the Mann–Whitney test statistic, U.[k]

With larger sample sizes the sampling distribution of U will be approximately normal. In this case the mean and standard deviation of this sampling distribution can be calculated as in the following box:

THE MANN–WHITNEY U-TEST

For *large* samples (either n_1 or n_2 greater than 20)
the sampling distribution of the test statistic, U,
is approximately normal,
with mean

$$\mu_u = \frac{n_1 n_2}{2}, \tag{7.4}$$

and standard error, $SE(U)$

$$= \sigma_u = \sqrt{\frac{n_1 n_2 (n_1 + n_2 + 1)}{12}} \tag{7.5}$$

A standardized value for the test statistic Z_{calc} in units of standard errors can be derived as before.

THE STANDARDIZED TEST STATISTIC FOR THE MANN–WHITNEY U-TEST

This is

$$Z_{calc} = \frac{U - \mu_u}{\sigma_u} \tag{7.6}$$

To make the test decision, the resulting Z_{calc} is compared with the theoretical sampling distribution. For small samples this is given by the special table; for large samples the table for the standard normal distribution (partially reproduced in table 2.7) is used.[l]

---

[k] Lindley and Scott, *Statistical Tables*, table 21, pp. 66–7. The table gives the lower percentage point of the distribution.

[l] For the complete table of the normal distribution see Lindley and Scott, *Statistical Tables*, table 4, pp. 34–5.

An illustration of the Mann–Whitney U-test

The calculations are illustrated in the upper panel of table 7.3 using the hypothetical data for series IV from table 7.1. The significance level is taken as 5 per cent in a two-tailed test with no direction predicted. If we start with the Harvard sample we get $U=45$ and $W=110$. If we had started instead with the Yale sample the respective results would be 55 and 100.[4]

We start with the procedure for making the decision on the basis of the published table for small samples. Because of the form in which the tables are constructed it is conventional to take the *lower* of the two possible values for the test; in this case, 45 for the Mann–Whitney test (or 100 for the Wilcoxon rank sum test).[5]

If we consult the table for two samples each of 10, we see that the critical value for the 5 per cent level is 27. This is the largest value that falls in the critical region. *For any value of the test statistic, U less than or equal to 27, the null hypothesis should be rejected.* For any value of U greater than 27 the null hypothesis cannot be rejected. Thus for variant IV, U is 45; this is markedly greater than 27 and so H_0 cannot be rejected.

The values of U for all four variants are given in column (2) of the lower panel of table 7.3. For the two extreme variants, I and IV, we find as expected that H_0 is easily rejected for I ($U=0$), but cannot be rejected for IV ($U=45$). For the intermediate variants H_0 cannot be rejected either for III ($U=32$) or for II ($U=30$) since these test statistics are both greater than 27.

It will be seen that the difference between U and the critical value is quite small in the case of II, and that it leads to a different result from the one obtained in §7.2.1 with the runs test, according to which H_0 should be rejected for II. The issue of different test results is discussed briefly in §7.2.4 after the introduction of one further non-parametric test.

With larger samples we would not be able to use the tables and would instead rely on the computer. To see how this procedure works we repeat the exercise using a statistical program (SPSS). The standardized value of the test statistic, Z_{calc}, calculated by the program is shown in column (4) of the lower panel of table 7.3. A quick check shows that it is equal to the results given by (7.6) based on the formulae for μ_u and σ_u in (7.4) and (7.5).[6]

The corresponding two-tailed significance levels are reported in column (5) of the lower panel of table 7.3.[7] The significance levels are 0.00 (zero probability of getting this result if H_0 is true) for I and 0.739 (73.9 per cent probability of getting this result if H_0 is true) for IV. The significance levels for II and III are lower but still well outside the critical region at 0.143 and 0.190, respectively. We thus reach the same decisions as we made when

Table 7.3 The Mann–Whitney U-test and the Wilcoxon rank sums test

1 Calculation of test statistics for two independent samples:
(imaginary data, series IV, table 7.1)

(1) Rank of Harvard students	(2) Number of Yale students with higher rank	(3) Rank of Yale students	(4) Number of Harvard students with higher rank
19	9	20	10
17	8	18	9
15	7	16	8
13	6	14	7
11	5	12	6
9	4	10	5
7	3	8	4
5	2	6	3
3	1	4	2
1	0	2	1
$W = \overline{100}$	$U = \overline{45}$	$W' = \overline{110}$	$U' = \overline{55}$

2 Test statistics, significance values, and results for all four series in table 7.1

(1)	(2)	(3)	(4)	(5)	(6)
		Test statistics			
	Mann– Whitney	Wilcoxon	Standardized value	Exact significance	
Series	U	W	Z	(2-tailed)*	Decision
I	0	55	-3.780	0.000 (0.0%)	*Reject H_0*
II	30	85	-1.512	0.143 (14.3%)	*Cannot reject H_0*
III	32	87	-1.361	0.190 (19.0%)	*Cannot reject H_0*
IV	45	100	-0.378	0.739 (73.9%)	*Cannot reject H_0*

Note:
* Probability of obtaining this value of U (or W) if the null hypothesis is correct. Both sample sizes are less than 20, so the exact distribution of the test statistic can be used rather than the normal approximation.

using the tables, but with the precise prob-values we have more information.[8]

7.2.3 The Kolmogorov–Smirnov test

The key idea underlying this third test is that if the two independent samples have been drawn from the same population, their **cumulative frequency distributions** will be essentially similar because they should both show only random deviations from the common population distribution.[m] The test is sensitive to any kind of difference there might be between the two distributions, for example differences in means or other measures of central tendency, in dispersion, or in skewness.

The null hypothesis is thus that there is no difference between the two samples. It is designed for use with continuous data and is more conservative (less likely to reject the null hypothesis) with discrete data. Therefore, if H_0 is rejected in an application of the Kolmogorov–Smirnov test with discrete data the researcher can have more confidence in the decision.

The test statistic is based on D, the *maximum* difference between the two cumulative frequency distributions, expressed as a proportion. If the research hypothesis is simply that there is a difference between the two samples, D is calculated without regard to sign for a two-tailed test. If H_1 predicts the direction of the difference, D is the maximum positive or maximum negative difference for a one-tailed test. The actual test statistic is not D, but $n_1 \times n_2 \times D$, where n_1 and n_2 are the sample sizes.

The particular sampling distribution used for the Kolmogorov–Smirnov test depends on whether the sample sizes are small or large, and whether they are of equal size. Published tables are available for selected sizes of small samples, indicating critical values for different levels of significance.[n] The table gives the upper percentage point, (i.e. the right-hand tail) and so differs in this respect from those referred to in the two previous sections. The decision rule thus changes and for this test is that the

---

[m] A cumulative absolute frequency distribution measures the number of observations below – or equal to – any selected value in the distribution; see §2.1.1 and §2.1.3. With ordinal data this would refer to the number in or below each ordered category (e.g. a classification of workers by social class). The corresponding cumulative *relative* frequency expresses this as a proportion (0.1, 0.2, etc.). The cumulative relative frequency could also be expressed as a percentage as in table 2.2 and table 2.3, or in fractions, but *for the purpose of the test statistic it must be in the form of a proportion.*

[n] Lindley and Scott, *Statistical Tables*, table 19, pp. 62–4 gives critical values for samples of $n_1 \leq n_2$ up to $n_2 = 20$, and for $n_1 = n_2$ from 20 to 100. The figures given for each significance level are for two-tailed tests and the corresponding value for a one-tailed test is obtained by moving to half the significance level. For example, for samples of $n_1 = n_2 = 10$, the critical value for a two-tailed test at 10 per cent is 60, and this would be the critical value for a one-tailed test at 5 per cent.

null hypothesis should be rejected if the test statistic, $n_1 n_2 D$, *is equal to or greater than* these values. Computer packages provide more exact prob-values and also cover large samples.

An illustration of the Kolmogorov–Smirnov test

The procedure for calculation of D is illustrated in the upper panel of table 7.4 using variant III of the imaginary data for the two groups of students. In this instance the available information is maximized by treating each rank (from 1 to 20) as a separate class interval, but the procedure can also be applied when the data are grouped (see §2.1.1). Because there are 10 items in each sample, the proportion of the total distribution represented by each entry is 0.1, and because there is only one entry in each class interval, each successive entry adds 0.1 to the cumulative relative frequency distributions shown in columns (3) and (4). The final row for each sample must be 1.

The difference between the two cumulative relative frequency distributions, D, is then calculated in column (5). If sign is ignored, the largest difference is 0.4, indicated by arrows in rows 6 and 16 (the fact that it occurs twice is irrelevant); and this is also the largest negative difference. The largest positive difference is 0.1 in the first row. The test statistic $n_1 n_2 D$ is then derived from this; in the present case this simply involves multiplying by 100, since $n_1 \times n_2 = 10 \times 10$.

The values of D for all four series, I to IV, are given in column (2) of the lower panel of table 7.4, and the corresponding test statistics, $n_1 n_2 D$, in column (3). We will deal first with the procedure for making a decision on the basis of the exact sampling distribution in the published tables. The significance level is taken as 5 per cent with no direction predicted.

The published table gives 70 as the critical value for samples of this size at the 5 per cent level. It is easily seen that the results for all four cases are the same as with the Mann–Whitney test. For the two extreme cases, the null hypothesis is rejected for I ($n_1 n_2 D = 100$) but cannot be rejected for D ($n_1 n_2 D = 10$). It also cannot be rejected for either of the intermediate cases, II ($n_1 n_2 D = 50$) or III ($n_1 n_2 D = 40$).

It is obvious that the last three results are falling progressively further from the critical region and thus that the probability of getting these results if H_0 is true is getting increasingly large. If we want to know the exact prob-values the exercise can be repeated using a computer. SPSS calculates a statistic it calls Kolmogorov–Smirnov Z (hereafter KS Z), for which the formula is

$$KS\ Z = D\sqrt{\frac{n_1 n_2}{n_1 + n_2}} \tag{7.7}$$

Table 7.4   The Kolmogorov–Smirnov test

1 Calculation of test statistic for two independent samples
(imaginary data, series III, table 7.1)

(1)	(2)	(3)	(4)	(5)
		Cumulative		$D=$
Ranking		relative frequency		Difference
Harvard	Yale	Harvard	Yale	Harvard–Yale
20		0.1	0.0	0.1 $<=$
	19	0.1	0.1	0.0
	18	0.1	0.2	−0.1
	17	0.1	0.3	−0.2
	16	0.1	0.4	−0.3
	15	0.1	0.5	−0.4 $<=$
14		0.2	0.5	−0.3
13		0.3	0.5	−0.2
	12	0.3	0.6	−0.3
11		0.4	0.6	−0.2
10		0.5	0.6	−0.1
9		0.6	0.6	0.0
	8	0.6	0.7	−0.1
	7	0.6	0.8	−0.2
	6	0.6	0.9	−0.3
	5	0.6	1.0	−0.4 $<=$
4		0.7	1.0	−0.3
3		0.8	1.0	−0.2
2		0.9	1.0	−0.1
1		1.0	1.0	0.0

2 Test statistics, significance values, and results for all four series in table 7.1

(1)	(2)	(3)	(4)	(5)	(6)
	Test statistic		Kolmogorov–	Significance	
Series	D	$n_1 n_2 D$	Smirnov Z	(2-tailed)*	Decision
I	1.0	100	2.236	0.000 (0.0%)	*Reject H_0*
II	0.5	50	1.118	0.164 (16.4%)	*Cannot reject H_0*
III	0.4	40	0.894	0.400 (40.0%)	*Cannot reject H_0*
IV	0.1	10	0.224	1.000 (100.0%)	*Cannot reject H_0*

Note:
* Probability of obtaining this value of D if the null hypothesis is correct. The significance
  levels quoted are an approximation.

Thus for case III, where $D=0.4$,

$$\text{KS } Z = 0.4 \times \sqrt{\frac{10 \times 10}{10 + 10}} = 0.4 \times 2.2361 = 0.8944$$

The values of KS Z for all four cases are reported in column (4) of the lower panel of table 7.4.[9] These are then used to calculate the approximate significance levels in column (5).

The prob-value for I is 0.00 (zero probability of getting this result if H_0 is true) and so H_0 must clearly be rejected. The prob-values then rise from 0.164 for II to 0.40 for III and finally – for the extreme case of IV – to 1.00 (100 per cent probability of getting this result if H_0 is true). The decisions listed in column (6) are thus identical to those made on the basis of the tables.[10]

7.2.4 Criteria for choosing between alternative tests

We have seen in the preceding sections that different non-parametric tests can be applied to the same data and lead to different decisions on whether or not the null hypothesis should be rejected. There are also circumstances where it is possible to use both parametric and non-parametric procedures to test a null hypothesis, and this again can result in different decisions. How should the choice between different tests be made?

The choice between alternative non-parametric tests can be made on the basis of a number of different criteria. One set of considerations includes the power of the tests (as defined in §6.3.2), the level of measurement, and the size of the sample(s). A second is the precise hypothesis that is to be tested. For example, some tests are more sensitive to differences in central tendency, others to differences in dispersion, others to *any* difference between the underlying populations (in central tendency or dispersion or skewness). For more detailed discussion of the relative merits of the different tests a specialist text on non-parametric tests should be consulted.[o]

With regard to the choice between parametric and non-parametric tests, two possible reasons were given at the outset of this chapter for choosing the latter. They involve fewer assumptions about the population distributions, and they do not require interval or ratio measurements. Against this, in cases where the underlying data are normally distributed and the measurements are at interval level, non-parametric tests are *less powerful*. This means that for a given sample size and a given level of significance, there is more risk of a Type II error (not rejecting the null

---

[o] We particularly recommend Sidney Siegel and N. John Castellan Jr., *Nonparametric Statistics for the Behavioral Sciences*, 2nd edn., McGraw-Hill, New York, 1988.

hypothesis when it is false). Thus, non-parametric tests should be reserved either for non-normal populations, or when very few data observations are available, or where information is presented in nominal or ordinal form.

Comparison of a t-test and a Mann–Whitney U-test

In chapter 6 (§6.7) a parametric difference of means *t*-test was used to compare the mean value of RELIEF in the two counties of Kent and Sussex. The conclusion drawn was that the null hypothesis of no difference between the two sample means could be rejected: the difference was statistically highly significant with a prob-value of only 0.6 per cent. If the same comparison test is made using the non-parametric Mann–Whitney test, the same decision is reached, with a statistically highly significant prob-value of 0.7 per cent.

However, this will not always be the case. If these two tests are run on the mean values in the same two counties of a different variable, INCOME, the tests yield *different* decisions. In the *t*-test, corrected for unequal variances, the prob-value is 15.6 per cent, and the null hypothesis of no difference between the two sample means could not be rejected in a two-tailed test at the 5 per cent level. In the Mann–Whitney test, by contrast, the prob-value is 4.5 per cent and H_0 would be rejected at the 5 per cent level. For this variable the non-parametric test is to be preferred in this instance because it cannot be established that the underlying populations from which the (relatively small) samples are drawn are normally distributed. It is not possible, therefore, to be sure that the conditions required for the parametric *t*-test are satisfied.[p]

7.3 The χ^2-test

In chapter 3 we considered the possibility of an association between the numerical values of two variables, and described a measure of the strength of that association, the correlation coefficient, r. We saw, for example, that the 24 Kent parishes with a relatively high (or low) level of UNEMP also had a relatively high (or low) level of RELIEF, with r=0.52 (§3.2.1). We also reviewed an alternative measure, Spearman's r_s, that could be used to assess the degree of correlation between ranked variables (§3.3).

We may, however, be interested in some features of a variable that are

---

[p] As a general principle, tests that throw away information, in this case by eliminating information on the scale of differences between values of INCOME, are less powerful. However, this does not always hold, as this feature may be over-ridden by other considerations. In difference of means tests, applied to data sets that have both very different variances and very different sample sizes, the *t*-test tends to be less powerful than non-parametric alternatives, such as Mann–Whitney.

not reflected in a numerical value or a rank order, but instead involve its classification into two or more categories. For example, a study of voting patterns in the United States in the presidential election of 1896 might classify voting both by degree of urbanization (large cities, other urban areas, rural areas) and by political choice (Democrat, Republican, Populist). It would then be possible to see whether there were any significant differences between voters related to their location. Or a historical demographer might classify women in a given locality on the basis of their fathers' occupation (merchant, farmer, craftsman, labourer), and of their own marital status (single, married, widowed, remarried). The purpose would be to see whether there was any relationship between their fathers' occupation and their own marital status.

Our aim in the remaining sections of this chapter is to explain some of the procedures that can be used when dealing with nominal (categorical) data of this sort. On some occasions a simple comparison of percentages may reveal such clear differences that nothing more is needed. But if the differences are small, or the relationship between different categories is more complex, then it would be necessary to adopt an appropriate statistical procedure.

We begin in §7.3.1 with a brief digression to introduce the basic idea of contingency tables or cross-tabulations used for such data. In §7.3.2 we discuss an application of the χ^2-test (lower case Greek chi, pronounced ki-squared) that can be used when it is desired to compare one or more samples with respect to a variable that is classified into two or more categories. This is a test of whether or not the differences between the categories are statistically significant. We also introduce a new theoretical probability distribution that is required for this test.

In §7.5 we will look at two other procedures that can be used when there is only one sample and the object is to test the observed distribution against some theoretical alternative. Finally, some of the corresponding non-parametric measures of the strength of association between the categories are discussed in §7.6.

7.3.1 Contingency tables or cross-tabulations

The χ^2-test is used where data are cross-classified in **contingency tables or cross-tabulations**. In their most general form these tabulations show the frequency with which the characteristics of one variable are associated with those for another variable for one or more samples of cases.

As an illustration of such a table we will use some data compiled from the records of the Retreat, an asylum established by Quakers in York in 1796, and famous for its promotion of moral therapy in place of the harsher treatments of the insane practised by many other institutions.[q] One of the points of interest is whether the success of the therapy changed over time as Quaker patients were joined by non-Quakers, and lay therapists were replaced as superintendents by qualified doctors. We can compare the outcomes under the regime of the first superintendent, George Jepson (1796–1823) with those of his successors Thomas Allis (1823–41), John Thurnam (1841–9) and John Kitching (1849–74). The first two were lay therapists, the latter two had medical qualifications.

A double classification of the patients can thus be made according to:

(a) the regime under which they were admitted, and
(b) which of three possible treatment outcomes was recorded in their case-books: Recovered, Improved or relieved, or Not improved.

The cases are the individual patients; the two variables are the superintendent's regime and the outcome. Note that both these variables are on the lowest level of data, the nominal level; in neither case is there any actual measurement beyond a simple count of the number of patients in each of the nominal categories.

In table 7.5 the information for this double classification is set out in the rows and columns of a contingency table. The data for Thurnam and Kitching have been combined to cover a longer period. The upper panel gives the absolute numbers of patients, and in the lower panel these figures are expressed as a percentage of the total number in the three samples.

Table 7.5 is described as a 3×3 table, because it has 3 rows and 3 columns. It has 9 **cells**, in which are entered the **observed frequencies** or **counts**. The dependent variable (the patient outcomes) is shown in the columns, and the possible explanatory variable (superintendent) in the rows. At the bottom are the **column totals** and on the right the **row totals**. These totals are also referred to more generally as **marginal totals**. The **grand total**, which is also the total number of observations (n) on which the table is based, is in the bottom right-hand corner.

7.3.2   The χ^2-test for a relationship between two variables

Cross-tabulations such as the one in table 7.5 show how the different samples (of patients admitted by the successive superintendents) compare with respect to the different categories of a variable (treatment outcomes). The table specifies the frequency with which the observations in each sample are associated with those for the treatment outcomes. The χ^2-test

---

[q] Anne Digby, *Madness, Morality and Medicine, A Study of the York Retreat, 1796–1914*, Cambridge University Press, 1985.

Table 7.5 Cross-tabulation of patients admitted to the York Retreat, by superintendent's regime and by treatment outcomes

	Treatment outcomes			
	Recovered	Improved	Not improved	Total
Numbers				
Superintendent				
Jepson (1796–1823)	117	31	11	159
Allis (1823–41)	96	29	22	147
Thurnam and Kitching				
(1841–74)	158	68	30	256
Total	371	128	63	562
Percentage				
Superintendent				
Jepson (1796–1823)	20.8	5.5	2.0	28.3
Allis (1823–41)	17.1	5.2	3.9	26.2
Thurnam and Kitching				
(1841–74)	28.1	12.1	5.3	45.5
Total	66.0	22.8	11.2	100.0

Source: Digby, *Madness,* p. 231. The classification excludes patients who died in the Retreat.

can then be applied to establish whether the observed **joint frequency distribution** in table 7.5 could have occurred by chance.[11] The use of the test for this purpose is sometimes referred to as a test of **independence** (or, conversely, of **association**) between the variables.

The χ^2-test involves a comparison of the observed frequencies (f_o) with those *that would be expected if there were no relationship between the variables* (f_e). At the core of this measure is the difference between the observed and the expected frequency in each cell.

The difference is squared (for familiar reasons – compare §2.3.2), and the squares are then standardized by dividing by the *expected* frequency in each cell.[r] Finally, this measure is summed over all cells. If f_o and f_e agree exactly, $\chi^2 = 0$. The greater the discrepancy between the observed and expected frequencies, the larger the value of χ^2.

---

[r] This ensures that the biggest contributions to χ^2 come from the biggest discrepancies between f_o and f_e, not from the cells with the largest number of cases.

THE χ^2-TEST

χ^2 is a measure of the difference between
the observed frequencies, f_o,
and
the frequencies that would be expected
if there were no relationship between the variables, f_e,

It is defined as follows:

$$\chi^2 = \Sigma \frac{(f_o - f_e)^2}{f_e} \tag{7.8}$$

The probability of getting a result greater than the calculated value of χ^2 can then be determined by reference to the appropriate theoretical probability distribution. This is one we have not yet encountered, the chi-square distribution, and is described in panel 7.1 and illustrated in figure 7.1.

The sampling distribution of χ^2 approximates this theoretical chi-square distribution very closely, provided the number of expected frequencies is at least equal to 5. However, if the number of expected frequencies in any of the cells is 5 or less (which can often happen if n, the total number of observations, is small) the distribution of the test statistic is *not* a good approximation of the theoretical chi-square distribution and the test has to be modified.

For a 2 × 2 table, this can be done by an alternative procedure known as **Fisher's exact test**. The outcome of this test is the probability of getting the observed results by chance. This probability can be assessed in the usual way; for example if the selected level of significance is 5 per cent, then a probability of less than 5 per cent would lead to rejection of the null hypothesis.

For larger cross-tabulations there is no easy correction that can be made. If there are a reasonably large number of cells and only a few have frequencies of 5 or less, it is possible to accept the results of the χ^2-test. However, if there are several cells with small frequencies it would be better to combine some of the categories in the original classification so as to eliminate the small frequencies.

Panel 7.1   The chi-square distribution

The concept of a theoretical probability distribution was first introduced in §5.4, where we discussed both the normal distribution and the *t*-distribution. We now need to refer to a further theoretical distribution, the **chi-square distribution** (pronounced ki-square). Like the *t*-distribution, it is related to the normal distribution, which can be thought of as its 'parent' distribution.

In formal terms the chi-square distribution is the sampling distribution of a random variable created by *squaring a single standard normal random variable* with mean zero and standard deviation of 1, and then summing all the squared terms.

Its basis is thus a statistic with which we are already familiar: take a random variable, X, which is normally distributed with a mean of μ and a standard deviation of σ. Then derive from this a standard normal variable

$$Z_1 = \frac{(X - \mu)}{\sigma}$$

This will have a mean of zero and a standard deviation of 1. Then square this to obtain Z_1^2. If a second independent variable is calculated in the same way, this will be Z_2^2, a third will be Z_3^2, and so on.

The total number of such squared terms is given by the parameter *k*, and *k* can have any value from 1 to infinity. If we designate the chi-square random variable as V, then

$$V = Z_1^2 + Z_2^2 + \dots + Z_k^2 \tag{7.9}$$

The precise shape of the distribution, including its mean and standard deviation, depends *solely* on *k*, which represents the number of degrees of freedom (df) of the chi-square distribution. Just as the normal curve was completely defined by two parameters, its mean and standard deviation, so the chi-square distribution is completely defined by this one parameter, *k*. A further property of this distribution is that the mean is also *k*, and the variance is $2k$.

Because the chi-square distribution is formed by the process of squaring a variable it can have only positive numbers, and when df is small the distribution is heavily skewed to the right. However as df increases the distribution becomes more symmetric, and at about 30 df it becomes effectively the same as a normal distribution. Some illustrative distributions are shown in figure 7.1.[*]

[*] The percentage points of the chi-square distribution are given for selected df from 1 to 100 in Lindley and Scott, *Statistical Tables*, table 8, p. 41.

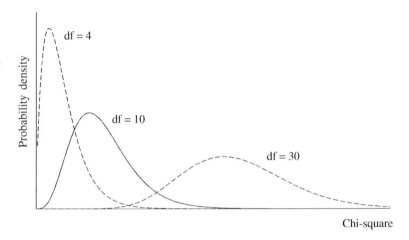

Illustration of the χ^2-test

To illustrate the χ^2-test we will now apply it to the data for the Retreat in
table 7.5. In accordance with the standard test procedure the null hypothesis is that there was no difference between the two outcomes with respect to
the regimes of the successive superintendents.

One research hypothesis might be that patients were less likely to
recover under the later superintendents than in Jepson's regime because
the admission of non-Quakers made a uniform therapeutic regime less
effective. Another might be that they were more likely to recover under
Thurnam and Kitching than under the previous lay regimes because of
benefits gained from the specifically medical expertise of the later superintendents. We adopt a 5 per cent significance level, and since direction
cannot be predicted it is effectively a two-tailed test.[12]

The test procedure *always* involves rejection of the null hypothesis if the
test statistic is *larger than* the critical value given by the sampling distribution for chi-square. Since χ^2 can never be negative there is no equivalent of
moving to the left-hand tail if the alternative to the null hypothesis points
in that direction; for example, if the research hypothesis is unequivocally
that later patients in the Retreat would show a lower recovery rate than
earlier ones.

However, if the researcher does feel able to predict direction, she can use
this to justify reporting a lower significance level than the one actually
achieved. Thus if the value obtained for χ^2 is large enough to indicate statistical significance at the 5 per cent level with no direction predicted, she
could report it as being significant at the 2.5 per cent level, *if direction had
been predicted in advance.*

The test statistic χ^2_{calc} measures the difference between the *observed* frequencies (shown in table 7.5) and the frequencies that would be *expected if there were no relationship between the two variables*.

Out of a total of 562 patients in the three samples, 371 (66.0 per cent) were classified as recovered. If there were no relationship between regime and outcome, *the same proportion* would be expected in all patients. The *expected* frequencies would thus be 66 per cent of the 159 patients admitted by Jepson, 66 per cent of the 147 admitted by Allis, and 66 per cent of the 256 admitted by Thurnam and Kitching.

This gives expected frequencies for the patients classified as recovered of 104.9, 97.0, and 169.0 to compare with the observed frequencies of 117, 96, and 158. Expected frequencies for the patients classified as improved (22.8 per cent) and not improved (11.2 per cent) can be derived in the same way. The full calculation of χ^2 is carried out in table 7.6, and produces a result for $\chi^2_{calc} = 9.64$.

In order to compare this with the theoretical chi-square distribution so as to make a decision regarding its significance, it is first necessary to determine the number of **degrees of freedom** associated with the cross-tabulation. This concept was first introduced in panel 5.3 in §5.4.2, and its application in the present context is explained in panel 7.2. We see from this that for the 3×3 tabulation of table 7.6 there are 4 degrees of freedom (df).

If we enter the published tables for the theoretical probability distribution of chi-square with 4 degrees of freedom (df) we find that for a 5 per cent significance level, the critical point is 9.488.[5] In other words, 5 per cent of the area under the curve lies to the right of this value. Any calculated value for the test statistic larger than that falls in the critical (rejection) region; any statistic lower than that falls in the region in which the null hypothesis cannot be rejected. Since the calculated test statistic is 9.64 it is greater than the critical value and the null hypothesis of no difference can be rejected.

It is thus established that there is a *statistically* significant association between the regimes of the successive superintendents and the results of treatment at the Retreat. As with all tests of statistical significance, the result is partly determined by the sample size. It is important to be aware that the *value of* χ^2_{calc} *is directly proportional to the size of the combined samples* used in the calculation. If the data in table 7.6 were all scaled down by half, the value of χ^2 would also be halved. It is thus relatively easy to get a large and statistically significant result with large samples.

[5] Lindley and Scott, *Statistical Tables*, table 8, pp. 40–1.

Table 7.6 χ^2-test for statistical significance: calculations using data for York Retreat, classified by superintendent's regime and treatment outcomes

Category	(1) Observed frequency f_o	(2) Expected frequency f_e	(3) Difference $(f_o - f_e)$	(4) Square of difference $(f_o - f_e)^2$	(5) Square of difference/ expected frequency $(f_o - f_e)^2/f_e$
Jepson					
Recovered	117	104.9	12.1	145.3	1.38
Improved or relieved	31	36.2	−5.2	27.5	0.76
Not improved	11	17.8	−6.8	46.3	2.60
Allis					
Recovered	96	97.0	−1.0	1.0	0.01
Improved or relieved	29	33.5	−4.5	20.4	0.61
Not improved	22	16.5	5.5	30.7	1.86
Thurnam and Kitching					
Recovered	158	169.0	−11.0	121.6	0.72
Improved or relieved	68	58.4	9.8	95.3	1.63
Not improved	30	28.7	1.3	1.6	0.06
Total	562	562.0	0.0	489.7	9.64

Note:
(1) See table 7.5.
(2) See text.

The test has shown that the differences are *statistically* significant. It could be, however, that it is only a very weak association, of no real historical interest for medical historians. It remains for historians of the institution to investigate the *strength* of the association, and to evaluate its underlying causes and consequences. A number of such measures of the strength of association will be considered in §7.6.

7.4 The one-sample runs test of randomness

The Wald–Wolfowitz runs test was introduced in §7.2.1 in the context of two independent samples. In this section we describe a different form of runs test that can be used by a researcher who has only a single sample and wishes to establish whether or not the observations in the sample occur in a random sequence, so that there is no relationship between each

Panel 7.2   The concept of degrees of freedom for a cross-tabulation

Let us begin by thinking of the simplest 2×2 cross-tabulation in which 2 row and 2 column totals have been entered, but all the cells are blank. If you were invited to choose a set of entries for the cells that would be consistent with these row and column totals you would be able to choose a value for only *one* cell. As soon as you had done this, all the others would be automatically determined since they must sum to the row and column totals. There are four cells, but 3 degrees of freedom have been lost and you have only 1 degree of freedom.

On the same basis if we are calculating the expected frequencies for a 2×2 cross-tabulation, then as soon as f_e has been calculated for any *one* cell, all the others are determined since they must sum to the row and column totals. There is thus only 1 degree of freedom in this case.

What happens if we have a larger table, for example, the 3×3 cross-tabulation in table 7.5? The expected proportion that would be classified as recovered if there were no association with the superintendent's regime was 66 per cent. We can thus calculate that for Jepson's 159 patients the expected number who would recover would be 105, and for those of Allis it would be 97. The corresponding figures for the 22.8 per cent of patients classified as improved would be 36 for Jepson and 34 for Allis.

Once these four expected frequencies have been calculated *the remaining five cells are all determined automatically.* From the row totals, we know that the expected numbers classified as not improved under Jepson must be $159 - (105 + 36) = 18$, and under Allis must be $147 - (97 + 34) = 16$.

From the column totals we then know that the expected figures for the three categories of Thurnam and Kitching's patients must be recovered: $371 - (105 + 97) = 169$; improved: $128 - (36 + 34) = 58$; and not improved: $63 - (18 + 16) = 29$. In this 3×3 table there are thus only *4 degrees of freedom.* We could start by filling some cells other than the four used in this illustration, but as soon as any four expected values have been calculated those of all the remaining cells would be predetermined.

More generally, the rule for cross-tabulations is that the number of degrees of freedom is equal to *one less than the number of rows, multiplied by one less than the number of columns.*

$$df = (r - 1)(c - 1) \qquad\qquad (7.10)$$

This is thus a further illustration of the principle stated in panel 5.3 in §5.4.2 that the number of degrees of freedom equals the number of observations less the number of constraints linking them.

observation and all previous or subsequent observations. Like all non-parametric tests, this one has the important advantage that it need not be assumed that the observations are normally distributed.

The definition of a run is exactly the same as before, but in this case the comparison is made between the number of runs shown by the sample data, and the number that would be expected if the sample were truly random. The test can be applied to any events that can be classified into two categories (heads or tails when tossing a coin, married or single if selecting from a group of women), and the *order in which the two categories occur is all that matters.*

The null hypothesis is that the order is random. The research hypothesis might simply be that the order is not random, in which case a two-tailed test would be made. Alternatively, however, the researcher might be interested in a proposition suggesting that some specified factor was causing the events to occur in clusters. In that case the research hypothesis would be that the number of runs should be fewer than would be expected if the data were random, and since direction is predicted a one-tailed test is required.

To illustrate the procedure, we take the imaginary case of an inspector who comes to visit a school and obtains from the principal an alphabetical list of surnames from which 25 pupils are to be selected for questioning. The selection is supposed to be made at random without regard to the intelligence of the pupils, although a measure of that is known to the school from internal tests. The agency employing the inspector thinks she may be colluding with the school, and so asks us to test whether the selection was truly random. The suspicion is not that too many of the more intelligent students are being selected at the expense of the less able, but rather that the inspector is somehow being guided to particular students in both categories who are expected to perform well because, for example, they are more articulate.

To test this we divide the 25 pupils into two categories (high and low) according to their test scores, and count the number of runs ($= r$) made up of pupils with high scores (H) and those with low scores (L) in the sample. If we find that H and L pupils were drawn in strict rotation (giving 25 runs, the maximum number possible with a sample of this size) we would strongly suspect that the choice was not random, and that the principal had influenced the selection in some way. We would be equally suspicious if the inspector chose first 13 H pupils in a row, and then 12 L pupils, so that there were only 2 runs.

In both these cases we would probably not need a statistical technique to tell us that we should reject the null hypothesis of a random sample. Such a procedure would be necessary, however, if the order is not at either of these extremes, and a runs test would be appropriate for this. If the sample is large, with either or both the number of events (H and L) greater than 20, then the distribution of r is approximately normal, with mean, μ_r, and standard deviation, σ_r, exactly as given previously by (7.1) and (7.2). The test statistic, Z_{calc} can thus be obtained as in 7.3. This can then be compared with the normal distribution (as in table 2.7) to obtain the prob-value for either a two-tailed or a one-tailed test.[t]

If the sample is small, with neither event (H or L) greater than 20, the required result can be obtained directly from a published table. The statisticians have worked out the sampling distribution of r that could be expected from repeated random samples, and we can refer to the tables of this distribution to establish what intermediate number of runs can be treated as consistent with a random sample.[u] With small samples we can either ask the computer to make the calculation or we can do it directly from the table. For larger samples the computer is obviously quicker.[v]

To see how the procedure works for a small sample we will consider four cases. I and II are those already mentioned, with $r = 25$ and 2, respectively. In III the sequence was

H LL HHH LLL HH LL HHH LLLL H LL HH

giving 11 runs, and in IV it was

LL HHH LLLL HHHH LLL HHH LLLL HH

giving 8 runs.[w]

Entering the table for the distribution of the number of runs for $n_1 = 12$ and $n_2 = 13$ and adopting the 5 per cent level, we find that the upper bound is 18 and the lower is 9. The upper bound indicates that if r is 19 or higher it is so large that the probability of obtaining it with a random sample is 5 per cent or less. Similarly, the lower bound indicates that if r is 8 or lower the probability of obtaining it with a random sample is 5 per cent or less.[13]

Accordingly, the null hypothesis cannot be rejected for values of r between 9 and 18, but can be rejected for any samples with r outside this range. Since three of our variants (I, II, and IV) fall outside this range it

---

[t] For the complete table of the normal distribution see Lindley and Scott, *Statistical Tables*, table 4, pp. 34–5.

[u] Lindley and Scott, *Statistical Tables*, table 18, pp. 60–2.

[v] Note that in order to perform the test with a computer package it may be necessary to recode the sequences from letters to numbers; for example by replacing all the Ls by a 1 and all the Hs by a 2.

[w] To simplify the illustration we have kept the number of both events constant in each case, but if a random selection had really been undertaken four times we would not expect that there would always be 12 Hs and 13 Ls on the list.

leaves only one, III, with 11 runs, for which the null hypothesis of a random sample cannot be rejected.

Note that the essence of this test is that it is based solely on the *order* in which the events occur, not on their *frequency*. It is the pattern of the ranking that informs us that the null hypothesis should be rejected for variants I, II, and IV. There is nothing in the frequencies (in every case 12 Hs and 13 Ls) to identify either the extreme lack of randomness in samples I and II, or the narrower difference in respect of randomness between III and IV.

It is also worth pointing out the difference between this test and the two-sample test described in §7.2.1. In the present test, perfect alternation (as in II) – and more generally a large number of runs – leads to rejection of the null hypothesis of randomness. By contrast, in the Wald–Wolfowitz runs test, perfect alternation (as in variant IV of table 7.1) – and more generally a large number of runs – means that the null hypothesis of no difference between the two samples *cannot* be rejected.

An illustration of the application of the runs test for randomness

For many centuries, and for millions of people, the state of the grain harvest each autumn was by far the most important element in determining their standard of living in the following year. Historians have naturally been very interested in the annual grain yield, and because grain prices were recorded much more frequently than grain yields, have often attempted to infer information about harvest fluctuations from the data on prices.

One particular issue that has claimed their attention is the very striking tendency of prices to run in clusters, with years of above-average prices following each other in sequence before giving way to a run of below-average prices. One possibility is that these are simply the result of random fluctuations in weather conditions, but two more interesting explanations have been proposed to account for the clusters.

The first is that runs of good and bad yields were caused by the need to set aside a substantial proportion of each year's crop for next year's seed. In a bad year the rural population would be forced to maintain their required minimum standard by consuming part of next year's seed corn; in a good year more could be set aside, and seed sown more liberally. In this way each year helped to generate a second year of similar quality until the sequence was broken by some larger shock induced by abnormal weather. This hypothesis in turn implies that the observed runs in prices simply reflect an underlying pattern in the (unknown) yields, with runs of low prices matching runs of above-average yields, and vice versa.[14]

The rival hypothesis is that the runs in prices are largely independent of the sequence of yields because of the possibility of grain storage. An exceptionally abundant harvest in one year will enable grain to be carried over not only for the next year, but also for subsequent years. Even if the following year was one of below average yields, prices might remain below average because grain was being sold from store. Thus there would be runs in prices that would not reflect corresponding runs in yields.

In the light of this analysis, one element in the investigation of the data on prices (and on yields where that exists) would be to establish whether or not the clusters of above and below average observations are random. Tony Wrigley applied a one-tailed runs test to French data on wheat yields and prices over the period 1828–1900, and showed that the null hypothesis of randomness could *not* be rejected for the *yields* (prob-value = 0.36), but was easily rejected for the *prices* (prob-value = 0.0028).[x]

When the same one-tailed test was applied to a series on wheat *prices* at Exeter over three subperiods between 1328 and 1789, the prob-values were respectively 0.0436, 0.0021 and 0.0003. As Wrigley noted, the null hypothesis can only just be rejected at the 5 per cent significance level for the first subperiod, but in the two other subperiods 'it is increasingly and ultimately extremely improbable that the runs were random' (p. 129).

On the basis of these findings Wrigley suggested that the presence of non-random runs in the price data, but not – for France – the data on yields, supported the storage rather than the seed corn hypothesis; and further, that the trend over time towards a stronger pattern of non-random fluctuations in prices also suggested that storage was the relevant factor since the impact of seed corn would have been most pronounced in medieval times.

This conclusion has been reinforced by the application of the runs test to data on both wheat yields and prices at the Winchester manors in the years 1283–1350. For yields the prob-value was 0.402, whereas for prices it was 0.0017. This suggested a high probability that the *yield* sequence was random but the *price* sequence was not. The contrast thus confirmed the message of the French yield data. Further support for the storage hypothesis was given by the application of this and other tests to data on butter prices. For butter, unlike wheat, the null hypothesis of random fluctuations in price could not be rejected, and this is what would be expected for a commodity that could not be stored.[y]

---

[x] E. A. Wrigley, 'Some reflections on corn yields and prices in pre-industrial economies', in E. A. Wrigley, *People, Cities and Wealth*, Blackwell, 1987, pp. 92–132.

[y] Randall Nielsen, 'Storage and English government in early modern grain markets', *Journal of Economic History*, 57, 1997, pp. 1–33. For further discussion of this issue see Karl Gunnar Persson, *Grain Markets in Europe 1500–1900*, Cambridge University Press, 1999.

7.5 One-sample non-parametric tests of goodness of fit

7.5.1 The one-sample χ^2-test

The χ^2-test introduced in §7.3.2 is applicable when the object is to test whether a null hypothesis of no association between two or more variables should be accepted or rejected. An alternative problem that might face an historian occurs when there is only *one* sample, and the point at issue is whether the observed distribution of the sample across certain categories is consistent with some alternative distribution specified by the researcher.

The procedure for making the test is identical to that already described in §7.3, except that the researcher has to specify the *expected* frequencies for comparison with the observed frequencies given by the sample. This is referred to as a test of **goodness of fit,** and is used to determine how well the observed observations fit the specified alternative. As with the previous χ^2-test, the expected frequency in each category should be at least 5.

The number of degrees of freedom is the number of rows (categories) in the distribution minus 1. Thus if there are 6 categories there will be 5 degrees of freedom since once five numbers have been entered in the table the final one is determined by the previous five and the total.

There are several possible alternative distributions that might be specified. One of the simplest is that the proportions are the same for all categories. For example, for a sample of cases reporting the day on which people were observed as being at work, the null hypothesis would be that the proportions should be the same for all six working days.[z] Other possibilities involve one of the theoretical distributions, such as the normal or the binomial. Alternatively the researcher might specify a particular empirical distribution; for example, that the ethnic distribution of the inmates of an institution is the same as their distribution in the general population, or that certain characteristics of a sample are the same as those for the population as a whole as given by a census.[15]

7.5.2 The one-sample Kolmogorov–Smirnov test

The Kolmogorov–Smirnov procedure described in §7.2.3 for comparing cumulative frequency distributions from two samples can also be adapted to provide a one-sample test of goodness of fit. The single sample provides

---

[z] See for example, Voth, *Time and Work*, p. 86.

the observed distribution and, as in §7.5.1, the researcher specifies an alternative theoretical distribution. The procedure can thus be used to test the null hypothesis that the sample observations are drawn from a population with the specified alternative distribution.

This alternative might be, for instance, a theoretical distribution such as the normal distribution. Or it might be that the distribution is uniform, so that the proportion of observations in each class interval is the same. In both these cases the computer will compile the alternative from the sample data. For example, it will calculate the normal distribution of a series with the same mean and standard deviation as the single sample, and then convert this to a cumulative frequency distribution.

It is also possible, however, for the researcher to specify the alternative by formulating a statistical model to represent some postulated theory of how the observations might be distributed. The issue would then be to test how well the observed data fit the predictions of the model.

The maximum difference between the observed and theoretical cumulative relative frequencies, D, is calculated as before, and provides the test statistic. Published tables of the sampling distribution of D can then be consulted to decide whether or not to reject H_0 at different levels of significance. The tables effectively cover all samples, regardless of size. In some versions, the critical values are tabulated for D; in other – more comprehensive – tables, for $D\sqrt{n}$, where n is the size of the single sample.[aa] For the latter, H_0 should be rejected if the value of $D\sqrt{n}$ is equal to or greater than the critical value on a one-tailed test with direction predicted. For a two-tailed test the critical value is applicable to half the given significance level.

To illustrate, assume that the test is applied to a sample of 70 observations with mean 35.5 and standard deviation of 20. The specified alternative is the normal distribution. D is found to be 0.0627 and $D\sqrt{n}$ is, therefore, 0.5244. Entering the table for the upper percentage points of the one-sample KS distribution, it will be seen that this is less than the value of 1.203 given for the 10 per cent significance level. It is thus not possible to reject the null hypothesis on a one-tailed test.

This test is superior in certain respects to the χ^2-test of goodness of fit. It can treat individual categories separately, whereas the χ^2-test may need to combine categories if the sample sizes are small.

[aa] Lindley and Scott, *Statistical Tables*, table 23, p. 70 has this form, and it is this value which SPSS reports under the name of Kolmogorov–Smirnov Z.

7.6 Non-parametric measures of strength of association

In §3.2 the correlation coefficient, r, was introduced as a measure of the *strength* of association between two interval level variables, X and Y. r has the very convenient property that it takes a value of 0 when there is no (linear) correlation between the two variables, and of +1 or –1 when there is perfect positive or negative correlation. However, it has two limitations. First, it can be used only with interval data. Secondly, inferences about the corresponding estimate of the strength of the relationship between the variables in the *population,* ρ (lower case Greek rho) require the assumption that the population distribution is normal.

In §3.3 we introduced one alternative to r, Spearman's rank correlation coefficient, r_s, for use with ranked data. This is a non-parametric measure of strength of association, though the term was not mentioned at that stage. We will now introduce, but not discuss in detail, four further non-parametric measures of strength of association which are not subject to the limitations affecting the correlation coefficient, and are appropriate for use with nominal and ordered data arranged in contingency tables.

Unfortunately these non-parametric measures can be awkward to interpret and compare. They do not all take a value of unity when there is perfect correlation; a few do, but for some the upper limit is more than 1, for others it is less than 1. Moreover, for some measures the upper limit depends on the number of rows and columns in the contingency table. There is also an untidy inconsistency with respect to notation: some of these measures of strength of association are conventionally described by Roman letters, whereas Greek letters are used for others; and some are calculated as squared measures whereas others are not.

7.6.1 Four measures of association: φ, Cramer's V, the contingency coefficient C, and Goodman and Kruskal's tau

We will mention four of these measures, the first three of which are based on χ^2. Their starting point is the fact (as noted in §7.3.2) that the χ^2-test for the statistical significance of a relationship varies directly with the size of the sample. For example, if the sample given in table 7.5 had covered 1,124 rather than 562 patients, the value calculated for χ^2 would also double, from 9.64 to 19.28. A simple correction for this is to divide χ^2 by the size of the sample. This leads to a measure denoted φ (lower case Greek phi)

$$\phi = \sqrt{\frac{\chi^2}{n}} \tag{7.11}$$

If the contingency table has only 2 *rows* (i.e. it is a $2 \times k$ table), the maximum value ϕ can take will be 1, but in any other case the upper limit can be substantially greater than 1.

An alternative introduced by Cramer is derived by dividing χ^2 by the product of the sample size and whichever of $r - 1$ and $c - 1$ is the smaller

$$V = \sqrt{\frac{\chi^2}{n \times \min(r - 1, c - 1)}} \tag{7.12}$$

where 'whichever is the smaller' is represented by min (for minimum). Thus in a 4×3 table there are fewer columns than rows, so the lower of $(r - 1)$ and $(c - 1)$ would be $(3 - 1) = 2$, and V would be equal to $\sqrt{\dfrac{\chi^2}{2n}}$, which is the same as $\phi/2$. The advantage of Cramer's V is that the maximum value it can take is always 1.

A third measure of association based on χ^2 is the contingency coefficient, denoted by C, and calculated as

$$C = \sqrt{\frac{\chi^2}{\chi^2 + n}} \tag{7.13}$$

C is easily computed once χ^2 has been calculated, but suffers from the limitation that its upper limit depends on the number of categories in the contingency table, although it is always less than 1. For example, if it is a 2×2 table the upper limit is 0.707, if it is a 3×3 table the maximum value is 0.816, and so on.

The final measure we will refer to is known as Goodman and Kruskal's tau, where tau is the name for the Greek letter τ. This measure of association is calculated on a quite different basis, and involves a procedure (which we need not consider here) for using values of the independent variable to predict values of the dependent variable.

If there is no association between the variables, the explanatory variable is no help in predicting the dependent variable and $\tau = 0$. If there is perfect association between the variables the explanatory variable would be a perfect predictor and $\tau = 1$. This version of the measure is denoted τ_b because A columns of the explanatory variable are used to predict B rows of the dependent variable.

In some circumstances, however, the researcher may simply be interested in the strength of association between the two variables without regarding either one as the possible explanatory variable. It is then possible to calculate an alternate version, denoted τ_a, in which the procedure is reversed and the B rows are used to predict the A columns. Except for the extreme cases of zero and perfect correlation, the numerical values of τ_a and τ_b will not be the same.

An illustration of the use of Cramer's V

Cramer's V was used by Ann Kussmaul in her fascinating study of farming patterns in early modern England as indicated by the seasonality of marriage. The predominant form of economic activity in a sample of 379 non-market parishes was determined by reference to the timing of marriages. Very broadly, in those parishes in which the majority of marriages occurred in the autumn after the harvest had been gathered in, economic activity was classified as predominantly arable (A-type). In those in which weddings were typically celebrated in spring and early summer following the birth of lambs and calves in late winter and early spring, activity was classified as predominantly pastoral (P-type).

Those parishes that showed little tendency to peaks in marriages in either of the two great agricultural seasons were classified as places of rural industry (X-type). Finally, a small number of parishes that displayed both high spring and high autumn peaks were classified as heterogeneous (H-type).[bb]

One of many features of rural England that Kussmaul was able to examine on the basis of this classification of data drawn from the marriage registers was the extent to which these rural patterns had changed over time. What was the strength of the association between the types of economic activity in successive periods? To establish this she uses Cramer's V. If the seasonal typing of the parishes in successive periods were completely independent, V would equal -1.0; if activity in one period were completely determined by activity in the previous period, V would equal $+1.0$. This measure was calculated for 12 successive periods from 1541–80 to 1801–40.

Table 7.7 reproduces Kussmaul's data for one such pair of periods, 1661–1700 and 1701–40. Calculating the expected frequencies and applying (7.8), χ^2 is found to be 168.59. Cramer's V can then be obtained by means of (7.12) as

$$V = \sqrt{\frac{168.59}{379 \times (4-1)}} = \sqrt{\frac{168.59}{1137}} = \sqrt{0.1483}$$
$$= +0.38$$

[bb] Ann Kussmaul, *A General View of the Rural Economy of England 1538–1840*, Cambridge University Press, 1990. This brief description of the classification does not do justice to the depth and subtlety of the work.

Table 7.7 Cross-tabulation of 379 parishes in England by seasonal type in 1661–1700 and 1701–1740

	Seasonal type in 1701–40				
	X	A	P	H	Total
Seasonal type in 1661–70					
X	57	31	16	5	109
A	17	92	3	15	127
P	21	17	50	7	95
H	6	25	7	10	48
Total	101	165	76	37	379

Source: Kussmaul, *General View*, p. 77. For the classification of parishes by seasonal type see text.

By the final pair of periods, 1741–80 and 1781–1820, the strength of the association over time had risen to +0.60. The full set of calculations thus shows the constancy of seasonal typing rising steadily from the late eighteenth century, as parishes settled into increasingly specialized patterns.[cc]

Notes

[1] A number of such measures of political power are discussed in Allan C. Bogue, 'Some dimensions of power in the thirty-seventh Senate', in William O. Aydelotte, Allan C. Bogue and Robert W. Fogel (eds.), *The Dimensions of Quantitative Research in History*, Oxford University Press, 1972. For example, one measure attributed more power to Senator A than Senator B, if the number of times A voted with the majority on a set of proposals when B was in the minority was greater than the number of times B voted with the majority when A was opposed. All senators could then be ranked on the basis of the total number of their positive power relationships in all possible pairings.

[2] The value given for Z_{calc} in table 7.2 incorporates a small correction to the formula given in (7.3). The computer program (in this instance SPSS) has added +0.5 to the numerator when Z_{calc} is negative, and −0.5 when it is positive. The scale of the correction is thus equal to $0.5/\sigma_r$, and since σ_r is determined solely by the size of the two samples (see (7.2)) the correction diminishes as the sample sizes increase. In table 7.2 the sample sizes are the same for each variant, and so the correction is constant at 0.230.

It is thus a correction that is effective when using the approximation of the sampling distribution to the normal distribution with small samples. When Z_{calc} is negative the correction makes it smaller; when it is positive the correction makes it

[cc] Kussmaul, *General View*, pp. 76–8. For other examples of the use of Cramer's V by Kussmaul, see pp. 68 and 134–6.

larger. It thus moves the critical value further into the respective tails, making it more difficult to reject the null hypothesis.

[3] Given the lower of the two possible values for U, the corresponding minimum value of W can be obtained as follows:

$$W = \frac{n_1(n_1 + 1)}{2} + U$$

where n_1 is the size of the sample with which the calculation of U was started.

[4] It is not actually necessary to repeat the procedure with the other sample as the starting point since there is a simple relationship between U and U', the sum obtained by starting with the second sample: $U' = (n_1 n_2) - U$, where n_1 and n_2 are the numbers in the respective samples. W' is then easily derived from U' by the formula for W and U in n. 3.

[5] We have specified a two-tailed test so the research hypothesis is simply $H_1: \mu_{u1} \neq \mu_{u2}$. If, however we had selected a two-tailed test with direction predicted it might have been $H_1: \mu_{u1} < \mu_{u2}$, in which case we could have moved to the 2.5 per cent level. The table gives a critical value for this level of 23. Since the decision rule would be the same (reject H_0, for any value of U equal to or less than this), it would be harder to reject the null hypothesis. The other possibility is $H_1: \mu_{u1} > \mu_{u2}$. To test this alternative it is necessary to move to the higher of the two possible values for U obtained by starting with the other sample (for example, to $U' = 55$ for series D). With this as the research hypothesis the decision rule would be to reject the null hypothesis if U' (rather than U) is equal to or less than the critical value.

[6] As can easily be seen, the value of Z is the same (though the sign is different) whichever sample one starts from. The fact that U and U' give the same absolute result for Z (though with different signs) can be seen from the following example. For variant B and two samples each of 10 observations, $\mu_u = \frac{1}{2}(n_1 n_2) = \frac{1}{2}(100) = 50$. Since $U = 45$, the numerator of $Z = U - \mu_u = 45 - 50 = -5$. If we take the higher value for U of 55 the numerator is $55 - 50 = +5$. The sign of Z is relevant only if direction is predicted, i.e. if H_0 is that the mean of one of the samples is larger (smaller) than the other.

[7] Because our examples are based on small samples SPSS is able to report two measures of significance. One is described as 'exact significance' and this is the only one quoted in table 7.3. It is based on the exact sampling distribution of the test statistic for small samples, and is thus consistent with the critical values given for these samples in the published tables. The other is described as 'asymptotic significance' and is the approximation based on the normal distribution. For large samples this is the only measure of significance available; it becomes progressively more accurate as the sample size increases.

[8] For an example of the use of the Mann–Whitney test by an historian see James H. Stock, 'Real estate mortgages, foreclosures, and Midwestern agrarian unrest, 1865–1920', *Journal of Economic History*, 44, 1984, pp. 89–106. Stock used this non-parametric test (see pp. 97–9) to explore the relationship of three qualitative levels of agrarian protest (ranked across 12 Midwestern states) with the corresponding rankings of various measures of the levels and volatility of farm debt in those states. The null hypothesis of no relationship between debt and unrest was rejected at the 1 per cent level.

See also Hans-Joachim Voth, *Time and Work in England, 1750–1830*, Oxford University Press, 2001, pp. 88–94, 227–8. Voth assembled evidence of people being at work on different days of the week from statements by witnesses who appeared before the Old Bailey in London between 1749 and 1763. He calculated the Mann–Whitney U to test whether Monday was statistically different from other days of the week (because workers were observing the practice of St Monday); and also to test whether work was markedly less frequent on the 46 days of the year that were the old Catholic holy days. In both cases the null hypothesis of no difference was rejected.

[9] The test reported in table 7.4 is a two-tailed test. If a one-tailed test is required, it is necessary only to divide the reported prob-value for KS Z by 2. There is, however, an alternative presentation of the one-tailed test statistic, known as χ^2, calculated as

$$4D^2 \frac{n_1 n_2}{n_1 + n_2}$$

This is equal to four times the square of KS Z. The χ^2 test statistic is compared to the chi-squared distribution with 2 degrees of freedom; this distribution will be described in §7.3. The critical value of the χ^2 test statistic at the 5 per cent level is

$$1.36 \sqrt{\frac{n_1 + n_2}{n_1 n_2}}$$

and there are corresponding values for other levels of significance.

[10] This test (referred to simply as the Smirnov test) was applied by Michael Anderson, *Family Structure in Nineteenth Century Lancashire*, Cambridge University Press, 1971, pp. 56–61 and 206–7. Anderson worked with the χ^2 version mentioned in n. 9. He used the procedure to compare how close family members lived to each other in his study town of Preston. The actual pattern of residence of members of the same family could be determined for a small subsample from the addresses in the census enumerator's books; the alternative was obtained by allocating people to numbered areas on a map by means of a random number table. The propinquity of the Preston families was shown to be statistically significant at the 0.01 per cent level when the exercise was based on related pairs of kin; but it was not quite significant at the 5 per cent level when it was done with a larger sample using individuals with the same surname and birthplace.

For a slightly different application of the test see David Loschky and Ben D. Childers, 'Early English mortality', *Journal of Interdisciplinary History*, 24, 1993, pp. 85–97. In this case the two-sample Kolmogorov–Smirnov test was used to compare pairs of life tables for years before and after 1500. The authors' primary aim was to establish whether there were any statistically distinguishable differences in the crude death rates implied by the pre-1500 and post-1500 tables. They were able to reject with great confidence (prob-value <0.01) the hypothesis that the samples of pre- and post-1500 data were drawn from the same underlying population.

[11] A subtly different application of the χ^2-test, which uses precisely the same procedure, is referred to as a **test of homogeneity**. The object of such a test is to establish whether two or more samples have the *same proportion* of cases possessing some particular characteristics. For example, a social historian might be interested in testing whether three regions in antebellum Virginia are homogeneous with respect to the proportion

of households in each region in respect of four categories of use of house servants: no servants, employed wage servants, owned slaves, and rented slaves. There is no suggestion of any association between the respective regions and the type of servant used.

[12] There is one issue that might be puzzling for some readers. The χ^2-test is intended for two or more independent samples, but the data for the Retreat are not at first sight samples: they are comprehensive records of all patients admitted to the institution. A statistician's response would be to say that each of the three sets of patients could nevertheless be thought of as a sample drawn from an infinite population composed of all the people who might have been admitted to the Retreat in the period of the particular superintendent. On this basis it is possible to apply the theories of sampling and sampling distributions introduced in chapter 5; see also §9.2.3.

[13] If we want to establish the exact prob-values we can use the computer to obtain the values of Z_{calc} (from (7.3)) and then establish either one-tailed or two-tailed significance levels by reference to the table of the normal distribution. For cases I–IV the values of Z are respectively, 4.510, –4.494, –0.810, and –2.038, giving prob-values for a two-tailed test of 0.000 for both I and II, –0.810 for III, and 0.042 for IV. If a one-tailed test is required these prob-values would be halved.

[14] For the hypothesis on seed corn see W. G. Hoskins, 'Harvest fluctuations and English economic history, 1480–1619', *Agricultural History Review*, 12, 1964, pp. 28–46 and Hoskins, 'Harvest fluctuations and English economic history, 1620–1759', *Agricultural History Review*, 16, 1968, pp. 15–31.

[15] See for example, Alan Armstrong, *Stability and Change in an English County Town, A Social Study of York, 1801–51*, Cambridge University Press, 1974, pp. 203–5. Armstrong drew a 10 per cent sample from the Census enumerators' books for York for both the 1841 and 1851 Censuses, and used a χ^2-test to compare the sample distribution by age, gender, and birthplace with the distributions shown by the Census. For the 1851 sample, the null hypothesis of no difference was accepted at the 5 per cent level for age and sex structure but not for birthplace. There was a deficiency of Irish-born because the sampling procedure had omitted the institutions and large lodging-houses in which many of the Irish resided.

See also Gary Magee, *Productivity and Performance in the Paper Industry*, Cambridge University Press, 1997, pp. 62–4. Magee compared the regional distribution of papermaking patents with the distribution that would be expected if patenting activity were directly proportional to the number of paper mills in each region.

7.7 Exercises for chapter 7

1. Which non-parametric test is best suited to the following data sets? In each case, write a sentence explaining your selection.

   (i) Data are available on the ranking of two variables within a population, but with no evidence on the scale of differences between them.

   (ii) Data are available on the ranking of two variables within a population, and the data set includes information on the scale of differences between them.

   (iii) Data are available on the ranking of two attributes for a particular sample; you wish to determine whether the rankings are statistically different.

(iv) Data are available on the distribution of attributes for two independent samples; you wish to determine whether there is a significant difference between the two subsets.

(v) Data are available on the frequency of an attribute for two independent samples; you wish to determine whether the samples are drawn from the same population.

2. In his testimony to a 1909 government inquiry into the effects of part-time work on child health, Mr Robert Morley, President of the Halifax District Trades and Labour Council, handed in data on the heights and weights of 40 boys aged 12–13, 20 of whom worked in a woollen factory half-time, and 20 of whom were in school full-time. In the following table, we have combined these data into a single measure of physical development, the body–mass index.

	Schoolboys			Factory boys	
	March 1908	October 1908		March 1908	October 1908
A1	16.84	17.14	B1	16.86	15.86
A2	20.62	20.97	B2	17.77	16.69
A3	17.02	17.35	B3	17.93	16.50
A4	16.08	15.73	B4	19.77	19.17
A5	17.87	18.63	B5	18.29	18.02
A6	17.09	16.95	B6	17.00	17.29
A7	17.84	17.99	B7	16.89	16.58
A8	16.83	17.00	B8	18.15	16.32
A9	20.03	21.30	B9	16.11	16.45
A10	16.71	18.84	B10	17.99	18.08
A11	16.09	17.00	B11	20.54	20.52
A12	15.77	15.69	B12	19.06	18.42
A13	17.04	16.74	B13	19.50	18.49
A14	17.85	18.56	B14	16.33	16.51
A15	14.47	14.78	B15	17.23	16.71
A16	18.90	19.36	B16	17.44	16.83
A17	18.36	20.15	B17	14.91	14.41
A18	15.34	16.38	B18	16.74	15.67
A19	15.47	15.99	B19	16.01	14.71
A20	15.08	15.78	B20	16.96	15.84

Note:

The body–mass index is calculated as $(703 \times \text{weight in lb})/(\text{height in feet})^2$.

Source: British Parliamentary Papers, *Report on Partial Exemption from School Attendance* (Cd. 4887, 1909), p. 281.

The data were used to support Mr Morley's argument that 'the effect of half-time [labour] is nearly universally bad'.

Apply the Wald–Wolfowitz runs test to determine whether the statistics bear out this interpretation.

(i) Use the body–mass index for March 1908 to determine whether these boys were drawn from the same population.

(ii) Then use the change in the body–mass index between March and October to test whether there are any systematic differences in the change in the body–mass index between the two groups after the beginning of half-time work.

3. The sequence of US presidential administrations (R indicates Republican, D indicates Democratic) since the Civil War has been as follows:

1865–1932: R R R R R D R D R R R R D D R R R
1932–2000: D D D D D R R D D R R D R R R D D

(i) *By hand*, use the runs test for randomness to determine whether there is evidence that the incumbent party has an advantage in successive elections over the entire period, 1865–2000.

(ii) Are your results any different if you subdivide the period into two parts: 1865–1932, and 1932–2000?

4. The density of retailers in different parts of Manchester in 1871 was as follows (higher scores indicate a greater density; the average for the whole of Manchester being 1):

Bakers: 2.04, 1.30, 1.50, 2.10, 1.68, 0.87, 1.80, 1.12, 1.22
Butchers: 1.40, 0.82, 1.01, 1.27, 0.95, 0.86, 1.11, 0.58, 0.95

Source: Roger Scola, *Feeding the Victorian City: The Food Supply of Victorian Manchester, 1770-1870*, Manchester University Press, 1992, p. 299.

(i) Do these figures support the hypothesis that there was no difference in the distribution of butchers and bakers in these regions? Choose the appropriate non-parametric test and make all necessary calculations *by hand*.

(ii) Test the hypothesis that butchers were more concentrated in some parts of Manchester than others.

5. Evaluate the hypothesis that average wealth holdings in the neighbouring counties of Berkshire and Buckinghamshire are drawn from the same population. Apply the parametric difference of means test as well as the non-parametric Mann–Whitney and Kolmogorov–Smirnov tests.

What differences do you detect between these test results? Which is to be preferred and why? Consider both historical and statistical reasons in your answer.

6. A survey of households in Liverpool in 1927-9 recorded information on the first occupation of children after leaving secondary school and on the occupation of their fathers.

Occupations of father	Child's occupation			
	Professional and business	Clerical and commercial	Manual labour	All occupations
Professional and business	321	323	122	766
Clerical and commercial	98	229	52	379
Manual labour	131	323	115	569
All occupations	550	875	289	1,714

Source: D. Caradog Jones (ed.), *The Social Survey of Merseyside*, 3, Liverpool University Press, 1934, pp. 178–180.

(i) Do the data support the report's conclusion that, 'the occupational grade of the parent has considerable weight in the determination of the occupational grade of the child'?

(ii) Do the data support the inference that the children of 'higher social class' (as measured by a higher occupational grade) are more likely to enter higher occupations?

(iii) Would your responses to (i) and (ii) differ if you were asked to evaluate whether children of each occupational class were more likely to be selected from the same occupational class as their father?

(iv) Would your responses to (i) and (ii) differ if the survey were based on a sample of 171 (i.e. one-tenth as large)?

Write a few sentences explaining what these figures indicate about the extent and pattern of social mobility in inter-war Britain.

7. *By hand*, construct a contingency table of occupational structure by region, using the Steckel data set. (*Hint*: the table will be 5 × 4.) Express the cross-tabulations as both counts and relative frequencies.

(i) *By hand*, calculate the χ^2 test statistic. Compare to the critical point at an appropriate level of significance, being careful to specify correctly the number of degrees of freedom.

(ii) Does the evidence support the hypothesis that the occupational structure was identical in all US regions in 1850?

(iii) How would you test the hypothesis that occupational structure was identical in all regions outside the North-East? What do you find?

8. *By hand*, use the one-sample Kolmogorov–Smirnov test on the data for Cambridge parishes in the Boyer relief data set to determine whether there are statistically significant differences between their populations. (*Hint*: order your data from lowest to highest.) Report your findings.

Why does it matter that you order the data properly before undertaking the calculation?

9. Using the data constructed for question 7, calculate the four measures of strength of association discussed in §7.6.1. Report your findings. Do the four tests reach the same conclusion about the strength of association between region and occupational structure? How do you explain any differences?

10. Can you think of a historical case in which data are available for *related* samples? (*Hint*: look at the exercises for this chapter.)

PART III

Multiple linear regression

CHAPTER 8

Multiple relationships

In this chapter we once again take up the subject of regression, first introduced in chapter 4, and this will now be our central theme for the remainder of this book. In chapter 4 we dealt only with simple regression, with one dependent and one explanatory variable. In the present chapter we will extend the model to see what happens when there is *more than one* explanatory variable. We introduce this idea in §8.1, and explain various aspects of the concept of **multiple regression** in §8.2. The related concepts of **partial** and **multiple correlation** are covered in §8.3.

In chapter 9 we will examine some of the underlying ideas in more depth, and will also deal with some of the issues arising from the fact that the data underlying our regressions are typically drawn from samples and so are subject to sampling error. Two further extensions of the basic linear regression model, the use of dummy variables and of lagged values, are then introduced in chapter 10.

8.1 The inclusion of additional explanatory variables

Extension of a regression to include several explanatory variables is frequently desirable, because it is usually appropriate to formulate and discuss relationships in which the behaviour of the dependent variable is explained by more than one factor.

The basic idea is very simple. In the initial treatment of the relationship between two variables (**bivariate regression**) in §4.2.1 there was one dependent variable (Y), which was influenced by one explanatory variable (X). In **multiple regression** we can have more than one explanatory variable $(X_1, X_2, \ldots, X_n)$, each of which may exercise an influence on the single dependent variable.

Where previously the (linear) relationship was expressed as

$$Y = a + bX \qquad (8.1)$$

it might now be

$$Y = a + b_1 X_1 + b_2 X_2 - b_3 X_3 \qquad\qquad (8.2)$$

Thus in an analysis of the level of *per capita* relief payments by English parishes in 1831, Y would be RELIEF and X_1 might still be UNEMP, as in §4.2.3, but additional explanatory variables could also be incorporated in the investigation to assess their effect on RELIEF. For example, X_2 might be FARMERS, the proportion of labour-hiring farmers in the total number of parish taxpayers; and X_3 might be LONDON, a measure of the distance of the parish from London, used as a proxy for the cost of migration. The signs before the explanatory variables indicate that Y is expected to rise as X_1 and X_2 rise, but to fall as X_3 rises.

The fundamental underlying theoretical principles and statistical procedures required for the estimation of multiple regression equations, and for the evaluation of the coefficients, are essentially the same as those already discussed in earlier chapters in relation to simple regression. The formulae and calculations naturally become more laborious and complicated with the inclusion of additional explanatory variables, and the computations can be left to the statistical computer programs.

There are, however, a few points relating to the interpretation of the results of multiple regression and correlation that it will be helpful to discuss.

The notation and terminology used for simple regression and correlation is adapted as shown in the right-hand column of table 8.1. As will be seen, the introduction of additional explanatory variables produces four new terms. In the following sections we will look at these terms and consider some of the more important changes in *interpretation* involved when dealing with **multivariate** relationships.

8.2 Multiple regression

8.2.1 The coefficient of multiple determination, R^2

As with simple regression it is desirable to have a measure of *the proportion of the variation in the dependent variable* that is *explained by the several explanatory variables* included in a multiple regression model. This measure is called the **coefficient of multiple determination.**

The logic and definitions are exactly the same as with the coefficient of determination (covered in §4.3.2), but it is referred to as R^2 rather than r^2. Subscripts can be added to show which variables were included; for example, $R^2_{Y.X_1 X_2 X_3}$ would indicate that the coefficient had been calculated for the regression of Y on three explanatory variables, X_1, X_2, and X_3.

Table 8.1 Notation for simple and multiple correlation and regression

One explanatory variable (simple or bivariate)		Two or more explanatory variables (multiple or multivariate)
r^2	Coefficient of determination	R^2 Coefficient of multiple determination (see §8.2.1 and §8.2.8)
b	Regression coefficient	$b_1, b_2, \ldots$ Partial regression coefficients (see §8.2.2–8.2.6)
r	Correlation coefficient	$\left. \begin{array}{l} r_{YX_1 \cdot X_2} \\ \\ r_{YX_2 \cdot X_1} \end{array} \right\}$ Partial correlation coefficients (see §8.3.1–8.3.3)
		$R_{Y \cdot X_1 X_2}$ Multiple correlation coefficient (see §8.3.4)

THE COEFFICIENT OF MULTIPLE DETERMINATION, R^2

R^2 is a measure of the *proportion of the variation*
in the dependent variable

explained by
the several explanatory variables
in a multiple regression.

The value of R^2 always lies between 0 and 1, and the higher it is the more the variation in Y that has been explained (sometimes referred to as an indication of 'the goodness of fit'). However, the total variation in Y (which is the denominator in the calculation of R^2) is unaffected by the number of explanatory variables, whereas each additional explanatory variable will add a term to the numerator. As a consequence of this, the addition of another explanatory variable will almost always raise the value of R^2, and will certainly never reduce it. A small correction to R^2 to take account of the number of explanatory variables used is described in §8.2.8.

8.2.2 Partial regression coefficients

With multiple regression there is one **partial regression coefficient** $(b_1, b_2, \dots, b_k)$ for each of the k explanatory variables. In (8.2) there were three such coefficients.

When there was only one regression coefficient, it was interpreted (see §4.2.1) as the measure of the influence of the explanatory variable (X) on the dependent variable (Y). If the value obtained for b was, say, $+2$, this meant that for every 1 unit that X increased, Y increased by 2 units. What is the corresponding interpretation for each of the partial regression coefficients? It is basically the same interpretation but with one additional – and very important – element.

The use of partial regression coefficients is an extremely powerful analytical device that enables us to examine the influence of each of the explanatory variables in turn *while controlling for the influence of the others.*

PARTIAL REGRESSION COEFFICIENTS

The partial regression coefficient
for each of the explanatory variables
is a measure of

the influence of that particular variable
on the dependent variable

*while the influence of all the other explanatory variables
is held constant.*

In experimental sciences it is possible to achieve this effect directly. For example, a plant scientist can compare the yield of a new variety of seed with that obtained from an older variety, by planting them in adjoining beds with identical soil quality, sunlight, and rainfall, and controlling for all other relevant factors (such as weeding or application of fertilizer). He can thus isolate the effects of the new variety of seed. A medical scientist can test a new drug by administering it to a groups of patients while giving a placebo to a second (control) group selected so as to be as similar as possible in terms of factors such as age, sex, and health status.

In historical studies and the social sciences this ability to assess the influence of one particular variable while controlling for the influence of others can normally be achieved only indirectly, by the application of

Table 8.2 Average monthly data on welfare expenditure, homelessness, temperature bands, and food costs (imaginary data)

(1) MONTH	(2) Y WELFARE (dollars)	(3) X_1 HOMELESS (%)	(4) X_2 TEMP (Band)	(5) X_3 FOODCOST (Jan = 100)
Jan	6,500	5.0	3	100
Feb	6,500	5.5	3	105
Mar	3,000	2.5	2	96
Apr	2,500	1.5	2	99
May	2,000	0.5	1	84
Jun	1,500	3.5	1	83
July	1,000	1.5	1	80
Aug	500	1.0	1	77
Sept	3,000	4.5	2	77
Oct	3,500	5.0	2	70
Nov	4,500	5.5	2	75
Dec	5,000	4.5	3	79

appropriate statistical procedures, of which multiple regression is the most powerful.

8.2.3 Controlling for the influence of a second explanatory variable

To illustrate this very important procedure consider the hypothetical data given in table 8.2. A charity mission operating in Chicago has information in its records on the amount spent each month, averaged over a period of years in the 1930s (WELFARE). These outlays covered the costs of providing accommodation and clothing, operating a soup kitchen, and dispensing medicines. A PhD student writing a dissertation on the history of the mission is trying to explain the variation from month to month. She initially finds data for a possible explanatory variable: the number of people who were sleeping rough expressed as a percentage of the city's population (HOMELESS).

She begins by plotting a scatter diagram of WELFARE and HOMELESS as shown in figure 8.1(a), and finds what appears to be a strong positive relationship. The regression line (with the t-ratios – see §6.4.2 – given in brackets) is[a]

---

[a] For simplicity of presentation the results of the regression are given to the nearest whole number and the t-ratios are rounded to one decimal place.

Figure 8.1 Scatter
diagrams for
hypothetical data
on WELFARE and
HOMELESS

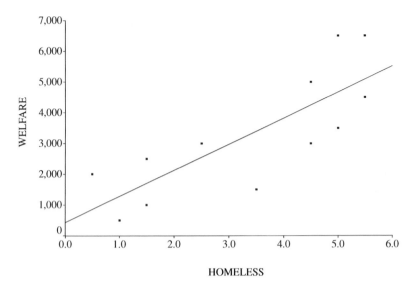

(a) Scatter diagram and regression line for all observations

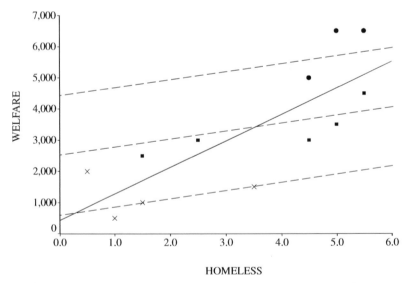

(b) Scatter diagram identifying the effect of TEMP on the relationship between
    WELFARE and HOMELESS

$$\text{WELFARE} = 431 + 848\,\text{HOMELESS} \qquad (8.3)$$
$$(0.5) \quad (4.2)$$

with $r^2 = 0.63$. The regression coefficient on HOMELESS is highly significant (with a t-ratio of 4.2 corresponding to a prob-value of 0.2 per cent), and indicates that welfare disbursements responded quite strongly to the proportion of the population sleeping rough, with *a rise of 848 dollars for every 1 unit increase in homelessness.* (Since the units for HOME-LESS are percentages, a rise of 1 unit would be a rise of one percentage point; for example, from 2.0 per cent to 3.0 per cent.)

However, comments by the director of the mission suggested to the researcher that homeless people were more likely to seek refuge in the shelter when the weather was bad. She therefore decided to add information on weather to the regression. As a measure for this she is able to use a record of monthly average temperatures (TEMP) grouped in three bands, warm (coded as 1), cold (2), and very cold (3). When account is taken of this second explanatory variable a very different picture emerges. The multiple regression equation (with t-ratios in brackets) is

$$\text{WELFARE} = -1{,}245 + 260\,\text{HOMELESS} + 1{,}910\,\text{TEMP} \qquad (8.4)$$
$$(2.3) \quad (1.6) \qquad\qquad (5.1)$$

The coefficient of multiple determination, R^2 is now 0.91. This indicates that the new model can explain 91 per cent of the variation in welfare expenses, a marked improvement on the 63 per cent explained by the model with only one dependent variable. Other changes are even more striking.

Compared to (8.3), the coefficient on HOMELESS has dropped from 848 to 260. Thus *when the effect of temperature is held constant* the partial regression coefficient shows that benefit payments rise by only *260 dollars for every 1 percentage point increase in homelessness.* Furthermore, the t-ratio on HOMELESS is now well under 2, and the coefficient is no longer statistically significant even at the 10 per cent level (prob-value = 13.7 per cent). By contrast, the coefficient on the new variable, TEMP, has a t-ratio of over 5 and is highly significant (prob-value = 0.1 per cent).

To see why the estimate of the response to homelessness has changed so sharply look at figure 8.1 (b). This has exactly the same data as figure 8.1 (a), but this time the points on the scatter diagram also distinguish the three different levels of payment according to the temperature bands. It can be seen immediately that:

- in summer months when the temperature was warm (band 1, marked with a cross) the outlays on WELFARE were relatively low

- in winter months when it was very cold (band 3, marked by circles) outlays were relatively high, and
- in early spring and autumn (band 2, marked by squares) they were at an intermediate level.

It is thus the additional factor of the amount spent in response to the changes in temperature that is largely responsible for the steep slope of the bivariate regression line of WELFARE on HOMELESS shown in both diagrams.

The distinction between the omission of a relevant explanatory variable from a regression model and its inclusion is thus very striking:

- If it is omitted, its effect on the dependent variable is simply *ignored*.
- When it is included, its effect is *held constant*.

Figure 8.1 (b) also shows three dotted straight lines, one for each temperature band. Each line has the same slope, determined by the partial regression coefficient on HOMELESS of 260 given by the multiple regression equation.[b] These lines illustrate the essence of multiple regression. In the present example, each of the dotted lines can be thought of as the relationship one would find between WELFARE and HOMELESS *while controlling for the temperature level*.

The top dotted line with an intercept of 4,485 is thus in a rough sense the simple regression line we would get if the *only* available observations on WELFARE and HOMELESS were the three circles (i.e. the expenditures by the mission when the temperature was in band 3).[c] Corresponding comments apply to the two other dotted lines for the squares and crosses.

8.2.4 Understanding the impact of additional explanatory variables

Not every additional explanatory variable will have as startling an impact on the rest of the regression model as the addition of TEMP. To see this point in practice, imagine that our researcher, before her attention turned to weather as a potential explanator of welfare expenses, had collected information on the cost of food over the year. She found a monthly index number for food costs in Chicago (FOODCOST) and decided to enter this as an additional explanatory variable.

The values of the index are presented as X_3 in table 8.2. Costs fell

---

[b] The lines are also equidistant, but that is not a general feature; it applies in this example only because the temperature bands move up in equal steps of 1.

[c] The value of the intercept is obtained by substituting the level of TEMP in the multiple regression equation when HOMELESS = 0. For example, when TEMP is in band 3 it becomes

$$-1{,}245 + (260 \times 0) + (1{,}910 \times 3) = -1{,}245 + 5{,}730 = 4{,}485$$

throughout the year. When she re-ran her initial regression with FOOD-COST as a second explanatory variable, the results were:

$$\text{WELFARE} = -6{,}182 + 846\,\text{HOMELESS} + 77.5\,\text{FOODCOST} \quad (8.5)$$
$$\phantom{\text{WELFARE} = -6{,}182 + }(3.0)\quad(5.9)\phantom{\text{HOMELESS} + }(3.3)$$

With the addition of this variable the R^2 has increased from 0.63 to 0.83.

The impact of adding the cost of food to the regression is revealing. The overall explanatory power of the equation has, once again, risen considerably. Clearly, the added variable is helping to explain more of the variation in the level of WELFARE over the year. Moreover, the high t-statistic on FOODCOST indicates that it is a statistically significant explanatory variable (the prob-value is 0.9 per cent).

But what is really interesting is that the coefficient on HOMELESS has barely changed at all from the simple regression model of (8.3). Moreover, its t-statistic, far from collapsing with the addition of a new statistically significant coefficient, has actually risen (from 4.2 to 5.9, or from a prob-value of 0.2 per cent to one below 0.05 per cent). The addition of FOOD-COST has sharpened the relationship between welfare payments and the level of homelessness.

Why has this happened? Why is the impact of this alternative second variable so very different from the addition of TEMP? The answer is to be found in the *relationships among the explanatory variables*. In the case of HOMELESS and TEMP, the reason why the addition of TEMP to the equation has such a startling effect on HOMELESS is that the two variables were not only strongly related to WELFARE, but were also strongly related to each other.

The correlation between HOMELESS and TEMP is 0.73, indicating a strong degree of interdependence between them.[d] So when TEMP was added to the equation, it essentially replicated much of the information previously provided by HOMELESS. Once it is also recognized that TEMP was more strongly correlated with WELFARE than was HOMELESS, it becomes clear that TEMP has more power to explain the behaviour of the dependent variable. In effect, the addition of TEMP swamps HOMELESS as an explanatory variable.

In contrast, the movements of HOMELESS and FOODCOST were almost completely independent of each other.[e] The correlation of the two variables is only 0.0026. The addition of the new variable thus provided new

[d] When two explanatory variables are highly correlated with each other, they are sometimes referred to as being highly **collinear**.

[e] When two explanatory variables exhibit independence, as measured by a very low correlation, they are sometimes referred to as **orthogonal** to each other.

and independent information that the regression model could use to explain WELFARE. This information did not replicate any of the information contained in the movement of HOMELESS; its addition therefore did not alter the relationship between HOMELESS and WELFARE contained in (8.3).

Two morals emerge from this simple example. First, the effect of controlling for additional explanatory variables is a matter of empirical analysis and cannot be determined *a priori*. Second, it is important for the historian to understand the underlying structure of the model being tested. The regression equation produces parameter values net of interdependences among the variables; but in many cases, it is these interdependencies that are important for a full understanding of the historical process being analysed.

A good start to a better understanding of the connections among the explanatory variables is to ask the computer to construct a correlation matrix, which sets out the simple correlation coefficients for each pair of variables (including the dependent variable) in tabular form (see table 8.3 in §8.3.1 for an example). A full discussion of how these simple correlations may be used to measure the impact of controlling for an additional explanatory variable is presented in the analysis of partial and multiple correlation in §8.3.

8.2.5   The Ballantine for multiple regression

The case of multivariate regression can be illustrated using the Ballantine, first introduced in chapter 4.[1] Figure 8.2, on p. 527, depicts the Ballantine for a regression in which two explanatory variables (X_1, X_2) influence the behaviour of the dependent variable, Y. Each circle represents the variation in the variables.[f] The variation in Y is indicated by the yellow circle; the variation in X_1 by the blue circle; the variation in X_2 by the red circle.

Note that there are significant overlaps between the three circles. These represent the extent of common variation among variables. The green area indicates the overlap between X_1 and Y, independent of X_2; the orange area, the overlap between X_2 and Y, independent of X_1. The purple area indicates the overlap between X_1 and X_2, independent of Y; the brown area indicates where all three variables overlap.

The coefficient of multiple determination, R^2, measures the extent to which the variation in the dependent variable, Y, is explained by the variation in the explanatory variables, X_1 and X_2. The explained sum of squares

---

[f] For convenience, each of the three circles is drawn to the same size. This is not meant to imply that the variance of each variable is the same. However, as noted in §4.4, having circles of equal size makes the analytical interpretation of the Ballantine easier.

in this case is equal to the sum of the green, orange, and brown areas. The yellow area shows the unexplained sum of squares, that part of Y that is not explained by the behaviour of X_1 or X_2. The R^2 is thus equal to the ratio of the green, orange, and brown areas to the total area of the yellow circle.

Although all three areas determine the value of R^2, only that part of the overlap that is unique to each variable is used to determine the partial regression coefficient. Thus, only the information contained in the green area is used to determine the value of b_1, the coefficient on X_1. Similarly, only the orange area is used to determine the value of b_2, the coefficient on X_2.

The regression analysis ignores the information contained in the brown area, since it is impossible to allocate it between X_1 and X_2. This is the reason why the regression coefficient on X_1 changes with the addition of a second explanatory variable. It is less that some part of the original explanatory power of X_1 is displaced onto X_2, but rather that the addition of X_2 compromises the original structure of the relationship between X_1 and Y.

One further effect of the inclusion of a second variable will be that the relationship between Y and X_1 is now estimated with less information (the size of the overlap is smaller). This means that the accuracy with which we can measure the value of the regression coefficient declines – the standard error of b_1 increases, and its t-statistic drops.

The Ballantine clearly indicates what is happening in the case of the Chicago welfare mission. In the original regression formulation in §8.2.3 it was assumed that only the proportion of homelessness among the population influenced outlays on welfare. In terms of the Ballantine, the green and brown areas in combination were used to determine b_1 and R^2.

When TEMP was added to the regression, more information (in the form of the orange area) was added to the overall model of welfare outlays. A higher proportion of the yellow circle is thus overlapped, and R^2 rises. At the same time, less information was used to estimate the value of b_1, which now depends on the green area alone, producing both a different coefficient and a different standard error. With the addition of TEMP, not only does the coefficient on HOMELESS change (indicating a high degree of correlation between the temperature on the street and the number of people sleeping rough), but its statistical significance declines.[8]

The Ballantine further indicates that the impact on b_1 of introducing an additional explanatory variable will be greater, the higher the degree of correlation between X_1 and X_2. In figure 8.3(a), on p. 527, the two variables are independent (or **orthogonal** to each other). There is no overlap between them. Thus, the addition of X_2 to a regression of Y on

---

[8] The simple correlation of TEMP and HOMELESS is 0.73.

X_1 will have no impact on the estimation of the regression coefficient, b_1. This is an extreme form of the situation that arose when we added FOOD-COST to the simple regression of WELFARE on HOMELESS in the example of the Chicago welfare mission.[h]

In contrast, figure 8.3 (b) on p. 527 depicts a Ballantine in which there is considerable overlap between the two variables. The brown area is very large relative to the green area, indicating that the addition of X_2 will reduce the contribution of X_1 to Y significantly. A situation when two (or more) explanatory variables are highly correlated (or **collinear**) with each other is known as **multicollinearity**; its implications for the assessment of the regression results are discussed in detail in §11.4.2.

8.2.6 The least squares criterion in multiple regression

The actual derivation of the partial regression coefficient in multiple regression models becomes more complex as the number of explanatory variables increases. In a simple bivariate regression everything can be understood in terms of two dimensions (as in chapter 4). For a model with three variables (Y, X_1, and X_2) it is necessary (and possible) to think in terms of a three-dimensional diagram. Think, for example, of the corner of a room: the X_1 axis is where one wall meets the floor; the X_2 axis is where the adjoining wall meets the floor, and the Y axis is where the two walls meet.

Then think of a collection of balloons floating above the floor at varying heights and at varying distances from the two walls. For each balloon, the distance from each wall represents the values of the two explanatory variables, and the height above the floor represents the value of the dependent variable, a picture roughly illustrated in figure 8.4 (a).

Finally, imagine a flat plane such as a piece of cardboard that is to be suspended in the middle of the space containing the balloons, as in figure 8.4 (b). Some of the balloons will be above the plane (shaded as before), some below (unshaded). The statisticians' least squares calculation then finds the 'best fitting' position for the plane by minimizing the sum of squares of the distance (deviations) of the balloons *from the plane*. The analysis is exactly analogous to the procedure discussed in §4.2.2 in which the least squares criterion was used to select the best fitting *line* in the context of a two-dimensional scatter diagram.

The plane can slope up or down independently in two directions: either from top to bottom or from front to back. The angle of the slope in one direction (from front to back) measures the effect of X_1 *while X_2 is held con-*

---

[h] Complete orthogonality would require that the simple correlation of X_1 and X_2 be 0.00; in the case of HOMELESS and FOODCOST, the correlation was 0.0026, implying a very small overlap between the blue and red circles.

stant; the angle of the slope in the other direction (from top to bottom) measures the effect of X_2 *while X_1 is held constant.*

It is in this sense that multiple regression holds one explanatory variable constant, while measuring the effect of the other. It was reflected in figure 8.1 (b) by the dotted parallel lines (each with the same slope) showing the effect of homelessness while controlling for the influence of the temperature.

If there are more than two explanatory variables, all but one have to be held constant in the calculation of the partial regression coefficient for the remaining variable. This makes the calculations quite complex, and we can be grateful that computers do them for us.

8.2.7 Standardized beta coefficients

The influence of each explanatory variable in a linear multiple regression model is measured by the partial regression coefficients *in whatever units the explanatory variable is itself measured.* In the example of the Chicago mission, one would say that WELFARE would increase by 260 dollars if HOMELESS increased by 1 *percentage point*; but by 1,910 dollars if TEMP increased by 1 *unit*.

Each of these is an absolute measure of the effect on the dependent variable, but it is not possible to form any impression from them of their *relative* importance as influences on expenditure on WELFARE. A suitable relative measure can be obtained by standardizing the coefficients.[2] Thus for any explanatory variable, X_k, its partial regression coefficient b_k is standardized by multiplying it by the ratio of the standard deviation of its explanatory variable (s_X) to the standard deviation of the dependent variable (s_Y).

THE STANDARDIZED BETA COEFFICIENT

The beta coefficient
is a measure of the *relative* effect
of each of the partial regression coefficients
in comparable units.

For any explanatory variable, X_k,

$$beta_k = b_k \frac{s_X}{s_Y} \tag{8.6}$$

where s_X is the standard deviation of the relevant explanatory variable, X_k, and s_Y is the standard deviation of the dependent variable, Y.

Figure 8.4 Least squares deviation from the regression plane with two explanatory variables

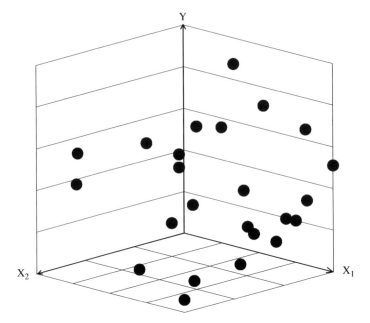

(a) Three-dimensional scatter diagram for a dependent variable and two explanatory variables

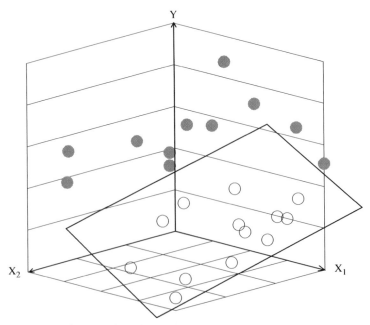

(b) Three-dimensional diagram with regression plane

The beta coefficient thus measures how many standard deviations of movement in Y are caused by a change of 1 standard deviation in each of the explanatory variables. For the Chicago mission, for example, when the two explanatory variables were HOMELESS and TEMP, the standardized betas were 0.24 and 0.76, respectively. For HOMELESS and FOODCOST they were 0.79 and 0.45.

8.2.8 The adjusted coefficient of multiple determination, $\bar{R}^2$

When the coefficient of multiple determination, R^2, was introduced in §8.2.1 it was noted that the introduction of an additional explanatory variable would always raise its value. It is appropriate to make a correction for the number of explanatory variables used in the model. This is done in terms of the degrees of freedom (see panel 8.1), given by the size of the sample and the number of parameters to be estimated (excluding the intercept term).

The resulting **adjusted coefficient of multiple determination** is called $\bar{R}^2$ (R bar squared).

THE ADJUSTED COEFFICIENT OF MULTIPLE DETERMINATION, $\bar{R}^2$

$\bar{R}^2$ is equal to R^2 *corrected for*
the number of explanatory variables plus the intercept:

$$\bar{R}^2 = 1 - \left((1 - R^2) \frac{n - 1}{n - k} \right) \tag{8.7}$$

where k = the number of explanatory variables plus the intercept,
and the number of df = k − 1.

In the simple Chicago mission example used in §8.2.3, the addition of TEMP raised R^2 from 0.63 to 0.91. Correcting the latter for the additional explanatory variable leads to only a small reduction, with $\bar{R}^2 = 0.88$.

In general, if the sample size is large, there will be very little difference between R^2 and $\bar{R}^2$, but if the model is based on a small sample and has a large number of explanatory variables, the difference can be substantial. This is a warning that in such a case there may be too few degrees of freedom to estimate a reliable relationship.

Panel 8.1   The degrees of freedom in a regression equation

The concept of degrees of freedom (df) was first encountered in the context of the t-distribution (§5.4.2 and panel 5.3) and again in connection with cross-tabulations for χ^2-tests (§7.3.2 and panel 7.2). In the context of the coefficient of a regression line, the number of degrees of freedom is determined by the size of the sample reduced by the number of items of information used in specifying the required unknown values.

Consider, for example, a series for which there are only two observations. It would then be possible to find a linear relationship between that series and *any* independent variable (however bizarrely unrelated it might be), and this would give a perfect fit. The equation for this line would have two parameters (the intercept, and the slope or regression coefficient) and would pass *exactly* through the two points; there would be no degrees of freedom.

If a third observation was added the line would be unlikely to pass exactly through all three points, but it might still be a reasonably good fit because there is still effectively only one 'free' observation to explain; there is only one degree of freedom. With each additional observation the number of degrees of freedom would increase, and so would the opportunity for the intercept and slope of the regression line to change. The number of degrees of freedom thus indicates the number of 'free' observations used to calculate the particular statistic.[*]

For example, in simple regression with one independent variable, using a sample of n observations, it is necessary to estimate 1 constant and 1 regression coefficient, leaving n–2 degrees of freedom. In multiple regressions with k independent variables it is necessary to estimate 1 constant and k regression coefficients, leaving $n - (k + 1)$ degrees of freedom. Thus with a sample size of 20, and 4 independent variables, there would be 15 degrees of freedom.

[*] This explanation is based on Peter E. Kennedy, *A Guide to Econometrics*, 3rd edn., Blackwell, 1992, pp. 66–7.

8.2.9   Interpreting the intercept term

The intercept, or constant term, indicates the intersection of the regression line with the vertical axis. It shows the value of the dependent variable when all of the explanatory variables are set equal to zero. But care needs to be exercised when drawing inferences from the intercept. In many cases, the explanatory variables cannot take the value of zero by construction (the temperature band in table 8.2, for example) or by observation (the homeless rate in table 8.2). In many other cases the data over which the regression is run do not include the value of zero (or even a value close to zero) for the dependent variable.

This suggests that the intercept is estimated by extrapolating from the known values of the sample to values outside the sample. Such out of sample extrapolation is often dangerous, since the underlying relationship between the explanatory variables and the dependent variable may be very different for a different range of data. When zero is an unrecorded value for the dependent variable (Y), great caution needs to be used in interpreting the predicted or fitted value of the dependent variable ($\hat{Y}$).

Even when the value of the intercept meets the requirements of relevance and can therefore be ascribed meaning, it is still important to understand what it does mean. The classic example of a meaningful intercept term involves a regression of household food expenditure on family earnings and the number of boarders (paying guests) in the household. People do not stop eating even if income falls to zero; they continue to buy food for themselves, even if they no longer have a boarder to feed. Thus, even if both explanatory variables are zero, the dependent variable still takes on a positive value.

In this case, the intercept therefore makes economic sense. Moreover, since the sample is likely to include some observations in which the household has no boarders, and in which unemployment reduces earnings to zero or close to it, the intercept makes statistical sense and is not contaminated by out of sample bias.

But what is the positive intercept actually measuring? The family that buys food is either paying for it out of past savings, or from money lent or given by family or friends, or is buying it on credit, to be paid for out of a future pay packet. These are factors that influence food expenditure, but which are excluded from the list of explanatory variables. Some statisticians generalize from this case to suggest that the value of the intercept merely indicates *the impact of all the variables excluded from the regression.*

This is a rather dubious claim (especially since, as §8.2.3 shows, excluded variables can also influence the coefficients on the included variables). However, it does point up the general proposition: that thought needs to be given to the meaning behind an intercept. It should not be interpreted automatically as the default value of the dependent variable when all the explanatory variables have a value of zero.

We can illustrate these issues by focusing on the intercepts in two of our case studies. In Benjamin and Kochin's analysis of inter-war Britain, unemployment is regressed on two variables, the ratio of unemployment benefits to wages, and the deviation of log output from its trend. Each of these could in theory take on zero values. Indeed, the observed value of the second variable was close to zero for some years but the benefit/wage ratio never was. So, although the intercept of 5.19 might be interpreted as the minimum level of unemployment in inter-war Britain (i.e. 5.19 per cent) without an insurance scheme and with 'full employment', it is important to recognize that such an interpretation requires that the model be extrapolated outside of its sample range to produce such a number.

In Hatton and Williamson's time-series model of Irish emigration, the intercept is –11.61, implying that if all the dependent variables were zero, the model would predict Irish immigration at this rate (i.e. a negative intercept would mean that migrants would be entering rather than departing from Ireland). It is hard to make sense of this term. Not only is the concept of Irish immigration to Ireland hard to accept, especially if the migrant stock of Irish abroad is set equal to zero, but so too is the concept of universal zero unemployment and zero relative wages.

8.3 Partial and multiple correlation

8.3.1 The interpretation and order of partial correlation coefficients

Just as the partial regression coefficient measures the effect of one variable while holding the others constant, so the **partial correlation coefficients** control for the influence of the other variables specified in the relationship.

The basic principles are the same as in simple correlation, but the notation changes slightly to show which variables are included in the correlation and which are held constant. Thus $r_{YX_1 . X_2X_3}$ indicates the correlation of Y and X_1, *while controlling for the influence of* X_2 and X_3.

> **PARTIAL CORRELATION COEFFICIENTS**
>
> The partial correlation coefficient
> is a measure of
> the strength of the linear relationship
> between two variables,
>
> *while controlling for the influence of the other variables*
> included in the correlation.

The number of control variables on the right of the point determines what is called the **order** of the partial correlation coefficient. Thus simple correlation, which *ignores* any other variables, is called a **zero-order correlation**. With two control variables, as in the example in the previous paragraph, it is a **second-order correlation (or partial)**, with three it is a **third-order**, and so on.

Consider, for example, the inter-relationship between five variables from the Poor Law data set for a sample of 311 parishes: RELIEF, UNEMP, FARMERS, GRAIN, and LONDON. As a first step in the analysis of the relationships between these five variables a statistical computer program might be used to calculate the zero-order correlation between all possible pairs; in this case there would be 10 pairs. The results are typically presented in a matrix of five rows and five columns, as in the upper panel of table 8.3, together with the two-tailed significance levels of the coefficients.

With each of these simple (bivariate) correlations no account is taken of any possible effect of the three remaining variables. In order to do this it is necessary to calculate first-, second-, and third-order partials, taking various combinations of two variables while controlling for one, two, or three of the others.

The lower panel of table 8.3 shows two of the **third-order partials**. In the first, RELIEF is correlated with UNEMP while controlling for FARMERS, GRAIN, and LONDON. In the second, RELIEF is correlated with LONDON, while controlling for the three remaining variables.

These tables can then be scrutinized to see how the coefficients change with the introduction of the various control variables. For example, the simple (bivariate) correlation coefficient for RELIEF and LONDON was −0.35; when the influence of the three other variables was controlled for, the third-order coefficient dropped to −0.26.

This partial correlation procedure can thus help one to get a better understanding of the possible causal links within a set of related variables. It not only measures the strength of the various combinations of relationships, but can also be a very effective way of detecting hidden relationships. Whereas the OLS regression coefficients indicate the net effect of the relationships among the explanatory variables, partial correlation coefficients enable the researcher to diagnose more completely the process by which the regression coefficients are generated.

They can also help to uncover spurious relationships, by revealing when an apparent relationship between X_1 and Y is actually the result of two separate causal relationships between these two variables and a third variable, X_2. The fact that the actual causal relationship is not between X_1 and Y would emerge through the calculation of a first-order partial correlation coefficient in which X_1 was correlated with Y *while controlling for X_2*.

Table 8.3 Correlation coefficients and partial correlation coefficients for five variables (data relate to 311 parishes in England and Wales)

(a) Zero-order correlation coefficients

		RELIEF	UNEMP	FARMER	GRAIN	LONDON
RELIEF	r	1.000	0.439	0.198	0.365	−0.347
	Sig		0.000	0.000	0.000	0.000
UNEMP	r		1.000	0.113	0.196	−0.170
	Sig			0.047	0.001	0.003
FARMER	r			1.000	0.385	0.150
	Sig				0.000	0.008
GRAIN	r				1.000	−0.372
	Sig					0.000
LONDON	r					1.000
	Sig					

(b) Third-order partial correlation coefficients
i Correlation of RELIEF and LONDON
controlling for FARMER, GRAIN, and UNEMP

		RELIEF	LONDON
RELIEF	r	1.000	−0.256
	Sig		0.000
LONDON	r		1.000
	Sig		

ii Correlation of RELIEF and UNEMP
controlling for FARMER, GRAIN, and LONDON

		RELIEF	UNEMP
RELIEF	r	1.000	0.383
	Sig		0.000
UNEMP	r		1.000
	Sig		

Table 8.4 Zero-order and partial correlations between church attendance, population density, and church density in England in 1851[a]

	258 rural districts	318 urban districts
Zero-order correlations		
1 ATTEND and POPDENS	0.353**	−0.536**
2 ATTEND and CHURCHES	0.572**	−0.418**
First-order partial correlations		
3 ATTEND and POPDENS		
controlling for CHURCHES	0.099	−0.617**
4 ATTEND and CHURCHES		
controlling for POPDENS	0.379**	0.532**

Notes:
[a] Note that log values are used for both POPDENS and CHURCHES in the urban analysis.
** indicates $p < 0.001$.
Source: Crockett, 'Variations in churchgoing rates'.

An illustration of the use of partial correlation coefficients

An excellent illustration of the way in which the inter-relationship between variables can be illuminated by the use of partial correlation coefficients is found in a recent study of attendance at church in Victorian England.[i] Using the rich data available in the 1851 Religious Census, Alasdair Crockett examines the inter-relationship between three variables. These are an index of churchgoing based on total attendances at all churches on Sunday 30 March 1850, expressed as a percentage of the total population (which we will call ATTEND); population per square kilometre (POPDENS); and churches per square kilometre (CHURCHES). His data cover a cross-section of 258 registration districts in rural England and 318 urban districts.

He presents the results of a series of zero-order and partial, first-order correlations between these three variables across the rural and urban districts, which we have reproduced in table 8.4.

The zero-order correlations in rows 1 and 2 of the table show both POPDENS and CHURCHES positively correlated with ATTEND among rural districts, and both negatively correlated with ATTEND among urban districts. All these correlations are statistically significant, with prob-values less than 0.001.

[i] Alasdair Crockett, 'Variations in churchgoing rates in England in 1851: supply-side deficiency or demand-led decline?', in Alasdair Crockett and Richard O'Leary (eds), *Religion in Modernity: Patterns and Processes in Europe and America*, Cambridge University Press, forthcoming.

However, when we turn to the partial correlations it is evident that in rural England there is no remaining statistically significant positive association between ATTEND and POPDENS once the third variable, CHURCHES, is controlled for (row 3). In contrast, the strong positive association between ATTEND and CHURCHES persists when POPDENS is controlled for (row 4). Crockett concludes from this that population density appeared to be positively associated with churchgoing across rural England only *because of its underlying relationship with church density*.

The story revealed by the first-order correlations for the urban districts is also interesting. The strong negative association between ATTEND and POPDENS (row 1) is still evident when CHURCHES is controlled for (row 3). However, when POPDENS is controlled for, the relationship between ATTEND and CHURCHES is strongly *positive* (row 4). It only appeared to be *negatively* correlated (row 2) because of the underlying relationship with population density.

8.3.2   Removing the influence of the control variable

How are the control variables actually held constant? The essential principle can be explained for the case of a first-order coefficient, i.e. where there is one control variable in a total of three variables. To illustrate the explanation let us continue with the churchgoing variables, with the aim of calculating the partial correlation coefficient between ATTEND and POPDENS while controlling for CHURCHES.

The basic technique starts with the calculation of two *simple* regression lines, in each of which the *control variable appears as the explanatory variable*:

> In the first POPDENS is regressed on CHURCHES
> In the second ATTEND is regressed on CHURCHES

The first of these fitted regression lines explains as much of the variation in POPDENS as can be attributed to CHURCHES. The remaining, unexplained, variation is reflected in the residuals. ATTEND will be one factor contributing to these residuals.

The second regression line explains as much of the deviation in ATTEND as can be attributed to CHURCHES. The remaining, unexplained, variation is again reflected in the residuals. POPDENS will be one factor contributing to these residuals.

With these two regressions CHURCHES has been allowed to explain as much of the variation in the two other variables as it can. The final step is then to *correlate the residuals* from the two regressions. This gives the desired measure of the relationship between POPDENS and ATTEND that is independent of any influence from CHURCHES.

On the basis of these correlations, Crockett advances a spatial interpretation of English churchgoing in the nineteenth century that focuses on the different geographies of church density in rural and urban parishes. Rural parishes were more spread out and many parishioners had long distances to walk on a Sunday. This constrained church attendance and explains the insignificant partial correlation between POPDENS and ATTEND after correcting for CHURCHES. In contrast, geographic isolation played no role in an urban environment replete with churches and chapels of many denominations.

Crockett instead argues that the strong negative correlation of POPDENS and ATTEND after correcting for CHURCHES in urban districts is better explained by the effects of industrialization on the propensity to attend church. In Crockett's terminology, rural church attendance was limited by supply factors, and urban church attendance by demand factors.

8.3.3 Calculation of partial correlation coefficients

The derivation of the formula for the calculation of partial coefficients will not be explained here. It is sufficient to note that the required measurement of the correlation between the residuals is obtained from the simple correlation coefficients among the several variables for which there is a multiple relationship.

Assume, for example, that there are three variables, Y_1, X_2, and X_3, for which there are three simple (zero-order) correlation coefficients, $r_{Y_1 X_2}$, $r_{Y_1 X_3}$, and $r_{X_2 X_3}$. (For simplicity the Xs and Ys will be omitted in the subsequent paragraphs.)

The first of the (first-order) partial correlation coefficients is $r_{12.3}$. This measures the strength of the relationship between Y_1 and X_2 when any influence of X_3 has been removed. The formula is

$$r_{12.3} = \frac{r_{12} - (r_{13})(r_{23})}{\sqrt{(1 - r_{13}^2)(1 - r_{23}^2)}} \qquad (8.8)$$

The second partial coefficient $r_{13.2}$ similarly measures the relationship between Y_1 and X_3 when any influence of X_2 has been removed. It can be derived in the same way by an appropriate re-arrangement of the simple correlation coefficients.

This formula can be used to explain what happened in our example of the Chicago welfare mission. The impact of adding a second explanatory variable to the basic regression of WELFARE on HOMELESS differed, depending on whether FOODCOST or TEMP was included. This impact is essentially the difference between the zero-order partial correlation between WELFARE and HOMELESS, and the two first-order partials, controlling for FOODCOST and TEMP, respectively.

The matrix of *zero-order* partial correlations among our variables looks like this[j]

	HOMELESS	FOODCOST	TEMP
WELFARE	0.7960	0.4495	0.9368
HOMELESS		0.0026	0.7271
FOODCOST			0.4521

If we plug these figures into (8.8) for the two cases, we find that the *first-order* partial correlation between WELFARE and HOMELESS controlling for FOODCOST is 0.8898, an increase compared to the zero-order correlation of 0.7960. The calculation is

$$\frac{0.7960 - (0.4495)(0.0026)}{\sqrt{[1-(0.4495)^2] \times [1-(0.0026)^2]}} = \frac{0.7948}{\sqrt{0.7979 \times 0.9999}} = 0.8898$$

By contrast, the corresponding first-order partial correlation between WELFARE and HOMELESS controlling for TEMP is only 0.4782, a much lower value than the zero-order correlation.

This contrast explains why the strength of HOMELESS in the regression in (8.3) fell dramatically with the addition of TEMP as an explanatory variable, but rose slightly when FOODCOST was added.

In general, the explanatory power of an explanatory variable will *increase* with the addition of a new variable that is *weakly correlated to it*; and will *fall* with the addition of a new variable that is *strongly correlated* to it.

8.3.4   The coefficient of multiple correlation, R

Finally, we may want to know how much of the variation in the dependent variable is provided by all the explanatory variables taken together, rather than by each separately. This is given by the **coefficient of multiple correlation.**

THE COEFFICIENT OF MULTIPLE CORRELATION, R

R is a measure of the
*closeness of the linear relationship
between all the variables*
taken together.

The letter R is used for this measure, with subscripts to indicate which variables have been included in the calculation. Thus $R_{Y \cdot X_1 X_2 X_3}$ would indicate the correlation of Y with three other variables.

[j] We have simplified the presentation by comparison with table 8.3 by omitting both the own correlations (e.g. WELFARE with WELFARE) and the statistical significance.

Numerically, for any given set of variables, R is simply the square root of the corresponding coefficient of multiple determination, R^2 (see §8.2.1). By convention R is always presented as positive, but the *sign* of the overall correlation coefficient has no meaning, since some of the explanatory variables may be positively correlated and others negatively. R can vary between 0 and 1. A value of 0 indicates no linear relationship, but – as with the two-variable case – it is always possible that there is a strong non-linear relationship.

Notes

[1] The name Ballantine was originally given to the shape of interlocking circles because of the similarity between figure 8.2 and the advertising logo of P. Ballantine & Co., a producer of beer and ales in Newark, New Jersey in the nineteenth century. The Ballantine logo consisted of three interlocking rings, each symbolizing the essential characteristics of Ballantine ale. Before Prohibition, these characteristics were identified as Purity, Strength, and Flavor; after the repeal of the 18th Amendment in 1933, the ring of Strength was renamed the ring of Body.

[2] For examples of the use of beta coefficients to compare the relative magnitudes of the effects on the dependent variable of different explanatory variables see William A. Sundstrom and Paul A. David, 'Old-age security motives, labor markets and farm family fertility in antebellum America', *Explorations in Economic History*, 25, 1988, pp. 190–2; and Michael Edelstein, *Overseas Investment in the Age of High Imperialism*, Columbia University Press, 1982, pp. 102–9.

8.4 Exercises for chapter 8

1. Write a paragraph interpreting the following results from a multiple regression model explaining a government's VOTE share in each General Election since 1945 in terms of the current economic GROWTH rate (per cent per annum), the current level of UNEMPloyment (per cent per annum), the current level of INFLTION (per cent per annum), and the number of STRIKES in the previous year. Be sure to discuss the meaning of the regression coefficients and associated t-statistics, the intercept term, and the coefficient of multiple determination.

$$\text{VOTE}_t = 45.5 + 5.4\,\text{GROWTH}_t - 1.2\,\text{UNEMP}_t - 2.6\,\text{INFLTION}_t - 5.1\,\text{STRIKES}_{t-1}$$
$$\qquad\quad (8.3)\ \ (4.2) \qquad\qquad (3.6) \qquad\quad (2.1) \qquad\qquad\quad (1.4)$$
$$R^2 = 0.65$$

2. You wish to build a model of family size in Irish counties in the early twentieth century. Use the Hatton and Williamson cross-section data set to test the hypotheses that family size is directly related to religion (CATHOLIC), age (AGE), and literacy (ILLITRTE).

(i) Test the hypotheses independently, by calculating the simple (zero-order partial) correlation coefficients for the variables across Irish counties in 1911.

(ii) Test the hypotheses jointly by calculating the partial correlation coefficients, holding the other variables constant.

(iii) Test the hypotheses by running a multiple regression of FAMSIZE on the three variables.

Compare the results. What points of similarity and dissimilarity do you find between the three approaches? Explain your findings.

3. Use the Ballantine methodology to interpret what happens in the Benjamin and Kochin model of unemployment when the number of explanatory variables is increased from one to two. Does it matter in which order the variables are added? Use the Ballantine method to illustrate what is happening when YEAR is added as a third variable in the equation. (*Hint*: look at the correlation matrix of all three variables.)

4. How would you respond to a critic of regression methodology who suggests that the analysis of partial correlations produces all the information you need to test hypotheses and evaluate relationships between variables, without any of the costs implicit in formal modelling?

5. Boyer's preferred OLS equation to explain county-by-county variation in RELIEF payments is reproduced in table 15.1 ('reduced-form model'). Generate beta coefficients for this regression. How does converting the results in this way alter our perception of the importance of the variables in explaining parish-by-parish variation in relief payments *per capita*?

6. What would you infer from a result in which the R^2 is positive but small, while the $\bar{R}^2$ is small but negative?

7. You run two regressions. In the first, the $\bar{R}^2$ is high, but the individual t-statistics on each variable are low. In the second, the individual t-statistics are high, but the overall $\bar{R}^2$ is low. Write a paragraph interpreting these results.

8. You run two variants of the same basic regression. In the first version, the coefficient on variable X_2 is -0.3 with a t-statistic of 1.41; in the second version, the coefficient is $+0.25$ and the t-statistic is 1.02. How do you interpret these differences? What do they tell you about the status of X_2 in the regression as a whole?

9. Are the following statements true or false? Explain your reasoning.

(i) In a regression, if the values of X_3 are doubled, the coefficient on X_3 will also be doubled.

(ii) In a regression, if the values of Y are halved, the coefficients on each X will also be halved.

(iii) In a regression of Y on log X, the regression coefficient is b. If the regression were re-estimated using Y on X, the regression coefficient would be log b.

(iv) In a regression, if every value of Y is larger by 5 units, the value of the intercept will be larger by 5 units.

(v) The addition of an orthogonal variable will raise R^2 but lower $\bar{R}^2$, whereas the addition of a collinear variable will raise both.

10. Evaluate the following propositions concerning R^2:

(i) 'The correct way to test for the relevance of an additional explanatory variable is to compare the level of R^2 before and after its inclusion. So long as the R^2 goes up, the additional variable should be included in the regression.'

(ii) 'The whole purpose of running regressions is to explain as much as possible about the behaviour of the dependent variable. This means getting the best fit from the data. The essence of the OLS model is to minimize the least squares, i.e. to minimize the residual sum of squares from a regression. Since the R^2 statistic is simply the ratio of the explained to the total sum of squares, it follows logically that the best approach to regression estimation is to maximize the value of R^2.'

CHAPTER 9

The classical linear regression model

This chapter builds on our previous work and takes a succession of giant strides towards realistic quantitative analysis of relationships between two or more variables. After completing this material it will be possible to examine a large range of potential historical problems, and to read critically many of the studies in history and the social sciences that make use of regression and related quantitative techniques.

We will begin in §9.1 with a brief discussion of the concept of a 'model' and of the associated methodology of quantitative research into the relationships between two or more variables. The basic technique of linear regression (discussed in chapters 4 and 8) is then extended in §9.2 to examine the reasons why the observed values of the dependent variable deviate from the regression line, and to consider the implications of these deviations. In §9.3 a new test statistic, the F-test, is introduced and used to test the significance of the multiple regression as a whole. Finally, §9.4 is devoted to a further useful summary statistic, the standard error of the estimate.

9.1 Historical research and models of relationships between variables

One of the principal features of quantitative research in the historical and social sciences is the attempt to analyse and explain the behaviour of some particular variable. The social historian may wish to explore changing patterns of racial discrimination; the urban historian may study the growth of cities. For the economic historian the subject may be the factors that influenced the supply of – and demand for – wheat or cotton or hogs, or the choice made by women between staying at home and going out to work. The political historian may investigate the voting behaviour of the electorate, or the effect of an incumbent president on congressional elections; for the demographer it may be the trends and fluctuations in fertility and mortality or in international migration.

In each of these and many similar problems a quantitative analysis begins with the **specification of a model**.[a] This is the researcher's formulation of the relationship between the phenomenon that she wishes to analyse, and other factors that she thinks will help to explain that phenomenon. In our earlier terminology she has one dependent variable, and attempts to specify which are the relevant explanatory variables, and how they are related to the dependent variable.

In most historical writing this is, of course, done implicitly. The non-quantitative historian does not say in as many words: 'here is the model I have formulated to explain why the number of criminal offences first increased and then declined', but her discussion of the issue is, in effect, an attempt to do this.[1]

The distinctive feature of the quantitative approach is first, that the relationships are made explicit; secondly, that they can be measured and tested. Whether or not this is a better approach depends largely on how well the relationships can be specified by the researcher, and how accurately the major relevant variables can be measured. Even if the results are statistically poor, the exercise will probably help to clarify the crucial issues.

The specification of the model will thus determine:

(a) The variables to be included.
(b) The researcher's *a priori* expectations about the *sign* of the regression coefficients, i.e. whether a rise in an explanatory variable will be associated with a rise or a fall in the dependent variable.
(c) The mathematical form of the relationship between the variables (for example, whether it is linear or has some other particular non-linear form).

Once a model has been specified, the subsequent stages in the analysis are the estimation and the evaluation of the model. **Estimation** is the collection of the necessary data and the application of appropriate statistical procedures to obtain estimates of the size and sign of the regression coefficients (i.e. the values for b_1, b_2, etc.). **Evaluation** is then the application of the hypothesis testing procedures to decide whether the estimates are reliable and statistically significant, and of historical or other criteria (including common sense) to decide whether they are meaningful and important.

---

[a] This is also referred to as the formulation of a **maintained hypothesis**.

9.1.1 Quantitative methods and historical judgement

A great deal of the material covered in this text is precise and mechanical. If one is required to calculate the mean and variance of a series, or a correlation coefficient for two variables, there is only one correct answer.

When dealing with confidence intervals and hypothesis testing there may be a little more scope for judgement – both when setting significance levels and when evaluating minor divergences about the chosen level – but the basic procedures are laid down and otherwise leave little room for disagreement. However, when it comes to the formulation of quantitative models to analyse and explain the behaviour of a particular variable, the position changes dramatically. Elements of the procedures will still involve precise mathematical or statistical calculations, but the fundamental approach is entirely dependent on the judgement of the researcher, and there is no uniquely correct answer.

It is helpful to stress this, because as soon as one starts to read the books and articles that use these methods it becomes evident that many topics remain highly controversial. Where authors disagree strongly, quantitative methods seldom resolve disputes. This may seem surprising given the apparent precision of quantitative measurements and techniques. But no model of the relationship between variables can ever be precisely or comprehensively specified. It is always possible to question the specification of the model, and to suggest other formulations that might be more satisfactory.

It then becomes necessary to judge the merits of the competing models, and here, too, there is enormous room for discretion and disagreement. There are likely to be differences in the choice of explanatory variables or in the way they are measured. Furthermore, it is seldom the case that all the relevant criteria point unambiguously in the same direction. One model may have a high R^2, but the regression coefficients may have large standard errors so that they are not statistically significant at acceptable levels. The rival model may have lower standard errors on the coefficients but perform less well on other tests, such as the ability of the model to predict the movement in the variable outside the period for which the regression was calculated.

A fundamental aim of this chapter (and of the further discussion in §12.5 and §12.6, and in the case studies in chapters 14 and 15) is thus to help readers understand (a) how these differences arise, (b) why the various criteria for evaluating the merits of different models may give conflicting verdicts, and (c) how the approach may be of considerable benefit to historical understanding even when the results are not conclusive.

9.2 Deviations of the dependent variable from the estimated regression line

In the preliminary consideration of the fitting of the regression line by the ordinary least squares (OLS) procedure in §4.2 we were of course aware that many of the observations of the dependent variable (Y) *did not lie* on the fitted line.

The measurement of the goodness of fit (r^2) given in §4.3 explicitly distinguished between:

(a) the part of the deviation of Y_i from $\overline{Y}$ which was explained by the regression line ($=\hat{Y}_i-\overline{Y}$), and

(b) the part which remained unexplained ($=Y_i-\hat{Y}_i$).

It is now necessary to consider more carefully the reasons for these deviations from the regression line and to examine their implications. The reasons why the observed values of Y do not all lie neatly on the regression line can be broadly divided into two groups.

9.2.1 Errors of measurement and specification

The first group of reasons consists of errors of measurement and specification.[b] These can take several forms, including:

(a) *The dependent variable, Y, may be measured incorrectly.* This might, for example, be the result of inaccuracies in the collection or processing of the data, or of ambiguities about the precise definition of Y.

(b) *Relevant explanatory variables may be omitted from the model.* This could happen because it did not occur to the researcher to include them; or because the necessary data were not available; or because they consist of aspects such as tastes or attitudes that are not readily measurable.

(c) There may be other forms of *mis-specification of the model,* including:

   (i) Assuming a linear relationship between the variables when it is actually non-linear.[c]

   (ii) Including irrelevant explanatory variables, because the researcher wrongly thought they were important.

   (iii) Assuming that a *time-series relationship is constant over time* (so that there is no change in the intercept or regression coefficients) when it is actually changing.

---

[b] The technical aspects of 'model specification', i.e. of the formulation of a relationship between a dependent variable and one or more independent variables, are examined in §11.2 and there is a discussion of the more general issues in §12.5 and §12.6.

[c] The specification of non-linear models will be discussed in chapter 12.

(iv) Assuming that a *cross-section relationship is constant across all the households, parishes, or other units of observation* (so that the same intercepts and regression coefficients apply to all units) when there is actually a structural difference between two groups of units (e.g. between states in the north-east of the United States and those on the frontier).

(v) Assuming that there is a *one-way relationship from the explanatory to the dependent variable* when there is actually a two-way relationship. For example, consumer demand for a product may be influenced by its price, but the price may – at the same time – be influenced by the volume of demand.

9.2.2 Stochastic (random) factors and the error term, *e*

However accurately and fully the researcher specifies a relationship, there will always be additional random factors that occur irregularly and unpredictably, and will have an impact on the dependent variable. These are referred to as **stochastic** factors and make up the second group of reasons why the observed values of Y do not all lie neatly on the regression line.

Stochastic factors may be relatively large events such as strikes, wars, riots, fires, droughts, or epidemics. Or they may be factors which are individually trivial and beyond analysis (for example, the individual attitudes or erratic behaviour of a particular parish officer on a particular occasion), but collectively can have an important effect on the actual value of the dependent variable.

More generally, it is characteristic of the human behaviour with which we are concerned in history and the social sciences that it is *not* absolutely uniform and consistent. Individuals and groups do not always respond in an identical way to any given stimulus.

These stochastic factors are thus equivalent to additional explanatory variables that, even if they were measurable, could not be sufficiently identified to be incorporated in the model of the relationship. We deal with them by means of the concept of an **error term**.

When a simple linear relationship between two variables was initially specified, it was expressed as

$$Y = a + bX \tag{9.1}$$

In order to recognize both the existence of possible errors of measurement and specification, and the potential importance of the stochastic factors, statisticians prefer to add to this an additional 'error term' designated by e.[d]

---

[d] Some authors refer to the error term as a disturbance or a stochastic term, and it is also designated in some texts by u or by the Greek letter ε (epsilon).

The effect of doing this is to transform the model from an **exact** or **deterministic relationship** to a **stochastic** one. This is an extremely important distinction, and represents the adaptation of a purely statistical method to the stochastic nature of almost all social phenomena.

The estimated relationship thus becomes

$$Y = a + bX + e \qquad (9.2)$$

This adds an additional (random) variable that covers *all* the possible reasons for the deviation of Y_i from the value $\hat{Y}_i$ indicated by the regression line.

Since the value of this random variable, e_i, cannot be actually observed in the same way as the other explanatory variables, certain assumptions have to be made about how it might behave. These assumptions are of critical importance to the evaluation of the model.

9.2.3 Sampling and the regression line

Before considering these assumptions it will be helpful to emphasize that we are essentially dealing with a characteristic sampling problem, created because our data consist of a single sample drawn from a much larger population containing many more observations.

This is not always immediately obvious. Say, for example, that the issue to be considered is the relationship between emigration from Ireland and wages in the United States, to see whether wages are a possible explanatory variable. The researcher may have available aggregate national data on these two variables for the period 1877–1913. He would perhaps not immediately think of this as a 'sample' in the same sense as the Boyer data from a handful of parishes, or a poll of a small sample of adults across the country to ask about their voting intentions in a forthcoming presidential election.

But if he is interested in the way in which decisions about migration are influenced by the prevailing level of wages, then the information generated by the specific experience of the particular individuals who emigrated from Ireland in the years 1877–1913 can be thought of conceptually as a sample from the **infinite population.** This infinite population would consist of all the possible migration decisions made by all those who contemplated emigrating in the sample period or in other periods, or who might do so in the future. It is thus necessary to determine how reliable this sample information is as a measure of the underlying population.

As before, Greek letters are used to indicate this 'true' regression line for the *population*, replacing a by α (alpha), b by β (beta), and e by ε (epsilon).

$$Y = \alpha + \beta X + \varepsilon \tag{9.3}$$

We do not know the values of α and β for the population; all we have are the estimates of a and b in the regression line derived from the sample. It is thus necessary to establish how reliable a is as an estimate of α, and how reliable b is as an estimate of β. In order to do this we must revert to the issue of the error term.

9.2.4 Assumptions about the error term

Imagine that it is possible to draw a very large (theoretically infinite) number of successive samples from a given population, each showing the relationship between two variables, X and Y.[e] For example, Y could be the quantity of meat supplied to urban markets by cattle farmers, and X the price of beef. A possible set of hypothetical outcomes is illustrated in figure 9.1 (a). For every value of X on the horizontal axis, there are numerous different values of Y.

Consider any single value of X, say X_1. When the price of beef (X) is at this particular level, some quantities supplied (Y) occur repeatedly in different samples, others only very occasionally. Those values that occur more than once rise vertically above each other, illustrated by the dashed line drawn at the mean value, μ_1. When all the samples had been completed we would be able to plot a distribution of all the possible values Y could take when beef prices have a value of X_1. The hypothetical result pictured in figure 9.1 (a) shows this distribution as smooth and symmetrical, with a narrow range between the left- and right-hand tails of the distribution, and thus a low variance.

Similarly, when the beef price has the higher value X_2, there would again be a distribution of values for Y, but in this case it is assumed that it is spread out over a much greater range, and thus has a higher variance. It has a higher mean value (μ_2) and is strongly skewed to the right. And for X_3, there is yet another pattern of distribution, with an m-shape that is neither smooth nor symmetrical, and with two modes. The mean, μ_3, is higher than for X_2, but the dispersion (variance) is narrower.

There could thus be a separate hypothetical distribution of the values of Y for every value of X, each with its own shape and its own mean and variance. The preceding discussion of the error term explains why these differences occur, so that there is not a single uniform value of Y for each

---

[e] This would be analogous to the exercise specified in question 7 of chapter 5, except that the information assembled from the successive samples would be the values of the two variables which are assumed to be related, not the sample means of a single variable.

Figure 9.1 The population of Y for different values of X

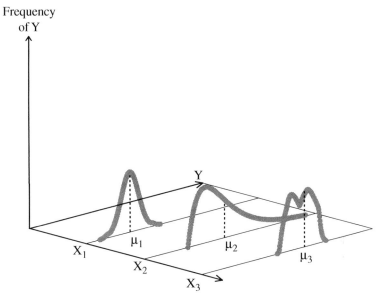

Frequency of Y

(a) Hypothetical populations

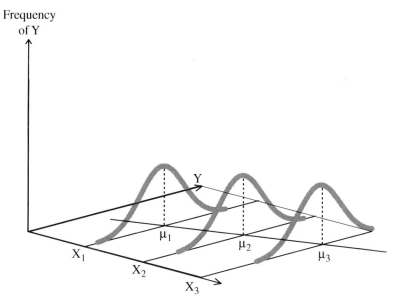

Frequency of Y

(b) The form of the population of Y *assumed* in simple linear regression

value of X. The differences between the distribution of Y at X_1, X_2, and at X_3 are thus determined by the behaviour of the corresponding error terms, e_1, e_2, and e_3.

In practice, of course, we do not have the luxury of the information about the population which could be obtained from an infinite number of samples; we have only a single sample, and thus a single value of Y for each value of X. But it is nevertheless necessary to know something about the possible distribution of the error terms in order to fit the best possible regression line to the sample data. To get round this problem the statisticians *assume* that the error term, e, is a random variable, and that its distributions obey certain simple and plausible rules. These key assumptions about the error term are illustrated in figure 9.1 (b), and are set out more formally in panel 9.1.

Panel 9.1   Assumptions of the classical linear regression model

The four basic *assumptions* of classical linear regression (CLR) are that for any particular model:

1.   The mean value of the random error, e, is zero ($\mu = 0$) for all values of X.
2.   The variance of the random error, e, is the *same* for all values of X, and is equal to the population variance, σ^2.
3.   Values of e for different values of X are *statistically independent* so that if, say, Y_1 is large, there is no reason to think that this will have any effect on Y_2, making it more likely to be either large or small.
4.   The mean values of Y all lie on a *straight* line. This is the *population regression line.*

In addition, it may optionally be assumed that the values of Y are *normally distributed* about their mean for each value of Y, and thus that the values of the random error, e, are also normally distributed about their mean. This assumption is often made, (and is adopted in figures 9.1 (b) and 9.2) but it is *not* required for the estimation of the coefficients in the most widely used form of regression analysis, the classical linear OLS model.

However, the normality assumption is required in order for hypotheses about the values of the coefficients to be tested by standard procedures for statistical inference, such as those to be discussed in §9.3.[*]

[*] The reason for this was explained in §6.2.1.

Figure 9.2 The true (population) regression line and the estimated (sample) regression line

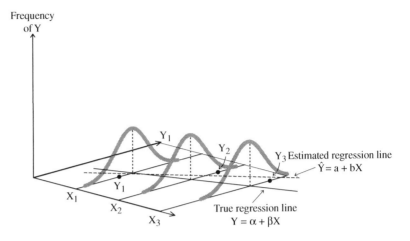

If we had the information for all possible values of the relationship between X and Y we could fit the true population regression line, $Y = \alpha + \beta X$. Since we have only the sample information the best that can be done is to estimate the sample regression line, $\hat{Y} = a + bX$, *assuming* that the distribution of the error term is as specified in panel 9.1.

Since the true population regression line is not actually known, the error terms representing the deviation of the actual values of Y from the true regression line cannot be measured. We can, however, observe the deviations of the estimated regression line from the sample values of Y.

The relationship between this estimated regression line and the true (unknown) regression line that would be given by the population data is shown in figure 9.2. The values of Y observed in the sample are Y_1, Y_2, and Y_3, and the estimated regression line passes through the values $\hat{Y}_1$, $\hat{Y}_2$, and $\hat{Y}_3$. Because of the random error terms, e_1, e_2, and e_3, the values of Y predicted by the true regression line differ from the observed values of Y. These error terms reflect the combined effect of the errors of measurement and specification discussed in §9.2.1, and the stochastic factors considered in §9.2.2.

The best model
When the four basic assumptions of the classical linear regression model all hold, the OLS model is the best approach to regression analysis. In the language of the statistician, the OLS model is BLUE, which stands for the **best linear unbiased estimator** of the regression.

To see what is meant by BLUE, recall from §5.2 the discussion of the sampling distribution of a sample statistic. In the case of a regression coefficient, b, the mean of its sampling distribution is said to be **unbiased** if it is equal to the true (unknown) population coefficient, β. If the assumptions underlying an OLS regression model are correct, then the estimates of its regression coefficients satisfy this condition.

This does not mean that the estimate formed from the particular sample we happen to have will equal the true β; the only estimate that would do this would be the average of all the estimates we would get if we could repeat the sampling process an infinite number of times. If there is more than one unbiased estimator, the one which is called the **best,** or the most **efficient,** is the one whose sampling distribution has the *smallest variance,* that is, is concentrated in a narrow range, not spread widely either side of the mean.

In essence, the notion of the OLS estimator as BLUE is that the performance of least squares regression could not be beaten by any other type of estimation technique (such as maximum likelihood) fitted to the same data. The OLS regression will provide the best and most appropriate fit to the data, as long the conditions set out in panel 9.1 are met.[f] The coefficients are measured accurately and have the lowest possible standard errors (and thus the highest possible t-statistics).

The OLS model will therefore give the model its best possible showing as an explanation for the behaviour of the dependent variable. But it is still necessary to ask: How good is the model as a whole? Just as we need to evaluate the performance of a single explanatory variable by measuring its statistical significance, we should also evaluate the model as a whole by measuring its statistical significance. This is the theme of the next section.

9.3 A significance test for the regression as a whole

The use of the t-test was introduced in chapters 5 and 6. In §6.7.3 it was applied to an example of a simple linear regression to test whether the relationship between the dependent variable, Y, and the explanatory variable, X, was statistically significant. The null hypothesis was that $\beta = 0$, meaning that the true (population) coefficient was zero so that there was no relationship between the two variables.

The principles of the test are exactly the same for a multiple regression model with more than one explanatory variable. The standard error can be calculated for each separate regression coefficient, and for each such coefficient a separate decision can be made as to whether or not the

---

[f] What happens if any of these assumptions are violated is discussed in chapter 11.

coefficient is statistically significant. It is also possible to test the *overall* significance of the estimated regression line. This involves a new test, and we introduce this in the following section. It is then applied to the regression model in §9.3.2 and 9.3.3.

9.3.1 The *F*-test and the *F*-distribution

The basic *F*-test is concerned with two independent sample variances, s_1^2 and s_2^2, each drawn from a normal population, and the point at issue is whether the variances of these two populations, σ_1^2 and σ_2^2, are the same. The null hypothesis would be $\sigma_1^2 = \sigma_2^2$, where the alternative hypothesis is that σ_1^2 is *greater than* σ_2^2. This involves a one-tailed test.

F_{calc} is measured as the ratio of the two sample variances, and by convention the larger variance is taken as the numerator of the ratio, so that the value of the test statistic must be equal to, or greater than 1. The greater the difference between the two population variances, the greater F_{calc} will be.

The sampling distribution for the probability of getting a result greater than F_{calc} follows the theoretical *F*-distribution outlined in panel 9.2 and illustrated in figure 9.3. The distribution is skewed, not symmetrical: one tail stretches out to the right to incorporate the small probability of getting exceptionally large values. The skewness varies according to the *degrees of freedom* of the two sample estimates, generating a family of curves for different sample sizes.

F-TESTS

The *F*-test is the ratio of two sample variances, s_1^2 and s_2^2, where $s_1^2 > s_2^2$.

$$F = \frac{s_1^2}{s_2^2} \tag{9.4}$$

9.3.2 *F*-tests of the statistical significance of the regression as a whole

One important and widely quoted use of the *F*-test is as a test of the *overall* explanatory power of the regression as measured by the coefficient of multiple determination, R^2 (see §8.2.1). If R^2 is not statistically significant it means that none of the explanatory variables are linearly associated with the dependent variable.[g]

---

[g] Another use of the *F*-test is in hypothesis testing of statistical differences between sample variances; see panel 6.1.

Panel 9.2   **The theoretical *F*-distribution**

This is the last of the four theoretical probability distributions we shall consider and is derived from the chi-square distribution described in panel 7.1 of §7.3.2.[*] The theoretical *F*-**distribution** is the sampling distribution of the *ratio of two independent chi-square random variables*, divided by their respective degrees of freedom, k_1 and k_2.

Using the same notation as in (7.8) of panel 7.1, if the first chi-square random variable is

$$V_1 = Z_1^2 + Z_2^2 + \dots + Z_{k1}^2 \qquad (9.5)$$

and the second independent chi-square random variable is

$$V_2 = Z_1^2 + Z_2^2 + \dots + Z_{k2}^2 \qquad (9.6)$$

then

$$F = \frac{V_1/k_1}{V_2/k_2} \qquad (9.7)$$

The shape of the *F*-distribution depends solely on these two parameters: k_1 in the numerator and k_2 in the denominator of the ratio. The distribution can take any value between 0 and infinity, and for small values of k_1 and k_2 it is skewed, with a long tail to the right. As the two parameters become large, however, the *F*-distribution approximates to the normal distribution. It is illustrated for selected values of k_1 and k_2 in figure 9.3.

Published tables for the *F*-distribution are given in many statistical texts, though they are usually heavily abridged since it is necessary to cover a range of combinations of the two degrees of freedom (k_1 and k_2) for each proportion of the distribution (for example, the upper 5 per cent).[**]

---

[*] The other two are the *Z*- and *t*-distributions encountered in §5.4.

[**] D. V. Lindley and W. F. Scott, *New Cambridge Statistical Tables*, 2nd edn., Cambridge University Press, 1995, pp.50–5 give the upper percentage points (right-hand tail) of the *F*-distribution for proportions from 10 per cent to 0.1 per cent for various combinations of df.

As explained in §9.3.1, the *F*-test involves the test of a ratio of two sample variances. In this case the two variances are the explained and the unexplained variation obtained from the regression equation. When there is only one explanatory variable in the model this reduces to the *t*-test already described in §6.7.3.[h] When there are two or more, it is a single test of the hypothesis that all the true regression coefficients (βs) are zero. The test statistic is F_{calc}.

THE *F*-TEST FOR THE STATISTICAL SIGNIFICANCE OF THE REGRESSION AS A WHOLE

The *F*-test is a test of the null hypothesis
that *all the true regression coefficients are zero,*

so that there is no (linear) relationship
between the set of explanatory variables
and the dependent variable.

$$F_{calc} = \frac{\sum(\hat{Y}_i - \bar{Y})^2/(k-1)}{\sum(Y_i - \hat{Y}_i)^2/(n-k)} \tag{9.8}$$

where k is the total number of explanatory variables plus the intercept,
and n is the sample size.

F_{calc} can be compared in the usual way with the theoretical probability of getting this particular result as determined by the theoretical *F*-distribution (see panel 9.2) at the chosen level of significance, where the required degrees of freedom are $k-1$ and $n-k$. If F_{calc} is greater than the theoretical (tabulated) value of *F* the null hypothesis is rejected. In other words, we reject the proposition that all the βs taken together are zero and have no influence on the dependent variable.

9.3.3 The relationship of *F* and R^2

When the coefficient of determination, r^2, was introduced in §4.3 it was defined as the ratio of the explained to the total (explained plus unexplained) variation. It will be seen that the first term in the numerator of the formula given above for F_{calc} is the explained variation, and the first term in the denominator is the unexplained variation. It can be shown by simple

---

[h] It can be shown that for any individual regression coefficient the two tests are formally equivalent and that $F = t^2$.

Figure 9.3 The
F-distribution for
selected degrees
of freedom

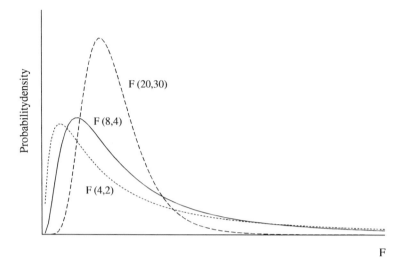

manipulation of these terms that the relationship between F_{calc} and the
equivalent coefficient of multiple determination, R^2, is as follows

$$F_{calc} = \frac{R^2/(k-1)}{(1-R^2)/(n-k)} \qquad (9.9)$$

If the regression model explains very little of the variations in the dependent variable, R^2 will be very small and therefore, as the above formula
shows, the value of F_{calc} will be very low. Conversely, the stronger the relationship specified in the model, the higher the value of F_{calc}. Thus a high
value of F_{calc} is generally also an indicator of strong overall relationships
between the dependent variable and the set of explanatory variables as a
whole.

9.4 The standard error of the estimate, SEE

The **standard error of the estimate** (SEE) is another useful summary statistic that is automatically calculated by most statistical programs. It measures the standard deviation of the residuals from the regression line and
provides the basis for **a confidence interval for a prediction** based on the
regression line. It is formally equal to the square root of the sum of the
unexplained variation divided by the number of degrees of freedom.

THE STANDARD ERROR OF THE ESTIMATE, SEE

SEE is a measure of the
standard deviation of the unexplained variation

$$SEE = \sqrt{\frac{\Sigma(Y_i - \hat{Y}_i)^2}{n-2}} \qquad (9.10)$$

It is used to calculate a confidence interval
around the regression line.

9.4.1 Confidence interval for a prediction of the mean value of a dependent variable

The first value we might wish to predict on the basis of a regression equation is the *mean* value of the dependent variable. Take, for example, a simple linear regression model relating the unemployment rate in each of a series of years (UNEMP) to a single explanatory variable, the benefits available to those unemployed, measured as a ratio to the average wage (BWRATIO):

$$UNEMP = a + b_1 \, BWRATIO + e \qquad (9.11)$$

The coefficients from this regression could be used to calculate the *mean* value of UNEMP that would be predicted for any given value of BWRATIO (say, X_0).[i] However, the regression line in (9.11) is estimated on the basis of only one set of observations and thus represents only *one sample* from the population of all possible relationships between the two variables. Other samples would give different values for the constant, a, and the regression coefficient, b_1, and thus different answers to the calculation.

It is thus necessary to have a confidence interval for this prediction of the mean value of UNEMP when BWRATIO $= X_0$, and to specify the desired level for this, say 95 per cent.

---

[i] Note that X_0 is *not* one of the specific values taken by the explanatory variable. It is any value chosen by the researcher, and may well lie outside the actual range of values for BWRATIO used in the estimation of the regression line if the aim is to predict what UNEMP might be at some other level.

CONFIDENCE INTERVAL FOR THE PREDICTION OF THE MEAN VALUE OF Y

For the 95 per cent confidence interval
the prediction of the mean value
of Y is based on
the standard error of the estimate, SEE.

For any value, X_0, the mean value of Y_0 equals

$$(a + b_1 X_0) \pm t_{0.025} SEE \sqrt{\frac{1}{n} + \frac{(X_0 - \bar{X})^2}{\Sigma(X_i - \bar{X})^2}} \qquad (9.12)$$

Note two features of (9.12). First, if the mean value of UNEMP is calculated when the value of X_0 chosen for BWRATIO is equal to *the mean value of that series*, then $X_0 = \bar{X}$. The numerator in the second term under the square root $(X_0 - \bar{X})$ thus becomes 0, and the confidence interval simplifies to SEE $\frac{1}{\sqrt{n}}$.

Second, when X_0 is *not* equal to the sample mean value of X, then the further it is from $\bar{X}$ in either direction, the larger that second term under the square root becomes, and so the greater the width of the confidence interval around the predicted mean value of UNEMP. This widening of the interval as the value of the explanatory variable moves away from its mean value is illustrated in figure 9.4 (where a broken vertical line is drawn through $\bar{X}$).

Thus while an estimated regression line can be used to extrapolate to periods (or cases) outside the sample, it is essential to be cautious in attempting to predict the mean value of Y for a value of X that is any distance away from the sample mean of X.

Illustration of the calculation of a confidence interval
The calculation underlying figure 9.4 can be used to illustrate the procedure for obtaining the confidence intervals. The values of UNEMP and BWRATIO are taken from the data set for unemployment in inter-war Britain. The value of the standard error of the estimate, SEE, is calculated according to (9.10). The unexplained sum of squares in the numerator of the equation is 305.17.[j] The data cover the 19 years from 1920 to 1938, so

---

[j] This and other statistics quoted in this section were calculated in table 6.1 and §6.7.3, but would also be given by any computer package used to estimate the regression line.

Figure 9.4 95 per cent confidence interval for a prediction of the mean value of UNEMP

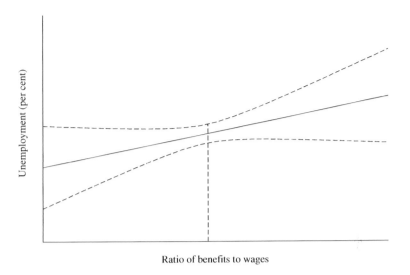

n − 2 is 17. The standard error of the estimate is thus

$$SEE = \sqrt{\frac{305.17}{17}} = 4.24$$

The next step is to obtain the values required for (9.12). This has three components in addition to SEE. First, the regression line specified in (9.11) must be estimated to obtain the values for the constant, a, and the regression coefficient, b_1. These are found to be 6.40 and 15.64, respectively.

Secondly, the table for the theoretical t-distribution (see table 5.1) shows that for 17 degrees of freedom, the two-tailed value of t at the 5 per cent level is 2.110. Thirdly, the values in the final term of (9.12) must be derived. Let us take X_0 at a value of 0.10, a little below the lowest value of BWRATIO observed in the sample. $\overline{X}$, the mean value of BWRATIO in the sample, is 0.467, and the sum of the deviations of X from its mean, $\Sigma(X-\overline{X})^2$, is 0.222. Since n is 19, the required term is

$$\sqrt{\frac{1}{n} + \frac{(X_0 - \overline{X})^2}{\Sigma(X_i - \overline{X})^2}}$$

$$= \sqrt{\frac{1}{19} + \frac{(0.10 - 0.467)^2}{0.222}} = \sqrt{0.053 + \frac{0.135}{0.222}} = \sqrt{0.660}$$

$$= 0.813.$$

The full calculation of the 95 per cent confidence interval for $X_0 = 0.10$ on the basis of (9.12) is thus

$$Y_0 = a + b_1 X_0 \pm t_{0.025} \text{SEE} \sqrt{\frac{1}{n} + \frac{(X_0 - \bar{X})^2}{(X_i - \bar{X})^2}}$$

$$= 6.40 + (15.64 \times 0.10) \pm 2.110 \times 4.24 \times 0.813$$

$$= 7.96 \pm 7.27$$

$$= 0.69 \text{ to } 15.23.$$

At this distance from the mean level of BWRATIO the width of the confidence band around a forecast of the mean value of the unemployment is thus rather large.

The same procedure was followed for a range of alternative values of X_0 to derive the full set of confidence intervals drawn in figure 9.4.

9.4.2 Confidence interval for a prediction of a specific value of a dependent variable

There is a second question we could ask on the basis of the regression equation. Instead of predicting the *mean* value of UNEMP we may wish to predict a *single value*, given a particular value for BWRATIO (X_0).

The answer to this question will be exactly the same, because the values for a, b, and X_0 are exactly the same. But the error around that answer will be greater because we are trying to estimate only one value for Y, rather then the mean of all possible Ys.

CONFIDENCE INTERVAL FOR THE PREDICTION OF A SPECIFIC VALUE OF Y

For the 95 per cent confidence interval
the prediction of a specific value
of Y is based on
the standard error of the estimate, SEE.

For any value, X_0, the value of Y_0 equals

$$(a + b_1 X_0) \pm t_{0.025} \text{SEE} \sqrt{\frac{1}{n} + \frac{(X_0 - \bar{X})^2}{\Sigma(X_i - \bar{X})^2} + 1} \qquad (9.13)$$

Compared to (9.12), (9.13) has an additional term under the square root, = 1. Therefore, the confidence interval (or prediction interval) will always be larger for this prediction of a specific value of the dependent variable than for the prediction of the mean value.

As the sample size gets larger, the first two terms under the square root in (9.13) approach zero, leaving just the final term, 1.[k] The confidence interval thus approaches $t_{0.025}$ SEE. It is for this reason that SEE is called the *standard error* of the estimate.

Note

[1]   For a provocative statement of a leading quantitative economic historian's views on 'covert theory', see Robert W. Fogel, 'The specification problem in economic history', *Journal of Economic History*, 27, 1967, pp. 283–308.

9.5 Exercises for chapter 9

1. Is an estimate BLUE if:
  (i)   The dependent variable is always in error by ±5 per cent?
  (ii) The dependent variable is in error by ±5 per cent for the bottom half of the distribution, but by ±15 per cent for the top half?
  (iii) The dependent variable is under-measured for the lower half of the distribution, but over-measured for the upper half?
  (iv) The dependent variable is always in error by ±5 units?
  (v)   The dependent variable is measured as only half of its true value for all observations?

2. Which of the following series used as an explanatory variable are subject to stochastic errors and which to systematic errors? In each case, write a sentence explaining your reasoning.

  (i)   A series on incomes based on tax data, given tax evasion by the rich
  (ii) A series on poverty based on reported income, given welfare fraud by the poor
  (iii) A series compiled by a census taker who leaves out every other house
  (iv) A series compiled by census subjects who round their ages to the nearest fifth year
  (v)   A series compiled by a government official who inverts every number, e.g. writing 75 not 57
  (vi) A series compiled by a government official who inverts every other number

[k] The first term diminishes because as n gets larger, 1/n gets smaller. The second term diminishes because the bigger the sample, the more cases of X there are to include in the sum of the deviations of X_i from in the denominator. $\Sigma(X_i - \bar{X})^2$ thus gets larger and larger relative to $(X_0 - \bar{X})^2$.

(vii) A series compiled by a researcher who misreads data as lb per inch, rather than kg per cm

(viii) A series compiled by a researcher who misreads data as being expressed in numbers, rather than in logs

(ix) A series that uses urban prices rather than rural prices to explain farm consumption patterns

(x) A series that measures urban prices by collecting data only from large retailers.

3. Write a brief paragraph discussing the following proposition:

Since the data on which the regression is being estimated are a sample drawn from the population, it must therefore follow that the estimators (coefficients) for that regression are themselves sample statistics – just one of many possible that could be drawn from the sampling distribution. It is important to recognize, therefore, that minimizing least squares gives the best fit to this particular set of numbers, but that this is not necessarily the best fit for any other sample, let alone for the population as a whole.

4. The error term is not only assumed to have zero mean and to be symmetrically distributed, it is also assumed to be independent of both the explanatory variables and the dependent variable. Why are the last two assumptions necessary to maintain unbiasedness?

5. Calculate *by hand* the value of F for the regression coefficient of disturbances on wheat prices in chapter 4, question 3. Compare this with the appropriate test statistic, being sure to identify the correct numbers of degrees of freedom. Does this suggest that the regression is statistically significant? Compare your findings with the answer to question 4 in chapter 6.

6. In chapter 6, question 7, a question was raised about whether the variances of birth rate were (a) the same for Bedfordshire and Essex, and (b) the same for Buckinghamshire and Sussex. Set up an F-test of these two hypotheses and report your finding (use the formula in equation 9.4).

In chapter 6, question 8, the number of parishes in each sample was increased. Maintain this fiction here. What difference do the larger samples make to (a) the value of the F-statistic, and (b) its statistical significance?

7. Run the following regression on the Benjamin–Kochin data set:

$$UNEMP = a + b\,BWRATIO + e$$

(i) Confirm that the reported value of the F-statistic is equal to the square of the t-statistic and that the statistical significance of the two tests are identical.

(ii) Construct a new variable, by adding 10 units to unemployment for each observation. Re-run the basic regression above and report the results.

(a) What do you notice about the statistical significance of the intercept?

(b) What do you notice about the relationship between the F- and t-statistics?

(c) What do you notice about the overall statistical significance of the equation? What does this tell you about the relationship between the F-test and the intercept?

(iii) Now run a variant of the basic regression, separating out the component parts of BWRATIO in the form

$$UNEMP = a + b_1 \, BENEFIT + b_2 \, WAGE + e$$

(a) Report the F-statistic and its significance.

(b) Use the formula (9.9) to explain why the value of the F-statistic has fallen so much, despite the small increase in R^2.

8. How would you use the F-test to determine the statistical significance of the R^2 statistic? (*Hint*: use (9.9).)

9. Calculate *by hand* the standard error of the estimate (SEE) for the regression coefficient of disturbances on wheat prices in chapter 4, question 3.

(i) What is the 95 per cent confidence interval around the predicted number of disturbances at a wheat price of 100 shillings per qtr?

(ii) Will this be larger or smaller than the 95 per cent confidence interval around the predicted number of disturbances at 85 shillings per qtr? (*Hint*: this second question should *not* require a second calculation.)

10. Using the Benjamin–Kochin data set:

(i) Apply the procedure of §9.4.1 to calculate the confidence interval around the predicted value of UNEMP for the full Benjamin–Kochin model, namely

$$UNEMP = a + b_1 \, BWRATIO + b_2 \, DEMAND + e$$

at the mean of BWRATIO.

(ii) Calculate the 95 per cent confidence interval around the value of BWRATIO in 1920.

(iii) How would your results differ if you were measuring the 95 per cent confidence interval around the mean value of DEMAND and the value of DEMAND in 1920, respectively?

(iv) How do your results influence your interpretation of the Benjamin–Kochin explanation of inter-war unemployment?

CHAPTER 10

Dummy variables and lagged values

In chapter 8 the simple linear regression model was extended to cover the introduction of two or more explanatory variables, and in chapter 9 the model was given its essential stochastic form.

In the present chapter two further extensions are described. First, §10.1 is devoted to the use of **dummy variables**. This is a procedure developed to enable us to include in a regression a variable that cannot be measured in the same way as a continuous numerical value (for example, income, or age at marriage) but is instead represented by two or more categories (for example, single, married, or widowed). This special form of a nominal (or categorical) scale is known as a dummy variable.

Secondly, in §10.2 we develop the implications of the idea that it may be appropriate for one or more of the explanatory variables to refer to an earlier period than the one to which the dependent variable relates. Such **lagged values** recognize the fact that there may be a delay before the changes in the explanatory variable make their full impact.

10.1 Dummy variables

10.1.1 Dummy variables with two or more categories

In historical research we often want to take account of factors in a regression that are not measurable in the usual way, but can be expressed as representing one of two (or more) categories. This is a special form of a nominal scale and is called a **dummy variable**. In this chapter we consider such variables only when they are introduced as *explanatory* variables. It is also possible for the *dependent* variable to be a dummy variable, and this will be discussed separately in chapter 13.

A number of examples of dummy variables *with two categories* occur in the Poor Law data set, such as whether or not there was a workhouse in the parish (WORKHSE), or whether or not child allowances (CHILDALL) were paid. These are dealt with by assigning a value of 1 whenever the answer is Yes, and a value of 0 whenever the answer is No. Other examples of classifications into two nominal categories that could be represented by a dummy variable include male/female, urban/rural, graduate/non-graduate, and house owner/not house owner.

A corresponding procedure in the context of a time series would be to assign a value of 1 to every year in the period when there was some exceptional event such as a war, a strike, or an earthquake, and a value of 0 to all other years.

Dummy variables can also be applied to a nominal variable with *more than two* categories. For example, in a study of earnings it might be appropriate to distinguish four categories of social class: professional, skilled, semi-skilled, and unskilled. Similarly, in a political study of US policy in the period since the Second World War it might be useful to include the role of different presidents as one of the explanatory variables, assigning a separate dummy variable for each of the periods in which successive presidents had held office. Other multiple category variables for which dummy variables might be used include religion, occupation, region, or time period.

Whatever the number of categories, one of them must be selected as the **reference category** (also referred to as the **control category** or **benchmark**), and this reference category must be *omitted from the regression*. An alternative, but generally less satisfactory procedure, is to omit the intercept rather than the reference category. Failure to adopt one or other of these procedures is known as the **dummy variable trap**. It is essential not to fall into this trap, because what is measured if neither the control category nor the intercept is omitted is effectively an identity with a perfect linear relationship between the dummies and the intercept. In this situation; the r^2 becomes 1 and the standard errors on all the coefficients become 0. Clearly such results are nonsensical.

To illustrate the proper application of dummy variables, consider the data set for children leaving home in the United States in the decade 1850–60. One of the explanatory variables was the place of residence of the family in 1850, subdivided into four areas, the Northeast, North-central, South, and Frontier.[a] Northeast was selected as the reference category. There are then *three separate* dummies (one fewer than the number of categories), *each of which takes a value of either 1 or 0,* as follows.

---

[a] The Frontier area was defined as Minnesota, Iowa, Kansas, Oklahoma, Texas, and states further west: Richard H. Steckel, 'The age at leaving home in the United States, 1850–1860', *Social Science History*, 20, 1996, p. 512.

NCENTRAL = 1 for families living in North-central states   0 for all other families

SOUTH   = 1 for families living in the South   0 for all other families

FRONTIER = 1 for families living on the Frontier   0 for all other families

The omitted reference category of residence in the Northeast then acts as the benchmark against which the results for these three categories are compared.

Students have been known to think that in a case like this the values given to the dummy variables would be 3, 2, 1, and 0. So it must be stressed that the values assigned to each dummy are *always either 1 or 0,* irrespective of the number of categories for which there are dummy variables, and that the reference category is omitted.

Once these dummy variables have been formed they can be included in a regression in the same way as any other explanatory variable. For example, in the time series analysis a wartime/peacetime dummy variable would enable the researcher to include the occurrence of war as one of the explanatory variables, and thus to *control* for its effects on the dependent variable in the manner explained in §8.2.3 above.

The coefficients on the dummy variables can be tested for significance in the same way as those on numerical variables, and all the other regression procedures, such as the calculation of the coefficient of multiple determination, R^2, or the F-test, are made and interpreted in the usual way.

An illustration of the use of dummy variables

The following regression equation is taken from a paper on the influence of London on wages paid in 1903 in a cross-section of districts in southern England.[b] The districts were classified in five groups according to their distance from London. The first four categories were for intervals of 25 miles (0–25 miles, 25–50 miles, and so on). The fifth category covered districts more than 100 miles from London, and was used as the control group.

$$\text{WAGE} = a + b_1 \text{LON } 0\text{–}25 + b_2 \text{LON } 25\text{–}50 + b_3 \text{LON } 50\text{–}70 + b_4 \text{LON } 75\text{–}100 + b_5 \text{GRAIN} + e \qquad (10.1)$$

where

WAGE = weekly summer cash wage in shillings for agricultural labourers in southern England

[b] George R. Boyer, 'The influence of London on labor markets in southern England, 1830–1914', *Social Science History*, 22, 1998, pp. 257–85.

LON   = dummy variables measuring distance from London in 25-mile intervals

GRAIN = dummy variable = 1 for districts located in counties specializing in grain production.

The regression results (with their t-statistics in parentheses) were:

Constant	a	13.71	(64.71)
LON 25	b_1	3.11	(8.77)
LON 25–50	b_2	1.17	(4.21)
LON 50–75	b_3	0.74	(2.65)
LON 75–100	b_4	0.48	(1.50)
GRAIN	b_5	−1.40	(7.37)
	R^2	0.357	
	N	239	

The author's comment (italics added)[c] was:

in 1903, weekly [agricultural] wages in districts within 25 miles of London were 3.1s. higher *than those in districts more than 100 miles from London.* . . . weekly wages were 1.2s. *higher* in districts 25–50 miles from London, and 0.7s. *higher* in districts 50–75 miles from London, than in those districts more than 100 miles from the metropolis. Agricultural wages in districts 75–100 miles from London were not *significantly* different than wages in districts more than 100 miles from London.

This illustrates two aspects of the use of dummy variables very clearly. First, the four dummy variables enable districts to be subdivided into five categories, and the separate regression coefficients measure the effect on wages as the districts get progressively further from London. Secondly, the districts more than 100 miles from London are used as the reference category, and are thus the basis for comparison with wages in districts nearer to the capital.

10.1.2 Dummy variables as a change in the intercept

In this section we will extend the discussion of dummy variables to show how the coefficients on the dummy variables can be interpreted as a change in the *intercept* of the regression equation; in this context they are sometimes referred to as **intercept dummy variables.** This will clarify the procedure and will also be helpful as a preliminary to the slightly more complex aspects in the discussion of additional dummy variables below.

[c] Boyer, 'The influence of London', pp. 266 and 267.

Consider, for example, an enquiry into a sample of workers from which information can be derived on INCOME (measured in $ per week); EDUC, a continuous variable for the number of years of education each worker had received beyond primary school; and a nominal category, race, distinguishing whether the workers were BLACK or WHITE.

The model could specify a linear relationship with INCOME as the dependent variable and two explanatory variables: EDUC and BLACK. The latter is the intercept dummy variable for race, with white workers as the reference category. We then have

$$INCOME = a + b_1 EDUC + b_2 BLACK + e \qquad (10.2)$$

EDUC thus measures the effect on INCOME of number of years of education, while controlling for race. BLACK measures the *difference* it makes to INCOME being a black rather than a white worker, while holding EDUC constant (i.e. effectively assuming both black and white workers have had the same number of years of education).

If the regression equation is computed in the usual way there will be a constant, a, and coefficients for EDUC and BLACK. Imagine that the latter turns out to be –40. There are effectively two versions of the regression equation. For all white workers, BLACK = 0, so –40 × 0 = 0, and the equation reduces to

$$INCOME = a + b_1 EDUC + e \qquad (10.3)$$

For all black workers, however, BLACK = 1, so –40 x 1 = – 40. Since this is a constant it can be added to (or, rather, because in this case it is negative, deducted from) the intercept, and the equation can be written as

$$INCOME = (a - 40) + b_1 EDUC + e \qquad (10.4)$$

If these two regressions are plotted on a graph (as in figure 10.1, using hypothetical figures) there are two parallel lines, one for white workers (whose incomes are marked by a cross) and one for black workers (marked by a square). The regression line for white workers has an intercept at a = 190, the one for black workers has an intercept at (a − 40) = 150. The difference in intercept thus represents the effect of being a black worker (controlling for EDUC). It indicates that a unit change in the dummy variable (from 0 for white workers to 1 for black workers) reduces INCOME for black workers as compared to white workers by $40 per week.

If the enquiry had subdivided the workers into four categories rather than two (say, white, Asian–American, African–American, and Hispanic), three dummy variables would be needed. There would then be four parallel lines, one for the reference category, and three others above or below that,

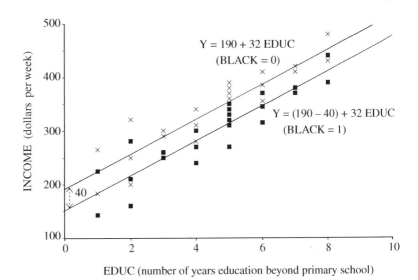

Figure 10.1 An intercept dummy variable

EDUC (number of years education beyond primary school)

their position relative to the intercept depending on the sign and size of the coefficients on the respective dummy variables.

10.1.3 Additional dummy variables

It may occur to the researcher that gender may also have an influence on INCOME. If information on this topic had been collected in the enquiry as well, the linear regression model could be reformulated with a second dummy variable for FEMALE, so that the reference category is now white males

$$INCOME = a + b_1 EDUC + b_2 BLACK + b_3 FEMALE + e \quad (10.5)$$

The workers can thus be subdivided into four categories, with the two dummy variables given the values of 1 or 0 as appropriate, and there would be a separate equation for each category. For example, the equation for white female workers would be

$$INCOME = a + b_1 EDUC + (b_2 \times 0) + (b_3 \times 1) + e \quad (10.6)$$

which reduces to

$$INCOME = a + b_1 EDUC + 0 + b_3 + e \quad (10.7)$$

The intercept for white female workers would thus be $(a + b_3)$. Treating the other three categories in the same way (and omitting the error term), the right-hand side of the four regressions can be summarized as

	Males	Females
White	$(a+0+0)+b_1 EDUC$	$(a+0+b_3)+b_1 EDUC$
Black	$(a+b_2+0)+b_1 EDUC$	$(a+b_2+b_3)+b_1 EDUC$

The intercept for white males is a and, as before, the coefficients b_2 and b_3 are added to this intercept to determine the difference it makes to INCOME if a worker is in one of the other categories (controlling for EDUC). Thus for any level of EDUC, INCOME for male black workers will differ from that for male white workers by b_2; INCOME for female white workers will differ by b_3; and INCOME for female black workers will differ by b_2+b_3. We might expect to find that both b_2 and b_3 are negative.[d]

10.1.4 Interaction between two dummy variables

It will be seen, however, that under this procedure INCOME for females is constrained so that it *always* differs from that for males by the amount of the single coefficient, b_3, regardless of whether the workers are black or white. An alternative procedure, which avoids this constraint, involves the introduction of **interaction terms**. These are a special type of dummy variable formed by *combining* variables, in this case two dummy variables.

In this example, three new dummy variables, combining the categories of race and gender, would be formed in place of the two previous ones for the separate categories. The regression model becomes

$$\text{INCOME}=a+b_1 EDUC+b_2 BLACK\text{–}MALE +$$
$$b_3 BLACK\text{–}FEMALE +$$
$$b_4 WHITE\text{–}FEMALE + e \tag{10.8}$$

The fourth category, white males, serves as the control.

In order to assign a value of 1 to these new compound variables, *both* elements must be satisfied. For example, BLACK–MALE will take a value of 1 only for workers who are both black and male; for all other workers it will be 0. With this approach the right-hand side values for the four categories (omitting the error term) are now

	Males	Females
White	$(a+0+0+0)+b_1 EDUC$	$(a+0+0+b_4)+b_1 EDUC$
Black	$(a+b_2+0+0)+b_1 EDUC$	$(a+0+b_3+0)+b_1 EDUC$

---

[d] For an application of this approach to the measure of wage discrimination against women in the United States see Claudia Goldin, *Understanding the Gender Gap. An Economic History of American Women*, Oxford University Press, 1990, pp. 84–7.

The difference in income between males and females is no longer forced to be the same regardless of race; it is now possible to determine by how much INCOME for each of the gender/race combinations will differ from that for white males (controlling for EDUC).

These interaction terms between intercept dummy variables need not be restricted to combinations of only two variables. If, for example, the enquiry had also assembled data on whether the workers were urban or rural it would be possible to form a term for categories such as female, black, rural, workers and to compare their income (controlling for EDUC) with a reference category of white, male, urban, workers.

10.1.5 Interaction between dummy and numerical variables

The previous subsection explained the formation of interaction terms between two or more dummy variables. For the example used, it was shown that this enables the researcher to determine (i) the effect on INCOME of number of years of education, while controlling for combinations of race and gender, and (ii) the *difference* it makes to INCOME being in any one of the race/gender combinations compared to the income of a white, male worker, while holding EDUC constant.

This is effectively a model of a single linear relationship between INCOME and EDUC, with a different intercept and regression line for each race/gender category. If the regression lines were plotted there would be three parallel lines, i.e. they would all have the same *slope*, given in the example above by b_1, the common coefficient on EDUC for all the different categories.

It may be, however, that the researcher thinks that there should be a *different* linear relationship between INCOME and EDUC for the different categories. In this case it is not only the intercepts that would shift as the categories changed, there would also be a change in the slope of the regression line.

This can be done by introducing a **slope dummy variable**, formed by *interacting a dummy variable with a numerical or continuous variable*. To simplify the illustration we will omit the gender category and revert to the initial linear relationship, repeating (10.2)

$$INCOME = a + b_1 EDUC + b_2 BLACK + e \qquad (10.2)$$

We now modify this by introducing a further **interaction term** or **interaction variable**, obtained by *multiplying* the numerical variable by the dummy variable.[1] The modified (but still linear) relationship is then

$$INCOME = a + b_1 EDUC + b_2 BLACK + b_3 EDUC \times BLACK + e \qquad (10.9)$$

For all white workers, both BLACK and EDUC×BLACK are zero. So the coefficients b_2 and b_3 are eliminated and the coefficient on EDUC remains as b_1. However, for all black workers BLACK = 1, and so EDUC× BLACK = EDUC. The intercept becomes $(a + b_2)$, and the coefficient on EDUC becomes $(b_1 + b_3)$.

The regression for white workers thus reduces to

$$\text{INCOME} = a + b_1 \text{EDUC} + e \qquad (10.10a)$$

whereas that for black workers is

$$\text{INCOME} = (a + b_2) + (b_1 + b_3)\text{EDUC} + e \qquad (10.10b)$$

To illustrate this we use another hypothetical data set. For white workers the details are exactly the same as for figure 10.1, but for black workers they are different. Fitting the regression line corresponding to (10.9) we get the following results. For white workers

$$\text{INCOME} = 190 + 32 \text{ EDUC}$$

and for black workers

$$\text{INCOME} = 190 + 32 \text{ EDUC} - 65 \text{ BLACK} - 5 \text{ EDUC} \times \text{BLACK}$$
$$= (190 - 65) + 27 \text{ EDUC}$$

The corresponding regression lines for the separate groups are shown in figure 10.2. As can be seen, the line for black workers has both a different intercept and a different slope.

The degree of discrimination revealed by this second data set is thus greater than that in the data underlying figure 10.1. In that case each additional year of post-primary education had the same effect on the incomes of the two groups of workers: incomes rose by \$32 for each extra year. In figure 10.2 that is still true for white workers, but for black workers the return to an extra year of education is only \$27. In addition when we control for the effects of education there is a bigger gap: the difference between the two intercepts is now \$65 rather than \$40.

However, this formulation of the two regression lines immediately raises an awkward question: has anything been achieved by working through the procedure for interacting a dummy variable with a numerical variable? We have simply ended with two separate regressions. Why could we not simply have formed two separate regressions to begin with?

The answer is that *in this case* we would get exactly the same estimates from the regression with the EDUC×BLACK interaction term as we would from two separate regressions, one for white and a second for black workers. In order for it to be worthwhile using the interaction between a

Figure 10.2 A slope and an intercept dummy variable

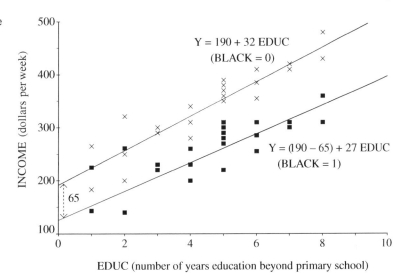

INCOME (dollars per week)

$Y = 190 + 32$ EDUC
(BLACK = 0)

$Y = (190 - 65) + 27$ EDUC
(BLACK = 1)

65

EDUC (number of years education beyond primary school)

numerical variable and a dummy variable, the regression model must include at least *one other numerical variable that is not interacted*. To illustrate this we could add an additional explanatory variable to (10.2) to cover experience (EXP), measured by the length of time each worker has held his/her current job.

If EXP is not interacted with BLACK, the slope coefficient for EXP is assumed to be the same for both groups of workers: INCOME for a black worker is assumed to benefit in exactly the same way from an extra year of experience as for a white worker. This restriction would *not* be imposed if two separate regressions were estimated, and the parameters derived from the separate models would be less **efficient** (as defined at the end of §9.2.4) than those produced by the single equation with an interaction term for the other numerical variable (EDUC).

10.2 Lagged variables

In all our previous discussions of time-series regressions we have implicitly assumed that all the observations relate to the same year. What do we do if we think it appropriate to include among the explanatory variables a variable referring to an earlier year, say 1949, when the dependent variable and the other explanatory variables all refer to 1950?

For example, an economic historian might consider that the expenditure on new machinery (INV) undertaken by firms in any year depends partly on the cost of borrowing as measured by the current interest rate

(INT) and partly on the value of goods sold (SALES) in the *previous year*. Using the subscripts t for the current year, and $t-1$ for the year one before that, the regression would be specified as

$$INV_t = a + b_1 INT_t + b_2 SALES_{t-1} + e_t \qquad (10.11)$$

$SALES_{t-1}$ is an example of what is known as a **lagged variable**. Lagged variables are treated in exactly the same way as any other explanatory variables and in a simple model such as the above do not require any special procedures. Their use is not restricted to annual time periods; the periods might equally be months or quarters if the required data are available.

When the effects of a variable are spread over several time periods in this way the resulting model is known as a **distributed lag model**. Such models are particularly common in economic analysis, where it is assumed that firms, households, or other agents need time to assemble and react to the information which influences their actions. However, these models might also be used in other contexts.

For example, a political historian might think that voters' political choices are influenced by the economic conditions they experienced in the year before an election and not just by the conditions prevailing in the year of the election. She might then model this by including lagged values of relevant economic variables, such as income or inflation.[2] Other possible explanatory variables reflecting successes or failures in foreign policy, or major political scandals, might be similarly lagged.

One question that is immediately posed by such models is the length of time over which this influence from the past is effective. One assumption, which avoids the need to select a specific period, is that the effects last forever: all previous periods are relevant. This is known as an **infinite** distributed lag model. Alternatively, the researcher may assume that the effect lasts for only a fixed period of time, say five years.

For example, the model for INV in (10.11) might be altered to specify that INV is affected by SALES both in the current year and also in each of the five preceding years

$$INV_t = a + b_1 INT_t + b_2 SALES_t + b_3 SALES_{t-1} + b_4 SALES_{t-2} +$$
$$b_5 SALES_{t-3} + b_6 SALES_{t-4} + b_7 SALES_{t-5} + e_t \qquad (10.12)$$

However, the choice of five lagged values is rather arbitrary since the theory of investment on which the model is based does not really provide guidance on this issue. Furthermore, equations like this might be difficult to estimate for two reasons. First, each time period involves a separate regression coefficient, and thus one additional parameter that has to be estimated; and each one uses up one further degree of freedom. In addition, the use of lagged variables uses up observations at the beginning of the period. For example, if the data set starts in 1850 but one of the explanatory variables is lagged by five years, the first value for the dependent variable will be 1855, and the number of years in the sample is reduced by five. If the distributed lag stretches back over many periods, or if the sample is small, this could be a serious problem.

Secondly, it is likely that there will be a close linear relationship between SALES in the current year and SALES in each of the previous years, so that the model is subject to the technical problem known as **multicollinearity**.[e]

We will discuss one technique for circumventing these difficulties in §10.2.2, but before we come to that it will be convenient to discuss first the ways in which it is possible for the lagged value *of the dependent variable* to appear as an explanatory variable on the right-hand side of the regression equation.

10.2.1 Lagged dependent variables

There are two main ways in which a **lagged dependent variable** can enter the regression model as one of the *explanatory* variables. The first and most important is because the researcher considers that the level of the dependent variable in any one period may be *influenced by its own level in previous periods*.[f] The justification for this is the belief that there is a strong element of habit, persistence, or inertia underlying many decisions.

For example, a model might specify that household expenditure on consumption (CONSUMP) is influenced by household income (INCOME) in the current and previous periods and also by consumption in the previous period. The case for this would be partly that households seek to maintain the level and pattern of spending to which they are accustomed, and partly that they need time to determine whether any shock to their income is transitory or permanent. The model would thus have lagged values of both the dependent and explanatory variables

$$\text{CONSUMP}_t = a + b_1 \text{CONSUMP}_{t-1} + b_2 \text{INCOME}_t + b_3 \text{INCOME}_{t-1} + e_t \tag{10.13}$$

Similarly, in models of emigration it is common to assume that previous emigration is a powerful influence, a process known as 'chain migration'. Former migrants from one's own country may encourage the next

---

[e] Multicollinearity will be discussed more fully in §11.4.2.

[f] When a model assumes in this way that the dependent variable is influenced by its own past values this is referred to as **autoregression**. Special care is necessary when interpreting the results from such a model because the inclusion of a lagged dependent variable violates the assumptions underlying the standard OLS regression model. This issue is further discussed in §11.3.3.

generation to emigrate in a variety of ways. They can reduce some of the uncertainty involved in moving to a foreign country, they may send back money for fares, and they can help with accommodation and the search for employment when the new immigrants arrive.

In their study of Irish emigration to the United States, for example, Hatton and Williamson suggest that this important influence can be captured either by the lagged dependent variable or by a variable that measures the total stock of Irish emigrants already in the receiving countries.[8] In their test of the model they formulate to explain Irish emigration, they include both the lagged value of the dependent variable $IRISHMIG_{t-1}$, and the current value of the stock of migrants, $MIGSTOCK_t$.

To simplify the presentation here we will combine all their other explanatory variables into a single variable that we call OTHER, and this version of their model is thus

$$IRISHMIG_t = a + b_1 IRISHMIG_{t-1} + b_2 MIGSTOCK_t + b_3 OTHER_t + e_t \qquad (10.14)$$

The second way in which the lagged value of the dependent variables can appear as one of the explanatory variables is when an equation is transformed by mathematical manipulation. This is typically done in order to overcome some problem in the original regression equation. There are a number of procedures that have this result, and in §10.2.2 we shall look at one of these to illustrate how it leads to a role for the lagged value of the dependent variable on the *right-hand side* of the equation.

10.2.2 Distributed lag models

Recall in relation to (10.12) above that the introduction of many or all past values of an explanatory variable in addition to the current value could give rise to two problems: too few degrees of freedom, and multicollinearity between the different terms for the same variable, in that example between current SALES and SALES for each of the five previous years.

One way to overcome the first of these problems is to impose some particular pattern on the coefficients on the successive lagged terms for the explanatory variable. This pattern effectively incorporates the researcher's view as to how the impact of the successive values of the lagged term might change over time, and means that it is no longer necessary for these coefficients to be estimated by the regression equation; they are already given.

There are many ways in which this can be done. One of the most common is to assume that the coefficients *decline geometrically*.[3] Assume

---

[8] Timothy J. Hatton and Jeffrey G. Williamson, 'After the famine: emigration from Ireland, 1850–1913', *Journal of Economic History*, 53, 1993, pp. 581–3.

that λ (lower case Greek lambda) is the **rate of decline of the distributed lag** and is a positive number with a value greater than 0 but less than 1. We can incorporate this in an infinite version of (10.12)

$$INV_t = a + b_1 INT_t + b_2 SALES_t + b_2 \lambda SALES_{t-1} +$$
$$b_2 \lambda^2 SALES_{t-2} + \ldots + b_2 \lambda^n SALES_{t-n} + e_t \qquad (10.15)$$

Assume, for example, that $\lambda = 0.5$. Then $\lambda^2 = 0.25$, $\lambda^3 = 0.125$, $\lambda^4 = 0.0625$, and so on. The closer λ is to 1, the slower the rate of decline in the coefficients on the successive terms for the lagged explanatory variable; the closer it is to zero, the more rapid the decline. The result of choosing this pattern is thus that the effect of more distant terms becomes progressively weaker, which in many contexts seems intuitively plausible. It would not require many periods before the effect of the lagged explanatory variable was so negligible that it could effectively be ignored.

Whereas (10.12) required the estimation of eight parameters: an intercept and seven regression coefficients, b_1 to b_7, (10.15) requires only four. These are the intercept, the coefficients b_1 on INT and b_2 on SALES, and λ. The problem of losing too many degrees of freedom has thus been reduced or eliminated, and the precise number of lagged periods to include in the model has effectively been finessed. However, it would still be an extremely difficult model to estimate, and because the parameters b_2 and λ are multiplied together it could not be done by the standard OLS procedure.

Fortunately, there is an ingenious way out of this problem, known in honour of its author as **Koyck's transformation**. This is described in panel 10.1 and leads to the following version of the model

$$INV_t = (1 - \lambda)a + b_2 SALES_t + \lambda INV_{t-1} + (e_t - \lambda e_{t-1}) \qquad (10.19)$$

The transformation has thus achieved a simple linear relationship, and solves all three of the problems encountered above:

- There are only three parameters to be estimated: the intercept, a; the regression coefficient on current SALES, b_2; and the rate of decline of the distributed lag, λ.
- The successive values of the lagged explanatory variable have been eliminated from the model so there is no longer a problem of multicollinearity.
- It is not necessary for the researcher to specify the precise length of the distributed lag.

A further notable feature of (10.19) is that, as indicated at the end of §10.2.1, the manipulation or transformation of the equation has had the result of entering the lagged value of the dependent variable (INV_{t-1}) as one of the explanatory variables. The interpretation of the regression coefficients on this and other terms in the model is discussed in §12.3.1.

There is inevitably a price to be paid for the substantial advantages gained from this transformation and the new model raises a number of technical issues in relation to the assumptions underlying the standard estimating procedures. Discussion of these technicalities would, however, take us beyond the scope of this book.[4]

Panel 10.1   Koyck's transformation

To see how Koyck's transformation can be applied we will simplify equation 10.15 by omitting the other explanatory variable, INT. The model becomes

$$INV_t = a + b_2 SALES_t + b_2 \lambda SALES_{t-1} + b_2 \lambda^2 SALES_{t-2} + \ldots$$
$$+ b_2 \lambda^n SALES_{t-n} + e_t$$
$$= a + b_2 (SALES_t + \lambda SALES_{t-1}$$
$$+ \lambda^2 SALES_{t-2} + \ldots + \lambda^n SALES_{t-n}) + e_t \qquad (10.16)$$

It follows, that there must be an exactly corresponding relationship for INV in year $t-1$

$$INV_{t-1} = a + b_2 (SALES_{t-1} + \lambda SALES_{t-2} + \lambda^2 SALES_{t-3} + \ldots$$
$$+ \lambda^n SALES_{t-n}) + e_{t-1} \qquad (10.17)$$

We come now to the transformation or manipulation. If every term in (10.17) is multiplied by λ, and the resulting equation then deducted from (10.16), we get

$$INV_t - \lambda INV_{t-1} = [a + b_2 (SALES_t + \lambda SALES_{t-1} +$$
$$\lambda^2 SALES_{t-2} + \ldots + \lambda^n SALES_{t-n}) + e_t] -$$
$$[\lambda a + b_2 (\lambda SALES_{t-1} + \lambda^2 SALES_{t-2} +$$
$$\lambda^3 SALES_{t-3} + \ldots + \lambda^{n+1} SALES_{t-n} +$$
$$\lambda e_{t-1})] \qquad (10.18)$$

All except two of the terms in SALES cancel out, because $\lambda SALES_{t-1} - \lambda SALES_{t-1} = 0$, and similarly for all the other terms in SALES except the first ($SALES_t$) and last ($SALES_{t-n}$). The latter is so far in the distant past that its coefficient, λ^{n+1}, can effectively be treated as zero, leaving only the current year in the model.

If we now move the lagged term for INV_{t-1} from the left-hand side of (10.18) to the right-hand side (with the appropriate change in sign from $-$ to $+$), we have drastically reduced (10.16) to

$$INV_t = (1 - \lambda)a + b_2 SALES_t + \lambda INV_{t-1} + (e_t - \lambda e_{t-1})$$
$$(10.19)$$

Notes

[1]   We may note here that it is also possible to form an interaction variable as the product of two numerical variables. One way in which this can be done will be covered in §12.1, where we consider the possibility of specifying a non-linear relationship (such as a parabola) that includes X^2 as one of the explanatory variables. Since X^2 is obtained by multiplying a numerical variable, X, *by itself*, a squared term such as this can equally be thought of as a further type of interaction variable. The final type is then one in which one numerical variable is multiplied by another, as in the example of AGRIC and LAND which is discussed in §14.2.2. In both these forms of interaction variable the effect is that the slope of the regression relationship is changing *continuously*.

[2]   See, for example, Howard S. Bloom and H. Douglas Price, 'Voter response to short-run economic conditions: the asymmetric effect of prosperity and recession', *American Political Science Review*, 69, 1975, pp. 1240–54. Their model of voting in the United States from 1896 to 1970 included a measure of income designed to represent 'the change in the "average" voter's real spending power prior to each election'. The best available measure of income as perceived by the voter was judged to be the 'percentage change in real per capita personal income during the year *preceding* each election' (p. 1243, italics added).

[3]   This geometric pattern is also known as a **Koyck distributed lag**. This is an attractive specification of the influence of past events at a constant rate over time. However, this may not be the most appropriate form of lag. There are many other patterns which have been suggested, including an arithmetic lag, in which the impacts declines linearly, and a polynomial lag, which can take various shapes, for example one in which the impact first rises for earlier values of the variable and then falls.

   To illustrate this last pattern, consider a change in the rate of interest that is thought to build up to its maximum effect on INV over two years and then to die away. The appropriate polynomial for a model with INV_t as the dependent variable would make the effect larger for a change in period $t-1$ than for one in t, larger still for a change in $t-2$ than for one in $t-1$, but then progressively smaller for a change in $t-3$ and all earlier periods.

[4]   There is a further point that might be made. Although Koyck's transformation solves certain problems, it is purely a mathematical manipulation and can be criticized because it does not have any theoretical justification. There are, however, a number of alternative models that do have a basis in economic theory, including the adaptive expectations model and the stock adjustment (or partial adjustment) model. Economic historians can find further discussion of these models in most econometric textbooks.

10.3 Exercises for chapter 10

1. You are setting up a model of the relationship between voter turnout by US state and a series of state-specific characteristics (such as average income per head; age distribution of the population; racial composition of

the population; share of union workers in the labour force; size of the government sector in the economy). The data for the model are drawn from five successive elections between 1968 and 1984; a number of the explanatory variables are in the form of dummy variables. Specify the dummy variables for the regression if:

(i) The age distribution of the population distinguishes 18–24-year-olds; 24–45-year-olds; 45–65-year-olds; over 65-year-olds.

(ii) The racial composition distinguishes Caucasian; African–American; and Asian–American.

(iii) The year of the vote is being tested as an independent cause of variation in voter turnout.

(iv) You wish to test whether turnout varies by age differently from election to election.

(v) You wish to test whether unionization of the government sector affects election outcomes.

2. Let us imagine that a historian believes that certain counties were more generous in their provision of poor relief than others and that this is a significant explanation of the variation in relief payments across Southern parishes. She finds qualitative support for this hypothesis for Sussex in the archives.

Use the dummy variable technique to test the hypothesis that Sussex parishes were more generous than all others, holding other parish characteristics constant. What do you find? Does the researcher's insight stand up to statistical scrutiny? What is the impact on the coefficients and standard errors on the other variables in the Boyer equation?

3. The researcher, emboldened by her findings, sets out to test the more general hypothesis that county was an important determinant of variation across all Southern parishes.

Once again, use the dummy variable procedure to test this hypothesis. Be certain to exclude one county to avoid the dummy variable trap. Which county did you choose as the default and why? Do the coefficients and standard errors on the additional variables bear out the researcher's hypothesis? How do you interpret the size and signs of the coefficients?

Examine the coefficients and standard errors on the other variables. Do these new results cause you to re-evaluate Boyer's interpretation?

4. In §10.1.1, we reported the results of Boyer's analysis of the influence of proximity to London on agricultural wage levels in Southern England in 1903. Use the dummy variable procedure to repeat the exercise for 1831, using the information in Boyer's relief data set on agricultural wages (INCOME), distance from LONDON, and specialization in GRAIN

production. In order to ensure consistency in variable definition over time, you will need to construct the following variables:

WAGE, which can be calculated by dividing INCOME by 2.6 to convert annual income in pounds to the weekly wage in shillings

GRAIND, which is equal to 1 if the value of the continuous variable GRAIN is greater than 20, and 0 otherwise

LON 0–25, which is equal to 1 if the distance from London is less than 25 miles and 0 otherwise

LON 25-50, which is equal to 1 if the distance from London is ⩾25 miles but <50 miles, and 0 otherwise

LON 50-75, which is equal to 1 if the distance from London is ⩾50 miles but <75 miles, and 0 otherwise

LON 75–100, which is equal to 1 if the distance from London is ⩾75 miles but <100 miles, and 0 otherwise.

Compare your results to those reproduced in the text. Was the influence of London stronger or weaker in 1831 than in 1903? Is the wage gradient steeper or shallower? Is the influence of grain specialization similar? How might you account for any differences?

5. How might you set up the model in question 4 to determine whether the influence of grain on agricultural wages varied by distance from London? Generate the appropriate new variables and test the hypothesis by regression. (*Hint*: re-read §10.1.4 on interactive dummy variables.) Report your results.

6. Benjamin and Kochin, in their analysis of British unemployment between 1920 and 1938, estimated the following equation:

$$UNEMP = a + b_1 \, BWRATIO + b_2 \, DEMAND + e$$

A critic of this model suggests that changes in the benefit–wage ratio on unemployment would not have been contemporaneous, as suggested in their formulation, but would have affected the labour market only after a lag of one year.

(i) Use the data on the web site to test the hypothesis. Report your findings.

(ii) How might you extend the model to test whether the impact of both the benefit–wage ratio and the DEMAND variable on unemployment was concentrated in the current rather than the previous year, using only a single regression? Run the appropriate regression and report and interpret your results.

7. What lag structure (including the number of lags, and for which periods), if any, would you recommend adopting in the following models?

(i) A quarterly version of Benjamin and Kochin's unemployment model, in which data are available four times a year.

(ii) A model of US presidential elections, in which the aim is to understand the vote share of a sitting President by county.

(iii) A model explaining the level of the Irish migrant stock in Australia, 1880-1913.

(iv) A model explaining individual earnings relative to each worker's level of schooling and work experience.

(v) A model explaining the impact of the Stock Market collapse of October 1987 on later values of the Dow–Jones (or FTSE) index of share prices.

8. Hatton and Williamson, in their time-series analysis of Irish emigration, 1877–1913, estimate the following equation:

$$\text{IRISHMIG}_t = a + b_1 \log \text{EMPFOR}_t + b_2 \Delta \log \text{EMPFOR}_{t-1} +$$
$$b3 \log \text{EMPDOM}_{t-1} + b_4 \log \text{IRWRATIO}_{t-1} +$$
$$b_5 \text{MIGSTOCK}_t + b_6 \text{IRISHMIG}_{t-1} + e$$

(i) Using the data on the web site, estimate the regression, making sure that you can retrieve the same results as reproduced in table 14.1. (*Hint*: be careful to take logs of the variables where necessary and also to use lagged variables where necessary.)

(ii) Now re-estimate the equation to determine the effect of assuming that the impact of the migrant stock is also lagged by one year. How much difference does it make to the value and statistical significance of the coefficients on MIGSTOCK and the other variables?

(iii) The lag of the dependent variable is included in the estimating equation. Why? What would be the impact on the equation if this variable were dropped? Report the impact on the coefficients and statistical significance of the variables in the model. Also report the impact on the regression diagnostics, such as the R^2 and the standard error of the equation.

What do these differences suggest about the importance of the lagged dependent variable to Hatton and Williamson's interpretation of Irish emigration, 1877–1913?

9. A critic of Hatton and Williamson's cross-section model of Irish migration by county suggests that the model fails to take chain migration into account. The suggestion is that emigration from each county will tend to be heavily influenced by the level of county emigration 10 years earlier.

Reconfigure the Hatton–Williamson model to test the hypothesis. How does the addition of lagged values of CNTYMIG for 1891, 1901, and 1911 affect our understanding of the process of migration? Is there evidence of a 'chain' at work? Is the impact of other variables substantially altered? Is the revision persuasive? (*Hint*: to produce the value of CNTYMIG, lagged 10 years, instruct the computer to construct a new variable (e.g. LAGMIG) which will be equal to the value of CNTYMIG lagged 32 observations.)

10. A researcher reports the results from a regression of expenditure on new machinery on sales and the interest rate as follows:

$$INV_t = 155.3 + 15.6 \, INT_t + 20.3 \, SALES_{t-1}$$

where the variables are as defined in §10.2. It is unclear from the discussion of these results whether the relationship between investment and sales is to be interpreted as a Koyck distributed lag model, in which this year's investment is determined by the history of sales over many previous years, or as a statement that this period's investment depends on last year's sales.

As a commentator on these results, how would you interpret the coefficients on both INT and SALES if the underlying relationship between INV and SALES were (a) a one-period lag, or (b) an infinite distributed lag?

Violating the assumptions of the classical linear regression model

We have thus far been developing the methodology of classical linear regression (CLR) using the ordinary least squares (OLS) system of estimation. This is a very powerful technique for uncovering the relationships among variables. Yet it has its limitations. It is clearly important to understand what these limitations are, to see how they affect the outcomes of the regression, and to suggest some procedures both to identify and to correct for these effects. That is the purpose of this chapter.

11.1 The assumptions of the classical linear regression model

The best way to proceed is first to indicate the main criteria that a model must satisfy in order to qualify as a good estimator, that is, to be what the econometricians call the **best linear unbiased estimator** (BLUE), and then to state the conditions under which OLS methods meet these criteria.

We have previously defined BLUE in §9.2.4 but repeat it here for convenience. In the case of a regression coefficient, b, the mean of its sampling distribution is said to be **unbiased** if it is equal to the true (unknown) population coefficient, β. If the assumptions underlying an OLS regression model are correct, then the estimates of its regression coefficients satisfy this criterion.

This does not mean that the estimate formed from the particular sample we happen to have will equal the true β; only that the average of all the estimates we would get if we could repeat the sampling process an infinite number of times would do so. If there is more than one unbiased estimator, the one which is called the **best**, or the most **efficient**, is the one whose sampling distribution has the *smallest variance*, that is, is most closely concentrated around its mean.

The conditions required for OLS to satisfy the criteria for BLUE fall into three categories.

11.1.1   The model is correctly specified

The most fundamental assumption of the classical regression approach is that the relationship between the dependent variable (Y) and the explanatory variables $(X_1, X_2, ... X_n)$ is correctly modelled:

(a) The OLS approach assumes that the relationship between the dependent and explanatory variables is **linear.** In a simple bivariate regression, the regression line is a straight line; in a multivariate regression, the relationship between the dependent variable and each of the explanatory variables is a straight line (see §11.2.1).

(b) The list of explanatory variables is complete and none is redundant. There are no omissions of relevant explanators, no inclusion of irrelevant variables (see §11.2.2).

(c) The relationship between the dependent and explanatory variables is stable across all observations (whether across individuals or over time) (see §11.2.3).

11.1.2   The error term is appropriately specified

The relationship between dependent and explanatory variables is inexact. To begin with, the regression model is not trying to measure identities or formulas. Secondly, it is simply not possible to include all the variables that *may* influence an outcome. Finally, some observations may be measured imprecisely. The combination of all of these factors is that the observations (and their relationship to the dependent variable) are measured with error. In the OLS model, this **error** (or **disturbance**) **term,** *e*, is *assumed* to have certain properties:[a]

(a) The mean value of the error term across all observations is zero (see §11.3.1)

(b) Each of the error terms has the same variance (the assumption of **homoscedasticity**) (see §11.3.2)

(c) The individual error terms are uncorrelated with each other (see §11.3.3).

11.1.3   The variables are correctly measured and appropriately specified

The OLS model also relies upon certain assumptions about the nature of the dependent and explanatory variables. In particular, it assumes that:

---

[a] These three assumptions were previously stated in panel 9.1, together with the linearity assumption in paragraph (a) of §11.1.1.

(a) The explanatory variables are correctly measured, i.e. that they are not systematically distorted so as to be always too high or always too low (see §11.4.1).
(b) The explanatory variables are not systematically correlated with each other (they are not **collinear**) (see §11.4.2).
(c) The explanatory variables are not systematically correlated with the error term (see §11.4.3).

The rest of this chapter shows what happens when these various assumptions are not maintained. We shall also suggest some simple tools for detecting and correcting these violations of the classical linear regression model. However, there are two important points it is worth noting at the outset. First, not all deviations from the list of fundamental assumptions are equally disastrous. Second, not all violations are easily detectable or correctable. Some can be identified or corrected only with techniques far beyond the scope of this simple introduction; some cannot be corrected at all without finding new and better data.

11.2 Problems of model specification

11.2.1 Non-linear models

The OLS model assumes linear relationships between X and Y. But what if the relationship is non-linear? Figure 11.1 provides an extreme version of the problem, using fictional data on the marginal (extra) cost of producing an additional statistical textbook. The true relationship between cost (Y) and output (X) has a U-shape (one of a family of curves known as *parabolas*), but the regression line that we have estimated from the data is a straight line.

The results are evidently unsatisfactory. The coefficient on X is clearly **biased** from its true value; it is very poorly defined (the standard error will be very high); moreover, it is very sensitive to changes in the sample. Thus, if those observations beyond the vertical line ZZ were missing, the slope of the linear regression line would become negative. Certainly, this regression would be worse than useless for the textbook publisher, whose marketing and pricing policies would be severely distorted if they were based on this inappropriate model specification.

How does one detect non-linearities? When there are only two variables, the best starting point is to plot the **residuals from the regression** (the difference between the observed and predicted values of the dependent variable) and see if they show any obvious patterns. Thus, in our textbook analysis, the residuals when plotted against output will follow an inverted U-shape; against marginal cost, they will trace an inverted L-shape.

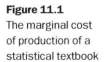

Figure 11.1
The marginal cost
of production of a
statistical textbook

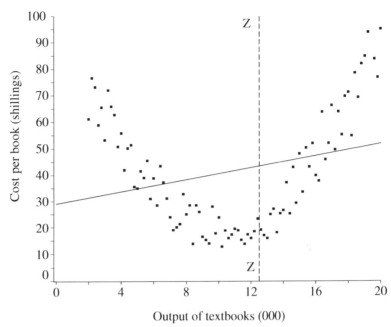

When there is more than one explanatory variable, this may not be a reliable methodology. In this case, the simplest method may be to split the sample into subgroups according to the size of the explanatory variable suspected of having a non-linear impact on Y, and run separate regressions for each subgroup. In the absence of non-linearities, the coefficients should not be significantly different from each other.

Not all non-linearities are as severe in form or consequence as the textbook example in figure 11.1. But without correction, all will produce biased and **inefficient** estimates of the 'true' relationships among the variables. Fortunately, most are amenable to the solution of transforming the variables. The procedures for doing this are explained and illustrated in detail in chapter 12 (§12.2).

11.2.2 Omitted and redundant variables

It is clearly not sensible to leave out variables that are important for understanding a historical development; it may not be so obvious why it matters if we add irrelevant variables. We can explain both with the aid of the Ballantine.

The Ballantine for examining the case of the **missing** variable is shown in figure 11.2 (a), on p. 528. The diagram indicates that the best model for estimating Y includes both X_1 and X_2. If the model is properly specified, the green area (and only the green area) will be used to estimate the impact of X_1 on Y; the orange area (and only the orange area), the impact of X_2 on Y; the brown area (for reasons given in §8.2.5) is ignored. In this case, the estimators will be unbiased. But, if X_2 is omitted, X_1 will use the information in both the green and brown areas to estimate the relationship with Y, generating biased regression coefficients.[b] The extent of the bias will be directly related to the extent to which the two circles overlap (i.e. the extent to which X_1 and X_2 are collinear).[c]

The Ballantine for examining the case of the **redundant** variable is shown in figure 11.2 (b), on p. 528. In this case, the true model for estimating Y uses only information about X_1; the coefficient is estimated using the information in the green and brown areas. However, an additional variable (or set of variables) X_2 is added spuriously; it has no real impact on Y, although because of its strong collinearity with X_1, it will overlap with Y in the brown (and orange) areas.

This overlap reduces the information available to the regression model for the estimation of the coefficient on X_1. The resulting coefficient is not biased (since the green area uses information unique to X_1), but it is inefficient: it has a higher variance than would result in the correctly specified model (the green area being smaller than the green–brown area, the coefficient is measured with too little information).

Thus, omission is more hazardous than redundancy. But this sort of logic may lead to 'kitchen-sink' regression analysis in which every measurable variable is included in a regression on the off-chance that it will turn out to be important. The problem, as may readily be imagined, is that the more redundant variables are added, the more the efficiency of the relevant explanatory variable will suffer. In the extreme, the coefficient on X_1 will have such a large standard error that it will appear to be statistically insignificant, and will be ignored when explaining the evolution of the dependent variable.[d]

[b] At the same time, because it uses more information to estimate the coefficient, it will have a smaller variance. This indicates the danger of comparing t-statistics from different regressions to determine which is the superior specification.

[c] Obviously, if X_1 and X_2 are orthogonal (see §8.2.5), the Ballantine circles will not overlap and omission of one variable will not generate bias in the evaluation of the other. If the researcher is interested only in a hypothesis test of the impact of X_1 on Y, the omission of orthogonal variables is acceptable. However, if the purpose is to explain the behaviour of Y, omission of X_2 will constitute a mis-specification since the model does not capture all the influences on Y.

[d] You may wish to add a fourth circle to the Ballantine of figure 11.2 (b) that intersects points A and B; this will reduce the total amount of information used to link X_1 to Y to a thin sliver, effectively reducing its explanatory power to almost nothing.

The appropriate antidote is the use of common sense. Only include those variables that can, for reasons of theory or history, be considered likely to affect the dependent variable. But at the same time never leave out something that is likely to be important. If needs be, use a proxy to capture an explanatory variable for which no actual data exists.[e]

Thus, if the aim of the regression is to model the growth and fluctuations of US imports over time, it would be essential to include a measure of the relative prices of domestic and imported goods. If such a term is excluded, the coefficients on the other variables (income, population, etc.) will be biased. If no such series has ever been constructed, it is vital that the researcher either undertakes the task of construction, or that he finds a substitute that moves together in a systematic way with the true relative price series (such as the relative price deflator of national incomes in the United States and the rest of the world).[f]

11.2.3 Unstable parameter values

Suppose that we are measuring the relationship between consumer demand for a luxury good (e.g. DVD players) and average household income. It is perfectly possible that there is a threshold level of income below which no households can afford the luxury good. Above that threshold, households will choose whether or not to purchase the good; the higher the income, the higher the proportion of households who make the choice. Thus, the demand curve will not be continuous across all income levels; there will be a distinct kink at the threshold level. Running a linear regression across all income groups will therefore produce a biased estimate of the coefficient on income (see figure 11.3 (b)).

Similarly, in the case of the relationship between benefits and unemployment in inter-war Britain, government policies setting the requirements for receiving the dole did not remain stable over time. In 1931, the government introduced the so-called Anomalies Regulations, which made it more difficult for certain categories of unemployed workers to claim benefits. For example, the burden of proof that someone was genuinely seeking work was shifted onto the claimants; single persons were expected to travel to seek work; and married women wishing to receive benefits had to satisfy substantially more demanding contributory requirements. Clearly, we would not expect the same relationship between BWRATIO and UNEMP to exist before and after the introduction of such restrictions.

---

[e] There are also formal statistical tests for omitted variables. These are discussed in advanced econometrics textbooks.

[f] More formally, the substitute should be collinear with the missing series; for further discussion see §11.4.2.

Figure 11.3
Illustration of the
use of dummy
variables to allow
for structural
changes

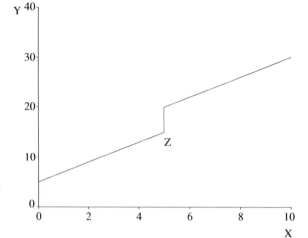

(a) Introduction of
an intercept dummy
variable

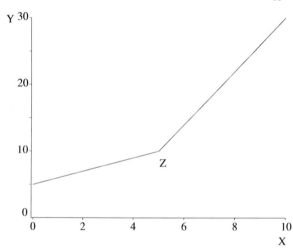

(b) Introduction of
a slope dummy
variable

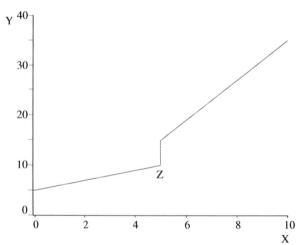

(c) Introduction of
both an intercept
and a slope dummy
variable

These are both examples of **structural change** in the parameter values of the system being modelled. Failure to incorporate evidence on structural change is an important source of error in the estimation of empirical models. In many cases (as in the example of British unemployment), a knowledge of history will reduce such errors. The timing of structural change will be known and can be factored into the basic regression. But not in all cases: in time-series analysis, it may not be known when such a regime change took place; in cross-section, a threshold effect may only be suspected. Moreover, it may be that a suspected structural break in the regression model turns out not to be important at all in the specification of the model.

How then does one determine whether there has been a structural break and whether it matters? Most tests involve splitting the sample into two (or more) subgroups: before and after the regime change in the case of time-series data, above and below the threshold in the case of cross-section data. The basis regression is then run on the subgroups and the results are compared.

The procedure followed most frequently is the **Chow test**, which runs an *F*-test on the two sub-samples in comparison to the pooled sample to determine if they are derived from the same underlying population. We will not here elaborate on the mechanics of the test; most statistical packages can be commanded to perform a Chow test. The packages will determine whether the model 'passes' the Chow test or not; if the *F*-statistic is deemed to be statistically significant, the regression fails the null hypothesis of parameter stability. The conclusion is then that there has been a structural break in the model, and that it matters.[1] We will reintroduce the Chow test in §14.1.2 when discussing parameter stability in relation to Benjamin and Kochin's model of inter-war unemployment.

What procedures are available for dealing with structural change? If there is a discrete structural change in the system (as in the case of the Anomalies Regulations) or a series of structural breaks over time, it is possible to use dummy variables to capture the change in the parameter values. As explained in §10.1, dummy variables can be used to alter the intercept of an equation, the slope of an equation, or both. Three simple cases are shown in figure 11.3.

In figure 11.3 (a) there is a change in the level of the variable Y at point Z. The slope of the relationship is the same before and after the structural break. In this case, an intercept dummy variable, taking the value 0 before the break and 1 thereafter, will be sufficient to capture the impact of the structural break on the system.

Thus, the model takes the following shape

$$Y_i = a_0 + a_1 D_i + b_1 X_i \tag{11.1}$$

where $D_i = 0$ if $X_i < X_t$
$ = 1$ if $X_i \geq X_t$

In figure 11.3 (b) the slope changes after the break (this is equivalent to the threshold effect of the DVD case). This is commonly referred to as a **piecewise linear regression**. In this case, it is necessary to add a slope dummy variable, obtained by the interaction of the relevant dummy variable and the explanatory (numerical) variable thought to be affected by the structural break. The dummy variable will have a value of 0 up to the threshold, and of 1 at and above it. In this case, the model takes the following shape

$$Y_i = a_0 + b_1 X_i + b_2 (X_i - X_t) D_i \tag{11.2}$$

where $D_i = 0$ if $X_i < X_t$
$ = 1$ if $X_i \geq X_t$

In figure 11.3 (c) the entire relationship changes after the break: both slope and intercept are different. It is therefore necessary to incorporate both an intercept dummy and a slope dummy. In this case, it is imperative that the regression also includes the untransformed variables (the constant and X). Thus, the model takes the following form

$$Y_i = a_0 + a_1 D_i + b_1 X_i + b_2 (X_i - X_t) D_i \tag{11.3}$$

where $D_i = 0$ if $X_i < X_t$
$ = 1$ if $X_i \geq X_t$

The dummy variables should be evaluated in the same way as any other variable in the regression. Clearly, if they are not statistically significant, the source of the structural change has been misdiagnosed. Alternatively, it may be that the Chow test is identifying some other problem in the construction of the model.

11.3 Problems of error specification

11.3.1 Non-zero errors

Although error terms with a mean value which is *not zero* are commonly cited as a violation of the basic assumptions of the CLR model, the only important consequence of a regression having a non-zero mean is that the coefficient on the constant (intercept) term will be biased. The slope coefficients are unaffected. As noted in §8.2.9, for many regression models the constant term has little or no significance (in some cases, indeed, it has no practical meaning at all). Clearly, where the constant does have a meaningful interpretation, the researcher needs to exercise care in evaluating whether the error term has a biased mean, but otherwise this violation can be safely ignored.

It is sometimes suggested that the CLR model requires that errors should also be *normally* distributed. This, however, is not the case. The OLS regression produces unbiased and efficient coefficient estimates (is BLUE) whether the errors are distributed normally or not. The only loss associated with non-normality is that the *t*- and *F*-statistics used for hypothesis testing can be applied only to large samples (say, above 30 observations). Thus, the problem arises only when a researcher is dealing with small samples (as, for example, when running regressions over annual observations between 1921 and 1938). But she should be cautious in such a situation in any case; there is more than one trap to jeopardize the unwary when data are scarce.

11.3.2 Heteroscedasticity

Heteroscedasticity is a complicated term that describes a fairly simple violation of the assumptions of classical linear regression methods. The CLR approach assumes that the *variance of the error term is equal across all observations*; this is known as **homoscedasticity** (equal spread). **Heteroscedasticity** (unequal spread) arises when the *variance of the error term differs* across observations.

In figure 11.4 it can easily be seen that the variance of the error (the breadth of the error distribution) in Y becomes progressively larger as X increases. This case of heteroscedastic errors may be compared to figure 9.1 (b), where the error term is shown, by assumption, as homoscedastic. Note that the violation of the CLR assumption occurs only when the error term shows a clear, systematic, pattern of distortion; random differences in the size of the error term across observations do not constitute heteroscedasticity.

Heteroscedasticity may arise for a number of reasons.

(a) In time-series analysis, it may arise because of a process of learning by experience, or, as econometricians commonly say, *error-learning*. If for example, the numbers of errors your class makes on statistics exams declines as you take more of them, the error term in a regression of

Figure 11.4
Heteroscedastic
error terms

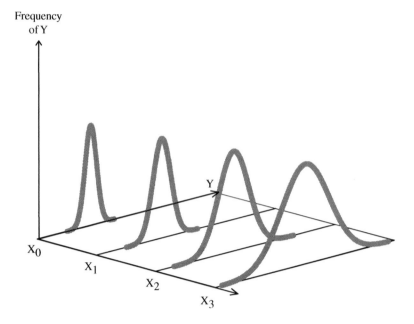

average class mark over time will be heteroscedastic. Similarly, if data collection methods in, for example, the recording of unemployment statistics improve over time, the error term of an equation seeking to explain the behaviour of unemployment will show heteroscedasticity.

The converse of this, decay in the quality of measurement over time, will also produce heteroscedastic errors; as will the impact of fatigue on productivity over time among individuals of varying robustness.

(b) In cross-section analysis, the most common source of heteroscedasticity originates in differences in scale or behaviour across reporting units. Thus, for example, the ratio of consumption expenditures to income tends to become more variable at higher incomes, as spending becomes more discretionary (the capacity of households to save rises with income, but different households exhibit differential levels of thrift).

Similarly, the dispersion of average local expenditures across parishes will tend to be greater in larger than in smaller counties, since the opportunity for divergent behaviour is greater, the larger the number of separate decision-makers.

In both cases, cross-section regressions applied to such data will be contaminated by heteroscedastic errors.

Regression coefficients produced under conditions of heteroscedasticity remain unbiased; however, they are inefficient, in that the variance associated with the coefficients will be larger than if the errors were homoscedastic. This will increase the confidence interval around any estimated coefficient, creating problems for testing hypotheses. In the extreme, variables that are statistically significant explanators of the dependent variable may be dismissed as irrelevant because their standard errors are too high, all because of the exaggerated impact of heteroscedasticity on the error term.

Because of this it is important to test for heteroscedasticity *before* testing for statistical significance. The first step is usually to examine the residuals from the estimating equation. These can be plotted against the (rank-ordered) level of whatever explanatory variable is thought to be responsible for distorting the error term. If the residuals show a distinct (upward or downward) trend on the graph, this is *prima facie* evidence of heteroscedasticity and needs closer scrutiny.

Formal tests are provided by most regression packages. The Goldfeld–Quandt, Breusch–Pagan, and White tests are all commonly employed, both to diagnose formally the presence of heteroscedasticity and, in the case of the White procedure, to create a heteroscedastic-corrected error term which permits the use of standard techniques for testing statistical significance. A similar test is used by Hatton and Williamson in their analysis of Irish emigration by county in the late nineteenth century (see §14.2.2).

11.3.3   Autocorrelation

The CLR approach requires that the errors associated with each observation are independent. If there is *a systematic relationship among the errors*, this is known as **autocorrelation**.

The most common environment for autocorrelation to occur is in time-series analysis. In this case, the error in one time period is influenced by the error in a previous period, which is in turn influenced by the error in a period before that, and so on. The structure of errors when mapped against time will show a systematic pattern, rather than a random distribution as required by the CLR model. Time-series autocorrelation is also referred to as **serial correlation**.

Serial correlation of errors happens if a shock to the system being described by the regression model creates echo or ripple effects over more than one period. A collapse of the stock market, for example, will reverberate through the financial and economic system for some time after its initial shock, because it takes time for market expectations to recover. Buyers and sellers of stocks may be more cautious in response to good economic news for some time to come; they may also be more sensitive to bad economic news in the future, making any after-shocks more devastating than would normally have been the case.

This example indicates that serial correlation may arise because of *inertia* (or path dependence), in which current behaviour is strongly influenced by past events. It may also occur because the economic system is slow to rebound from random shocks. The economy of the American South, for example, took a very long time to recover from the shock of the Civil War on the market-place. The plantation system of the cotton economy was severely disrupted by the war (and subsequent slave emancipation), which required a long period of institutional adjustment of market institutions after 1865. So, too, was the market for American cotton abroad, which faced competition from Brazilian and Egyptian suppliers who had begun to supply Britain during the Union blockade of Confederate exports.

Serial correlation may also arise for more mundane reasons. Data are often manipulated before publication in ways that create systematic interdependence among errors. When information is missing for certain observations, the gaps are often filled by interpolation between reported data points, or by extrapolation from known information. If a data series shows sharp peaks and troughs, it may be smoothed by the use of moving averages to reveal the underlying trend; similarly, if there are strong seasonal fluctuations in a series, researchers may have employed seasonal correction before publishing the data. In each of these cases, the errors are redistributed from their original (true) structure, and serial correlation results.

Some typical patterns of autocorrelated errors are shown in figure 11.5. Four types are displayed. In (a) and (b), each successive term is *positively* correlated to the last. In (a), the errors oscillate around a zero mean – this pattern might emerge when modelling a business cycle or some other system in which there are regular, fluctuating errors. In (b), the degree of correlation is higher and cumulating – the errors become consistently larger over time.

The cumulative effect is also seen in (c), but in reverse. Here the process starts with a large shock at the beginning of the period; the *negatively* correlated errors cause a gradual decumulation in the error term. Finally, (d) illustrates another pattern of negative serial correlation, consistent with a situation in which the aftermath of an original, positive shock follows a

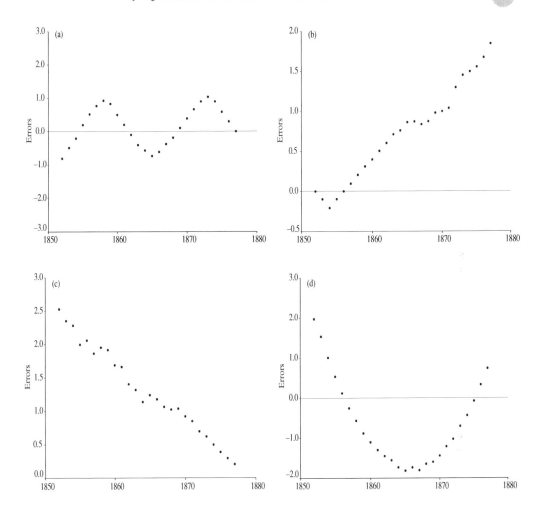

Figure 11.5

Typical patterns of autocorrelated errors

distinctly non-linear trajectory over time, diverging from the linear specification implicit in OLS regression.

Although autocorrelation is normally associated with time-series data, it may also crop up in cross-section analysis. In this case, the error associated with one observation (one Irish county, or one Poor Law district) is systematically related to the error in another observation (or observations). Such **spatial autocorrelation** could occur in migration analysis, for example, if there were information chains which linked one county (say, Dublin) to another (say, Limerick). In this case, a shock to the level of emigration of Dubliners would also increase emigration from Limerick. Similarly, if the authorities in charge of setting Poor Law rates in one Kent parish were influenced by rate-setting in other parishes in the county, it would no longer be appropriate to assume that the error term in a regression analysis of Poor Law rates was free of autocorrelation.[2]

The problem of autocorrelation for OLS regression with time-series data is illustrated in figure 11.6. In this case, we have assumed systematic positive serial correlation, such that the errors grow over time (as in figure 11.5 (b)). We have shown two possible outcomes relative to the true relationship between X and Y. In the top line, we have begun from the assumption that there is a positive shock to the relationship (i.e. the error term at time zero is positive); since the error in the next period is positively correlated with the original shock, it too will be positive, as will be the next, and so on. Thus, the estimated OLS regression line deviates progressively further from the true OLS line over time.

Because the error terms are systematically biased upwards, the measured observations are also larger than their true values (in the sense of the values predicted by the true underlying relationship between X and Y, as represented by the middle line). In the bottom line, we have assumed the same structure of autocorrelated errors, but imposed them from a different starting point in which the original shock was negative. Again, the error term shows a systematic bias from its non-zero mean, generating observations that are consistently and progressively too low relative to the true OLS line.[8]

It is quite clear that serial correlation creates biased estimates of the true relationship between X and Y. Moreover, for any given system of autocorrelation, the direction of bias is entirely dependent on the size and direction of the original shock to the system. Unless the serial correlation is eradicated, the results of any such regression may be severely misleading.

Autocorrelation is by far the most harmful of the mis-specifications of the error term; fortunately, it has proven to be among the easiest to diagnose and to take care of. The procedure for correcting autocorrelation is to identify the structure of autocorrelated errors and remove it from the error term, leaving only random errors behind.

As always, the first step is to diagnose the problem. This may be achieved by visual inspection of the residuals to identify any obvious pattern. The difficulty with visual inspection, of course, is less in determining whether a pattern exists than in deciding whether it is significant enough to warrant correction. However, most regression analyses provide a direct test, known

---

[8] The alternative regression lines gradually converge towards the true relationship because the influence of shocks tends to diminish over time.

Figure 11.6
Autocorrelation

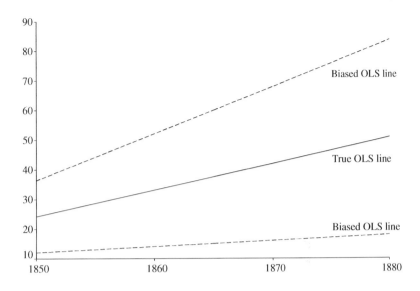

as the **Durbin–Watson**, which produces a test statistic (the DW or *d* statistic) that may be used as benchmark against which to judge the extent of serial correlation.

If there is no autocorrelation, the value of *d* will be approximately 2.0. The further *d* is from 2.0 the more probable it is that autocorrelation contaminates the data set. However, there is also an indeterminate range of *d*, in which autocorrelation may or may not exist. Given the seriousness of the outcome, it is probably best to be conservative and to correct for autocorrelation, even when the test statistic remains in the indeterminate range.

What if the Durbin–Watson test indicates autocorrelation? The first response should be to ensure that the problem is not one of model or variable mis-specification, as is frequently the case. Possible culprits include non-linearities or missing explanatory variables. If the researcher is satisfied that this is a *bona fide* case of autocorrelation, any of the standard correction procedures provided by the computer package may be applied.

The most common are the Cochrane–Orcutt procedure, Durbin's two-stage method, and the Hildreth–Lu technique. If the true underlying error term of the regression is normally distributed, each of these correcting procedures is equivalent. Each of the procedures generates both an estimate of the degree of autocorrelation (ρ, lower case Greek rho) as well as error-corrected coefficient estimates. In terms of figure 11.6, each procedure will take steps to reconstruct the error term to its random component, amend the observation estimates accordingly, and effectively rotate the regression line away from its biased location towards the true relationship.[3]

The Durbin–Watson procedure is an inappropriate test of autocorrelation *in the case of autoregression* (including autoregressive transformations of data such as the Koyck lag model; see §10.2.1). When a regression includes the lagged dependent variable as a regressor, the value of the Durbin–Watson statistic is biased towards 2, so that the null hypothesis of serial correlation would invariably be rejected. It is necessary therefore to find an alternative procedure.

A number of other procedures have been developed, of which one of the most frequently cited is the Breusch–Gordon Lagrange Multiplier test. We discuss this briefly in our analysis of Hatton and Williamson's work on Irish emigration in chapter 14, which uses this procedure to test for the extent of serial correlation in an autoregressive framework.[h]

11.3.4 Outliers

A potential further problem results when one (or more) of the errors in the error term is unusually large, relative to the rest of the distribution. While this does not formally contravene any of the assumptions of the CLR model it does have some negative consequences, especially for OLS estimation, and should not be ignored.

A potential warning sign of this problem is the presence of **outliers** in a sample. These are observations in a data set *that do not conform to the patterns suggested by the remainder of the sample.*[i] They are unusual observations.

Two types of outlier may be identified. One occurs when the value of an explanatory variable for an observation is very different from the remaining values in the sample. The other occurs when the dependent variable for an observation is very different from that predicted by the regression model (it is measured with a large residual).

Both types of outlier may seriously affect regression results. An unusual value of an explanatory variable relative to the rest of the sample may constitute a **leverage point**, giving it unusual influence over the value of the regression coefficient. Thus, in the bivariate model of figure 11.7 (a), most of the data points are clustered together in the centre of the distribution, while one observation clearly diverges. The slope of the OLS regression line in this example depends entirely on the position of that one data point.

---

[h] One test that was much used in previous econometric work to test for serial correlation in autoregression is Durbin's h. However, recent analysis suggests that this is an inappropriate procedure.

[i] For a preliminary analysis of the problem, see §3.1.3.

The second type of outlier is depicted in figure 11.7 (b), in which one observation is measured with a large error. The least squares method will cause the regression to pivot towards that observation, as it searches to minimize the aggregate value of the residuals ('the sum of squares'), thus distorting the results. Once again, a single observation has a large influence on the regression results.

Thus, the key issue is not whether an observation is an outlier *per se*, but whether it is an **influential observation** – i.e. whether it has unusual influence on the regression model.

Not all influential observations are equally harmful. Indeed, it is often pointed out that the existence of explanatory variables far from the centre of the sample is a good thing, because it gives the regression model more information with which to discern patterns in the relationship among variables. As a general rule, the more tightly clustered the values of a particular explanatory variable, the more poorly defined its coefficient estimate.

The real problem is not with leverage points (unless it can be shown that they are misleading), but with **rogue observations.** These are observations that do not belong with the rest of the data set, not because one or more of the explanatory variables were unusual, but rather because the model linking X and Y is not the same for that observation as for the rest of the data. Rogue observations carry the potential to distort parameter estimates, invalidate test statistics, and may lead to incorrect statistical inference.

How should we test for outliers and determine whether they are good or bad influences?

Clearly, the first step is to determine whether there are any *influential observations* in the data set. The crucial question is whether the regression model is significantly changed by the presence of any single observation. This can be addressed by comparing the model results with and without each data point in sequence. Tests can determine whether the absence of an observation causes any regression coefficient to change by a significant amount (the dfBeta test), or whether it significantly affects the measurement of the dependent variable (the dfFits test).

Let us say that a model has been tested and one or more observations are revealed to be influential. What should be done about them? It is tempting to discard the observations entirely. But, because of the potential value of leverage points, this should be resisted. Rogue observations are more clearly expendable. But how can they be distinguished?

Possible leverage points are often identified by graphing a scatter plot of the data and searching for unusual observations.[j] But there are clear limits

---

[j] This was done in figure 3.2, in our preliminary discussion of the problem.

Figure 11.7 Outliers

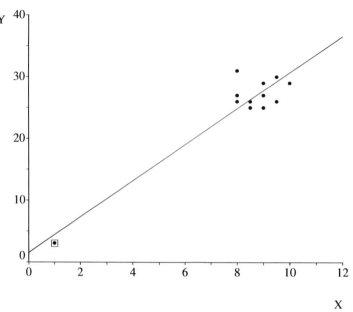

(a) An outlier as a leverage point

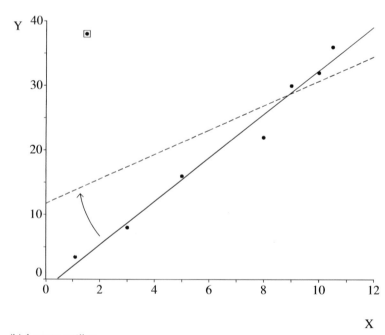

(b) A rogue outlier

to the usefulness of graphical aids, especially when dealing with more complicated multivariate models, where it may be difficult to spot an outlier by eyeballing. More helpful are tests (such as Hadi's) that systematically examine the distributional parameters of the data set and determine whether any observations fall into the upper or lower tails.

There are also a number of tests for outliers due to error in the estimating equation.[k] One is to include observation-specific dummies in the regression, and to test whether the coefficients on these are statistically significant. Ideally, this test should be run over all observations, in order to pick up any outlier – it is a test of the entire system, not just of one apparent odd case.

Regardless of the outcome of these tests, if outliers are identified, the best course is to abandon OLS estimation, and to utilize one of the various regression methods that have been developed to accommodate outliers. These are known as **robust regressions**, implying that their results are robust to problems of this sort. There are a variety of robust estimators, almost all of which use weighting techniques to reduce the emphasis on high-error observations. All are superior to OLS methods in this situation. They may be run over the entire data set and their results compared to the OLS specification. If the robust regression method generates very different results, it suggests some further problems with the data. For an illustration, see the robust regression we run in §14.1.2 to test the Benjamin and Kochin model.

11.4 Problems of variable specification

11.4.1 Errors in variables

Both the dependent and the explanatory variables may suffer from measurement errors, arising from incomplete information, mistakes in reporting or recording of information, or flawed responses to survey questions. Lord Stamp's famous quotation about the accuracy of official Indian statistics is worth quoting here, as it is broadly applicable to the historical statistics of many other countries:[l]

> The Government are very keen on amassing statistics – they collect them, add them, raise them to the nth power, take the cube root and prepare wonderful diagrams. But what you must never forget is that every one of those figures comes in the first instance from the *chowty dar* (village watchman), who just puts down what he damn well pleases.

---

[k] Visual inspection of the regression residuals is not one of them, since the pivoting of the OLS line to minimize the total sum of squares will tend to mask individually large residuals (see figure 11.7 (b)).

[l] Sir Josiah Stamp, *Some Economic Factors in Modern Life*, P. S. King & Son, 1929, p. 258.

This, fortunately, over-states the extent of the problem, but it is clearly right to be wary about the implications of any such errors in measurement on our regression results.

We can divide the problem between errors in the dependent variable and errors in the explanatory variables. In both cases, it is important to distinguish **stochastic** from **systematic** errors.

Stochastic errors, which originate in rounding of data, accidental inaccuracies in reporting or recording, or other random variability, may be thought of as increasing the size of the error term, while maintaining its fundamental characteristics of being symmetric around a zero mean.

Systematic errors, which arise from consistent distortion in the reporting or recording of information, are more troublesome. They clearly add to the size of the error term, but also destroy its fundamental characteristics. Statistical analysis can provide no solutions to this type of error, nor any guide to its possible impact on regression results, other than to say that any regression working with data that is systematically distorted will produce results that are also systematically distorted, perhaps to the point of uselessness.

It is therefore imperative that researchers should try to understand the data and any possible sources of such systematic error, and should attempt to make corrections to the data before running a regression. If, for example, it is known that the measurement of US imports was biased downwards between 1861 and 1865 because of blockade running during the Civil War, it is important that a correction be made for this before running a regression on (say) the relationship of imports to incomes and relative prices over 1840–1900. This correction might be made by adding 20 per cent to the level of imports in that period (the best guess of the extent of smuggling). Since the correction is a best guess, it will obviously be imprecise. It might be thought that this is merely substituting one error for another. However, there is a crucial difference: it is substituting a stochastic for a systematic error, and this is clearly a move in the right direction.

Similarly, if it is known that a vital explanatory variable is missing from a data set, it is imperative that a proxy be introduced to capture its effect on the dependent variable. If this is not done, all the other explanatory variables will be biased. The proxy, once again, cannot be measured with absolute accuracy, but if it is properly chosen, the added error it introduces to the regression will be stochastic, and its addition will correct for the systematic error created by the absence of the vital explanatory variable.

In what follows, we assume that systematic errors have been expunged and that the only remaining errors in variables are random or stochastic.

Error measurement in the *dependent* variable is not very important. The error term will be larger, suggesting an increase in the imprecision of the regression as a whole, which will show up as a fall in the R^2. The standard errors of the regression coefficients will be higher, leading to smaller *t*-statistics, but the coefficients themselves will be unbiased.

Error measurement in the *explanatory* variables is more problematical. The error is added to the error term. This not only makes it larger and the regression less precise, it also destroys the fundamental assumption that the error term is independent of the explanatory variables. Clearly, if X is in error and this error is added to *e*, then X and *e* must be correlated. When a regression is run over Y, X, and an error term, *e*, the coefficient on X will be biased; the greater the extent of measurement error, the greater the extent of the bias.

The solutions to errors-in-variables problems are far from perfect. The most common solution involves **instrumental variables (IV)** estimation.[m] An instrumental (or proxy) variable is one that is highly correlated to the explanatory variable in error, but which is not correlated with the error term of the equation. This sounds good in theory, but is very hard to apply in practice. Not only are good proxies difficult to find, it is even harder to determine that they are indeed independent of the error term, as required by theory. For this reason, many researchers are disposed to ignore the problem, on the basis that most measurement errors are small, and that attempting to correct them may cause more problems that leaving them alone.

There are however a couple of approaches which are worth pursuing in cases where the errors-in-variables problem is too large to ignore.

One possibility that is widely canvassed in time-series analysis is substituting a lagged value of the explanatory variable in question. Lagged and current values are likely to be correlated with each other; as long as their errors are not so correlated, the lagged variable will be an appropriate instrumental variable.

The most efficient approach to errors-in-variables problems in cross-section analysis is the Durbin method. This solution operates by ranking the explanatory variable by size (from 1, the lowest, to n, the highest) and using the rank order $(1, 2, \ldots, n)$ as its proxy replacement.

11.4.2 Multicollinearity

Multicollinearity is a term that was originally introduced to capture the effect of a perfect, or exact, linear relationship between two (or more) of the explanatory (right-hand) variables in a regression.

[m] Kennedy discusses the instrumental variables approach in a Ballantine framework in Peter E. Kennedy, *A Guide to Econometrics*, 3rd edn., Blackwell, 1992, pp. 143–5.

We have already met this problem in the form of the 'dummy variable trap' (see §10.1.1). The problem could also arise if, in a regression on county-level Irish migration, both AGRIC (the share of the labour force in agriculture) and NONAG (the share of the labour force employed outside agriculture) were included; or if a regression of aggregate relief payments per county were to include both the number of persons receiving relief and the average payment per recipient. But, as these examples make clear, the chances of encountering perfect linear relationships outside of design flaws in the model are rare.

Given the rarity of this situation, the term **multicollinearity** is now generally applied more broadly to situations in which *two or more explanatory variables are highly, rather than perfectly, correlated with each other.*

Within our data sets, there are numerous cases where we would expect to find significant correlations among variables. In the cross-section analysis of migration by Irish county, for example, we might well expect RELIEF and HOUSING to be significantly related to each other, as well as URBAN and AGRIC. Neither would be perfectly collinear, but statistical tests will reveal high correlation coefficients across the data set.

What will happen as a result of such multicollinearity? In the extreme case of perfect collinearity, the computer will generate coefficient estimates that are indeterminate with standard errors that are infinite. Indeed, if any regression produces such a result (see, for example, question 3), it is an indication that the researcher has either fallen prey to multicollinearity, or has fallen into the dummy variable trap. The solution is easy: the offending supernumerary variable must be identified and dropped from the list of right-hand variables.

What about the weaker, but more frequent, case of high but imperfect collinearity? The standard errors will be very high relative to the size of the coefficient, generating a low t-statistic, and suggesting that the explanatory power of the affected variable will be weak. The reported confidence interval around the measured coefficient will be large; frequently, it will include zero, suggesting that the variable is without statistical significance. In cases of true *multi*-collinearity (in which *more than two* explanatory variables are highly correlated with each other), the statistical significance of all affected variables will be pushed towards zero. At the same time, the overall explanatory power of the equation, as measured by R^2, may be very high (e.g. 0.9 or higher).

But not all cases of insignificant t-statistics can be blamed on multicollinearity. In many cases, it may simply be that there is no systematic relationship between X and Y. How can one distinguish between these two cases?

One indication is the presence of a high R^2 but few significant t-statistics. If the regression packet also reveals that the F-test rejects the null hypothesis that all coefficients are simultaneously zero, then that is added reason to be suspicious.

Another simple test is to examine the correlation coefficients across explanatory variables to see if they are jointly determined. An r of 0.75 or above is a frequently recommended diagnostic measure. But, more obviously, one should think about the variables being included in a model and try to avoid introducing explanatory variables that are clearly measuring the same, or very similar aspects, of a problem, hypothesis, or model.

A third strategy is to run a series of **stepwise** regressions, in which additional explanatory variables are added one at a time, recording all possible combinations of regression results. The changes in the coefficients at each permutation of the variables can be used to infer the structure of collinearity.

It is not always possible to avoid including two or more variables that are collinear. For example, in measuring the level of Irish emigration across counties, it is highly relevant to determine whether counties dominated by agriculture in the post-famine era were more likely to shed excess labour, and also to discover whether counties with a higher level of urbanization had better networks of communication and information that promoted emigration. Agriculture and urbanization may be highly (negatively) correlated with each other, but they are measuring different, separable factors that may have influenced migration, and the costs of including both are lower than the costs of leaving either out.

If we exclude either one, we jump from the frying pan of multicollinearity into the fire of specification bias. In the absence of one variable, the other would take on the added burden of explanation. Moreover, the coefficient on the variable left in would be biased (it would be a mix of the two 'true' coefficients). If both are left in, the coefficients remain unbiased, only their statistical significance is adversely affected. Of course, if one variable is left out and the other remains statistically insignificant, this might tell us that neither variable was important to begin with, even if they were collinear.

In the end, multicollinearity has to be accepted as an occupational hazard of running regressions. In some sense, its existence represents a minor morality play, indicating the limitation of quantitative methods and emphasizing that running regressions is no substitute for historical reasoning and appropriate, logical, model-building.

11.4.3 Simultaneity

If we run a regression of Y on X, we are asserting that Y is the dependent variable and X is its explanator. There is a strict causal link from the right-hand side of the equation to the left.

But (as we have already noted in §4.1.1) it is not difficult to think of circumstances when the relationship between X and Y is not unidirectional. In such cases, Y is influenced by X but X is also influenced by Y. The classic example relates to the market for a particular commodity. Increases in the supply of this commodity will tend to reduce its price (as its scarcity declines, people have to pay less to purchase it). At the same time, however, as the price of the commodity falls, its supply tends to drop (as producers shift towards manufacturing other items that will generate more revenue). Price is determined by supply (and demand); at the same time, supply (and demand) are determined by price.

This is the case of **simultaneous equations**, in which there is no truly independent, or **exogenous**, variable determined outside the framework of the model. All variables are, to a greater or lesser extent, **endogenous** – that is, determined within the model. The explanatory variables are no longer independent of the error term (since a shift in the error term directly changes the dependent variable, which in turn changes the explanatory variable because of the feed-back effect), thus violating one of the principal assumptions of the classical linear regression.

Simultaneity generates biased estimates of the relationship between X and Y. Moreover, the bias does not disappear as the sample size increases (it is therefore also inconsistent). In the extreme case, this arises because it is simply not possible to characterize the relationships between X and Y with a single estimating equation. The extent of bias will depend on the degree of correlation between the explanatory variables and the error term: the higher the correlation, the greater the bias.

What can be done about simultaneity? If the extent of such bias is small, it is tempting to do nothing. In other words, if the extent of feed-back from Y to X is very limited, the extent of correlation of the X and e will be small, and the bias in the estimated coefficient on X will also be small.

If, however, the problem is considered to be more significant, then one of two solutions may be followed. The first is to model the system more appropriately and then estimate the relationships as a system, rather than as a series of separate regressions. Such an approach, however, falls far beyond the limits of this book. A more limited response is to use single-equation methods, but to do so as a two-part procedure. This is the technique known as **two-stage least squares** (2SLS). It is a special case of the instrumental variables approach, which was introduced previously to indicate a solution to the errors-in-variables problem.[n]

The 2SLS procedure operates by locating an instrumental variable that can substitute for the biased explanatory variables in the simultaneous equation. The logic of the 2SLS procedure is to correct the biased explanatory variable by expunging it of the feed-back impact from the dependent variable. The best way to do this is to treat the contaminated variable (X) as itself a dependent variable, and regress it against the other explanatory variables in the system (since the formal dependent variable is not included in this first stage of the estimating system, the feed-back effects are necessarily excluded).[4]

The predicted values of X from this regression are then used either as instrumental variables in the original estimating equation, or alternatively (and more simply) substituted for the original values of X in the equation. The results from this second stage of the procedure will be consistent (i.e. unbiased over large samples); moreover, most econometricians consider it to be the best solution to the problem of simultaneity in small samples as well. In the final chapter (§15.1.1) we will examine the use of this technique by Boyer to deal with the problem of simultaneity in his model of the Poor Law and the agricultural labour market.

We have treated each of the violations of the CLR model separately. However, although our analysis implies that each problem of mis-specification may be treated in isolation, most practitioners recommend that more general strategies be employed that investigate the model as a whole. We discuss this and other aspects of best-practice model evaluation in §12.6.

Notes

[1] An alternative methodology for identifying structural breaks is to run the regression over one subgroup, and then apply the estimated coefficients to the known explanatory variables to forecast the value of the dependent variable in that part of the sample thought to lie beyond the structural break or threshold. The measured values are then compared to the forecast; if the measured values fall outside the predicted confidence interval, this is *prima facie* evidence of parameter change.

[2] Note that autocorrelation may occur because of specification problems in either model or variable selection. We observed an example of model mis-specification in our discussion of the U-shaped cost curve in §11.1.1, where we noted that the residuals from figure 11.1 follow an inverted U-shape against firm size. This situation is

[n] Both errors-in-variables and simultaneous equations raise the same problem of correlation between X and e, although the causal connection is significantly different in each case.

similar to that depicted in figure 11.5 (d) and represents a clear case of autocorrelation. A similar outcome may result from excluding a relevant explanator from a regression, especially if the missing variable follows a systematic pattern over time. In these cases, the correct procedure is to correct for the mis-specification; if this is done properly, it should also take care of the autocorrelation.

3   The analysis in this chapter assumes first-order autocorrelation, i.e. that the correlation across errors is from this period to the last, and so on. In quarterly data, it may be that the error in this quarter's data is correlated not to the last quarter's error, but to the error from one year (four quarters) ago. If this is the case, the DW statistic will not diagnose the problem. More advanced textbooks discuss the procedures appropriate to this situation.

4   Simultaneity is not to be confused with the situation of *reverse causation* in which a model is compromised because the causation really runs in the opposite direction from that specified by the researcher; see, for example, the discussion of such a possibility in relation to Benjamin and Kochin's model in §14.1.1. Reverse causation is a problem of model mis-specification that arises not from contraventions of the statistical properties of the CLR model, but rather from a fundamental misreading of the historical evidence. It is another instance of the principle that correlation need not imply causation.

11.5 Exercises for chapter 11

1. Take the Boyer birth rate data set and run a regression of

$$BRTHRATE = a + b_1 INCOME + b_2 DENSITY + b_3 INFTMORT +$$
$$+ b_4 CHILDAL3 + b_5 CHILDAL4 + b_6 CHILDAL5 +$$
$$b_7 HOUSING + b_8 ALLOTMNT + b_9 COTTIND + e.$$

(i) Check that your results are the same as those reprinted in table 15.2.

(ii) Instruct the computer to generate residuals (i.e. $\hat{Y}_i - Y_i$) from the estimating equation. Plot these residuals against the value of (a) BRTHRATE; (b) INCOME; and (c) POP.

Describe and interpret your findings. Are there any indications of model mis-specification in these results?

2. With the aid of the combined Boyer data set, construct a model that tests the importance of omitted and redundant variables for evaluating regressions. For example, in a model explaining INCOME, you might choose to exclude LONDON; alternatively, you might choose to include COUNTY (as a continuous, rather than as a dummy, variable). Be sure to include the impact of both problems on t-statistics and R^2. Is it correct to assert that the impact of omitted and redundant variables is larger, the smaller the number of explanatory variables included in the regression?

3. Examine the correlation matrix of variables in the Hatton–Williamson cross-section data set.

(i) Are there indications of possible multicollinearity in the matrix? Which variables strike you as especially of concern? What difference does it make if you remove one of the pair of variables from the equation? (*Hint*:you will need to remove each in turn.) Is the impact felt solely on that one variable or are others affected? Explain your findings.

(ii) Instruct the computer to construct a new variable, RURAL, which is equal to (1 − URBAN). Now run an equation of CNTYMIG on the appropriate variables, including both RURAL and URBAN. What is the result?

4. In your own words, write a paragraph making clear the distinction between the concepts of autocorrelation and autoregression.

5. Write a brief essay, identifying what you consider to be the most likely sources of error in historical statistics, being sure to indicate which errors are most serious for statistical analysis and how you might try to evaluate their significance.

6. A researcher uses the Boyer relief data set to construct a model explaining the cross-section pattern of wealth per person across early nineteenth-century English parishes. The model is simply a linear regression of WEALTH on three variables, LONDON, DENSITY, and GRAIN. Is there any reason to suspect that the data may be contaminated by heteroscedasticity?

As a preliminary test, you examine the variance of wealth across parishes in the data set. What do you find and how do your findings compare with your prior expectations? (*Hint*: instruct the computer to group the parish data by size, rather than trying to analyse the problem using parishes singly.)

As the next step, you re-examine the researcher's model for signs of heteroscedastic disturbances. Run the regression model and examine the residuals to determine whether there are signs of heteroscedasticity, and if so whether:

(a) they conform with the preliminary analysis of the variance of wealth
(b) they appear to be serious.

Write a brief report to explain your findings.

7. Test the Benjamin–Kochin data set for signs of serial correlation in:

(i) the behaviour of the benefit–wage ratio over time.

(ii) the behaviour of unemployment over time.

(iii) a regression of unemployment on the benefit–wage ratio.

Explain your method and interpret your findings.

8. Generate a scatter-plot of the Irish emigration rate for 1876–1913. Are there any years that appear idiosyncratic?

Develop a methodology for testing whether these are leverage points, rogue observations, or are not influential observations at all. Use the basic Hatton–Williamson time-series regression model as your basis for evaluating these observations.

What do you find and how, if at all, do your findings modify our understanding of the history of Irish migration in this period?

9. What is the appropriate dummy variable model for the following examples of structural change?

(i) Clerical workers earned the same income as artisans in London in 1913, but chose to live in more expensive housing.

(ii) Clerical workers earned the same income as artisans in London in 1913, but chose to spend more of each extra pound on housing.

(iii) The number of overseas holidays is higher for business executives than for clerical staff; fortunately for the executives, since they earn more, they can afford it.

(iv) The number of overseas holidays has increased significantly now that ordinary families can afford to travel abroad.

(v) Once ordinary families found they could afford to travel abroad, they gained a taste for foreign culture and the growth of overseas holidays has accelerated.

10. A critic of Hatton and Williamson's time-series analysis of Irish emigration, 1877–1913, notes that there was a structural break in the relationship between relative wages and emigration around 1896. Before 1896, relative wages were falling, whereas after 1896 they rose. However, Irish emigration rates continued to decline.

You wish to evaluate this critique. Take the following steps:

(i) Graph the pattern of relative wages to determine whether there is a change in behaviour after 1896.

(ii) Use a dummy variable test to determine whether there is a significant difference in the relationship between the relative wage and Irish emigration after 1896 (see chapter 10, question 8 for the basic regression equation).

The dummy variable test focuses on the stability of only one explanatory variable. You wish to evaluate the stability of the entire model over the period. In order to do so, you choose the Chow test. A working description of the test may be found in §14.1.2.

(iii) Use the Chow test to evaluate whether there is a structural break in the emigration model in 1896. What do you find?

(iv) Compare the coefficient estimates from the two subsamples with the regression run over the entire period.

What is your overall response to the critic? How, if at all, does this alter our understanding of Irish emigration in this period?

PART IV

Further topics in regression analysis

CHAPTER 12

Non-linear models and functional forms

In all the preceding discussion of regression and correlation, both simple and multiple, we have always assumed and tested for *linear* relationships. This means that in a simple bivariate regression, the regression line is always a straight line; in a multivariate regression, the relationship between the dependent variable and *each* of the explanatory variables is a straight line. However, we were warned in §11.1.1 that the results obtained by applying the classical linear regression (CLR) model might be seriously distorted if the actual relationship between the variables was *not* linear.

One illustration of such a **non-linear association** was given for cost data in figure 11.1. As another, we can take the familiar relationship between age and height. Data for males in Britain from birth to age 34 are plotted as a scatter diagram in figure 12.1.[1] We see a changing pattern with an initial period of rapid increase between birth and 2 years, then steady growth with a slight acceleration from about 12 to 16 years, and after that a period of stability from an age of about 16 or 17. If we extended the chart to later ages we would find a slight decrease in height from about 40 years of age, and this would become more pronounced as osteoporosis takes its toll in old age.

It is, of course, possible to fit a straight line to these data, but as figure 12.1 shows, this is clearly a very poor way to model this relationship over the whole of the life cycle, and it becomes increasingly less appropriate after age 16. Can we do better?

In §12.1 we discuss various forms that might be adopted to model non-linear relationships. Then in §12.2 we explain the procedures available for transforming some of these non-linear models so that they can be estimated by familiar OLS procedures. §12.3 is devoted to the interpretation of the regression coefficients when the basic relationship between the explanatory and dependent variables is non-linear, and §12.4 looks at the

Figure 12.1 A non-linear relationship between age and height

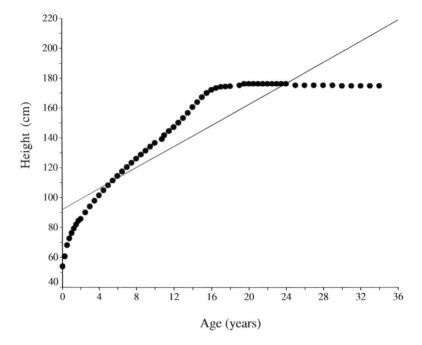

procedures for fitting log-linear and non-linear trends to time series. §12.5 reviews some of the principles that might guide a researcher in choosing to specify a particular non-linear relationship, and illustrates these by examples from the historical literature. Finally, §12.6 discusses how to judge whether the model specified represents a suitable way of interpreting the data and conforms to the empirical realities.

12.1 Different forms of non-linear relationships

Our study of linear relationships was built on models such as

$$Y = a + b_1X_1 - b_2X_2 + e \tag{12.1}$$

When we turn to non-linear models there are a number of possible alternatives, each of which specifies a different type of relationship. Some of the most common relationships are listed below; in each case a and b (and for (12.7), g and h) are constants, and X and Y are variables.[a]

---

[a] If any of these relationships were used to model data in regression analysis, the model would also have to include an error term.

- A quadratic curve or parabola $\quad Y = a + b_1 X + b_2 X^2$ $\hspace{2cm}$ (12.2)[b]

- A reciprocal or inverse curve $\quad Y = a + b\dfrac{1}{X}$ $\hspace{2cm}$ (12.3)

- A geometric curve $\hspace{2.5cm} Y = aX^b$ $\hspace{2cm}$ (12.4)

- A multivariate version of (12.4) $\;\; Y = aX_1^{b_1} X_2^{b_2}$ $\hspace{1.5cm}$ (12.5)[2]

- An exponential curve $\hspace{2cm} Y = ab^X$ $\hspace{2cm}$ (12.6)

- A logistic curve $\hspace{2.8cm} Y = \dfrac{h}{g + ab^x}$ $\hspace{1.7cm}$ (12.7)

Some illustrative non-linear relationships are shown in figures 12.2–12.6. The shape and position of many of these curves depend primarily on the value taken by the parameter, b. For example, the **geometric curve** in figure 12.2 slopes upwards and to the right if b is positive, but downward and to the left if b is negative. Similarly, the **exponential curve** in figure 12.3 slopes upward and to the right if b is greater than 1, but downward and to the left if b is positive but less than 1.

All four **reciprocal curves** in figure 12.4 are drawn for values of a equal +2 or −2, and for b equal +3 or −3. As X increases the curves fall if b is positive, and rise if it is negative, and they get progressively closer to the value of the a, though they never quite reach it.[c]

The crucial parameters governing the shape of the four **quadratic curves** shown in figure 12.5 are b_1 and b_2. The curves depicted in figure 12.5 (a) slope upwards if both parameters are positive, and slope downwards if both are negative. In figure 12.5(b), we have drawn two curves for which the parameters have opposite signs. The left-hand curve has a positive value of b_1 and a negative value of b_2; the right-hand curve has a negative value of b_1 and a positive value of b_2. The intercept is determined by the value of a, in the same manner as with a linear regression.[d]

The slope of each curve is determined by the relative value of b_1 and b_2, in the form of $(b_1 - 2 b_2 X)$. For the two curves in figure 12.5 (a), the higher the value of this expression, the steeper the slope. The fact that X is

---

[b] Equation (12.2) has a single explanatory variable, X, which appears as X and also squared. It is one of a family of curves (known as *polynomials*). A quadratic might have additional explanatory variables (X_2, X_3, and so on). A higher-order polynomial will have higher powers than X^2; for example, the cubic equation will have a term in X^3, and the model might be: $Y = a + b_1 X_1 + b_2 X_2^3$. Any polynomial will be non-linear.

[c] The mathematical name for a curve such as this, that approaches progressively closer to a line without ever reaching it, is an asymptote.

[d] In each case, we have set a = 400; $b_1 = 45$; and $b_2 = 1.5$. Only the signs have been changed.

Figure 12.2
Geometric curves:
$Y = aX^b$

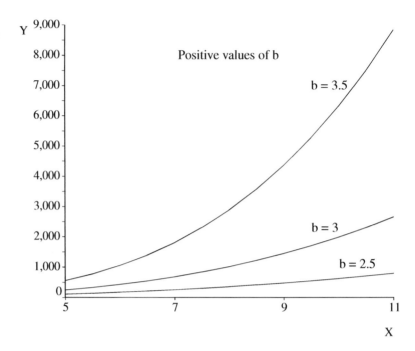

Positive values of b

b = 3.5

b = 3

b = 2.5

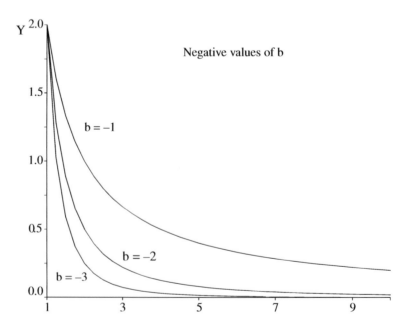

Negative values of b

b = −1

b = −2

b = −3

Figure 12.3
Exponential curves:
$Y = ab^x$

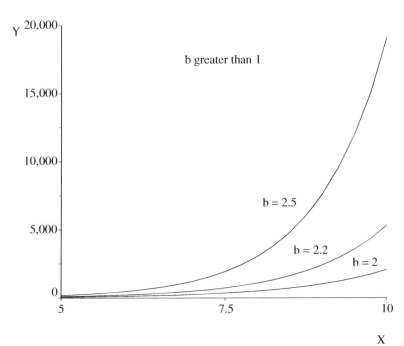

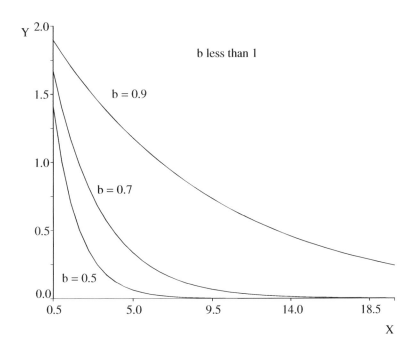

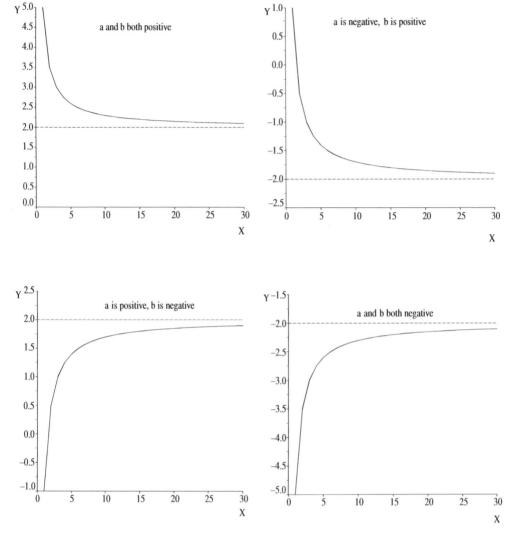

Figure 12.4
Reciprocal curves:
$Y = a + b/X$

included in this expression ensures that the relation between X and Y is non-linear; as X rises, the value of the expression and, therefore, the slope of the curve will change.

In the case of the lower panel, figure 12.5 (b), the location of the turning point, at which the slope of the curve changes (either from positive to negative, or vice versa), is when X equals the ratio of $(b_1/2b_2)$. In the left-hand curve, b_1 equals 45 and b_2 is -1.5; thus, the curve reaches its *maximum* when X equals 15. In the right-hand curve, b_1 is -45 and b_2 equals 1.5; the curve reaches its minimum when X equals 15.[e]

[e] Note the similarity between the top curve in figure 12.5 (a) and the geometric curve with $b > 0$; and also the similarity between the lower curve in figure 12.5 (b) below the turning point and the exponential curve with $b < 1$.

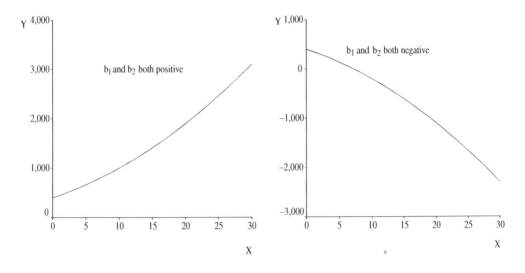

(a) Rising and falling without turning points

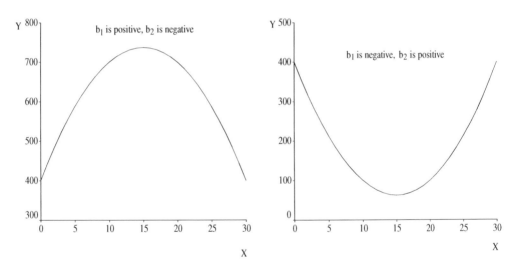

(b) Maximum and minimum turning points

Figure 12.5

Quadratic curves:
$Y = a + b_1 X + b_2 X^2$

The final non-linear relationship to be considered is the logistic. The most general form of the **logistic curve** is given in (12.7). With four constants and the variable, X, there are numerous possible permutations, and we will mention only a selection of the various shapes the curve can take. If the constants g and h are both positive, b is greater than 1, and the power x in the denominator is negative, then the logistic curve slopes *upward* from left to right in an elongated S-shape (also known as a sigmoid curve). If the

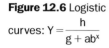

Figure 12.6 Logistic curves: $Y = \dfrac{h}{g + ab^x}$

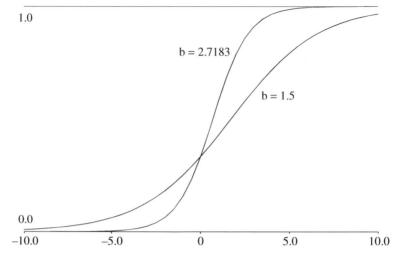

value of b, or the sign of x or h changes – for example, if b is less than 1; or if all three of them are changed – for example, h negative, b less than 1 and x positive – the logistic curve slopes *downward* from left to right in the shape of a backward-elongated S.

The constants g and h determine the upper and lower limits of the arms of the S-shape at each end of the curve. For the upper limit, four special cases are of interest; in each case the lower bound is zero. The four cases and the resulting upper limits are:

Value of g	Value of h	Upper limit of curve
0	>0	∞
1	>0	h
>1	>0	h/g
1	1	1

The constant, a, determines the point at which the curve begins to rise; the greater a is, the further to the right will be the point at which the curve begins to bend upwards. The final constant, b, determines the slope of the curve: the greater it is, the steeper the slope.

Figure 12.6 shows two logistic curves, for both of which g and h = 1, so that the upper limit of both curves is 1. The two curves have the same value of a (= 2), but different slopes: for one b = 1.5 and for the other b = e (the exponential constant introduced in §1.6.2, with a value to four decimal places of 2.7183). The reason for choosing this value for b is explained below.

One particular variant of the logistic curve is of special importance. In this form g, h, and a are all set equal to 1, x is negative, and b is taken as equal to e. The equation is thus

$$Y = \frac{1}{1 + e^{-x}} \tag{12.7a}$$

It can also be shown by manipulation that this is identical to[3]

$$Y = \frac{e^x}{1 + e^x} \tag{12.7b}$$

This form of the logistic curve, with a lower limit of 0 and an upper limit equal to 1, plays a central role in the procedures we will discuss in chapter 13.

All these relationships look very much more difficult than the simple linear regressions, and of course the underlying mathematics is more complicated. However, for our purposes the basic ideas essentially follow through from the linear to the non-linear models. The procedures and measurements for non-linear regression are thus very similar to those already explained in chapters 4 and 8.

There are, however, two important additional aspects of the procedures for non-linear relationships that must be considered. The first relates to the method of estimation, the second to the interpretation of the regression coefficients.

12.2 Estimation of non-linear regression models

For the purposes of undertaking regression analysis the non-linear models can be divided into three groups: the first group require only a simple substitution, and then can be fitted by the same ordinary least squares (OLS) procedure that we have been using for linear relationships. The second group can also be estimated by the OLS procedure, but only after any non-linear explanatory variables have been transformed into logarithms.

The third group are intractably non-linear, i.e. there is no suitable transformation that can be applied. These include the logistic curve, (12.7), and models in this group may also be created by certain features of the error term.[f] As a result the underlying regressions are too complex to be solved in the usual way and require more elaborate procedures, one of which (maximum likelihood) is discussed briefly in panel 13.1 in the next chapter.

---

[f] For example, if (12.5) were modelled with an additive rather than a multiplicative error, so that the model was $Y = aX_1^b X_2^b + e$ rather than $Y = aX_1^b X_2^b e$, then it would be intractably non-linear.

In the remainder of this section we will review examples of non-linear models in the first two groups.

12.2.1 Two groups of non-linear models

The first group of non-linear models
The first group covers models such as those shown in (12.2) and (12.3). These can easily be fitted by the same OLS procedure that is used for linear relationships (see §4.2.2). All that is required is to define a new variable in place of any terms in X which are non-linear, for example, X^2 or $1/X$.[8] If the non-linear term is X^2 we simply square all the observations in the series for X and give the resulting series a new name, say Z. Similarly, if the non-linear term is $1/X$ we simply work out the reciprocal of X, and call that Z.

If this new series, Z, is substituted in the original equation there is then a standard linear relationship, and we can proceed in the usual way, with all the advantageous properties of the OLS regression. For example, the quadratic in (12.2),

$$Y = a + b_1 X + b_2 X^2 + e, \tag{12.2}$$

becomes

$$Y = a + b_1 X_1 + b_2 Z + e \tag{12.2a}$$

in which there are no non-linear terms. This procedure is adopted in §12.4 to fit a non-linear trend to a time series. Similarly, the reciprocal model in (12.3) becomes

$$Y = a + bZ + e \tag{12.3a}$$

This simple procedure can be followed for all models in which the *nonlinearity occurs only in the X variables*, not in the regression coefficients.

The second group of non-linear models
The second group covers models such as those shown in (12.4). These can also be estimated by the regular OLS procedure but it is first necessary *to transform the explanatory variables into logs*, and these logarithms are then substituted for the original variables. Recall from §1.6 that

(i) two numbers can be multiplied by taking the sum of their logs, e.g.

$$\log (a \times b) = \log a + \log b;$$

---

[8] Terms such as X^2 or $1/X$ are described as 'non-linear' because if any one of them is included in an equation it automatically means that the regression relationship is no longer a straight line (or the multivariate equivalent such as a plane) but has some form of curve.

and

(ii) a number raised to a power equals the exponent × the log of the number, e.g.

$$\log X^3 = 3 \times \log X.$$

By applying both these transformations the geometric curve $(12.4)^h$ can be expressed in logs as follows

$$\log Y = \log a + b(\log X) + e \tag{12.4a}$$

This is called a **double logarithmic** (or log-log) model, because *both X and Y are in logs.*[i] An example of a geometric curve (with $b = -3$) is shown in figure 12.7 (a) and its double logarithmic transformation is given in figure 12.7 (b). The procedure to be followed for estimating a model of this type is set out in §12.2.2.

The alternative to this is a **semi-logarithmic** model. This can take several forms. In one, *X is in logs but Y is not*

$$Y = a + b \log X + e \tag{12.8}$$

Lin-log models of this form are frequently used to model relationships. Hatton and Williamson specified a multivariate model of this form in their study of migration, and Benjamin and Kochin also used this form in their analysis of inter-war unemployment.[j] We will look more closely at their models in chapter 14.

In another, sometimes described as an inverse semi-log model, *Y is in logs but X is not*

$$\log Y = a + b X + e \tag{12.9}$$

---

[h] The multivariate version in (12.5) is essentially the same but has one extra term in $\log X_2$. The transformation is thus: $\log Y = \log a + b_1 (\log X_1) + b_2 (\log X_2)$.

[i] Some writers also refer to this as a log-linear model because – as can be seen in figure 12.6 – it is linear when plotted in logs. However, this usage may cause confusion, and we prefer to reserve the term log-linear for semi-logarithmic models such as (12.6a) and (12.9), where only the explanatory variable is in logs. By extension, the semi-log model (12.8), where only the dependent variable is in logs, is sometimes called a lin-log model. Using the terms in this fashion has the advantage of indicating immediately whether the logged variables are on the left-hand side of the equation (log-linear), the right-hand side (lin-log), or both (log-log).

[j] See Timothy J. Hatton and Jeffrey G. Williamson, 'After the famine: emigration from Ireland, 1850–1913', *Journal of Economic History*, 53, 1993, p. 581; and Daniel K. Benjamin and Lewis A. Kochin, 'Searching for an explanation for unemployment in interwar Britain', *Journal of Political Economy*, 87, 1979, p. 453.

Figure 12.7 Double
logarithmic
transformation of a
geometric model

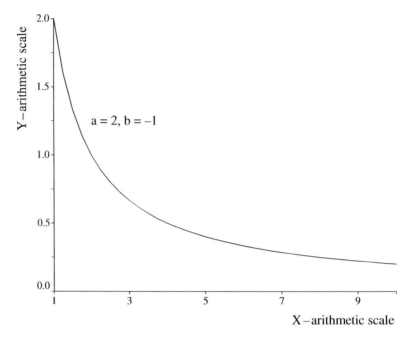

(a) The original curve: $Y = aX^b$

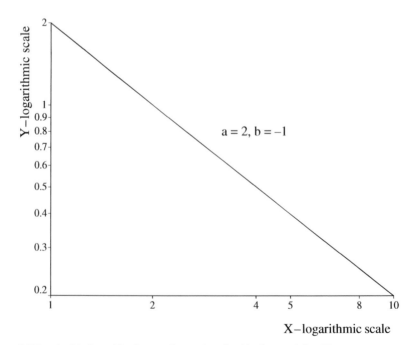

(b) The double logarithmic transformation: $\log Y = \log a + b(\log X)$

Models of this form are less common, but are used, for example, in studies of earnings, with the log of the wage taken as the dependent variable and factors such as age, education, and a dummy variable for union membership as the explanatory variables.[k]

A third version of the semi-log (or log-linear) model is obtained by transformation of the exponential curve (12.6), giving an equation in which *both Y and the coefficient b are in logs, but X is not*

$$\log Y = \log a + (\log b)X + e \tag{12.6a}$$

An exponential curve (with $b = 2.5$) and its semi-log transformation are shown in figure 12.8 (a) and (b).

This transformation of the exponential curve is not often used to model relationships in the social sciences. Its importance derives from the fact that it is the model used to fit a long-run trend to a time series. The trend obtained in this way will be linear in the logs (though not when converted back to ordinary numbers), and is generally recommended in preference to either the moving average described in §1.8 or the simple linear trend introduced in §4.2.5.

The procedure for fitting this and other non-linear trends is described in §12.4. Fitting this particular log-linear trend has the further advantage that the annual compound rate of growth of the series can be obtained very simply from the regression coefficient, and this is explained later in this chapter (see panel 12.1).

12.2.2 Estimating the double logarithmic and semi-logarithmic models

The first step in the procedure for fitting a regression based on the double logarithmic model (12.4a) is to calculate two new variables by taking the logarithms of the original variables. We will refer to each of these new variables by an asterisk (*) to indicate its relationship to the original variable:

$$Y^* \equiv \log Y$$

and

$$X^* \equiv \log X$$

By substituting these three new variables in (12.4a) we get a standard linear regression

$$Y^* = a^* + bX^* + e \tag{12.4b}$$

where a^* is the logarithm of the intercept, a.

***

[k] This is the form used, for example, by Barry Eichengreen and Henry A. Gemery, 'The earnings of skilled and unskilled immigrants at the end of the nineteenth century', *Journal of Economic History*, 46, 1986, pp. 441–54.

Figure 12.8 Semi-logarithmic transformation of an exponential model

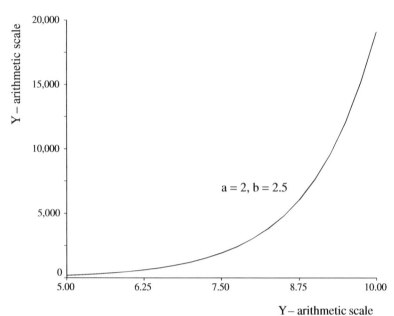

a = 2, b = 2.5

(a) The original curve: $Y = ab^X$

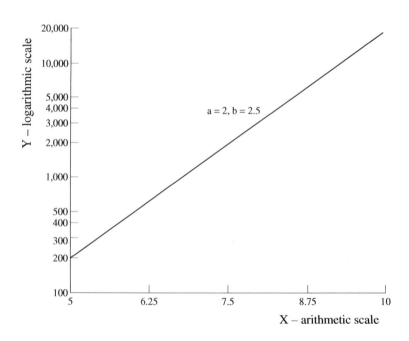

a = 2, b = 2.5

(b) The semi-logarithmic transformation: $\log Y = \log a + X(\log b)$

Suppose, for the purpose of illustration, that the linear regression in (12.4b) has been computed by the standard OLS procedure; the intercept, a*, is found to be 0.69315 and the regression coefficient, b, is 1.75. These parameters can be substituted in the *original* transformation (12.4a) to get

$$\log Y = 0.69315 + 1.75 \log X \qquad (12.4c)$$

In practice, the relationship would usually be reported in this logarithmic form. However, it is possible to get back to ordinary numbers by finding the exponential of 0.69315 (which $= 2$) and reversing both the logarithmic transformations. This gives

$$Y = 2X^{1.75} \qquad (12.4d)$$

Essentially the same procedure is followed for the estimation of the semi-log models, except that there is only one new variable to be created in each case: $X^* \equiv \log X$ for the model of (12.8), and $Y^* \equiv \log Y$ for the model of (12.9). In neither case is the intercept a in log form.

12.3 Interpretation of non-linear relationships

The second essential feature of non-linear models that must be considered relates to the interpretation of the regression coefficients. In the initial discussion of linear relationships in §4.2 it was noted that the regression coefficient measured the slope of the line. In a simple linear model such as $Y = a + bX + e$, the coefficient b on the explanatory variable informs us that when X changes by 1 unit, Y changes by b units; the units being whatever X and Y are measured in.[1]

In slightly more formal terms, if we use the symbol Δ (capital Greek delta) to represent 'a small change', then we can say that in a linear relationship, $\Delta Y = b\Delta X$, and if ΔX is 1 unit then ΔY is b units. What is the corresponding interpretation of the regression coefficient when any of the variables is in log form?

12.3.1 Interpretation of the regression coefficients for logarithmic models

It follows from the properties of logs summarized in §1.6.2 that a change in the log of a variable is a *proportionate* rather than an absolute change. Using the same symbol, Δ, then such a proportionate change in Y would be $\Delta Y/Y$, and similarly for X. We then have three cases to consider.

---

[1] As one particular application of this rule, note that if the regression coefficient, b, is expressed as a logarithm – as in (12.6a) – then its value will depend on whether the author has taken a natural logarithm to base e, as is usually done, or a log to base 10 (see §1.6.2).

(a) The first case is the double logarithmic (log-log) model in which both the dependent and the explanatory variable are in logs. In this form the regression coefficient informs us that when there is a small *proportionate* change in X there will be a small *proportionate* change in Y equal to b. So

$$\frac{\Delta Y}{Y} = b\frac{\Delta X}{X}$$

and if the proportionate change in X is 1 per cent, the proportionate change in Y will be b per cent.

Economists will recognize that if this relationship is re-written

$$b = \frac{\Delta Y}{Y} \div \frac{\Delta X}{X} \tag{12.10}$$

it shows that b defines an **elasticity**. Thus if this double logarithmic model was applied to the demand for a commodity, in which Y was some measure of quantity and X was the price, the regression coefficient, b, would measure the price elasticity (and would have a negative sign).

In other contexts this expression for the regression coefficient, b, can also be interpreted as the constant rate of growth of Y associated with a constant rate of growth of X. In the example used in §12.2.2 in relation to (12.4c) above, b was 1.75. This means that when X grows at 1 per cent p.a., Y grows at 1.75 per cent p.a.

(b) The second case is the semi-log (lin-log) model such as (12.8) in which the explanatory variable, X, is in log form but not the dependent variable, Y. In this case the interpretation of the regression coefficient, b, is that when there is a small *proportionate* change in X, there will be an *absolute* change of b units in Y. So

$$\Delta Y = b\frac{\Delta X}{X}$$

If, for example, the proportionate change in X is 0.01 (or 1 per cent) then the absolute change in Y will be 0.01b; this is the same as b/100.

(c) Thirdly, we can consider the alternative form of semi-log (log-lin) model in which the dependent variable, Y, is in log form but not the explanatory variable, X; for example (12.9). In this case the regression coefficient tells us that when there is an *absolute* change in X, there will be a *proportionate* change in Y of b. So

$$\frac{\Delta Y}{Y} = b\Delta X$$

and if ΔX is 1 unit the proportionate change in Y will be b units, corresponding to a percentage change of 100b per cent.

The possible combinations of units for X and Y are summarized in table 12.1. Columns (1) and (2) indicate the form in which X and Y are specified by the model. Columns (3) and (4) show how this affects the meaning of the change in X and the resulting change in Y. Note that absolute units are measured in the same units as the relevant variable.

12.3.2 Elasticities

It is often interesting to establish the elasticity implied by a particular regression model. This is the ratio of the proportional change in the dependent variable to the proportional change in the explanatory variable, or

$$\frac{\Delta Y}{Y} \div \frac{\Delta X}{X}$$

As noted above (see (12.10)) when the model is specified as a double logarithmic relationship, the elasticity can be read directly from the regression coefficient, b. However, it is only for this model that b is identical to the elasticity; it does *not* hold for any other model.

In every other case, if the researcher wants to determine the elasticity she can always do so, but it requires an additional manipulation of the regression coefficient. For example, in the case of the lin-log model considered in paragraph (b) above, where it is the explanatory variable X that is in

Table 12.1 Absolute and proportionate regression coefficients

Type of model	(1) X measured in	(2) Y measured in	(3) Change in X	(4) Resulting change in Y
1 Linear models, e.g. $Y = a + b_1 X_1 - b_2 X_2$	numbers	numbers	1 unit	b units
2 Semi-logarithmic models, e.g. $Y = a + b \log X$	logs	numbers	1%	b/100 units
OR $\log Y = a + b X$	numbers	logs	1 unit	$(b \times 100)\%$
3 Double logarithmic models, e.g. $\log Y = \log a + b \log X$	logs	logs	1%	b%

logs, a small proportionate change in X produces a small absolute change in Y, and

$$b = \Delta Y \div \frac{\Delta X}{X} \qquad (12.11)$$

This can be converted to an elasticity by dividing both sides by Y to get

$$\frac{b}{Y} = \frac{\Delta Y}{Y} \div \frac{\Delta X}{X} \qquad (12.12)$$

Similarly, in the alternative form of log-lin model considered in paragraph (c) above, where it is the dependent variable Y that is in logs, a small absolute change in X $(=\Delta X)$ produces a small proportionate change in Y

$$\left(= \frac{\Delta Y}{Y} \right)$$

and so

$$b = \frac{\Delta Y}{Y} \div \Delta X \qquad (12.13)$$

In order to convert this into an elasticity it is necessary to multiply both sides by X, giving[4]

$$bX = \frac{\Delta Y}{Y} \div \frac{\Delta X}{X} \qquad (12.14)$$

We have thus established that for a semi-log model in which the explanatory variable is in log form, the elasticity is measured by b/Y. For the alternative semi-log model in which the dependent variable is in log form, the proportionate change in Y caused by a proportionate change in X, or elasticity, is measured by bX.

In the same way it can be shown that for a standard linear model the elasticity is

$$b \frac{X}{Y}$$

and for the reciprocal model it is

$$-b \frac{1}{XY}$$

It is important to note, however, that all these measures of elasticity differ in one vital respect from the measure associated with the double logarithmic model. In that model the elasticity is *constant* irrespective of the values of X and Y. In all the other models the elasticity is *variable* and its precise value will depend on the value of X and Y. So when these elasticities are reported, the single result given is typically calculated *at the mean values* of the variables.

12.3.3 Long-run multipliers

There is one final point to be made regarding the interpretation of regression coefficients. It arises in relation to the distributed lag models discussed in §10.2.2. It was noted that a model could be specified that allowed all or many past values of an explanatory variable to influence the dependent variable. This was illustrated by (10.15) in §10.2.2, in which all past values of SALES appeared as separate explanatory variables. It was shown that such a model was difficult to estimate but that the problems could be overcome by a transformation such as (10.19) (see panel 10.1). For convenience this equation is reproduced here

$$INV_t = (1 - \lambda)a + bSALES_t + \lambda INV_{t-1} + (e_t - \lambda e_{t-1}) \qquad (12.15)$$

In this form of the model only the current value of SALES is shown on the right hand side. In this case the regression coefficient, b, measures the change in INV caused by a change in SALES in the current period, and is referred to as an **impact multiplier.** The total effect of the change in SALES in all previous periods, or **long-run multiplier** (which we will refer to as $\bar{b}$ to distinguish it from the short-run coefficients), is not given directly by (12.15). However, it can easily be derived as

$$\frac{b}{1 - \lambda}$$

where b is the coefficient on the current SALES, and λ is the rate of decline of the distributed lag and is given by the coefficient on the lagged dependent variable, INV_{t-1}.[5]

12.4 Fitting a trend to a time series

In this section we continue the discussion of the measurement of long-run trends first introduced in §1.8. We begin by looking at the log-linear trend and then turn briefly to other forms of non-linear trend.

12.4.1 Fitting a log-linear trend

The semi-log transformation of the exponential model (12.6a) is widely used in the study of time series to fit a trend to the series. A **log-linear trend** of this nature *grows at a constant rate*, and will appear as a straight line *when plotted in logs*. It thus differs from the linear trend described in §4.2.5; this was also linear but in the original numbers, not in logs.

The log-linear (or semi-logarithmic) trend is fitted to the data by treating the *log of the relevant series* (Y) as the dependent variable and *time* as the explanatory variable (X). As explained in §4.2.5, it makes no difference to the resulting trend whether time is measured by successive dates (1920, 1921, …) or by any other series that increases by 1 unit each year (1, 2, 3, …), though the coefficients will be different.

To illustrate the procedure we can fit a log-linear trend to the series for NNP (real net national product in £ million) for 1920–38 used by Benjamin and Kochin in their analysis of inter-war unemployment in the UK.[m] We do so using the actual years (YEAR) as the explanatory variable. The model is thus

$$\log NNP = \log a + \log b \; YEAR + e \tag{12.16}$$

The computer estimates this regression as

$$\log NNP = -26.084 + 0.01781 \; YEAR$$

This measure of the trend in NNP would normally be left in logs and plotted in that form. If, however, it were desired to convert back to ordinary numbers, the procedure for 1920 would be

$$\log NNP = -26.084 + (0.01781 \times 1920) = 8.1135$$
$$\text{so } NNP = \exp(8.1135) = \text{£3,339.2 m}$$

and similarly for other years.

This procedure for fitting a log-linear trend has the further important advantage that the regression coefficient provides a direct measure of the **annual compound rate of growth** of the series. This method of calculating the rate of growth of a time series is described in panel 12.1, and compared with alternative methods.

Where a time series relates to periods of less than a year, regression analysis can be used not only to fit a long-run trend, but also to eliminate the seasonal variations in the series by means of dummy variables. This makes it possible to analyse the three separate components of the series: long-run trend, seasonal variation, and residual cyclical and random fluctuations. This procedure is explained in panel 12.2.

12.4.2   Fitting non-linear trends

The log-linear trend described in the previous subsection is appropriate only if it provides a good fit to the data. This may be judged by inspection or by suitable statistical tests such as the value of R^2 and of the standard

---

[m] This is the series given in the data set and used previously when fitting a linear trend in §4.2.5.

errors. There will, however, be many series for which a linear trend is not a good fit, and it is then necessary to fit a more complex model.

To illustrate one such case, we revert to the series used in §1.8 for miles of railway track added in the United States from 1831 to 1913 (RAILWAY); this was shown together with its fitted trend in figure 1.3. To model this we use a quadratic in which a term in X^2 is added to the model used previously (see (12.16)). For this version we take TIME as the explanatory variable, using a sequence of numbers from 1 to 83. The model is thus

$$\log \text{RAILWAY} = \log a + \log b_1 \text{ TIME} + \log b_2 (\text{TIME})^2 + e$$

$$(12.22)$$

This belongs to the first group of non-linear models described in §12.2, and so can be converted to a linear form by simply replacing the term in $(\text{TIME})^2$ by the corresponding squared values. Thus for 1832, $(2)^2$ becomes 4, for 1833 $(3)^2$ becomes 9, and so on all the way to the final year, where $(83)^2$ is replaced by 6,889. We now have a standard linear model with two explanatory variables that can be estimated by OLS. When the computer does this, the results (with t-statistics in brackets) are

$$\log \text{RAILWAY} = 4.7799 + 0.1185 \text{ TIME} - 0.00095 (\text{TIME})^2$$
$$(25.23) \quad (11.39) \qquad (7.88)$$

The trend in actual miles can then be derived for each year by applying these results and finding the exponential.[n] For example, for 1881 (which is 51 in the series for TIME) the trend value is found from

$$\log \text{RAILWAY} = 4.7799 + (0.1185 \times 51) - (0.00095 \times (51)^2) = 8.3653$$
$$\text{so RAILWAY} = \exp(8.3653) = 4,295 \text{ miles}$$

and similarly for all other years. This is the long-term trend in construction of railway track that was fitted to the data in figure 1.3.

The key to understanding why this model produces a trend which first rises and then falls, is to notice the effect of the term for $(\text{TIME})^2$. Its coefficient, $\log b_2$, is *smaller than* the coefficient on TIME, $\log b_1$, *but is negative*. In the early years of the series, the positive impact of b_1 outweighs the negative effect of b_2, even though TIME is much smaller than $(\text{TIME})^2$. But in later years, $(\text{TIME})^2$ becomes so large relative to TIME that eventually its negative coefficient dominates, and the trend starts to decline.

To illustrate this effect, we can compare the above calculation for 1881 with comparable calculations for 1891, when the trend value was close to

[n] These results are rounded to simplify the presentation, but the calculations are very sensitive to the precise coefficients, and the illustrations for 1881 and other years were done with figures to 7 decimal places: $b_1 = 0.1185348$ and $b_2 = -0.0009457$.

Panel 12.1   Measurement of the compound rate of growth

A great advantage of the procedure for fitting a log-linear trend described in §12.4.1 is that the regression coefficient provides a direct measure of the **annual compound rate of growth** of a series.

To illustrate, it should be evident from (12.16), and the calculation made on the basis of the regression results for 1920, that the value of log NNP will rise each year by a fixed absolute amount equal to the regression coefficient, b (since the intercept does not change and the value of YEAR by which the coefficient is multiplied always increases by exactly 1). In the example used the fixed amount (in logs) was 0.01781.

Recall from §1.6 and panel 1.1 that an equal *absolute* change in the logarithm of a variable represents a constant *proportional* change in the variable. It follows, therefore, that if log NNP is growing each year by a *constant amount* of 0.01781, then NNP must be growing at a *constant rate* equal to the exponential of that amount, which is 1.01797. Thus the annual compound rate of growth can be obtained very simply from the exponential of the coefficient by subtracting 1 and multiplying by 100. The growth rate of NNP is therefore 1.797 per cent p.a.[*]

It is important not to confuse this use of the coefficient on the log-linear model with the coefficient on the log-log model interpreted in §12.3.1 as the constant rate of growth of Y associated with a constant rate of growth of X. The difference in this case is that X represents time and is not growing at a constant *rate*, but by a constant absolute *amount* of one year each year.

The strength of this measurement of the rate of growth is that it is based on the log-linear trend that has been fitted to *all* years in the series.[**] An alternative procedure often adopted to measure the compound rate of growth is to select two years, say the first and the last in the series, and calculate the growth between these two points by means of the compound interest formula

$$X_t = X_0 \left(1 + \frac{r}{100} \right)^t \tag{12.17a}$$

---

[*] Note that when the rate of growth is small, a close approximation to the compound growth rate can be obtained more simply from the regression coefficient itself (multiplied by 100). In the present example b = 0.01781 so the approximation would be 1.78 per cent p. a.

[**] The linear trend fitted in §4.2.5 was also based on all points in the series, but the growth rate cannot be obtained directly from the regression, and because the trend is not linear in the logs, the slope of the line does not correspond to a constant rate of growth. The growth rate can be calculated by applying the compound interest formula to two selected years, but it will vary according to the years selected.

where X_0 and X_t are the values of the series in the two selected years, r is the rate of growth, and t the number of years between X_0 and X_t over which the growth is to be calculated.

In order to solve (12.17a) it must first be converted to logarithms, giving

$$\log X_t = \log X_0 + \left[t \times \log\left(1 + \frac{r}{100} \right) \right] \qquad (12.17b)$$

so

$$\log\left(1 + \frac{r}{100} \right) = \frac{\log X_t - \log X_0}{t}$$

For NNP in 1920 and 1938, X_0 is £3,426m, X_t is £4,807m and t = 18. Substituting these values in (12.17b) gives $\log (1 + r/100) = 0.01882$. We then take the exponential of this to get $(1 + r/100) = 1.01899$. By subtracting 1 and multiplying by 100 we obtain the compound rate of growth of 1.90 per cent p.a.

This procedure amounts, in effect, to simply drawing a straight line through the two selected dates and ignoring what happens to the series in all other years. In this case the two methods give broadly similar results. However, the use of the compound interest formula can give misleading results, particularly if the two selected dates occur at different points in the business cycle – for example, if the first is a year of depression and the second at or close to a peak year.

Calculation of the growth rate from the coefficient in the log-linear trend model is, in general, more reliable, and is recommended as the best-practice procedure. This is, of course, subject to the proviso that a log-linear trend is a good fit for the particular series. If the long-run growth of the series is not constant, then a single estimate of the growth rate is not appropriate, and other procedures must be adopted to find the relevant growth rate for different segments of the curve.

To conclude this discussion of growth rates we report a very helpful rule of thumb. This states that the product of (i) the annual compound rate of growth of a series and (ii) the time it will take for that series *to double* if it is growing at that rate, is approximately equal to 70. Thus, if we know that, say, the population of a country is growing at 5 per cent p.a., we can immediately say that the population will double in 14 years. Conversely, if we want to know what rate of economic growth would be required in order to achieve a doubling of the average standard of living within a period of 20 years, we can immediately calculate that it would need to be 3.5 per cent p.a.

Panel 12.2   Decomposition of a time series by means of a log-linear trend and seasonal dummy variables

In §1.8 we described a procedure for decomposing a time series for periods of less than a year into a trend, a pattern of regular seasonal variation, and a residual cyclical or irregular fluctuation. We can now introduce an alternative – and in some respects more satisfactory procedure – using regression analysis, first to fit the trend and then, with the aid of seasonal dummy variables, to ascertain the seasonal adjustment factors.

To illustrate the method we will again take the quarterly data on bankruptcy in eighteenth-century England (BANKRUPT) compiled by Hoppit and used in table 1.2. In the first stage, the long-run trend in the series is estimated by fitting a semi-log model with TIME as the explanatory variable. The model is

$$\log \text{BANKRUPT} = \log a + \log b\ \text{TIME} + e \qquad (12.18)$$

If this is estimated for the period from 1777QI to 1787QIV, using successive numbers 1, 2, 3, … for each quarter to represent TIME, the computer obtains

$$\log \text{BANKRUPT} = 4.9237 - 0.0032\ \text{TIME}$$

The trend value for 1777QI (in ordinary numbers) would thus be $\exp[4.9237 - (0.0032 \times 1)] = \exp(4.9205) = 137.07$; for 1777QII it would be $\exp[4.9237 - (0.0032 \times 2)] = \exp(4.9173) = 136.63$, and so on.

Having calculated the trend, in the second stage the log of BANKRUPT is regressed on its trend (TRENDB) and the seasonal dummy variables. The trend is converted back to ordinary numbers because it is again a semi-log model (see (12.6a)), with only the dependent variable in logs.

Dummies are created for three of the four quarters, leaving the fourth as the control quarter. Thus, if QIV is taken as the control quarter, the dummy variables are

DQI   which has a value of 1 for every 1st quarter, 0 otherwise
DQII   which has a value of 1 for every 2nd quarter, 0 otherwise, and
DQIII which has a value of 1 for every 3rd quarter, 0 otherwise.

Each of the coefficients on the dummies captures the effect of its own seasonal variations on the pattern of bankruptcy, relative to the pattern in the control quarter.

The model is thus

$$\log \text{BANKRUPT} = \log a + \log b_1 \text{TRENDB} + \log b_2 \text{DQI} \\ + \log b_3 \text{DQII} + \log b_4 \text{DQIII} + e \quad (12.19)$$

Estimation of the model gives the following results, with t-statistics in brackets.

$$\log \text{BANKRUPT} = 4.00 + 0.0072 \text{ TRENDB} + 0.0057 \text{ DQI} \\ (7.99)\ (1.85) \qquad\qquad (0.10) \\ + 0.0273 \text{ DQII} - 0.3170 \text{ DQIII} \\ (0.474) \qquad\quad (5.52)$$

The t-statistics show that the seasonal dummy for the third quarter is highly significant, though those for the first and second quarters are not. Together with the F-test (for which the prob value is 0.000) there is clear evidence of a strong seasonal pattern in bankruptcies in this period.

Since we have used a semi-log model the seasonal coefficients are in logs, and are multiplicative rather than additive. The first step in calculating the quarterly adjustment factors is thus to obtain their exponentials (and their relationship then becomes additive). The second step is to convert these from adjustments relative to the control quarter, QIV, into the actual adjustments required.

To do this we need some simple algebra, based on the following four equations:

$$\text{DQI} \ = 1.0057 \text{ DQIV} \qquad\qquad\qquad (12.20a)$$

$$\text{DQII} = 1.0277 \text{ DQIV} \qquad\qquad\qquad (12.20b)$$

$$\text{DQIII} = 0.7283 \text{ DQIV} \qquad\qquad\qquad (12.20c)$$

$$\text{DQIV} = 4 - (\text{DQI} + \text{DQII} + \text{DQIII}) \qquad (12.21)$$

The first three of these equations are simply statements of the value of the seasonal dummies relative to QIV, based on the exponentials of the regression coefficients. Equation (12.21) incorporates the rule that the four adjustment factors must sum to 4; in other words, their average must be exactly 1 so that the annual totals will not be changed by the removal of the seasonal pattern.

Since all four equations relate to DQIV we can substitute the first three in (12.21) to get

$$\text{DQIV} = 4 - (1.0057 \text{ DQIV} + 1.0277 \text{ DQIV} + 0.7283 \text{ DQIV})$$

We then take all the terms in DQIV to the left-hand side

$$DQIV(1 + 1.0057 + 1.0277 + 0.7283) = 4$$

so

$$DQIV = 4/(3.7617) = 1.0633$$

We now know the seasonal adjustment factor for QIV. Therefore the factor for QI is $1.0057 \times 1.0633 = 1.0694$, and similar calculations for QII and QIII complete the exercise. The full set of seasonal adjustments is set out below, with those previously calculated in chapter 1 given for comparison. The differences are not large and lie within the 95 per cent confidence intervals derived from the t-statistics.

| Seasonal dummies | 1.0694 | 1.0928 | 0.7745 | 1.0633 |
| Previous method | 1.0939 | 1.0548 | 0.7712 | 1.0802 |

As before, the original series is divided by these factors to obtain a series with the seasonal variations removed, and that in turn can be divided by the trend to reveal the remaining fluctuations without either trend or seasonal variation.

its peak level; and with 1901, by when it had declined. Since the constant term is always the same we ignore that and concentrate on the two remaining terms. Since TIME increases in each case by 10 years, the change in the term $\log b_1$ (TIME) will always be $10 \times 0.11853 = 1.1853$. It remains to work out the change in the second term and to calculate the net effect of the two terms. The former is done in columns (2) and (3) of table 12.2, the latter in column (4).

This calculation shows that between 1881 and 1891 the combined effect was an increase of 0.1261; between 1891 and 1901 it was a fall of -0.063. The corresponding exponentials are 1.1344 and 0.9389. This is a (multivariate) semi-log model with only the dependent variable in logs, so these exponentials represent the *ratios of the dependent variable*. The final result is thus that the ratio of 1891 to 1881 is 1.1344, corresponding to an *increase* in the trend value by 13.44 per cent, from 4,295 to 4,873 miles. By contrast the ratio of 1901 to 1891 is 0.9389, corresponding to a *decrease* over the second period by 6.11 per cent, from 4,873 to 4,575 miles.

The exercise also underlines the fact that although the net change in the two explanatory variables can be used to calculate the percentage change in

Table 12.2 Calculation of change in fitted trend, miles of railway track added in the United States, 1881, 1891, and 1901

	(1) Change in $\log b_1$ (TIME)	(2) $\log b_2$ (TIME)^2	(3) Change in $\log b_2$ (TIME)^2	(4) Net change in log RAILWAY
1881	...	$(-0.00095 \times 2601) = -2.4599$	...	...
1891	1.1853	$(-0.00095 \times 3721) = -3.5191$	-1.0592	0.1261
1901	1.1853	$(-0.00095 \times 5041) = -4.7674$	-1.2483	-0.0630

Notes:
(1) and (2) calculated from results of trend fitted by (12.22)

$$\log \text{RAILWAY} = 4.7799 + 0.1185\, \text{TIME} - 0.00095\, (\text{TIME})^2$$

with TIME measured by a series running from 1 (for 1831) to 83 (for 1913).
(4) = (1) + (3).

the trend over any period, this will *not be a constant rate of growth*; it will vary according to the position of the selected dates on the fitted trend.

Inspection of the *t*-statistics and other tests suggests that this quadratic provides a reasonably good fit for this series. If it did not, we could explore higher-order polynomials such as cubics or quartics (i.e. models with terms in X^3 or X^4). These additional terms would act in a similar fashion to the term in $(\text{TIME})^2$, and would eventually produce additional turning points in the trend.[6]

Alternatively we could try other curves. In his classic study of the trends in a large number of production series for the United Kingdom, United States, and other countries Simon Kuznets fitted a variety of non-linear functional forms including parabolas and logistic curves.[o] The logistic is appropriate for many production series that start at a low level, rise rapidly for a time, and then level off as a result of factors such as declining prices and profitability as a consequence of the entry of other producers, saturation of the market, and competition from new products. The upper and lower bounds of this process are captured by the coefficients g and h discussed in §12.1.

12.5 Modelling a relationship

The process of fitting a suitable trend to a time series can be thought of as a special case of the more general problem of finding an appropriate

[o] Simon Kuznets, *Secular Movements in Production and Prices,* Houghton Mifflin, 1930.

functional form with which to model the relationship between a dependent variable and one or more explanatory variables. How do we know which of the possible non-linear relationships is the best one to choose once we have decided that the most appropriate relationship is not linear? More generally, when should we choose a non-linear rather than a linear relationship?

We begin with a discussion of some general principles that might help to inform this decision, and then look at how these have been implemented in practice by authors investigating a wide variety of topics. We conclude the chapter by returning to the general question of how to evaluate the specification of a model, a conceptual issue that embraces not only matters of non-linearity, but other issues, such as the selection of variables and how best to evaluate the success or failure of the model when confronted with historical data.

12.5.1 Choice of functional form

The range of possible functional forms that might be selected is quite large, and it should be emphasized at the outset that it is not confined to the precise forms specified earlier in this chapter. For example, if a multivariate double logarithmic model is derived by transformation of the geometric curve given in (12.5), the result is

$$\log Y = a + b_1 \log X_1 + b_2 \log X_2 + e \tag{12.23}$$

This could obviously be extended by the inclusion of more explanatory variables, but it is not necessary that *all* of these should be in logs. In exactly the same way, a researcher might work with a variant of the lin-log model specified in (12.8) in which some of the right-hand-side variables are in logs and others are not.

There are a number of reasons why logs might be used for some variables in these models but not for others. Logs would not normally be used for dummy variables; and there is the technical consideration that it is possible to express only positive values in logs, so a variable with a range that includes values of 0 or less must necessarily be left in ordinary numbers.[p] A more substantial reason would be the view that some particular variable should be entered in the model in ordinary numbers because its relationship to the dependent variable was absolute, not proportional.

---

[p] Some researchers who wish to use logs, but who are confronted with data points equal to 0, have been known to add a small positive number (e.g. 0.001) to all the values in the series to permit a logarithmic transformation.

There is an example of this in Hatton and Williamson's time-series model of Irish emigration, where all but one of the explanatory variables is in logs (see §14.2.1). The exception is the measure of the proportion of the total Irish population already living abroad (MIGSTOCK). The reason why this is not converted to logs is that it is the *level* of this variable that is seen as relevant to the flow of immigrants, not its rate of change. Another case occurs in a model of wage determination in post-war Britain, where the authors included both unemployment and the log of unemployment as explanatory variables in an otherwise log-log model, because they believed that its level as well as its rate of change would have an important influence on the rate of change in wages.[7]

The issue of when it is appropriate to include linear and non-linear variables in the same regression equation is part of the general debate over functional form.[q] How do we know which of the many possible functional forms is the right one for a particular application? Is the log-linear model appropriate, or is the double log model superior? The problem is compounded by the likelihood that a number of different non-linear forms *could* fit the same data without clear evidence of statistical superiority, as indicated by traditional goodness of fit measures such as R^2 and t-statistics.[r]

The decision on whether or not to take logs of explanatory and/or dependent variables is only one of the issues to be considered in deciding on the form in which a model is to be specified. A second is the use of lagged variables, a procedure that might be adopted for the reasons discussed in §10.2. Yet another is the procedure that should be adopted to deal with the effects of common trends in time series. This problem frequently arises because of the risk of spurious correlation when both dependent and explanatory variables are moving together over time.[8] In a growing economy, for example, the process of growth will be experienced by many economic and social factors, and a regression that does not account separately for this is likely to obtain a high but misleading R^2.

There are several methods available for dealing with this problem of **trendedness.** One is to fit a suitable trend to every affected variable, and then work with the deviations from the trend (as discussed in §1.8.2) rather than the original series. Another is to include time as one of the explanatory variables so that this variable picks up the effects of the changes over time. However, neither procedure is generally recommended.

---

[q] There are advanced procedures, such as RESET, discussed in most econometrics textbooks, that test whether the most appropriate functional form for the data is linear or non-linear.

[r] As can be seen, for example, by comparison of figure 12.2 when $b > 0$ with figure 12.5 (a), when both b_1 and $b_2 > 0$; or of figure 12.2 when $b = -2$, with figure 12.3 when $b = 0.7$.

A better solution involves working with the differences of successive values of the time series rather than the actual values.[9] For example, if the value of NNP in 1924 was £3,622m and in 1925 it was £3,840m, then the **first difference** is £218m. This would be designated as ΔNNP, where Δ (capital Greek delta) is the symbol used earlier in this chapter for a small change. The **second difference** is then the first difference of the first difference, denoted by Δ^2NNP. In general, first differencing of a time series is sufficient to eliminate a linear long-run trend, and second differencing would eliminate a non-linear trend with a quadratic term such as X^2.

12.5.2   Some general principles

Given this range of choices, what should determine our selection of variables and the functional form in which the model is specified?

The essential answer, the golden rule, is that the *choice should be based on some consideration of general principles combined with knowledge of the data and of the behaviour of the relevant variables*. An appropriate analytical framework should always be the starting point of any investigation. But this need not be a grand or formal theory. It may be, as with models of the economy derived from the great structure of Keynesian macro-economics, or rival monetarist theories, which lead to a complete set of equations for variables such as consumption, investment, and prices.[10] But more often what is required is much less sophisticated than this.

Economic principles regarding the relationship between price and quantity in supply and demand functions, or between profit maximization and industry performance, have been fertile sources of ideas for quantitative analysis. Other disciplines similarly provide broad principles and generalizations. Thus, some writers have suggested Durkheim's theory of *anomie* as a promising basis for a quantitative investigation of suicide; a study of infant mortality might start from the analysis and reasoning of medical scientists and epidemiologists; a proposition regarding relative deprivation might be applied in an investigation of social unrest. In other cases, the basis for a regression model may be found even more simply in ideas put forward as no more than common sense.

The analytical framework underlying the choice of functional form and the selection of variables should be set out explicitly in advance of the estimation, and the expected signs – and if possible the size – of the coefficients should be indicated. As will be seen, this is the procedure followed in all four of the case studies discussed in chapters 14 and 15.

What should *never* be done is to take a bunch of possible relationships, grab as many variables as possible, and set the computer to run regressions until it comes up with a few that might be judged satisfactory. Results obtained in this way can have no credibility; neither low standard errors nor high R^2s are worth anything in such circumstances. If a model has no underlying principle there is absolutely no reason to believe that any relationship obtained by the regression reflects any sort of causal relationship between the dependent and explanatory variables.

The implementation of these general ideas can now be illustrated by a few examples from recent literature. In each case we have space to identify only one or two principal features of the models, and our brief comments do not do justice to the richness of the analytical frameworks developed in these studies. In each case, we are focusing on the specific issue of including and specifying a non-linear relationship in the model, although it should be clear that the examples chosen have been selected for their general sensitivity to the imperatives of model specification.

12.5.3 Implementing the principles: some examples from economic history

We start with a very specific issue. An historian has found a set of apprenticeship contracts in the local archives. They contain information on various matters, including the length of the contract, the date it was signed, the occupation and location of the master, the age of the apprentice, and certain details about issues such as probation, pay, and schooling. How should this information be analysed?

A basic economic principle, known as the *diminishing marginal productivity of labour*, states that under competitive conditions a firm should continue to hire labour up to the point where the cost of an extra worker is equal to the additional revenue he will produce. If the same principles are applied to the demand for apprentices on the part of the master – under a system with variable contract lengths – it might be expected that the duration of the contract would be related positively to the cost of the arrangement to the master (in wages paid, board, working time lost while training the apprentice, and so on), and negatively to the value of the output produced by the apprentice.

It is also necessary to consider the contract from the point of view of the apprentice. Here the analysis can build on ideas derived from human capital theory. The essence of this theory is that investments are made in human resources in order to raise their productivity, and thus in time their earnings. The forms of such investment in human capital include formal schooling and on-the-job training, as well as broader factors such as good health and nutrition. The implication of this theory is that apprentices will be willing to sign on for longer contracts, the more they expect their future earnings to be increased by the training received during the apprenticeship.

Working from these ideas Gillian Hamilton was able to develop a successful model of the duration of apprenticeship contracts in late eighteenth- and early nineteenth-century Montreal.[s] Most factors in her model entered the regression as linear explanators. But theoretical considerations recommended the addition of age-squared as a variable to test for non-linear effects in age. Younger boys were both less mature and less experienced, so that employers would require longer service contracts to ensure full recompense for the expense of training. Moreover, the risks that the apprentice would under-perform were highest for the very young, about whom the employer had little or no prior knowledge. The reported coefficient on age is negative while that on the square of age is positive, indicating that contracts became increasingly short, the older the apprentice.[t]

One way for employers to find out something about the potential risk was to require a probationary period before negotiating a contract. Hamilton found that contract lengths were much shorter for probationers, as theory would suggest. Moreover, boys who were sponsored by a guardian served longer terms, consistent with the hypothesis that information was a key ingredient in contract bargaining. The signs and significance of other variables in the regression equation further support the underlying theory, with lengthier contracts for apprentices who negotiated money at the end of the apprenticeship (a form of head-right), or access to schooling or church during it.[11]

A further illustration of the value of human capital theory in historical applications may be found in the analysis of the earnings of immigrants into the United States compared to those of native-born workers in the same occupations. The theory tells us that earnings will be systematically related to variables that affect individual productivity, such as education, work experience, and age. Moreover, it indicates that the relationships will be non-linear, albeit in different ways. Thus, there are diminishing returns to each additional year of experience; whereas the returns to added years of education are likely first to rise (as literacy and learning skills are developed), and then to fall (as knowledge becomes less functional). For manual workers, the relationship between age and earnings certainly has a strong

[s] Gillian Hamilton, 'The market for Montreal apprentices: contract length and information', *Explorations in Economic History*, 33, 1996, pp. 496–523.

[t] The respective coefficients are -2.033 and $+0.043$. Thus at age 10 their combined effect on the length of contract is $(10 \times -2.033) + (100 \times 0.043) = -16.03$. At age 20 it is $(20 \times -2.033) + (400 \times 0.043) = -23.46$, a reduction in contract length of only 7.4, not 10, years. The implied shape of the age–duration relationship is similar to that of an exponential curve (figure 12.3) with a value of b of about 0.9.

quadratic component, with productivity potential rising during early adulthood and falling after middle age, because of factors such as declining physical strength.[12]

Accordingly, models of earnings have been specified with non-linear functional forms, typically by taking the log of earnings as the dependent variable, and by squared terms for age, years of work experience, and – for immigrants – years in the United States, among the explanatory variables. This log-lin formulation thus measures the proportional effect on earnings of these and other variables.[13] One advantage of using age and age squared terms in the human capital variables is that it permits a range of possible functional forms, depending on the sign and size of the coefficients.

Human capital theory, complemented by the pioneering work of sociological investigators such as Seebohm Rowntree in the late nineteenth century, also provides strong foundations for life-cycle theories of income, consumption, and wealth accumulation. A simple model of the path of income and consumption over the life cycle leads to the hypothesis that there will be a strong but changing association between age and accumulated savings (or wealth), leading to hump-shaped wealth–age profiles. While income first rises and then falls over an individual's lifetime, consumption needs tend to remain relatively stable. Elderly individuals, whose human capital has depreciated with time, are likely to find that their earnings are insufficient to cover living expenses. Workers are therefore motivated to save for retirement during the peak earning years.

In any such life-cycle model, a non-linear specification with terms in age and age squared would be required to produce the postulated turning point in the relationship between age and wealth (or savings). When such models are estimated, the regression coefficients on age are typically found to be statistically significant, and the coefficient on age is large relative to the one on age squared, but it is positive whereas the latter is negative. The result of this specification is that the positive term with the large coefficient initially outweighs the negative term, and predicted wealth rises with age. But eventually (as with the exercise fitting non-linear trends in §12.4.2), age squared becomes so much larger than age that despite its smaller coefficient the negative term dominates, and predicted wealth starts to decline.[14]

Normally the turning point in historical studies is found somewhere in late middle-age. At this stage in the life cycle, ageing begins to lower productivity and reduces earning capacity. Consumption, however, continues and households run down their stock of assets to pay for it. The speed of decumulation is likely to increase as the worker moves from middle to old age, either because of formal retirement, or because of reduced opportunities for finding work at good pay.

Life-cycle models focus primarily on the path of total consumption over time. But historians are also interested in understanding the patterns of spending, across income groups and across products. One of the fundamental relationships in the study of demand analysis is the way in which expenditure on particular commodities varies with the income level of the household. This is known as the Engel curve, after a nineteenth-century statistician who established that as the standard of living of the household rises, the proportion of expenditure devoted to food decreases, while the proportion devoted to luxuries increases. Engel curves do not necessarily maintain the same shape for different commodities. This point was made by Prais and Houthakker in a pioneering econometric study of spending patterns of British working- and middle-class households in the late 1930s.[14]

Prais and Houthakker found that spending on some commodities was linearly related to income – a unit change in income produced the same increase in spending for the poor and the comfortably off. For other goods and services, the relationship between expenditure and income was clearly non-linear. However, even within the general category of non-linear relationships, there were a variety of responses, demanding a range of different non-linear specifications. Thus, expenditure on household appliances rose more rapidly than income, suggesting an exponential curve with b greater than 1. By contrast, expenditure on food rose more slowly than income, suggesting a geometric curve with b less than 0. Here is a classic case in which theory tempered by common sense and practical familiarity guided the choice among functional forms.

Micro-economic theories useful to historians are not limited to studies of the individual. There is also a large literature devoted to the behaviour of firms and industries. One very fertile area has been the study of production functions and cost functions, which provide a theoretical specification of the determinants of production or of costs suggesting the use of the double logarithmic form in empirical work. These models have been used to understand the changing structure of American industry in the nineteenth century and its implications for the rate of productivity growth; to compare the productivity and profit performance of state-owned and private utility companies in nineteenth-century Britain; and as the basis for a study of possible explanations for the higher level of productivity attained by the United States, among other topics.[15]

For our final example in this section, we take a subject where a very different form of non-linear relationship applies. A combination of theo-

[14] S. J. Prais and H. S. Houthakker, *The Analysis of Family Budgets*, Cambridge University Press, 1955, pp. 87–100.

retical insights and empirical observation, and of ideas drawn from epi-
demiological work on the spread of disease, stimulated modelling of the
diffusion of new technologies in terms of an S-shaped logistic curve, with
the dependent variable measuring the proportion of firms adopting the
innovative technology.

The general proposition is that there is an initial period of slow growth
when the product or process is first introduced by a small number of more
innovative firms; more rapid diffusion (comparable to contagion) as the
advantages of the technology become more widely known; and a final
phase in which diffusion slows down once the majority of potential users
have installed the technology. Factors underlying this pattern include the
initial lack of information about the advantages of the innovation and the
costs of acquiring this other than by observing the experience of early
adopters, and the gradual reduction of uncertainty as a common perception of the value of the innovation is formed.

For innovations to which these factors apply, these trends are effectively
modelled by a logistic curve, where the parameter, b, measures the speed of
diffusion, and is itself related positively to the profitability of the innovation and negatively to the capital investment required to adopt it.[16] A very
similar model is used in relation to demand for household appliances. In
this context, it is suggested that the speed of diffusion is determined by
whether the innovation merely increases the amount of discretionary time,
as with time-saving appliances such as vacuum cleaners and washing
machines – in which case diffusion is slow; or actually enhances its quality,
as with time-using appliances such as radios and TV sets – in which case
the appliances spread much more rapidly.[17]

Not all theories emanate from economics, of course. It is a strength of
economic history that it is able to draw upon a well-established array of
testable theories. But theory need not be formal to establish hypotheses
against which to judge the empirical evidence. Indeed, some critics of
model-building in economic history have suggested that its theoretical
base is too dependent on a narrow range of assumptions, arguing that the
less formal and more inductive theorizing of other disciplines has its
advantages.

12.5.4 Implementing the principles: some examples from demographic, social, and political history

In the study of past demography, a keen understanding of empirical realities, much of it shaped by graphical analysis, and much originating before
the spread of the computer, has influenced the application of more sophisticated quantitative modelling. Two of the central issues in population

history are the decline in birth and death rates, and the association of these trends with the processes of industrialization and modernization. We mention only a few studies here out of the wide array of quantitative analyses of the demographic transition.

The pioneer of quantitative demography was William Farr, the first Statistical Superintendent of the General Registry Office in London who, during his tenure from 1838 to 1880, wrote a series of reports evaluating the so-called 'laws of mortality'. Among these was Farr's Law, which posited a mathematical relationship between the crude death rate (the ratio of total deaths to population) and urban density. The best fit to the data for registration districts outside London in the 1860s was a geometric model, with b equal to 0.122. Farr's Law has been criticized by more recent scholars, but it represented an important first step towards understanding mortality patterns in mid-Victorian Britain.[18]

A more elaborate model of late-nineteenth-century mortality in Britain has been estimated on data for a sample of 36 towns. As one component of this study, a double logarithmic specification was adopted in which the log of age-specific mortality was regressed on the three sets of explanatory variables, all in logs. These covered measures of density, of public health indicators such as expenditure on sanitation and water, and a measure of nutritional status proxied by the volume of food affordable with the level of real income in the different towns.[v]

A comparative analysis of child mortality in Britain and America at the end of the nineteenth century analysed differences across occupations, focusing primarily on the influence of environment and income. Environment was proxied by the proportion of workers in each occupation who lived in urban centres; this was entered in the regression as a linear variable. Income, however, was entered in log form, 'since we expect to observe diminishing returns in the mortality effects of income gains'.[w]

An earlier study of fertility analysed the number of surviving children under the age of four among a survey of American workers in the late nineteenth century. Among the variables included in the model were measures of household income, the industry and occupation of the (male) household head, whether the wife was working, the ethnicity of the husband, the age of the wife, and the square of wife's age. The last two variables were included to capture 'the curvilinear relationship of fertility to age of woman'. The analysis found that the age variables were large and highly

---

[v] Robert Millward and Frances N. Bell, 'Economic factors in the decline of mortality in late nineteenth century Britain', *European Review of Economic History*, 2, 1998, pp. 263–88.

[w] Samuel H. Preston and Michael R. Haines, *Fatal Years: Child Mortality in Late Nineteenth-Century America*, Princeton University Press, 1991, pp. 194–8.

significant, sketching a parabolic relationship between age and number of children.[x]

Another area in which general principles have been developed on the basis of less formal theorizing is social and political history. Among the many manifestations of social and political disorder are large-scale social movements such as protest meetings, riots, boycotts, and lynchings, as well as more individual actions such as crimes against property, drug addiction, and suicide. On the basis of official records and contemporary newspaper accounts it is generally possible to find information that can be used for quantitative analysis, though the nature of such evidence always requires very careful consideration.[19] Given suitable data, what general principles might inform such analysis?

Sociologists and political theorists have suggested a variety of explanations for such actions. The most straightforward views attribute disorders directly to hardships associated with factors such as high food prices or unemployment. A more general category of explanations includes propositions about the breakdown of existing social norms and constraints, and the creation of discontinuities as a result of developments such as urbanization and industrialization; the impact of rising well-being in encouraging the growth of previously limited expectations; and awareness of relative deprivation between rich and poor or between black and white. Other explanations draw on more general notions of the pursuit of collective self-interest and class solidarity, notably those deriving from Marxist ideas of class-consciousness.

When any of these broad ideas are applied to a specific issue they have, of course, to be supplemented by additional, historically specific, explanatory variables. Thus a study of protests and demonstrations in rural England in the early nineteenth century will need to consider factors such as the effect of enclosures or the introduction of new machinery. Similarly, a study of strikes in a particular period will need to take into account the prevailing labour legislation, the strength and experience of the trade unions, the economic circumstances of the firm or industry in that period, and so on.

There is a voluminous theoretical and empirical literature in this field, and though many studies give careful consideration to the available quantitative data, there are fewer that take the further step of applying a formal statistical technique to explore the suggested hypotheses. We will discuss just one contemporary study to illustrate what can be achieved when regression analysis is used.[20] The issue for consideration is the nature of

---

[x] Michael Haines, *Fertility and Occupation: Population Patterns in Industrialization*, Academic Press, 1979, pp. 212–23.

the relationship between crime and economic conditions.[21] Most theories in the literature of criminology and the related social sciences predict a strong positive relationship for crimes against property, as did Dorothy Thomas in the work reported in §3.2.4. However, in recent years several quantitative studies have found a relationship that was weak or even negative, especially when unemployment was taken as the explanatory variable.[y] In an attempt to explain this, current research has emphasized the existence of two diverse channels relating the state of the economy to crime rates.

An increase in prosperity makes more goods available and so creates more *opportunity* for crime. However, a fall in prosperity leads to an increase in dissatisfaction (or hunger or alienation or sense of deprivation) and so creates a greater *motivation* for crime. Thus if the former is the dominant factor, crime and prosperity will be positively related; if the latter predominates, there will be an inverse relationship.

An analysis made in the late 1980s of crime in post-war England and Wales used regression analysis to explore these connections in depth, focusing especially on short-run fluctuations.[z] The problem of spurious correlation in time series (mentioned in §12.5.1) was overcome by specifying the regression model entirely in first differences of the log of the variables; this is equivalent to measuring the annual growth rates of both the dependent and the explanatory variables (see panel 12.1). Real personal consumption *per capita* was taken as the main measure of economic conditions, and an interesting subsidiary result of the study was that once the effect of personal consumption is taken into account, unemployment fails to add anything extra to the explanation of any type of crime. Other explanatory variables included the proportion of young males in the population, the weather, police strength, and beer consumption.

The primary finding was that economic factors did have a major influence on trends in both property crime and crimes against the person. For crimes such as burglary, robbery, and theft there was a strong tendency for the crime rate to move inversely with the cycles of prosperity and depression, and a similar association was found for the United States, Japan, and France. By contrast, crimes against the person – such as violence and sexual offences – tended to move in the opposite direction, increasing as economic conditions improved.

[y] See the review of the issue in D. Cantor and K. C. Land, 'Unemployment and crime rates in the post-World War II United States: a theoretical and empirical analysis', *American Sociological Review*, 44, 1979, pp. 588–608.

[z] Simon Field, *Trends in Crime and their Interpretation: A Study of Recorded Crime in England and Wales*, HMSO, 1990.

The implication of this finding is thus that for property crime the motivation effect was the most powerful, while for personal crime the opportunity effect dominated. The study explores some of the reasons why this might be so, and also looks at lagged effects to explain the difference between short-term and long-term patterns.

Turning next to the politics of democracy, a variety of issues have been the subject of quantitative analysis. These include voter participation, the effects of incumbency, and – in the United States – the presidential 'coattails' effect; but perhaps the most interesting is the famous proposition associated with President Clinton: 'It's the economy, stupid'. The underlying notion is that a vote represents a rational choice between alternatives, and that one of the fundamental factors which influences that choice is the state of the economy and its impact on the individual voter.[22]

One of the more persuasive of several attempts to investigate this relationship is the multivariate regression model proposed by Bloom and Price.[aa] Their model postulates that voting behaviour is determined by both long- and short-run forces, and is tested on data for US elections for the House of Representatives from 1896 to 1970. It is a linear model, with the dependent variable represented by the deviation of the Republican share of the two-party vote in those elections from the share that would be expected on the basis of a measure of long-run party identification. The explanatory variable is simply the percentage change in real *per capita* income during the year preceding each election, but two separate regressions are estimated, for periods with Republican and Democratic presidents respectively.

The model does not assume that economic conditions are the sole determinants of voting behaviour. Other factors, such as foreign policy and candidates' personalities, are clearly relevant and must be regarded as omitted variables in the terminology of §11.2.2. They are thus represented by the error term as sources of the unexplained variation in the dependent variable, but as long as they are not correlated with the changes in the explanatory variable their omission will not bias resulting estimates of the impact of economic factors on the vote.

In addition to the test over the full set of 37 elections, the regression was run separately for elections preceded by declining income and those preceded by rising income. One of the principal findings is that the relationship between voting and economic conditions is asymmetric. Politicians

---

[aa] Howard S. Bloom and H. Douglas Price, 'Voter response to short-run economic conditions: the asymmetric effect of prosperity and recession', *American Political Science Review*, 69, 1975, pp. 1240–54.

are punished by the voters for economic downturns, but are not rewarded for economic upturns.

If the economy can influence the outcome of elections it is natural to consider the possibility that politicians may seek to influence the economy for political reasons. This aspect of political debate has stimulated numerous quantitative studies of the 'political cycle'. What are the motivations of political parties when formulating their economic policies? Were periods with Republican (or Labour) administrations more or less likely to be associated with low inflation, full employment, rapid growth, and small budget deficits than periods when Democrats (or Conservatives) were in office?

According to the 'opportunistic' theory, political parties have no policy preferences of their own, and simply choose economic policies that maximize their chances of election. The rival 'partisan' theory postulates that left-wing parties are more strongly motivated to promote growth and reduce unemployment than to curb inflation, and that these priorities are reversed for right-wing parties. In recent developments these models have been further refined by the incorporation of rational expectations.

A comprehensive study of this issue by Alesina *et al.* has formulated a series of predictions based on variants of these models, and tested them in a large set of multivariate regressions for the United States, United Kingdom, and other industrial democracies. For target variables such as output, inflation, and the money supply their concern is with rates of growth and so the dependent variable is formulated in logs, but for other targets such as unemployment and the budget deficit it is the level that is relevant and so the relationship is linear. The key explanatory variables are lagged values of the dependent variable, and dummy variables for the periods when the various political parties were in office. The major conclusion, for both the United States and other countries, is that the post-war data generally support the rational partisan theory, particularly with respect to growth and unemployment.[bb]

12.6 Model specification

The models that we have analysed in the previous section have all demonstrated the golden rule of empirical analysis – the establishment of an appropriate analytical framework, derived from a close understanding of the relevant theory, tempered with appreciation of any historical realities

---

[bb] Alberto Alesina, Nouriel Roubini and Gerald D. Cohen, *Political Cycles and the Macroeconomy*, MIT Press, 1997. For a quantitative analysis of the same issues of policy formation in the United Kingdom see Paul Mosley, *The Making of Economic Policy*, Harvester Press, 1984.

that warrant modifications to the framework before it is confronted with the data.

Model specification is not simply about choosing and fine-tuning a model to determine which explanatory variables should be chosen and in what form they should appear in the regression. It is also about determining whether the model so chosen is appropriate, whether it represents a suitable way of interpreting the data, and whether or not it conforms to the empirical realities. After all, there are often competing theories of a particular process or event and we need to establish the appropriate criteria for determining which is the best model.

Controversy exists among quantitative historians, as it does among those working in the cultural and literary end of the discipline. There is no universal consensus, even about theory, and certainly not about implementation. Debates have raged among economic historians over the pace of industrialization in eighteenth- and nineteenth-century Britain, over the economic impact of slavery in the antebellum United States, over the causes of the global Great Depression in the 1930s. Quantitative analysis has often clarified the terms of the debate. Initial disagreement has frequently stimulated improvements in the data base and in model specification, and these have helped to bring about a convergence among critics. Nevertheless, some disputes do remain unresolved.

There are, however, even among disputants, some generally accepted rules of engagement – some agreement about what constitutes best practice. Much of the common ground actually concerns worst practice – what ought never to be done when testing a hypothesis or model. We have already indicated that 'kitchen-sink' regression procedures, in which everything is thrown into the model and variants of the basic regression are run until an acceptable outcome is reached, are to be avoided. About this, there is consensus.[23]

Nonetheless, the use of specification searches to identify the best representation of the model remains common. When a model is run, the researcher pays particular attention to the R^2 of the equation as a whole, to the signs of the regression coefficients and their standard errors, and to diagnostic statistics such as the Durbin–Watson statistic for serial correlation. Often, the researcher is unsure whether a particular variable should be entered in logs or not, or whether lags of the variable should be included. It seems straightforward just to add more terms to determine whether they are statistically significant or not, or to correct for some warning of serial correlation in the DW statistic by running a Cochrane–Orcutt regression. The criticism of this approach is, however, that continual reassessment of the regression equation in this fashion compromises the very statistics used to evaluate the success of the model. If the specification search is motivated by a desire to maximize the value of R^2 and t-statistics, then it is inappropriate to employ them as neutral arbiters of the success or failure of a model.

How, then, should a conscientious reader approach an article to determine whether the researcher has resisted the temptations of specification searches in his work? How should a reader approach empirical controversies? Clearly, we have suggested that traditional arbiters of success, such as R^2 and t-statistics, may mislead. This is not to say that authors who only report such matters are obviously guilty of worst practice, nor that we should automatically throw out their results. But readers would be wise to look for evidence that the research has been undertaken in a less problematical way.

Best-practice methodology focuses on mis-specification searches, i.e. the use of the various instruments discussed in chapter 11 to determine whether the model, or its empirical implementation, suffers from fatal errors of omission or commission. Almost all such tests focus on the properties of the residuals from the regression; the best work indicates that these residuals have been evaluated for problems, such as serial correlation, heteroscedasticity, omitted variables, structural change, etc. Ideally, these tests should be carried out simultaneously, in order to minimize the possibility that the test statistics for each procedure are themselves contaminated by the order in which they are carried out.

If any of the tests do reveal clear evidence of a problem, the researcher should show evidence of having considered the possibility that the model is mis-specified and needs revision, rather than having immediately turned to one of the many tools at her disposal for 'correcting' for the problem.

Obviously, the menu of possible specification errors depends on the type of regression exercise – cross-section models should be tested for some problems, and time-series models for others. But such tests are an essential ingredient of good model-building and should be evaluated by readers.

Any model is, of course, only as good as the data on which it is based. Problems can arise in many ways, including errors of measurement or of omission in the underlying source, errors in drawing samples from the data, and errors in the procedures subsequently adopted to record or process the data. Even if a series is reliable for one purpose, it may be unsuitable if used as a measure of a different concept.[cc] Careful scrutiny of

---

[cc] For example, unwillingness of victims to report crime may mean that an accurate measure of recorded crime is a very poor measure of the crimes actually committed; evasion of tax may

all data before they are used for regression analysis is thus something to which historians must give the highest priority, and visual inspection of the data can be particularly valuable.

It is also very unwise to run regression models borrowed from other studies on a data set that might well have very different properties. Thus, the tendency among some economists to employ historical data in order to run regressions derived from contemporary economic theory as a test of the general validity of the theory, without any attempt to examine the empirical and institutional differences between past and present, is to be deplored.[dd] As a general conclusion, the more information about the procedures employed in evaluating the data *before* and *after* the regression is run, the sounder are likely to be the results and the more convinced the reader should be of their value.

Assume, however, that two researchers have both shown exemplary commitment to the principles of best-practice modelling, but have nonetheless produced divergent results. Are there any other clues that might assist the reader in choosing between them?

One procedure that is often invoked as a good way to test the strength of a model is out-of-sample prediction. This involves reserving some of the data points from the sample, running the model over the rest, and using the regression results to predict the value of the dependent variable *outside* the period over which the regression was estimated. If the model is a good one – *and if the underlying structural conditions have not changed* – the predictions should compare well with the actual values over this additional period. Clearly, if one model has better predictive powers than another over the same omitted sample, this is indicative of model superiority.

Another comparative strategy employed by some researchers is the development of a general model that incorporates both rival interpretations of the event or process being studied. The general model is then gradually pared down as empirically marginal features are discarded, or as rival elements are tested for mis-specification and found wanting.

mean that an accurate measure of income assessed for taxation is a very poor measure of the income actually received by taxpayers.

[dd]The point might be illustrated by studies of the labour market, where theories of wage determination formulated in the late twentieth century might be totally inappropriate in relation to earlier periods in which both the role of trade unions and the size of firms were very different. More fundamentally, human behaviour itself is not immutable. Modern mores and codes of conduct that underpin current theories of individual action in economics, politics, and other disciplines are likely not to have applied in the distant past. See also the more detailed discussion of quantitative studies of historical changes in Larry W. Isaac and Larry J. Griffin, 'Ahistoricism in time-series analysis of historical process: critique, redirection and illustrations from US labor history', *American Sociological Review*, 54, 1989, pp. 873–90.

Both of these initiatives require that the researcher follow a particular empirical strategy; they cannot easily be invoked by readers *ex post*. The reader is left with a less definitive, and possibly more subjective set of comparisons – does the underlying theory in one model seem more plausible than another? Does one empirical application seem more relevant in a specific historical setting than another? Do the regression coefficients in one model make more sense than those in another? The procedure of looking at coefficients and using them to examine the purported relationships between variables can be most illuminating and is often ignored by researchers. Often, the best question to ask of any model is simply: 'Do I believe the results?'

In chapters 14 and 15, we shall focus on four case studies that use regression techniques. Part of what we will be looking for is evidence of the use of diagnostic tools, both formal and informal, to evaluate the overall soundness of the model specification being used.

Notes

[1] We are indebted to Roderick Floud for these data. They are taken from J. M. Tanner, R. H. Whitehouse and M. Takaishi, 'Standards from birth to maturity for height, weight, height velocity and weight velocity: British children, 1965 (Part I)', *Archives of Disease in Childhood*, 41, 1966, pp. 454–71; and I. Knight and J. Eldridge, *The Heights and Weights of Adults in Great Britain*, HMSO, 1984.

[2] If the symbols are changed, economists may recognise (12.5) as the familiar Cobb–Douglas production function, in which output (Q) is determined by inputs of labour (L) and capital (K): $Q = A L^{\alpha} K^{\beta}$. The two features of this specification are (i) the equation is non-linear in variables but linear in parameters, and (ii) the effect of the explanatory variables is multiplicative, not additive.

[3] The manipulation is based on the rules for powers given in §1.6.1, in particular, the rule that any number raised to the power 0 is equal to 1. Thus $e^x \times e^{-x} = e^{x-x} = e^0 = 1$, and we can substitute $e^x \times e^{-x}$ for 1 in both the numerator and the denominator of (12.7a). We therefore get

$$Y = \frac{e^x \times e^{-x}}{e^x \times e^{-x} + e^{-x}} = \frac{e^x \times e^{-x}}{e^{-x}(e^x + 1)} = \frac{e^x \times e^{-x}}{e^{-x}(1 + e^x)}$$

The terms in e^{-x} in the numerator and the denominator then cancel out, to leave the version in 12.7b.

[4] The following points may help some students to see more easily why it is necessary to *multiply* by X. First, the definition of an elasticity, which was initially given as

$$\frac{\Delta Y}{Y} \div \frac{\Delta X}{X}$$

may be re-written as

$$\frac{\Delta Y}{Y} \times \frac{X}{\Delta X}$$

which in turn is the same as

$$\frac{\Delta Y}{\Delta X} \times \frac{X}{Y}$$

Secondly, the definition of b in this semi-log model, which was initially given as

$$\frac{\Delta Y}{Y} \div \Delta X$$

can similarly be re-written as

$$\frac{\Delta Y}{Y} \times \frac{1}{\Delta X} = \frac{\Delta Y}{\Delta X} \times \frac{1}{Y}$$

Multiplication of the second term in this revised definition by X then gives the required elasticity.

[5] $b/1 - \lambda$ gives the value for the long-run multiplier because the sum of all the coefficients on current and past values for SALES in the untransformed (10.15) in §10.2.2, can be written as $b(1 + \lambda + \lambda^2 + \ldots + \lambda^n)$ and the mathematicians tell us that the expression in brackets is an example of a geometric progression which sums to $1/1 - \lambda$.

[6] See, for example, Robert Woods, *The Demography of Victorian England and Wales*, Cambridge University Press, 2000, pp. 377–8, where a third-order polynomial is used to plot the relationship between population density and distance from centre of London. The trend shows an initial rise in density as distance increases and then a decline. In quadratics and higher-order polynomials, the number of turning points is always one less than the size of the highest power.

[7] Richard Layard and Stephen Nickell, 'The labour market', in Rudiger Dornbusch and Richard Layard, *The Performance of the British Economy*, Oxford University Press, 1987, pp.131–79; see especially p.139.

[8] When the problem is confined to two or more of the explanatory variables it represents a form of multicollinearity, a problem briefly discussed in §11.4.2.

[9] Recent developments in time-series statistics have produced even better procedures, such as error-correction mechanisms, but these are too advanced for this text.

[10] For an example of a relatively simple Keynesian model see T. Thomas, 'Aggregate demand in the United Kingdom 1918–1945', in Roderick Floud and Donald McCloskey (eds.), *The Economic History of Britain since 1700, II, 1860 to the 1970s*, 1st edn., Cambridge University Press, 1981, pp. 332–46. A much more advanced and comprehensive model covering the same period is developed in Nicholas H. Dimsdale and Nicholas Horsewood, 'Fiscal policy and employment in inter-war Britain; some evidence from a new model', *Oxford Economic Papers*, 47, 1995, pp. 369–96.

[11] An earlier investigation of servant indentures in colonial America also found some evidence of non-linearity. In this case, age was entered as a series of dummy variables for each year, giving flexibility to the measured relationship between age and length of indenture. The coefficients on the dummies fell from 2.75 for those aged less than

15 to 0.17 for age 19, showing that age and length of indenture were negatively related, while the change in the coefficient for each successive year showed that the relationship was not linear. David Galenson, *White Servitude in Colonial America*, Cambridge University Press, 1981, pp. 97–113.

[12] For a stylized representation of the age–earnings profile derived from data on US households in 1889–90, see Hartmut Kaelble and Mark Thomas, 'Introduction', in Y. S. Brenner, H. Kaelble and M. Thomas (eds.), *Income Distribution in Historical Perspective*, Cambridge University Press, 1991, pp. 19–23.

[13] These points are illustrated by Timothy J. Hatton, 'The immigration assimilation puzzle in late nineteenth-century America', *Journal of Economic History*, 57, 1997, pp. 34–63; and Christopher Hanes, 'Immigrants' relative rate of wage growth in the late 19th century', *Explorations in Economic History*, 33, 1996, pp. 35–64.

[14] Severals models of asset accumulation have found this relationship with age. See, for example, J. R. Kearl, Clayne L. Pope and Larry T. Wimmer, 'Household wealth in a settlement economy: Utah, 1850–1870', *Journal of Economic History*, 40, 1980, pp. 477–96; and Livio Di Matteo, 'Wealth accumulation and the life-cycle in economic history: implications of alternative approaches to data', *Explorations in Economic History*, 35, 1998, pp. 296–324.

[15] On American industry see Jeremy Atack, 'Economies of scale and efficiency gains in the rise of the factory in America, 1820–1900', in Peter Kilby (ed.), *From Quantity to Quiddity*, Wesleyan University Press, 1987, pp. 286–335; and John A. James, 'Structural change in American manufacturing, 1850–1890', *Journal of Economic History*, 43, 1983, pp. 433–59. James Foreman-Peck and Robert Millward, *Public and Private Ownership of British Industry 1820–1990*, Oxford University Press, 1994, pp. 197–239, is a masterly study of the performance of public and private industry. The Anglo-American productivity gap is analysed in S. N. Broadberry and N. F. R. Crafts, 'Britain's productivity gap in the 1930s: some neglected factors', *Journal of Economic History*, 52, 1992, pp. 531–58.

[16] The classic study is Z. Griliches, 'Hybrid corn: an exploration in the economics of technical change', *Econometrica*, 25, 1957, pp. 501–22. See also the application to the diffusion of the stationary high-pressure engine in Cornish mining in the early nineteenth century in G. N. von Tunzelmann, *Steam Power and British Industrialization*, Oxford University Press, 1978, pp. 252–64.

[17] For the application of the logistic curve to expenditure on household durables see Sue Bowden and Paul Turner, 'The demand for consumer durables in the United Kingdom in the interwar period', *Journal of Economic History*, 53, 1993, pp.244–58. The suggested explanation for the logistic pattern is given by Sue Bowden and Avner Offer, 'Household appliances and the use of time: the United States and Britain since the 1920s', *Economic History Review*, 47, 1994, pp. 725–48.

[18] For a critical evaluation of Farr's Law see Woods, *Demography of Victorian England and Wales*, pp. 190–202. Woods also analyses the evidence for a relationship between the incidence of specific diseases, such as measles and tuberculosis, and population density using log-linear models, see pp. 317–25.

[19] See, for example, the exemplary studies of the surviving sixteenth-century judicial records of suicide in S. J. Stevenson, 'The rise of suicide verdicts in south-east England, 1530–1590: the legal process', *Continuity and Change*, 2, 1987, pp. 37–75; of violent crime in J. S. Cockburn, 'Patterns of violence in English society: homicide in Kent, 1560–1985', *Past and Present*, 130, 1991, pp. 70–106; and of the concept of 'crowds' in Mark Harrison, *Crowds and History, Mass Phenomena in English Towns, 1790–1835*, Cambridge University Press, 1988.

[20] Some other examples include Edward Shorter and Charles Tilly, *Strikes in France 1830–1968*, Cambridge University Press, 1974; Neil Sheflin, Leo Troy and C. Timothy Koeller, 'Structural stability in models of American trade union growth', *Quarterly Journal of Economics*, 96, 1981, pp. 77–88; A. R. Gillis, 'Crime and state surveillance in nineteenth-century France', *American Journal of Sociology*, 95, 1989, pp. 307–41; and E. M. Beck and Stewart E. Tolnay, 'The killing fields of the deep South, the market for cotton and the lynching of blacks, 1882–1930', *American Sociological Review*, 55, 1990, pp. 526–39.

[21] For an application of a linear regression model of the relationship between crimes against property and fluctuations in prices in the seventeenth and eighteenth centuries, see the major study by J. M. Beattie, *Crime and the Courts in England, 1660–1800*, Oxford University Press, 1986, pp. 199–237. Prices are measured by the Schumpeter–Gilboy index; the regressions are run separately for urban and for rural parishes in Sussex, and for Surrey, and also distinguish wartime and peacetime periods. The general finding is that there was a clear positive relationship between the fluctuations in prosecutions and in prices (with an R^2 of 0.41 for Surrey and of 0.52 for Sussex), but there were some variations over time and between urban and rural parishes.

[22] The early history of research on this topic is reviewed in one of the seminal modern studies, Gerald H. Kramer, 'Short-term fluctuations in US voting behavior, 1896–1964', *American Political Science Review*, 65, 1971, pp. 131–43. Subsequent studies in the United States include Edward R. Tufte, *Political Control of the Economy*, Princeton University Press, 1978; Gregory B. Markus, 'The impact of personal and national economic conditions on the presidential vote: a pooled cross-sectional analysis', *American Journal of Political Science*, 32, 1988, pp. 137–54; and Robert S. Erikson, 'Economic conditions and the Congressional vote: a review of the macrolevel evidence', *American Journal of Political Science*, 34, 1990, pp. 373–99. For some of the corresponding studies of the United Kingdom see James E. Alt, *The Politics of Economic Decline*, Cambridge University Press, 1979, pp. 113–38.

[23] No doubt part of the reason for this approach lies in the preference among researchers and readers for providing positive results, i.e. finding that a hypothesis is consistent with the data. Were the criteria for judging intellectual quality to include analyses that demonstrate that a model is inconsistent with the data, researchers would have less incentive to employ specification searches until 'good' R^2 and t-statistics were produced.

12.7 Exercises for chapter 12

1. Plot the following time-series relationships from the Benjamin–Kochin data set:

   (i) The level of benefit.
  (ii) The wage rate.
 (iii) The unemployment rate.

In each case, identify the most appropriate functional form to fit these shapes. (*Hint*: choose from the list in §12.1, but note that (iii) involves a polynomial form.)

For each of these three series, estimate a regression model using your chosen functional form. Report your results.

Now predict the residuals from the fitted regression line. If your intuition about the right shape is correct, there should be no obvious non-linear relationship in the residuals when graphed against time. What do you find?

2. In a model of earnings by age for household heads in the United States in 1889–90, the fitted regression line is

$$\text{EARNINGS} = 425.1 + 12.6\,\text{WORKAGE} - 0.3\,\text{WORKAGE}^2$$

where WORKAGE is measured as the actual age in years – 15.

   (i) Draw the curve of this relationship *freehand* (and without using the computer), indicating the direction of slope at younger and older ages.
  (ii) Calculate the age at which earnings begin to decline. What are the average earnings at this age?
 (iii) Can the average worker expect to earn more on retirement (at age 65) than when he started work at age 15?

3. In a model of death rates by age for the Massachusetts population in 1865, the fitted regression line is

$$\text{MORTALITY} = 57.8 - 3.78\,\text{AGE} + 0.06\,\text{AGE}^2$$

where MORTALITY measures the death rate per 1,000 people.

   (i) Draw the curve of this relationship *freehand* (and without using the computer), indicating the direction of slope at younger and older ages.
  (ii) Calculate the age at which the death rate is (a) at its peak; and (b) at its lowest level.

(iii) What is the expected death rate for this population: At the age of 10? At the age of 70?

4. Evaluate the following propositions about non-linear models, indicating whether they are true or false and explaining why:

(i) 'Logarithmic transformation is appropriate for multiplicative non-linear relationships; substitution is appropriate for additive non-linear relationships.'

(ii) 'The advantage of the linear trend model is that, since it is a straight line, it produces a constant growth rate to the data.'

(iii) 'The linear growth rate is measured as the elasticity of the dependent variable against time.'

(iv) 'The number of turning points in a polynomial series is always one less than the size of the power; thus there is 1 turning point in a quadratic equation, 2 in a cubic, etc.'

(v) 'Equation (12.15) indicates that the long-run multiplier will always be larger than the impact multiplier.'

5. You review a regression result of the following form:

$$Y = 5 + 2X_1 - X_2$$

What is the predicted value of Y, given that $X_1 = 2, X_2 = 3$ if:

(i) The model is linear in all terms?
(ii) The model is double-logarithmic?
(iii) The model is semi-logarithmic of the lin-log form?
(iv) The model is semi-logarithmic of the log-lin form?
(v) The model is semi-logarithmic of the exponential form?

What is the impact of a unit change in X_1 in each of these cases?

6. Using the Hatton–Williamson time-series data set on Irish emigration:

(i) Draw a graph of the total emigration rate by year for 1880–1913.
(ii) Fit a linear trend to the data on total emigration by year, 1880–1913.
(iii) Fit a log-linear trend to the data on total emigration by year, 1880–1913.

Compare the results of the two regressions. Which provides the superior fit?

7. Using the log-linear trend regression estimated for question 6:

(i) Work out the implied growth rate for the emigration rate from 1880-1913. How does this compare to the growth rate calculated using the compound growth rate formula (12.17b)?

Would you consider that a great deal of information has been lost by apply-ing the short-hand formula in this case?

(ii) Re-run the log-linear regression for IRMIG over the years, 1877–1913. Report your results and work out the implied growth rate of the emigration rate. How does this rate compare to that cal-culated from the compound growth formula, fitted to the end-points alone?

Would you consider that a great deal of information has been lost by apply-ing the short-hand formula, in this case?

Are there any general lessons about the applicability of the compound growth-rate formula to be learned from a comparison of your findings for the two periods?

8. Use the basic Benjamin–Kochin (OLS) regression to calculate the elastic-ity of unemployment with respect to the benefit–wage ratio.

(i) Re-run the Benjamin–Kochin equation with the logarithm of UNEMP as the dependent variable. What is the elasticity of unem-ployment with respect to the benefit–wage ratio at the mean?

(ii) Re-run the Benjamin–Kochin equation with the logarithm of BWRATIO as the explanatory variable. What is the elasticity of unemployment with respect to the benefit–wage ratio at the mean?

(iii) Re-run the Benjamin–Kochin equation with the logarithm of UNEMP as the dependent variable and the logarithm of BWRATIO as the explanatory variable. What is the elasticity of unemployment with respect to the benefit–wage ratio at the mean?

(iv) Re-run the Benjamin–Kochin model as an OLS equation, with lagged UNEMP as an additional right-hand-side variable. How much different is the long-run multiplier of the benefit–wage ratio on unemployment from the impact multiplier? What is the long-run elasticity?

9. As a test of the Benjamin–Kochin model of inter-war British unemploy-ment, you decide to use out-of-sample prediction. The strategy you decide to pursue is to run the basic model over the period between 1920 and 1935 and evaluate how well it predicts the value of unemployment in 1936–8. What do you find? (*Hint*: you will need to instruct the computer to predict the fitted values from the regression for the additional years; many pro-grams will do this automatically, but do check.) How do the results compare both to actual unemployment and to the predicted value of unemployment from the regression for 1920–38?

You also wish to use out-of-sample prediction to determine whether an alternative model is superior. This model is:

$$UNEMP = a + b_1 \, BENEFIT + b_2 \, WAGE + b_3 \, DEMAND + e$$

Once again, you wish to compare the fitted values for 1936–8 from a regression run over 1920–35 to the actual unemployment rates in those years and to the fitted values from a regression run over the entire sample. Report your results and draw any appropriate inferences.

What does this exercise suggest about the relative strengths of the two models for explaining inter-war unemployment in Britain?

10. Set up a model explaining the time-series behaviour since the Second World War of any ONE of (a) US imports of oil; (b) the divorce rate in the United Kingdom; (c) the level of foreign aid from the G7 countries to African states. Be sure to specify the explanatory variables to be used in the model; the form of the relationship between each explanatory variable and the dependent variable; and what you would look for when analysing the results.

CHAPTER 13

Logit, probit, and tobit models

In our analysis of regression models thus far, we have employed models that implicitly assume that the *dependent* variable is continuous, rather than discrete, and complete, rather than restricted. But many variables that historians are interested in studying do not share these characteristics. If the historian wishes to analyse why a state voted Republican or Democrat in a presidential election, or why some households decided to invest in the stock market in 1929 and others did not, or which country a family decided to migrate to, she is dealing in every case with responses that can take on only a small number of possible values. Similarly, other variables are limited in the range of values they can take – a labour historian investigating individual variation in the length of the working year in weeks will find many more values in her data set, but none above 52 or less than 0.

Such variables are known as **limited dependent variables**. Dependent variables that can take on only a small number of discrete values (such as 0, 1, 2) are known as **qualitative dependent variables**; those that are continuous, but restricted in their range (e.g. never becoming negative), are known as **censored variables**. Because of the restriction on the value of the dependent variable, these and other such questions involve different estimating strategies and require different regression techniques from the standard OLS approach.

In §13.1, we discuss the nature of limited dependent variables in more detail and indicate why standard OLS models are inappropriate for this class of data. In §13.2, §13.3, and §13.4, we introduce two models (known as logit and probit) that are more suited to limited dependent variables and apply them to the simple case of a binary dependent variable. In §13.5, we extend these models to cases in which the dependent variable can take on more than two discrete values. Finally, in §13.6, we focus on the problems of censored dependent variables and briefly discuss two models (known as the tobit and two-stage models) that have been developed expressly for this case.

13.1 Limited dependent variables

13.1.1 Three cases of limited dependent variables

The first case is when the dependent variable is limited by the fact that *it is a categorical or qualitative dummy variable.* As with the dummy explanatory variables discussed in §10.1, dummy *dependent* variables may be restricted so that they can take only the values of 0 or 1 (referred to as **binary** or **dichotomous**); or there may be a larger but still finite number of possible values.

Examples in historical research of a binary dependent variable include: political variables, such as whether an elected representative voted 'yes' or 'no' in a parliamentary vote; economic variables, such as whether or not a worker experienced unemployment last year; and social variables, such as whether or not a widow has remarried. In each case, the response would be coded as 0 (for the negative outcome) or 1 (for the positive).[a]

Alternatively, there may be more than two possible outcomes. The dependent variable may, for example, take the values 0, 1, 2, and 3 (or more).[b] This would be appropriate in a model of occupational status of urban workers, distinguishing between white collar, blue collar, unskilled, and professional employment; or of mode of transport to work (walk, bicycle, automobile, bus, train, etc.).

The second case occurs when the dependent variable is limited because, although it is continuous, *it can take values only within the range of 0 to 1.* For example, the proportion of all debates in a parliamentary session in which an elected representative votes together with her party of affiliation can range from 0 (never) to 1 (always); the proportion of the previous year that a worker was unemployed can range from 0 (not at all) to 1 (all the time); the proportion of households that owns an automobile can range from 0 (nobody) to 1 (everybody). In each case, these variables are calculated as the ratio of positive outcomes to total outcomes and may be expressed as the **average or expected value** of the outcome for the group or individual (see panel 13.1).

The third case arises when a continuous dependent variable is limited *because it is bounded in one direction or the other.* For example, some households may own more than one car, but no household can own fewer than no cars. Thus, the lower limit of automobile ownership is zero. Variables

---

[a] It would be possible to reverse the order and code negative responses as 1, but the standard convention is as described here. However, students are advised to make sure that the historian has followed convention before interpreting regression results.

[b] These are sometimes referred to as either polychotomous or polyotomous variables, but we eschew such linguistic barbarisms.

Panel 13.1   Expected values and probability theory

The term **expected value** is derived from probability theory. It refers to the value that would be expected if a random observation were chosen from the population. It is equal to *the sum of all the possible values, weighted by their individual probabilities.*

Take a game of coin tossing in which you are paid $1 for every head and nothing for a tail. The expected value of your gain from a single coin toss (assuming a fair coin) will be the sum of each value, multiplied by its chance of occurring. In this simple case, it is $1 $\times$ 0.5 + $0 $\times$ 0.5, which equals $0.50. Clearly, you would receive either $1 or nothing for any given toss, but if a very large number of tosses were made, this would be the most likely average of all the values (as in our discussion of sampling distributions in §5.2.1).

This probabilistic exercise can be extended to non-random occurrences. Thus, if half the population owned cars and half did not, the expected value of automobile ownership would be 0.5, an impossible value for any single individual, but the average value across the population as a whole. It is clear that the expected value in this case could range from 0 (no-one owns a car) to 1 (everyone does), and includes any value within these boundaries.

The reason for introducing the term expected value in this chapter is that logit and probit models are framed in terms of probability theory. The dependent variable in the regression formulations is identified as the *probability of an event*, e.g. the probability of a household owning a car given their income, family size, wealth, etc. The regression predicts the expected value of car ownership for households sharing these characteristics.

whose values are bounded in this way are known as **censored**. Most such variables are censored from below, that is they cannot fall below a certain level (usually, they cannot take on negative values). Less commonly, variables are censored from above. One example is the measurement of household savings in a given period, which cannot be greater than the total income received.[c]

[c] A related problem occurs if a sample excludes observations according to some criterion, such as a minimum height requirement in a sample of army recruits, or maximum family size in a survey of household expenditures. Such cases are known as **truncated samples**. Their solution requires more complex econometric theory than is possible in this text. Unhappily, truncated samples do occur with some frequency in historical research and researchers should always be careful to consider the problem.

All these situations complicate regression analysis. OLS methods are generally inappropriate for qualitative and limited dependent variables, and alternative procedures should be employed. The most common approaches used in quantitative analysis of such cases are the so-called logit, probit, and tobit models. These were developed to deal with some of the complexities of modelling limited dependent variables. Twenty years ago they were rarely applied in historical analysis. However, with the explosion in computing power in recent years they are now included in all major computer packages, and there has been an upsurge in their popularity. They have been used to analyse such a wide array of issues in social, political, demographic, and economic history it is hardly necessary to provide examples, but a few references are given to illustrate the range of subjects to which these models have been fruitfully applied.[1]

13.1.2 Why linear models are not appropriate for limited dependent variables

As an illustration of the method of logit and probit models and their superiority over OLS procedures, let us develop a simple example. Figure 13.1 shows the pattern of automobile ownership for a fictitious sample of households in Detroit in 1919. Families either own a car or they do not. Automobile ownership is thus a binary variable, taking the value of 1 (own) or 0 (not own). The explanatory variable in this simple bivariate model is income. The data points (marked by circles) thus lie on one of two horizontal lines.

It is evident from the graph that the frequency of automobile ownership rises with income. The best-fitting OLS regression is superimposed on the data. The slope of the straight line indicates the increased likelihood of a household owning a car as income rises. But the linear model has two serious problems.

First, it produces awkward results. For households with an income below $1,540, it predicts negative ownership; for households with income above $8,815, it predicts a probability of owning a car in excess of one. Neither outcome is possible. Moreover, the standard errors around the OLS coefficients are likely to be high, given the inability of a linear model to fit the pattern of a dependent variable strung along two parallel lines.

Secondly, the OLS regression suffers from heteroscedasticity: the size of the error term will be different for those who own automobiles and those who do not.[2] Since automobile ownership is related to the level of income, it therefore follows that the variance of the error term depends on the value of the explanatory variable. This contradicts the assumption of

Figure 13.1
Pattern of
automobile
ownership,
Detroit, 1919

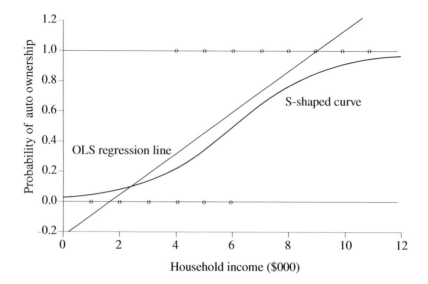

homoscedasticity, one of the fundamental conditions of the classical linear regression model (see panel 9.1 and §11.3.2).

The linear model is clearly not ideal. What should we use instead? The first step is to drop the assumption of linearity and instead apply a functional form for the regression line that is more consistent with the data. We have already employed this tactic in chapter 12 when dealing with non-linear variables. In essence, the solution to the problem of dichotomous variables merely extends the logic of curve-fitting to cover the special case of limited dependent variables.

Figure 13.1 clearly shows that the best way to fit a curve to the observations on Detroit automobile ownership is to use a sigmoid shape – an elongated S-shaped curve that approaches zero at its lowest values and one at its highest. A large number of functional forms take on this shape. However, most analysis is based on the cumulative distribution function of one of two theoretical distributions.

A **cumulative distribution function (cdf)** is an ogive (see §2.1.3) fitted to the density function of a particular distribution; for example, the density function of the standard normal distribution explained in §5.4.1. The cdf is generated by adding up (cumulating) the successive values of the density function from its lowest to its highest value.

One such cdf is the **logistic curve**.[3] We have already met this in chapter 12 and seen in figure 12.6 that it demonstrates the required S-shape. It is this curve that is fitted to the data in figure 13.1.

Figure 13.2
Cumulative
distribution function
of the standardized
normal distribution

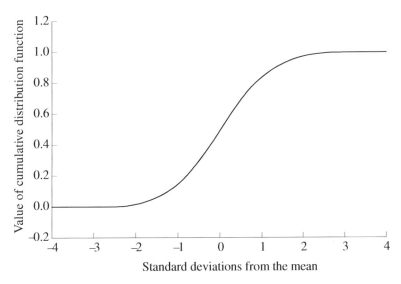

The standard normal distribution also takes on the S-shape when it is changed from a density function to a cumulative distribution. To see why this is so, recall from §2.6.2 that in the standardized normal distribution, the area under the curve sums to one. The speed with which the *cdf approaches one* will be slow at the start of the distribution (the extreme furthest left from the mean) and at the end (furthest right from the mean), where the slope of the normal curve is low and thus the successive increments in the cdf are small. The speed will reach its maximum in the middle of the distribution where the slope is greater, and the increments are large. This is reflected in the shape of the cdf of the normal curve – shallow at the extremes and steepest in the middle – as depicted in figure 13.2.

The regression strategy is to take one of these forms and fit it to the data. Regression models that assume a logistic distribution function are known as **logit** models. Those that assume a normal distribution function are known as **probit** models.[d] Every major computer program allows the researcher to estimate either probit or logit models on any given data set. We focus on each of these models in turn, beginning with the logit model.

---

[d] It would in some respects be more appropriate to refer to the probit model as the normit, reflecting its origin in the normal curve, just as the logit is derived from the logistic curve.

13.2 Estimating the logit model: coefficients, absolute effects, and elasticities

13.2.1 The logit regression model

Consider an analysis of household ownership of automobiles, in which the dependent variable is binary (either owning a car or not). The relevant explanatory variables might include family income, the size of the family, location, etc.

Were the researcher to choose a linear regression model, this would be formulated as

$$Y_i = a + b_1 X_1 + b_2 X_2 + b_3 X_3 + e \tag{13.1}$$

where

$Y_i = 1$ if the household owned an automobile

and

$Y_i = 0$ if the household did not own an automobile

The dependent variable may be interpreted as the probability of owning a car. However, as we have already seen, the linear model is inappropriate to this case; and so she adopts the logit model instead.

This model assumes that the probability of owning a car is distributed according to the **logistic function**. This is a variant of the logistic equation, the particular derivation of which was explained in §12.1

$$Y = \frac{e^x}{1 + e^x} \tag{13.2}$$

The term e^X stands for 'e raised to the power X', where e is the exponential constant $= 2.7183$ and the variable X is referred to as the exponent (see §1.6).[e]

The special feature of the logistic function is that the X in (13.2) is replaced by the *constant and all of the explanatory variables in the relevant regression equation*. For example, for the model specified in (13.1), the logistic function would be

$$Y = \frac{e^{a + b_1 X_1 + b_2 X_2 + b_3 X_3}}{1 + e^{a + b_1 X_1 + b_2 X_2 + b_3 X_3}} \tag{13.3a}$$

This is a very cumbersome expression to work with, and in order to simplify it we will replace the intercept, all the explanatory variables and their

---

[e] An alternative way of writing 'e to the power X' is exp(X), and this variant is occasionally seen in articles and textbooks. In this chapter, we will retain the use of e^x.

coefficients by the single letter, w. w is not a conventional symbol, but is simply used here as a convenient shorthand expression. Equation (13.3a) thus becomes

$$Y = \frac{e^w}{1 + e^w} \tag{13.3b}$$

We can now apply this procedure to the specific form of the logit model. The logit model relates to each individual unit in the sample, in this case the households that either own or do not own a car. It assumes that the probability of owning a car is distributed according to the logistic function, which takes the value

$$P(Y_i = 1) = \frac{e^w}{1 + e^w} \tag{13.4}$$

where $P(Y_i = 1)$ indicates the probability of the ith household owning an automobile.

The probability of the ith household not owning a car is similarly $P(Y_i = 0)$, which equals $1 - P(Y_i = 1)$. Substituting this in (13.4) gives

$$P(Y_i = 0) = 1 - \frac{e^w}{1 + e^w} \tag{13.5a}$$

By a process of manipulation, this can be simplified either to[4]

$$P(Y_i = 0) = \frac{1}{1 + e^w} \tag{13.5b}$$

or to

$$P(Y_i = 0) = \frac{e^{-w}}{1 + e^{-w}} \tag{13.5c}$$

The method by which this set of equations, (13.4) and (13.5c), is solved is known as **maximum likelihood**. Essentially, the procedure chooses the value of the model parameters, a and b_i, to provide the best fit to the distribution of the dependent variable. An intuitive explanation is provided in panel 13.2.

The parameters so chosen are the **logit coefficients**.

13.2.2 Interpreting logit coefficients

The computer reports the logit results in standard format – a constant term plus coefficients on each explanatory variable. The computer also reports the standard errors (and/or t-statistics) for each term. In many cases historians are happy simply to reproduce the logit coefficients and t-statistics,

Panel 13.2   Maximum-likelihood models

In previous chapters, our regression analysis has been based on the application of classical linear regression models, such as OLS. Not all applications are amenable to CLR models, however, and econometricians have developed alternative methodologies. Among the most important of these is a class of models based on **maximum-likelihood** techniques.

Maximum-likelihood models are mathematically very complex, requiring sophisticated calculus tools well beyond the level of this text. Since they are now part and parcel of every statistical computer package, there is no need to work through their formal mechanics. Nonetheless, it is helpful to understand the general methodology involved, and we can explain the procedure intuitively.

The basic approach of maximum-likelihood models is to fit a specified model to a specific set of data. The researcher chooses the model and then asks the computer to select the parameters of the model that *best replicate the data set*. The model selection is taken from the range of probability distributions, including the normal distribution, the lognormal, the logistic, etc. Each of these has specific attributes (mean, variance, skewness, etc.) that govern its shape and position. The model may be chosen on theoretical grounds (it reflects the process by which the events recorded in the data were produced), empirical grounds (it looks like the distribution of the data), or practical grounds (it is easy to estimate).

Note, however, that each distribution has an infinite number of possible outcomes, depending on the specific mix of attributes (parameters). Every normal curve, for example, has the same basic bell-shape, but different means and variances will produce different variants of the basic shape (as illustrated in figure 2.5).

The maximum-likelihood model is designed to find out which combination of parameters best fits the sample data; in other words, to find which combination maximizes the likelihood of reproducing the data. The model searches among the possible parameter values until the optimal combination is found. The chosen parameters are the maximum-likelihood estimates for this particular model fitted to this particular data set.

Let us use a simple example. We randomly draw ten individuals from the entire US population to assist a sports manufacturer decide how many left-handed golf clubs to produce. We signify right-handed people by 0 and left-handed as 1. The results of the survey are $(0, 0, 1, 1, 0, 0, 0, 0, 1, 0)$. What distribution of attributes is most likely to produce this outcome? We assume

Figure 13.3

Maximum-
likelihood function

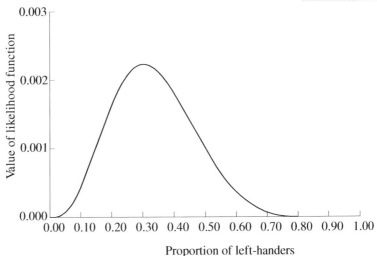

that there is only one parameter that matters, namely the proportion of left-handed people in the population. We symbolize this proportion by p. What proportion is likely to produce this result?

Clearly, it cannot be that all Americans are either left- or right-handed; thus the **likelihood** of $p=0$ and $p=1$ are both zero. If the proportion were 0.1 (1 in 10), each occurrence of a right-handed observation would occur with a probability of 0.9, and each occurrence of a left-handed with a probability of 0.1. Since the individuals were chosen randomly from a very large population, each observation is independent, such that the probability of drawing this specific sample is the *product* of each separate probability.

Thus, if $p=0.1$, the likelihood of generating our sample is

$$0.9 \times 0.9 \times 0.1 \times 0.1 \times 0.9 \times 0.9 \times 0.9 \times 0.9 \times 0.1 \times 0.9 = 0.0004783$$

Similarly, if $p=0.2$, the likelihood would be:

$$0.8 \times 0.8 \times 0.2 \times 0.2 \times 0.8 \times 0.8 \times 0.8 \times 0.8 \times 0.2 \times 0.8 = 0.0016777$$

which is a little higher than with $p=0.1$.

The likelihood can be applied to every other value of p between 0 and 1. The distribution of probabilities from such a process is depicted in figure 13.3. The distribution reaches its peak at $p=0.3$, as we would anticipate.

This picture sketches the **likelihood function**. The formula for the likelihood function in this case is:

$$L(p) = \prod_{y_i=1} p \times \prod_{y_i=0} (1-p) \tag{13.6}$$

where $\prod_{y_i=1}$ indicates the product of all the positive terms and $\prod_{y_i=0}$ the product of all the negative terms. Dealing with product terms can be complicated, especially when working with more complicated distributional forms. Generally, therefore, researchers prefer to use the logarithm of the likelihood function, or the **log-likelihood function**, which is additive rather than multiplicative in the terms. This is defined for our simple example as:

$$\log L(p) = \sum_{y_i=1} \log p + \sum_{y_i=0} \log(1-p) \tag{13.7}$$

which may be re-written as:

$$\log L(p) = n_1 \log p + (n - n_1)\log(1-p) \tag{13.8}$$

where n and n_1 indicate the total number of observations and the number of positive observations, respectively.

Both the likelihood and the log-likelihood functions reach their highest values when $p = 0.3$. This is the **maximum-likelihood estimate** of p for this class of distribution and this particular sample.

The example establishes the methodology commonly applied in maximum-likelihood models:

(a) Select the distribution most appropriate to the data being investigated.
(b) Establish the likelihood function for given parameters of the distribution.
(c) Determine the value of the parameters that maximize the value of the likelihood function, given the data.

The parallels between our simple model and the general problem involving dichotomous dependent variables should be clear. A given sample produces a series of observations that are binary, taking the value of 0 or 1. We interpret these values as probabilities and try to determine what factors influence the particular distribution of 0s and 1s among the sample.

In the case of the logit model, the assumed distribution of the data is the logistic. The likelihood function is constructed by assigning (13.4) and (13.5c) to the positive and negative outcomes respectively. Thus, the log-likelihood function may be written as

$$\log L = \sum_{Y_i = 1} \log \frac{e^w}{1 + e^w} + \sum_{Y_i = 0} \log \frac{e^{-w}}{1 + e^{-w}} \qquad (13.9)$$

The computer iterates around the possible values of the parameters embedded in w until it finds that combination that maximizes the value of the function, i.e. comes closest to mimicking the actual distribution of outcomes in the sample. This produces the maximum-likelihood estimates of a, the constant, and b_i, the coefficients, as reported in column (1) of table 13.2.

and to limit inferences to the sign and significance of each coefficient.[f] The signs and the standard errors of logit coefficients may be interpreted in exactly the same way as for OLS regressions. For example, if the sign of a coefficient is negative, it indicates that the dependent variable falls as the explanatory variable increases in value. If the t-statistic falls below a critical level, it indicates that the logit coefficient is not statistically significantly different from zero at a certain level of α. Similarly, the larger the t-statistic, the smaller the confidence interval around the reported coefficient.[g]

However, in other cases, an historian may not consider it sufficient to establish the sign and significance of the logit coefficients. She may also be interested in making comparisons across coefficients, to determine which explanatory variable has a greater impact on a particular outcome. Alternatively, she may wish to discover how big an impact a certain change in the explanatory variable (say, income) has on the value of the dependent variable (say, the probability of owning a car). In order to accomplish any of these tasks, it is necessary to understand exactly how the logit coefficient is to be interpreted.

It may be obvious from the way this has been stated, that interpreting logit coefficients is not as straightforward as it is with an OLS regression. Unlike the OLS formulation, the coefficient, b_k, is not a direct measure of the change in the dependent variable, $P(Y_i = 1)$ for a unit change in explanatory variable, X_k. Moreover, we cannot simply substitute the value of X_k

[f] Note, however, that no empirical meaning can be ascribed to the constant term in a logit function.

[g] Some programs also produce prob-values for the logit coefficients.

into the equation and read off the value of the dependent variable directly, as with OLS formulations. The information can be abstracted, but it requires some manipulation of the coefficients.

To understand what is at issue, let us return to our sample of Detroit households in 1919. We have estimated a logit model for the pattern of automobile ownership with income as the sole explanatory variable, X_1. The coefficient on income is found to be 0.6111; the constant term is -3.6921. We wish to know the predicted level of automobile ownership at a certain income, say, \$2 thousand. The **value of the logit function** at that income level can be calculated by substituting the coefficients and the value of the explanatory variable into the regression equation, $a + b_1 X_1$. This produces

$$-3.6921 + (0.6111 \times 2) = -2.4699$$

Clearly, this figure cannot be the expected probability of owning a car, since that must lie between 0 and 1. How can we move from what we see (the value of the logit function), to what we want to know (the probability of car ownership at $X_1 = 2$)?

The first step in answering this question is to note that if we divide (13.4) by (13.5b) we get

$$e^w = \frac{P(Y_i = 1)}{P(Y_i = 0)} \tag{13.10a}$$

where e^w is the expected value of the dependent variable from the regression.[5] The ratio of the two probabilities on the right-hand side of the equation is known as the **odds ratio**.

THE ODDS RATIO

This is the ratio of the

probability of a positive outcome, $P(Y_i = 1)$,
to the
probability of a negative outcome, $P(Y_i = 0)$.

It is thus equal to

$$\frac{P(Y_i = 1)}{P(Y_i = 0)} \tag{13.10b}$$

If we take the logarithm of both sides of (13.10a), the left-hand side becomes w, and the right-hand side equals the natural logarithm of the odds ratio, usually referred to as the **log odds ratio**.[6] Thus,

$$w = \log_e \left(\frac{P(Y_i = 1)}{P(Y_i = 0)} \right) \tag{13.11}$$

To complete the derivation, recall that w is our shorthand term for the complete set of explanatory variables, $a + b_k X_k$. Thus, *the log odds ratio is equal to the estimated value of the logit function at a given set of explanatory variables.*

THE LOG ODDS RATIO

This is the
logarithm of the odds ratio.

It is equal to

$$\log_e \left(\frac{P(Y_i = 1)}{P(Y_i = 0)} \right) \tag{13.11}$$

and since this equals w,

the log odds ratio is thus also equal to
*the value of the logit function
at a given set of X_k.*

In our hypothetical Detroit sample, the measured value of the logit function, w, at $X_1 = \$2$ thousand was -2.4699. In order to transform this into the *predicted* probability of owning an automobile, $P(Y_i = 1)$, which we may represent by $\hat{P}_Y$, we have to undertake the following steps:

(i) Take the exponent of -2.4699; this equals 0.0846. This step transforms the log odds ratio into the odds ratio proper (e^w, as in (13.10a)).
(ii) Divide 0.0846 by 1.0846; this produces 0.078. This step extracts the value of $P(Y_i = 1)$ from the odds ratio (using $e^w/(1 + e^w)$), as previously shown in (13.4).

Thus, $\hat{P}_Y$ at an income level of \$2 thousand is 0.078, or 7.8 per cent. We can use the same procedure to calculate $\hat{P}_Y$ for any other income level in the sample.[h]

---

[h] The procedure is the same, no matter how many explanatory variables there are in the regression.

The procedure may also be used to calculate the *average* level of automobile ownership for the sample as a whole from the logit regression. This could be accomplished by first estimating $\hat{P}_Y$ for each observation and then calculating its average. However, such a laborious process is unnecessary, since the average value of $\hat{P}_Y$ is precisely equal to the mean of $P(Y_i = 1)$ for the sample as whole (which we designate as $\bar{P}_Y$). Thus, $\Sigma\hat{P}_Y/n = \bar{P}_Y$. This result is the maximum-likelihood equivalent of the standard OLS finding that the sum of all the deviations from the regression line is equal to zero; the logit regression provides the best fit to the data on average.[7]

THE AVERAGE PREDICTED VALUE OF P_Y

The *average predicted value*
of the dependent variable
for all the observations from the logit regression is

$$\frac{1}{n}\sum_i \hat{P}_{Y_i}$$

This is
precisely equal to
the sample mean of the dependent variable, $\bar{P}_Y$.

The procedure outlined in this subsection shows how to calculate the probability of a given outcome for a certain *level* of an explanatory variable. But it does not permit us to measure the impact of a *change* in the explanatory variable on the outcome. Thus, we can work out what the chances of owning a car are for any given level of income, but we do not yet know how to calculate how much the chances will change as income rises. In the next three subsections, we will focus on this second issue.

Our discussion of the effects of a change in an explanatory variable will distinguish between the impact on the dependent variable, $P(Y_i = 1)$ of an *absolute* change in an explanatory variable and of a *proportionate* change. The former would be most appropriate if the aim is to discover which explanatory factor had the largest influence on a particular decision. The latter would be most appropriate if the aim is to understand how sensitive a decision is to a given change in one or more explanatory factors. We will discuss the effects of an absolute change in §13.2.3 and §13.2.4, and will deal with the proportionate changes in §13.2.5.

13.2.3 Absolute changes: marginal effects and impact effects

The impact on the dependent variable, $P(Y_i = 1)$, of an *absolute change* in an explanatory variable, X_k, can be measured in two different ways. The **marginal effect** measures the impact of an *infinitesimal* change in X_k. This impact is commonly indicated by the expression, $\partial P_Y / \partial X_k$.[i]

THE MARGINAL EFFECT

This is the
impact on the dependent variable, $P(Y_i = 1)$,
of
an infinitesimal change in an explanatory variable, X_k.

It is indicated by the expression

$$\frac{\partial P_Y}{\partial X_k}$$

The alternative **impact effect** measures the *change in $P(Y_i = 1)$ relative to a (larger) finite change in X_k.* The impact effect of an absolute change in X_k is commonly indicated by the expression, $\Delta P_Y / \Delta X_k$, where Δ (capital Greek delta) is the mathematical symbol for a finite change. It is usually calculated for a change of one unit in X_k, although the impact of other finite changes may also be estimated. Since $\Delta P_Y / \Delta X_k$ is a ratio (unlike $\partial P_Y / \partial X_k$), the scale of the impact effect differs as ΔX_k changes. If the effect is measured for a change of one unit then $\Delta X_k = 1$, and the impact effect is simply equal to ΔP_Y.

---

[i] $\partial P_Y / \partial X_k$ is the mathematical symbol representing a very small change in $P(Y_i = 1)$ caused by a very small change in one explanatory variable, X_k, while any other explanatory variables are held constant. (For the mathematically inclined, it is the partial derivative of the logistic function with regard to X_k at the point of measurement.) Note that it must be thought of as a single expression; unlike $\Delta P_Y / \Delta X_k$, it is *not* a ratio of a numerator to a denominator, in which the value of the denominator can change from one calculation to another.

THE IMPACT EFFECT

This is the
change in the dependent variable, $P(Y_i = 1)$,
relative to
a finite change in an explanatory variable, X_k.

It is indicated by the expression

$$\frac{\Delta P_Y}{\Delta X_k}$$

The difference between these two measurements can be illustrated with reference to a diagram of the logistic curve. Figure 13.4 reproduces the fitted values of the logit regression of automobile ownership on income for our Detroit sample. It is constructed by calculating the logit value, w, for each observation, using the coefficient values of a and b_1 (-3.6921 and 0.6111), and then converting these to predicted values of automobile ownership for each household, using the procedure laid down in steps (i) and (ii) in §13.2.2.

We have identified two points, A and B, on the logit curve. These show the predicted level of automobile ownership ($\hat{P}_Y$) when income (X_1) equals $2 and $3 thousand respectively. The line joining the points indicates the change in $\hat{P}_Y$ for a one-unit change in X_1 (in this case, $\Delta X_1 = \$1$ thousand). *The slope of this line indicates the impact effect on P_Y of a unit change in X_1.* In terms of the expression for the impact effect, the size of ΔX_1 is one unit; ΔP_Y will be equal to the change in $\hat{P}_Y$ between A and B.

The other way to measure the slope is to fit a line that is *tangential* to the curve at a particular point, say A. The slope of this line is exactly equal to the slope of the curve at that point. It is indicated on figure 13.4 as a dotted line. *The slope of this line indicates the marginal effect on P_Y of an infinitesimal change in X_1.* Both ∂X_1 and ∂P_Y are very small (too small for the eye to see, perhaps). However, the comparative changes of X_1 and P_Y may be evaluated by extrapolating from the infinitesimal to a finite change by moving along the slope of the dotted line.

What the slopes tell us

There are two points to note regarding the slopes. First, the slope of the dotted line and the solid line in figure 13.4 are different. Our two different methods of measuring the change in P_Y resulting from an absolute change

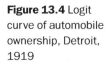

Figure 13.4 Logit curve of automobile ownership, Detroit, 1919

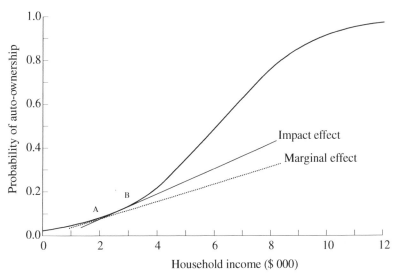

in X_k thus produce two different estimates (this can be seen by comparing the size of the increase in P_Y occasioned by a one-unit change in X_k along the two lines). *The marginal effect and the impact effect will be different for the same logistic curve, when measured at the same level of X_k.*

It is therefore important to determine when to use one measure rather than the other. The general rule of thumb is that the researcher is interested in measuring the effect of the smallest meaningful change in the explanatory variable. If we are dealing with a continuous variable, such as income, this suggests calculation of the effect of an infinitesimal movement in X_k (the marginal effect). On the other hand, if we are dealing with a discrete explanatory variable, whose values change by one unit at a time (a dummy variable, for example, whose value changes from 0 to 1), it is more appropriate to measure the impact of a one-unit change in X_k (the impact effect). The marginal effect can be calculated for a discrete variable, but the relevance of measuring the impact of an infinitesimal change in a variable that can move only by one unit at a time is clearly limited.

Second, *the size of both the marginal effect and the impact effect depend on the level of X_k at which they are estimated.* In the linear OLS model, the slope of the regression line remains the same throughout the sample. This is clearly not true of the logit function. The slope of both the solid and the dotted lines will vary depending on where they are measured on the logit curve. If we measured the impact effect of a change from $4 to $5 thousand dollars, we would find that the slope of the line joining the two points on the logit curve would be steeper than the solid line joining A and B.

Likewise, the slope of the dotted line also varies along the curve. This can be seen by comparing the tangency lines at A and B in figure 13.4. It happens that the slope (and therefore the size of the marginal effect) is largest at the middle of the logit curve (i.e. when the predicted value of $P(Y_i = 1) = 0.50$). The further we move from the middle of the curve, the more the slope will diminish (and the marginal effect will decline in value). The varying slopes are due to the inherent non-linearity of the logit curve.

It is therefore important not to place too much emphasis on the measurement of either the marginal or the impact effect of a change in an explanatory variable at a single point on the curve. But on the other hand, researchers have no wish to report a whole battery of results for each individual, or for each possible permutation of the explanatory variables. They invariably do provide one indicator of the effect of an absolute change, and this is usually the *average* marginal, or *average* impact, effect for all observations. This collapses the multiplicity of possible outcomes into a single index, which gives equal weight to the effect of a change in, say, income on car ownership for every household in the sample.

13.2.4　Calculating the marginal and impact effects

Having explained these two terms, we must now show how the change in $P(Y_i = 1)$ is calculated, both for an individual case (in the Detroit example, a particular household with a certain income), and for the sample as a whole (all households). We begin with an explanation of the procedure for calculating the marginal effect of a change in an explanatory variable.

The marginal effect for an individual case
The first form of impact defined in §13.2.3 was the **marginal effect.** For the ith individual household this is equal to $\partial P_{Yi}/\partial X_k$. It can be shown that[8]

$$\frac{\partial P_{Yi}}{\partial X_k} = P(Y_i = 1) \times P(Y_i = 0) \times b_k \qquad (13.12)$$

where $P(Y_i = 1)$ and $P(Y_i = 0)$ are the predicted values of the ith household owning and not owning a car at the chosen value of X_k, and b_k is the logit coefficient.

In order to apply this formula it is necessary to calculate $P(Y_i = 1)$ by the procedure laid down in §13.2.2, and $P(Y_i = 0)$ can be obtained directly from this. For the Detroit sample the required sequence of steps when income is $2 thousand is as follows:

(i) Log odds ratio   = Value of logit function at $X = \$2$ thousand

   $= -3.6921 + (0.6111 \times 2)$

   $= -2.4699$

(ii) Odds ratio $= \exp(-2.4699)$

   $= 0.0846$

(iii) Value of $P(Y_i = 1)$ $=$ Odds ratio/$(1 +$ Odds ratio$)$

   $= 0.0846/1.0846$

   $= 0.078$

(iv) Value of $P(Y_i = 0)$ $= 1 - P(Y_i = 1)$

   $= 1 - 0.078$

   $= 0.922$

The marginal effect on automobile ownership of a change in income for a household whose income is $2 thousand can thus be calculated by substituting these results in (13.12) to get $0.078 \times 0.922 \times 0.6111 = 0.044$.

The marginal effect for the sample as a whole
This completes the calculation of the marginal effect for an individual case, but it is also necessary to obtain the effect for the *sample as a whole*. The marginal effect of a change in X_k for the whole sample is equal to the *average of all the individual marginal effects*. Thus,

$$\frac{\partial P_Y}{\partial X_k} = \frac{1}{n} \sum_i \frac{\partial P_{Y_i}}{\partial X_k} \tag{13.13a}$$

On the basis of (13.12), this can be re-written as

$$\frac{\partial P_Y}{\partial X_k} = b_k \times \sum_i \frac{\hat{P}_{Y_i} \times (1 - \hat{P}_{Y_i})}{n} \tag{13.13b}$$

where $\hat{P}_{Y_i}$ indicates the predicted probability of owning an automobile for the ith household, and $(1 - \hat{P}_{Y_i})$ is the predicted probability of the household not owning an automobile. The second term in the equation is less daunting than it may appear; it is simply the average across all the observations of the product of the predicted probabilities of owning and not owning a car.

In the specific case of the Detroit sample, the logit coefficient on income is 0.6111; the sample mean of the product of the individual probabilities is 0.1542. So the marginal effect of an infinitesimal change in income on automobile ownership is calculated as $0.6111 \times 0.1542 = 0.0942$.

There remains the question of how the reported value of the marginal effect should be interpreted. Is 0.0942 a large number or a small one? Without a point of comparison, it is hard to tell. In a bivariate model, therefore, with only one explanatory variable, the marginal effect is of limited interest. In a multivariate model, however, it provides a means to compare the impact on the dependent variable of very small changes in each of the explanatory variables. One variant of this approach that is often to be found in logit (and probit) exercises is the publication of the ratio of the marginal effects, indicating the relative strength of the explanatory variables in influencing the behaviour of the dependent variable.

The impact effect for an individual case

As an illustration of how to calculate the alternative measure of the **impact effect**, we measure the impact of a change in X_k of precisely one unit. The procedure to be followed is an extension of the procedure for calculating the value of $\hat{P}_Y$ at any given level of X_k. It therefore requires further manipulation of the log odds ratio, introduced in (13.11).

Recall that the log odds ratio is equal to the value of the logit function predicted by the regression model at any specified value of X_k. Our task now is to see how the log odds ratio responds to a change in X_k, and how we should translate this change into the impact on the ultimate dependent variable, the probability of $P(Y_i = 1)$. One way to work this out would be to recalculate the value of the logit function replacing X_k with its new value and then go through the procedure for extracting the value of $P(Y_i = 1)$ as in §13.2.2 or the calculation just made for the marginal effect.

However, there is a slightly quicker route to a solution. The crucial element in this revised procedure is to recognize that the coefficient b_k measures *the change in the log odds ratio* for a *unit change* in X_k, while holding all other variables constant. Thus,

$$b_k = \Delta \log_e \left(\frac{P(Y_i = 1)}{P(Y_i = 0)} \right) \tag{13.14}$$

The *new value of the log odds ratio* after the change is thus *equal to the original value plus the regression coefficient.*

We can illustrate the procedure with reference to our Detroit sample, and we again take the individual household with an income of $2 thousand.[9] The predicted value of $\hat{P}_Y$ for this household has already been calculated (in §13.2.2) at 0.078. The sequence of steps to calculate the new predicted value of $\hat{P}_Y$ for an increase in income of one unit ($1 thousand) is as follows:

(i) New value of log odds ratio $=$ original value $+$ logit coefficient on income

$$= -2.4699 + 0.6111$$
$$= -1.8588$$

(ii) New value of odds ratio $= \exp(-1.8588)$
$$= 0.1559$$

(iii) New value of $P(Y_i = 1)$ $=$ new odds ratio/$(1 +$ new odds ratio$)$
$$= 0.1559/1.1559$$
$$= 0.1349$$

(iv) Change in $P(Y_i = 1)$ $=$ new value of $P(Y_i = 1) -$ old value
$$= 0.1349 - 0.0780$$
$$= 0.0569.^j$$

The impact effect of a unit change in the explanatory variable is thus 0.0569. This might also be represented as a percentage, by multiplying by 100 to produce 5.69 per cent.

The impact effect for the sample as a whole

The final version required is the calculation of the impact effect for the sample as a whole. The impact effect of a unit change in X_k for all households in the sample is measured by the *average of the individual impact effects* for each sample observation. Thus,

$$\frac{\Delta P_Y}{\Delta X_k} = \frac{1}{n} \sum_i \frac{\Delta \hat{P}_{Y_i}}{\Delta X_k} \tag{13.15a}$$

In the unit case, where $\Delta X_k = 1$ for all observations, this simplifies to

$$\frac{\Delta P_Y}{\Delta X_k} = \frac{1}{n} \sum_i \Delta \hat{P}_{Y_i} \tag{13.15b}$$

On the face of it, this requires the tedious process of going through steps (i) through (iv) above for every household in the sample.

---

^{j} Researchers sometimes report **odds-ratio coefficients** rather than logit coefficients when presenting their results. These are exactly equivalent: the odds-ratio coefficient is simply the exponential of the logit coefficient. But, if the results are reported in this way, it becomes possible to reduce the number of steps to calculate the change in $\hat{P}_Y$ for a unit change in X_k. The new value of the odds ratio (step (ii)) is equal to the odds-ratio coefficient *multiplied* by the original odds ratio. The remaining steps are the same.

Fortunately, however, both theory and the computer come to the researcher's rescue. Another way of expressing (13.15b) is as the difference between P_Y *before and after* a unit change in X_k, averaged over all observations. Theory tells us that the average value of P_Y *before the change* is precisely equal to the sample mean of P_Y in the original data set $(\overline{P}_Y)$. The difficulty comes from the need to measure the average value of P_Y *after the unit change* in X_k.

This is where the computer comes to the rescue. It can be directed to calculate the logit value of $[a + b_k \times (X_k + 1)]$ for every observation; it can then convert these log odds ratios into the new value of $P(Y_i = 1)$ for each observation by following steps (ii) and (iii). The simple average of these individual probabilities provides the new value for the sample as a whole which, when compared to the original sample mean of $P(Y_i = 1)$ produces the logit estimate of the impact effect of a unit change in X_k for the sample as a whole.

When this calculation is undertaken for the fictitious Detroit sample, the average predicted value of $\hat{P}_Y$ after a unit change in income is found to be 0.249. The sample mean of automobile ownership $(\overline{P}_Y)$ is 0.175, so the change is 0.074. This indicates that the rate of automobile ownership in the sample as a whole increases by 0.074 (or by 7.4 per cent) for an increase in household income of $1 thousand.

Some researchers are content to report the marginal effect alone (sometimes using the term, 'marginal probability'), or the impact effect alone. Others go beyond this calculation to produce estimates of the *proportionate impact* on the dependent variable of a *proportionate change* in the explanatory variable. We have already met these proportionate changes in chapter 12 in the form of elasticities, and these represent a very helpful source of additional information which can be derived from the logit model.

The next section explains the procedure for extracting elasticities from the logit regression results.

13.2.5 Proportionate effects: logit elasticities

In §12.3, an elasticity was defined as the ratio of the proportionate change in the dependent variable, Y, to a proportionate change in the explanatory variable, X_k. In this case, the dependent variable is P_Y, so that the formula may be written as

$$\eta_k = \frac{\Delta P_Y}{P_Y} \div \frac{\Delta X_k}{X_k} \tag{13.16a}$$

where η_k (lower case Greek eta) is the symbol for the elasticity. The terms may be reordered to produce an alternative formula

$$\eta_k = \frac{\Delta P_Y}{\Delta X_k} \times \frac{X_k}{P_Y} \qquad (13.16b)$$

Equation (13.16b) shows that the calculation of the elasticity involves two separate elements: the ratio of *the changes in* P_Y and X_k, and the ratio of *the values of* X_k and P_Y. The first element measures the slope of the relationship between P_Y and X_k; the second element measures the location at which this slope is to be calculated.

Since there are two ways to measure the slope of the logit curve at a given point, it follows that there are two ways to calculate the elasticity.[k] For the **point elasticity**, the first element is the marginal effect,

$$\frac{\partial P_Y}{\partial X_k}$$

calculated in the previous section.

For the **unit elasticity**, the first element is the impact effect, ΔP_Y, calculated for a *unit change* in the explanatory variable ($\Delta X_k = 1$).

The second element of (13.16b), X_k/P_Y, is the same for both the unit and the point elasticity. For an individual observation, it is the ratio of the value of the explanatory variable, X_k, and the predicted value, $\hat{P}_Y$, at that point. For the sample as a whole, we once again take advantage of the finding that the average predicted value of $\hat{P}_Y$ is equal to $\bar{P}_Y$, the sample mean of $P(Y_i = 1)$. The average value of each explanatory variable is also equal to its sample mean, $\bar{X}_k$.

We will begin with the calculation of the point elasticity *for the entire sample* (i.e. the average elasticity for all households). The formula is

$$\eta_k = \frac{\partial P_Y}{\partial X_k} \times \frac{\bar{X}_k}{\bar{P}_Y} \qquad (13.17)$$

The formula for the first term was previously given in (13.13b) as $b_k \times \sum_i \frac{\hat{P}_{Y_i} \times (1 - \hat{P}_{Y_i})}{n}$. If we substitute this into (13.17), we get the formula for the point elasticity

$$\eta_k = b_k \times \sum_i \frac{\hat{P}_{Y_i} \times (1 - \hat{P}_{Y_i})}{n} \times \frac{\bar{X}_k}{\bar{P}_Y} \qquad (13.18)$$

---

[k] We have adopted the terms 'point' and 'unit' to distinguish the two elasticities, but it should be noted that some authors simply refer to 'the elasticity' without specifying exactly which they have measured.

THE POINT ELASTICITY

This measures the ratio of
a *proportionate change* in the dependent variable, P_Y,
to
a *proportionate change* in the explanatory variable, X_k,

when the change in X_k is infinitesimal.

For the sample as a whole
it is measured at the means by

$$\eta_k = b_k \times \sum_i \frac{\hat{P}_{Y_i} \times (1 - \hat{P}_{Y_i})}{n} \times \frac{\overline{X}_k}{\overline{P}_Y} \qquad (13.18)$$

The corresponding calculation for the unit elasticity starts from the formula

$$\eta_k = \frac{\Delta P_Y}{\Delta X_k} \times \frac{\overline{X}_k}{\overline{P}_Y} \qquad (13.19)$$

However, we saw in (13.15b) that for the sample as a whole, the first term on the right-hand side was equal to

$$\frac{1}{n} \sum_i \Delta \hat{P}_{Y_i}$$

This term can be substituted in (13.19) to give the formula for the unit elasticity for the sample as a whole

$$\eta_k = \frac{1}{n} \sum_i \Delta \hat{P}_{Y_i} \times \frac{\overline{X}_k}{\overline{P}_Y} \qquad (13.20)$$

We may return once again to our Detroit example to illustrate the application of these two formulae. In §13.2.4 we measured the marginal and impact effects of a change in income for the sample as a whole at 0.0942 and 0.074, respectively. These may be converted to point and unit elasticities by multiplying by the ratio of the sample means of income ($\overline{X}_k = \$2.95$ thousand) and car ownership ($\overline{P}_Y = 0.175$). The point elasticity is thus measured at 1.5885; the unit elasticity at 1.2474.

THE UNIT ELASTICITY

This measures the ratio of
a *proportionate change* in the dependent variable, P_Y,

to

a *proportionate change* in the explanatory variable, X_k,

when X_k *changes by one unit.*

For the sample as a whole
it is measured at the means by

$$\eta_k = \frac{1}{n} \sum_i \Delta \hat{P}_{Y_i} \times \frac{\bar{X}_k}{\bar{P}_Y} \tag{13.20}$$

However, the point elasticity may mislead if the change in the explanatory variable is not small. This would always be the case, for example, if we were estimating the effect of a change in a dummy explanatory variable from 0 to 1. Under these circumstances, it is clearly better to calculate the unit elasticity, even if its derivation is more complicated.

At this stage it may be helpful to summarize the rather complex set of procedures for interpreting logit coefficients. We do so in two ways. First, with the aid of figure 13.5, which provides a simple flow diagram incorporating all the relevant formulae for measuring the effect of the absolute and proportionate changes for the sample as a whole.

Secondly, to show how these formulae and procedures work out in practice, we have also given in table 13.1 some stylized results from the simple bivariate model of car ownership in Detroit.

Column (1) in table 13.1 indicates the level of income at thousand-dollar intervals of the income distribution, from $1 thousand to $10 thousand. The remaining entries follow logically from this information by the formulae adopted above. The final row in the table gives the results for the sample as a whole; it is a weighted average of the figures reported in the income specific rows.[1] This row summarizes the average response of automobile ownership to changing income across all observations.

The non-linearity of the logit function is clearly revealed in the table. The measurement of the impact of both the absolute and proportionate

---

[1] It is a weighted, rather than a simple, average because the income is not distributed evenly across all income levels in the original data set.

Figure 13.5 Flow chart for deriving logit results for the sample as a whole

$$\text{Logit coefficient } b_k = \Delta\log\left[\frac{P(Y_i = 1)}{P(Y_i = 0)}\right]$$

$$\log \text{ odds ratio } (= w). \quad \text{Value at } b_k = a + b_k\overline{X}_k$$

$$\text{Odds ratio} = \exp(\log \text{ Odds ratio}) = \exp(w)$$

$$\text{Probability of } Y_i = 1 = P(Y_i = 1) = \hat{P}_{Y_i}$$

$$= \frac{\text{Odds ratio}}{1 + \text{Odds ratio}} = \frac{\exp(w)}{1 + \exp(w)}$$

$$\text{For sample as a whole} = \frac{1}{n}\Sigma_i\hat{P}_{Y_i} = \overline{P}_Y$$

Infinitesimal change   *Unit change, $\Delta X_k = 1$*

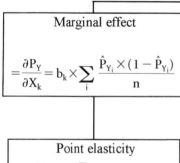

Marginal effect

$$= \frac{\partial P_Y}{\partial X_k} = b_k \times \sum_i \frac{\hat{P}_{Y_i} \times (1 - \hat{P}_{Y_i})}{n}$$

Point elasticity

$$= \frac{\partial P_y}{\partial X_k} \times \frac{\overline{X}_k}{\overline{P}_Y}$$

$$= b_k \times \sum_i \frac{\hat{P}_{Y_i} \times (1 - \hat{P}_{Y_i})}{n} \times \frac{\overline{X}_k}{\overline{P}_Y}$$

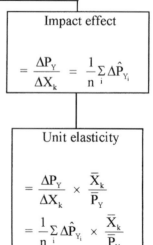

Impact effect

$$= \frac{\Delta P_Y}{\Delta X_k} = \frac{1}{n}\Sigma_i\Delta\hat{P}_{Y_i}$$

Unit elasticity

$$= \frac{\Delta P_Y}{\Delta X_k} \times \frac{\overline{X}_k}{\overline{P}_Y}$$

$$= \frac{1}{n}\Sigma_i\Delta\hat{P}_{Y_i} \times \frac{\overline{X}_k}{\overline{P}_Y}$$

Table 13.1 Deriving the findings from a logit regression (hypothetical data)

(1) Income ($000)	(2) Logit value	(3) Odds ratio	(4) Predicted value of Y	(5) Marginal effect	(6) Impact effect	(7) Point elasticity	(8) Unit elasticity
1	−3.081	0.046	0.044	0.026	0.034	0.584	0.777
2	−2.470	0.085	0.078	0.044	0.057	1.127	1.458
3	−1.859	0.156	0.135	0.071	0.088	1.586	1.964
4	−1.248	0.287	0.223	0.106	0.123	1.899	2.204
5	−0.637	0.529	0.346	0.138	0.148	1.998	2.133
6	−0.026	0.975	0.494	0.153	0.149	1.857	1.808
7	0.586	1.796	0.642	0.140	0.126	1.530	1.369
8	1.197	3.309	0.768	0.109	0.091	1.135	0.950
9	1.808	6.097	0.859	0.074	0.059	0.775	0.620
10	2.419	11.233	0.918	0.046	0.036	0.500	0.388
Average for the sample as a whole							
2.95	−1.889	0.212	0.175	0.094	0.074	1.588	1.247

Notes:

(2) is the predicted value of the logit function from the regression, $a + bX$, where X is income, $a = -3.6921$, and $b = 0.6111$.

(3) is the exponent of (2).

(4) is calculated using the formula $OR/(1 + OR)$, where OR is the value of the odds ratio in (3).

(5) is $(4) \times [1 - (4)] \times$ the regression coefficient, b [$= 0.6111$].

(6) is the difference between successive values of (4) (the value in row 10 is the difference between 0.918 and the value of (4) if $X = 11$).

(7) is $(5) \times (1) \div (4)$.

(8) is $(6) \times (1) \div (4)$.

All columns are subject to rounding error.

changes clearly varies within the sample; the point elasticity, for example, is 0.58 at an income level of $1 thousand, rising to almost 2.0 at $6 thousand, and declining steadily to 0.50 at $10 thousand.

For this reason, although our calculations thus far have focused primarily on the average effect of changing income for the sample as a whole, it is clear that such a summary calculation hides a great deal of information about the behaviour of automobile ownership in our data set. The averages are clearly useful, but it will often be desirable for a researcher to go behind them to investigate changes at specific points of the logistic curve. For example, she may be interested in the responsiveness of automobile ownership to changes

in income for the median household, or she may wish to compare the behaviour of ownership for lower- and upper-income families. The non-linearity
of the logit function ensures that these valuations will diverge, as table 13.1
makes clear.

13.2.6 Non-linearity and the measurement of change

Because of the non-linearity of the logit curve, it is worth discussing briefly
the mechanics of evaluating changes in X_k on the predicted value of $P(Y_i = 1)$
at particular points of the curve. It happens that the procedures deviate from
those laid down in the previous sections and summarized in table 13.1 only
in one dimension – the evaluation of $\hat{P}_Y$ in the various formulae.

When dealing with the average behaviour across the entire sample, we
can apply the sample mean, $\bar{P}_Y$, in the calculation of marginal and impact
effects and of point and unit elasticities. This is, however, no longer per-
missible when dealing with local, rather than average, estimates. If we wish
to calculate the point elasticity for the *median* income level, we must substitute the predicted value of $\bar{P}_Y$ at that particular value of X_k, using the
regression coefficients to generate the logit value, w, and working from
there to calculate $\hat{P}_Y$, according to the steps set out in §13.2.5. The other formulae in §13.2.4 and §13.2.5 must similarly be revised, by substituting
local estimates of $\hat{P}_Y$ for $\bar{P}_Y$ in each case.

The calculation of the impact effects and the unit elasticities is set out
below for households at various points of the income distribution. We have
chosen the median ($2,420) and the upper and lower quartiles of the
Detroit sample ($1,500 and $3,750, respectively). Readers are encouraged
to follow the calculations through, using the procedures set out in table
13.1, and also to calculate the marginal effects and point elasticities on their
own. In both cases, the underlying proposition that motivated this exercise
is borne out – the impact effects and elasticities show considerable variation within the sample.

	$\Delta P_Y / \Delta X_1$	$\times$	$X_1 / \hat{P}_Y$	$=$	η_1
Lower quartile:	0.044		1.50/0.059		1.119
Median income:	0.069		2.42/0.099		1.688
Upper quartile:	0.114		3.75/0.198		2.159

Such variability in predicted outcomes is likely to be true for all logit
models, because of the inherent non-linearity of the logistic curve. The
greater the degree of variation in the outcome being modelled over the
sample, the greater the effect of the non-linearity. If we have an outcome
that does not vary very much within the sample, however, the potential for
divergent results within the sample will be correspondingly small.

Once we have moved from average to local measurements of change, it is also possible to introduce new levels of change in the explanatory variable, other than the unit effect. One such measure that is sometimes cited is the change in Y for *a change of 1 standard deviation* in the explanatory variable. The s.d. of income in the Detroit sample is 2.05, so the measured change in $\hat{P}_Y$ would be 0.2124, or 21.24 per cent.[m]

13.2.7 Goodness of fit

Researchers are often interested in the goodness of fit for a regression equation. Since the logit model does not use least squares methods, it is not possible to estimate the R^2 directly. Instead, it is necessary to construct other measures of the goodness of fit, which have become known as pseudo R^2 measures.

As explained in panel 13.1, the optimal evaluation of the parameters of the logit model is determined by maximizing the value of the **log-likelihood function**. It is this function that is the basis for constructing the pseudo R^2 measures. Since there is no ideal value of the log-likelihood function against which the model estimate can be compared (corresponding to the explanation of 100 per cent of the variance in an OLS model), the goodness-of-fit measure compares the value of the model estimate to the value of the log-likelihood function *if the model explained nothing of the variation in* P_Y. This estimate is known as the **base likelihood**.

Let the maximum log likelihood be symbolized as $\log L_1$ and the log value of the base likelihood as $\log L_0$.

The first goodness-of-fit measure is defined as

$$\text{pseudo } R^2 = 1 - \frac{1}{1 + [2(\log L_1 - \log L_0)/n]} \tag{13.21}$$

where

$$\log L_0 = n_1 \log\left(\frac{n_1}{n}\right) + n_0 \log\left(1 - \frac{n_1}{n}\right) \tag{13.22}$$

for a sample of size n with n_1 positive outcomes and $(n - n_1) = n_0$ negative outcomes. The minimum value that pseudo R^2 can take will be zero, but the maximum is always less than 1. The precise upper bound varies with the ratio n_1/n, and this limits its usefulness as a measure of the goodness of fit of a logit model.

---

[m] The crucial change is in step (i). The new value of the log odds ratio will be $-1.8894 + (0.6111 \times 2.05) = -0.6366$. The rest of the sequence proceeds accordingly.

This has led to the introduction of a number of alternative measures of goodness of fit, one of which is McFadden's R^2. This is calculated as

$$\text{McFadden's } R^2 = 1 - \frac{\log L_1}{\log L_0} \tag{13.23}$$

This will always lie between 0 and 1 and can theoretically attain a value of 1.[n] However, it is not likely to do so in practice because of the usual problems with cross-section regressions.[o]

The comparison of likelihood estimates can help us further understand the results of the logit model. One use to which the comparison of L_1 and L_0 has been put is to determine whether the model adds explanatory power over a simple prediction that the same probability of a positive outcome applies to all observations, regardless of the values of the related explanatory variables. The **log-likelihood ratio**, calculated as $2(\log L_1 - \log L_0)$, is the logit equivalent of the F-test for the joint statistical significance of coefficients in the OLS model (see §9.3.2). The name of the test is often abbreviated to $-2 \log \lambda$ (lower case Greek lambda). The test statistic of the log-likelihood ratio is distributed as a chi-square with $(k-1)$ degrees of freedom, where k is the total number of explanatory variables in the regression.

THE LOG-LIKELIHOOD RATIO, $-2 \log \lambda$

This ratio is a test of the
overall statistical significance of the coefficients
of the logit model.

It is a test of the null hypothesis that
the set of explanatory variables
have no effect on the
probability of a positive outcome.

---

[n] A perfect fit would require that the model precisely match the distribution of $(Y_i = 0)$ and $(Y_i = 1)$ for all observations, in which case the value of $\log L_1$ would be zero.

[o] Another method of measuring goodness of fit in logit models, which begins from a similar premise, is to calculate the number of correct predictions of positive outcomes. Great care needs to be taken when interpreting such measures, for technical reasons that are beyond the scope of this text.

13.3 Estimating the logit model: an illustration

13.3.1 An illustration of the logit model

To illustrate the procedures described in §13.2, let us now consider a fuller version of our fictitious sample of Detroit households in 1919, with two additional explanatory variables, family size and wealth. The data have been coded and entered into the computer. We wish to analyse why some households own cars (AUTO = 1) and others do not (AUTO = 0). Our hypothesis is that ownership will be influenced by three factors: household income (INCOME), family size (FAMSIZE), and, as a measure of accumulated wealth, home ownership (HOME).

INCOME is a continuous variable, measured in thousands of dollars; HOME is a binary dummy variable, taking the value of 1 if the household owns its home outright and 0 otherwise; FAMSIZE is a categorical variable, whose (discrete) values range from 2 to 8. The regression is estimated over 1,000 observations. The average level of car ownership in the sample is again 17.5 per cent.

The results of the logit model are shown in column (1) of table 13.2. The coefficients are clearly all statistically significant; the very high value of the log-likelihood ratio, $-2 \log \lambda = 420.02$, confirms that the equation is a powerful device for explaining the variation of automobile ownership.[p] This is also reflected in the high value of the two goodness-of-fit measures, the pseudo R^2 and McFadden's R^2. Each of these values is derived from the comparison of the values of the base log-likelihood function (log $L_0 = -463.7264$) and the maximum log-likelihood function (log $L_1 = -253.717$).

Statistics aside, the regression makes intuitive sense as well. The coefficients are all of the appropriate sign: the probability of owning a car increases with income and home ownership, but is negatively related to family size (reflecting the greater claim on household income of a large family).

The impact of the sign on the dependent variable is similarly reflected in column (2) of table 13.2, which translates the logit coefficients into **odds-ratio coefficients**. The odds-ratio coefficient is equal *to the exponential of the logit coefficient* (for example, for INCOME, exp(0.6476) = 1.9109). As noted in footnote *j* on p. 405, the odds-ratio coefficients can be used to calculate the revised odds ratio resulting from a unit change in the explanatory variable.

---

[p] The critical value of the chi-squared distribution with 3 degrees of freedom at the 1 per cent level is 6.635.

Table 13.2　Detroit automobile ownership, 1919: the full logit model (hypothetical data)

	Dependent variable: AUTO					
	(1) Logit model	(2) Odds-ratio coefficients*	(3) Marginal effect**	(4) Impact effect**	(5) Point Elasticity**	(6) Unit Elasticity**
INCOME	0.6476	1.9109	0.0935	0.0542	1.576	0.914
	(11.353)	(11.353)				
FAMSIZE	−0.9601	0.3828	−0.1386	−0.0610	−4.619	−2.034
	(8.011)	(8.011)				
HOME	2.2405	9.3980	0.3235	0.2358	0.342	0.223***
	(9.092)	(9.092)				
CONSTANT	0.7285					
	(1.137)					
$\text{Log } L_0 =$	−463.726	pseudo $R^2 = 0.2958$				
$\text{Log } L_1 =$	−253.717	McFadden's $R^2 = 0.4529$				
$-2 \log \lambda =$	420.02					

Notes:

* No constant term is reported for the odds-ratio specification, since the expected value of the dependent variable is completely independent of the intercept term.

** These effects and elasticities are reported for the sample averages.

*** The unit elasticity for HOME is evaluated at the sample mean of the dummy variable (0.185).

Figures in parentheses are *t*-statistics.

If the logit coefficient is negative, the odds-ratio coefficient will be less than 1, indicating that the odds ratio declines as the explanatory variable rises. This is the case with FAMSIZE, showing that the probability of a household owning a car diminishes as the size of the family increases. By contrast, the odds-ratio coefficients on INCOME and HOME are both above 1, indicating that the odds ratio moves in the same direction as the explanatory variable, i.e. that the probability of owning a car rises with income and wealth. It should be noted that the *t*-statistics on these two variants of the logit model are identical, as are the other statistical indicators, such as $-2 \log \lambda$.

The sign is an important part of any model, but we also wish to know how much of a difference the explanatory variables make to the outcome of the model. How big a change in income is necessary to increase car ownership by a certain amount? Is this a large or a small amount, relative to our expectations? To address these questions, table 13.2 displays the relevant marginal and impact effects, and the point and unit elasticities, for the sample as a whole. It is worth making a few points about these results.

First, the equation has three different types of explanatory variable, for each of which one or more of the various measures of the effect of absolute and proportional changes is most appropriate. For INCOME, which is a continuous variable, the impact of a change in income is best measured by the marginal effect and the point elasticity, although application of the unit variants is also feasible.

For HOME, which is a binary dummy variable, the impact effect is most appropriate. A comparison between the predicted value of automobile ownership when HOME = 0 and when HOME = 1 will indicate the sensitivity of $P(Y_i = 1)$ to changes in home ownership. In this case, it is not possible to work with sample means, but with predicted values before and after the change in HOME.[9] Also, because the change in HOME is from a base of 0, it is not possible to calculate the unit elasticity at that point (since $X_k = 0$, the formula for the unit elasticity must also be zero).[10]

FAMSIZE is a discrete, non-binary variable. In this case it is again best to measure the effect of changes in FAMSIZE on automobile ownership using the impact effect. In this case, however, since it is not a binary variable, it is possible to calculate the impact of a unit change in FAMSIZE for all households from the reported level of FAMSIZE in the data set. Thus, for households with two family members, we can evaluate the impact of adding a further person to the household on the expected probability of owning a car, and can do the same for all other observations. Since we are beginning from the sample mean of X_k, we can use $\bar{P}_Y$ in the formulae. Moreover, since FAMSIZE is non-zero, it is feasible to calculate the unit elasticity.

Second, it is important to recognize that all such calculations are made for a change in one explanatory variable, *holding all other variables constant*. Thus, the point elasticity for an infinitesimal change in income incorporates only direct effects of income change on car ownership and pays no attention to indirect effects created by the impact of changing income on HOME or FAMSIZE.

It is also possible to extend the results of table 13.2 by calculating the effects and elasticities for households at particular points on the logit function. This would be especially relevant for understanding the dynamics of automobile ownership at different income levels, but it is also possible to

---

[9] This is, of course, because the change in HOME is not being measured at its sample mean, which is neither 0 nor 1.

evaluate the impact of changing family size. The procedure for calculating these local effects is the same as outlined in §13.2.6.[11]

13.3.2   Estimating the logit model using grouped data

Although the logit model is usually run using information on individual units, it can also be run over aggregated data, in which the individual observations are combined into groups. If specified properly, the group model will produce broadly the same results as the same equation run over all the individual data. However, if group estimation is used it is essential that the grouping of individual observations is appropriately structured.

The rules for proper aggregation are: for continuous variables, any grouping is appropriate, so long as it is consistent; for discrete variables, there must be as many groups as there are values (thus, two for HOME and seven for FAMSIZE in the Detroit data set). Were we to designate nine groups for INCOME, the total number of groups (or cells) would be $(2 \times 7 \times 9) = 126$.

The dependent variable in group estimation is the ratio of positive to total outcomes *in each cell.* It is the odds ratio for the group of observations that share this particular combination of attributes (home ownership, family size, and income, in the case of the Detroit survey). If all the households in that cell own a car, its value will be 1; if none do, it will be 0; if some proportion does, it will fall between 0 and 1. The group logit regression is thus an example of estimation using a dependent variable that is continuous within the bounds of 0 and 1. The logic of the approach can thus be generalized to other similar data, such as the proportion of an individual's decision or experiences over a given period that falls into one of two categories.

As an illustration of the group logit approach, we have run the basic automobile regression across nine income classes, subdivided by home ownership and family size. There were 126 possible data cells altogether, of which 36 were empty (no observations met this combination of characteristics). The grouped logit model was run over the 90 inhabited cells, using the weighted least squares methodology included in the STATA statistical program. The results are as follows

$$\text{AUTO} = 0.7031 + 0.6496\,\text{INCOME} - 0.9570\,\text{FAMSIZE} + 2.2377\,\text{HOME}$$
$$\quad\;\; (1.099)\quad (11.453)\qquad\qquad (7.994)\qquad\qquad (9.078)$$

$$\log L_1 = -253.725; -2\log \lambda = 420.00; \text{McFadden's } R^2 = 0.4529.$$

It will be seen that there is very little difference from the results of table 13.2, run over the original 1,000 observations, indicating the power of the grouped methodology when properly applied.[12]

13.4 Estimating the probit model

13.4.1 The probit model

We introduced this chapter by discussing the logit and probit models together. There is very little to choose between them in terms of model specification and parameter selection. The probit, being based on the normal distribution, has a slightly more elongated S-shape, but for most purposes the difference is too small to be a basis for choosing one model over the other. The models are very close substitutes. For this reason, neither dominates in empirical work, and historians are just as likely to report probit results as logit results.

When an historian uses the probit model, most of the reported results will be identical or nearly identical to the results of the logit specification. This is true for the value of the likelihood function at its maximum, as well as for any tests of goodness of fit or model specification, such as the log-likelihood ratio or the various pseudo R^2 measures. Similarly, the t-statistics will be the same in the two models. However, one set of results will look very different. These are the coefficient estimates themselves.

The **probit coefficients** are *systematically* smaller than those produced by the logit model. The divergence is due to the different shape of the normal and logistic distributions and is invariant to the data set being analysed. The ratio of the coefficients on the probit and logit models is equal to the *ratio of the standard deviation* of their underlying distributions.

The probit, being based on the standard normal distribution, has zero mean and unit variance, and thus its standard deviation is also 1. The logistic curve also has zero mean, but its variance is equal to $\pi^2/3$, and so its standard deviation is equal to $\sqrt{\pi^2/3}$, which is approximately 1.8138. The s.d. ratio of probit : logit is thus 1:1.8138, which is approximately equal to 0.5513. The coefficients on the probit model are, therefore, *on average* 0.55 times the value of those on the logit model.[13]

As an illustration of these propositions, we have re-estimated our estimating equation for automobile ownership in our fictitious Detroit survey (see §13.3.1) using a probit regression. The probit results are as follows

$$AUTO = 0.1942 + 0.3575 \text{ INCOME} - 0.4957 \text{ FAMSIZE} + 1.2589 \text{ HOME}$$
$$(0.599) \quad (12.428) \qquad\qquad (8.045) \qquad\qquad (9.274)$$

$$\log L_1 = -253.708; -2 \log \lambda = 420.04; \text{McFadden's } R^2 = 0.4529.$$

The value of the log-likelihood function, the log-likelihood ratio, and the McFadden R^2 measure are very similar to the results reported in table 13.2. The ratio of the probit to the logit coefficients ranges from 0.52 to 0.56; the t-statistics are identical in the two formulations.[14]

13.4.2 Interpreting the results from a probit model

The most difficult aspect of working with probit models is interpreting the meaning of the coefficients. The source of the difficulty is that the probit is based on the cumulative standardized normal distribution, the interpretation of which is far from straightforward. Moreover, as with logits, the probit model does not directly predict the expected value of the dependent variable. The logit model generates an estimate of the log of the odds ratio; the probit model produces another, and more complex, variable, usually known as the probit index. It is indicated by the symbol Φ (upper case Greek phi).

The **probit index** is derived from the *constant and the coefficients of the probit model, evaluated at the mean of all the explanatory variables.* For the model of automobile ownership in §13.4.1, the mean for INCOME is $2.95 thousand, for FAMSIZE it is 5.831 persons, and for HOME it is 0.185. So the value of the probit index is

$$0.1942 + (0.3575 \times 2.95) + (-0.4957 \times 5.831) + (1.2589 \times 0.185) = -1.4084$$

How do we transform this result into something more familiar and useful? As with the logit model, we can calculate the impact of two forms of absolute change in an explanatory variable, and two forms of proportionate change.

We begin with the calculation of the *impact effect* of a unit change in X_k, the explanatory variable, INCOME. The coefficient on INCOME in the probit regression, given in §13.4.1, is 0.3575. This probit coefficient has a special interpretation: it indicates that *a unit increase in income raises the probit index by 0.3575 standard deviations.* The impact of such a change on the expected value of automobile ownership will vary according to where on the standardized normal distribution this change of 0.3575 s.d. takes place.

To measure this we need to translate the value of the probit index into the expected value of AUTO, and this is done by means of the published tables of the area under the standardized normal distribution, an excerpt from which was presented in table 2.7. The value of the cumulative area to $Z = 1.4084$ is 0.9205.[r] In order to calculate AUTO we need to find the value in the tail beyond Z. This is equal to $1 - 0.9205 = 0.0795$, which gives us $\hat{P}_Y$, the average expected level of car ownership at the means of the explanatory variables.

---

[r] D. V. Lindley and W. F. Scott, *New Cambridge Statistical Tables*, 2nd edn., Cambridge University Press, 1995, table 4, p. 34 by interpolation between the values for Z of 1.40 (0.9192) and 1.41 (0.9207) to get 0.9205. Because the table is symmetrical, the area in the lower tail beyond -1.4084 is identical to the area in the upper tail beyond $+1.4084$.

The value of the probit index *after a unit change in INCOME* is equal to the original value of the probit index plus the regression coefficient on INCOME, which equals $-1.4084 + 0.3575 = -1.0509$. In the same way as before, this can be translated into an expected value of AUTO using the table for the standardized normal distribution. This gives an area to Z of 0.8533, so the new value is $(1 - 0.8533) = 0.1467$. The original value was 0.0795, so the absolute increase in the level of car ownership is $0.1467 - 0.0795 = 0.0672$. The estimate of the *impact effect* of a unit change in INCOME, calculated at the means of all the explanatory variables, is thus 0.0672.

The alternative measure, the *marginal effect* $(\partial P_Y/\partial X_k)$, is derived by multiplying the probit coefficient for the relevant explanatory variable (in this case 0.3575) by a tabulated statistic we have not previously encountered: the height of the normal density function, valued at the probit index.[15] For a probit index of -1.4084 the figure is 0.1480, so the marginal effect is equal to $0.3575 \times 0.1480 = 0.0529$.

We turn next to the two elasticities. As with the logit elasticities in §13.2.5 the calculations involve two elements: the ratio of the proportionate changes in P_y and X_k, and the ratios of the values of P_y and X_k. For the sample as a whole, the latter are again taken at their mean values, i.e. at $\bar{X}_k$ and $\hat{P}_Y$.

The *unit elasticity* can thus be calculated in the usual way (see (13.19)) as the ratio of the change in the dependent variable (ΔP_Y) to the change in the explanatory variable (ΔX_k), multiplied by the ratio of the two variables at their mean values $(\bar{X}_k/\hat{P}_Y)$. We have already calculated $\Delta P_Y = 0.0672$ and $\hat{P}_Y = 0.0795$. We know that the mean level of the explanatory variable, $\bar{X}_k$, is \$2.95 thousand, and for a unit change ΔX_k is 1. So the unit elasticity is $(0.0672/1) \times (2.95/0.0795) = 2.4936$.

The alternative *point elasticity* is similarly calculated by multiplying the marginal effect $(\partial P_Y/\partial X_k)$ by the ratio of the two variables at their mean values. The first term was calculated above as 0.0529 so the point elasticity is $0.0529 \times (2.95/0.0795) = 1.9633$.

The difference in scale between the point and unit elasticity measurements is the probit equivalent of the difference between the slope of the marginal and impact effects in the logit function, as shown in figure 13.4.

These probit calculations are indicative of the procedure. However, they are based on only one point on the normal distribution function. Since this function is no less non-linear than the logistic curve, we have to be careful about generalizing from local results to the sample as a whole. As with the logit estimates of the average effects and elasticities, if we wish to know the effect of a change in X_k for the overall sample, the correct procedure is to take the average effect of a given (infinitesimal or unit) change for each observation. And, as with the logit model, theory and the computer make this a relatively straightforward exercise. Once again, the average value of $\hat{P}_Y$ for the observations as a whole is $\bar{P}_Y$. And once again, the computer will calculate the effect of a change in the explanatory variable on the probit index for each observation, from which the impact on $P(Y_i = 1)$ for the sample as a whole can be calculated.

13.5 Multi-response models

At the start of the chapter, we stated that categorical dependent variables need not be binary. Survey questions may elicit a more complicated array of responses than a simple 'yes' or 'no', indicating the strength of support for a proposition (e.g. perhaps, probably, rarely). Consumers may face a greater selection of choices than simply 'buy' or 'not buy', such as deciding which brand of automobile to favour. Voters may have to choose between more than two parties at the ballot box (e.g., Liberal, Conservative, Labour in the British election of 1910; Democrat, Republican, Progressive in the US election of 1912). The class of regression techniques that has been developed to analyse cases such as these, where there are more than two possible outcomes, is known as **multi-response models**.[5]

Multi-response models may be divided into two types, depending on whether a ranking of the dependent variable is ordered or random. **Ordered response models** are applied to situations in which the categories reflect a natural ordering of alternatives. A survey of household spending habits may generate responses such as 'never', 'sometimes', 'often', 'always'. Infant mortality rates at the county level may be classified as 'low', 'average', 'high', relative to the national norm. Workers may choose between working 'full-time', 'part-time', or 'not at all'. In each case, the value of the dependent variable reflects a ranking of alternatives; it is not random, as it would be if the categories were (say) 'blue', 'red', 'green', and 'yellow'.

Although ordered variables are ranked, they cannot be analysed by OLS methods, because the numbers assigned to the different ranks are essentially arbitrary. Thus, the distance between 'never' and 'sometimes' is not necessarily the same as that between 'often' and 'always'. Instead, the **ordered logit** or **ordered probit** models are used, depending on whether the underlying distribution is assumed to be logistic or standard normal.[16]

---

[5] In what follows, we leave the technical details to econometrics texts and the method of solution to the computer package.

The second type of response model applies where the assigning of values to states is random rather than ordered. In such cases the appropriate multi-response model is either the **multinomial logit** or the **multinomial probit** model. A model investigating emigration from Ireland might analyse the pattern of migrant destinations according to a set of individual and locational characteristics. A dichotomous model of Irish emigration that distinguished only between those who did not emigrate and those who did, could be extended by subdividing the latter by assigning 1 to those who went to the United Kingdom, and 2, 3, and 4 to emigrants to the United States, Canada, and the Antipodes, respectively. Similarly, a study of automobile ownership in Detroit in 1919 might try to model brand selection, by assigning 1 to Ford, 2 to Chevrolet, 3 to Buick, etc. In both cases, the order by which the values are assigned is random, so clearly the ordered probit model would be inappropriate.[17]

In the case of multinomial models, there is a significant difference between the logit and probit alternatives, in contrast to their use in binary choice models. The logit model, although less computationally awkward, has one significant drawback. This is known as the **independence of irrelevant alternatives**. It arises because of the assumption in the logit model that all options are equally likely.

Let us assume that the model of Irish emigration is recast by separating the Antipodes into Australia and New Zealand. The logical expectation would be that this change would have no impact on the measured probabilities of emigrating to the *other* destinations. Unfortunately, in the multinomial logit model, this is not the case; all the probabilities will decline by the same proportion. Thus, unless all categories of the dependent variable are equally likely, the multinomial logit may be inappropriate.

The alternative is to use multinomial probit, which does not assume independence of the error term across alternative states. Its disadvantage is its high computational complexity and expense, limiting analysis to fewer than five categories.

13.6 Censored dependent variables

13.6.1 A censored continuous dependent variable

Finally, we discuss the situation in which the density of the dependent variable, while continuous, is **censored** or incomplete. Censoring takes place either from above (a variable cannot take on a value more than, say, 10) or from below (it cannot take a value below, say, 5). The most common form of censoring is when the minimum value of a variable is 0.

The effect of censoring on OLS estimation is shown in figure 13.6. In 13.6 (a), the dependent variable is censored *from above*. The maximum value that the worker can choose to work is 50 hours. They may wish to work longer hours, but are constrained by union, workplace, or government rules. In the scatter diagram the hours desired by the worker are represented by the hollow circles; whereas, for hours desired in excess of 50, the *actual* hours worked are given by the filled circles. Because the OLS regression line omits the censored values in excess of 50 hours it clearly provides a biased estimate of the impact of wages on hours of work demanded. The true regression line would omit these 'imposed' values but would include the values in excess of 50 hours desired by the workers.

Similarly, the result of censoring *from below* is shown in figure 13.6 (b). The scatter diagram shows the results of a survey of consumer spending on life insurance at different levels of household income. It is evident that expenditure on insurance is positively related to income for those who could afford to purchase a policy. But many households in the survey bought no life insurance at all. They cannot buy negative amounts of life insurance, so their expenditures are censored *from below* at zero. Because the OLS regression line includes the censored values it is once again clearly biased. The true line for the regression of expenditure on life insurance on income would omit these zero values.

The extent of the bias in this case will depend on the frequency of the uninsured and their distribution by income (and similarly for the censored hours of work). If the proportion of censored observations is small, the bias will be minor and OLS regression techniques may still be used. Likewise, if the relationship between income and being uninsured is stochastic, the bias from using OLS methods will be small.

It is tempting to consider running an OLS regression on the uncensored observations alone. But temptation should be resisted. The coefficient estimates will be biased, as inspection of figure 13.6 makes clear.

13.6.2   The tobit model

The issue of censoring was first analysed systematically by James Tobin in his study of the purchase of automobiles, refrigerators, and other consumer durables by US households in the 1950s.[1] Tobin observed that many households bought no durables during the survey year, indicating that a linear regression model would be inappropriate.

---

[1] James Tobin, 'Estimation of relationships for limited dependent variables', *Econometrica*, 1958, 26, pp. 24–36.

Figure 13.6 OLS model with censored observations

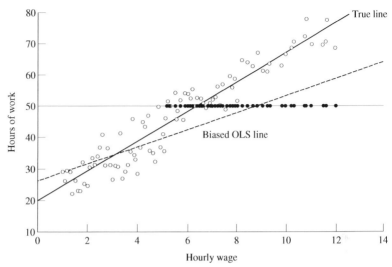

(a) Censored from above

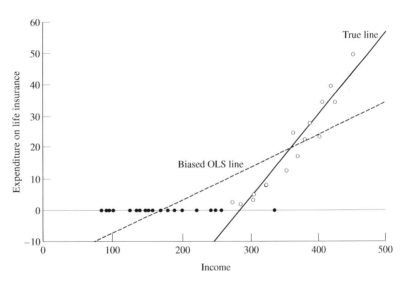

(b) Censored from below

The model that Tobin developed to deal with the problem of censored dependent variables has become known as the **tobit**. Very simply the tobit model sets up the regression problem in the following form:

$$Y_i = w + e \tag{13.24}$$

where w again stands for the constant and all the explanatory variables with their coefficients in the regression equation, and

$$Y_i = Y_i \text{ if expenditure is positive}$$

and

$$Y_i = 0 \text{ if expenditure is zero}$$

The tobit approach thus distinguishes the decision to buy from the decision of how much to buy. Note that the structure of (13.24) is similar to that of (13.1), simply substituting a continuous variable for the binary choice in the first restriction. The tobit model may thus be seen as an extension of the logit-probit method.[u]

The model is solved simultaneously using maximum-likelihood methods, by setting up a likelihood function with two elements, one relating to the zero observations, the other to the positive outcomes. Each part of the likelihood function is based on the standard normal distribution.

The **tobit coefficients** have a dual interpretation. They measure the impact of a change in the explanatory variables both on the probability of making a purchase and on the size of the purchase made. By solving as a single system, the tobit does not allow for differential effects of the set of explanatory variables on the two components of the household decision. Rather it asserts that the variables that determine whether to buy operate in the same way to determine how much to buy. So, in the case of our Detroit households, the sensitivity of expenditure on automobiles is the same throughout the income distribution; but those families below a certain income level, although desirous of a car, cannot buy one because it is not available at their offer price.

Since Tobin's pioneering work, deeper understanding of the underlying theory behind censored regressions has unearthed some problems with the tobit solution. In particular, it produces biased coefficient estimates if the explanatory variables are not normally distributed. This is a serious

---

[u] Tobit models may be applied to censoring from above as well as below. They may also be adapted to cases in which the dependent variable is constrained from above and below (e.g. when hours of work cannot fall below 20 or rise above 50).

problem if income, a notoriously non-normally distributed variable, is a primary explanator, as it often is in models of consumption patterns.[v]

Moreover, it is now understood that even under ideal conditions, the coefficient estimates produced by the tobit model do not measure the expected change in the dependent variable for a given change in an explanatory variable. Rather, the coefficient on income is a mixture of two separate (and separable) elements on automobile ownership: the raising of some households above the income level at which purchase of a car is possible, and the desire to spend more money on a car for those who could already afford one.

13.6.3 Two-part censored models

An alternative to the tobit specification, which uses only one regression to deal with censoring, is to subdivide the problem into two parts. Thus, in the case of consumer durable expenditure, the problem is separated into (a) the decision to buy, and (b) the decision on how much to buy for those who choose to. Similarly, if we were investigating workers' participation in strikes, we could separate out the decision to join a strike from the duration of the strike.

The first stage of the two-part model is a model of binary choice, in which the dependent variable is dichotomous, taking the value of 0 or 1. It can be estimated by the logit or probit model (most empirical work uses the latter). The second stage uses interval level quantitative information (how much was spent, the length of the period on strike) *only for those observations that took the value of 1 in the first part.* For this stage a straightforward OLS regression is run on those observations.

Thus, the coefficients on, say, the decision to purchase an item are allowed to differ from the coefficients on how much to buy. This is especially useful if it is thought that the mix of explanatory variables that influence the decision to buy are systematically different from those that determine how much to spend. It is also an advantage over the standard tobit specification, that neither the probit nor the OLS require that all explanatory variables be normally distributed.

To indicate the contrasts between the tobit and the two-part specification, we have extended our fictitious Detroit survey to incorporate information on the value of cars owned. The results of the two regressions are

---

[v] If income is distributed log-normally, it is possible to rescue the tobit specification by using the logarithm of income instead, but other variables in the regression model may also be non-normal.

Table 13.3 Detroit automobile ownership, 1919: censored models (hypothetical data)

	(1)	(2)	(3)
		Two-stage model	
	Tobit model	Probit equation	OLS equation
Dependent variable:	CARCOST	AUTO (all)	CARCOST (if AUTO=1)
INCOME	235.6741 (14.857)	0.3575 (12.428)	116.3986 (10.663)
FAMSIZE	−230.4858 (6.673)	−0.4957 (8.045)	71.3988 (2.660)
HOME	650.3871 (8.425)	1.2589 (9.274)	60.3503 (1.116)
CONSTANT	−326.3432 (1.672)	0.1942 (0.559)	344.8536 (−2.251)
	pseudo R^2 0.1272	−2 log λ 420.02	R^2 0.4165

Note:
Figures in parentheses are *t*-statistics.

shown in table 13.3. The most striking difference between the single-equation and the two-stage model is in the interpretation of the two secondary explanatory variables, HOME and FAMSIZE. Whereas the tobit regression suggests that the value of the automobile dropped as family size increased and rose as wealth increased, the two-stage model permits a more sophisticated interpretation.

A comparison of the probit and the second-stage OLS equations in columns (2) and (3) of the table indicates that HOME was primarily a determinant of whether a family purchased a car or not, but was not a statistically significant factor in explaining the value of the car owned. A bigger family size reduced the probability of owning a car for any given level of income or wealth; but for those with incomes above the threshold, a larger family translated into a more expensive (perhaps larger?) car. It seems clear that the two-part specification permits a richer interpretation of the data than the tobit.

Notes

[1] The following are a few recent examples of studies that use logit or probit procedure for the analysis of binary dependent variables. The effects of early industrialization on the employment of children, in Sara Horrell and Jane Humphries, '"The exploitation of little children": child labor and the family economy in the industrial revolution', *Explorations in Economic History*, 32, 1995, pp. 485–516. The retirement and related decisions made by a sample of Union army veterans in 1900 and 1910, in Dora L. Costa, *The Evolution of Retirement*, University of Chicago Press, 1998. The probability of dying from or contracting disease for a sample of Civil War recruits during their military service, in Chulhee Lee, 'Socio-economic background, disease and mortality among Union army recruits: implications for economic and demographic history', *Explorations in Economic History*, 34, 1997, pp. 27–55. The probability of voting for or against tariff repeal in the British Parliament in the 1840s, in Cheryl Schonhardt-Bailey, 'Linking constituency interests to legislative voting behaviour: the role of district economic and electoral composition in the repeal of the Corn Laws', *Parliamentary History*, 13, 1994, pp. 86–118.

[2] This can be easily shown by rewriting the OLS regression, $Y_i = a + bX_i + e_i$ in the form $e_i = Y_i - a - bX_i$. When $Y_i = 1$, the error term is equal to $(1 - a - bX_i)$; when $Y_i = 0$, it is equal to $(-a - bX_i)$. The error term will be larger for households for whom $Y_i = 1$ than for those for whom $Y_i = 0$.

[3] The logistic curve is the cdf of the hyperbolic-secant-square (sech^2) distribution.

[4] We can derive (13.5b) by re-writing (13.5a)

$$P(Y_i = 0) = 1 - \frac{e^w}{1 + e^w}$$

as follows

$$P(Y_i = 0) = \frac{1 + e^w}{1 + e^w} - \frac{e^w}{1 + e^w} = \frac{1 + e^w - e^w}{1 + e^w} = \frac{1}{1 + e^w}$$

to produce (13.5b).

Similarly, we may derive (13.5c) as follows, recalling from §1.6.1 that the multiplication of powers is achieved by addition of the exponents, so that $e^w \times e^{-w} = e^{w-w}$, then

$$P(Y_i = 0) = \frac{1 + e^w}{1 + e^w} - \frac{e^w}{1 + e^w}$$

$$= \frac{1 + e^w - e^w}{1 + e^w} = \frac{e^w e^{-w} + e^w - e^w}{1 + e^w}$$

$$= \frac{e^w e^{-w}}{e^w e^{-w} + e^w} = \frac{e^w e^{-w}}{e^w (1 + e^{-w})}$$

$$= \frac{e^{-w}}{1 + e^{-w}}$$

which produces (13.5c).

5 Dividing (13.4) by (13.5b) is equivalent to multiplying (13.4) by the reciprocal (inverse) of (13.5b), i.e.

$$\frac{e^w}{1+e^w} \times \frac{1+e^w}{1} = e^w$$

to produce (13.10).

6 To see why the logarithmic transformation of e^w produces w, we apply the rules for the log of a number raised to a power (see §1.6.2) to the expression $\log_e(e^w)$ to produce $w \times \log_e e$. Since $\log e$ to the base $e = 1$, this gives w.

7 However, the individual predicted values of car ownership ($\hat{P}_{Y_i}$) from the regression almost never take on the exact value of the original data, although they are constrained to the range (0,1). In the Detroit data set, the fitted values range from 0.04 to 0.95. The logit function, although clearly superior to a linear specification, nonetheless produces only an approximation to the actual distribution of data points.

8 Equation (13.12) can be obtained by calculating the derivative of the logit function with respect to X_k. For an individual household, this gives

$$\frac{\partial P_{Y_i}}{\partial X_k} = \frac{e^w}{(1+e^w)^2} \times b_k = \frac{e^w}{(1+e^w)} \times \frac{1}{(1+e^w)} \times b_k \qquad (13.12a)$$

From (13.4) the first term is equal to $P(Y_i=1)$, and from (13.5b) the second term is equal to $P(Y_i=0)$. Hence $\partial P_{Y_i}/\partial X_k = P(Y_i=1) \times P(Y_i=0) \times b_k$.

9 It was suggested previously that the impact effect is best calculated for discrete variables, such as a dummy explanatory variable. In our simple bivariate model, we have no dummies; we therefore calculate the impact effect for a unit change in income. The procedure set out in the text may be generalized to the case of a discrete variable. The one significant difference in the procedure for binary dummy variables is that the absolute effect is measured by comparing $\hat{P}_Y$ for the cases when the dummy equals one and zero. When calculating the impact effect of a change in a dummy variable for the sample as a whole, it is necessary to set the dummy variable to zero for all observations to provide the base-line for comparison, and then to compare this result to the case when the dummy variable is set to one for all observations.

10 The unit elasticity may either be measured by comparing the impact effect of moving from 0 to 1 relative to the average value of the dummy in the sample as a whole, or by using the average value of the dummy as the starting point for estimating the impact effect, e.g. moving from 0.185 to 1.185 and using 1/0.185 as the second term in the elasticity formula.

11 One cautionary note. It is important to ensure that the selection of the values of X_k are internally consistent. Thus, if the researcher is working through the effects of changing income at the lower quartile of INCOME in the sample, it is essential that she use the average values of FAMSIZE and HOME *at this income level*, rather than the lower quartiles of each variable, which would be inconsistent and, therefore, inappropriate.

12 For an interesting illustration of the logit model applied to group data see Konrad H. Jarausch and Gerhard Arminger, 'The German teaching profession and Nazi party

membership: a demographic logit model', *Journal of Interdisciplinary History*, 20 (Autumn 1989), pp. 197–225. The authors analyse the proportion of teachers who joined the Nazi party by various demographic and social characteristics, including religion, sex, and birth cohort. Since all of their variables are categorical, there is absolutely no difference between running such a regression on the various cells of the cross-tabulations, weighted by the number of observations in each, and running a regression that counts each individual separately.

[13] In practice, because the distributions do not share precisely the same shape and because observations are not drawn equally from all parts of the distribution, the actual ratio of the two coefficient estimates will vary around 0.55, normally falling in the range, 0.475–0.625. The larger the sample, the more likely it is that all parts of the distribution will be sampled, and the closer the ratio of coefficients will be to 0.55. The smaller the sample variance, the greater is the distortion. The other factor that influences the ratio of the coefficients is the proportion of positive outcomes in the sample. If $P(Y_i = 1)$ is either very large or very small, the distortion is likely to be larger.

[14] We note in passing that the probit approach run over properly structured grouped data produces very similar results to those obtained using the full data set. When we ran a grouped probit regression using the same 126 groups as in §13.3.2, the following results were obtained:

$$\text{AUTO} = 0.1596 + 0.3625 \text{ INCOME} - 0.4919 \text{ FAMSIZE} + 1.2559 \text{ HOME}$$
$$(0.458) \quad (12.400) \qquad\qquad (7.995) \qquad\qquad (9.241)$$

$$\log L_1 = -253.615; \quad -2\log\lambda = 420.22;] \quad \text{McFadden's } R^2 = 0.4531.$$

[15] The height of the normal density function is calculated from the formula:

$$\frac{1}{\sqrt{2\pi}} \exp\left(-\frac{1}{2}z^2\right)$$

where π is the constant pi and z is the probit index. The table is reproduced in G. S. Maddala, *Introduction to Econometrics*, 2nd edn., Prentice-Hall, 1992, pp. 610–11.

[16] An insightful application of an ordered response model to analyse successive votes in the US Senate in 1929–1930 on the introduction of the Smoot–Hawley tariff is found in Colleen M. Callahan, Judith A. McDonald and Anthony Patrick O'Brien, 'Who voted for Smoot–Hawley?' *Journal of Economic History*, 54, 1994, pp. 683–90. The variable VOTE has a value of 2 for a representative who voted yes for both the initial passage of the bill in May 1929 and the final passage in June 1930; 1 if he or she voted in favour of initial passage but against final passage; and 0 if the representative voted no on both occasions.

[17] One example of a model that uses multinomial logit regressions is Robert A. Margo, 'The labor force participation of older Americans in 1900: Further Results,' *Explorations in Economic History*, 30, 1993, pp. 409–23, in which the procedure was used to distinguish between not working, being currently employed, and being in long-term unemployment. Another is Daniel A. Ackerberg and Maristella Botticini,

'The choice of agrarian contracts in early Renaissance Tuscany: risk sharing, moral hazard, or capital market imperfections?', *Explorations in Economic History*, 37, 2000, pp. 241–57, in which the distinctions were between owner-occupation of land, fixed-rent contracts, and share contracts.

13.7 Exercises for chapter 13

1. Which model (logit, tobit, or neither) is more appropriate for regression analysis of the following variables?

  (i)   Whether a household owns or rents their dwelling
  (ii)   How much a household pays in rent for their dwelling
  (iii)   How much debt a household still owes on its (owned) dwelling
  (iv)   Whether a person voted in the last election
  (v)   Which party a person voted for in the last election
  (vi)   What proportion of all eligible voters voted in the last 10 elections
  (vii)   What proportion of all votes were cast for a particular party in the last 10 elections
  (viii)   How many votes were cast for the same party in the last 10 elections.

2. Using the AUTO data set on the web page, run a logit regression of HOME, with INCOME and FAMSIZE as the regressors. The regression result (with t-statistics in parentheses) should be

$$\text{HOME} = 0.027 + 0.2170\ \text{INCOME} - 0.4196\ \text{FAMSIZE}$$
$$(0.03) \quad (2.99) \qquad\qquad (-2.45)$$

Report the values of the pseudo R^2 and the two log-likelihood values.

     You wish to work out the level of HOME when INCOME is $2 thousand and $5 thousand. Report your answer, showing the requisite steps.

3. Use the regression analysis of HOME ownership to:

  (i)   Calculate the impact effect of an increase in INCOME on HOME at $2 thousand and $5 thousand, respectively. Report your answer, showing the requisite steps. Express this result as an elasticity.
  (ii)   Calculate the marginal effect of an increase in INCOME on HOME at $2 thousand and $5 thousand, respectively. Report your answer, showing the requisite steps. Express this result as an elasticity.

4. You wish to use the Steckel data set to test certain hypotheses about the causes of migration in antebellum America. The hypotheses include:

  (a)   Literacy is a positive influence on migration
  (b)   Migration tends to fall as households age

(c) Larger families are less able to migrate, because of the increased expense

(d) Immigrants, who have already migrated once, are more likely to migrate again

(e) Urban households are more likely to migrate than rural

(f) The absence of a wife increases the probability of moving

(g) Migration tends to be more frequent in some regions than others

(h) Unskilled workers tend to move less often than other occupations

(i) Migration is less frequent for households without property

(j) For those with property, the wealthier the family, the less likely they are to move.

(i) Set up a model to test the hypotheses. (*Note*: you will need to instruct the computer to generate new dummy variables in order to test hypotheses (c), (d), (e), and (i)).

Use the logit procedure to test these hypotheses. Record your results and write a brief essay interpreting them. How effective is the model at explaining household migration? Which hypotheses are supported and which are not? Be sure not only to examine the signs and significance of the coefficients, but pay attention to the historical significance of the results. (*Hint*: think about the elasticities.) Is this a complete model of household migration?

(ii) Run a probit regression and compare the results to the logit formulation. Analyse any differences.

5. Take the probit results from question 4 and use them to interpret the value of the probit index at the mean of the variables. Apply the method introduced in §13.6 to calculate the impact effect of a unit change in the value of real estate on the probability of migration at the mean. Compare the result of this exercise to the impact effect of a unit change in PROPERTY using the logit coefficients.

6. A researcher wishes to analyse why some Southern parishes built workhouses while others did not. Her maintained hypothesis is that workhouses tended to be built in large, rich, densely settled parishes. These parish characteristics are captured by POP, WEALTH, INCOME, and DENSITY.

(i) Set up a logit model to test the hypotheses and report the results.

(ii) Re-organize the data into groups and re-run the logit model. Set up your groups carefully, using the criteria established in §13.3.2. Report your results, being sure to identify any differences from the ungrouped results.

7. Set up a model using the Steckel data set to investigate the relationship between the value of the household's real property and the characteristics of the family. Motivate your selection of explanatory variables.

   (i) Evaluate your model using standard (OLS) regression methods. Report your results.
   (ii) Evaluate your model using a tobit regression. Report your results.
   (iii) Evaluate your model using the two-part procedure, applying a logit or probit equation to establish the determinants of holding any real estate, and an OLS regression to evaluate the determinants of the level of real estate for propertied households. (*Hint*: generate a dummy variable for positive wealth holding.) Report your results.

Interpret the differences between these results. Are there empirical reasons for preferring one formulation over the others? What do these various formulations tell us about the determinants of wealth holding in antebellum America?

8. A researcher argues that the provision of child allowances varied from parish to parish according to the affluence of the parish (WEALTH, INCOME), its economic structure (GRAIN, COTTIND), and whether or not there was a local workhouse.

   (i) Set up a probit model to test the hypotheses and report the results. Does the regression support the argument?

The researcher further argues that the number of children at which allowance is paid is influenced by the same variables. In order to test this hypothesis, it is necessary to generate a multinomial variable, which takes the value of 0 if no child allowance is paid; 1 if allowance begins with 3 children; 2 if it begins with 4 children; and 3 if it begins with 5 or more children.

   (ii) Run an ordered probit regression to analyse this second hypothesis. What do the results tell us? Are the results consistent with the simpler model? Does the new version add any information for our understanding of the provision of child allowances in Southern parishes?

9. Is the mean household or the median household a more relevant organizing entity for limited dependent variable analysis? Justify your choice.

10. Instruct the computer to set up a multinomial of occupation in the Steckel data set. Run a multinomial logit equation of occupation on region, degree of urbanization, and ethnic origin. What do you find? How would you interpret the regression results?

PART V

Specifying and interpreting models: four case studies

CHAPTER 14

Case studies 1 and 2: unemployment in Britain and emigration from Ireland

We noted in chapter 1 that the most important of our three aims in this text was to enable our readers to read, understand, and evaluate articles or books that make use of modern quantitative methods to support their analyses of historical questions. We selected four specific case studies that we have referred to and used as illustrations at various points in preceding chapters. In this and the following chapter we want to look more closely at each of these studies, and to see in particular how their models were specified, how any technical problems such as autocorrelation or simultaneity were handled, and how the regression coefficients, standard errors (and *t*-ratios or prob-values), and other statistical results were interpreted and related to the historical issues addressed in the articles.

The present chapter covers two studies investigating the causes of unemployment in inter-war Britain and of the nineteenth-century emigration from Ireland to the United States and other countries. Chapter 15 is devoted to the impact of the Old Poor Law on relief payments, earnings, and employment in England in the 1830s, and to the factors that influenced children's decisions to leave the family home in the United States in the mid-nineteenth century. We assume that students will by now have carefully read the case studies and thought about the institutional and historical questions with which they deal. The comments that follow are thus concerned primarily with their statistical aspects, and we will refer to the historical background only where this is necessary to give a context for the statistical issues.

Each of these studies is briefly introduced in appendix A and the variables used are described and listed in tables A.1–A.5. Each series is given an abbreviated name written in capital letters, and we shall refer here to the series by these names (as we have done throughout the text) rather than by the symbols or alternative references used in the original studies.

In specifying the models in the following sections we shall also continue our previous practice of referring to the constant as a, and to all other coefficients as b_1, b_2, and so on, even if this differs from the notation adopted by the authors. And we shall continue to use the term 'log' rather than 'ln' to indicate a natural logarithm.

14.1 Inter-war benefits and unemployment in Great Britain

We begin with the earliest and simplest of the models in our four articles, the one used by Benjamin and Kochin in their 1979 paper to study the effect of the unemployment benefits paid to the millions who were out of work in inter-war Britain (see §A.1 in appendix A for their basic hypothesis and table A.4 for details of the data set).[a] We look first at their procedure and then, in §14.1.2, at some of the criticisms that their paper evoked.

14.1.1   The Benjamin and Kochin model

Benjamin and Kochin argued that the dominant explanation for the high level of unemployment in inter-war Britain was not – as often suggested by other writers – the depressed level of overall demand. Their central hypothesis was that it was the generous payment of benefits to those on the dole (compared to the amount they would have received in wages if in work) that was primarily responsible.

Benjamin and Kochin's basic model is a single equation specifying a linear relationship between the dependent variable, UNEMP, and two explanatory variables: BWRATIO (the replacement rate, measured as the ratio of BENEFITS to WAGES), and DEMAND (measured by the difference between log output and the trend of log output, and thus equivalent to the ratio of output to its trend)

$$\text{UNEMP} = a + b_1 \text{BWRATIO} + b_2 \text{DEMAND} + e \qquad (14.1)$$

They estimate this model using ordinary least squares (OLS), and report the following results (p. 453), with t-statistics shown in parentheses[1]

$$\text{UNEMP} = 5.19 + 18.3\,\text{BWRATIO} - 90.0\,\text{DEMAND} \qquad (14.2)^2$$
$$(2.64) \quad (4.46) \qquad\qquad (-8.30)$$

$$R^2 = 0.84, \quad \bar{R}^2 = 0.82, \quad \text{DW} = 2.18, \quad \text{SEE} = 1.90$$

---

[a] Unless otherwise noted all page references in §14.1 are to Daniel K. Benjamin and Lewis A. Kochin, 'Searching for an explanation of unemployment in interwar Britain', *Journal of Political Economy*, 87, 1979, pp. 441–78.

We can see immediately that the *t*-ratios are all well in excess of 2 and thus all the coefficients are statistically significant (see §6.7.3 and (6.15)). The coefficients are also correctly signed: positive for BWRATIO (a rise in the relative level of benefits increases UNEMP) and negative for DEMAND (the higher output is relative to its trend value, the lower the level of UNEMP).

The size of the coefficients appears to give greater predictive importance to DEMAND than to BWRATIO. However, since coefficient size depends crucially on the size of the explanatory variable, it makes sense to scale the two coefficients by calculating standardized beta coefficients (see §8.2.7). The betas are 0.4533 for BWRATIO and 0.8422 for DEMAND, indicating that a change of one standard deviation in DEMAND has a much greater impact on UNEMP than a change of one standard deviation in BWRATIO.

The coefficient of multiple determination, R^2, is very high at 0.84, and because there are only two explanatory variables the adjusted $\bar{R}^2$ is only marginally lower than this. The model thus accounts for 82 per cent of the variation in inter-war unemployment. However, we should not attach too much importance to this since a high R^2 is not uncommon with time-series data in which many variables may fluctuate together even if not causally related. The value of DW, the Durbin–Watson statistic, is close to 2, thus indicating that there is no problem of autocorrelation (see §11.3.3). SEE is the standard error of the estimate, as defined in (9.10) and §9.4.

Benjamin and Kochin (pp. 453–5) also consider the possibility that there might be a problem of mis-specification if the direction of causation runs in the opposite direction from that assumed by their model. They discuss two mechanisms that might lead to such reverse causation, in which case a high level of unemployment would be the *cause* of a high benefit–wage ratio rather than an effect. However, they conclude that neither was operating in inter-war Britain.

The first mechanism might have occurred if high levels of unemployment caused low levels of wages and thus raised the BWRATIO. They dismiss this possibility on the grounds that most of the variation in the inter-war BWRATIO was caused by movements in BENEFITS rather than in WAGES; and also show that if BENEFITS and WAGES are entered separately in an alternative specification of the model, the coefficient on the former remains strongly significant (with a *t*-ratio of 4.04) whereas the latter is insignificant (with a *t*-ratio of –0.82).

The second mechanism might have occurred if the level of benefits had been influenced by the level of unemployment. Benjamin and Kochin argue that there is no evidence in the parliamentary debates to suggest that this was a relevant consideration, and that the most important determinant of the scale of benefits was the current and prospective financial condition of the Fund from which they were paid.[3]

In addition to the primary model in (14.1), they also experiment with a variety of other specifications (p. 453, n. 16). These include one in which the relationship between UNEMP and BWRATIO is modelled as non-linear, thus allowing for the possibility that the ratio of benefits to wages might have a very different impact on UNEMP at different levels of BWRATIO. In another a **time trend** (a series which simply increases by 1 unit each year) was added to (14.1);[b] and in others the primary model was estimated for different time periods, omitting successively 1920, 1920–1, 1920–2 and 1920–3. They find, however, that the results of all these alternative functional forms are statistically very similar to those given by (14.1).

Benjamin and Kochin (pp. 464–70) use the regression coefficients on BWRATIO and DEMAND from (14.1) to estimate the effect of the unemployment benefit scheme. Unfortunately, their model involves a complication which means that the coefficient on BWRATIO cannot be taken in the usual way to measure its impact on the dependent variable, and the manner in which they deal with this involves some rather complicated economic and mathematical reasoning that goes well beyond the scope of this text. We simply note that their final conclusion is that over the period as a whole 'the insurance system raised the average unemployment rate by about five to eight percentage points' (p. 468), and thus had a very substantial effect.

14.1.2 Parameter stability and outliers in the Benjamin and Kochin model

The publication of this paper unleashed a flurry of criticisms. Many of these concerned either historical and institutional questions, such as the administration and actual working of the unemployment insurance scheme, or aspects of the data, such as the appropriate measure of benefits relative to wages. There were, however, a number of interesting points concerned with the statistical procedures, and we will look briefly at the most important of these.

One pair of critics, Ormerod and Worswick, argue that the estimated coefficient on BWRATIO (and hence the estimate of its effect on UNEMP) is 'very sensitive to small changes in the sample period' and thus 'casts serious doubts on the validity of their results'.[c] They show a scatter diagram

---

[b] A time trend can be regarded as a proxy for any unmeasured (or unmeasurable) variables that might affect the dependent variable and have a similar upward or downward trend.

[c] P. A. Ormerod and G. D. N. Worswick, 'Unemployment in inter-war Britain', *Journal of Political Economy*, 90, 1982, pp. 400–9, quotation at p. 402.

for UNEMP and BWRATIO in which the observation for 1920 appears to be a clear outlier, and the remaining years fall into two groups. The observations for 1921–9 lie on one straight line with a *negative* slope, and those for 1930–8 on another line, again with a *negative* slope, though for these years a very slight one.[d] A negative slope is, of course, the opposite of what Benjamin and Kochin find, since their regression coefficient on BWRATIO is positive.

In order to demonstrate the sensitivity of the BWRATIO coefficient to the sample of years for which the equation is estimated, Ormerod and Worswick re-estimate the equation successively omitting the years from 1920. Their first alternative is thus for 1921–38, the second for 1922–38, and so on for 10 equations ending with 1930–8.

As one test of sensitivity they take a 95 per cent confidence interval around the original regression coefficient on BWRATIO of 18.3, giving them a range from 10.6 to 26.1.[e] They then show that six of the 10 coefficients on BWRATIO estimated for their 10 alternative sample periods fall *outside* this range.[f]

As a further test Ormerod and Worswick examine the robustness of the Benjamin and Kochin results when a time series is added to their 10 alternative time periods.[4] The 95 per cent confidence interval is considerably larger in this case (because the standard error on the regression coefficient, BWRATIO, for the period 1920–38 is much larger) and the range when the time trend is included is from 4.3 to 33.6. None of the coefficients for periods starting in 1923 or later falls within this range, and only one is statistically significant.

In their vigorous reply, Benjamin and Kochin reject these tests of the stability of their coefficients as being inappropriate.[g] In their place, they apply two other tests for parameter stability. The first is a dummy variable test, based on the equation for a piecewise linear regression, introduced in §11.2.3. This test takes the basic regression and adds a slope dummy variable, equal to the interaction of the explanatory variable whose stability is being tested (in this case, the benefit–wage ratio) and a categorical variable

---

[d] You have already plotted this scatter diagram in question 3 of chapter 3.

[e] The 95 per cent confidence interval corresponds broadly to 2 standard errors (SE) either side of the estimate; it can be calculated as shown in §5.6.3, using (5.16). Ormerod and Worswick give the SE as 3.87, and their confidence interval is thus $18.36 \pm 2 \times (3.87)$.

[f] Ormerod and Worswick, 'Unemployment', table 3, p. 405.

[g] Daniel K. Benjamin and Levis A. Kochin, 'Unemployment and unemployment benefits in twentieth-century Britain: a reply to our critics', *Journal of Political Economy*, 90, 1982, pp. 410–36; see especially pp. 412–15.

set at 0 below the threshold of change and 1 above. The revised equation is thus

$$UNEMP = a + b_1 BWRATIO + b_2 DEMAND +$$
$$b_3 DUMMY*BWRATIO + e \qquad (14.3)$$

The test statistic is the t-statistic on b_3, evaluated at standard levels of significance. If the t-statistic falls below the critical level, then the model does not indicate structural change and the null hypothesis of stability should not be rejected. Since Benjamin and Kochin are testing for general parameter stability, rather than the existence of a single structural break, they ran the dummy variable test over a range of subperiods, beginning with 1921–38 and changing the beginning period by one year up to 1930–8. In no case did the t-statistic on b_3 pass at the 5 per cent level of significance.

The dummy variable test asks whether a single parameter is stable over the regression sample. The **Chow test** asks whether the entire model is stable, i.e. whether all the parameters are stable. The Chow procedure divides the sample into two (or more) subperiods, running the same regression over each, and then comparing their results to those from a regression run over the entire sample. The comparison is based not on parameter values, but on the overall explanatory power of the equations, as measured by the unexplained variation, or residual sum of squares (RSS), first introduced in §4.3.2.[h]

Let us identify the RSS for the entire sample as RSS_1; for the two sub-samples, we use RSS_2 and RSS_3. The test statistic for the Chow test is:

$$F = \frac{(RSS_1 - RSS_2 - RSS_3)/k}{(RSS_2 + RSS_3)/(n_2 + n_3 - 2k)} \qquad (14.4)$$

where n_2 and n_3 indicate the number of observations in the subsamples and k is the number of explanatory variables in the original (and by extension, the subsample) regression.

This calculated statistic may be compared to the critical value of the F-statistic from any published F-table. The critical value (F_{mn}) is reported for two degrees of freedom, one for the denominator and one for the numerator. The df in the Chow test are equal to k and $(n_1 + n_2 - 2k)$, respectively. If the calculated F is larger than the critical value at the appropriate level of significance, then the null hypothesis of model stability is rejected; if F falls below the critical value, the null hypothesis is not rejected.

Benjamin and Kochin once again ran the Chow test over a range of possible subsamples in order to test for general model stability. In no case do

---

[h] The unexplained variation is also referred to as the error sum of squares (ESS).

they find the calculated *F*-statistic to be greater than the critical value at the 5 per cent level of significance, indicating that the null hypothesis of parameter stability should not be rejected.

The starting point for Ormerod and Worswick's criticism was that 1920 appeared to be a clear outlier. This suggestion has also been made by other historians critical of Benjamin and Kochin's results. To our knowledge, no one has formally evaluated whether 1920 really is an outlier.[5] In §11.3.4, we discussed the general problem of outliers and influential observations. In that section, we distinguished 'good' outliers from 'bad' outliers, suggesting that leverage points, in which the values of explanatory variables are significantly different from the rest of the sample, may provide valuable information about the model as a whole. In contrast, rogue observations marred by large prediction errors should be discarded.

Is 1920 a good or a bad outlier? A scatter-plot of the data on UNEMP and BWRATIO certainly marks it out as a leverage point, and this is confirmed by a more formal statistical test, due to Hadi, which determines whether the value of the observation falls into the tail of the sample distribution as a whole. The values of BWRATIO for 1920 and 1921 are significantly different from the rest of the sample at the 5 per cent level (the Hadi test detects no outliers in either UNEMP or DEMAND).

To determine whether any observations in the Benjamin–Kochin data constituted outliers due to estimation error, we ran two tests. A dummy variable test, which evaluated the statistical significance of observation dummies in the estimating equation, identified 1921 and 1930, but not 1920, as outliers at the 5 per cent level. A second test involves running the regression for as many times as there are data points, dropping each observation in turn, and predicting the value of the dependent variable for the missing variable. This is a variant of the method of out-of-sample prediction. An observation is identified as an outlier if the difference between the predicted and actual values of the dependent variable is statistically large.[6] The null hypothesis of no difference between the reported and predicted unemployment rates was rejected for a larger number of observations, including 1921, but excluding both 1920 and 1930.[i] On this basis, 1920 does not appear to have been an estimation outlier, while 1921 clearly was.

Thus it appears that 1920 was a leverage point, but not a rogue observation. 1921, on the other hand, may have been both. But how did these data points influence the overall equation? The substance of Ormerod and Worswick's critique is that the high and significant value of the coefficient

---

[i] The other outliers by this criteria were 1924–6 and 1936–8.

on BWRATIO was largely determined by the influence of 1920 on the relationship between the benefit–wage ratio and unemployment. Is this criticism appropriate?

The two standard tests (dfBeta and dfFits, described in §11.3.4) reveal 1920 and 1921 to have been influential observations.[j] The dfBeta statistics indicate that the coefficient on BWRATIO was significantly different from the rest of the sample for both years; the dfFit value confirms that this difference in coefficients was substantial enough to cause a statistically significant difference in the predicted dependent variable. Thus, the dfFit values are consistent with the suspicion that unemployment in 1921 was generated by a process different from the rest of the sample, while 1920 was not.

What should be done about such outliers? The temptation is to throw them away, but this would clearly be inappropriate in the case of 1920 – the reason why that year is influential is not that it is a rogue observation, but rather that one of its explanatory variables falls into the tail of the distribution. Dropping 1920 would jettison valuable information about the model as a whole. The judgement on 1921 is more mixed, however, since it shows up as an outlier in both categories. There may be a case for excluding 1921 – curiously, since it was not identified by Benjamin and Kochin's critics as a rogue observation.[k]

The alternative to discarding either or both observations is to apply **robust regression** techniques to the data (§11.3.4). Robust regressions use weighting procedures to reduce the power of influential observations. Purely for illustration, we have run one over the entire Benjamin and Kochin data set, with the following results

$$\text{UNEMP} = 4.87 + 18.83 \text{ BWRATIO} - 91.35 \text{ DEMAND}$$
$$(2.49) \quad (4.62) \qquad\qquad (-8.37)$$

which is essentially identical to the result in (14.2).[l]

---

[j] As with all such tests, it is imperative that they be run over the entire sample; 'cherry-picking' certain observations, such as 1920–1, for special evaluation is inappropriate.

[k] If 1921 is excluded, the OLS regression result becomes:

$$\text{UNEMP} = 2.61 + 23.21 \text{ BWRATIO} - 84.77 \text{ DEMAND}$$
$$(1.38) \quad (5.99) \qquad\qquad (-9.08)$$

$$R^2 = 0.89, \ \bar{R}^2 = 0.88 \ \text{SEE} = 1.56$$

It is not possible to generate a Durbin–Watson statistic since the data are no longer continuous.

[l] Or rather, to our results as given in n. 2. Note that robust regression techniques do not product standard goodness-of-fit measures.

Benjamin and Kochin's response to their critics was not the last word on the origins of unemployment in the inter-war period, as might be predicted from the tone of the debate.[m] More sophisticated econometric modelling of the inter-war labour market has been undertaken, both by advocates of a benefit story and by those who find it unpersuasive. Much of the debate has continued to work with annual observations, although some scholars have attempted to increase the degrees of freedom of such models by introducing quarterly data.[7]

However, much the most intriguing developments in inter-war labour history have emerged from micro-economic analysis of survey data for the 1920s and 1930s. The pioneering work was undertaken by Barry Eichengreen, who sampled the records of the *New Survey of London Life and Labour* that was undertaken between 1928 and 1932. With this data, Eichengreen was able to test Benjamin and Kochin's hypothesis about the influence of rising benefits on labour supply decisions for individual workers, rather than generalizing from market aggregates.

Eichengreen's conclusions offered a substantial revision of the benefit argument. For household heads, who dominated employment in this period, the ratio of benefits to wages played almost no role in determining whether they were in work or out of work. But for non-household heads the replacement rate did matter, perhaps causing their unemployment rate to rise to as much as double what it would have been had replacement rates stayed at 1913 levels. However, since these secondary workers accounted for only a very small part of the London labour force, the weighted average of the two effects was small, leading Eichengreen to conclude that, 'it does not appear that the generosity of the dole had much effect on the overall unemployment rate'.[n]

14.2 Emigration from Ireland

Our next and more elaborate case study is the 1993 article by Hatton and Williamson examining the massive emigration from Ireland to the United States and other destinations after the famine (see §A.2 in appendix A for a brief introduction and table A.3 for details of the data set).[o] The overall rate

---

[m] There are clearly several respects in which their modelling procedure would not conform with what is today regarded as best practice in the sense of §12.6, but the article reflects standard practice of the time it was written.

[n] Barry Eichengreen, 'Unemployment in inter-war Britain: dole or doldrums?', in N.F.R. Crafts, N. H. Dimsdale and S. Engerman (eds.), *Quantitative Economic History*, Oxford University Press, 1991, pp.1–27, quotation at p. 22.

[o] All page references in this section are to Timothy J. Hatton and Jeffrey G. Williamson, 'After the famine: emigration from Ireland, 1850–1913', *Journal of Economic History*, 53, 1993, pp. 575–600.

of emigration fluctuated sharply from year to year, and also displayed a very clear long-term trend. After the immediate post-famine flood had abated, the trend rate remained very high at around 15 per 1,000 of the total Irish population in the 1860s and 1870s, and then declined to about 8 per 1,000 in the years immediately before the First World War.

Hatton and Williamson explore the causes of that emigration, attempting to explain both the decline over time in the long-term trend, and also the annual fluctuations. Following the tradition of earlier studies of migration they look for the principal causes in the economic conditions in Ireland, notably wages and employment, and assume that potential migrants compare these with the prospects offered to them in the United States and other possible destinations. These forces are supplemented by other economic and social conditions such as age, urbanization and access to land, poverty, religion, and literacy. The basis of the modelling strategy adopted by Hatton and Williamson is to specify comprehensive models covering as many as possible of these factors, and then to use the results of the regression analysis to establish their relative importance.

For some of the relevant variables this can best be done in a time-series model; for other variables more information is available in selected years in which the data can be analysed by a model that combines cross-sectional information for Irish counties over time. We look at each of these in turn.

14.2.1 The time-series model of Irish emigration

The first model, based on annual time-series data for the years 1877–1913, is set out below, using the symbol Δ (capital Greek delta) to indicate 'change in', and the subscripts t and $t-1$ to indicate the current and previous year

$$\begin{aligned} \text{IRISHMIG}_t = a &+ b_1 \Delta \log \text{EMPFOR}_t + b_2 \Delta \log \text{EMPDOM}_t + \\ & b_3 \Delta \log \text{IRWRATIO}_t + b_4 \log \text{EMPFOR}_{t-1} + \\ & b_5 \log \text{EMPDOM}_{t-1} + b_6 \log \text{IRWRATIO}_{t-1} + \\ & b_7 \text{MIGSTOCK}_t + b_8 \text{IRISHMIG}_{t-1} + e \quad (14.5) \end{aligned}$$

The model thus specifies that IRISHMIG, the rate of emigration per 1,000 of the population, is partly determined by *changes* between the current and previous periods in three variables, foreign employment, domestic employment, and the relative wage, and partly by the *lagged levels* of those same variables.[8] A further explanatory variable is the proportion of the total Irish population already living abroad; this is intended to capture the effects of chain migration, in which one generation of emi-

Table 14.1 Determinants of total Irish emigration rates, time-series data, 1877–1913

	(1) Coefficient	(2) t-statistics
Constant	−11.61	2.56
$\Delta \log \text{EMPFOR}$	108.95	4.52
$\log \text{EMPFOR}_{t-1}$	64.57	2.63
$\log \text{EMPDOM}_{t-1}$	−17.24	2.65
$\log \text{IRWRATIO}_{t-1}$	13.16	3.88
MIGSTOCK_t	22.87	2.29
IRISHMIG_{t-1}	0.44	3.46
R^2	0.86	
Residual sum of squares	80.05	
Durbin–Watson	1.90	
LM(1)	0.15	

Source: Hatton and Williamson, 'Emigration', p. 584.

grants assists the movement of the next generation by the provision of information, and financial and psychological support.

The model also includes the lagged value of the dependent variable, a procedure explained in §10.2.1. The dependent variable is not in log form, but six of the eight explanatory variables on the right-hand side are expressed as logs, so the model is semi-logarithmic (lin-log).

They estimated their model for total emigration, and also for emigration to particular regions, and for males and females. We focus here on the total. In reporting their results Hatton and Williamson omit two of the variables, ΔIRWRATIO and ΔEMPDOM, because the coefficients on these were never statistically significant. The remaining results are reproduced in table 14.1.

We see that all the t-ratios are well in excess of 2, and thus the regression coefficients on all these terms are statistically significant at the 5 per cent level or better. The high R^2 enables Hatton and Williamson to claim that 'Irish emigration can largely be explained by the variables included in [table 14.1], which account for four-fifths of the variance in the emigration rate' (p. 584).

The value of the Durbin–Watson statistic is close to 2, implying an absence of first-order autocorrelation. However, since it is known that the

Durbin–Watson test is biased against finding autocorrelation if a lagged dependent variable is included on the right-hand side, Hatton and Williamson also include the results from a second test for serial correlation, the Lagrange Multiplier (LM(1)) test, that is appropriate for autoregressive models.

This test (also known as the Breusch–Gordon test) is run by regressing the residuals from (14.5) against their lagged values and the other explanatory variables from the original equation. The R^2 from this second equation, multiplied by the degrees of freedom of the equation $(n-k)$ produces a test statistic – known as LM(1) – that has a chi-squared distribution with $(n-k)$ degrees of freedom. The value of LM(1) in this case is 0.15, well below the critical value at any reasonable level of significance, indicating that the null hypothesis of serial correlation can be rejected with confidence. This indicates that the R^2 of the test regression is very low, which implies that lagged residuals are not explaining current residuals. There is therefore no evidence of serial correlation.[p]

Hatton and Williamson conclude from the regression results that the effect of the overseas employment rate is very powerful. 'In the short run, a 10 per cent change in the employment rate (for example, a change in the unemployment rate from 10 to 1 per cent) would raise the emigration rate by more than 11 per 1,000' (p. 584).[q] To see how they derive this result from (14.5) we need to recall that this relationship in their model is semi-logarithmic: ΔEMPFOR is in logs, IRISHMIG is not.

Reference to our discussion of non-linear regression coefficients in §12.3 and table 12.1 indicates that in the case of a relationship of this form a change of 1 per cent in X causes a change in Y of b/100 units. The relevant value of b in this case is the regression coefficient on ΔEMPFOR in table 14.1, which is +108.95, so b/100 is 1.0895. However, Hatton and Williamson have chosen to refer to a change in X (in this case, EMPFOR) of 10 per cent rather than 1 per cent, so we must make a corresponding adjustment to the change in Y, and multiply b/100 by 10. The result is, therefore, that a 10 per cent change in EMPFOR would raise the emigration rate by 10.895 per 1,000 population or, in round numbers, by 11 per 1,000, controlling for the effects of the other variables in the model.[9]

---

[p] The other statistic reported in table 14.1 is the residual sum of squares (RSS), which indicates how much of the variance in the dependent variable is not explained by the regression. It is used by Hatton and Williamson to enable comparisons between (14.5) run on total emigration, and other versions run on slightly different data sets.

[q] Remember that EMPFOR is measured as 1 minus the proportion of the labour force unemployed each year. A fall in unemployment from 10 to 1 per cent is equivalent to a rise in *employment* from 90 per cent to 99 per cent, i.e. by 10 per cent.

Since Hatton and Williamson are interested in the long-term trend as well as the annual fluctuations, they also formulate an alternative *long-run version* of the model. In this the long run is characterized by the elimination of any impact from short-term changes in wage and employment rates, or in the emigration rate. This is achieved by setting ΔEMPFOR, ΔEMPDOM, and ΔIRWRATIO equal to zero, and by regarding IRISHMIG$_t$ and IRISHMIG$_{t-1}$ as equal. Making these changes (after which the time scripts are no longer needed), and moving the second term for IRISHMIG to the left-hand side, the model becomes[r]

$$(1 - b_8)\ \text{IRISHMIG} = a + b_4 \log \text{EMPFOR} +$$
$$b_5 \log \text{EMPDOM} + b_6 \log \text{IRWRATIO} +$$
$$b_7 \text{MIGSTOCK} + e \qquad (14.6a)$$

Dividing all terms on both sides by $(1 - b_8)$ we get

$$\text{IRISHMIG} = \frac{a}{1 - b_8} + \frac{b_4}{1 - b_8} \log \text{EMPFOR} +$$

$$\frac{b_5}{1 - b_8} \log \text{EMPDOM} +$$

$$\frac{b_6}{1 - b_8} \log \text{IRWRATIO} +$$

$$\frac{b_7}{1 - b_8} \text{MIGSTOCK} + e \qquad (14.6b)$$

Recalling the symbol $\tilde{b}$ adopted to distinguish the long-run coefficient (see §12.3.3) we can thus say that the *long-run* effect on IRISHMIG of a change in the foreign employment prospects is measured by

$$\tilde{b}_4 = \frac{b_4}{1 - b_8}$$

where b_8 is the coefficient on the lagged dependent variable estimated from the full model in (14.5), and similarly for the other variables in (14.6b).[s]

We thus have the long-run multiplier,

$$\tilde{b}_4 = \frac{b_4}{1 - b_8}$$

[r] The left-hand side is written as $(1 - b_8)$ IRISHMIG. This is the same as IRISHMIG$-b_8$IRISHMIG.
[s] This procedure for deriving long-run multipliers was also described in §12.3.3.

where b_4 is the coefficient on EMPFOR, given in table 14.1 as 64.57; and b_8 is the coefficient on IRISHMIG, given as 0.44.[f] So

$$\tilde{b}_4 = \frac{64.57}{1 - 0.44} = 115.3$$

and

$$\frac{\tilde{b}_4}{100} \text{ is } 1.153$$

As in the previous case we are determining the effect of a 10 per cent rather than a 1 per cent change, so must multiply this by 10. The result is, therefore, 11.5, or roughly the same magnitude as the short-run effect, as noted by Hatton and Williamson (p. 584).

Hatton and Williamson then turn to the effect of a sustained rise of 10 per cent in IRWRATIO, the foreign-to-domestic wage ratio, and find that this 'would lead ultimately to an increase in the emigration rate of 2.35 per 1,000' (p. 584). Since the form of this relationship is exactly the same as the previous one, the calculation follows the same lines. Replacing b_4 by b_6 we get

$$\tilde{b}_6 = \frac{13.16}{1 - 0.44} = 23.5$$

and so

$$\frac{\tilde{b}_6}{100} \text{ is } 0.235$$

Multiplying this by 10 for a 10 per cent change gives 2.35.

Hatton and Williamson also run a separate regression (not reproduced in the text) to determine whether migration rates are affected by relative wages, or by Irish wages alone. The regression also determines the relative weights of the home and foreign wage levels on the decision to migrate (see p. 585). In this alternative regression, the logs of the Irish and overseas wages are entered as separate explanatory variables. Hatton and Williamson report that the test results easily pass the chi-squared test at the 5 per cent level, indicating that the coefficients are indeed of equal value and opposite signs.[10]

The necessary data for direct measurement of EMPDOM were not available, and it was proxied by a series for the percentage deviation of Irish farm output from trend. The calculation of the long-run effect of a 10 per

---

[f] The $t-1$ time subscripts on both variables in table 14.1 are irrelevant when considering the long-term model.

cent change in this variable follows the same lines as those for EMPFOR and IRWRATIO, and is about –3 per 1,000 (p. 585).

For the final variable, the migrant stock, Hatton and Williamson calculate that the long-run impact was that 'for every 1,000 previous migrants an additional 41 were attracted overseas each year' (p. 585). In this case the MIGSTOCK variable was not entered in the model in logarithmic form so we are dealing with a simple linear relationship (as in the first row of table 12.1). A change of 1 unit in MIGSTOCK will cause a change of b units in IRISHMIG (both measured per 1,000 population) and the long-run impact is derived as

$$\frac{22.87}{1 - 0.44} = 40.8$$

Hatton and Williamson conclude from this part of their analysis that the principal cause of the long-run downward trend in Irish emigration was the increase in Irish real wages relative to those available to potential migrants in the United States and other receiving countries. They measure the actual fall in IRWRATIO between 1852–6 and 1909–13 at about 43 per cent, which would have 'lowered the long-run emigration rate by as much as 10 per 1,000, accounting for much of the secular decline in the emigration rate that we observe in the data' (p. 586).[u] They further conclude, on the basis of the value of R^2 in (14.5), that over 80 per cent of the variation in the short-run fluctuations in emigration is explained by the combination of variables (other than ΔEMPDOM and ΔIRWRATIO) specified in their model.

14.2.2 The panel model of Irish emigration

In order to throw further light on the composition of the emigrants, Hatton and Williamson compiled a second data set based mainly on Census of Population data for each of 32 Irish counties for each of the census years, 1881, 1891, 1901, and 1911. A few variables that they initially thought might be relevant were excluded because they were found to have very little significance, and the final data set covers the dependent variable and 10 explanatory variables. These are listed and defined in the lower panel of table A.3.

An important advantage of their approach is that it covers a large range of variables and is thus able to control for the full set of characteristics simultaneously (p. 591). Some previous studies have drawn conclusions from

---

[u] Their wage data cover only the period from 1876 and they estimate the decline from 1852–6 by extrapolation of the later rate. The long-run effect on IRISHMIG of a change in IRWRATIO of 43 per cent would be $43 \times 0.0235 = 10.1$ per 1,000.

simple relationships between emigration and one potentially relevant characteristic, but this effectively ignores the possible contribution of other characteristics.[v] For example, it has been observed that emigration rates varied
greatly across different regions, and it has been suggested that emigration
was associated with religion and republicanism. However, without the controls provided by a full regression model it is impossible to say how far
poverty, illiteracy, and differences in religion contributed to higher rates of
emigration, since these variables were themselves correlated across regions
and counties. Similarly, the flow abroad was lower from the more industrialized areas of Ireland, but without a comprehensive regression model we
cannot say whether it was the presence of industry, the level of wages, or just
the extent of urbanization that acted as a deterrent to emigration.

The dependent variable is CNTYMIG, the proportion per 1,000 of the
county population that emigrated. The explanatory variables cover a range
of economic, demographic, religious, and social factors suggested by the
extensive literature on Irish emigration. The emigration rate is expected to
be higher in counties that have a larger proportion of their population who
were in the prime emigration age group of 15–34 (AGE), or were living in
towns of 2,000 or more (URBAN), or who were CATHOLIC. It is expected
to be lower in counties that have a larger proportion who were illiterate
(ILLITRTE). Poverty is measured by two variables: the proportion living in
the lowest grades of HOUSING, and the percentage receiving poor
RELIEF. Both these are expected to be positively associated with emigration. High rates of emigration are also expected to be associated with large
families, and the average size is measured by FAMSIZE.

Among the economic variables, the economic composition of the labour
force is measured by AGRIC, the proportion of the county labour force
working in agriculture. Access to land is proxied by LANDHLDG, the proportion of county agricultural holdings of less than 5 acres, but this variable
is not entered in the model on its own. Instead an interaction variable is
created by multiplying LANDHLDG and AGRIC. This was done 'to give it a
greater weight in the more agricultural counties' (p. 591). The potential
income gain from migration is measured by CYWRATIO, the ratio of the
foreign real wage to the agricultural real wage in the county. This variable is
entered in the cross-sectional model in logarithmic form to facilitate comparison with the time-series results. None of the other variables are in logs.

Hatton and Williamson use a pooled or panel model to analyse these
data. Models of this type are discussed in more detail in panel 14.1. Their

---

[v] The critical distinction between controlling for other variables and simply ignoring them was
  discussed in §8.2.3.

Table 14.2 Determinants of Irish county emigration rates, panel data, 1881–1911

	(1) Coefficient	(2) t-statistics
Constant	−45.92	4.20
AGE	13.60	0.88
URBAN	3.02	0.50
AGRIC	16.39	2.38
LANDHLDG–AGRIC	−41.98	3.26
log CYWRATIO	6.43	2.12
RELIEF	1.96	4.40
HOUSING	7.69	1.45
FAMSIZE	7.93	5.24
CATHOLIC	−4.97	1.79
ILLITRTE	1.53	0.19
R^2	0.70	
Residual sum of squares	1420.9	
HETERO	0.73	

Source: Hatton and Williamson, 'Emigration', p. 593.

model uses data for 32 counties for each of four census years, and is thus a pooled data set of 128 observations. They initially included year dummies to allow for the possibility that the coefficients would not be stable across all four dates, but this was found not to be the case and the year dummies were omitted.[11]

The results of this pooled model are given in table 14.2, again focusing exclusively on total emigration. R^2 is 0.70 and the model thus explains 70 per cent of the variation in CNTYMIG, a good performance by the standard usually attained in cross-sectional regressions.

HETERO reports a test statistic for heteroscedasticity. The test employed by Hatton and Williamson is a variant of the Lagrange Multiplier tests (such as the Breusch–Pagan and White tests) introduced in §11.3.2. The test statistic is derived by running the square of the residuals from the fitted regression equation against a constant and the fitted values of the dependent variable. If there is heteroscedasticity, this regression should show a systematic relationship between the size of the residual and the size of the fitted value.

The test statistic of the null hypothesis of homoscedasticity is nR^2, where n is the number of observations and R^2 is the coefficient of

Panel 14.1   Pooled or panel data

Hatton and Williamson's use of a data set that combines a series of *cross-sections* of information on individual units *over time* is known as either a **pooled** or a **panel** data set. Panel data may include information on a group of individual observations (individuals, households, firms) over time (these are sometimes known as **longitudinal** data), or on aggregates, including administrative units such as parishes, counties, states, or countries.

The virtue of panel data is that they provide more degrees of freedom within which to explore relationships among variables; they also allow for more sophisticated integrated treatment of variability across space and time. The challenge of panel data is that the assumptions of independence among explanatory variables that underpin much regression analysis are less likely to apply, resulting in the need for more complex econometric procedures.

Obviously, such sophisticated econometric procedures are beyond the scope of this simple text. However, since panel data are becoming increasingly common in historical work, some simple observations are worthwhile.

The linear regression approach to a panel data set suggests the following model:

$$Y_{it} = b_{it} X_{it} + e_{it} \tag{14.7}$$

where the subscript indicates unit i in time period t. However, such an open-ended formulation is likely to be too general.

Two alternative specifications are commonly employed in panel data analysis – the fixed effects model and the random effects model.

The **fixed effects model** posits that the b coefficients are constant for all units and time periods. Sometimes, these models allow the intercept to vary across either time or across units (i.e. the effects are fixed for units at any one time, but may vary by unit from one cross-section to the next; or, they are fixed in any given time period, but may vary by units within the panel). Such models employ dummy variables to allow the intercept to change accordingly.

Hatton and Williamson apply an unrestricted fixed effects model in their pooled regression analysis of county level Irish emigration, 1881–1911. They included year dummies for 1881, 1891, 1901, and 1911 to test whether emigration patterns were different in each year, irrespective of the behaviour of the explanatory variables. In other words, they were testing for the existence of some undefined, but time-specific parameters. Hatton and Williamson report that these year dummies were statistically insignificant. They therefore employ the unrestricted pooled regression, with a single intercept term.

The **random effects model** rejects the notion that shifts in the regression line arising from unknown influences can be captured by dummy variables and posits instead that these unknown factors should be incorporated in the error term. Thus the regression model takes the form:

$$Y_{it} = a_i + bX_{it} + e_i + u_{it} \qquad (14.8)$$

where u_i represents a second error term representing the individual variance of experience within the sample.

The random effects model is especially relevant to cases in which the raw data represent a sample from the population, where the purpose of the regression is to infer behaviour patterns for the population as a whole from the sample, and when the sample observations may suffer from stochastic error. However, random effects models may be hard to reconcile with the assumption of independence of errors across observations that is fundamental to the classical linear regression approach. For this reason, more complex econometrics are often applied to random effects models.

In cases (such as Hatton and Williamson's) where the observations include information on the entire population under study, the fixed effects model is generally considered to be more appropriate. This can be estimated using OLS techniques.

Panel data techniques exist not only for basic regression, such as in Hatton and Williamson's use of OLS procedures, but also for probit, logit, and tobit analysis. Tests for violations of the CLR model (such as heteroscedasticity, autocorrelation, etc.) are generally available for panel analysis. This is an approach that is becoming more routine in regression packages and more frequent in social science and historical research.

determination. This test statistic is distributed as a chi-square, with 1 d.f. The value of HETERO reported in table 14.2 is 0.73. The tabulated critical value of the chi-square at the 5 per cent level of significance is 3.841, indicating that the null hypothesis should not be rejected.

We can now look briefly at the results of this model. For the relative wage we can interpret the regression coefficient in the same way as we did with short-run semi-logarithmic time-series relationships in the previous section. A 10 per cent change in CYWRATIO will cause a change in CNTYMIG of $10 \times b/100$ units. Since b is given in table 14.2 as 6.43 (with a *t*-ratio of 2.12) it can be said 'that a 10 per cent rise in the relative wage would raise the emigration rate by 0.64 per 1,000' (p. 592.) As Hatton and Williamson note, this estimate is noticeably smaller than the corresponding short-run coefficient estimated on time series, and much lower than the long-run time-series coefficient. The coefficient on the former is given in table 14.1 as 13.16 so the effect of a 10 per cent rise would be $13.16 \div 100 \times$ by $10 = 1.32$; the latter was found in the preceding section to be 2.35.

Since the model specifies a simple linear relationship between the dependent variable and all the remaining explanatory variables, the interpretation of the regression coefficients on each of these variables is straightforward. A change in an explanatory variable of 1 unit will cause a change in CNTYMIG of b units; that is of b per 1,000 of the population, because this is the unit in which the dependent variable is measured. Since all except one of the explanatory variables are measured as proportions (or in the case of RELIEF as a percentage), we can thus say that a change of 1 per cent (equivalent to a change in a proportion of 0.01) will have an effect on CNTYMIG of b units.

The exception is FAMSIZE, where the unit is average number of persons per family. This variable has a large and highly significant coefficient which 'implies that a one-person reduction in average family size would lower the emigration rate by 7.93 per 1,000. This would support those who have argued that demographic forces continued to influence emigration in the late nineteenth century. High birth rates led to large families which precipitated a large flow of emigration' (p. 593).

If we look next at the other economic factors, we can see that the coefficients on AGRIC, and on the interaction variable created by the product of LANDHLDG and AGRIC, are both large and statistically significant. For the former alone a 1 per cent rise in the proportion of the labour force in agriculture would raise the emigration rate by 16.4 per 1,000, for the latter a rise of 1 per cent would lower the rate by as much as 42 per 1,000. The interaction variable can be interpreted as indicating that the higher the proportion of smallholdings, the smaller was emigration, controlling for the share of the labour force in agriculture. As Hatton and Williamson conclude: 'these results strongly suggest that lack of opportunities in agriculture (including opportunities to obtain or inherit a small farm) was an important cause of emigration' (p. 592).[12]

Turning now to the remaining variables we find from the coefficient on AGE in table 14.2 that a 1 per cent rise in the proportion of the population in the prime emigration age group would raise the rate by 13.6 per 1,000, but that this coefficient is not statistically significant. However, Hatton and Williamson report this result in a somewhat different form from usual.

What they say is: 'the point estimate for the proportion of the population between 15 and 34 indicates, plausibly, that emigration would be 13.6 per 1,000 higher *for this group than for the population as a whole*' (p. 592, italics ours). How do they get to this?

Note that the total migration rate may be expressed as the weighted average of two migration rates – that for 15–34-year-olds and that for the rest of the population. Let p be the proportion of the population aged 15–34; since the proportion must sum to one, the rest of the population is $1-p$. If the migration rates of the two groups are M_1 and M_2, we can express total migration (MIG) as:

$$MIG = M_1(p) + M_2(1-p) \qquad (14.9a)$$

This may be re-written as

$$MIG = M_1(p) + M_2 - M_2(p) = M_2 + (M_1 - M_2)p \qquad (14.9b)$$

If we were to run a regression with MIG as the dependent variable and p as the explanatory variable, we would have

$$MIG = a + b(p) + e \qquad (14.10)$$

By comparing (14.9b) and (14.10) it is easily seen that b, the coefficient on p in the regression, is an estimate of $(M_1 - M_2)$, i.e. of the difference between the migration rate of those aged 15–34 and that of the remainder of the population.[w] Hence we could report the regression coefficient, b, as the amount by which the migration rate for 15–34-year-olds exceeds the rate for the rest of the population: 13.6 per 1,000. (This is not quite what Hatton and Williamson suggested, which was the rate by which migration for 15–34 year-olds exceeded the overall migration rate.) Alternatively, the coefficient could be reported in the usual way by noting that an increase in the proportion of the population aged 15–34 by 1 unit (for example, from 0.33 to 0.34) would raise the migration rate by 13.6 per cent (for example, from 11 per 1,000 to 12.5 per 1,000).

It follows from the principle captured by (14.9) and (14.10) that the coefficients on any other explanatory variable that *relates to a proportion of the relevant population* (for example, share of the labour force in manufacturing, share of the housing stock which is owner-occupied) can also be interpreted in this way. Thus, the coefficient on URBAN in table 14.2 indicates that the migration rate of urban inhabitants was 3.02 per 1,000 higher than that for non-urbanites; while the migration rate for Catholics was on average 4.97 per 1,000 lower than for non-Catholics. All such coefficients are, of course, estimated holding other characteristics constant.

___

[w] Also note that the intercept term is an estimate of M_2.

URBAN has the expected positive sign but the effect of urbanization is only 3.0 per 1,000 and the coefficient is again not significant. Of the two poverty variables, RELIEF is highly significant, but the effect on emigration is relatively small: a rise of 1 per cent in the proportion of the population receiving poor relief would raise the emigration rate by 1.96 per 1,000. HOUSING has a smaller impact: a 1 per cent increase in the proportion of families living in the worst types of housing would raise the emigration rate by 0.08 per 1,000.[x]

Finally we see that the sign of the coefficient on CATHOLIC is negative, and that on ILLITRTE is positive. In both cases this is the opposite of what was expected, though the coefficient is insignificant in the latter case (p. 594).

14.2.3 The impact of the explanatory variables on changes in emigration over time

In order to assess the importance of the different explanatory variables it is necessary to relate the size of the regression coefficients to the *actual change* in the variables that occurred during the late nineteenth century. The regression model may find that a variable has a very large and statistically significant coefficient, as was the case with the interaction variable AGRIC–LANDHLDG. But if the value of that variable remains broadly constant over the period, then it is of little importance as an explanation for the changes in emigration.

In order to assess the combined impact of the actual changes in their 10 explanatory variables and the indications of the effect of those changes given by the regression coefficients, Hatton and Williamson measure the contribution of each variable to the decline in county emigration rates over the period 1881–1911 (p. 595). They do this by calculating the (unweighted) mean value across the 32 counties for each of the variables, and then obtaining from this the *change* in the mean value. They then multiply this change by its corresponding regression coefficient. The effect of doing this is to replace the previous indications of the effect of an arbitrary 1 per cent or 10 per cent change by an approximation to the actual change that occurred over time.

We repeat their procedure in table 14.3 for the change from 1881 to 1911; they also report their results for the shorter period 1881–1901. The results indicate that the main contribution to the decline in county emigration of 9.5 per 1,000 over the four decades was made by FAMSIZE, and by

---

[x] RELIEF is expressed in percentage terms. Hence a 1 per cent rise in RELIEF is a unit rise in its value; the impact is calculated as 1.96×1. HOUSING, in contrast, is expressed as a proportion. A 1 per cent rise in HOUSING is a 0.01 unit increase in its value; the impact is calculated as 7.69×0.01, which equals 0.0769, or 0.08 when rounded to the second decimal place.

Table 14.3 Decomposition of changes in Irish emigration rates, 1881–1911

	(1)	(2)	(3)	(4)	(5)
	Mean value		Change	Regression	Effect on
	1881	1911	1881–1911	coefficient	emigration rate
CNTYMIG	16.552	7.027	−9.525		
AGE	0.320	0.318	−0.002	13.60	−0.03
URBAN	0.177	0.214	0.037	3.02	0.11
AGRIC	0.663	0.646	−0.017	16.39	−0.28
AGRIC–LANDHLDG	0.078	0.105	0.027	−41.98	−1.13
log CYWRATIO	0.629	0.501	−0.128	6.43	−0.82
RELIEF	2.509	1.801	−0.708	1.96	−1.39
HOUSING	0.458	0.246	−0.212	7.69	−1.63
FAMSIZE	5.098	4.641	−0.458	7.93	−3.63
CATHOLIC	0.811	0.814	0.003	−4.97	−0.01
ILLITRTE	0.252	0.111	−0.141	1.53	−0.22
Total change in county emigration rates estimated from regression coefficients					−9.03
Actual change in CNTYMIG as above					−9.52

Notes:
(1) and (2) from the original Hatton and Williamson data set, not the version rounded to 2
 decimal places in 'Emigration', p. 598.
(3) = (2) − (1)
(4) from table 14.2, column (1)
(5) = (3) × (4). These results differ very slightly from those reported by Hatton and
 Williamson, p. 595 because of rounding.

the three variables reflecting living standards: CYWRATIO, RELIEF, and HOUSING. The decline in average family size reduced the emigration rate by 3.6 per 1,000, and the other three variables taken together by 3.8 per 1,000. By contrast, the two agricultural variables together contributed only a modest 1.4 per 1,000.

Hatton and Williamson observe that there may seem to be a discrepancy between these panel findings and the time-series results, 'which laid stress on the importance of relative wage rates in driving Irish emigration' (p. 595). However they argue that wage rates can be viewed as a summary statistic representing various aspects of living standards. In the time-series model these other aspects are absent, and so the full impact of living standards is attributed to the relative wage term. In the cross-sectional model

Table 14.4   Restricted model of Irish county emigration rates, panel data, 1881–1911

	(1) Coefficient	(2) t-statistics
Constant	−54.42	10.07
CYWRATIO	11.91	4.15
FAMSIZE	12.17	10.58
R^2	0.57	
Residual sum of squares	2145.9	
HETERO	0.66	

Source: Hatton and Williamson, 'Emigration', p. 596.

these aspects are directly represented and so the effect of relative wages is diminished.

To test this assertion, Hatton and Williamson run a revised version of their panel model. In this they omit those aspects of living standards other than the relative wage, and also the minor variables that were not statistically significant or were found to have little or no effect. This alternative model thus contains only two of the original explanatory variables: CYWRATIO and FAMSIZE.

We report their results for total emigration in table 14.4. They show how with this very restricted specification the relative wage term captures some of the effects previously attributed to the other measures of living standards. The impact of a 10 per cent increase almost doubles from 0.64 to 1.19 per 1,000, about the same as the short-run coefficient in the time-series equation of 1.32, and about half the long-run coefficient of 2.35. They conclude from this that the results of the time-series and cross-section models 'can be largely reconciled' (p. 596).

Notes

[1] At the time this paper was published it was not yet standard practice to give actual prob-values. The significance of regression coefficients was indicated by reporting either the standard errors or the *t*-statistics (i.e. the ratios of the regression coefficients to their standard errors) or, occasionally, both. Note also that the *t*-ratios in this paper are expressed with the same sign as the coefficient; in Hatton and Williamson's paper discussed below, the *t*-ratios are expressed as absolute values. While it is more accurate to report the sign, it is no longer standard practice, largely because the sign is irrelevant to the interpretation of statistical significance.

[2] We regret that we have not been able to reproduce Benjamin and Kochin's results precisely. When (14.2) is run on the data on the web site (with the two explanatory variables taken to 5 decimal places) the result is

$$UNEMP = 5.13 + 18.36 \, BWRATIO - 91.24 \, DEMAND$$
$$\quad\quad\quad (2.27) \quad (4.75) \quad\quad\quad\quad (-8.82)$$

$$R^2 = 0.86, \quad \bar{R}^2 = 0.84, \quad D\text{–}W = 2.22, \quad SEE = 1.80$$

Note that the results reported in Ormerod and Worswick are slightly different again. None of the discrepancies is large enough to affect the interpretation of the model, and in what follows we report the original results from Benjamin and Kochin.

[3] Benjamin and Kochin also reject the possibility of simultaneity (see §11.4.3), whereby unemployment influences the replacement rate at the same time as the replacement rate causes unemployment, though they do so without the benefit of a formal test, such as the two-stage least squares model introduced in §15.1.1 and panel 15.3.

[4] Ormerod and Worswick recognize that Benjamin and Kochin had experimented with the addition of a time period for the full period 1920–38, but had found that the coefficient on the time trend was itself insignificant and that there was little impact on the estimated value of the other coefficients. However, they say that this conclusion is correct only for the full period, not for the shorter subperiods.

[5] Strictly, tests for parameter stability are not the same as tests for outliers, although Benjamin and Kochin's variant of the Chow test does go some way to providing a formal statistical test of the status of 1920.

[6] The test statistic in this case is whether the reported unemployment rate falls within 2.131 standard errors of predicted unemployment, where 2.131 is the t-statistic at the 5 per cent level with 15 df.

[7] Timothy J. Hatton, 'A quarterly model of the labour market in interwar Britain', *Oxford Bulletin of Economics and Statistics*, 50, February 1988, pp. 1–25; Nicholas H. Dimsdale, S. Nickell, and N. J. Horsewood, 'Real wages and unemployment in Britain during the 1930s', *Economic Journal*, 99, June 1989, pp. 271–92.

[8] For a separate paper showing how this model is formally derived from appropriate economic principles, see Timothy J. Hatton, 'A model of UK emigration, 1870–1913', *Review of Economics and Statistics*, 77, 1995, pp. 407–15.

[9] Note that Hatton and Williamson's procedure for calculating the impact of a 10 per cent change in each explanatory variable is an extrapolation from the impact of an infinitesimal change. An alternative method for calculating the effect of a given per cent change in EMPFOR would be to multiply the coefficient b_4 by the change in the value of log EMPFOR. Thus, a 10 per cent increase in EMPFOR (e.g. from 90 to 99 per cent) would generate a 10.38 per cent increase in IRISHMIG (Δlog EMPFOR = $0.09531 \times 108.95 = 10.384$).

[10] In contrast, Hatton and Williamson enter the home and foreign *employment* rate as separate variables in the main regression. They do this because they believe that potential migrants interpret information about the labour market in Ireland and

abroad in different ways, so that it would be inappropriate to combine the two elements into one ratio (see p. 582).

[11] To include year dummies one of the four census years would be chosen as the control year, say 1881, and three separate year dummies would be created, which we can call 1891, 1901, and 1911. The year dummy 1891 would take a value of 1 for all observations relating to 1891, and 0 otherwise; 1901 would be 1 for all observations relating to 1901, 0 otherwise; 1911 would be 1 for all observations relating to 1911, 0 otherwise.

[12] The interaction variable would normally be constructed as the product of the two component variables. Unfortunately, at a late stage of their work, Hatton and Williamson changed the value of their AGRIC variable without changing the interaction term. The unchanged values are included in the data set on the web page to enable readers to reproduce the published regression results. As can be seen by constructing the correct interaction variable, this discrepancy makes little difference to the results.

CHAPTER 15

Case studies 3 and 4: the Old Poor Law in England and leaving home in the United States, 1850–1860

15.1 The effects of the Old Poor Law

This case study is concerned with two cross-sectional models formulated to investigate the operation of the Old Poor Law in the south of England in the early nineteenth century. As noted in the brief introduction of this subject in §A.1 in appendix A, the rapid increase in the cost of relief during and after the Napoleonic Wars provoked fierce criticism of the system adopted to assist the poor in these decades. In his 1990 book Boyer explored several aspects of this topic, and we review two of these. The first is his analysis of the effect of the system of poor relief on the working of the agricultural labour market; specifically, the relationship between relief payments, the wages paid to farm labourers, and the rate of unemployment (pp. 122–49).[a] Details of the data set that he created for this purpose are set out in table A.1 in appendix A.

The second theme is Boyer's investigation of the proposition advanced – most famously – by Malthus, that relief payments related to the number of children in the labourer's family were a major cause of a high birth rate and a rapid growth of population (pp. 150–72). The data set used for the investigation of this topic is listed in table A.2.

The institutional framework for this debate is, of course, specific to the conditions in the south of England in the early nineteenth century, but the underlying issues are of enduring relevance. Many of the points at issue will be recognized by anyone familiar with recent discussions in the United States and other countries about the adverse effects of benefit payments and the policies adopted to get people 'off welfare'.

---

[a] Unless otherwise noted all page references in this section are to George R. Boyer, *An Economic History of the English Poor Law*, Cambridge University Press, 1990.

15.1.1   Relief payments, wages, and unemployment

The hypotheses and the two models

The questions that Boyer wishes to address relate essentially to the steep increase in total and *per capita* relief expenditure over time. The Royal Poor Law Commission appointed to investigate the problem reported in 1834 that the principal cause of the increase was the system of outdoor relief that enabled able-bodied labourers to obtain relief without having to endure the rigours of life in a workhouse. This and other criticisms of the Old Poor Law were later challenged by Blaug, Digby, and other historians.[1]

Ideally this debate should be investigated by a time-series approach that models the rise in relief payments in relation to the behaviour of various competing explanatory factors. The data necessary for this do not exist, but Boyer argues that most of the relevant hypotheses can be tested indirectly by a cross-sectional regression to explain variations in relief across parishes (p. 126).

For example, one hypothesis advanced by those who challenged the Commission's analysis is that the rise in relief was due to falling rural incomes, caused by a decline in employment opportunities for women and children in cottage industries because of the competition from the rapidly developing factory sector. Another is that it was a response by rural parishes to the increased demand for labour in urban areas and the consequent need to pay higher rural wages: farmers used the Poor Law to supplement wages, effectively passing some of the burden of their labour costs on to other ratepayers.

If these and other changes increased *per capita* relief expenditures *over time*, then we should also find that *at any point in time* parishes with fewer opportunities for cottage industry, or those with more competition from urban industry, had higher *per capita* relief expenditures than parishes in a more favourable position with respect to these factors, other things being equal.

Boyer compiled a large cross-sectional data set covering a sample of 311 parishes from 20 counties in southern England. In addition to the measure of RELIEF there are seven numerical variables and a further seven dummy variables. With one exception the observations all relate either to the census year 1831 or to the following year, when rural parishes completed an elaborate questionnaire distributed by the Royal Poor Law Commission.[b]

---

[b] The sample parishes were selected on the basis of the completeness of their returns to the Commission, but – for the reasons mentioned in n. 2 of chapter 5 – Boyer believes that there is no obvious bias as a result of this (pp. 129, 149).

The first problem that Boyer faced in specifying his model is created by the interdependence of several of the key hypotheses advanced by contemporaries and later historians (p. 127). It is widely held that both wage rates for agricultural labourers (INCOME) and unemployment among labourers (UNEMP) were determinants of RELIEF, but at the same time it is also claimed that RELIEF led to lower INCOME and higher UNEMP. Moreover, Boyer's approach assumes that labour-hiring farmers were able to choose what they considered would be for them the most profitable combination of the three variables: the wages they paid, the employment they offered during non-peak seasons, and the level of benefits paid through the Poor Law to unemployed labourers.

These three variables, INCOME, UNEMP, and RELIEF are referred to as **endogenous**, meaning that they are determined *within* the system of relationships Boyer is modelling. By contrast, the hypothesized explanatory variables are referred to as **exogenous** or **pre-determined**. Exogenous variables are determined outside the model in question, and cannot be affected by any changes in the other variables within the system of relationships.

Given this mutual interaction between the three endogenous variables there is clearly a problem of **simultaneity**, and thus a violation of one of the assumptions of the classical linear regression (CLR) model (see §11.4.3). In these circumstances it is not appropriate to use a single-equation model to explain cross-parish variations in relief expenditures, and Boyer adopts two alternative procedures; one known as a **reduced-form** model, the second as a **simultaneous-equations** or a **structural** model (p. 133). A full explanation of these two types of model is not possible at the level of exposition appropriate to this book, but a very elementary introduction to what is involved is given in panels 15.1 and 15.2 for those who wish to know a little more. The panels should be read *after* completing this section.

Ordinary least squares (OLS) can be used to estimate the reduced-form equations, but because of the effects of the simultaneity in the relationships this procedure should not be employed to estimate a simultaneous-equations model. Instead Boyer adopts the alternative **two-stage least squares** (2SLS) procedure introduced in §11.4.3. Panel 15.3 gives a brief explanation of the procedure. Once the model has been estimated by 2SLS, the interpretation of the regression results is exactly the same as for models estimated by OLS.

The reduced-form model
Strictly speaking, the reduced-form model is derived from the structural model in the manner explained in panel 15.2 and illustrated (with a different example) in the appendix to this section. However, in the present

context it is convenient to follow Boyer in beginning with the simpler reduced-form equations. He specifies three separate reduced-form equations. In each of these, one of the three endogenous variables is the dependent variable, while the remaining two simultaneously determined endogenous variables are *omitted* from the equation.

For example, in (15.1) we have a simple linear relationship with RELIEF as the dependent variable and twelve explanatory variables. INCOME and UNEMP do not appear in this *reduced-form equation.*

$$
\begin{aligned}
\text{RELIEF} = a + b_1\text{COTTIND} + b_2\text{ALLOTMNT} + \\
b_3\text{LONDON} + b_4\text{FARMERS} + b_5\text{DENSITY} + \\
b_6\text{CHILDALL} + b_7\text{SUBSIDY} + b_8\text{WORKHSE} + \\
b_9\text{ROUNDSMN} + b_{10}\text{LABRATE} + b_{11}\text{GRAIN} + \\
b_{12}\text{WEALTH} + e \qquad (15.1)
\end{aligned}
$$

The identical list of explanatory variables appears in the corresponding reduced-form equations for INCOME and UNEMP. These equations thus escape the problem of simultaneity by successively taking one of the endogenous variables as the dependent variable and excluding the two remaining endogenous variables from any role in the equation.

This solves the simultaneity problem, but it does so at the cost of making it impossible to test the hypothesis that RELIEF, INCOME, and UNEMP were mutually determined, and that this interaction was a major cause of the long-term increase in expenditure on relief. In order to do this, it would be necessary to specify a model with three equations in which all three endogenous variables are *simultaneously* determined. The crucial rule for such models is that there must be as many independent equations as there are endogenous variables.

Unfortunately, Boyer is compelled to eliminate the equation for UNEMP, and he therefore specifies a simultaneous-equations model with only two endogenous variables and two equations.[2] The effect of excluding UNEMP in this way is that it ceases to be endogenous to the model and can be treated as another exogenous variable.

The simultaneous-equations model

The two equations in this *simultaneous-equations model* are given (p. 134) as

$$
\begin{aligned}
\text{RELIEF} = a + b_1\text{COTTIND} + b_2\text{ALLOTMNT} + \\
b_3\text{LONDON} + b_4\text{FARMERS} + b_5\text{WEALTH} + \\
b_6\text{WORKHSE} + b_7\text{UNEMP} + b_8\text{INCOME} + e \quad (15.2)
\end{aligned}
$$

and

$$INCOME = a + b_1 COTTIND + b_2 ALLOTMNT +$$
$$b_3 LONDON + b_4 CHILDALL + b_5 SUBSIDY +$$
$$b_6 LABRATE + b_7 ROUNDSMN + b_8 DENSITY +$$
$$b_9 RELIEF + e \qquad\qquad (15.3)$$

Two features of this model should be noted. First, when one of the endogenous variables is the dependent variable, the other is *not* omitted (as was the case in the reduced-form model) but appears on the right-hand side as an explanatory variable. We thus have INCOME in (15.2) and RELIEF in (15.3).

Because INCOME is included on the right-hand side of (15.2) it is not necessary to include also those explanatory variables that help to explain INCOME but do not directly affect RELIEF. This explains why the four variables in (15.1) that represent specific forms of outdoor relief (CHILDALL, SUBSIDY, LABRATE, and ROUNDSMN) are omitted from (15.2). They are expected to have a negative effect on INCOME, but are not a direct determinant of the overall level of RELIEF.

Secondly, unlike the reduced-form model, the equations in the simultaneous-equations model for RELIEF and INCOME ((15.2) and (15.3)) do not share the same explanatory variables. FARMERS is included in (15.2) to test whether parishes in which labour-hiring farmers had greater political power were able to pass on to other ratepayers more of the cost of maintaining their workers, thus leading to higher RELIEF. However, this power is not regarded as a determinant of INCOME, and so this variable does not appear in (15.3). GRAIN is designed to be a proxy for the extent of seasonality in the demand for labour and is omitted from (15.2) because it should affect RELIEF only through its effect on UNEMP, which is already entered in the equation. And as noted in the previous paragraph, the four variables representing forms of outdoor relief are included as determinants of INCOME but not of RELIEF.

We can now turn to the discussion of the results of the regression procedures.

The regression results

Boyer gives a very full discussion of the role of the different explanatory variables (pp. 134–8). He also includes two useful tables (p. 135) comparing the direction of impact that each variable is predicted to have according to the various hypotheses in the Poor Law literature (these are known as the *expected signs* of the coefficients) with the actual effect shown by the results of the regressions. The expected results are shown as positive ($+$), negative

Panel 15.1   Simultaneous-equations models

A **simultaneous-equations** (or **structural**) model relates each of the endogenous variables to some specified combination of exogenous and endogenous variables. The crucial rule is that there must be as many independent equations as there are endogenous variables.

Boyer's model supposes that labour-hiring farmers were able to jointly determine RELIEF and INCOME so as to maximize their profits. We thus have two linear equations and two **endogenous** variables, RELIEF and INCOME, which are determined by the model (p. 134). (As noted in §15.1.1 it was not possible to include UNEMP in the model; if it could have been included, as Boyer initially proposed, there would have been three dependent variables and a set of three equations.)

There are a large number of **exogenous** or predetermined variables (for example, COTTIND, ALLOTMNT, and WEALTH) which are taken as given outside the model. To simplify the presentation at this point we shall refer to all of the combinations of exogenous variables that Boyer enters in any specific relationship as though they were 1 single variable, called EXOG 1, EXOG 2, and so on. Thus EXOG 1 covers the seven explanatory variables set out in full in (15.2) of §15.1.1, and similarly for EXOG 2 and (15.3). We then have the following equations

$$\text{RELIEF} = a_1 + b_1 \text{EXOG 1} + b_2 \text{INCOME} + e \qquad (15.2a)$$

$$\text{INCOME} = a_2 + b_3 \text{EXOG 2} + b_4 \text{RELIEF} + e \qquad (15.3a)$$

There are three important features to note about this model.

(a) Unlike all the other models we have considered hitherto, this model consists of a *set of two equations* that must be considered together and contains *two* dependent variables.

(b) The relationships are *interdependent*, as indicated by the model: changes in INCOME will lead to changes in RELIEF, and at the same time changes in RELIEF will cause changes in INCOME.

(c) Because this interdependence or simultaneity is present in the relationships, one of the assumptions of classical linear regression (CLR) is violated (see §11.4.3). For this reason the simultaneous-equations model cannot be reliably estimated by the ordinary least squares (OLS) procedure. Boyer adopts an alternative technique known as **two-stage least squares** (2SLS), explained in panel 15.3.

Panel 15.2 Reduced-form models

The equations in a reduced-form model are obtained by solving the simultaneous-equations model so that the endogenous variables are expressed as functions of the exogenous variables. An illustration of what is meant by 'solving the simultaneous-equations model' is given in the appendix to this section on pp. 491–5.

In the reduced form there is a single equation for each endogenous variable, with *only the exogenous variables* on the right-hand side. None of the endogenous variables appear simultaneously as explanatory variables. Using the same summary term, EXOG, for a set of explanatory variables as in panel 15.1, the reduced-form equations would emerge as

$$\text{RELIEF} = a_1 + b_1 \text{EXOG } 3 + e \tag{15.4}$$

$$\text{INCOME} = a_2 + b_2 \text{EXOG } 3 + e \tag{15.5}$$

Equation 15.1 and the two corresponding equations for INCOME and UNEMP are of this type though they were not derived in precisely this way from the corresponding structural model. All these reduced-form equations can be estimated in the standard way by ordinary least squares (OLS).

The change from the simultaneous-equations to the reduced-form model not only changes the right-hand side to exclude the endogenous variables, it also changes the value of the parameters, i.e. of the constant and the regression coefficients. This happens because in the reduced-form model the coefficients measure both

(a) the direct effect of the respective exogenous variables on the endogenous variables, and

(b) their indirect effects through the changes in the endogenous variables which react simultaneously on each other.

This change in the parameters is further discussed and illustrated in the appendix to this section.

Panel 15.3   Estimation by two-stage least squares

As the name implies, this procedure involves estimation in two stages, each of which is done by ordinary least squares (OLS). We will give here a brief description of the 2SLS procedure, as it would be used to estimate the simultaneous set of equations, (15.2) and (15.3).

The first stage

In the first stage an equation is estimated for each of the endogenous variables in the model, in this case for RELIEF and INCOME. These equations contain *all the exogenous variables* in the model, that is, both the seven on the right-hand side of (15.2), and the additional five from (15.3) that are not already entered in (15.2). The endogenous variables on the right-hand side of these equations are *not* included at this stage.

What we are doing, in effect, is to estimate a reduced-form equation for RELIEF in which the influence of its own exogenous explanatory variables is combined with the influence of INCOME as represented indirectly by *its* exogenous variables.[*]

The second stage

In the second stage the original equations (in this case, (15.2) and (15.3)) are estimated separately, by OLS. The endogenous variables on the right hand side are now included in the estimation, but they are measured not by their *actual* values, as given in the relevant data set, but by their *predicted* values as given by the first stage of estimation. The *predicted* values are obtained in exactly the same way as those that were calculated for $\hat{Y}$ in the very simple regression model in table 4.2 of §4.3, though of course there are many more variables and regression coefficients in (15.2) and (15.3).

Thus (15.2) is estimated with its list of seven explanatory variables and the predicted value of INCOME; (15.3) is estimated with its list of eight explanatory variables and the predicted value of RELIEF. The statistical computer package will calculate these predicted values as part of the first-stage procedure, and the program can then be instructed to use these predicted values to estimate the second-stage equations by OLS in the standard way. The computer package will also correct the standard errors in the second stage, which would otherwise be biased.

---

[*] This can be thought of as a special case of the **instrumental variable** technique (see §11.4.1) in the sense that all the exogenous variables are taken together to create an instrumental variable.

(−), or uncertain (?); the actual results are either positive (+) or negative (−) or not statistically significant (0).

We reproduce in table 15.1 the results Boyer reports for both models for RELIEF and INCOME. R^2 is 0.30 for the reduced-form equation for RELIEF and 0.36 for INCOME. This is quite satisfactory for cross-sectional models, which typically yield lower coefficients of multiple determination than time-series models. In the latter, aspects of the change through time are typically common to many variables, creating a broadly similar pattern of variation for dependent and explanatory variables. By contrast, with cross-sectional models, there are likely to be many other factors at work in the individual cases (in this instance parishes) that will influence the dependent variable (see §3.2.3).[3]

Boyer reports both the t-ratios and the prob-values.[c] The two are, of course, different ways of assessing the same issue. For example, ALLOTMNT (in the reduced-form equation for RELIEF) has a very low t-statistic (0.13) and a correspondingly high prob-value 0.899; in other words there is a probability of 89.9 per cent of getting a value greater than t if the null hypothesis of no association between RELIEF and ALLOTMNT is correct, and the null hypothesis therefore cannot be rejected.

By contrast the t-ratio for LONDON is very high (3.85) and there is a correspondingly low prob-value of 0.0001; in other words there is only a 0.01 per cent probability of getting a value greater than t if there is no association, and the null hypothesis can be rejected.

More generally, as would be expected from the discussion of this matter in §6.3.5, we see that coefficients with a t-ratio of 2 or higher have a corresponding prob-value of 0.05 or lower and are thus significant at the 5 per cent level or better. Those (such as COTTIND) with a t-statistic a little under 2 are significant at the 10 per cent level though not at the 5 per cent level. As a more precise indicator, the prob-value allows more discretion in the assessment of regression results.

We turn now to the values obtained for the regression coefficients. All the relationships are linear so the results should all take the form 'a small absolute change in X will cause a small absolute change in Y of b units'. It is necessary to bear in mind, however, that many of the explanatory variables are dummy variables, and that some of the numerical variables are measured in proportions or percentages.

The first quantitative result given by Boyer is that *per capita* relief expenditures were between 1.7 shillings and 3.4 shillings *lower* in parishes with

---

[c] The two parallel lines either side of t in table 15.1 are known as a modulus. This simply indicates that the author is stating the prob-value without regard to the *sign* of t.

Table 15.1 The agricultural labour market and the Old Poor Law, simultaneous-equations and reduced-form models, cross-section data, c. 1831

	(1)	(2)	(3)	(4)	(5)	(6)
	Reduced-form model			Simultaneous-equations model		
	Coefficient	t-statistic	Prob>|t|	Coefficient	t-statistic	Prob>|t|
1 Dependent variable RELIEF (in shillings)						
Constant	11.20	4.92	0.0001	32.75	1.51	0.133
COTTIND	−1.70	1.75	0.082	−3.40	1.79	0.075
ALLOTMNT	0.10	0.13	0.899	−0.85	0.95	0.342
LONDON	−0.04	3.85	0.0001	−0.08	2.12	0.035
FARMERS	5.30	2.46	0.015	8.39	3.29	0.001
WEALTH	−0.30	1.64	0.103	−0.002	0.01	0.993
DENSITY	−0.55	1.11	0.268			
CHILDALL	5.52	5.31	0.0001			
SUBSIDY	−0.11	0.11	0.912			
GRAIN	0.29	3.11	0.002			
WORKHSE	1.24	1.41	0.158	0.75	0.70	0.484
ROUNDSMN	1.10	0.88	0.381			
LABRATE	1.24	1.30	0.195			
UNEMP				0.34	3.48	0.001
INCOME				−0.49	−0.75	0.454
R^2	0.304					
2 Dependent variable INCOME (in £)						
Constant	35.67	26.54	0.0001	38.91	24.14	0.0001
COTTIND	−2.83	4.93	0.0001	−3.30	5.36	0.0001
ALLOTMNT	−0.85	1.82	0.070	−0.88	1.78	0.076
LONDON	−0.06	9.57	0.0001	−0.07	9.28	0.0001
FARMER	1.99	1.56	0.119			
WEALTH	0.07	0.67	0.503			
DENSITY	−0.65	2.21	0.028	−0.86	2.80	0.006
CHILDALL	−1.36	2.21	0.028	−0.19	0.24	0.810
SUBSIDY	−0.40	0.67	0.503	−0.39	0.64	0.523
GRAIN	−0.09	1.67	0.097			
WORKHSE	0.70	1.36	0.175			
ROUNDSMN	0.49	0.66	0.508	0.91	1.17	0.244
LABRATE	0.004	0.01	0.994	0.16	0.26	0.793
RELIEF				−0.19	2.33	0.020
R^2	0.363					

Source: Boyer, *Poor Law,* pp. 139 and 140.

cottage industry than in those without (p. 138). This follows directly from the coefficients on the dummy variable for COTTIND. The range of values is given by the point estimates for COTTIND in the reduced-form and simultaneous-equation models, and the sign indicates that the effect on RELIEF was negative. As with all the other dummy variables in the model there are only two categories, and so there is a straight comparison between those parishes that have cottage industry and the control category that do not. The subsequent statements about the effects of COTTIND and ALLOTMNT on INCOME (p. 140), and of CHILDALL on INCOME (p. 142) are obtained in precisely the same way.

Boyer qualifies the results based on dummy variables, particularly for ALLOTMNT. These are included in the model to test the hypothesis that a further cause of the rise in *per capita* relief expenditure was the need to compensate labourers for the loss of land caused by enclosures and other forms of engrossment. However, because 'dummy variables measure the occurrence of a phenomenon rather than its magnitude, one cannot always make meaningful time-series inferences from their cross-sectional coefficients' (p. 127). In this case, the typical amount of land lost by labourers was much larger than the size of the average allotment, and therefore 'the coefficient from the cross-sectional analysis understates the long-term effect of labourers' loss of land' (p. 143).

The next set of quantitative estimates is a little more complicated. Boyer observes that distance from LONDON (a proxy for the cost of migration) had a negative effect on both RELIEF and INCOME. A 10 per cent increase in LONDON resulted in a reduction in RELIEF of between 1.5 and 2.9 per cent, and in INCOME of between 1.3 and 1.4 per cent (p. 141). How does he get these results?

We know directly from the regression coefficients that a change in LONDON of 1 mile will lead to an absolute fall in RELIEF of between 0.04 and 0.08 shillings and in INCOME of between £0.06 and £0.07.[4] The values come from the two models reported in table 15.1 and all the coefficients are negative. However, Boyer has chosen to convert these absolute changes to relative ones, and he does this in relation to the *mean values* of the three variables.

The mean distance of all parishes from London is 65.1 miles, the mean of RELIEF is 18.0 shillings, and the mean of INCOME is £29.6.[d] A 10 per cent change in LONDON would thus be 6.51 miles, and the effect of this

---

[d] The mean values of RELIEF and INCOME (and of most of the other variables) are given by Boyer on p. 149. The mean distance from London is not given but can easily be calculated from the data set.

would be 6.51 times larger than the effects of a change of 1 mile. Multiplying the original coefficients by 6.51 gives a fall of between 0.26 and 0.52 shillings in RELIEF and between £0.39 and £0.42 in INCOME.

These absolute changes must then be related to the mean values to get the proportionate changes quoted by Boyer. 0.26 shillings is 1.5 per cent of the mean RELIEF expenditure of 18.0 shillings, and 0.52 shillings is 2.9 per cent. Similarly £0.39 is 1.3 per cent of the mean INCOME of £29.6, and £0.42 is 1.4 per cent. Similar roundabout procedures are used to derive proportionate effects for a number of the other coefficients discussed by Boyer, including those relating to specialization in grain and the political power of labour-hiring farmers (p. 141).

A different route must be followed to reach another type of result: the statement that 'the elasticity of relief expenditures with respect to the unemployment rate is 0.14' (p. 141). The starting point here is the positive coefficient on unemployment of 0.34 in the simultaneous-equations model for RELIEF. Since the model specifies a simple linear relationship between RELIEF and UNEMP, this means that a rise in UNEMP of 0.01 would increase RELIEF by 0.34 shillings. Using the symbol Δ (capital Greek delta) to represent a 'change in', we could express this as

$$\frac{\Delta Y}{\Delta X} = 0.34$$

However, as explained in §12.3.2 this is not the same as the *elasticity*, which is defined as the ratio of the proportionate changes in the two variables:

$$\frac{\Delta Y}{Y} \div \frac{\Delta X}{X}$$

If we re-arrange the terms we see that this definition can also be written as

$$\frac{\Delta Y}{\Delta X} \times \frac{X}{Y}$$

To obtain the elasticity it is thus necessary to multiply the coefficient of 0.34 by

$$\frac{X}{Y}$$

This can be done in relation to the mean values of the variables, respectively, 7.4 per cent for UNEMP and 18.0 shillings for RELIEF. We thus have

$$0.34 \times \frac{7.4}{18.0} = 0.14$$

Since this is not a *constant* elasticity (see again §12.3.2) its value would be different at other levels of the variables, but it is usual to evaluate the elasticity 'at the mean'.

Conclusions from the regressions

Boyer draws several interesting conclusions from his regressions. Those explanatory variables that proved not to be statistically significant are dismissed as being irrelevant to an explanation for the trends in relief expenditures. He finds, for example, that payment of allowances in aid of wages (measured by the dummy variables for LABRATE, ROUNDSMN, and SUBSIDY) did not increase unemployment rates or *per capita* relief expenditures, or reduce labourers' earnings; the existence of workhouses did not reduce unemployment rates (p. 143). The INCOME variable was also not statistically significant in the simultaneous-equations model for RELIEF and he notes: 'Surprisingly, the hypothesis that poor relief was used to supplement "substandard" wages was not supported by the data' (p. 142).

By contrast, the coefficients on GRAIN, COTTIND, and FARMER were all statistically significant and Boyer concludes: 'Crop mix, income from cottage industry, and the political power of labour-hiring farmers were important determinants of per capita relief expenditures' (p. 142). The negative coefficients on LONDON were statistically highly significant in the equations for both RELIEF and INCOME, supporting the view that the need to pay more in both wages and relief diminished as the relative pull of the capital weakened with distance.

Unlike Hatton and Williamson, Boyer does not have data that would enable him to quantify the changes in the explanatory variables over time, and thus make a formal quantitative assessment of the relative importance of the different forces comparable to table 14.3. Instead he draws on the historical literature to show that there were marked changes in three of the factors proposed as explanations for the rise in RELIEF (pp. 143–5). First, there was increased specialization in grain in the southeast of England in response to the rise in grain prices from 1760 to 1815. Second, the political power of labour-hiring farmers increased in southern parishes after 1760 as a result of changes in the economic and legal environment.

The third, and probably the most important, change was the combination of (a) the decline in employment opportunities and wage rates for women and children in cottage industry, and (b) the rapid increase in London wage rates. In order to secure an adequate labour force for the peak harvest season, farmers were compelled to respond to these two trends by offering improved incomes to their labourers in the form of an appropriate combination of wages and relief.

15.1.2   The Old Poor Law and the birth rate

One of the most frequent of the contemporary criticisms of the Old Poor Law was that the granting of outdoor relief to able-bodied labourers – and particularly the payment of child allowances to labourers with large families – was a powerful factor in promoting earlier marriage and higher birth rates. Malthus argued that this undermined one of the essential preventive checks to population growth, and would lead to subsistence crises. The Royal Poor Law Commission made this a further part of its condemnation of the system of outdoor relief.

A number of scholars have attempted to test the Malthusian hypothesis empirically. The most substantial of these studies, by Huzel, claimed to show that Malthus was wrong because the payment of child allowances was actually associated with relatively low birth and marriage rates.[5] However Boyer argues that there are problems with each of the tests applied by Huzel. His major criticism is that a test confined to comparisons across parishes of relief payments and birth rates fails to *control for* other possible determinants of differences in birth rates, and similarly for marriage rates and infant mortality (p. 152). A simple bivariate comparison simply *ignores* all the other potential causes of variation in these demographic variables across parishes. There is thus an omitted-variables problem in Huzel's formulation of the sort analysed in §11.2.2. To be satisfactory as a test of the Malthusian hypothesis, these other factors must be included, and controlled for, in a more comprehensive model.

The double log model

Boyer accordingly discusses the socio-economic determinants of fertility (pp. 155–61). The model is initially specified as a linear relationship (p. 159), but it is subsequently estimated as a double logarithmic specification,[e] and is set out below in this form. All the numerical variables are in logs, the variable names are as given in table A.2 in appendix A, and the sign on the coefficients indicates the expected impact of each of the explanatory variables. Only two variables are expected to have a negative effect: population pressure (DENSITY) and lack of accommodation (HOUSING).

$$
\begin{aligned}
\log \text{BRTHRATE} = a + b_1 \log \text{INCOME} - b_2 \log \text{DENSITY} - \\
b_3 \log \text{HOUSING} + b_4 \text{CHILDAL3} + \\
b_5 \text{CHILDAL4} + b_6 \text{CHILDAL5} + \\
b_7 \text{ALLOTMNT} + b_8 \text{COTTIND} + \\
b_9 \log \text{INFTMORT} + e \quad\quad (15.6)
\end{aligned}
$$

[e] The log-log transformation of the OLS regression is designed to assist comparison of the coefficients with the non-linear model of fertility that is introduced later in this section. The coefficients are reported in columns (1) and (4) of table 15.2.

The data set covers 214 parishes in 12 counties in southeast England, c. 1831. Equation (15.6) can be estimated by the ordinary least squares (OLS) procedure after substituting the logs of the numerical variables for the original values (see §12.2.2).

Data constraints mean that BRTHRATE has to be measured per 100 families residing in the parish, not per 100 women aged 15–64, and thus cannot take account of differences between parishes in the number of women of childbearing age. This creates two problems that Boyer can only note but not remedy (p. 158). First, variations across parishes in the ratio of births to families could be due simply to differences in the age distribution of married females.

Secondly, differential rates of migration away from the parishes might also be a cause of variation in measured BRTHRATE. If out-migration rates were higher from poor 'unpromising' parishes, then such parishes should have contained a relatively smaller share of young unmarried adults and married couples than more prosperous parishes. This would lead to a lower BRTHRATE for these parishes, other things being equal. 'Thus there might be a spurious positive relationship between birth rates and measures of parish prosperity, such as wage rates.' Furthermore, if generous child allowances were associated with poor parishes, there might also be a spurious negative relationship between birth rates and child allowances.

Boyer then confronts a further awkward problem (p. 161). This one is created by the fact that the denominator of INFTMORT (infant deaths per 100 live *births*) is also the numerator of the dependent variable (number of *births* per 100 families). Any errors in the measurement of births will lead to a spurious negative relationship between BRTHRATE and INFTMORT. He is able to find a way out of this dilemma, but it involves specifying a model in a form that falls into the intractably non-linear category mentioned in §12.2.[f] It can thus be estimated only by non-linear least squares, a procedure that falls outside the scope of this text.

Results from the regressions
Fortunately, however, the results of this procedure are interpreted in exactly the same way as those from OLS, and so there is no difficulty in evaluating them. They are given, together with those from (15.6), in table 15.2, again reporting both *t*-ratios and prob-values. As Boyer observes, the results of the two models are 'qualitatively similar' (p. 163) for all the variables except INFTMORT, and his discussion of the results is based on the non-linear model.[6] The *t*-statistics for this model show that all the variables

---

[f] The feature that makes the model non-linear occurs in the error term in Boyer's equation (2), p. 162.

Table 15.2   Determinants of birth rates, cross-section data, c. 1831

	(1)	(2)	(3)	(4)	(5)	(6)
	Double logarithmic model			Non-linear model		
	Coefficient	*t*-statistic	Prob>|*t*|	Coefficient	*t*-statistic	Prob>|*t*|
Constant	1.12	2.06	0.041	−2.81	4.28	0.0001
INCOME	0.45	2.95	0.004	0.44	2.40	0.017
DENSITY	−0.09	2.70	0.007	−0.10	2.52	0.013
INFTMORT	−0.06	1.17	0.242	0.38	5.82	0.0001
CHILDAL3	0.13	2.24	0.026	0.25	3.67	0.0003
CHILDAL4	0.11	2.15	0.033	0.17	2.64	0.009
CHILDAL5	0.09	1.50	0.124	0.17	2.25	0.025
HOUSING	−0.19	1.62	0.106	−0.28	1.94	0.054
ALLOTMNT	0.001	0.03	0.981	0.01	0.21	0.838
COTTIND	0.04	0.76	0.446	−0.06	0.91	0.364
R^2	0.124					

Source: Boyer, *Poor Law*, p. 163.

except COTTIND and ALLOTMNT were statistically significant. R^2 in the OLS specification is only 0.124, indicating that there was a great deal of random variation across parishes in birth rates and perhaps also that other factors – not represented in Boyer's model – were also important.

The important conclusion from this study is that the provision of child allowances did have a positive effect on birth rates, other things being equal, and that the quantitative impact was large. The regression coefficient for CHILDAL3 is +0.25. Since the dependent variable is in log form, this indicates that parishes that began allowances at three children had birth rates 25 per cent higher than those of parishes without allowances, controlling for INCOME and other factors. For parishes that began relief at four children, birth rates were 17 per cent higher; and the same differential was found for parishes that began at five or more children.

Three other Malthusian hypotheses are also supported by the regression results. Since these are all double logarithmic relationships the elasticities can be read directly from the coefficients, indicating that there would be a change of b per cent in BRTHRATE for every 1 per cent change in the explanatory variable (see §12.3.1 and table 12.1). Farm labourers' annual income had a positive effect on fertility, with an increase in INCOME of 10 per cent resulting in a rise in BRTHRATE of 4.4 per cent. Lack of accommodation and high population density both had a negative effect. The coefficient on HOUSING of -0.28 indicates that an increase of 10 per cent in the ratio of families to the number of houses would account for a fall in BRTHRATE of 2.8 per cent; and a 10 per cent increase in DENSITY would result in a reduction of 1.0 per cent.

These cross-section results show that child allowances, INCOME, HOUSING, and DENSITY all had a statistically significant impact on the birth rate, but – as always – it is also necessary to consider whether these factors were *historically* important. In the present context that can be done by ascertaining what their effect was in relation to the rise in the crude birth rate during the late eighteenth and early nineteenth century (pp. 167–71).

For this purpose Boyer assumes that there were no child allowances at the beginning of this period. To obtain an estimate of their effect at the end of the period he constructs an average across the different regions in England in 1824. The parishes in each region were subdivided into four categories: those not giving child allowances, and those giving allowances beginning at three, four, or five or more children. The impact of child allowances for each category is assumed to be the same in each region as in the southern parishes covered by the regression (zero for those not paying allowances, and 0.25, 0.17, and 0.17, for the other three categories). The regions were then weighted according to their population in 1821. The final result is a weighted average of 0.142. In other words, for England as a whole, the payment of child allowances caused birth rates to be 14.2 per cent higher in 1824, other things being equal, than they would have been in the absence of this form of relief (p. 168).

For the other explanatory variables Boyer obtains estimates of the percentage change over the four decades from 1781 to 1821, and multiplies these by the elasticities from the regression results for (15.6). The results are summarized in table 15.3. The table indicates that the five variables would have caused birth rate to rise by between 5.0 and 7.8 per cent. If child allowances had not been adopted the birth rate would have *declined* by between 6.4 and 9.2 per cent. According to Wrigley and Schofield the actual increase over this period was 14.4 per cent.[8]

As Boyer concludes, 'the early-nineteenth-century increase in birth rates cannot be understood without taking child allowance policies into account' (p. 171). Similarly, the abolition of child allowances following the introduction of the New Poor Law in 1834 was a major reason why birth

---

[8] E. A. Wrigley and R. S. Schofield, *The Population History of England, 1541–1871*, Edward Arnold, 1981, p. 529.

Table 15.3 Impact of child allowances and other factors on the increase in the English birth rate, 1781–1821

	(1) Percentage change 1781–1821	(2) Regression coefficient	(3) Effect on birth rate (%)
INCOME	+14	0.44	+6.16
DENSITY	+63	−0.10	−6.30
HOUSING	+10 to +20	−0.28	−2.80 to −5.60
CHILDALL	...	0.14	+14.20
INFTMORT	−9	0.38	−3.42
Total change in birth rate as a result of above factors			+5.0 to +7.8
Actual change in crude birth rate			14.4

Notes:
(1) From Boyer, *Poor Law*, p. 170;
(2) From table 15.2, column (4);
(3) = (1) multiplied by (2).

rates remained broadly stable between 1831 and 1851, despite a more rapid increase in workers' real incomes.

15.2 Leaving home in the United States, 1850–1860

Our final case study analyses an important aspect of the social evolution of the family and its relation to broader socio-cultural dynamics. The nineteenth century is generally recognized as a period in which the status of children underwent considerable change. Broader economic opportunities afforded by industrialization challenged the customary structure of the family economy, as children began more frequently to work outside the home, and as they found themselves able to marry and set up independent households at an earlier age.

Richard Steckel addresses a key part of this story by analysing the age at which youths left the family home. Steckel drew a sample of households from the manuscript schedules of the US Census for 1860; he then matched as many of these as he could back to the 1850 census manuscript schedules.[7] His sample incorporated information on almost 1,600 male-headed households, including many who had migrated *en famille* between 1850 and 1860. He then compared the names of the members of the household

Figure 15.1

Departures of children from home by age and sex, United States, 1850–1860

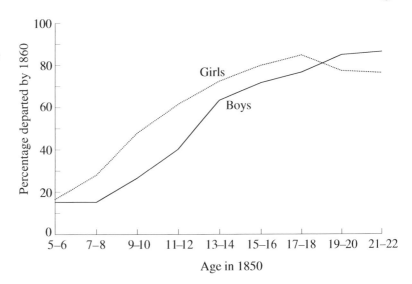

in the two years to determine which of the children who were listed in the census in 1850 were not present in the household 10 years later. This allowed Steckel to determine the probability that a child of a given age would leave the family home within the next 10 years.

The complexity of American migration patterns made it impossible to match all households from 1860 to 1850. Therefore, Steckel's data set is not a random sample of all US families, but rather focuses on households that were already established in 1850 and for which the household head survived until 1860. It excludes all households established between 1850 and 1860, as well as those in which all the children left before 1860. Nonetheless, consideration of other evidence leads Steckel to conclude that his results are representative of the circumstances governing the decision to leave the family home in this period.

The calculated departure rates are depicted in figure 15.1.[8] The graph shows the proportion of children of a given age in 1850 who had left the household by 1860. The horizontal axis is the age of the children in 1850; the vertical axis shows the departure rate over the next 10 years. It is important to emphasize that Steckel's data do not mean that 15.7 per cent of 5–6-year-old boys were leaving the family home in the 1850s, but rather that 15.7 per cent of those aged 5–6 in 1850 *left home sometime over the next 10 years.* The graph shows the departure rates of children aged from 5 to 22 in 1850.[9]

The graph shows a broadly sigmoid (or logistic) pattern of departures for both sexes. The leaving rate is low for 5–6-year-olds, rises steeply through the early teenage years, before reaching a high plateau for children over 17. It is evident from the graph that younger girls tended to leave the family home faster than boys, and also that women who remained in the household after 18 were less likely to leave than men of the same age.

15.2.1 Influences on leaving home

Steckel's analysis is revealing of the pace at which children left home at given stages of their life cycle. But it does not tell us what determined the decision to leave home. There is a large literature that discusses decisions to migrate and to leave home. Steckel examines this literature and establishes a series of hypotheses about the dynamics of early departure. These hypotheses focus on the relative costs and benefits of leaving home and staying within the family. He finds six major variables that may have influenced these costs and benefits:

- *Household wealth*: Wealthier families had more resources, which would allow children to stay at home longer, rather than leave in search of employment or a fortune. Moreover, greater household wealth enabled children to stay at home and gain more skills and education; it also raised the chances that the family had a business that could employ the child.
- *Gender*: Girls tended to leave home at a younger age than boys. This reflected a number of factors: a lower age at marriage for females; the greater opportunity for factory employment of young girls (and the greater opportunity for boys to find a job in the family business); the earlier maturation of girls; and the greater likelihood that boys would be offered additional schooling.
- *Location*: Since rents and other costs were higher in urban areas, the costs of leaving home were also higher, suggesting that children would stay at home longer in more urban settings. Also, migration tended to be more frequent on the frontier and it is probable that this extends to the age of leaving home as well.
- *Family structure*: The more children in a family, the greater the competition for household resources. It is therefore plausible to suggest that children of larger families who could find work outside the home would be encouraged to leave. Birth order might matter as well. In some cultures, the youngest (female) child is expected to stay at home to support ageing parents; in other cultures, it is the oldest (female) child that fulfils this function. Finally, the death of a parent may affect the resources available to the household, perhaps increasing the need of older (male and female) children to stay at home to maintain family status and wealth.
- *Ethnicity*: The children of foreign-born family heads may have retained

the culture of home-leaving of their parents, giving rise to different patterns compared to children of American parents.

- *Migration*: If households migrated with the employment of their children in mind, this would reduce the chances of children leaving the home at a later stage.

- *Literacy*: Migration studies often indicate that illiterate individuals are less likely to move, perhaps because they are less aware of the opportunities available elsewhere, perhaps because they lack the confidence to take risks, perhaps because their services are less in demand in new regions than those of skilled workers.

15.2.2 The logit model

In order to assess the importance of these various influences on the decision to leave home, Steckel models a regression in which the probability of leaving home within the period 1850–60 is the dependent variable. The independent variables take the values recorded in answers to questions asked at the 1850 Census and therefore relate to the situation of the household and its individual members in 1850.

The regression has the following form:

$$
\begin{aligned}
\text{LEAVE} = a + b_1\,&\text{PROPERTY} + b_2\,\text{LITRACYF} + \\
b_3\,&\text{MIGRATED} + b_4\,\text{LITRACYM} + b_5\,\text{DEATHM} + \\
b_6\,&\text{AGEM} + b_7\,\text{AGECHILD} + b_8\,\text{YNGERFAM} + \\
b_9\,&\text{OLDERFAM} + b_{10}\,\text{BORNENG} + b_{11}\,\text{BORNIRE} + \\
b_{12}\,&\text{BORNOTHR} + b_{13}\,\text{WHITECLR} + \\
b_{14}\,&\text{BLUECLR} + b_{15}\,\text{UNSKILD} + b_{16}\,\text{OTHROCC} + \\
b_{17}\,&\text{NCENTRAL} + b_{18}\,\text{SOUTH} + b_{19}\,\text{FRONTIER} + \\
b_{20}\,&\text{LARGEURB} + b_{21}\,\text{SMALLURB} + e \qquad (15.7)
\end{aligned}
$$

The dependent variable, LEAVE, is dichotomous, taking the value of 1 if a child who lived with the family in 1850 was not reported as present in 1860. The regression model used by Steckel to estimate the equation is a **logit**, as introduced in §13.2.1. The regression procedure effectively chooses the coefficient values to reproduce as closely as possible the observed distribution of binary values in the sample. Thus, it generates values of a and b_k which when positive will fit the distribution of leavers in the sample, and when negative will fit the distribution of stayers in the sample.

The explanatory variables were chosen to reflect the various hypotheses set out in §15.2.1. The importance of household wealth is tested by including the value of real estate owned in 1850 (PROPERTY). Steckel also includes information on the father's occupation (WHITECLR, BLUECLR, UNSKILD, OTHROCC) as further evidence of the household's economic standing. The significance of household structure and the intensity of competing claims on family resources is reflected in two variables that measure family composition – the number of children under the age of 10 (YNGERFAM), and the number of children who were 10 years and older (OLDERFAM) in 1850.

Other household characteristics include the literacy of each parent (LITRACYF, LITRACYM), whether or not the mother was still living (DEATHM), whether the family had migrated between 1850 and 1860 (MIGRATED), and the ethnic origins of the household head (BORNENG, BORNIRE, BORNOTHR). Steckel incorporated information on location, by region (NCENTRAL, SOUTH, FRONTIER), and by urban status (LARGEURB, SMALLURB). Finally, he includes the age of the child in 1850 (AGECHILD) and, as an indicator of the birth order of the child, the age of the mother in 1850 (AGEM).

None of the variables is transformed from their original value. There are thus no log values and no rates of change. The majority of the 21 explanatory variables are dummy variables. The only five which are continuous are: AGECHILD, AGEM, YNGERFAM, OLDERFAM, and PROPERTY. All of these are measured in actual numbers, except for PROPERTY, which is measured in thousands of dollars.

The dummy variables fall into two types:

One set represent simple binary observations – households either migrated (MIGRATED = 1) or they did not (MIGRATED = 0). The coefficient on MIGRATED therefore indicates the difference in the value of LEAVE between a household that did and did not migrate between 1850 and 1860. LITRACYM, LITRACYF, and DEATHM also take this form.

A second set represent more complex patterns. Thus, Steckel distinguished five categories of father's occupation. For reasons explained in §10.1.1, one of these categories (in this case, farmer) must be excluded from the regression to avoid the dummy variable trap. There are thus four occupational dummies in (15.7), each taking the value of (0,1). For example, a child whose father was a farmer would have 0 values for each of the four occupational dummies. If the father was a white collar worker, these dummies would take the values: WHITECLR = 1, BLUECLR = 0, UNSKILD = 0, OTHROCC = 0; and similarly for fathers in each of the three remaining occupations. The omitted occupation (farmer) is included in the constant term. Thus, the coefficient on WHITECLR indicates the difference in the value of LEAVE if the father were a white collar worker, *relative to the value of LEAVE if the father were a farmer.*

Similarly, there are three dummy variables for father's birthplace, for which there are four categories (the three listed above and the omitted category, born in the United States). A child with a US-born father would have 0 values for each ethnic dummy; a child with an English-born father would record 1 for BORNENG and 0 for the others; and similarly for the two remaining categories. There are four regional variables and three dummies (with Northeast being omitted); and there are three urban variables and two dummies (with rural as the omitted category). In each case, the omitted variables are in the constant term, and in each case, *the value of the coefficient on the dummy variable is relative to the value of LEAVE for the relevant omitted variable.*

Steckel divided his sample by sex into groups aged 5–11 and 12–18 in 1850.[10] There are over 1,000 observations for the younger age categories and 579 observations for the older. The sample was divided evenly between girls and boys. The results for each of these groups are shown in table 15.4.

Interpreting the coefficients

The logit model is a more complex regression model than the OLS (or even 2SLS) versions that have been used in the other case studies. The signs and the *t*-statistics may be interpreted in the standard way, but the coefficients do not predict the values of LEAVE directly and must be transformed into something more meaningful. In chapter 13, we discussed the transformation from logit coefficients into both marginal and impact effects and elasticities. Steckel's analysis is framed in terms of elasticities.

Two concepts of elasticity were introduced in §13.2.5: the point elasticity and the unit elasticity. The latter measures the ratio of a proportionate change in the dependent variable to a proportionate change in the explanatory variable, when the latter changes by one unit. It is the unit elasticity that Steckel has calculated, and that is reproduced in columns (3) and (6) in table 15.4. In what follows, we focus on the derivation of the unit elasticity on AGECHILD in column (6); that is, the proportionate response of LEAVE for a unit change in AGECHILD, calculated for the data set of boys aged 12–18.

As explained in the discussion of logit coefficients in §13.2.2, the basis for the calculation is the odds ratio, and its logarithm, the log odds ratio. In this case the mean value of LEAVE in the data set of boys aged 12–18 is 0.6511, and the proportion of stayers in the sample is $1 - 0.6511 = 0.3489$, so the odds ratio is $0.6511/0.3489 = 1.8662$.[h] The log of the odds ratio is

---

[h] The mean value of LEAVE corresponds to the mean value of $P(Y_i = 1)$ in the terminology employed in chapter 13, and the mean value of stayers corresponds to $P(Y_i = 0)$.

Table 15.4   The age at leaving home in the United States, 1850–1860, explaining the probability of departure, boys and girls aged 5–11 and 12–18

	(1)	(2)	(3)	(4)	(5)	(6)
	Boys aged 5–11			Boys aged 12–18		
	Coefficient	t-statistic	Elasticity	Coefficient	t-statistic	Elasticity
Constant	−2.971	−4.36	−2.412	−2.065	−2.05	−0.676
PROPERTY	−0.005	−0.21	−0.006	−0.013	−0.57	−0.010
LITRACYF	−0.219	−0.73	−0.017	0.263	0.62	0.007
MIGRATED	−0.120	−0.51	−0.013	0.401	1.23	0.016
Wife						
LITRACYM	0.156	0.64	0.019	−0.043	−0.12	−0.002
DEATHM	0.607	2.93	0.066	0.075	0.26	0.003
AGEM	−0.045	−2.85	−1.249	−0.073	−3.73	−0.952
Child						
AGECHILD	0.254	6.16	1.582	0.330	6.21	1.582
Family composition						
YNGERFAM	0.124	1.95	0.335	0.068	0.93	0.059
OLDERFAM	0.099	1.87	0.165	0.105	1.52	0.133
Foreign-born						
BORNENG	0.383	0.66	0.005	−1.340	−1.60	−0.005
BORNIRE	0.138	0.28	0.003	−0.384	−0.53	−0.002
BORNOTHR	0.099	1.87	0.165	0.105	1.52	0.133
Occupation						
WHITECLR	0.499	1.84	0.042	0.263	0.66	0.007
BLUECLR	0.754	3.63	0.108	0.088	0.29	0.004
UNSKILD	0.589	1.69	0.024	0.177	0.39	0.003
OTHROCC	0.926	2.22	0.020	0.621	1.20	0.008
Place of residence						
NCENTRAL	0.468	1.94	0.071	0.291	0.95	0.015
SOUTH	0.162	0.76	0.060	0.393	1.56	0.063
FRONTIER	0.778	2.72	0.066	0.006	0.02	0.000
LARGEURB	−0.718	−1.71	−0.027	−0.439	−0.96	−0.006
SMALLURB	−0.653	−1.14	−0.014	−1.222	−1.61	−0.009
−2 log λ		89.08			82.05	
df		21			21	
n		1135			579	

Table 15.4 (*cont.*)

	(1)	(2)	(3)	(4)	(5)	(6)
	Girls aged 5–11			Girls aged 12–18		
	Coefficient	*t*-statistic	Elasticity	Coefficient	*t*-statistic	Elasticity
Constant	−3.424	−5.15	−2.401	−2.722	−2.39	−0.614
PROPERTY	−0.033	−1.17	−0.035	0.010	0.32	0.004
LITRACYF	−0.338	−1.02	−0.019	−0.216	−0.51	−0.004
MIGRATED	−0.035	−0.15	−0.003	0.205	0.53	0.005
Wife						
LITRACYM	0.158	0.63	0.016	−0.227	−0.65	−0.008
DEATHM	−0.052	−0.24	−0.005	0.551	1.45	0.013
AGEM	−0.041	−2.68	−0.981	−0.023	−1.17	−0.200
Child						
AGECHILD	0.439	10.53	2.370	0.300	5.05	0.973
Family composition						
YNGERFAM	0.133	3.21	0.306	0.205	2.52	0.128
OLDERFAM	0.065	1.21	0.091	−0.112	−1.57	−0.093
Foreign-born						
BORNENG	−0.120	−0.20	−0.002	0.661	0.78	0.003
BORNIRE	0.378	1.00	0.011	0.617	0.74	0.003
BORNOTHR	0.419	0.76	0.006	−0.024	−0.03	−0.000
Occupation						
WHITECLR	−0.246	−0.91	−0.018	−0.152	−0.42	−0.003
BLUECLR	0.104	0.48	0.011	0.104	0.35	0.004
UNSKILD	0.605	1.97	0.028	0.061	0.10	0.001
OTHROCC	1.114	2.75	0.024	−0.737	−0.98	−0.003
Place of residence						
NCENTRAL	0.178	0.80	0.025	0.477	1.52	0.022
SOUTH	−0.100	−0.51	−0.030	0.362	1.38	0.038
FRONTIER	0.522	1.86	0.036	1.123	2.35	0.023
LARGEURB	−0.554	−1.52	−0.019	−1.272	−2.56	−0.011
SMALLURB	−0.521	−1.18	−0.014	−0.152	−0.22	−0.001
$-2 \log \lambda$		167.40			62.99	
df		21			21	
n		1038			579	

Source: Richard H. Steckel, 'The age at leaving home in the United States, 1850–1860', *Social Science History*, 20, 1996, pp. 521–2.

thus 0.6239. The coefficient on AGECHILD in column (4) of table 15.4 is 0.330, which represents the change in the log odds ratio for an increase of 1 year in AGECHILD. Adding the coefficient to the mean value of the log odds ratio produces $0.6239 + 0.330 = 0.9539$.

In order to work out what has happened to the value of LEAVE, we take the exponent of 0.9539 (to move from log to natural value), which equals 2.5958. This is the value of the odds ratio itself. Since the odds ratio is LEAVE/(1 − LEAVE), the value of LEAVE can be extracted from the odds ratio by calculating (odds ratio/1 + odds ratio) or, in this case, (2.5958/3.5958). This produces a revised value of LEAVE of 0.7219.

Thus, a unit change in AGECHILD changes LEAVE from 0.6511 to 0.7219, a proportionate increase of $0.0708/0.6511 = 0.1087$. Since the mean value of AGECHILD in this sample is 14.63, a unit increase of 1 year represents a proportionate increase of 0.0684. The unit elasticity is calculated as the proportionate change in LEAVE divided by the proportionate change in AGECHILD (see (13.10a) in §13.2.2); this is $0.1087/0.0684 = 1.589$.[i]

A complication arises when evaluating the elasticity of the dependent variable with respect to a change in the dummy variable, namely that a unit change in the dummy (from 0 to 1) cannot be expressed as a proportion of its base value. Steckel therefore measures the elasticity relative to the mean value of the dummy variable in the sample, i.e. the proportion of all households or individuals exhibiting this characteristic. In the case of LITRACYF, for example, the responsiveness of LEAVE to a unit change can be calculated by taking the exponent of $(0.6239 + 0.263)$ − the log value of the odds ratio at the sample mean plus the coefficient on LITRACYF – to generate the odds ratio, and then proceeding as above.

The new value of LEAVE is 0.7083, an increase of 8.78 per cent. The sample mean of LITRACYF is 0.08636; a unit increase in the dummy variable, expressed relative to its sample mean, is thus (1.08635/0.08635), or 1,258 per cent. The ratio of 8.78 to 1,258 produces the elasticity estimate of 0.007, as reported by Steckel. The relatively large coefficient on LITRACYF translates into only a modest effect on the dependent variable.

Conclusions from the logit model

What conclusions may be drawn from the logit analysis? Table 15.4 shows the importance of focusing on the elasticities rather than the actual coefficients when evaluating the results of a logit regression. As the table

---

[i] Steckel's estimate of the elasticity is 1.582, rather than the 1.589 cited here. The difference is very slight and is almost certainly the result of some rounding on either his part or ours.

shows, most of the elasticities associated with a unit change in the explanatory variables are small. As Steckel notes (p. 520) the *t*-statistics and other tests indicate that socio-economic variables were more powerful influences on the younger children than on those in the older age group.

The most important single influence on the timing and frequency of leaving home was clearly the age of the child. The large elasticity of AGE-CHILD suggests that a difference in the child's age of 1 year in 1850 increased the probability of leaving the home by almost 1.6 per cent for boys, and by as much as 2.4 per cent for young girls.

Yet, after holding this influence constant, some of the hypotheses set out in §15.2.1 received consistent support from the model. Thus, the coefficient on the number of young children in the household (YNGER-FAM) was large and significant for all cases except the older boys, suggesting that younger children tended to push older ones out of crowded homes. The age of the mother (AGEM) was also consistently significant, and inversely related to the decision to leave home: an additional year of age of the mother reduced the probability of leaving by about 1 per cent for both age-groups of boys and for young girls. If this is a proxy for birth order, the result is consistent with evidence from other societies that later-born children tended to remain with the family longer.

Older children might be forced out by younger siblings, but the oldest tended to stay behind, perhaps in their capacity as heirs apparent to the family estate. Similarly, father's occupation clearly had a strong influence on departure from the home, especially for younger children. The coefficients for all four occupations are positive, indicating that farm children (the control category) were generally least likely to leave home. For young boys the chances of leaving were markedly higher for the sons of blue collar workers, and lowest for those in unskilled and 'other' occupations; while the young daughters of unskilled workers were among the least likely to stay. For older children, the *t*-statistics on the occupation dummies for the father's occupation are uniformly low, indicating that this was not a significant influence on their decision to leave home.

Households resident on the American frontier were more likely to see their children leave, reflecting perhaps a combination of greater opportunities and a greater awareness of the advantages of going further west. Some part of the frontier effect can be attributed to other features of that area. As Steckel observes (p. 523) the frontier was less urbanized, and families living there had younger women as mothers, and had more children under 10 per family, than those in the Northeast. When these characteristics are controlled for, the expected chances of departure were higher for young boys on the frontier than in the Northeast (the control category) or the South, and were highest in the north-central states. For young girls the rate of departure was highest on the frontier, while for older girls it was higher there than in the northeast and north-central states, but even higher in the South.

Some of the other hypotheses received at best weak or inconsistent support from the logit results. Thus, living in an urban community clearly reduced the rate of leaving home relative to being in a rural setting for all categories, although the elasticities were small and only one coefficient was statistically significant. Similarly, the impact of the mother's absence from the household had a measurable effect only on the departure rate of young boys. The wealth of the household, as proxied by the value of its real estate, had little systematic impact on the decision to leave home; parental literacy and ethnicity were likewise unimportant. Previous relocation decisions also counted for little.

With so many variables being insignificant (in the regression on older boys, only two variables plus the constant are significant at the 10 per cent critical value), it might be asked whether the model as a whole has statistical power. The value of $-2 \log \lambda$ given at the base of table 15.4 tests the proposition, by providing a test of whether the logit regression is a better predictor of the odds ratio than a model in which the proportion of leavers is constant across all households (see §13.2.7). It is thus a joint test of the statistical significance of all the explanatory variables. The null hypothesis is that the explanatory variables have no effect on the odds ratio.

This statistic is distributed as a chi-square distribution with $(k-1)$ degrees of freedom, where k is the total number of regressors, including the constant. Steckel observes that the df for this test is 21.

For the sample of boys, 12–18, the baseline log-likelihood ($\log L_0$) is -374.468; the log-likelihood of the logit model is ($\log L_1$) -333.442. The test statistic is thus $-2\,(-374.468+333.442)=82.05$. The 1 per cent critical value of chi-square with 21 df is 38.93, indicating that we may safely reject the null hypothesis that the logit specification produced no added value. It is easily seen from table 15.4 that the logit specifications for the other samples also pass muster.

In chapter 13, we discussed the relative merits of the logit and probit specifications of models with dichotomous dependent variables. As a comparative exercise, we ran the probit regression using the Steckel data set for boys aged 12–18. The two models produce almost identical results, allowing for the systematic difference in the size of the coefficients explained in §13.4.1. The coefficient values in the logit formulation are about 1.81 times as large as in the probit regression (the ratio is not precise because of the slight difference in the shape of the two distributions and the non-linearity of the specifications); the *t*-statistics are almost identical. The value of the $-2 \log \lambda$ test is very similar in both specifications, as are the log-likelihood value and the two goodness-of-fit tests introduced in §13.2.7: the pseudo R^2 and McFadden's R^2. All in all, it appears that there is little to distinguish between the probit and logit specifications of this particular model.

Appendix to §15.1.1 Derivation of reduced-form equations from a simultaneous-equations model

This appendix is presented as an illustration of the procedure for deriving the reduced-form equations from a simultaneous-equations model. Each of the reduced-form equations has only the exogenous variables on the right-hand side. We also show how the regression coefficients of the reduced-form equations differ from those of the simultaneous-equations model, and how these two sets of parameters are related.

Consider a simple three-equation economic model in which there are three endogenous variables: consumption (CON), investment (INV), and national product (NNP), and two exogenous variables: national product in the previous period (NNP_{t-1}) and government expenditure (GOV). In terms of the model these variables are exogenous because last year's NNP is already determined and GOV is fixed by the public authorities without regard to the other variables in this model.

The first equation in the model specifies that the level of consumption depends on the level of national product. The second specifies that the level of investment depends partly on the current level of NNP and partly on its lagged value. To complete the model the third equation is an identity that says that NNP is equal to the sum of CON, INV, and GOV. The model thus says that changes in NNP will cause changes in CON, but also that changes in CON will cause changes in NNP, and there is a similar simultaneous relationship between INV and NNP.

To keep the algebra simple we omit the constants and the error terms. The simultaneous-equations model is then:

$$\text{CON} = b_1 \text{NNP} \tag{15.8}$$

$$\text{INV} = b_2 \text{NNP} + b_3 \text{NNP}_{t-1} \tag{15.9}$$

$$\text{NNP} = \text{CON} + \text{INV} + \text{GOV} \tag{15.10}$$

To derive the reduced-form equations from the structural equations we proceed as follows:

a *Substitute (15.8) and (15.9) in (15.10) and collect all the terms in NNP on the left-hand side*

$$NNP = [b_1 NNP] + [b_2 NNP + b_3 NNP_{t-1}] + GOV$$

$$NNP - b_1 NNP - b_2 NNP = b_3 NNP_{t-1} + GOV$$

$$(1 - b_1 - b_2)NNP = b_3 NNP_{t-1} + GOV$$

$$NNP = \frac{b_3}{1 - b_1 - b_2} NNP_{t-1} +$$

$$\frac{1}{1 - b_1 - b_2} GOV \qquad (15.11)$$

b *Substitute (15.11) in (15.8)*

$$CON = b_1 \left[\frac{b_3}{1 - b_1 - b_2} NNP_{t-1} + \frac{1}{1 - b_1 - b_2} GOV \right]$$

$$= \frac{b_1 b_3}{1 - b_1 - b_2} NNP_{t-1} + \frac{b_1}{1 - b_1 - b_2} GOV \qquad (15.12)$$

c *Substitute (15.12) in (15.9) and collect the terms in NNP$_{t-1}$*

$$INV = b_2 \left[\frac{b_3}{1 - b_1 - b_2} NNP_{t-1} + \frac{1}{1 - b_1 - b_2} GOV \right] + b_3 NNP_{t-1}$$

$$= \frac{b_2 b_3 + b_3(1 - b_1 - b_2)}{1 - b_1 - b_2} NNP_{t-1} + \frac{b_2}{1 - b_1 - b_2} GOV$$

$$= \frac{b_3(1 - b_1)}{1 - b_1 - b_2} NNP_{t-1} + \frac{b_2}{1 - b_1 - b_2} GOV \qquad (15.13)$$

We now have three reduced-form equations, (15.11)–(15.13), each of which has only the exogenous variables GOV and NNP$_{t-1}$ as explanatory variables. The equations all have very complicated regression coefficients. Of course if we estimate the equations we will not see these complicated coefficients, with separate results for b_1, b_2, and b_3. What we will get, for example if we estimate (15.13), is simply a regression coefficient for each explanatory variable; we will call them respectively c_1 and c_2:

$$INV = c_1 NNP_{t-1} + c_2 GOV \qquad (15.13a)$$

where c_1 is measuring **both** the direct effect of NNP$_{t-1}$ on INV (equivalent to b_3 in (15.11) in the full simultaneous-equations model) **and also** the combination of all the indirect effects involving b_1 and b_2. There are corresponding equations for (15.11) and (15.12):

$$\text{NNP} = c_3 \text{NNP}_{t-1} + c_4 \text{GOV} \qquad (15.11a)$$

and

$$\text{CON} = c_5 \text{NNP}_{t-1} + c_6 \text{GOV} \qquad (15.12a)$$

In the case of (15.13) these indirect effects on INV arise because:

(a) changes in INV lead to changes in NNP (as specified in (15.10))
(b) the resulting changes in NNP in turn lead to changes in INV (measured by b_2 in (15.9)), and
(c) also lead to changes in CON (measured by b_1 in (15.8));
(d) the resulting changes in CON in turn lead to further changes in NNP (as specified in (15.10)), and
(e) these changes in NNP have a further effect on INV (measured by b_2 in (15.9)).

Although the values of the parameters of the simultaneous-equations model (b_1, b_2, and b_3) are not directly revealed by the reduced-form equations, it may be possible to extract them from the values of the coefficients (c_1, c_2, c_3, etc.) in the reduced-form equations.

In the present case, for example, we can see from a comparison of the coefficient on GOV in (15.13a) with the corresponding coefficient in (15.13) that

$$c_2 = \frac{b_2}{1 - b_1 - b_2}$$

and similarly, from a comparison of the coefficients on GOV in (15.11) and (15.11a), we can obtain

$$c_4 = \frac{1}{1 - b_1 - b_2}$$

It follows, therefore, that $c_2 = c_4 \times b_2$, and thus that

$$b_2 = \frac{c_2}{c_4}$$

By a similar procedure using (15.12a) and (15.12) with (15.11) and (15.11a) we can obtain

$$b_1 = \frac{c_6}{c_4}$$

To complete the exercise, we can see from the comparison of the coefficients on NNP_{t-1} in (15.11) and (15.11a) that

$$c_3 = \frac{b_3}{1 - b_1 - b_2}$$

and since we now know c_3, b_1, and b_2, it is possible to work out what b_3 must be.

Notes

[1] Mark Blaug, 'The myth of the old poor law and the making of the new', *Journal of Economic History*, 23, 1963, pp. 151–84; Anne Digby, *Pauper Palaces*, Routledge & Kegan Paul, 1978.

[2] It was necessary for Boyer to eliminate UNEMP because *per capita* expenditure on relief is equal to the product of (a) the rate at which relief is paid, and (b) the frequency with which it is paid, and the latter factor is obviously correlated with the unemployment rate. This correlation makes it impossible to model the independent effect of the generosity of relief payments on unemployment. See further, Boyer, *Poor Law*, p. 133.

[3] Although Boyer does not report the R^2 from the 2SLS regressions, they are broadly similar to the OLS estimates (0.325 for RELIEF, 0.362 for INCOME).

[4] These are the values as reported after rounding to 2 decimal places. To reproduce the results as published by Boyer we need to work to 3 decimal places for the coefficient in the simultaneous-equation model for INCOME, i.e. with a coefficient of £0.065 rather than £0.07, obtained by replicating the regression. The other three regression coefficients are not sensitive to the additional decimal place.

[5] J. P. Huzel, 'Malthus, the Poor Law, and population in early nineteenth century England', *Economic History Review*, 22, 1969, pp. 430–52; and Huzel, 'The demographic impact of the old poor law: more reflexions on Malthus', *Economic History Review*, 33, 1980, pp. 367–81.

[6] In the first model the coefficient on INFTMORT is *negative* though not statistically significant, while in the second it is positive and highly significant. Boyer regards this as confirmation of the existence of a spurious negative relationship between BRTHRATE and INFTMORT in (15.6).

[7] In order to facilitate matching, Steckel sampled only households with at least one native-born child over 10 years old in 1860. Steckel's technique for matching was to look for households by the name of the household head in the two years. In cases where families stayed in the same state, this would be relatively simple, since there are indexes of the names of household heads for each state in 1850 and 1860. For those households that could not be located in the same state in 1850, Steckel was able to use the census manuscript information on the birthplace of all family members. The state in which any child aged 10 or above was born would be a good clue to the household's place of residence in 1850; Steckel then consulted the name index of household heads for that state in 1850 to effect a match.

[8] Steckel had to make one final correction in his calculation of average departure rates. The absence of a child in the household in 1860 could be caused by mortality as well as migration. Steckel used information on age-specific mortality rates to estimate the

number of absences due to death at each age. The expected death toll was then sub-tracted from the overall number of absences by age to generate departure rates. The figures shown in figure 15.1 are for departures without correction for mortality.

[9] Steckel excluded children under 5 in 1850, since their departure was probably domi-nated by premature mortality; he also excluded children over 22, because there were too few of them to generate statistically reliable data. Married children were also excluded from the sample.

[10] The separation by gender follows from the hypotheses in §15.2.1. The separation into age groups is designed to minimize the inconvenience of being able to separate out mortality from voluntarily leaving home in the dependent variable. Age-specific mortality rates are stable between the ages of 12 and 18, suggesting that the bias will be small. For younger children, however, the problem may be more severe. If we treat this as a stochastic error in the measurement of the dependent variable, this will have no effect on the coefficients in table 15.4 (see §11.4.1). The implicit assumption in Steckel's model is that child mortality is not systematically related to the explanatory variables such that it disguises the true relationship between voluntary departure and independent variables. Steckel receives support for this assumption from the rel-ative stability of the coefficients and elasticities in the two age-groups.

The four data sets

The following sections provide a brief description of the four data sets that are referred to throughout the book and form the basis for the case studies discussed in chapters 14 and 15. The original works should be consulted for further discussion of the historical aspects and for more detailed information about the sources. The data sets are not reproduced in this book but can be easily accessed without charge via a special page on the Cambridge University Press web site at www.cambridge.org/9780521806633.

Some of the series are entered in the regression models in the form of logarithms or as first differences, but all series are given in the data sets in their original form, and if any manipulation or transformation is required this must be done by users of the data set.

A.1 The iniquitous effects of the Old Poor Law

During the late eighteenth and early nineteenth centuries there was a rapid increase in expenditure on poor relief in England. Fierce criticisms of the system led eventually to the establishment of a Royal Commission and to the introduction of a New Poor Law in 1834. Many contemporary critics of the Old Poor Law attributed the remorseless growth of expenditure to the widespread adoption of systems of outdoor relief whereby those in need could receive financial assistance at home without being forced into the demeaning conditions of life in a workhouse.

A number of historians have proposed other explanations for the rising level of relief payments. Some see the problem as arising from increasing poverty among farm workers, due to the falling real value of wages paid to agricultural labourers; the removal by enclosure of allotments on which labourers could produce milk, potatoes, and other foods to supplement their wages; and the decline in home employment opportunities for women and children as the rise of factory-based textile industry wiped out cottage industry. Others have emphasized the ability of arable farmers to exploit their local political influence to get the parish to pay relief to labourers in the winter months, thereby shifting part of the cost of keeping seasonal workers in the parish on to non-farming ratepayers.

Apart from its cost to the taxpayer, the Old Poor Law was also alleged to have had many iniquitous effects, chief of which was the widely-held belief that the granting to able-bodied labourers of outdoor relief related to the number of their children encouraged a high birth rate, and was thus responsible for an excessively rapid growth of population. The most famous exponent of this view was Thomas Malthus, who argued that relief payments artificially reduced the cost of having children and so undermined the 'preventive check' to population growth in the form of late marriage or abstention. This Malthusian argument was adopted by the Royal Commission as one of its grounds for the reform of the Old Poor Law.

In chapters 4 and 5 of a study published in 1990, George Boyer addresses these two issues with specific reference to conditions in southern England.[a] He compiled two data sets covering a sample of parishes in the south of England in 1831. To investigate the factors that influenced the level of relief expenditure he used 15 series for a sample of 311 parishes; these are described in table A.1.[1] We added a further series, POP.

For the principal investigation of the birth rate he was able to obtain information for a sample of 214 parishes for 10 series. Four of these are already listed in table A.1 (INCOME, DENSITY, ALLOTMNT, and COTTIND); the remaining six are set out in table A.2. The first column of the data set indicates the county in which the parish is located, using a numerical code for the name of the county: 1 is Kent, 2 is Sussex, 3 is Essex, and so on. The full list of 24 county code numbers is reproduced with the data set. The next column identifies the parish, again using a numerical code for the name; the actual names are of little interest and this code is not reproduced.

The main source for both these data sets was the Rural Queries (the replies to 58 questions distributed among rural parishes in the summer of 1832 by the Royal Poor Law Commission) and the enumeration of population, occupations, and other data in the 1831 Census of Population.[2]

A.2 What explains the scale and timing of the massive emigration from Ireland after the famine?

In the period between the famine and the First World War more than 4.5 million men and women emigrated from Ireland. As a proportion of the

---

[a] George R. Boyer, *An Economic History of the English Poor Law*, Cambridge University Press, 1990.

Table A.1 Data set for investigation of relief payments in England in 1831

(a) Measured series for values c. 1831 unless otherwise noted

RELIEF   Relief expenditure of each parish per head of the population (in shillings)

INCOME   Annual income of adult male agricultural labourers in each parish (in £)

UNEMP   The ratio of the average number of unemployed labourers in each parish to the total number of wage labourers

LONDON   The distance to London from the centre of the county in which each parish was located (in miles)

FARMERS   The ratio of the number of labour-hiring farmers in each parish to the total number of parish ratepayers

GRAIN   The estimated percentage of adult males in each parish employed in grain production

DENSITY   The ratio of the total population of each parish to the acreage

WEALTH   The value of real property (land and buildings) in each parish in 1815 per head of the population (in £)

POP   The population of each parish

(b) Series for which the answer for each parish is either 'yes' (recorded as 1) or 'no' (recorded as 0)

COTTIND   Does cottage industry exist in the parish?

ALLOTMNT   Do labourers have allotments of farm land?

WORKHSE   Is there a workhouse in the parish?

CHILDALL   Does the parish pay child allowances?

SUBSIDY   Does the parish subsidize the wage rates of privately employed labourers?

LABRATE   Does the parish use a labour rate?*

ROUNDSMN   Does the parish use the roundsman system?**

Notes:

* Under the labour rate unemployed labourers were apportioned among all occupiers of property according to 'the extent of occupation, acreage rent or number of horses employed'.

** Under this system unemployed labourers were sent round the ratepayers in the parish with the expectation that they would be offered work.

Table A.2 Data set for investigation of the birth rate in southern England, c. 1826–1830*

(a) Measured series

BRTHRATE The ratio of births per 100 families in each parish in 1826–30

INFTMORT The ratio of deaths of infants aged 0–4 per 100 live births in each parish in 1826–30

HOUSING The ratio of families per inhabited house in each parish in 1831

(b) Series for which the answer for each parish is either 'yes' (recorded as 1) or 'no' (recorded as 0)

CHILDAL3 Does the parish begin payment of child allowances at three children?

CHILDAL4 Does the parish begin payment of child allowances at four children?

CHILDAL5 Does the parish begin payment of child allowances at five or more children?

Notes:
* In addition the following four series listed in table A.1 are also used in the study of birth rates: INCOME, DENSITY, ALLOTMNT, and COTTIND.

population this was more than double the rate of emigration from any other European country. The overwhelming majority went to the United States, but smaller numbers moved to Great Britain and a few also went to Canada, Australia, and New Zealand. In an article published in 1993 Timothy Hatton and Jeffrey Williamson explored several features of this emigration.[b] They investigated the trend over time, the annual fluctuations, and the possible characteristics within each county of Ireland that influenced the outflow, for example, religion, age structure, dependence on agriculture, and living standards.[3]

The authors compiled two basic data sets for this purpose. One consists of annual series for 1877–1913, the period for which the emigration and other data are thought to be reasonably reliable. The five basic series are listed in the top panel of table A.3; for some purposes these series are also subdivided by the country which received the emigrants or by gender; or they are used with various modifications, for example by taking the change in a series rather than its actual level, or by taking logs.

[b] Timothy J. Hatton and Jeffrey G. Williamson, 'After the famine: emigration from Ireland, 1850–1913', *Journal of Economic History,* 53, 1993, pp. 576–600.

Table A.3 Data set for investigation of emigration from Ireland, 1877–1913

(a) Annual series, 1877–1913

IRISHMIG   Number emigrating from Ireland each year per 1,000 of
            population. (In addition to total emigration, separate series are
            given in the data set for adjusted total emigration,* and also for
            total intercontinental emigration, emigration to the United States,
            and total male and total female emigration.)

EMPFOR   The foreign employment rate measured as 1 – the proportion
            unemployed each year. (For total emigration the foreign rate is
            calculated as a geometric weighted average of the rates for the
            United States (weight 0.7), Great Britain (0.2), Canada (0.05), and
            Australia (0.05), with the weights proportionate to the emigration
            shares.)

EMPDOM   The domestic (Irish) employment rate. This should in principle
            be measured in the same way as the foreign rate, but in the
            absence of a series for Irish unemployment a proxy was created by
            measuring the proportionate deviation of Irish agricultural
            output each year from its trend.

IRWRATIO   The ratio of the foreign real wage of builders' labourers to the
            corresponding domestic real wage for Ireland as a whole for each
            year. (For total emigration the foreign real wage is a weighted
            average calculated in the same way as for foreign employment.)

MIGSTOCK   The stock of previous emigrants already living abroad each year in
            the United States, Great Britain, Canada, Australia, and New
            Zealand, as a proportion of the total Irish population.

(b) Data for each county for each of the four census dates, 1881–1911

CNTYMIG   The proportion per 1,000 of the county population that
            emigrated

AGE   The proportion of the county population aged 15–34

URBAN   The proportion of the county population living in towns of 2,000
            or more

AGRIC   The proportion of the county male labour force in agriculture

LANDHLDG   The proportion of the county agricultural holdings less than 5
            acres

CYWRATIO   The ratio of the foreign real wage (defined and weighted as above)
            to the domestic real wage in agriculture in the county

Table A.3 *(cont.)*

RELIEF	The percentage of the county population receiving poor relief
HOUSING	The proportion of county families living in third- and fourth-class housing
FAMSIZE	The average family size in the county
CATHOLIC	The proportion of the county population who were Catholic
ILLITRTE	The proportion of the county population who were illiterate

Notes:

* Emigration from Ireland to Britain is believed to be seriously under-stated, so Hatton and Williamson construct an adjusted total using double the recorded flow to Britain.

The second set provides data for each of the 32 counties at four census dates (1881, 1891, 1901, and 1911) for 11 items, listed in the lower panel of the table.[4]

A.3 To what extent were generous unemployment benefits responsible for the high level of unemployment in inter-war Britain?

From 1921 until the outbreak of the Second World War in 1939 unemployment in Great Britain was at record levels: it averaged 14 per cent – far higher than it had been before 1913 or than it would be for any sustained period after 1948 – and it never fell below 9.5 per cent. Among various explanations which have been suggested for this high and persistent inability to provide work for such a large proportion of the labour force were the role of the trade unions and the excessive level of real wages; the overvaluation of sterling as a result of the decision to return to the gold standard with the pound valued at its pre-war rate against other currencies; structural problems arising from over-commitment to the old staple export industries such as coal, textiles, and shipbuilding; and a general lack of demand.

Then in 1979, in a highly controversial article, Daniel Benjamin and Levis Kochin injected a new factor into the debate.[c] Their suggestion was

[c] Daniel K. Benjamin and Levis A. Kochin, 'Searching for an explanation for unemployment in interwar Britain', *Journal of Political Economy*, 87, 1979, pp.441–78. They were not the first to argue that unemployment benefits contributed to a willingness to remain unemployed for a longer period, but the hypothesis had been displaced by alternative explanations and it was only with their article that it returned to prominence in the literature on the inter-war period.

that the persistently high level of unemployment 'was due in large part . . . to high unemployment benefits relative to wages'. Apart from the severe crises of 1921 and 1930–2, the high unemployment of other inter-war years 'was the consequence almost solely of the dole. The army of the unemployed standing watch in Britain at the publication of the *General Theory* was largely a volunteer army'.[d]

The insurance scheme that they highlighted had first been introduced in Britain in 1911, but only for a very small proportion of the workforce. An Act of 1920 extended coverage to almost all manual workers over the age of 16 (the two main exceptions were agricultural workers and domestic servants – both relatively stable sectors with low unemployment) and provided much more generous levels of benefit. There were numerous subsequent changes, but Benjamin and Kochin argue that the level of the benefits – together with various institutional features of the system – made the inter-war scheme 'more generous relative to wages than ever before or since'. In their view it was primarily this generosity that explains why unemployment was so much higher than in earlier or later periods.

Their paper provoked a flurry of historical and statistical criticisms, but most historians would now recognize that the benefit system did make some contribution to the severity of inter-war unemployment, though not by as much as Benjamin and Kochin had originally claimed.[5]

Their data set consisted of four annual primary series for the years 1920–38: UNEMP, WAGES, BENEFITS, and NNP.[6] They are defined in table A.4; all are taken from published sources.[7] From these they constructed two further series. BWRATIO is the replacement rate, and is a measure of the generosity of BENEFITS relative to WAGES (i.e. of the extent to which they are a replacement for wages). DEMAND is a measure of the effects of changes in aggregate demand calculated as the ratio of NNP to NNP*, its trend value.[e]

A.4   What influenced children's decision to leave home in the United States in the mid-nineteenth century?

Most children eventually leave home, but what are the factors that influence when and whether they do this? In order to find some of the his-

---

[d] The phrases quoted are from Benjamin and Kochin, p. 474; the reference to the *General Theory* is to the book which the famous economist, John Maynard Keynes, published in 1936 to explain his theory of the nature and causes of unemployment.

[e] The ratio of output to its trend is included in the regression model as the difference between the log of actual output (log NNP) and the log of its trend value (log NNP*). The use of logs in this way as a means of measuring proportions was explained in §1.6.3. The log-linear trend value for NNP* was estimated by using the procedure explained in §12.4.

Table A.4 Data set for investigation of unemployment in inter-war Britain, 1920–1938

(a) Annual series, 1920–1938

UNEMP	Total unemployment as a percentage of all insured employees
WAGES	Average weekly earnings (wages and salaries) of all full-time employees (in shillings)
BENEFITS	Weekly benefit entitlement of an adult male with one adult dependent and two dependent children (in shillings)
BWRATIO	The replacement rate, measured as the ratio of BENEFITS to WAGES
NNP	Real output measured by net national product (in £ million at 1938 factor cost)
DEMAND	The ratio of NNP to its trend value, NNP*

---

torical answers to these questions Richard Steckel extracted data from the manuscript schedules for the censuses of the United States for 1850 and 1860.[f] His analysis dealt with two issues: the average age at which the children left home and the factors that influenced them to make this decision, but our concern here is only with the data and procedures relating to the latter issue.

To obtain his data set Steckel initially drew from the manuscript schedules for the 1860 Census a random sample of households with at least one native-born child aged 10 or above still living at home. Those same households were then identified in the 1850 Census, using the state in which the child was born as a pointer to locate where the family had been enumerated in 1850. This information was obtained for 1600 male-headed households, and these yielded a national sample of unmarried children aged 5–29 who were recorded as living at home in 1850.

It was thus possible to determine from these matched samples of households which of the children living at home in 1850 were still there a decade later. To investigate what might have influenced the decisions of those who had departed, Steckel assembled information on a range of socio-economic and demographic characteristics of the father, the mother, the

---

[f] Richard H. Steckel, 'The age at leaving home in the United States, 1850–1860', *Social Science History*, 20, 1996, pp. 507–32. The manuscript schedules are the original household returns from which the published census reports were compiled.

Table A.5 Data set for investigation of decisions to leave home in the United States, 1850–1860

PROPERTY	The value of the father's real estate (in $1,000)
LITRACYF	Dummy variable = 1 if the father was illiterate, 0 otherwise
MIGRATED	Dummy variable = 1 if the household had migrated between 1850 and 1860, 0 otherwise
LITRACYM	Dummy variable = 1 if the mother was illiterate, 0 otherwise
DEATHM	Dummy variable = 1 if the mother had died before 1850, 0 otherwise
AGEM	The mother's age
AGECHILD	The child's age
YNGERFAM	The number of children in the family under the age of 10
OLDERFAM	The number of children in the family aged 10 and over
BORNENG	One of a set of four categories for ethnicity. It is a dummy variable that takes the value of 1 if the father was born in England, 0 otherwise. There are similar dummy variables for BORNIRE (born in Ireland) and BORNOTHR (born elsewhere). The control category is Native Born.
WHITECLR	One of a set of five categories for the father's occupation. It is a dummy variable that takes the value of 1 if the father was in a white collar occupation, 0 otherwise. There are similar dummy variables for BLUECLR (blue collar), UNSKILD (unskilled), and OTHROCC (other or occupation not given). The control category is Farmer.
NCENTRAL	One of a set of four categories for place of residence. It is a dummy variable that takes the value of 1 if the residence of the family in 1850 was in a North-central state, 0 otherwise. There are similar dummy variables for the SOUTH and FRONTIER. The control category is residence in a state in the Northeast.
LARGEURB	One of a set of 2 dummy variables for urbanization. It is a dummy variable that takes the value of 1 if the residence of the family in 1850 was in an urban area with a population of more than 25,000, 0 otherwise. There is a similar dummy variable for SMALLURB (with a population of less than 25,000). The control category is residence in a Rural area.

Note:
The terms dummy variable and control category are explained in §10.1.1.

child, and the household. All this information relates to the position in 1850 and was extracted from the Census schedules. The full list of characteristics is set out in table A.5.

The results are reported for 1,714 boys and 1,617 girls in two age groups, 5–11, and 12–18. In order to keep the working data set for this textbook to a manageable size we have reproduced only the information relating to 579 boys aged 12–18, but the identical procedures are used for the younger boys and for the girls, and the results for the whole sample are discussed in chapter 15.

It should be noted that the children are subdivided according to their age in 1850, so that there is some overlap between the two groups in respect of the age at which they eventually left home. The children aged 5–11 could have departed at any age from 6 (a 5-year-old who left in 1851) to 21 (an 11-year-old who left shortly before the census was taken in 1860). The corresponding range of age at departure for those in the group aged 12–18 would be 13–28. Steckel estimates that the mean age at which children left home for the sample as a whole was 26.5 years for males and 22 years for females.[8]

Notes

[1] For other quantitative studies of English poor relief see Mark Blaug, 'The myth of the old poor law and the making of the new', *Journal of Economic History*, 23, 1963, pp. 151–84; J. P. Huzel, 'Malthus, the poor law, and population in early nineteenth century England', *Economic History Review*, 22, 1969, pp. 430–52 and 'The demographic impact of the poor law: more reflexions on Malthus', *Economic History Review*, 33, 1980, pp. 364–81; and G. S. L. Tucker, 'The old poor law revisited', *Explorations in Economic History*, 12, 1975, pp. 233–52.

[2] The detailed replies from parishes were printed in four large volumes as Appendix B of the H. M. Commissioners for Inquiry into the Administration and Practical Operation of the Poor Laws, *Report, Appendix B1, Answers to Rural Questions* (H.C. 44), *Parliamentary Papers*, 1834, XXX–XXXIII; for the 1831 Census of Population of England and Wales see *Parliamentary Papers, 1833* (H.C. 149), XXXVI–XXXVIII. The data on the number of births and infant deaths listed in table A.2 were extracted by Boyer from unpublished parish returns for the 1831 Census located in the Public Record Office (PRO, HO 71).

[3] For good general discussions of the issues posed in analysis of emigration see J. D. Gould, 'European inter-continental emigration, 1815–1914: patterns and causes', *Journal of European Economic History*, 8, 1979, pp. 593–679; Gould, 'European inter-continental emigration: the role of diffusion and feedback', *Journal of European Economic History*, 8, 1980, pp. 267–315; and Dudley Baines, 'European emigration, 1815–1930: looking at the emigration decision again', *Economic History Review*, 47,

[8] Steckel, 'Leaving home', p. 517.

1994, pp. 525–44. For some more recent quantitative studies see Timothy J. Hatton and Jeffrey G. Williamson (eds.), *Migration and the International Labour Market, 1850–1939*, Routledge, 1994.

[4]   The main source for the annual migration series was Imre Ferenczi and Walter F. Willcox, *International Migrations: vol I, Statistics*, NBER, 1929. The annual home and foreign real wage series were compiled by Jeffrey G. Williamson, 'The evolution of global labor markets in the first and second world since 1830: background and evidence', *NBER Working Papers on Historical Factors in Long-Run Growth*, 36, NBER, 1992. The unemployment series are from J. R. Vernon, 'Unemployment rates in post-bellum America, 1869–1899', University of Florida, 1991, manuscript; Charles H. Feinstein, *National Income, Expenditure and Output of the United Kingdom, 1855–1965*, Cambridge University Press, 1972; Wray Vamplew (ed.), *Australian Historical Statistics*, Fairfax, Syme & Weldon, 1987, p. 153; and a series specially constructed by Hatton and Williamson for Canada. The county data were taken mainly from various volumes of the decennial *Census of Ireland*, Parliamentary Papers, or the *Emigration Statistics of Ireland*, Parliamentary Papers, for the four dates.

[5]   The main initial contributions to the debate were Michael Collins, 'Unemployment in interwar Britain: still searching for an explanation', *Journal of Political Economy*, 90, 1982, pp. 369–79; David Metcalfe, Stephen J. Nickell and Nicos Floros, 'Still searching for an explanation of unemployment in interwar Britain', *Journal of Political Economy*, 90, 1982, pp. 386–99; P. A. Ormerod and G.D.N. Worswick, 'Unemployment in inter-war Britain', *Journal of Political Economy*, 90, 1982, pp. 400–9; and Daniel K. Benjamin and Levis A. Kochin, 'Unemployment and unemployment benefits in twentieth-century Britain: a reply to our critics', *Journal of Political Economy*, 90, 1982, pp. 410–436. For later quantitative work on this topic see also Timothy J. Hatton, 'Unemployment benefits and the macroeconomics of the interwar labour market', *Oxford Economic Papers*, 35 (Supplement), 1983, pp. 486–505; and Barry Eichengreen, 'Unemployment in interwar Britain: dole or doldrums?', in N. F. R. Crafts, N. H. D. Dimsdale and S. Engerman (eds.), *Quantitative Economic History*, Oxford University Press, 1991, pp. 1–27.

[6]   Benjamin and Kochin also tested their hypothesis with additional series for juvenile unemployment (for 1924–35) and for male and female unemployment (for 1923–37), but these series are not reproduced in the data set.

[7]   Wages are from Agatha L. Chapman, *Wages and Salaries in the United Kingdom, 1920–1938*, Cambridge University Press, 1953; benefits from Eveline Burns, *British Unemployment Programs, 1920–1938*, Social Science Research Council, 1941; unemployment from official Ministry of Labour statistics reproduced in Board of Trade, *Statistical Abstract of the United Kingdom*, HMSO, 1936 and 1939, and net national product from Feinstein, *National Income*.

Index numbers

B.1 Price and quantity relatives

In §1.7 we noted that many of the series used in quantitative analysis of historical trends and fluctuations take the form of index numbers of the changes in either prices or quantities, and gave a few examples of controversies in which they have figured prominently. The aim of the present appendix is to outline the main principles involved in the construction of index numbers. Slightly more formal presentation of the principal concepts and definitions is also given in panels B.1 and B.2 for those comfortable with the algebra.

It may help to clarify the nature of a proper index number if we refer first to **price and quantity relatives**. These are not index numbers, although they look exactly like them because they also have one item in the series shown as 100. However these relatives are merely series that have been converted from an absolute to a relative basis. All that this involves is choosing some particular year for which the value of the series is taken as 100, and then expressing all the other items in the series as a ratio to the value in the chosen year. The advantage of doing this is that it makes it easier to see the relationship between values; fewer digits are required and the comparative dimension is more readily grasped.

To illustrate this simple procedure, data on the quantity of bituminous coal produced in the United States each year from 1900 to 1913 are given in column (1) of table B.1. The corresponding **quantity relative** is calculated in column (2) with 1900 as 100 and in column (3) with 1913 as 100. Both relatives are rounded to one decimal point. In the same way a **price relative** could be constructed from data on (say) the annual average price of a specific grade of raw cotton at New Orleans in cents per lb.

The important point to note about such relatives is that the relationship between any pair of years is completely unaffected by either the switch to

Table B.1   Bituminous coal output in the United States, 1900–1913, original data
and two quantity relatives

Year	(1) Output (000 tons)	(2) Relative (1900 = 100)	(3) Relative (1913 = 100)
1900	212,316	100.0	44.4
1901	225,828	106.4	47.2
1902	260,217	122.6	54.4
1903	282,749	133.2	59.1
1904	278,660	131.2	58.2
1905	315,063	148.4	65.9
1906	342,875	161.5	71.7
1907	394,759	185.9	82.5
1908	332,574	156.6	69.5
1909	379,744	178.9	79.4
1910	417,111	196.5	87.2
1911	405,907	191.2	84.8
1912	450,105	212.0	94.1
1913	478,435	225.3	100.0

Source: US Department of Commerce, *Historical Statistics of the United States,* series G13,
Washington, DC, 1949.

the relative form or the choice of year to take as 100. For example, the
output of coal in 1910 is always 60.3 per cent higher than the output in
1902, whichever column is used for the computation. Relatives are useful,
but they do not provide any additional information that is not already contained in the original series. The distinguishing feature of a proper index
number is that it does exactly that.

B.2 Two types of index number

Proper **index numbers** differ from such quantity or price relatives because
they combine data that would otherwise have to be considered separately,
and thus provide additional information that could not be accurately
measured in any other way. Assume for example, that we wish to construct
a measure of the overall industrial production of the United Kingdom
from 1770 to 1830. We would need to combine data on the output of cotton
goods, woollen goods, iron, coal, beer, leather, and other industrial prod-

ucts. In principle, a separate series should be included for every good produced in the United Kingdom in these years. However, that is not normally
practicable, and instead a representative sample of products would be
selected.

How then should the output data for these products be combined? It
would clearly not be sensible to simply add together a mishmash of figures
for tons of coal, yards of cotton cloth, gallons of beer, and so on. It is necessary to find some way of combining the data that circumvents the difficulty
created by the heterogeneity of the units in which the quantities are measured. Furthermore, there were enormous differences in the rates at which
individual industries increased production over this period. To take an
extreme example, the increase in the output of cotton yarn was a staggering
6,500 per cent, whereas that for beer was only a paltry 43 per cent. It is
therefore essential to combine the series in such a way that the overall index
reflects the relative importance of the various industries, and this requires
some definition of 'relative importance' and some system of weighting the
components.

There are a number of ways in which these requirements can be
satisfied, but in practice only two main types of index number are widely
used, and we will concentrate on these. One type uses the prices of a *fixed*
year to convert the component quantities to comparable values and simultaneously to weight them. This is known as a **Laspeyres quantity index**.
The *year used for the weights* is referred to as the **base year**.

The other type uses a *changing* set of prices to value the quantities and is
known as a **Paasche quantity index**. In both cases a weighted arithmetic
mean (see §2.2.2) is used to combine the different quantities. The *year
shown as 100* for the index is called the **reference year** and, as we shall see,
this may *not* be the same as the base year.

Each of these quantity indices has its corresponding price index. In the
Laspeyres price index the quantities of a fixed base year are used to weight
the component prices. In the **Paasche price index** a changing set of quantities is used to weight the prices. The price and quantity indices are thus
perfectly symmetrical.

In order to illustrate some of the key features of these two types of
index number we have invented a very simple data set in which there are
only two commodities, cotton cloth and beer. Table B.2 sets out all the relevant information on the prices and quantities of these two goods for
the three years, 1900, 1901, and 1902. The quantities refer identically to
the amounts produced in each year and the amounts consumed, and the
product of the prices and quantities in columns (3) and (6) can be interpreted as the value at current prices of the expenditure on the individual

Table B.2 Illustrative data for construction of price and quantity index numbers

	(1)	(2)	(3)	(4)	(5)	(6)	(7)
		Cotton cloth			Beer		Total
Year	Quantity (m units)	Price ($/unit)	Expenditure (m $)	Quantity (m units)	Price ($/unit)	Expenditure (m $)	expenditure (m $)
1900	1	10	10	2	15	30	40
1901	5	11	55	3	18	54	109
1902	10	12	120	4	20	80	200

Notes:
$(3) = (1) \times (2)$;
$(6) = (4) \times (5)$;
$(7) = (3) + (6)$.

commodities.[1] The corresponding aggregate expenditure is given in column (7).

We will look first at the Laspeyres type of index with fixed weights, and then in §B.5 at the alternative Paasche index with changing weights. To illustrate the procedures without excessive repetition we will refer from now on only to an index of *prices*, but everything said about the construction and properties of price indices in the remainder of this appendix is equally applicable to the corresponding indices of quantities. The only difference is that instead of using quantities to combine prices, a quantity index is formed by using prices to combine quantities. A number of possible price and quantity indices for the two goods are given in table B.3. The working for the price indices in (1)–(5) in the upper panel is given below; the construction of the corresponding quantity indices in the lower panel should be undertaken as an exercise.

B.3 Laspeyres index numbers with fixed weights

To begin with we will take 1900 as the base year. There are then two possible methods that can be used to construct a Laspeyres price index. The first is a ratio of *aggregates*. We can think of the quantities purchased in the base year as a fixed basket of goods, and then calculate what it would cost to buy this basket of goods at the prices prevailing each year. We thus work directly with the actual prices of each year (from columns (2) and (5) of table B.2), and the quantities of 1900 (from columns (1) and (4)).

Table B.3 Price and quantity indices for the data in table B.2 (1900 = 100)

	(1) Laspeyres (1900 weights)	(2) Laspeyres (1902 weights)	(3) Paasche (Given year weights)	(4) Fisher Ideal index	(5) Divisia index
Price indices					
1900	100.0	100.00	100.00	100.00	100.00
1901	117.5	113.75	114.74	116.11	116.12
1902	130.0	125.00	125.00	127.48	127.73
Quantity indices					
1900	100.0	100.00	100.00	100.00	100.00
1901	237.5	230.77	231.92	234.69	236.25
1902	400.0	384.62	384.62	392.23	394.06

An index with 1900 = 100 is formed by dividing the resulting aggregate cost for each year by the cost in the base year and multiplying by 100. The calculations are:

$$1900 \frac{(10 \times 1) + (15 \times 2)}{(10 \times 1) + (15 \times 2)} \times 100 = \frac{10 + 30}{10 + 30} \times 100 = \frac{40}{40} \times 100 = 100.0$$

$$1901 \frac{(11 \times 1) + (18 \times 2)}{(10 \times 1) + (15 \times 2)} \times 100 = \frac{11 + 36}{40} \times 100 = \frac{47}{40} \times 100 = 117.5$$

$$1902 \frac{(12 \times 1) + (20 \times 2)}{(10 \times 1) + (15 \times 2)} \times 100 = \frac{12 + 40}{40} \times 100 = \frac{52}{40} \times 100 = 130.0$$

In each case, the first term in the brackets is the price of the commodity; the second is the base-year quantity. It will be seen that this quantity (1 unit for cloth, 2 units for beer) does not change.

This is the index given in column (1) of table B.3. It has a very straight-forward interpretation: the cost of purchasing the 1900 basket of goods would be 17.5 per cent more at 1901 prices than it was at the actual prices prevailing in 1900, and it would be 30 per cent more at 1902 prices.

This aggregate method reveals most clearly the fundamental nature of an index number and should be carefully studied. However, it involves working with all the detail of the original prices and quantities, and in a real-life cal-culation there would of course be many more than two commodities.

It is usually simpler, therefore, to use a second method, in which the prices are first converted to price relatives with the fixed base year (in this case 1900) as 100. These relatives are then multiplied by an appropriate measure of the relative importance of the item to obtain a *weighted average of the price relatives*. For the present example the appropriate weights are the share of each product in total expenditure in the base year, as given by the data for 1900 in columns (3), (6), and (7) of table B.2.

In our example, the successive relatives are 100, 110, and 120 for cloth; 100, 120, and 133.33 for beer. Because the weights do not change in the Laspeyres index it is convenient to express them as a proportion, and then use these fixed proportions in the calculations for each year.[a] The 1900 proportion for cloth is thus $10/40 = 0.25$, and for beer it is $30/40 = 0.75$. The required index with $1900 = 100$ is then formed and the results obtained are identical to those given by the aggregate method:

$$1900 \quad (100 \times 0.25) + (100 \times 0.75) \quad = (25 + 75) \quad = 100.0$$

$$1901 \quad (110 \times 0.25) + (120 \times 0.75) \quad = (27.5 + 90) \quad = 117.5$$

$$1902 \quad (120 \times 0.25) + (133.33 \times 0.75) = (30 + 100) \quad = 130.0$$

The aggregate method and the weighted average of the price relatives appear to follow different routes but the underlying arithmetic operations are actually identical, and the two methods will always give the same result *provided that the year taken as 100 for the relatives is the same as the base year.* If it is not, the outcome is not an alternative measure of the change in prices, it is simply wrong. The way in which failure to observe this crucial condition will generate a meaningless result is demonstrated in the algebraic presentation in panel B.1.

With realistic data sets, the second method – using relatives – is generally easier to use, and is the method most commonly adopted for the construction of index numbers. Because the two methods give identical results, users of index numbers frequently refer to the shares in expenditure as though these were the true weights, but this is not correct. As is demonstrated in panel B.1, the true weights of the Laspeyres price index, regardless of whether it is compiled by the first or the second method, are the actual *quantities* in the base year.

This distinction matters for historians and other users of index numbers, because changes in expenditure shares reflect changes in both prices and quantities, whereas it is *only the changes in quantities* that are rel-

---

[a] Expressing the weights as proportions (rather than percentages) has the further advantage that the sum of the weights is 1, and it is thus unnecessary to divide the sum of the weighted relatives by the sum of the weights; compare (2.1a) in §2.2.2.

evant when analysing what effect different sets of weights might have on the movement in a price index.[b]

The appropriate quantities to use for the weights are determined by the nature of the price index. For example, for an index of farm prices it would be the quantities of the different farm products sold in the base year; for an index of the cost of living for pensioners it would be the quantities purchased by pensioners in the base year; for an index of share prices the number of shares issued by the company in the base year; and so on.

For index numbers, unlike relatives, the chosen base year is potentially a crucial determinant of the measurement. It is thus important that the year selected as the base for a price index should not be one in which the quantities were seriously distorted by wars, strikes, or other abnormal events. Indeed, it is quite common to base an index on an average of several years rather than a single year, in the expectation that this will minimize any distortions in the relative quantities.

However, even when the selection is confined to broadly 'normal' years, the results obtained with different base years may differ markedly because the relative quantities used as weights will change in response to the underlying economic processes.

B.4 The index number problem and chained indices

This possibility of obtaining different results with different base years brings us to the famous **index number problem**. When the increase in prices between 1900 and 1902 was measured using the Laspeyres formula with 1900 quantities as weights we found a rise in prices from 100 to 130, an increase of 30 per cent.

What happens if we repeat the calculation using 1902 quantities as weights? If we choose the second method, the price relatives for 1900 and 1901 must be recalculated *with 1902 = 100*. For 1900, they are 83.33 for cloth and 75 for beer; for 1901 they are 91.67 and 90. The respective 1902 expenditure shares are $120/200 = 0.6$ and $80/200 = 0.4$. The calculations are thus:

$$1900 \quad (83.33 \times 0.6) + (75 \times 0.4) \quad = (50 + 30) \quad = 80$$

$$1901 \quad (91.67 \times 0.6) + (90 \times 0.4) \quad = (55 + 36) \quad = 91$$

$$1902 \quad (100.0 \times 0.6) + (100 \times 0.4) \quad = (60 + 40) \quad = 100$$

[b] See, for example, the discussion of alternative weights in Charles H. Feinstein, 'Pessimism perpetuated, real wages and the standard of living in Britain during and after the industrial revolution', *Journal of Economic History*, 58, 1998, pp. 640–1.

Panel B.1   Laspeyres index numbers

The underlying structure of index numbers can be seen more clearly if we use some simple notation. Consider a bundle of commodities, such as those in table B.2, each of which has a price, P, and a quantity, Q. Subscripts (P_0, P_1, ...and Q_0, Q_1, ...) indicate the year to which the information relates. The value of the expenditure on any one commodity in year 0 at the prices of year 0 would be the product, P_0Q_0, and for the value of the expenditure on *all* commodities in that year we use the summation sign, Σ, and show this as ΣP_0Q_0.

What will a **Laspeyres price index** look like? If we take year 0 as base year, the *aggregate method* involves weighting the prices of each year (P_0, P_1, P_2 ...) by the quantities of the base year (Q_0). This is summed over all commodities. It is then expressed as an index – with year 0 as 100 – by dividing each year by ΣP_0Q_0 and multiplying by 100. This price index is set out in column (1) below. The corresponding **Laspeyres quantity index** is given in column (2).

Year	(1) Laspeyres price index	(2) Laspeyres quantity index
0	$\dfrac{\Sigma P_0Q_0}{\Sigma P_0Q_0} \times 100$	$\dfrac{\Sigma P_0Q_0}{\Sigma P_0Q_0} \times 100$
1	$\dfrac{\Sigma P_1Q_0}{\Sigma P_0Q_0} \times 100$	$\dfrac{\Sigma P_0Q_1}{\Sigma P_0Q_0} \times 100$
2	$\dfrac{\Sigma P_2Q_0}{\Sigma P_0Q_0} \times 100$	$\dfrac{\Sigma P_0Q_2}{\Sigma P_0Q_0} \times 100$

By running one's eye down the left-hand side of the successive formulae in column (1) it can be seen that for each year the prices of that year are being compared with prices in the base year, always using the quantities of the base year as weights. Similarly, on the right-hand side of the quantity index in column (2), the quantities for each year are being compared with quantities in the base year, using the prices of the base year as fixed weights.

The second method of constructing the same price index involves *weighting the price relatives* for each commodity by the base year share of that commodity in total expenditure. For example, for the price indices in years 1 and 2 (year $0 = 100$) this would be

$$\frac{\Sigma\left(\dfrac{P_1}{P_0}\right)P_0Q_0}{\Sigma P_0Q_0} \times 100 \quad \text{and} \quad \frac{\Sigma\left(\dfrac{P_2}{P_0}\right)P_0Q_0}{\Sigma P_0Q_0} \times 100$$

Since the P_0 in the denominator of the price relative for each separate commodity would cancel out with the P_0 in the expenditure share for that commodity, this will give a formula identical to the one in column (2) above. Similarly, in the corresponding formula for a quantity relative, the Q_0 in the denominator of the relative would cancel out with the Q_0 in the expenditure share, leaving exactly the same formula as the one in column (2) above.

The formula for the use of relatives demonstrates two important points about index numbers. First, the fact that the formula for the second method reduces in this way to the one used for the first method shows that the weights for the index *are actually the base year quantities*, and are *not* the base year expenditure shares. Secondly, it is easy to see that if the year taken as 100 for the relatives is *not* the same as the base year, then the terms would not cancel out in the formula above, and the result would be a meaningless expression.

For example, if the index is calculated using year 0 expenditure shares while the relatives have year 2 as 100, the result for year 1 would be

$$\frac{\Sigma\left(\dfrac{P_1}{P_2}\right)P_0Q_0}{\Sigma P_0Q_0} \times 100$$

$$= \frac{\Sigma\dfrac{P_1P_0Q_0}{P_2}}{\Sigma P_0Q_0} \times 100$$

and it would be impossible to give this a sensible interpretation.

This index has $1902 = 100$. In order to make it more easily comparable with the previous index calculated with 1900 weights it is helpful to express these results relative to 1900. If 1900 is scaled up from 80 to 100, then 1901 increases proportionately from 91 to 113.75, and 1902 from 100 to 125 (as in column (2) of table B.3). Note that this scaling procedure changes the reference year to 1900 but the *base year is not affected* by this: it remains

1902. We thus find that with 1902 weights the change in prices between 1900 and 1902 is not a rise of 30 per cent, but of only 25 per cent.

The fact that the increase in prices in our simple example is *greater* with 1900 weights than with 1902 weights is not accidental. The data used for our simple two-good economy exhibit one of the fundamental characteristics of a market economy: an inverse relationship between relative movements in prices and quantities. Cotton cloth shows a smaller increase in price than beer, and a larger increase in output. Inverse relationships of this type are an essential feature of index numbers, and one of which historians should always be acutely aware.

They are driven by powerful forces on both the supply and the demand sides of the economy. On the demand side, consumers generally tend to switch their consumption in favour of those goods that are becoming relatively cheaper. On the supply side, it is usually the case that the greater the output, the lower the cost, and so products with the largest expansion in output tend to have the smallest increase in price (the process known to economists as economies of scale). However the process is initiated, these two forces interact cumulatively: greater demand stimulates increased output, and higher output reduces prices and increases demand.

For any economy that experiences this process, a price index constructed with a base year *early* in the period under review will always show a greater increase in prices than one constructed with a *late* base year. This occurs because the early-year index gives a relatively larger weight to those products that show a relatively large increase in prices.

By contrast, by the end of the period, the production of those relatively more expensive goods will have declined in relative importance, and the quantity weights attached to them will be correspondingly lower than they were at the beginning of the period. In our simple example 2 units of beer were consumed for every 1 unit of cloth in 1900, but by 1902 the ratio was only 0.4 units of beer for every unit of cloth.

Exactly the same tendency applies to quantity indices. A quantity index constructed with a base year *early* in the period will always show a greater increase in quantities than one constructed with a base year *late* in the period. The more rapid the rate of structural change in an economy, the more important this phenomenon will be.

One of the most striking historical examples of this effect occurred in the period of exceptionally rapid economic change in the USSR between 1928 and 1937. At the beginning of this period the economy had relatively few machines and other capital goods, and consequently their price was relatively very high. By the end of the period of Stalin's programme of forced industrialization and collectivization, it was food and consumer goods that were scarce and expensive relative to machinery.[2] As a result of this structural shift there were marked discrepancies in the results according to whether index numbers of output used early or late years for their weights, and similarly for prices.

For example, a Laspeyres index of industrial production with early-year weights gave a relatively high weight to the initially relatively expensive – but fast-growing – machinery, and a low weight to the initially relatively cheap – but slow-growing – consumer goods. Conversely, late-year weights were relatively low for the machinery and relatively high for the consumer goods. One of the most reliable estimates of the GNP of the USSR for 1928 and 1937 showed an increase of 175 per cent when measured at the prices of 1928, compared to only 62 per cent when 1937 was taken as the base year.[3]

Given the possibility of more than one answer, what should the historian do in practice? In statistical terms, both early-year and late-year answers are *equally valid* and there is no justification for choosing one rather than the other.[4] Furthermore, the fact of a marked divergence between the early-year and late-year measures is a valuable signal to the historian that there has been significant structural change. Notwithstanding this, it may be desirable for some purposes to have a single measure of the change in prices or quantities, and there are a number of possible ways in which this can be accomplished.

Fisher Ideal and Divisia indices
One procedure that can be adopted in cases where the early-year and late-year indices show markedly different results, is to calculate what is known as the **Fisher Ideal** index. This is simply a geometric mean (see §2.2.1) of the results derived from the two alternative indices. For example, for the two price indices calculated with the data of table B.2, the Fisher Ideal price index would be 116.110 for 1901 and 127.475 for 1902.

This index also has a number of attractive statistical and theoretical properties. One of the former is that the product of a Fisher price index and the corresponding Fisher quantity index is exactly equal to the index of the value of total expenditure. The change in value can thus be perfectly decomposed into these two measures of price and quantity change.

Another procedure sometimes recommended is a **Divisia** index. Unlike the other indices we have considered, the Divisia is based on the *growth* of prices (or quantities) calculated over intervals as short as possible – with historical data this is usually a year.[5] The growth of each item in the index is calculated as the difference of the logs, and this difference is then weighted by the arithmetic average of its share in total expenditure at the beginning and at the end of each period over which growth is calculated. The growth of the index is then obtained as the exponential of this weighted average, and the series can then be reassembled as an index by starting at 100 and multiplying by the successive exponentials of the weighted averages.

The procedure may seem somewhat complicated, and we can illustrate it with a Divisia price index based on our simple example. From 1900 to 1901 the growth in prices is $(\log 11 - \log 10) = (2.3979 - 2.3026) = 0.0953$ for cloth, and $(\log 18 - \log 15) = (2.8904 - 2.7081) = 0.1823$ for beer.

The arithmetic mean of the weights for the beginning and end of this year are $0.5 \times (10/40 + 55/109) = 0.3773$ for cloth and $0.5 \times (30/40 + 54/109) = 0.6227$ for beer. So the weighted average growth for this year is $(0.3773 \times 0.0953) + (0.6227 \times 0.1823) = 0.1495$. The exponential of this is 1.16125, or a rate of growth of 16.125 per cent.

The corresponding calculation for the growth rate from 1901 to 1902 would be $(0.5523 \times 0.0870) + (0.4477 \times 0.1054) = 0.0952$ and the exponential of this is 1.0999, or a growth rate of 9.99 per cent.

Taking 1900 as 100, the Divisia price index would thus show an increase of 16.125 per cent on 100 to equal 116.12 for 1901; and a further increase of 9.99 per cent on this, to reach 127.73 for 1902. This gives an index (see column (5) of table B.3) that is fractionally higher in each year (relative to 1900) than the corresponding Fisher Ideal index. As can be seen from columns (1) and (2) of table B.3, it also falls between the indices with early-year and late-year weights.[c] For the corresponding quantity indices, given in the lower panel of table B.3, the differences are marginally larger (because the growth of the quantities is more rapid than the growth of the prices) but the overall pattern relative to the other indices is the same.

The Divisia indices should also provide a perfect decomposition of the change in value into changes in price and in quantity, but because growth is calculated over discrete intervals (rather than continuously), the decomposition is not exact.

Chained indices

The second way of dealing with the index number problem is to construct a **chained index** which links (or splices) a succession of shorter price indices in order to cover a longer span of time than would be appropriate with a single base year. These successive indices form a single continuous series, with a single reference year but a number of underlying base years. The actual procedure for doing this is usually no more than an arithmetic adjustment based on one or more overlapping years. In this way the new

---

[c] For the use of Fisher Ideal and Divisia indices with historical data, see N. F. R. Crafts, *British Economic Growth during the Industrial Revolution*, Cambridge University Press, 1985, p. 26.

Table B.4 Chained index numbers with changes in the reference year (imaginary data)

	(1) First subindex (1900 = 100)	(2) Second subindex (1902 = 100)	(3) Chained index (1900 = 100)	(4) Same index with a new reference year (1905 = 100)
1900	100		100	20
1901	150		150	30
1902	250	100	250	50
1903		120	300	60
1904		160	400	80
1905		200	500	100

subindex is brought up to the same level as the old subindex over those years, and the subsequent years are scaled proportionately, as illustrated in column (3) of table B.4.

There are two main reasons for adopting this procedure. The first is that over time it usually becomes impossible to continue the components of a single index. Some goods either cease to be produced (horse carriages) or their quality changes so radically (computers) that those in the market at the end of the period are no longer comparable with those produced at the beginning. It is then simply not possible to find market prices in the year 2000 which could be used to value directly either a carriage of the type constructed in 1800, or a computer of the type produced in 1950.

The second is that even when this extreme situation does not arise, a chained index provides a means of circumventing the index number problem by constantly revising the base year so that the quantities used are always up to date and thus fully relevant as weights for the constituent prices.[d] Each subindex is thus appropriate to its specific time period, and the gap between the early-year and late-year weights is too short to matter. For contemporary index numbers generated by official agencies this is now standard practice. Researchers working with historical series may not be

---

[d] The Divisia index can be interpreted as a chained index which is rebased in every time period; in our example every year.

able to do this if the data required are not available, but the chaining procedure should be considered whenever possible.[e]

It is worth repeating that the year shown as 100 in a chained index will
not be the base year except for – at most – one of the subperiods. All other
subperiods in the index will have their own base year. Since, as we have
already demonstrated, the actual base year can have a substantial impact on
any measurement derived from index numbers, it is highly desirable to
identify the true base year in any long-run historical series.

The way in which chaining can conceal the true base year is illustrated
by the example given in table B.4. One imaginary index is given in column
(1) for 1900–2 with 1900 as the base year, and a second in column (2) for
1902–5 with 1902 as base year. The two indices could then be spliced in
1902 as shown in column (3). The resulting spliced index is then converted
in column (4) to an index with 1905 as the reference year.

This final procedure has not altered the pattern of price change in any
way, but it has effectively suppressed the actual base year. The good historian should always take pains to uncover the truth, so that her evaluation of
the change in the indices is not distorted by misunderstanding of the true
base year used to weight the index.

B.5 Paasche index numbers with changing (given year) weights

The **Paasche** type of index number follows the same underlying principles
as the Laspeyres index, but instead of using the *fixed* quantities of a single
base year to weight the component prices it uses the *changing* quantities of
successive years. Thus each successive year in a time series (also referred to
as the **given year**) is compared with the selected reference year. So if 1900 is
chosen as the reference year for the data set of table B.2, the first item in the
Paasche index compares 1901 prices with 1900 prices, using 1901 quantities as the weights. The next item compares 1902 prices with 1900 prices,
using 1902 quantities as the weights, and so on.

If we use the aggregate method to make the calculation, we have first the
comparison of 1900 and 1901 *with 1901 weights*

$$1900 \frac{(10 \times 5) + (15 \times 3)}{(11 \times 5) + (18 \times 3)} \times 100 = \frac{50 + 45}{55 + 54} \times 100 = \frac{95}{109} \times 100 = 87.15$$

[e] For an example of such linking for a nineteenth-century series see Charles H. Feinstein,
'Pessimism perpetuated, real wages and the standard of living in Britain during and after the
Industrial Revolution', *Journal of Economic History*, 58, 1998, p. 634; and for linking of constituent series over a much longer period, Henry Phelps Brown and Sheila V. Hopkins, *A Perspective
of Wages and Prices*, Methuen, 1981, p. 40.

and then the comparison of 1900 and 1902 *with 1902 weights*

$$1900\,\frac{(10\times10)+(15\times4)}{(12\times10)+(20\times4)}\times100=\frac{100+60}{120+80}\times100=\frac{160}{200}\times100=80.00$$

Compared to the corresponding Laspeyres calculation in §B.3, the first term in the brackets is still the price of the commodity in the current year, but the second term for the quantity weights is no longer fixed: it changes from year to year. As result, we have two separate comparisons, one with 1901 as 100 and as base year, the second with 1902 as 100 and as base year.

The interpretation is again straightforward. The basket of goods purchased in 1901 would have cost 12.85 per cent less if it had been purchased at the prices prevailing in 1900. The basket of goods purchased in 1902 would have cost 20 per cent less if it had been purchased at 1900 prices.

In order to obtain a single continuous index we can select 1900 as the reference year (though it is not the base year) and then invert the previous results. This says, in effect, if 1900 is 87.15 when 1901 = 100, then if 1900 is raised to 100, 1901 becomes 114.74. Similarly, if 1900 is 80 when 1902 = 100, then if 1900 is raised to 100, 1902 becomes 125. This result is shown as column (3) of table B.3.

Alternatively, exactly the same result can be obtained by multiplying the price relatives by the expenditure shares of the given year. The first step is to calculate the required proportions and relatives. When 1901 is the given year, the respective shares of cotton cloth and beer are 55/109 = 0.5046 and 54/109 = 0.4954. It is again essential that the *reference year for the relatives must be the same as the base year*. As demonstrated in panel B.2, if this rule is not observed the result is completely meaningless. When 1901 is the given year, the price relatives are thus 10/11 × 100 = 90.91 for cloth and 15/18 × 100 = 83.33 for beer.

Secondly, as we have already seen with the aggregate method, the initial form of the Paasche index is not a single continuous index but a succession of binary comparisons. Thus if we simply take the first step of calculating a weighted average of the price relatives as given above – in the same way as we did for the Laspeyres index in §B.3 – the results we would get for 1900 and 1901 with 1901 = 100 are

$$1900\;(90.91\times0.5046)+\;(83.33\times0.4954)=(45.87+41.28)=\;87.15$$

$$1901\,(100.0\times0.5046)+(100.0\times0.4954)=(50.46+49.54)=100.0$$

In order to convert this into an index with 1900 = 100 it is again necessary to invert these results, raising 87.15 to 100 and 100 to 114.74. This is equivalent to taking *the reciprocal of the weighted average of the price*

Panel B.2 Paasche index numbers

The formula for the **Paasche price index** is set out in column (1) below, with year 0 taken as the reference year $= 100$. The corresponding **Paasche quantity index** is given in column (2).

Year	(1) Paasche price index	(2) Paasche quantity index
0	$\dfrac{\Sigma P_0 Q_0}{\Sigma P_0 Q_0} \times 100$	$\dfrac{\Sigma P_0 Q_0}{\Sigma P_0 Q_0} \times 100$
1	$\dfrac{\Sigma P_1 Q_1}{\Sigma P_0 Q_1} \times 100$	$\dfrac{\Sigma P_1 Q_1}{\Sigma P_1 Q_0} \times 100$
2	$\dfrac{\Sigma P_2 Q_2}{\Sigma P_0 Q_2} \times 100$	$\dfrac{\Sigma P_2 Q_2}{\Sigma P_2 Q_0} \times 100$

Running one's eye down the successive Paasche formula shows how for this index the weights change every year. Thus for each year in the price index the prices of that year are compared with the reference year prices, using the quantities of the given year as weights: Q_1 for year 1, Q_2 for year 2, and so on.

An important feature of the Paasche indices is that, strictly speaking, each given year should only be compared directly with the reference year. If, instead, a Paasche index is used to measure the change in prices between years 1 and 2 what we actually have is

$$\frac{\Sigma P_2 Q_2}{\Sigma P_0 Q_2} \div \frac{\Sigma P_1 Q_1}{\Sigma P_0 Q_1} \times 100 = \frac{\Sigma P_2 Q_2}{\Sigma P_0 Q_2} \times \frac{\Sigma P_0 Q_1}{\Sigma P_1 Q_1} \times 100$$

In our numerical example this corresponds to $125/114.74 = 108.94$ (see column (3) of table B.3). This change between years 1 and 2 is thus measured as the product of the change from year 2 to year 0 measured with year 2 weights, and the change from year 0 to year 1 measured with year 1 weights. Apart from its complexity this is awkward because the measured change is a combination of the 'pure' change in prices and the change in weights from year 2 quantities to year 1 quantities, and may be distorted by the latter.

The alternative method of calculating a Paasche price index is to take the reciprocal of the price relatives multiplied by the given year expenditure shares. For example, for the index for year 1 this would be

$$\left[1/\frac{\Sigma\left(\dfrac{P_0}{P_1}\right)P_1Q_1}{\Sigma P_1Q_1} \right] \times 100$$

As long as the prices are expressed relative to the given year, the P_1s in the denominator of the relative and the numerator of the expenditure share will cancel out to give

$$\left[1/\frac{\Sigma P_0Q_1}{\Sigma P_1Q_1} \right] \times 100$$

and when this is inverted the formula is identical to the one for year 1 in column (1) above.

Students (and others) often omit these two critical elements in the procedure for a Paasche index based on relatives. If the reciprocal is omitted, the index measures the prices of year 0 relative to those of year 1, instead of the reverse. If the price relative is not recalculated every year to have the given year as 100 the result is quite meaningless. For example, if the price relative for year 1 had been taken with year 0 as 100 the calculation would be

$$1/\frac{\Sigma\left(\dfrac{P_1}{P_0}\right)P_1Q_1}{\Sigma P_1Q_1}$$

$$=\frac{\Sigma P_1Q_1}{\dfrac{P_1{}^2Q_1}{P_0}}$$

a complex expression for which there is no intelligible interpretation.

It is because of possible pitfalls of this type that it is so important to think of index numbers in terms of a notation such as the one adopted in this panel. It is always possible to make an arithmetic calculation which looks correct on the surface, but it is only by scrutiny of its underlying structure that one can decide whether or not the index is sensible.

relatives and then multiplying by 100, and this is the form in which a Paasche index is often calculated. (It is presented in this form in panel B.2.)

We can go directly to this version of the procedure to calculate the index for 1902 with 1900 as the reference year. When 1902 is the given year, the respective shares in expenditure are $120/200 = 0.6$ and $80/200 = 0.4$, and the price relatives (now with 1902 as 100) are $10/12 \times 100 = 83.33$ for cloth, and $15/20 \times 100 = 75$ for beer. The full calculation is thus

$$[(1 \times 100)/(83.33 \times 0.6 + 75 \times 0.4)] \times 100 = [100/(0.50 + 0.30)] \times 100 = 125$$

This is an essential but rather convoluted procedure, and Paasche indices can be derived by an indirect route; indeed this is sometimes done without the researcher realizing that what he has calculated is in fact a Paasche index. The indirect route exploits the fact that the change in any series at current values is made up of a combination of either a change in a Laspeyres quantity index and a Paasche price index, or a change in a Laspeyres price index and a Paasche quantity index.

Thus, for example, if the current value series represented by the expenditure series in column (7) of table B.2 is expressed as an index with 1900 = 100, and then divided by the Laspeyres quantity index with 1900 weights (as in column (4) of table B.3), the result will be the Paasche price index exactly as calculated above for column (3) of that table.

There are thus three combinations of price and quantity indices by which we can obtain an exact decomposition of an increase in total expenditure. For our two-commodity example, the various possibilities for the fivefold increase between 1900 and 1902 are

- a Paasche price index (125) and a Laspeyres quantity index (400)
- a Laspeyres price index (130) and a Paasche quantity index (384.62)
- a Fisher Ideal price index (127.47) and a Fisher Ideal quantity index (392.23)

On the basis of the first of these decompositions one could say, therefore, that the increase in the value of total expenditure from 100 to 500 consisted of an increase in prices of 25 per cent and an increase in quantities (a rise 'in real terms') of 300 per cent. The fact that the other two methods would give a different partitioning between price and quantity is simply another manifestation of the index number problem.

Finally, it should be noted that in the perspective of a comparison of 1900 and 1902, the calculation of the Paasche price index for 1902 (with 1902 quantities as weights) is identically equal at 125 to the result that would be obtained using a Laspeyres price index with 1902 as the base year, because the latter also has 1902 quantities as weights. This can be seen in the figures for 1902 in the upper panel of table B.3 (and for the corresponding quantity indices in the lower panel, for which both are equal to 384.62).

For this reason the index number problem discussed in §B.4 is sometimes presented as the difference between a Laspeyres and a Paasche measure, but this arbitrarily assumes that the base of the former is an early year and the base of the latter a late year, neither of which is necessarily correct.

Notes

[1] The product of the prices and quantities might also be interpreted as the value of the output of beer and cloth produced. However, the measure of output relevant for the construction of a quantity index of output, such as an index of industrial production, would be the **value added,** i.e. for each constituent industry, the difference between the value at which its products are sold and the value of the raw materials, fuel, and other inputs which it purchased. The corresponding 'value added prices' are thus not the same as the prices at which the goods were purchased by consumers. The prices in table B.2 are assumed to be consumer prices and so we refer to the series in columns (3), (6), and (7) as the value of expenditure. It is measured at 'current prices', i.e. at the prices prevailing in each year.

[2] For a very clear and full discussion of these issues see Abram Bergson, *The Real National Income of Soviet Russia since 1928,* Harvard University Press, 1961, pp. 25–41; and Janet G. Chapman, *Trends in Consumption in the Soviet Union,* Rand Corporation, 1964, pp. 27–44.

[3] Bergson, *Real National Income,* p. 217. For illustrations of a substantial index number problem in relation to measures of industrial production in the United Kingdom between 1924 and 1948 and in the United States between 1909 and 1937, see W. E. G. Salter, *Productivity and Technical Change,* Cambridge University Press, 1960, pp. 151–2, 170.

[4] There are, however, substantial differences in the underlying *economic* interpretation of the alternative index number formulae. For an introduction to these principles see Robin Marris, *Economic Arithmetic,* Macmillan, 1958, pp. 227–83 or Dan Usher, *The Measurement of Economic Growth,* Basil Blackwell, 1980, pp. 12–64. The economic principles are discussed briefly in an historical context in N. F. R. Crafts, *British Economic Growth during the Industrial Revolution,* Cambridge University Press, 1985, pp. 25–8.

[5] The form of this index used for empirical work is an approximation to a theoretical version which cannot be applied in practice because it treats time as a continuous variable, whereas empirical work can be undertaken only with discrete periods of time such as a month or a year.

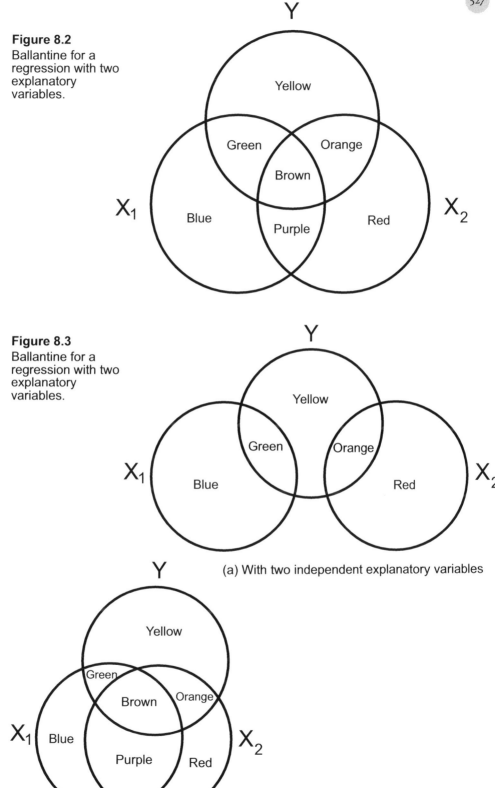

Figure 8.2
Ballantine for a regression with two explanatory variables.

Y

Yellow

Green   Orange

Brown

X₁   Blue   Purple   Red   X₂

Figure 8.3
Ballantine for a regression with two explanatory variables.

Y

Yellow

Green   Orange

X₁   Blue   Red   X₂

(a) With two independent explanatory variables

Y

Yellow

Green

Brown   Orange

X₁   Blue

Purple   Red   X₂

(b) With two explanatory variables which are not independent

Figure 11.2
Omitted and
redundant variables.

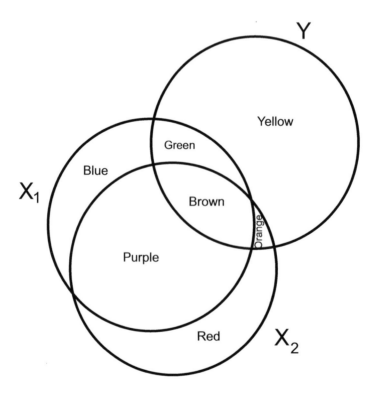

(a) Ballantine to show the effect of a missing variable

(b) Ballantine to show the effect of a redundant variable

Bibliography

Ackerberg, Daniel A. and Maristella Botticini, 'The choice of agrarian contracts in early Renaissance Tuscany: risk sharing, moral hazard, or capital market imperfections?, *Explorations in Economic History*, 37, 2000, pp. 241–57

Alesina, Alberto, Nouriel Roubini and Gerald D. Cohen, *Political Cycles and the Macroeconomy*, MIT Press, 1997

Alt, James E., *The Politics of Economic Decline*, Cambridge University Press, 1979

Anderson, Michael, *Family Structure in Nineteenth Century Lancashire*, Cambridge University Press, 1971

Armstrong, Alan, *Stability and Change in an English County Town, A Social Study of York, 1801–51*, Cambridge University Press, 1974

Ashton, T. S., *Economic Fluctuations in England, 1700–1800*, Oxford University Press, 1959

Atack, Jeremy, 'Economies of scale and efficiency gains in the rise of the factory in America, 1820–1900', in Peter Kilby (ed.), *From Quantity to Quiddity*, Wesleyan University Press, 1987, pp. 286–335

Baines, Dudley, 'European emigration, 1815–1930: looking at the emigration decision again', *Economic History Review*, 47, 1994, pp. 525–44

Beattie, J. M., *Crime and the Courts in England, 1660–1800*, Oxford University Press, 1986

Beck, E. M. and Stewart E. Tolnay, 'The killing fields of the deep South, the market for cotton and the lynching of blacks, 1882–1930', *American Sociological Review*, 55, 1990, pp. 526–39

Benjamin, Daniel K. and Levis A. Kochin, 'Searching for an explanation for unemployment in interwar Britain', *Journal of Political Economy*, 87, 1979, pp. 441–78

'Unemployment and unemployment benefits in twentieth-century Britain: a reply to our critics', *Journal of Political Economy*, 90, 1982, pp. 410–36

Bergson, Abram, *The Real National Income of Soviet Russia since 1928*, Harvard University Press, 1961

Blalock, H. M., *Social Statistics*, 2nd edn., McGraw-Hill, 1979

Blaug, Mark, 'The myth of the old poor law and the making of the new', *Journal of Economic History*, 23, 1963, pp. 151–84

Bloom, Howard S. and H. Douglas Price, 'Voter response to short-run economic conditions: the asymmetric effect of prosperity and recession', *American Political Science Review*, 69, 1975, pp. 1240–54

Bogue, Allan C., 'Some dimensions of power in the thirty-seventh senate', in William O. Aydelotte, Allan C. Bogue and Robert W. Fogel (eds.), *The Dimensions of Quantitative Research in History*, Oxford University Press, 1972

Bowden, Sue and Avner Offer, 'Household appliances and the use of time: the United States and Britain since the 1920s', *Economic History Review*, 47, 1994, pp. 725–48

Bowden, Sue and Paul Turner, 'The demand for consumer durables in the United Kingdom in the interwar period', *Journal of Economic History*, 53, 1993, pp. 244–58

Boyer, George, R., *An Economic History of the English Poor Law*, Cambridge University Press, 1990

'The influence of London on labor markets in southern England, 1830–1914', *Social Science History*, 22, 1998, pp. 257–85

Broadberry, Stephen N. and N. F. R. Crafts, 'Britain's productivity gap in the 1930s: some neglected factors', *Journal of Economic History*, 52, 1992, pp. 531–58

Burns, Arthur F. and W. C. Mitchell, *Measuring Business Cycles*, NBER, 1947

Burns, Eveline, *British Unemployment Programs, 1920–1938*, Social Science Research Council, 1941

Callahan, Colleen M., Judith A. McDonald and Anthony Patrick O'Brien, 'Who voted for Smoot–Hawley?', *Journal of Economic History*, 54, 1994, pp. 683–90

Cantor, D. and K. C. Land, 'Unemployment and crime rates in the post-World War II United States: a theoretical and empirical analysis', *American Sociological Review*, 44, 1979, pp. 588–608

Caradog Jones, D. (ed.), *The Social Survey of Merseyside*, 3, Liverpool University Press, 1934

Census of Population of England and Wales, 1831, *Parliamentary Papers, 1833* (H.C. 149), XXXVI–XXXVIII

Chapman, Agatha L., *Wages and Salaries in the United Kingdom, 1920–1938*, Cambridge University Press, 1953

Chapman, Janet G., *Trends in Consumption in the Soviet Union*, Rand Corporation, 1964

Cochran, W. G., *Sampling Techniques*, 3rd edn., Wiley & Sons, 1977

Cockburn, J. S., 'Patterns of violence in English society: homicide in Kent, 1560–1985', *Past and Present*, 130, 1991, pp. 70–106

Cohen, Jacob and Patricia Cohen, *Applied Multiple Regression/Correlation Analysis for the Behavioral Sciences*, Lawrence Erlbaum Associates, 1975

Collins, Michael, 'Unemployment in interwar Britain: still searching for an explanation', *Journal of Political Economy*, 90, 1982, pp. 369–79

Costa, Dora L., *The Evolution of Retirement*, University of Chicago Press, 1998

Crafts, N. F. R., *British Economic Growth during the Industrial Revolution*, Cambridge University Press, 1985

Crockett, Alasdair, 'Variations in churchgoing rates in England in 1851: supply-side deficiency or demand-led decline?', in Alasdair Crockett and Richard O'Leary (eds.), *Religion in Modernity: Patterns and Processes in Europe and America*, Cambridge University Press, forthcoming

David, Paul A. and Peter Solar, 'A bicentenary contribution to the history of the cost of living in America', *Research in Economic History*, 2, 1977, pp. 1–80

Deane, Phyllis and W. A. Cole, *British Economic Growth 1688–1959*, Cambridge University Press, 1962

Di Matteo, Livio, 'Wealth accumulation and the life-cycle in economic history: implications of alternative approaches to data', *Explorations in Economic History*, 35, 1998, pp. 296–324

Digby, Anne, *Pauper Palaces*, Routledge & Kegan Paul, 1978
  Madness, Morality and Medicine, A Study of the York Retreat, 1796–1914, Cambridge University Press, 1985

Dimsdale, Nicholas H. and Nicholas Horsewood, 'Fiscal policy and employment in interwar Britain; some evidence from a new model', *Oxford Economic Papers*, 47, 1995, pp. 369–96

Dimsdale, Nicholas H., S. Nickell and N. J. Horsewood, 'Real wages and unemployment in Britain during the 1930s', *Economic Journal*, 99, June 1989, pp. 271–92

Edelstein, Michael, *Overseas Investment in the Age of High Imperialism*, Columbia University Press, 1982

Eichengreen, Barry, 'Unemployment in interwar Britain: dole or doldrums?', in N. F. R. Crafts, N. H. Dimsdale and S. Engerman (eds.), *Quantitative Economic History*, Oxford University Press, 1991, pp.1–27

Eichengreen, Barry and Henry A. Gemery, 'The earnings of skilled and unskilled immigrants at the end of the nineteenth century', *Journal of Economic History*, 46, 1986, pp. 441–54

Erikson, Robert S., 'Economic conditions and the Congressional vote: a review of the macrolevel evidence', *American Journal of Political Science*, 34, 1990, pp. 373–99

Feinstein, Charles H., *National Income, Expenditure and Output of the United Kingdom, 1855–1965*, Cambridge University Press, 1972

    'Pessimism perpetuated, real wages and the standard of living in Britain during and after the industrial revolution', *Journal of Economic History*, 58, 1998, pp. 640–1

Ferenczi, Imre and Walter F. Willcox, *International Migrations: vol I, Statistics*, NBER, 1929

Field, Simon, *Trends in Crime and their Interpretation: A Study of Recorded Crime in England and Wales*, HMSO, 1990

Fogel, Robert W., 'The specification problem in economic history', *Journal of Economic History*, 27, 1967, pp. 283–308

Ford, A. G., *The Gold Standard 1880–1914, Britain and Argentina*, Oxford University Press, 1962

Foreman-Peck, James and Robert Millward, *Public and Private Ownership of British Industry 1820–1990*, Oxford University Press, 1994

Frickey, Edwin, *Production in the United States 1860–1914*, Harvard University Press, 1947

Galenson, David, *White Servitude in Colonial America*, Cambridge University Press, 1981

Gattrell, V. A. C. and T. B. Hadden, 'Criminal statistics and their interpretation', in E. A. Wrigley (ed.), *Nineteenth-Century Society, Essays in the Use of Quantitative Methods for the Study of Social Data*, Cambridge University Press, 1972, pp. 363–96

Gayer, A. D., W. W. Rostow and A. J. Schwartz, *The Growth and Fluctuation of the British Economy, 1790–1850*, Oxford University Press, 1953

Gillis, A. R., 'Crime and state surveillance in nineteenth-century France', *American Journal of Sociology*, 95, 1989, pp. 307–41

Goldin, Claudia, *Understanding the Gender Gap. An Economic History of American Women*, Oxford University Press, 1990

Gould, J. D., 'European inter-continental emigration, 1815–1914: patterns and causes', *Journal of European Economic History*, 8, 1979, pp. 593–679

    'European inter-continental emigration: the role of diffusion and feedback', *Journal of European Economic History*, 8, 1980, pp. 267–315

Granger, C. W. J. and C. M. Elliott, 'A fresh look at wheat prices and markets in the eighteenth century', *Economic History Review*, 20, 1967, pp. 257–65

Griliches, Zvi, 'Hybrid corn: an exploration in the economics of technical change', *Econometrica*, 25, 1957, pp. 501–22

H. M. Commissioners for Inquiry into the Administration and Practical Operation of the Poor Laws, *Report, Appendix B1, Answers to Rural Questions* (H.C.44), *Parliamentary Papers*, 1834, XXX–XXXIII

Haines, Michael R., *Fertility and Occupation: Population Patterns in Industrialization*, Academic Press, 1979

Hamilton, Gillian, 'The market for Montreal apprentices: contract length and information', *Explorations in Economic History*, 33, 1996, pp. 496–523

Hanes, Christopher, 'Immigrants' relative rate of wage growth in the late 19th century', *Explorations in Economic History*, 33, 1996, pp. 35–64

Harrison, Mark, *Crowds and History, Mass Phenomena in English Towns, 1790–1835*, Cambridge University Press, 1988

Hatton, Timothy J., 'Unemployment benefits and the macroeconomics of the interwar labour market', *Oxford Economic Papers*, 35 (Supplement), 1983, pp. 486–505

'A quarterly model of the labour market in interwar Britain', *Oxford Bulletin of Economics and Statistics*, 50, February 1988, pp. 1–25

'A model of UK emigration, 1870–1913', *Review of Economics and Statistics*, 77, 1995, pp. 407–15

'The immigration assimilation puzzle in late nineteenth-century America', *Journal of Economic History*, 57, 1997, pp. 34–63

Hatton, Timothy J. and Jeffrey G. Williamson, 'After the famine: emigration from Ireland, 1850–1913', *Journal of Economic History*, 53, 1993, pp. 575–600

(eds.), *Migration and the International Labour Market, 1850–1939*, Routledge, 1994

Hay, Douglas, 'War, dearth and theft in the eighteenth century', *Past and Present*, 95, 1982, pp. 117–60

Hoffmann, Walther G., *British Industry, 1700–1950*, Basil Blackwell, 1955

Hoppit, Julian, *Risk and Failure in English Business, 1700–1800*, Cambridge University Press, 1987

Horrell, Sara and Jane Humphries, '"The exploitation of little children": child labor and the family economy in the industrial revolution', *Explorations in Economic History*, 32, 1995, pp. 485–516

Hoskins, W. G., 'Harvest fluctuations and English economic history, 1480–1619', *Agricultural History Review*, 12, 1964, pp. 28–46

'Harvest fluctuations and English economic history, 1620–1759', *Agricultural History Review*, 16, 1968, pp. 15–31

Huzel, J. P., 'Malthus, the poor law, and population in early nineteenth century England', *Economic History Review*, 22, 1969, pp. 430–52

'The demographic impact of the old poor law: more reflexions on Malthus', *Economic History Review,* 33, 1980, pp. 367–81

Isaac, Larry W. and Larry J. Griffin, 'Ahistoricism in time-series analysis of historical process: critique, redirection and illustrations from US labor history', *American Sociological Review,* 54, 1989, pp. 873–90

Jackson, Robert V., 'Rates of industrial growth during the industrial revolution', *Economic History Review,* 45, 1992, pp. 1–23

James, John A., 'Structural change in American manufacturing, 1850–1890', *Journal of Economic History,* 43, 1983, pp. 433–59

Jarausch, Konrad H. and Gerhard Arminger, 'The German teaching profession and Nazi party membership: a demographic logit model', *Journal of Interdisciplinary History,* 20 (Autumn 1989), pp. 197–225

John, A. H., 'The course of agricultural change, 1660–1760', in L. Pressnell (ed.), *Studies in the Industrial Revolution,* University of London, 1960, p. 136

Kaelble, Hartmut and Mark Thomas, 'Introduction', in Y. S. Brenner, H. Kaelble and M. Thomas (eds.), *Income Distribution in Historical Perspective,* Cambridge University Press, 1991, pp. 1–56

Kearl, J. R., Clayne L. Pope, and Larry T. Wimmer, 'Household wealth in a settlement economy: Utah, 1850–1870', *Journal of Economic History,* 40, 1980, pp. 477–96

Kennedy, Peter E., 'The "Ballentine": a graphical aid for econometrics', *Australian Economic Papers,* 20, 1981, pp. 414–16

A Guide to Econometrics, 3rd edn., Blackwell, 1992

Knight, I. and J. Eldridge, *The Heights and Weights of Adults in Great Britain,* HMSO, 1984

Kramer, Gerald H., 'Short-term fluctuations in US voting behavior, 1896–1964', *American Political Science Review,* 65, 1971, pp. 131–43

Kussmaul, Ann, *Servants in Husbandry in Early Modern England,* Cambridge University Press, 1981

A General View of the Rural Economy of England 1538–1840, Cambridge University Press, 1990

Kuznets, Simon, *Secular Movements in Production and Prices,* Houghton Mifflin, 1930

Layard, Richard and Stephen Nickell, 'The labour market', in Rudiger Dornbusch and Richard Layard, *The Performance of the British Economy,* Oxford University Press, 1987, pp.131–79

Lee, Chulhee, 'Socio-economic background, disease and mortality among Union army recruits: implications for economic and demographic history', *Explorations in Economic History,* 34, 1997, pp. 27–55

Lewis, W. Arthur, *Growth and Fluctuations, 1870–1913,* Allen & Unwin, 1978

Lindley, D. V. and W. F. Scott, *New Cambridge Statistical Tables*, 2nd edn., Cambridge University Press, 1995

Loschky, David and Ben D. Childers, 'Early English mortality', *Journal of Interdisciplinary History*, 24, 1993, pp. 85–97

Maddala, G. S. *Introduction to Econometrics*, 2nd edn., Prentice-Hall, 1992

Maddison, Angus, *Monitoring the World Economy, 1820–1992*, OECD, 1995.

Magee, Gary, *Productivity and Performance in the Paper Industry*, Cambridge University Press, 1997

Margo, Robert, A., 'The labor force participation of older Americans in 1900: further results', *Explorations in Economic History*, 30, 1993, pp. 409–23

Markus, Gregory B., 'The impact of personal and national economic conditions on the presidential vote: a pooled cross-sectional analysis', *American Journal of Political Science*, 32, 1988, pp. 137–54

Marris, Robin, *Economic Arithmetic*, Macmillan, 1958

McCloskey, Donald N. and J. Richard Zecher, 'How the gold standard worked, 1880–1913', in Donald N. McCloskey, *Enterprise and Trade in Victorian Britain*, Allen & Unwin, 1981, pp. 184–208

Metcalfe, David, Stephen J. Nickell and Nicos Floros, 'Still searching for an explanation of unemployment in interwar Britain', *Journal of Political Economy*, 90, 1982, pp. 386–99

Millward, Robert and Frances N. Bell, 'Economic factors in the decline of mortality in late nineteenth century Britain', *European Review of Economic History*, 2, 1998, pp. 263–88

Mosley, Paul, *The Making of Economic Policy*, Harvester Press, 1984

Neal, Larry, *The Rise of Financial Capitalism*, Cambridge University Press, 1990

Nielsen, Randall, 'Storage and English government in early modern grain markets', *Journal of Economic History*, 57, 1997, pp. 1–33

Ormerod, P. A. and G. D. N. Worswick, 'Unemployment in interwar Britain', *Journal of Political Economy*, 90, 1982, pp. 400–9

Persson, Karl Gunnar, *Grain Markets in Europe 1500–1900*, Cambridge University Press, 1999

Phelps Brown, Henry and Sheila V. Hopkins, 'Seven centuries of the price of consumables, compared with builders' wage rates', *Economica*, 23, 1956, reprinted in Henry Phelps Brown and Sheila V. Hopkins, *A Perspective of Wages and Prices*, Methuen, 1981, pp. 13–59

Prais, S. J. and H. S. Houthakker, *The Analysis of Family Budgets*, Cambridge University Press, 1955

Preston, Samuel H. and Michael R. Haines, *Fatal Years: Child Mortality in Late Nineteenth-Century America*, Princeton University Press, 1991

Salter, W. E. G., *Productivity and Technical Change*, Cambridge University Press, 1960

Schofield, R. S., 'Sampling in historical research', in E. A. Wrigley (ed.), *Nineteenth-Century Society, Essays in the Use of Quantitative Methods for the Study of Social Data*, Cambridge University Press, 1972, pp. 146–90

Schonhardt-Bailey, Cheryl, 'Linking constituency interests to legislative voting behaviour: the role of district economic and electoral composition in the repeal of the Corn Laws', *Parliamentary History*, 13, 1994, pp. 86–118

Scola, Roger, *Feeding the Victorian City: The Food Supply of Victorian Manchester, 1770–1870*, Manchester University Press, 1992

Sheflin, Neil, Leo Troy and C. Timothy Koeller, 'Structural stability in models of American trade union growth', *Quarterly Journal of Economics*, 96, 1981, pp. 77–88

Shorter, Edward and Charles Tilly, *Strikes in France 1830–1968*, Cambridge University Press, 1974

Siegel, Sidney and N. John Castellan, Jr., *Nonparametric Statistics for the Behavioral Sciences*, 2nd edn., McGraw-Hill, 1988

Solomou, Solomos, *Phases of Economic Growth, 1850–1973, Kondratieff Waves and Kuznets Swings*, Cambridge University Press, 1987

Southall, Humphrey and David Gilbert, 'A good time to wed? Marriage and economic distress in England and Wales, 1839–1914', *Economic History Review*, 49, 1996, pp. 35–57

Spraos, John, 'The statistical debate on the net barter terms of trade between primary commodities and manufactures', *Economic Journal*, 90, 1980, pp. 107–28

Stamp, Sir Josiah, *Some Economic Factors in Modern Life*, P. S. King & Son, 1929

Steckel, Richard H., 'The age at leaving home in the United States, 1850–1860', *Social Science History*, 20, 1996, pp. 507–32

Stevenson, S. J., 'The rise of suicide verdicts in south-east England, 1530–1590: the legal process', *Continuity and Change*, 2, 1987, pp. 37–75

Stock, James H., 'Real estate mortgages, foreclosures, and Midwestern agrarian unrest, 1865–1920', *Journal of Economic History*, 44, 1984, pp. 89–106

Sundstrom, William A. and Paul A. David, 'Old-age security motives, labor markets and farm family fertility in antebellum America', *Explorations in Economic History*, 25, 1988, pp. 164–97

Szreter, Simon, *Fertility, Class and Gender in Britain, 1860–1914*, Cambridge University Press, 1996

Tanner, J. M., R. H. Whitehouse and M. Takaishi, 'Standards from birth to maturity for height, weight, height velocity and weight velocity: British children, 1965 (Part I)', *Archives of Disease in Childhood*, 41, 1966, pp. 454–71

Thomas, Brinley, *Migration and Economic Growth*, Cambridge University Press, 1954

Thomas, Dorothy Swaine, *Social Aspects of the Business Cycle*, Routledge, 1925

Thomas, T., 'Aggregate demand in the United Kingdom 1918–1945', in Robert Floud and Donald McCloskey (eds.), *The Economic History of Britain since 1700*, II, *1860 to the 1970s*, 1st edn., Cambridge University Press, 1981, pp. 332–46

Tobin, James, 'Estimation of relationships for limited dependent variables', *Econometrica*, 1958, 26, pp. 24–36

Tucker, G. S. L., 'The old poor law revisited', *Explorations in Economic History*, 12, 1975, pp. 233–52

Tufte, Edward R., *Political Control of the Economy*, Princeton University Press, 1978

US Department of Commerce, *Historical Statistics of the United States*, Series G13, Washington, DC, 1949

Usher, Dan, *The Measurement of Economic Growth*, Basil Blackwell, 1980

Vamplew, Wray (ed.), *Australian Historical Statistics*, Fairfax, Syme & Weldon, 1987

Vernon, J. R., 'Unemployment rates in post-bellum America, 1869–1899', University of Florida, 1991, manuscript

von Tunzelmann, G. N., *Steam Power and British Industrialization*, Oxford University Press, 1978

Voth, Hans-Joachim, *Time and Work in England, 1750–1830*, Oxford University Press, 2001

Williamson, Jeffrey G., *American Growth and the Balance of Payments 1820–1913, A Study of the Long Swing*, University of North Carolina Press, 1964

'The evolution of global labor markets in the first and second world since 1830: background and evidence', *NBER Working Papers on Historical Factors in Long-Run Growth*, 36, NBER, 1992

Winter, Jay, 'Unemployment, nutrition and infant mortality in Britain, 1920–50', in Jay Winter (ed.), *The Working Class in Modern British History*, Cambridge University Press, 1983, pp. 232–56

Wonnacott, T. H. and R. J. Wonnacott, *Introductory Statistics*, 5th edn., John Wiley, 1990

Woods, Robert, *The Demography of Victorian England and Wales*, Cambridge University Press, 2000

Wrigley, E. A.,   'Some reflections on corn yields and prices in pre-industrial economies', in E. A. Wrigley, *People, Cities and Wealth*, Blackwell, 1987, pp. 92–132

Wrigley, E. A. and R. S. Schofield,   *The Population History of England 1541–1871*, Edward Arnold, 1981

Subject index

(Page references for boxes with definitions of the main terms and concepts are shown in bold type.)

Name Index

Printed in Great Britain
by Amazon